CW00807386

SCIENCE AND JUDICIAL REASONING

Science, which inevitably underlies environmental disputes, poses significant challenges for the scientifically untrained judges who decide such cases. In addition to disrupting ordinary fact-finding and causal inquiry, science can impact the framing of disputes and the standard of review. Judges must therefore adopt various tools to adjust the level of science allowed to enter their deliberations, which may fundamentally impact the legitimacy of their reasoning. While neglecting or replacing scientific authority can erode the convincing nature of judicial reasoning, the same authority, when treated properly, may lend persuasive force to adjudicatory findings, and buttress the legitimacy of judgments. In this work, Katalin Sulyok surveys the environmental case law of seven major jurisdictions and analyses framing techniques, evidentiary procedures, causal inquiries, and standards of review, offering valuable insight into how judges justify their choices between rival scientific claims in a convincing and legitimate manner.

Katalin Sulyok is Lecturer at ELTE University, Budapest. She holds a master of laws degree from Harvard Law School, a PhD in international law and a bachelor degree in biology from ELTE University. Sulyok researches and teaches public international law and environmental law with a special research focus on the intersecting areas of law and natural sciences. She has also been working as head of department at the Office of the Ombudsman for Future Generations in Hungary.

CAMBRIDGE STUDIES ON ENVIRONMENT, ENERGY AND NATURAL RESOURCES GOVERNANCE

Cambridge Studies on Environment, Energy and Natural Resources Governance publishes foundational monographs of general interest to scholars and practitioners within the broadly defined fields of sustainable development policy, including studies on law, economics, politics, history, and policy. These fields currently attract unprecedented interest due both to the urgency of developing policies to address climate change, the energy transition, food security and water availability and, more generally, to the progressive realization of the impact of humans as a geological driver of the state of the Earth, now called the "Anthropocene."

The general editor of the series is Professor Jorge E. Viñuales, the Harold Samuel Chair of Law and Environmental Policy at the University of Cambridge and the Founder and First Director of the Cambridge Centre for Environment, Energy and Natural Resource Governance (C-EENRG).

Science and Judicial Reasoning

THE LEGITIMACY OF INTERNATIONAL ENVIRONMENTAL ADJUDICATION

KATALIN SULYOK

ELTE University, Budapest

CAMBRIDGE
UNIVERSITY PRESS

CAMBRIDGE
UNIVERSITY PRESS

University Printing House, Cambridge CB2 8BS, United Kingdom

One Liberty Plaza, 20th Floor, New York, NY 10006, USA

477 Williamstown Road, Port Melbourne, VIC 3207, Australia

314–321, 3rd Floor, Plot 3, Splendor Forum, Jasola District Centre,
New Delhi – 110025, India

79 Anson Road, #06–04/06, Singapore 079906

Cambridge University Press is part of the University of Cambridge.

It furthers the University's mission by disseminating knowledge in the pursuit of
education, learning, and research at the highest international levels of excellence.

www.cambridge.org
Information on this title: www.cambridge.org/9781108489669
DOI: 10.1017/9781108779173

© Katalin Sulyok 2021

This publication is in copyright. Subject to statutory exception
and to the provisions of relevant collective licensing agreements,
no reproduction of any part may take place without the written
permission of Cambridge University Press.

First published 2021

A catalogue record for this publication is available from the British Library.

ISBN 978-1-108-48966-9 Hardback

Cambridge University Press has no responsibility for the persistence or accuracy of
URLs for external or third-party internet websites referred to in this publication
and does not guarantee that any content on such websites is, or will remain,
accurate or appropriate.

To Gabor and Zsigmond

Contents

Tables

Foreword

In a series of lectures delivered in Sao Paulo in the early 1970s, French philosopher Michel Foucault, then at the apex of his influence, canvassed a theory of how legal procedures (*formes juridiques*) had shaped the very understanding of what is 'true' and how truth is to be established, not only in the context of a legal process but also beyond. The recourse to 'inquiry' in the legal process underpinned, according to Foucault's intriguing proposition, the conception of how truth should be established in other areas of knowledge. The testing ground relied on by Foucault was vast and diverse, from accounts in Greek tragedy, to medieval ordeals, to the social sciences (*sciences humaines*) of the nineteenth century.

Katalin Sulyok's impressive study of the role of science in judicial reasoning takes as a starting point the reverse road. She seeks to understand how scientific truth and argument can shape a specific form of legal inquiry, namely the judicial process. Her testing ground is the vast phenomenon that can be characterized as international environmental adjudication. Her approach has all the virtues of profound theoretical inquiry in international law with none of the frequent shortcomings in the actual technical and practical knowledge. She offers theory deeply grounded in practice, at a level which the practitioner will greatly appreciate, particularly on issues such as the analysis of causality, which have been largely overlooked. And she distils from a painstaking analysis of such practice an overall narrative which emphasizes the battleground between two claims to truth, those of science and law, which rely on different processes and, importantly, rest on different constituencies.

Her point is as simple as it is powerful: one of those constituencies (lawyers and, more specifically, judges) have no choice but to integrate science in judicial reasoning or else their decisions will lose credibility and legitimacy. This is a normative imperative, not merely a practical one, but its natural element is an inherent tension. The judge must pay attention to science, but they cannot 'outsource' their decision to the scientific constituency. The judicial decision thus remains a normative – not a factual – one. The means through which this difficult balance may be achieved are carefully identified and analysed, in their theoretical and practical context, relying on a body of practice which, until now, had only received partial consideration.

It is an outstanding work, which will guide research on this subject for years to come, and I very much welcome its publication in the Cambridge Studies on Environment, Energy and Natural Resources Governance.

J. E. Viñuales
Cambridge, 10 February 2020

Acknowledgements

This book is based on my doctoral dissertation written at my alma mater, Eötvös Loránd (ELTE) University Faculty of Law, concerning the ways in which international courts and tribunals interact with scientific knowledge. This research has grown out of, on the one hand, my thesis in biology written at ELTE Faculty of Natural Sciences and on the other hand my LLM thesis at Harvard Law School concerning the scientific fact-finding of US courts in toxic tort litigation, which was later awarded the Irving Oberman Memorial Award for the best environmental law paper of the academic year.

Due to my dual background in law and science, my research interests cover the intersecting areas of the two realms. This monograph is the first book-length answer given to the interdisciplinary question I have been intrigued by during my PhD research, namely, how courts could decide disputes over contested scientific facts in an efficient and legitimate way. The Henry Wheaton (J. B. Scott) Prize awarded for my doctoral dissertation by the *Institut de Droit international* made it possible for me to dedicate time to develop my research into the present monograph.

The inquiry laid out in this book is a combination of three distinct fields of knowledge to which I have been drawn simultaneously: environmental law, pubic international law, and natural sciences. In chronological order, I was first infected with love and respect for nature and natural sciences for which I am indebted to my science teachers and professors at all stages of my education, in particular to Béla Gál, Liz Pásztor, György Csizmazia, and most of all, Professor Peter Csermely.

My interest and passion for novel terrains of international law can be traced back to my experience at the Jessup Moot Court Competition, which I attended first as a participant at the International Rounds in Washington DC and later as a coach. I feel very fortunate to be part of the vibrant Jessup alumni community at ELTE Law School in Budapest, where I also have had the honour of co-coaching the ELTE Jessup Team winning the Jessup International Championship Round in 2019.

A major source of inspiration for some of the main ideas developed in this book has been my LLM studies at Harvard Law School, where I spent the academic year of 2015/2016 as a Fulbright scholar. I am very grateful to Professor Richard Lazarus for supervising my research on toxic tort jurisprudence and to Professor Sheila Jasanoff for her thought-provoking class on Science and Technology Studies. This most enriching period was made possible by the generous financial support of the scholarships provided by the former Head of State, László Sólyom, the Fulbright Commission, and Harvard Law School.

I would like to express my sincere gratitude for the inspiring environment and the infinite academic resources to the Lauterpacht Centre for International Law, the Max Planck Institute for Comparative Public Law and International Law in Heidelberg, as well as the Center for Environment, Energy, and Natural Resource Governance of Cambridge University, where I had the privilege of spending several visiting research periods to further refine this work. I am truly indebted to Jorge Viñuales for his continuous encouragement in this process, and for his advice and guidance throughout the years.

I am very grateful to my supervisors, Professor Pal Sonnevend and Professor Gabor Kardos, for their insights and help during my doctoral studies. This research could not have been conducted without the support of Professor Gyula Bándi and Professor Marcel Szabo, the incumbent and the former Ombudsman for Future Generations of Hungary, with whom I was working as head of department during a significant portion of this research.

Finally, I could not have succeeded with this book project without the love and support of my family. Most particularly, I am really thankful to my husband, Gabor Kajtar, for accompanying me on my academic and real-life journeys, and to my son, Zsigmond, who is literally a twin brother of this book. I am also very grateful to my parents, who have always encouraged me to follow my passion and from whom I inherited my love for books. Last but not least, many thanks go to Annamaria Balogh for her valuable help with the editing process.

Author Note

This book is based on a dissertation that was awarded the 2019 Henry Wheaton Prize instituted by the James B. Scott Competition of the *Institut de Droit international*.

Table of Cases

INTERNATIONAL TRIBUNAL FOR THE LAW OF THE SEA

WTO DISPUTE SETTLEMENT

EUROPEAN COURT OF HUMAN RIGHTS

INTER-AMERICAN COMMISSION OF HUMAN RIGHTS

INTER-AMERICAN COURT OF HUMAN RIGHTS

AFRICAN COMMISSION ON HUMAN AND PEOPLES' RIGHTS

Table of Cases

DOMESTIC CASE LAW

Abbreviations

AB	Appellate Body
ABC	Abyei Boundaries Commission
ACHR	American Convention on Human Rights
ACtHPR	African Court of Human and Peoples' Rights
ALOP	Appropriate level of protection
ARSIWA	International Law Commission's Articles on the Responsibility of States for Internationally Wrongful Acts
AUD	Australian Dollar
BIT	Bilateral Investment Treaties
CFI	Court of First Instance of the European Union
DES	Diethylstilbestrol
DSU	Understanding on Rules and Procedures Governing the Settlement of Disputes
EC	European Communities
ECHR	European Convention on Human Rights
ECtHR	European Court of Human Rights
ECJ	European Court of Justice
ECOWAS	Economic Community of West African States
EEZ	Exclusive economic zone
EIA	Environmental impact assessment
EPA	Environmental Protection Agency
EU	European Union
FAO	Food and Agriculture Organization
FCTC	WHO Framework Convention on Tobacco Control
GATT	General Agreement on Tariffs and Trade
GHG	Greenhouse gas
GMO	Genetically modified organism
ICJ	International Court of Justice
IACtHR	Inter-American Court of Human Rights

ICC	International Chamber of Commerce
ICRW	International Convention on the Regulation of Whaling
ICSID	International Center for Settlement of Investment Disputes
ILC	International Law Commission
ILO	International Labour Organization
IMO	International Maritime Organization
IPCC	International Panel on Climate Change
ISA	International Seabed Authority
ITLOS	International Tribunal for the Law of the Sea
IWC	International Whaling Commission
JARPA	Japanese Whale Research Program under Special Permit in the Antarctic
JARPA II	Second Phase of the Japanese Whale Research Program under Special Permit in the Antarctic
KHEP	Kishenganga Hydro-Electric Project
MTBE	Methyl tertiary butyl ether
MEA	Multilateral environmental agreement
MIT	Multilateral Investment Treaties
MOX plant	Mixed-oxide fuel plant
MPA	Marine Protected Area
MSR	Marine scientific research
NAFTA	North American Free Trade Agreement
NEWREP-A	New Scientific Whale Research Program in the Antarctic Ocean
NGO	Non-governmental organization
OAS	Organization of American States
OSPAR	OSPAR Convention for the Protection of the Marine Environment of the North-East Atlantic
PCA	Permanent Court of Arbitration
PCB	Polychlorinated biphenyl
PCIJ	Permanent Court of International Justice
RIAA	Reports of International Arbitral Awards
RR	Relative risk
SGR	Standards, guidelines and recommendations
SOA	Chinese State Oceanic Administration
SPS	Sanitary and phyto-sanitary measures
STS	Science and Technology Studies
TAC	Total allowable catch
TBT	Technical Barriers to Trade
UK	United Kingdom
UN	United Nations
UNCC	UN Compensation Commission
UNCITRAL	UN Commission on International Trade Law

UNCLOS	UN Convention on the Law of the Sea
UNEP	UN Environmental Programme
UNESCO	UN Educational, Scientific and Cultural Organization
UNSC	United Nations Security Council
US	United States of America
USD	US Dollar
USSR	Union of Soviet Socialist Republics
VCLT	Vienna Convention on the Law of Treaties
WHO	World Health Organization
WTO	World Trade Organization

PART I

The Three-Fold Challenge of Engaging with Science in International Environmental Adjudication

1

Introduction to a Comparative Study on Judicial Engagement with Science

Progress must and can be made in the social sciences to come abreast of the new advances in the physical sciences.

Philip C. Jessup[1]

I SCIENCE ENTERS INTERNATIONAL ENVIRONMENTAL ADJUDICATION

Science often entails connotations of 'objectivity', 'certainty', and the capability to discover the 'factual truth'. Judicial decisions, in turn, are routinely associated with resolving disputes in a 'final', 'neutral', and 'authoritative' way. Yet international environmental adjudicatory decisions, where scientific and legal authority get entangled with each other, suggest that neither science nor law can fully live up to these idealized expectations. What happens if science and law yield competing narratives as to the factual basis of a dispute? Who could and should resolve their conflict and how, based on what benchmarks? Would the uncertain, probabilistic nature of scientific input diminish the authority of a legal judgment based upon it? And can a legal judgment speak authoritatively if it contradicts elementary scientific knowledge? Overall, how can adjudicators do justice to both legal and scientific cognitive authority in science-based legal disputes?

This book interrogates these questions through the lens of international environmental adjudicative practice with a focus on what will be called science-intensive cases, that is, legal disputes with apparent scientific dimensions. It will provide a fine-grained analysis of the many layers of difficulties the presence of science poses for international judges both in terms of their procedures and their reasoning. Scientific evidence and science-based arguments are a hallmark of environmental adjudication, and our main purpose here is to show that they fundamentally impact the ways in which such disputes can be decided in a convincing and legitimate manner. Consequently, the diverse judicial tools that adjudicators employ to reflect on scientific knowledge will be analysed here through the prism of legitimacy.

[1] P. C. Jessup, *A Modern Law of Nations* (The Macmillan Company, 1948), p. 2.

That modern life is becoming ever more permeated with science and technology warrants no specific illustration. Less evident though is perhaps the fundamental impact that science and technology exert on social institutions,[2] adjudication being one of them. Scientific arguments and evidence enter the adjudicative process in a myriad of ways. Scientific facts are sometimes embedded in the primary rule upon which the controversy rests, as in the case of disputes revolving around environmental harm and causality. On other occasions, scientific results become relevant to the interpretation of notions in which law and science are closely interwoven.[3] Science is often 'indispensable in distilling the essence of what legal concepts such as 'significance' of damage, 'sufficiency', 'reasonable threshold', or 'necessity' come to mean in a given case'.[4] Yet even scientific experts themselves often differ on the content of these science-intensive terms,[5] which complicates matters further for adjudicators who are tasked with deciding legal disputes revolving around the meaning of these notions.

Environmental cases that entertain a set of highly complex scientific and techno-logical facts are gradually becoming the norm in environmental adjudication. Nevertheless, law and science are normally still regarded as 'distinct cultures'.[6] International law is no exception. In spite of the fact that one hardly finds an international environmental agreement not incorporating scientific or technical standards,[7] science and international law have been for the most part treated as 'virtual strangers'[8] both in scholarship and in adjudicatory practice.

This is all the more remarkable considering that discharging the judicial task has become a highly interdisciplinary exercise. Interdisciplinarity in this context is more than a fashionable buzzword. It goes beyond the regular practice of appointing experts and gathering scientific evidence in environmental disputes. The main proposition of this book contends that interdisciplinarity has far-reaching implica-tions for how judges ought to investigate and reason in science-heavy disputes. In short, interdisciplinarity imposes a heavy epistemic burden on judges. They have to develop a basic understanding of the scientific aspects of the dispute, as they alone

---

[2]   S. Jasanoff, 'Ordering knowledge, ordering society' in *States of Knowledge: The Co-production of Science and Social Order* (Routledge, 2004), pp. 13–45 p. 13.

[3]   Caroline Foster labels such cases as 'mixed questions of fact and law', see C. E. Foster, *Science and the Precautionary Principle in International Courts and Tribunals* (Cambridge University Press, 2011), pp. 137–48.

[4]   *Pulp Mills on the River Uruguay (Argentina v. Uruguay)* (2010) ICJ Rep 14, Joint Dissenting Opinion of Judges Al-Khasawneh and Simma, para. 17.

[5]   F. Francioni, 'The private sector and the challenge of implementation' in P.-M. Dupuy and J. E. Viñuales (eds.), *Harnessing Foreign Investment to Promote Environmental Protection* (Cambridge University Press, 2013), pp. 24–49 p. 26.

[6]   S. Jasanoff, 'In a constitutional moment: science and social order at the millennium' in B. Joerges and H. Nowotny (eds.), *Social Studies of Science and Technology: Looking Back, Ahead* (Kluwer Academic Publishers, 2003), pp. 155–80 p. 164.

[7]   J. Peel, 'Changing conceptions of environmental risk' in J. E. Viñuales (ed.), *The Rio Declaration on Environment and Development: A Commentary* (Oxford University Press, 2015), pp. 76–84 p. 78.

[8]   J. Klabbers, 'Changing futures? Science and international law' (2009) *Finnish Yearbook of International Law* 211–13 at 211.

bear the responsibility to render a final decision in the controversy. This imposes certain limitations on the extent to which judges may ask for epistemic support from natural scientists even when they choose to appoint experts. The imperative for judges to preserve their monopoly over the dispute resolution and to exert some form of control over scientific expertise precludes simply sharing this epistemic burden with experts by automatically relying on their opinion in the courtroom. As will be argued in this book, this epistemic obligation imposed on legal adjudicators fundamentally shapes the judicial task and influences the modalities in which judges can craft a convincing and therefore legitimate reasoning in science-intensive cases. Adjudicators may justify their decisions on scientific matters in a legal dispute in varied ways, by appealing either to scientific or non-scientific – legalistic or everyday – knowledge and authority. Uncovering the epistemic and practical conditionalities of each of these reasoning styles is among the main goals of this study.

International judges increasingly face scientific dilemmas as the number of science-intensive environmental disputes are steadily on the rise. It is not only environmental disputes that proliferate, but also available judicial fora that hear such cases. Environmental claims are brought before a growing 'patchwork of jurisdictions'[9] on the international level. These fora increasingly confront scientific facts, directly and indirectly, through weighing the parties' positions regarding techno-scientific matters.[10] Science inevitably underlies disputes concerning natural resource allocation, environmental liability, risk assessment requirements, violations of human rights guarantees serving to ensure a clean environment, and states' right to regulate environmental risks to the detriment of foreign investment or international trade. In light of this, one may intuitively think that the marked presence of science in litigation warrants[11] a significant role for scientific arguments in resolving such disputes. Yet a closer look at the landscape of international environmental adjudication reveals that scientific input is often marginalized or addressed only minimally by judges. Notably, international adjudicatory fora differ in their approaches to science-backed claims. While some hesitate to decide cases based on highly technical scientific evidence with reference to their lack of expertise, others go to great lengths to evaluate scientific inputs.

Despite the varying extent to which science is allowed to enter judicial deliberations, the fact remains that science represents a cross-cutting, universal concern for the entire course of adjudication. The entering of scientific arguments into dispute resolution fundamentally impacts several stages of the adjudicative process; more specifically, the ways in which the legally relevant aspects of disputes are framed, the techniques of

---

[9] T. Stephens, *International Courts and Environmental Protection* (Cambridge University Press, 2009), pp. 21–2.

[10] J. E. Viñuales, 'Observations sur le traitement des motifs scientifiques dans le contentieux environmental international' in F. Couveinhes Matsumoto and R. Nollez-Goldbach (eds.), *Les motifs non-juridiques des jugements internationaux. Actes de la 1ére journée de droit international de l'ENS* (Pedone, 2016), pp. 113–25 p. 114.

[11] For a similar position see J. E. Viñuales, 'Legal techniques for dealing with scientific uncertainty in environmental law' (2010) 43 *Vanderbilt Journal of Transnational Law* 437–503 at 478.

scientific fact-finding are selected, the causal inquiry is conducted as well as the extent to which adjudicators grant deference to litigants in making scientific findings.

This is, of course, not to suggest that the dynamics of environmental adjudication are solely shaped by the intrusion of scientific knowledge. In resolving environmental disputes, judges ought to manage feelings just as much as facts,[12] together with fears and value choices of the public. The role of science in adjudication, however, merits special attention because science has strategic importance in the judicial process. It enters adjudication as a source of ostensibly objective, extra-legal cognitive authority, to which the parties appeal supporting their arguments. This strategic value distinguishes scientific arguments from various other types of factual, policy, and legal arguments the parties invoke in a litigation. While scientific references may lend considerable persuasive force to the parties' arguments, science normally falls within the blind spot of international adjudicators. Judge Cançado Trindade summarized the ambivalent role science plays in adjudication by pointing out that 'conflicting evidence seems to make the paradise of lawyers and practitioners at national and international levels. It seems to make, likewise, the purgatory of judges and fact-finders, at national and international levels.'[13]

The role adjudicators assign to science in litigation is inevitably informed by the wider context in which society interacts with science. Present-day societies seem to have an ambivalent relationship with science. The beginning of the twenty-first century has seen a backlash against scientific authority in many parts of the world marked by, inter alia, a rise in anti-vaccination movements and a growing number of proponents of intelligent design, climate change denial, and populist agendas embracing scientific scepticism. In parallel to these constructed 'scientific controversies',[14] the same decades have experienced unprecedented techno-scientific breakthroughs such as 3D printing, gene therapy, smart technology, artificial intelligence, and climate engineering. Science transforms not only the way people are born into,[15] think about,[16] or sense the world,[17] but also alters how they feel belonging to communities,[18] perceive basic ethical rights and wrongs,[19] hold accountable sovereign

---

[12]   L. Squintani, J. Darpö, L. Lavrysen, and P.-T. Stoll, *Managing Facts and Feelings in Environmental Governance* (Edward Elgar, 2019).

[13]   *Pulp Mills*, Separate Opinion of Judge Cançado Trindade, para. 148.

[14]   D. Harker, *Creating Scientific Controversies* (Cambridge University Press, 2015).

[15]   See for example assisted reproductive technologies, such as in vitro fertilization.

[16]   J. Taylor, 'How technology is changing the way children think and focus' (4 December 2012) *Psychology Today*, available at https://bit.ly/36SRCKX (last accessed 10 January 2020).

[17]   W. G. Wright, 'Using virtual reality to augment perception, enhance sensorimotor adaptation, and change our minds' (8 April 2014) *Frontiers in System Neuroscience*, available at www.frontiersin.org /articles/10.3389/fnsys.2014.00056/full (last accessed 6 January 2020).

[18]   On the effects of social media on sense of community see Z. Zhang, 'Feeling the sense of community in social networking usage' (2010) 57 *IEEE Transactions on Engineering Management* 225–39.

[19]   Relevant examples include sense of equality, equal opportunity, and corresponding rights and obligations. A salient example is flagged by gender equality movements, which started off after World War I, when wartime industry made women workforce acceptable and desirable. This later

powers,[20] construe privacy,[21] and last, but perhaps most closely speaking to the narrower topic of adjudication, the extent to which people regard a football referee's judgment legitimate in the case of conflicting results from video referees.[22]

The opposing reactions given to scientific intrusion into modern life shape the extent to which science can impact social institutions, including adjudication. As one philosopher of science has put it, '[a]ttitudes to science range all the way from uncritical admiration at one extreme, through distrust, resentment, and envy, to denigration and outright hostility at the other'.[23] Judicial reactions given to the scientific aspects of disputes fluctuate to a similarly remarkable extent. Responses vary from affording automatic deference to expert evaluations, through attempting to reveal 'the' single scientific truth among rival scientific positions, to adopting various avoidance strategies that view science-intensive aspects non-justiciable or circumvent considering science in more subtle ways.

In light of the ubiquitous presence of techno-scientific matters in environmental adjudication and the diversity of adjudicatory reactions triggered thereby, the judicial treatment of science is well worth a specific study. Comprehensive analyses have already been offered to appraise how environmental concerns appear before various international courts,[24] yet no inquiry of comparable scope has been conducted to address how science itself exerts a transformative impact on the process of environmental adjudication. Earlier scholarly works have mainly focused on the role of science in environmental governance and policymaking,[25] not in litigation. In the

---

led to equal pay demands. Moreover, access to technology is a precondition for, and often important symbol of, gender equality, see M. Coker, 'Saudi women can now drive. Overcoming beliefs on gender will be harder' (24 June 2018) *New York Times*, available at www.nytimes.com/2018/06/24/world/middleeast/saudi-women-drivers.html (last accessed 6 January 2020).

[20] E. MacAskill, 'WikiLeaks publishes "biggest ever leak of secret CIA documents"' (7 March 2017) *Guardian*, available at https://bit.ly/2Atqp5d (last accessed 6 January 2020).

[21] Technology may alter the protected sphere of privacy both in the physical and the virtual sphere. A relevant example is provided by the emergence of new legal regulations banning drones from invading one's home and private life. See A. Satariano, 'G.D.P.R., a new privacy law, makes Europe world's leading tech watchdog' (24 May 2018) *New York Times*, available at www.nytimes.com/2018/05/24/technology/europe-gdpr-privacy.html (last accessed 6 January 2020).

[22] 'What is VAR, what are the rules, and how is it being used at World Cup 2018?' (26 June 2018) *Daily Telegraph*, available at www.telegraph.co.uk/world-cup/0/var-rules-used-world-cup-2018/ (last accessed 6 January 2020).

[23] S. Haack, *Defending Science within Reason: Between Scientism and Cynicism* (Prometheus Books, 2007), p. 17.

[24] Stephens, *International Courts and Environmental Protection*; C. P. R. Romano, *The Peaceful Settlement of International Environmental Disputes: A Pragmatic Approach* (Kluwer Law International, 2000); A. Boyle and J. Harrison, 'Judicial settlement of international environmental disputes: current problems' (2013) 4 *Journal of International Dispute Settlement* 245–76.

[25] J. Peel, *Science and Risk Regulation in International Law* (Cambridge University Press, 2010); M. Ambrus, K. Arts, E. Hey, and H. Raulus (eds.), *The Role of 'Experts' in International and European Decision-Making Processes* (Cambridge University Press, 2014); J. Peel, 'Changing conceptions of environmental risk' in J. E. Viñuales (ed.), *The Rio Declaration on Environment and Development: A Commentary* (Oxford University Press, 2015), pp. 74–85.

context of international adjudication, important contributions have been made with respect to scientific fact-finding,[26] and regarding the scientific engagement of a specific court or tribunal.[27] Yet thus far only a couple of articles have sought to survey judicial methods across multiple international jurisdictions,[28] and no comprehensive study has addressed the various ways in which judges treat and interact with scientific arguments in the practice of all major international jurisdictions. This book will now address this understudied aspect of international environmental adjudication.

Emphatically, the focus of this analysis lies not on the prospect for success of environmental considerations in a legal dispute, but on the reach and weight of scientific arguments in such disputes. Despite this strict analytical distinction between scientific arguments and environmental interests, the two are interlocked in the adjudicatory practice in many respects. Environmental claims almost always rely on scientific justification and evidence; therefore, their success often directly hinges on the receptivity of judges to such arguments. At the same time, scientific evidence and narrative can also be relied on by parties, who advance claims running against environmental protection goals. In either scenario, ambiguous and inconsistent engagement with scientific arguments is detrimental to every party as it

---

[26] L. Boisson de Chazournes, M. M. Mbengue, R. Das, and G. Gros, 'One size does not fit all: uses of experts before international courts and tribunals – an insight into the practice' (2018) 9 *Journal of International Dispute Settlement* 477–505; L. Boisson de Chazournes, H. Ruiz Fabri, M. M. Mbengue, R. Das, and G. Gros, 'The expert in the international adjudicative process: introduction to the special issue' (2018) 9 *Journal of International Dispute Settlement* 339–44; Foster, *Science and the Precautionary Principle in International Courts and Tribunals*; M. M. Mbengue, 'Scientific fact-finding at the International Court of Justice: an appraisal in the aftermath of the Whaling case' (2016) 29 *Leiden Journal of International Law* 529–50; M. M. Mbengue, 'International courts and tribunals as fact-finders: the case of scientific fact-finding in international adjudication' (2011) 34 *Loyola of Los Angeles International & Comparative Law Review* 53; C. E. Foster, 'New clothes for the emperor? Consultation of experts by the International Court of Justice' (2014) 5 *Journal of International Dispute Settlement* 139–73; C. E. Foster, 'The consultation of independent experts by international court and tribunals in health and environmental cases' (2009) 20 *Finnish Yearbook of International Law* 391–417; J. E. Alvarez, 'Are international judges afraid of science?: a comment on Mbengue' (2011) 34 *Loyola of Los Angeles International & Comparative Law Review* 81–98; C. Payne, 'Mastering the evidence: improving fact finding by international courts' (2011) *Environmental Law* 1191–220.

[27] C. Lévesque, 'Science in the hands of international investment tribunals: a case for "scientific due process"' (2009) 20 *Finnish Yearbook of International Law* 259–90; A. Ridell and B. Plant, *Evidence before the International Court of Justice* (British Institute of International and Comparative Law, 2009); A. Ridell, 'Scientific evidence in the International Court of Justice: problems and possibilities' (2009) 20 *Finnish Yearbook of International Law* 229–58; Mbengue, 'Scientific fact-finding at the International Court of Justice: an appraisal in the aftermath of the Whaling case'; M. A. Orellana, 'The role of science in investment arbitrations concerning public health and the environment' (2006) 17 *Yearbook of International Environmental Law* 48–72; L. Gruszczynski, *Regulating Health and Environmental Risks under WTO Law: A Critical Analysis of the SPS Agreement* (Oxford University Press, 2010).

[28] Viñuales, 'Observations sur le traitement des motifs scientifiques dans le contentieux environnemental international'; J. D'Aspremont and M. M. Mbengue, 'Strategies of engagement with scientific fact-finding in international adjudication' (2014) 5 *Journal of International Dispute Settlement* 240–72.

undermines procedural fairness and, as will be argued in this book, erodes the legitimacy of the adjudicatory process.

The transformational and far-reaching impact that science exerts on the entirety of the adjudicatory process has remained largely under-theorized in scholarship. This stands in stark contrast with the field of environmental governance and policy-making, where the role of scientific expertise has been subject to detailed scholarly commentary.[29] To illustrate the canonized role of science in policymaking, suffice it to refer to well-established notions such as 'science-based policy-making',[30] or 'regulatory science'.[31] Tellingly, no similar concept has been coined to address the fundamental role science plays in adjudication. To fill this gap, this study will view and address science as a common underlying thread in environmental disputes shaping the dynamics of the entire adjudicative process. Although science poses similar challenges for the judicial inquiry, it often triggers divergent solutions across jurisdictions. This variety of international adjudicatory reactions will be put at the centre of this inquiry. Understanding the limits and modalities of judicial engagement with science and portraying the different reasoning styles through which persuasive and legitimate judicial decisions can be crafted constitute the main objectives of this research.

II THE THREE-FOLD CHALLENGE OF USING SCIENCE IN ADJUDICATION: THE CONTEXT

The above mentioned theoretical foundations have two important implications for this study. First, the modalities of judicial engagement with scientific arguments will be analysed with regard to the wider context of the science – law interface – in order to reveal the inherent challenges in the interaction of these disciplines and the hidden possibilities to enhance their co-operation. Second, this study will view science as a linchpin concept, from the aspect of which many difficulties and shortcomings of science-heavy environmental adjudication can be adequately explained. This narrative entails that the presence of science will be seen as posing similar challenges along the entire process of adjudication. Consequently, the scope of this study shall encompass every judicial technique that serves to engage and interact with science in the adjudicatory process instead of focusing on certain specific judicial tools and techniques.

Turning first to the context of judicial interaction with science, this study will argue that three main challenges arise when judges who are not trained in science

---

[29] Peel, *Science and Risk Regulation in International Law*; Ambrus, Arts, Hey, and Raulus, *The Role of 'Experts' in International and European Decision-Making Processes*.

[30] Peel, *Science and Risk Regulation in International Law*, pp. 115–29; P. Pascual, W. Wagner, and E. Fisher, 'Making methods visible: improving the quality of science-based regulation' (2013) 2 *Michigan Journal of Environmental and Administrative Law* 429–72 at 429–72.

[31] S. Jasanoff, *The Fifth Branch* (Harvard University Press, 1990), pp. 76–9.

need to make legal sense of scientific arguments. Due to these difficulties scientific arguments do not lend themselves to straightforward judicial appraisal in an adjudicatory setting. Hence, in order to better understand the reasons for the apparent difficulties of science-intensive adjudication, one first ought to explore the broader context of environmental disputes. In this respect this study will identify epistemic, doctrinal, and legitimacy challenges. Epistemic challenges stem from the fact that science and law are both capable of lending cognitive authority to knowledge claims, and these authorities may be in conflict with each other. Doctrinal challenges emerge from the fundamental differences in the ways in which law and science conceive concepts of 'cause' and 'causation', the criteria for persuasive evidence, and their different levels of tolerance towards probabilistic evidence and ambiguity. Lastly, legitimacy challenges make it difficult for judges to preserve their monopoly over the resolution of disputes and to select the appropriate rationality to justify their reasoning.

In order to provide a deeper explanation for these challenges, the forthcoming analysis heavily draws on interdisciplinary insights. First, on natural science literature, which extensively deals with the problem of scientific uncertainty – a central feature underlying the doctrinal differences between law and science. Second, insights of the philosophy of science, especially Science and Technology Studies (STS) that analyse the epistemic complexities surrounding the use of scientific knowledge in a social context, will be relied on to provide a background to applicable epistemic challenges. These accounts focus on the interrelations of legitimacy, public authority, and accountability of both science and law.[32] They can, thus, help better understand the difficulties of reconciling society's two major 'authoritative institutions'[33] within the frames of legal adjudication. More particularly, insights from the philosophy of science shall inform our analysis regarding the appropriate limits of the judicial purview, and the extent of deference that adjudicators may justifiably accord to expert evaluations in the judicial review. Also, understanding the social preconditions of scientific research could help devise legal procedures that alleviate or, at best, do not exacerbate the epistemic difficulties of using science in an adjudicatory setting. For this reason, they will also guide our recommendations for how to select legitimate judicial reasoning styles in science-intensive cases.

III JUDICIAL ENGAGEMENT WITH SCIENCE: THE FRAMEWORK

This book is dedicated to examining the differing extent and ways in which international adjudicators engage with scientific facts and arguments in settling international environmental disputes. The focus of this analysis will be referred to as

---

[32] S. Jasanoff, 'Serviceable truths: science for action in law and policy' (2014) 93 *Texas Law Review* 1723 at 1723.
[33] Jasanoff, 'Serviceable truths', 1723.

'judicial engagement with science', which encompasses a host of practices, with which adjudicators assess, interact, and occasionally investigate the scientific dimensions of legal disputes.

To make this abstract concept more amenable to a fine-grained comparative analysis, judicial engagement with science will be evaluated with respect to four distinct stages of the adjudicatory process. This research will identify and comparatively assess the judicial techniques serving for engaging with science specifically at the following stages of adjudication:

(i) **Framing of the legally relevant issues to be decided.** Framing stands for a strategic choice of adjudicators allowing them to exclude certain scientific arguments from their inquiry.

(ii) **Scientific fact-finding.** These methods indicate the extent to which courts request and rely on expert evidence in reaching their decisions, and the procedures in which adjudicators handle and weigh uncertain and probabilistic scientific proofs.

(iii) **Causal inquiry.** The causal assessment indicates whether courts are willing to conduct a thorough, science-based causal inquiry or they would rather circumvent and substitute science in reaching their judgment on finding a causal link established.

(iv) **Extent and standard of judicial review.** The standard of review describes the degree of deference adjudicators afford to sovereigns' scientific claims. Different standards entail differing extent and depth of the judicial review in science-intensive disputes.

Each substantive chapter included in Part II will proceed along the above four levels of analysis when examining the case law of relevant international courts and tribunals. The structure of this four-stage framework also duly reflects that these judicial techniques are part of the same process and hence are influenced by the same factors and underlying assumptions about the appropriate weight and role of scientific arguments in a judicial decision. For this reason, this research posits that in order to comment on the role assigned to science in legal decision-making, these judicial techniques should be examined taken together and not in isolation from each other. Scholarly contributions have already been offered with regard to some of the components of the above analytic framework, more specifically, concerning scientific fact-finding,[34]

---

[34] Boisson de Chazournes, Mbengue, Das, and Gros, 'One size does not fit all – uses of experts before international courts and tribunals'; Boisson de Chazournes, Ruiz Fabri, Mbengue, Das, and Gros, 'The expert in the international adjudicative process'; Foster, *Science and the Precautionary Principle in International Courts and Tribunals*; Mbengue, 'Scientific fact-finding at the International Court of Justice: an appraisal in the aftermath of the *Whaling* case'; Mbengue, 'International courts and tribunals as fact-finders'; Foster, 'New clothes for the emperor?'; Foster, 'The consultation of independent experts by international court and tribunals in health and environmental cases'; Alvarez, 'Are international judges afraid of science?: a comment on Mbengue'; Payne, 'Mastering the evidence'.

causation,[35] and the standard of review.[36] Yet none of these accounts extends its scope to all four stages of the adjudicatory process, which will be in the centre of analysis in this book.

The analytical chapters will address the scientific engagement techniques of seven major international jurisdictions. These chapters aim to supply practical information for practitioners and scholars about the array of acceptable scientific references before each of the relevant jurisdictions. The analysis will also appraise the extent to which science-based arguments offered by the parties shape the adjudicatory inquiry of the respective judicial body. The comparative part of the study, which is set forth in Part III, will then provide a comprehensive classification of the various adjudicatory techniques identified in the analytical chapters using judicial engagement with science as a benchmark. It may be apt to note at the outset that the comparative analysis will also encompass references to relevant adjudicatory solutions of the UN Compensation Commission, and the US-Marshall Islands Nuclear Claims Tribunal as well as domestic climate change litigation and toxic tort case law. Highlighting some good adjudicatory practices of science-intensive judicial inquiry seeks to foster cross-fertilization between fora that decide environmental disputes at all levels.

As will be seen, no unified approach towards scientific arguments manifests itself in the fragmented international adjudicatory landscape. In fact, two opposite trends can be discerned from the judicial tools applied along the four relevant stages of adjudication. On the one hand, certain practices impede or even preclude the intrusion of science into adjudicatory assessment and thereby downplay the role of science in judicial inquiry. On the other hand, other tools aim to incorporate and accommodate science in adjudicatory analysis. The forthcoming analysis will provide a typology of judicial techniques that serve one of these opposite trends of interacting with science in the courtroom.

Finally, even though the study is dedicated to a specific aspect of international adjudication, that is, techniques of judicial engagement of science, it seeks to avoid the proverbial trap of conveying only a specialist's narrative, which is famous for knowing 'more and more about less and less'.[37] To that end, the book will address

---

[35]   I. Plakokefalos, 'Causation in the law of state responsibility and the problem of overdetermination: in search of clarity' (2015) 26 *European Journal of International Law* 471–92.

[36]   L. Gruszczynski and W. Werner (eds.), *Deference in International Courts and Tribunals: Standard of Review and Margin of Appreciation* (Oxford University Press, 2014); L. Gruszczynski, 'Standard of review and scientific evidence in WTO law and international investment arbitration' in L. Gruszczynski and W. Werner (eds.), *Deference in International Courts and Tribunals: Standard of Review and Margin of Appreciation* (Oxford University Press, 2014), pp. 153–73; M. Ioannidis, 'Beyond the standard of review: deference criteria in WTO law and the case for a procedural approach' in L. Gruszczynski and W. Werner (eds.), *Deference in International Courts and Tribunals: Standard of Review and Margin of Appreciation* (Oxford University Press, 2014), pp. 91–112.

[37]   The adage ('A specialist is a man who knows more and more about less and less') is generally attributed to William J. Mayo, quoted in *Reader's Digest*, November 1927 as cited by J. Pauwelyn, 'The WTO 20 years on: "global governance by judiciary" or, rather, member-driven settlement of

broader implications of adjudicatory engagement with science, most notably, how to craft persuasive and legitimate judicial reasoning in complex science-based matters and what are the desirable forms and limits of a more direct judicial engagement with science. These issues shall also be informative and relevant for contexts outside the narrower field of international environmental disputes, such as domestic environmental adjudication or science-intensive litigation in other branches of international law.

IV SCIENCE AND THE LEGITIMACY OF JUDICIAL REASONING: THE FOCUS

Scientific authority can lend significant epistemic support for judicial findings. An eminent example, predating most of modern environmental disputes, is the landmark *Brown* v. *Board of Education* decision of the US Supreme Court, which in its famous footnote eleven cited several psychology studies to debunk the entrenched and highly politicized view that the segregated school system provided 'separate but equal' education opportunities for African Americans.[38] Transforming scientific knowledge into legal authority is, however, not always smooth nor automatic. Most of the conundrums occur when scientific research is nascent in the respective field, or relevant studies cannot be produced during the short timeframe of court proceedings, when litigants challenge the merits of party-submitted scientific evidence, or relevant expert input remains inherently ambiguous and volatile. Sometimes it is the judicial conduct that disrupts drawing on the epistemic authority of science. This is typically the case when judges circumvent scientific issues, disregard expert input, and provide only opaque or lousy evidentiary assessments. What clearly emerges from the review of case law is that judges' attitude is decisive for the extent to which science can assist in judicial decision-making.

The ultimate goal of conducting a comparative analysis into the various judicial engagement practices is to identify different reasoning techniques with which judges can adequately reflect on and account for the scientific aspects of disputes in their appraisal. It will be posited that the ways of engaging with science in the adjudicatory reasoning has direct bearing on the legitimacy of the decision reached. Thus far, the legitimacy of judicial reasoning was mostly theorized and assessed in light of how adjudicators apply and interpret the *law*.[39] Yet this inquiry seeks to uncover an under-theorized aspect of legitimacy, namely, how the presence of cognitively authoritative *scientific facts* affects the modalities of crafting a persuasive judicial reasoning. Do epistemically authoritative scientific arguments in a legal dispute

---

(some) trade disputes between (some) WTO members?' (2017) 27 *European Journal of International Law* 1119–26 at 1122.

[38] *Brown* v. *Board of Education of Topeka*, 347 U.S. 483 (1954).

[39] N. Grossman, 'Solomonic judgments and the legitimacy of the International Court of Justice' in N. Grossman, H. G. Cohen, A. Føllesdal, and G. Ulfstein (eds.), *Legitimacy and International Courts* (Cambridge University Press, 2018), pp. 43–61 p. 61.

undermine crafting convincing legalistic justifications? Or are they an asset, or even a necessary element in deciding disputes authoritatively? Is scientific legitimacy a prerequisite to legal legitimacy? Or legal legitimacy can be constructed irrespective of scientific knowledge? To what extent could or should legal adjudicators engage with the underlying science in their reasoning? And if so, what are the available reasoning techniques to do so in a legitimate way? This study is dedicated to providing some answers to these legitimacy queries with regard to international adjudicatory reasoning in science-heavy cases. The detailed analysis in this respect will be set forth in Part III.

This study seeks to contribute to the recently expanding scholarly discussion on the legitimacy of international adjudication by identifying the modalities of crafting persuasive and legitimate judicial reasoning in science-intensive cases. An increasing number of scholarly contributions analyse the legitimacy of a given international adjudicative body or that of international courts in general,[40] the legitimacy of international environmental governance,[41] international environmental adjudication,[42] or that of international environmental law.[43] However, none of these has interrogated specifically and comprehensively how the presence of science, as a source of extra-legal cognitive authority, may impact the legitimacy of adjudicatory reasoning in the environmental practice of major international fora.

The legitimacy of adjudicatory decisions will be perceived as a product of proper argumentation, and therefore, this survey will focus on different types of reasoning techniques with which adjudicators can justify their choices in science-intensive cases. The central yardstick in this respect is not that using *more* science would necessarily result in better-reasoned judgments. Rather, the legitimacy of science-intensive judgments hinges, in view of this study, on *how* adjudicators reflect on the scientific aspects of disputes in their reasoning. The book identifies four types of benchmarks that international fora use in their reasoning to justify the acceptance or rejection of a particular scientific claim. It differentiates between legal, scientific,

---

[40] N. Grossman, H. G. Cohen, A. Føllesdal, and G. Ulfstein (eds.), *Legitimacy and International Courts* (Cambridge University Press, 2018); N. Grossman, 'Legitimacy and international adjudicative bodies' (2009) 41 *George Washington International Law Review* 107–80; A. von Bogdandy and I. Venzke (eds.), *In Whose Name? A Public Law Theory of International Adjudication* (Oxford University Press, 2014); K. J. Alter, L. R. Helfer, and M. R. Madsen (eds.), *International Courts Authority* (Oxford University Press, 2018).

[41] V. Galaz et al., 'Global governance dimensions of globally networked risks: the state of the art in social science research' (2017) 8 *Risk, Hazards & Crisis in Public Policy* 4–27 at 18–20; E. Hey, 'International institutions and global environmental governance' (2006) 100 *American Society of International Law Proceedings* 303–16.

[42] C. Voigt (ed.), *International Judicial Practice on the Environment: Questions of Legitimacy* (Cambridge University Press, 2019).

[43] J. Brunnée and S. J. Toope, *Legitimacy and Legality in International Law* (Cambridge University Press, 2010), pp. 126–219; D. Bodansky, 'The legitimacy of international governance: a coming challenge for international environmental law?' (1999) 93 *American Journal of International Law* 596.

hybrid, and intuitive benchmarks, and discusses the benefits and trade-offs each of these argumentative techniques entail in terms of factual accuracy, epistemic non-arbitrariness, practical feasibility, and preserving the judicial monopoly over adjudicatory function. It also offers solutions for remedying applicable shortcomings of each reasoning style.

A key proposition of this study will argue that notwithstanding the manifold challenge judicial engagement with science entails, science can also be an important ally for adjudicators. If treated properly, science can support the persuasiveness and legitimacy of adjudicatory decisions. Yet if apparent scientific dimensions are marginalized or omitted from the judicial assessment, the presence of cognitively authoritative scientific arguments would hinder the persuasiveness of adjudicatory reasoning. Proper scientific engagement is especially consequential in times of increasing competition between jurisdictions, and rising suspicion and backlash against globalized institutions. Well-reasoned engagement with science, in turn, would ultimately support the legitimacy of adjudicatory fora, which are facing heightened scrutiny and expectations for impartial and unbiased treatment of cases.

The above points to the ultimate questions that need to be addressed in this inquiry, namely, how exactly is a court of law supposed to answer a legal question put before it once that question tends to be inextricably linked to, and even stemming from, uncertain scientific facts? How can adjudicators best comply with the simple-sounding task of deciding whether a breach has taken place, while they also observe epistemic non-arbitrariness and preserve the judicial control over scientific expertise, thereby securing persuasiveness and legitimacy for their decisions? The ensuing chapters seek answers to these queries by mapping the argumentative space of international judges, which yields a convincing and legitimate decision that also respects the cognitive authority of science.

V INTERNATIONAL ENVIRONMENTAL ADJUDICATION: THE SCOPE OF THIS STUDY

The presence of scientific evidence and arguments is of course not confined to environmental disputes but occurs in various legal contexts ranging from intellectual property law to criminal law. This study will only focus on disputes entertaining an environmental component, broadly understood. Narrowing down the scope of inquiry is justified on both practical and theoretical grounds. As to practical reasons, the recent proliferation of adjudicative bodies dealing with international environmental disputes coupled with a corresponding surge in the number of such cases renders any in-depth comparative case law analysis to be of considerable length even with such a confined scope. From a doctrinal point of view, environmental disputes arguably form a distinct category of international cases due to the peculiar normative principles and distinctive competing interests they feature. All these reasons justify examining scientific engagement of judges with respect to decisions that are as homogenous as possible as to their relevant factual and normative background.

Various definitions have been proposed for the term 'international environmental disputes' with differing scope.[44] This study builds on a rather broad definition encompassing all international 'disputes with environmental components'.[45] Importantly, 'environmental disputes' in such a broad sense cannot be equated with cases entertaining 'purely' environmental claims, since environmental questions never appear in isolation from other substantive questions of law in a dispute.[46]

By now a wide array of international adjudicatory bodies confront science-based environmental claims in various contexts. As environmental considerations have markedly permeated into other branches of international law, such as regimes of trade and investment law, human rights law, as well as maritime law, specialized judicial bodies of these fields have been used as 'borrowed fora'[47] for hearing environmental claims. This seems to further undermine efforts of gathering momentum[48] for the establishment of a specialized international environmental court, which has been proposed by scholars, but was ultimately abandoned largely due to the lack of sufficient support from states.[49]

As a result, a comprehensive analysis on the judicial techniques of scientific engagement in environmental disputes shall embrace several international courts and tribunals. The scope of this study accordingly extends to decisions of the International Court of Justice, inter-state and investment arbitration tribunals, regional human rights courts, the World Trade Organization's dispute settlement mechanism, and the case law of the International Tribunal for the Law of the Sea. From the respective jurisprudence, those disputes will be subject to scrutiny, where scientific arguments played, or could have played, a role in the litigation. The EU judiciary, although it has an impressive environmental case law, is not included in

---

[44]   Stephens proposes to define the concept as 'any legal or factual disagreement between states which involves one or more questions of environmental protection or natural resource use or management'. T. Stephens, 'International environmental dispute settlement' in J. E. Viñuales (ed.), *The Rio Declaration on Environment and Development: A Commentary* (Oxford University Press, 2015), pp. 604–5; Cesare offers the following definition: 'A conflict of views or of interests between two or more states, taking the form of specific opposing claims and relating to an anthropogenic alteration of an ecosystem, having detrimental effect on human society and leading to environmental scarcity of natural resources.' Cesare P. R. Romano, *The Peaceful Settlement of International Environmental Disputes A Pragmatic Approach* (Kluwer Law International, 2000), p. 29.

[45]   Pierre-Marie Dupuy and Jorge E. Viñuales point out that instead of 'environmental disputes' the more exact definition would be 'disputes with environmental components'. P.-M. Dupuy and J. E. Viñuales, *International Environmental Law* (Cambridge University Press, 2018), p. 247.

[46]   P. Sands, *Litigating Environmental Disputes: Courts, Tribunals and the Progressive Development of International Environmental Law* (OECD Global Forum on International Investment, 2008), p. 4.

[47]   Dupuy and Viñuales, *International Environmental Law*, p. 247.

[48]   S. Bruce, 'The project for an international environmental court' in C. Tomuschat, R. P. Mazzeschi, and D. Thürer (eds.), *Conciliation in International Law* (Brill, 2017), pp. 133–70.

[49]   P. Sands, 'International environmental litigation and its future' (1998) 32 *University of Richmond Law Review* 1619 at 1639.

the scope of this analysis. European Union courts are of a *sui generis* nature, as they are situated between the domestic and the international legal order with regard to their main functions. Moreover, the underlying body of normative rules, that is, the environmental law of the European Union, features idiosyncratic rules and principles, which provide an elaborate normative basis for adjudication. For all these reasons, including these courts among the relevant fora would have likely strained the present comparative framework.

To delineate the scope of this analysis we ought to further distinguish legal adjudication from various non-legal dispute settlement mechanisms. Decisions resulting from diplomatic means of dispute settlement,[50] and various non-compliance procedures[51] will not be included in the assessment. Adjudication in the context of the study stands for the legal proceedings of international courts and tribunals aiming to decide environmental disputes with a binding decision. Therefore, non-binding recommendations of non-judicial organs, such as the World Bank Inspection Panel or the World Heritage Committee, are excluded from the scope of this research.

Finally, this book will not address decisions that were handed down by domestic courts on the basis of international environmental conventions, such as judgments arising from the application of the Convention on Supplementary Compensation for Nuclear Damage and the International Oil Pollution Compensation Fund.[52] Furthermore, as this research zeroes in on judicial reasoning, those international environmental disputes will not be subject to further study that were settled out-of-court with an *ex gratia* payment, such as the arbitration following the incident of the Cosmos 958[53] or the *Gut Dam* case.[54]

VI STRUCTURE OF THE BOOK

This inquiry is structured into three main parts. Part I sets out the analytic framework of the comparative case law analysis and sheds light on the wider context of judicial

[50] T. Stephens, 'The settlement of disputes in international environmental law' in S. Alam, M. J. H. Bhuiyan, T. Chowdhury, and E. Techera (eds.), *Routledge Handbook of International Environmental Law* (Routledge, 2012), pp. 175–87 pp. 181–2.

[51] See for example T. Treves, 'The settlement of disputes and non-compliance procedures' in T. Treves, L. Pineschi, A. Tanzi, C. Pitea, and F. R. Jacur (eds.), *Non-Compliance Procedures and Mechanisms and the Effectiveness of International Environmental Agreements* (T. M. C. Asser Press, 2009), pp. 499–518.

[52] Further examples for such multilateral liability regimes are the 1992 Convention for Oil Pollution Damage and the 1992 International Convention for the Establishment of an International Fund for Compensation for Oil Pollution Damage. For a detailed discussion of related decisions of national courts see M. Fitzmaurice, 'Principle 13 liability and compensation' in J. E. Viñuales (ed.), *The Rio Development on Environment and Development* (Oxford University Press, 2015), pp. 351–81 pp. 362–6.

[53] For more details on the settlement of the Cosmos 958 incident see E. Louka, *International Environmental Law Fairness, Effectiveness, and World Order* (Cambridge University Press, 2006), p. 476.

[54] The case was settled between the United States and Canada, see R. Lefeber, *Transboundary Environmental Interference and the Origin of State Liability* (Kluwer Law International, 1996), pp. 90–1.

engagement with science in the practice of international courts and tribunals. Chapter 1 serves as introduction by laying out the context, the framework, the scope, and the focus of the comparative analysis. Chapter 2 lays out in detail the analytic framework of the study and addresses the three-fold challenge judges face in using scientific input and arguments in an adjudicatory setting.

Part II puts forth a detailed substantive analysis of the scientific engagement techniques of seven major international jurisdictions. Chapters 3–8 therefore detail how science takes on a particular significance in the practice of each relevant fora and how respective international adjudicators engage with the scientific arguments raised along the four stages of the adjudicative process. The environmental case law of the International Court of Justice (Chapter 3) and the case-practice of inter-state environmental arbitration (Chapter 4) will be analysed first. This will be followed by an analysis of the practice of regional human rights courts (Chapter 5), the World Trade Organization dispute settlement mechanism (Chapter 6), the awards rendered in investor-state dispute settlement proceedings (Chapter 7), and the decisions of the International Tribunal for the Law of the Sea (Chapter 8).

Part III comparatively assesses the techniques of judicial engagement as identified in the previous part and strives to provide a fine-grained narrative and understanding of the many ways in which science impacts and interacts with the adjudicatory process and, more particularly, with judicial reasoning. Chapter 9 first describes parallel trends of incorporating and downplaying the scientific dimensions of disputes in current international environmental adjudicatory practice. Specific argumentative techniques will be identified with which adjudicators seek to reflect on the scientific dimensions of disputes. Chapter 10 provides a typology of the different reasoning techniques with a focus on the interrelations between the presence of cognitively authoritative scientific knowledge and the legitimacy of adjudicatory reasoning. It then addresses applicable benefits and shortcomings of each reasoning style and identifies judicial good practices of crafting convincing and epistemically legitimate reasoning to justify judicial choices between competing science-based arguments. Chapter 11 offers some concluding remarks.

2

The Rules of Judicial Engagement with Science: A Three-Fold Challenge

Troposphere, whatever. I told you before I'm not a scientist. That's why I don't want to deal with global warming, to tell you the truth.

Justice Antonin Scalia[1]

To shed light on the context of using science in environmental adjudication this study sets off by enumerating the challenges of using scientific input in a legal setting from a theoretical point of view. Understanding the cartography of relevant forces that are at play in channelling scientific expertise into legal decision-making helps explain the reasons for the many difficulties, one may even say deficiencies, of science-intensive environmental adjudication. This chapter will then introduce the analytic framework of the book, which is designed to evaluate and comparatively assess the varied judicial reactions given to the intrusion of science into the adjudicatory process. Finally, it will reveal a fundamental relationship between the inevitable presence of science in environmental disputes and the persuasiveness and legitimacy of adjudicatory reasoning in such cases – the main concern of this study.

The title of this chapter refers to 'Rules of Engagement' with science with a slightly provocative undertone. This term is understood here as referring to a set of rules governing proper interaction between scientific and legal authority in the adjudicatory process. Despite possible connotations of this concept in other legal contexts, the relationship between science and law is, emphatically, by no means inimical. Rather, the term engagement presupposes their cooperative alliance. Indeed, the active partnership of the two sides is inevitable in science-intensive litigation. The success of law's engagement with science in the courtroom is predicated upon the ability of the two disciplines to develop a clear understanding of what can be reasonably expected from the scientific and the legal sides and what roles each of them ought to fulfil. Forging such an interdisciplinary co-operation meets with inherent challenges, which will be the focus of the ensuing analysis.

---

[1] *Massachusetts v. Environmental Protection Agency*, US Supreme Court, 2 April 2007, 549 US 497 (2007), transcript of oral hearing.

The scope of this comparative study extends to environmental cases, which are defined here in a broad sense, including all legal disputes featuring environmental components.[2] International environmental disputes are brought before a growing array of international fora that hear science-based environmental claims in various legal contexts. The following remarks seek to capture the shared challenges these fora face when appraising science-intensive claims of litigants in international environmental disputes.

I THE THREE-FOLD CHALLENGE OF USING SCIENCE IN AN ADJUDICATORY SETTING

Scientific disputes virtually always feature legal claims supported by scientific arguments and legal texts that incorporate technical notions. The interpretation of these is an intricate judicial task owing to the close interconnection and inextricable linkage of law and facts in such disputes. This peculiar construction of science-intensive cases necessarily entails that rendering judicial judgment becomes an interdisciplinary exercise. As will be argued here, this feature is more than a high-sounding but empty label. Interdisciplinarity has deep implications for the way in which judges ought to investigate scientific claims in their inquiry and reflect on scientific insights in their reasoning.

The term interdisciplinarity stands for integrating information, techniques, perspectives, and concepts from two or more specialized fields of knowledge in order to solve problems whose solutions are beyond the scope of a single discipline.[3] Adjudicating science-intensive claims falls under this definition, as answering the questions put before judges warrants both legal and scientific expertise. What is significant risk of environmental harm? What does ecological necessity mean? What is the cause of an injury? To answer these legally relevant questions, judges must rely on expertise, and have to co-operate with scientists in the courtroom to uncover the factual bases of these queries. And herein lies the crux of the problem. Judges must maintain an appropriate balance in their interdisciplinary co-operation, as they alone are vested with the power and responsibility to act as the *final* arbiter of disputes and, hence, they cannot be spirited by cross-disciplinary epistemic partnership and blindly rely on what they receive from scientific experts.

Flowing from the interdisciplinary nature of their task, adjudicators are faced with idiosyncratic challenges in scientific disputes, which shape their attitude towards interacting with science during the adjudicative process. It is argued here that interdisciplinarity in the courtroom entails three types of interconnected, though analytically distinct, challenges. On the one hand, epistemic challenge arises owing to the extra-legal cognitive authority of science, which may be in conflict with legal

---

[2] Dupuy and Viñuales, *International Environmental Law*, p. 300.

[3] For a similar definition of interdisciplinary research see Institute of Medicine, *Facilitating Interdisciplinary Research* (The National Academies Press, 2005), p. 26.

logic and rationality. On the other hand, there is a doctrinal challenge flowing from the fact that science and law use different concepts of reliable evidence, causation, and they have different levels of tolerance towards uncertainty. Finally, a peculiar set of legitimacy challenges flows from the delicate task of allocating competences between judges and experts in the adjudicatory process. Should adjudicators be willing to rely on expert evidence they may inadvertently delegate their judicial function to non-elected experts. Whereas if they choose to assess a science-intensive claim irrespective of expert input, they run the risk of making epistemically arbitrary judgments, which undermines the legitimacy of their reasoning. We shall now turn to discuss these difficulties in more detail.

1 *Epistemic Challenge: Clash of Cognitive Authorities*

Science and law have both emerged as two disciplines that are capable of lending cognitive (epistemic) authority to knowledge claims.[4] They are both means of inquiry seeking to understand different aspects of the same reality. Science produces knowledge claims just as do other social practices. This is particularly salient when science enters the adversarial process of legal dispute resolution. In such cases, a struggle follows suit over the power to draw the boundary between science and non-science. The stakes are particularly high as the party who can successfully appeal in its argument to science would also be able to harness the cultural authority attached to it.[5]

When these two major branches of human inquiry get entangled with each other in the context of adjudication, numerous epistemic complexities arise. Epistemology, also known as the theory of knowledge, studies the ways and means of human understanding and inquiry; and is particularly concerned with identifying the conditions of forming knowledge and justified beliefs. Epistemic intricacies have a major impact on the ways in which adjudicators are willing and able to engage with scientific input. Hence, any detailed examination of the latter requires a brief overview of the epistemic difficulties inherent in using science in a legal setting.

First, truth claimed by science can sometimes be in conflict with that of law. Suffice it to refer to mainstream scientific[6] and politico-legal[7] discourse on climate change, which run in diametrically opposite directions in certain cultures. In an adjudicatory context, such conflicts ought to be resolved by judges, who may lack requisite knowledge and training (i.e. epistemic competence) to adjudge the validity

[4] D. L. Faigman, 'Where law and science (and religion) meet' (2014) 93 *Texas Law Review* 1659 at 1659.
[5] T. Gieryn, 'Boundaries of science' in S. Jasanoff, G. E. Markle, and T. Pinch (eds.), *Handbook of Science and Technology Studies* (Sage, 1995), pp. 393–443, p. 437.
[6] International Panel on Climate Change, *Fifth Assessment Report* (2014).
[7] Oliver Milman, 'US federal department is censoring use of term "climate change", emails reveal' (7 August 2017) *Guardian*, available at https://bit.ly/3dp3rLj (last accessed 6 January 2020).

of knowledge claims of the scientific realm. This generates considerable tensions in science-intensive adjudication, where experts produce (scientifically authoritative) scientific input, which needs to be translated into legitimate (thus, legally authoritative) judgments by scientifically non-trained adjudicators.

Second, science and law are also mutually dependent on each other in the courtroom. What will be counted as an acceptable, reliable scientific knowledge claim for purposes of the legal proceedings is co-produced by legal and scientific authority. Whether a certain expert opinion will be rubberstamped by judges, as reliable 'scientific evidence' is a 'product created by both science and law'.[8] This means that whether a given piece of scientific evidence will be accepted as a basis of judicial findings is not a direct consequence of the scientific correctness and soundness of that evidence, but depends just as much on how skilfully advocates present it in the courtroom, and also, what tests adjudicators apply to scrutinize the claim at hand.

The close interaction between law and science is perhaps best illustrated by the process of cross-examination, which serves to 'authenticate' scientific expert opinions for purposes of the adjudicatory inquiry. This can be traced back to law's epistemological model, which seeks to reveal the truth in an adversarial argumentation process.[9] As a result, only those pieces of expert evidence would withstand judicial scrutiny that survive cross-examination. Yet, practitioners' hindsight confirms that the testifying experience of the expert at hand is critical to the success of cross-examination given the 'unforgiving'[10] and high-pressure atmosphere of the questioning process. This entails, in the extreme, that scientifically and legally authoritative claims may oppose each other. To take a few examples, this may happen when unfounded or biased scientific positions are fostered by experienced experts presenting their opinions in a (legally) persuasive way; or vice versa, when the evidence presented by scientists, who are not endowed with good oratory skills to explain their research in an easily understandable way to laymen, would be found unpersuasive and incoherent by the end of cross-examination irrespective of the scientific validity and correctness of the opinion. As is made clear from the foregoing, the privilege of judges to determine 'who is entitled to speak authoritatively'[11] in the courtroom may backfire and seriously undermine the authority of adjudicatory findings if those saliently run against scientific authority.

Third, scientific knowledge claims are hierarchically not subordinate but juxtaposed to those produced by legal logic and rationality. The cognitive authority of science may intimidate adjudicators from touching upon the scientific dimensions of a legal dispute. The fundamental problem with such an overly cautious judicial

---

8   D. Walton and N. Zhang, 'The epistemology of scientific evidence' (2013) 21 *Artificial Intelligence and Law* 173–219 at 182.

9   Walton and Zhang, 'The epistemology of scientific evidence', 182.

10 N. Blackaby and A. Wilbraham, 'Practical issues relating to the use of expert evidence in investment treaty arbitration' (2016) 31 *ICSID Review* 655–69 at 658.

11 A. Briggle and C. Mitcham, *Ethics and Science* (Cambridge University Press, 2012), p. 257.

approach is that scientific and legal concepts are closely intertwined in many key notions of environmental law, such as significant environmental harm or reasonable environmental risks; and the scientific dimensions cannot be analytically dissected from the legally relevant aspects of these concepts. Adjudicators who are intimidated by the cognitive authority of science would then be prevented from discharging the judicial function to decide a science-intensive dispute featuring claims blending science and law together. Yet legal epistemology never requires absolute certainty from judges, therefore, it is perfectly in line with the adjudicatory task to decide cases even if the respective judge only formed a justified belief about the factual bases of the case.[12] Nevertheless, scientific uncertainty seems to occupy a special cachet in the eyes of adjudicators, as it often paralyses their inquiry. Whereas factual uncertainties do not seem to pose an insurmountable obstacle for judges to reach such justified beliefs in other areas of law, where applicable forms of uncertainty are akin to common sense experience, for example, in the case of evidentiary difficulties in many tort situations. Further implications of such intimidating effect of science's authority will be addressed later in this chapter.

Fourth, science as an extra-legal cognitive authority may challenge the discretionary monopoly of judges over resolving the dispute. This leads to dilemmas about the desired division of competence between scientific experts and judges and to corresponding concerns about inadvertent delegation of the judicial function, which will be further elaborated on later in this section. Epistemic dilemmas also arise with respect to setting the appropriate extent of deference with which adjudicators assess highly technical and scientific claims of the parties. These will impact adjudicators' choices as to the standard of review. Divergent standards of review that are applied in international environmental adjudication will be elaborated on later in Section II, Subsection 4.1.

Further to that, in light of the above it comes as no surprise that using scientific arguments in a legal dispute has considerable strategic value for both litigants and adjudicators. The coming chapters will explore the ways in which science plays a strategic role in each of the adjudicative fora examined in this study. Suffice it to note at the outset that parties employ science-based arguments to harness the persuasive force of science in a variety of contexts. Adjudicators may also avail themselves of tactical uses of science. A stark example is offered by the ways in which they select the legally relevant aspects of the dispute that are deemed decisive in rendering their decision. This judicial exercise will be examined among various framing techniques and will be addressed in Section II, Subsection 1 in more detail. On a more abstract level, the subjectivity inherent in drawing the boundaries of legally relevant issues in a dispute leads to competing conceptions of the scope of judicial purview. As a corollary of such demarcation, framing separates 'scientific'

---

[12]   D. Dwyer, *The Judicial Assessment of Expert Evidence* (Cambridge University Press, 2008), p. 70; A. Legg, *The Margin of Appreciation in International Human Rights Law* (Oxford University Press, 2012), p. 146.

questions that are reserved for experts from legal ones that can only be assessed by adjudicators. This brings us to a discussion on the extent of judicial review and the scope of the adjudicatory task. A general overview of these issues is provided later in this chapter under Section II, Subsection 4.2.

To better understand the forces shaping the relationship between science and society it is essential to emphasize the culturally and historically situated nature of scientists and scientific authority. A most tangible proof of the socially embedded nature of science is provided by the history of natural sciences. The Middle Ages often saw natural scientists as heretic, whereas during the Enlightenment, science was, on the other extreme, regarded as the promised land of gaining certain knowledge about the world. Disappointment over such false hopes has been coupled in the twentieth century with distrust stemming from the destructive and horrifying applications of techno-scientific knowledge in times of war. The extreme complexity of scientific knowledge has led at the beginning of the new millennium to a post-truth era, when science and scientists are regarded by many as weak and irrelevant actors, or even worse, as agents of manipulation. All of this gains relevance for the present purposes inasmuch as the expectations of judges towards scientific experts are inevitably informed by the wider cultural and social context of adjudication.

Insights from the philosophy of science also reveal the social conditions of producing scientific knowledge. These accounts focus on mundane influences, which scientists are exposed to ranging from political pressure through expert bias to power relations embedded in peer-review processes and even to intentional fraud of forging appealing results. A more subtle symptom of the social aspect of scientific knowledge production manifests in the existence of epistemic communities,[13] that is, scientists working in policy relevant fields who may hold shared beliefs and values about the desirability of certain normative decisions, which underlie and may influence their analytic reasoning.[14] The presence of expert communities is particularly salient in environmental lawmaking, where their influence on regulatory and administrative processes has already been subject to commentary in international law.[15]

Any impartial inquiry into the interrelations of science and law cannot deny that science, as all other forms of human enterprise, is fallible and occasionally may even be biased. Ample critical analyses point to examples where science and technology function as a tool of power politics and domination or serve political agendas or industrial vested interests.[16] Scholars of STS also warn that such 'politicized' use of

---

[13]   P. M. Haas, 'Epistemic communities' in J. Krieger (ed.), *The Oxford Companion to International Relations* (Oxford University Press, 2013), pp. 351–9.

[14]   P. M. Haas, 'Ideas, experts and governance' in M. Ambrus, K. Arts, E. Hey, and H. Raulus (eds.), *The Role of Experts in International and European Decision-Making Processes* (Cambridge University Press, 2014), pp. 19–43, pp. 29–32.

[15]   Peel, *Science and Risk Regulation in International Law*, pp. 76–9.

[16]   W. G. Werner, 'The politics of expertise': applying paradoxes of scientific expertise to international law' in M. Ambrus, K. Arts, E. Hey, and H. Raulus (eds.), *The Role of 'Experts' in International and*

science is an inherent corollary of science's cognitive authority. The famous words of Bruno Latour – 'give me a laboratory, and I will raise the world'[17] – allude to a host of social practices with which scientists may successfully claim monopoly over the creation of scientific, and therefore true, facts, while being insulated from critiques of the lay public in their laboratory, which functions not only as a physical work-place, but also as a cultural place, where authoritative knowledge claims are produced via methods not intelligible for the public. This may seed distrust in scientifically lay judges towards scientific claims. Yet, as will be argued in this book, such distrust does not justify the downplaying of science in adjudication neither from a theoretical nor a practical point of view.

There are further myths that need to be debunked if one would like to clarify what science can, and cannot, deliver to adjudication. Critical STS studies[18] point out that science can in no way be seen as the realm of 'pure' knowledge claims. The scientific process is in fact value-laden just as are scientists, who hold personal values and beliefs. Nevertheless, acknowledging that science and researchers are not value-neutral ought not to be fatal to the trustworthiness of science. The process of scientific research remains essentially consensual, where exactly the diversity of views and beliefs held by experts promotes uncovering social prejudice, and there-fore is key to foster a working culture that minimizes biased results.[19] Critical accounts also uncover the culturally embedded nature of objectivity – a label that is often attributed to natural sciences as a distinguishing feature separating science from other practices of inquiry. Hence, objectivity should be seen as a socially constructed and context-dependent attribute of science.[20] Moreover, there are many other social practices engaged in empirical inquiry besides science, such as history or investigative journalism, as they all make 'informed conjectures about the possible explanation of the phenomena that concern them'.[21] Viewing from this

European Decision-Making Processes (Cambridge University Press, 2014), pp. 44–62 p. 51; Haas, 'Ideas, experts and governance'.

[17] B. Latour, 'Give me a laboratory and I will raise the world' in K. Knorr-Cetina and M. Mulkay (eds.), *Science Observed: Perspectives on the Social Study of Science* (Sage, 1983), pp. 141–70.

[18] K. Popper, *The Logic of Scientific Discovery* (Routledge, 2005); R. K. Merton, 'The normative structure of science' in N. W. Storer (ed.), *The Sociology of Science* (University of Chicago Press, 1973), pp. 267–78; T. Gieryn, 'Boundaries of science'; T. Kuhn, *The Structure of Scientific Revolutions* (University of Chicago Press, 1962, 1970 ed.); A. Irwin, 'STS perspectives on scientific governance' in E. J. Hackett, O. Amsterdamska, M. Lynch, and J. Wajcman (eds.), *The Handbook of Science and Technology Studies* (MIT Press, 2008), pp. 583–607; S. Jasanoff, 'Genealogies of STS' (2012), 42 *Social Studies of Science* 435–41; Jasanoff, 'In a constitutional moment: science and social order at the millennium'; S. Jasanoff, *Science and Public Reason* (Routledge-Earthscan, 2012); S. Jasanoff, *Science at the Bar* (Harvard University Press, 1995); Jasanoff, *The Fifth Branch*; S. Jasanoff, 'The practices of objectivity in regulatory science' in C. Camic, N. Gross, and M. Lamont (eds.), *Social Knowledge in the Making* (University of Chicago Press, 2011), pp. 307–38; Jasanoff, 'Serviceable truths'; Faigman, 'Where law and science (and religion) meet'.

[19] N. Oreskes, *Why Trust Science?* (Princeton University Press, 2019), pp. 136–8.

[20] Jasanoff, 'The practices of objectivity in regulatory science'.

[21] Haack, *Defending Science within Reason: Between Scientism and Cynicism*, p. 97.

perspectives, it becomes apparent that the core standards of good and trustworthy evidence are not inherent in the scientific enterprise.[22] It follows that merely using the label scientific in the context of a piece of evidence as a synonym for being reliable, or legitimate in an adjudicatory context, would be a sign of misconceived respect for natural sciences. Yet again, accepting these premises does not equal to denying existing differences between objective knowledge claims and subjective beliefs. It only entails that the real question concerns who is entitled to set the standards of science and based on what considerations. Similarly, accounts from the philosophy of science do not render superfluous the legitimate efforts to identify and single out spurious claims of pseudo-sciences.

Overall, emphasizing the social character of scientific research in this book intends only to dissolve widely held false beliefs picturing scientists making pure, objective, and therefore true scientific knowledge in their isolated ivory tower in an atmosphere of disinterestedness. Challenging this pedestal on which natural science has often been put may encourage a closer judicial engagement and interaction with the underlying scientific facts. Importantly, however, such involvement is only desirable to the extent that it does not lead to replacing scientific knowledge with common-sense rationality or epistemically arbitrary choices. Emphatically, revealing the social character of scientific knowledge production does not in any way justify carving out scientific aspects of disputes from the judicial inquiry. Neither does it legitimate neglecting expert advice. Despite all the imperfections and pitfalls of scientific research, science undoubtedly remains one of the most (if not *the* most) successful human endeavours aiming to understand the world. It has produced a vast amount of empirically true results, which proved to be fundamentally beneficial to humanity. Hence, marginalizing science in adjudication would not only be inappropriate from an empirical point of view, but would also seriously undermine the persuasive force of respective judicial decisions. Amid rapid development of science and in times when technology becomes embedded in everyday life to an unprecedented extent, establishing appropriate methods of handling and reflecting on scientific input seems to be a prerequisite to render persuasive judgments.

For all these reasons, insights from the philosophy of science will be informative for this inquiry inasmuch as they reveal the reasons why harnessing the cognitive authority of science is so essential not only for litigants but also for adjudicators in crafting their judicial reasoning. Further to that, STS accounts analytically explain the motivations behind frequent efforts challenging scientific integrity in a litigious context. Lastly, they help better understand the causes of the apparent difficulties of science-intensive adjudication and, therefore, may guide us to offer solutions for better incorporating science in the adjudicatory process.

---

[22] Haack, *Defending Science within Reason: Between Scientism and Cynicism*, p. 23.

2 Doctrinal Challenges: Structural Differences between Law and Natural Sciences

Ideally, judges should be able to retain control over incorporating scientific knowledge in legal decision-making processes, in other words, over the translation of scientific facts into legal determinations. For fulfilling this mandate adjudicators ought to be better acquainted with the basic characteristics and specificities of the scientific 'language'. This section will therefore address the perplexing differences in the vocabulary of law and natural sciences, which give rise to what is termed here doctrinal challenges.

Truism holds that 'law and science speak two different languages',[23] and indeed, a closer examination reveals several structural differences between their fundamental concepts and ways of reasoning. These divergences pose doctrinal difficulties for evaluating scientific facts in a legal setting; specifically, for integrating scientific facts into causal inquiry and into evidentiary assessments, and for crafting legal justification for accepting or rejecting a certain scientific claim during judicial review.

Arguably, many deficiencies of science-intensive adjudication stem from the ignorance of how science works.[24] Against this backdrop, a central proposition of this study holds that better understanding the inherent characteristics of science and scientific inquiry would facilitate a more in-depth and meaningful judicial engagement with scientific input by revealing what it is that science can actually deliver to adjudicators. In this vein, the following section explores these fundamental differences between law and natural sciences. Namely, the difference in the way law and science conceive fundamental rules governing their inquiry (i.e., their 'laws'), in how they treat concepts of 'cause' and 'causation', their different approaches to what constitutes valid evidence, the divergent modes of their persuasion, and their different levels of tolerance towards uncertainty.

2.1 'Laws of Nature' vs. 'Laws of Culture'

The most salient difference perhaps between the legal and the scientific realm concerns the character of their 'laws'. On a certain level of generality laws of natural sciences appear to be descriptive, while 'man-made' laws pursue prescriptive functions. Readers will be familiar with Kepler's laws of planetary motion, or Newton's laws on motion, and will be aware of the fact that these do not operate as normative rules. While scientific laws describe how the world works, legal rules are

---

[23]   E. Vos, 'The European Court of Justice in the face of scientific uncertainty and complexity' in M. Dawson, B. De Witte, and E. Muir (eds.), *Judicial Activism at the European Court of Justice* (Edward Elgar, 2013), pp. 142–66.

[24]   Harker makes the argument that 'when it comes to drawing conclusions about the state of a particular scientific issue, many of our most common mistakes stem from ignorance of how science works rather than ignorance of the science itself'. See Harker, *Creating Scientific Controversies*, p. 10.

preoccupied with how the world ought to be ordered.[25] A related difference concerns the role of exemptions in the structure of respective laws. While exceptions from a general rule are commonplace among legal laws and do not touch upon their validity, exceptions are alien to laws of science and would invalidate the given law.

Yet contrasting science and law as purely normative versus purely descriptive realms is vulnerable to analytical challenges. There exist some commonalities between 'laws of nature' (i.e. scientific laws) and 'laws of culture' (i.e. legal laws) that should be borne in mind. Importantly, they are both results of social practices inasmuch as scientific laws are also produced by social communities. Scientific laws have to be agreed on by the relevant scientific community and be canonized in light of the prevailing paradigm.[26] To put it differently, scientific laws ultimately also gain their validity from the scientific community, just as norms of law are produced through legislative processes, according to a set of mutually agreed rules of the legislature.

2.2 Causes and Causal Inference

Law and science use different conceptions of cause and causation. Causes of legal relevance are of narrower scope than naturally occurring factors (natural causes) leading to the same outcome. Although there is a virtually infinite number of naturally occurring factors, not all of them are equally relevant for the purposes of law.[27] Reflecting these qualitative differences in approach to causal arguments, H. L. A. Hart and Tony Honoré distinguish between causally relevant factors ('causes') and 'mere conditions'.[28] Those factors identified as causal have legal relevance, while mere conditions do not form part of legal inquiry. Accordingly, typical causal questions in law interrogate whether a specific harm was caused by a certain human conduct or omission.[29]

Legal regimes, therefore, adopt certain tests to establish the causes they regard as legally appreciable among the various conditions of an outcome.[30] Common-law tort law developed an especially sophisticated theory of causation, which also inspired the causal inquiry of international courts and tribunals. In tort law, a conduct is a factual cause of a harm when the harm would not have occurred absent the conduct.[31] This definition allows that there can be several factual causes of an outcome; as long as a conduct is necessary for the outcome, it is regarded as

---

[25] Faigman, 'Where law and science (and religion) meet', 1661.
[26] Jasanoff, 'Serviceable truths', 1725.
[27] Examples from everyday experiences are weather conditions 'causing' slippery road before a car accident, or an enduring drought that 'generates' dry leaves feeding a bush fire illustrates this point.
[28] H. L. A. Hart and T. Honoré, *Causation in the Law*, 2nd ed. (Oxford University Press, 1985), p. 113.
[29] Hart and Honoré, *Causation in the Law*, p. 84.
[30] Hart and Honoré, *Causation in the Law*, pp. 112–13.
[31] The American Law Institute, *Third Restatement of the Law of Torts for Physical and Emotional Harm* (The American Law Institute Publishers, 2010), § 26.

a factual cause (cause-in-fact, or but-for cause).[32] Therefore a particular conduct need only be 'a' cause and not 'the' (*sine qua non*) cause of the harm for qualifying as a factual cause. A causal agent is regarded as a cause-in-fact if, but for its presence, the result would not have occurred or would have occurred later.[33] Other causal agents that complement the necessary causal sets are regarded as background causes.[34]

More complicated causal scenarios also arise. In exceptional cases there are multiple acts, each of which would have been a factual cause of the outcome alone in the absence of the other act. This situation is known in tort law as the multiple sufficient causes scenario,[35] where each of the multiple sufficient causes should be regarded as a cause-in-fact, even though none is by itself a but-for cause of the harm. This scenario is often called causal overdetermination.[36] Multiple sufficient causes are to be distinguished from multiple causes, as the latter simply accounts for a scenario when there are multiple but-for causes of a certain outcome.[37] Multiple sufficient causal sets can also emerge consecutively, in what is called the pre-emptive causes scenario.[38] In that case, the supervening act or omission, the so-called duplicative factor, cannot be regarded a factual cause,[39] as the harm would have occurred anyway. The textbook example of duplicative factors is hitting an already deceased man by car.

The concept of causation in law is different in many respects from the causal concepts used in science.[40] As one commentator has put it, the scientific understanding of causation is 'more complex than the law legitimates'.[41] The but-for test of legal causation favours a mechanistic understanding of causation, which is predicated upon the metaphor of a causal chain consisting of discrete events, where each

---

[32] The American Law Institute, *Third Restatement of the Law of Torts for Physical and Emotional Harm*, §26 Comment b.

[33] Sander Greenland, 'Relation of probability of causation to relative risk and doubling dose: a methodological error that has become a social problem' (1999) 89(8) *American Journal of Public Health* 1166.

[34] The American Law Institute, *Third Restatement of the Law of Torts for Physical and Emotional Harm*, §26 Comment d.

[35] The American Law Institute, *Third Restatement of the Law of Torts for Physical and Emotional Harm*, at §27, §27 Comment a.

[36] S. Steel, *Proof of Causation in Tort Law* (Cambridge University Press, 2015), pp. 18–20; Plakokefalos, 'Causation in the law of state responsibility and the problem of overdetermination'.

[37] The American Law Institute, *Third Restatement of the Law of Torts for Physical and Emotional Harm*, §26 Comment j.

[38] The American Law Institute, *Third Restatement of the Law of Torts for Physical and Emotional Harm*, §26 Comment k.

[39] The American Law Institute, *Third Restatement of the Law of Torts for Physical and Emotional Harm*, §26 Comment k.

[40] T. A. Brennan, 'Causal chains and statistical links: the role of scientific uncertainty in hazardous-substance litigation' (1987) 73 *Cornell Law Review* 469 at 471.

[41] Carl F. Cranor, 'The challenge of developing science for the law of torts' in R. Goldberg (ed.), *Perspectives on Causation* (Hart Publishing, 2011), pp. 261–81, p. 261.

event is dependent upon the previous one.[42] However, in fact, elements of the 'chain' might be independent of the first triggering action and hence, the causal process is better conceived as a 'complex set of conditions'.[43] Consequently, judges often run into difficulties when they try to select a certain event from the hypothetical chain of events to be the cause of the injury. Moreover, lawyers often fall prey to the *post hoc ergo propter hoc* way of reasoning,[44] that is, to causally attribute subsequent effects to prior events in an automatic way.

Finally, law and science differ also in their methods of reasoning. Consistent with their thinking in terms of the metaphor of a causal chain, lawyers tend to apply deductive reasoning.[45] However, this approach in itself creates the illusion of causality, since it is necessarily loaded with causal assumptions.[46] Scientists, in contrast, normally use inductive reasoning,[47] which is built on a series of specific observations and seeks to draw its final conclusion on their basis. The conclusion thus reached in scientific research remains always probabilistic.

2.3 Standard of Required Proof, Acceptance of Probabilistic Evidence

Legal regimes establish a particular standard of proof to determine the required level of proof above which a causal claim is to be accepted as valid and legally appreciable. Tort law systems, for instance, use the preponderance of evidence standard, that is, the balance of probability.[48] By contrast, there is no generally agreed standard for proof of causality in science.[49] The different approaches towards proof of causation might be attributable to the fact that scientists actually 'disprove the null hypothesis',[50] instead of proving their actual hypothesis. A null hypothesis stands for the negation of a hypothesis. If, for instance, a given hypothesis assumes a causal relation between two factors, the null hypothesis would posit that they are in fact random variables. The basis of scientific inquiry is thus the *rejection* of the null hypothesis by collecting statistically significant evidence for that.

The scientific method of inquiry has important ramifications on the way of persuasion in science. In contrast to legal reasoning, which attaches persuasive force to argumentation approaching the 'truth', a scientifically persuasive reasoning

---

[42]   Brennan, 'Causal chains and statistical links', 485–6.
[43]   Hart and Honoré, *Causation in the Law*, p. 72.
[44]   Lecture of Bostjan Zupančič entitled Causation, the English language transcript of which has been provided to the author by courtesy of Judge Zupančič.
[45]   Brennan, 'Causal chains and statistical links', 482.
[46]   Brennan, 'Causal chains and statistical links', 482.
[47]   Brennan, 'Causal chains and statistical links', 481, 490.
[48]   Steel, *Proof of Causation in Tort Law*, p. 50.
[49]   P. Feldschreiber, L.-A. Mulcahy, and S. Day, 'Biostatistics and causation in medicinal product liability suits' in R. Goldberg (ed.), *Perspectives on Causation* (Hart Publishing, 2011), pp. 179–94 p. 190.
[50]   Brennan, 'Causal chains and statistical links', 511.

moves away from falsity.[51] This impacts the preferred points of reference in the two realms: scientific inquiry is built upon replicable experiments, while legal inquiry relies on discrete events and experience to provide persuasive evidence.[52]

There is also a striking difference in the approach of lawyers and scientists towards probabilistic evidence. While statistical evidence is treated as normal in science, it is conceived only as 'a second best' option in law.[53] The robustness of evidence in science is assessed in terms of the level of significance ('p'), which is conceived to be a statement of probability. Scientists therefore attach a confidence interval to every result, which indicates the range in which the parameter lies in a given percentage of the time. As a scientific consensus, the 95 per cent confidence interval stands for a statistically significant finding.

In contrast to that, judges often do not want to engage in probabilistic reasoning[54] and tend not to regard the preponderance rule as a purely mathematical question according to which a statistical chance bigger than 50 per cent automatically results in a finding of causation. One reason for this difference might be that this so-called naked statistical evidence approach can easily lead to counter-intuitive results. The *Smith* v. *Rapid Transit* case well illustrates the dilemmas of basing the preponderance rule solely on one mathematical probability calculation.[55] In the case at hand, a bus pushed the plaintiff's car off a road on which one company, Rapid Transit, had the exclusive right to run a coach service. The court was not ready to accept that Rapid Transit was the actual tortfeasor based on purely mathematical calculations of probability. Evaluating the conclusion of the court, one commentator emphasizes the importance of subjective belief embedded in the preponderance rule, as it requires 'that the factfinder believe(s) that [X] actually occurred not merely that probably [X] (occurred)'.[56] As such belief may be grounded in other factors than mere statistical calculations the preponderance standard functions as an essentially subjective standard.

2.4 Comfort with Uncertainty in Law and in Science

A most striking difference between the scientific and legal realm manifests itself in the markedly diverging roles attached to uncertain knowledge claims. While scientists consider uncertainty as part of the normal parameters of their discipline, legal adjudicators often find uncertainty an obstacle to fulfilling their ultimate task of becoming ascertained about the factual conditions of their legal assessment.

---

[51]   H. Kritzer, 'The arts of persuasion in science and law: conflicting norms in the courtroom' (2009) *Law and Contemporary Problems* 41–61 at 48.
[52]   Kritzer, 'The arts of persuasion in science and law: conflicting norms in the courtroom', 48.
[53]   Brennan, 'Causal chains and statistical links', 490.
[54]   Brennan, 'Causal chains and statistical links', 490–91.
[55]   *Smith* v. *Rapid Transit*, Supreme Judicial Court of Massachusetts, 4 January 1945, 317 Mass 469, 470.
[56]   Steel, *Proof of Causation in Tort Law*, p. 92.

2.4.1 UNCERTAINTY IN SCIENCE. Scientific facts underlying environmental harm are highly complex and uncertain, furthermore, their effects are temporally and spatially spread out.[57] In scientific literature,[58] the concept of scientific uncertainty, in the broad sense, means that human knowledge will always remain imperfect when it comes to understanding and describing highly complex natural phenomena. In the narrow sense, scientific uncertainty stands for the fact that scientific research can only provide probabilistic results, as some uncertainty always remains as to the precise value of a given parameter. Throughout this book, uncertainty will be used in this narrow sense, referring to the statistical, probabilistic nature of scientific results. Note that scientific uncertainty is an inherent feature of even the most accurate scientific result and therefore cannot be equated with the insufficiency[59] or contradicting nature of relevant evidence, as is suggested by a more colloquial understanding of uncertainty.

Environmental law scholars repeatedly take note of the challenges that scientific uncertainty poses in their field,[60] yet legal literature rarely engages in more in-depth discussion on the specific sources of uncertainty. Hence a brief taxonomy of these sources should follow to demonstrate the factors that make science essentially and irreducibly uncertain. Better understanding the root causes of uncertainty helps fully face the extent and nature of the problems it entails. Moreover, to reach an optimal decision, judges should be able to evaluate the emerging forms of uncertainty and to attach different weight to different kinds of ambiguities. Importantly, scientific uncertainty should not be conceived as a monolithic concept and it is crucial for adjudicators to develop a deeper understanding of uncertainty in order to be able to distinguish between reducible and irreducible forms thereof. The ensuing discussion will depict a fine-grained picture on the various forms of uncertainty to raise awareness of the heterogeneity of the phenomenon.

Scientific uncertainty can be traced back to certain attributes of scientific facts and the scientific inquiry that produces them, which are usually termed as 'types' or 'sources' of uncertainty. These sources vary across different fields of natural sciences and environmental sciences literature provides various classifications of scientific uncertainty. Instead of attempting to provide an all-encompassing review of these

---

[57]   R. J. Lazarus, *The Making of Environmental Law* (University of Chicago Press, 2004), p. 20.
[58]   J. D. Brown, 'Prospects for the open treatment of uncertainty in environmental research' (2010) 34 *Progress in Physical Geography* 75–100 at 77.
[59]   Adjudicatory decisions brought under the SPS Agreement explicitly stress that scientific uncertainty is to be distinguished from the insufficiency of evidence. For more details see Gruszczynski, *Regulating Health and Environmental Risks under WTO Law: A Critical Analysis of the SPS Agreement*, pp. 187–8.
[60]   D. A. Farber, 'Uncertainty' (2011) 99 *Georgetown Law Journal* 901–59 at 901; C. Smith, 'Policy implications of uncertainty' (2011) 369 *Philosophical Transactions of the Royal Society A: Mathematical, Physical and Engineering Sciences* 4932–37 at 4932; Peel, *Science and Risk Regulation in International Law*, pp. 378–9; in the context of WTO law see Gruszczynski, *Regulating Health and Environmental Risks under WTO Law: A Critical Analysis of the SPS Agreement*, pp. 30–4.

taxonomies, here is a summary of the major categories of uncertainty present in environmental sciences, as these forms of ambiguity are the most typical in environmental adjudication:

    (i)   uncertainty due to natural variability over time or space;
   (ii)   uncertainty due to extremely high complexity of natural systems;
  (iii)   model uncertainty;
  (iv)   uncertainty due to limitations of measurement devices;
   (v)   uncertainty due to insufficient or ambiguous data;
  (vi)   judgment uncertainty;
 (vii)   linguistic uncertainty; and
(viii)   unknown unknowns in science.

i Natural Variation across Time and Space

This type of uncertainty arises in systems that change in ways that are difficult to predict[61] and, thus, are exceptionally hard to account for in models. An apposite example of the difficulties entailed in natural variation is making predictions on a species' population size. This prediction is inevitably uncertain as populations vary depending on many factors, such as availability of food, abundance of predators, or disease spread. For all these reasons, any predictions as to future population sizes will always be burdened with uncertainty flowing from background natural variation. Moreover, this type of uncertainty makes the detection of environmental trends difficult even in light of data collected for decades.[62]

ii Extremely High Complexity of Environmental Systems

Simply put, a great deal of uncertainty is a result of the extremely high complexity of environmental systems, which are not fully understood. It is virtually impossible to describe all relevant connections and feedbacks in ecosystems. Food web research well illustrates this challenge. In a marine ecosystem, which comprises dozens of species, up to 28 million different pathways could be drawn linking two particular species in the food web.[63] Such extreme level of complexity can only be represented in models where the system is grossly simplified. This in turn entails a great deal of uncertainty as to any real convergence between model results and the real behaviour of the system.

    Lessons learnt from prior food web research conducted to aid fisheries management[64] also warn us that indirect connections between species are often overlooked by scientists. This may result in fundamentally mistaken policies. To

---

[61] H. M. Regan, M. Colyvan, and M. A. Burgman, 'A taxonomy and treatment of uncertainty for ecology and conservation biology' (2002) 12 *Ecological Applications* 618–28 at 618.

[62] C. N. Cook, M. B. Mascia, M. W. Schwartz, H. P. Possingham, and R. A. Fuller, 'Achieving conservation science that bridges the knowledge-action boundary: achieving effective conservation science' (2013) 27 *Conservation Biology* 669–78 at 671.

[63] P. Yodzis, 'Must top predators be culled for the sake of fisheries?' (2001) 16 *Trends in Ecology & Evolution* 78–84 at 80.

[64] P. Yodzis, 'Diffuse effects in food webs' (2000) 81 *Ecology* 261.

take an example, if one considers only direct inter-species connections, it seems to be an intuitively appealing option to cull top predators in order to increase attainable yields of an industrially important target fish species. However, in complex food webs, where fish predators also prey on the target species on lower levels of the food chain, the population of the target species will be, in fact, decreased if top predators are removed from the ecosystem, since these predators may also prey on the fish predator itself. Consequently, decreasing the number of top predators via culling will decrease the population of the target species, which is exactly the opposite of the desired outcome. With regard to the extreme complexity of living networks, this cause of uncertainty remains pervasive and dominant in scientific results.

iii Model Uncertainty

A certain extent of irreducible uncertainty results, on the one hand, from the necessary simplification inherent in every model that describes natural processes.[65] Such simplification may lead to omitting a variable from the model, which will later on prove to be a relevant factor in the system's behaviour. On the other hand, uncertainty may also arise from constructing imprecise models of relatively known processes. This takes place for instance when scientists describe essentially stochastic natural systems with deterministic models.[66]

Moreover, uncertainty may also flow from the fact that we do not always know all the relevant processes of the real world, which may give rise to multiple working hypotheses for the same phenomenon, and thus, different models for representing the same process.[67] This type of uncertainty is well illustrated by the historic example of modelling ozone depletion in the 1980s. Initially, there were three conflicting scientific theories for explaining the decay of atmospheric ozone: a dynamic, a solar, and a chemical theory.[68] However, all these models dismissed the role of heterogeneous reactions, which later turned out to be precisely the driving mechanism behind ozone hole formation.

Another subset of model uncertainty is called parametric uncertainty and arises from using uncertain parameters in a model,[69] for example when a model relies on uncertain thresholds of an otherwise known relationship.[70] Parametric uncertainty may also be a result of certain abstractions used in a model generating parameters

---

[65] Regan, Colyvan, and Burgman, 'A taxonomy and treatment of uncertainty for ecology and conservation biology', 620.

[66] D. Ludwig, M. Mangel, and B. Haddad, 'Ecology, conservation, and public policy' (2001) 32 *Annual Review of Ecology and Systematics* 481–517 at 489.

[67] M. R. Payne et al., 'Uncertainties in projecting climate-change impacts in marine ecosystems' (2016) 73(5) *ICES Journal of Marine Science: Journal Du Conseil* 1274.

[68] J. O'Reilly et al., 'Characterizing uncertainty in expert assessments: ozone depletion and the West Antarctic ice sheet: characterizing uncertainty in expert assessments' (2011) 2(5) *Wiley Interdisciplinary Reviews: Climate Change* 731.

[69] Payne et al., 'Uncertainties in projecting climate-change impacts in marine ecosystems', 1277.

[70] A. Grubler, Y. Ermoliev, and A Kryazhimskiy, 'Coping with uncertainties: examples of modeling approaches at IIASA' (2015) 98 *Technological Forecasting and Social Change* 214.

that cannot be directly equated with biological interpretation.[71] As alluded to above, many forms of model uncertainty cannot be fully eliminated and, thus, it emerges as one of the most pervasive type of uncertainty.

iv Measurement Error

Measurement error manifests in three main types: operator error, instrument error, and systematic error.[72] Operator error can be traced back to imperfections in handling the measurement device, and instrument error stands for random problems with the device itself. Systematic errors arise from biased sampling procedures, which may be a result of unintentional erroneous calibration of the device at hand or consistent, incorrect recordings of the results. Observational bias may also be triggered by entrenched theories, which can influence the observation itself. The observer's error can largely be eliminated with appropriate training, and systematic errors rooted in theoretical grounds can also be reduced if properly recognized by observers.

v Ambiguity of Resulting Data

Uncertainty also arises from the fact that observations and modelling often can only provide scarce or ambiguous data. Estimation error may also occur, which stands for inaccuracies in data due to the erroneous choice of statistical methods.[73] The absence of long-term consistent data sets is indeed one of the regular challenges that regulatory scientists face.

vi Judgment Uncertainty: Subjective Elements in Drawing Inference

In lack of proper data, scientists need to make extrapolations and interpolations, which inevitably include making subjective judgments.[74] Subjective inferences may bring significantly biased results. This gives rise to a specific source of scientific uncertainty, called judgment uncertainty.[75] A classic example of such bias can be witnessed in the history of recording the ozone hole. Initially, scientists consistently dismissed data evidencing a growing ozone hole[76] when the data contradicted every accepted scientific theory on ozone dynamics. Scientists also warn that due to psychological factors one may have a preference for making less ambiguous statements or for processing information selectively to confirm the observer's expected outcome.[77] These subjective elements all influence the scientific conclusions offered by experts.

---

[71] Payne et al., 'Uncertainties in projecting climate change impacts in marine ecosystems', 1277.

[72] Regan, Colyvan, and Burgman, 'A taxonomy and treatment of uncertainty for ecology and conservation biology', 619.

[73] J. Harwood and K. Stokes, 'Coping with uncertainty in ecological advice: lessons from fisheries' (2003) 18 *Trends in Ecology & Evolution* 617–22 at 618.

[74] Regan, Colyvan, and Burgman, 'A taxonomy and treatment of uncertainty for ecology and conservation biology', 618, 621.

[75] O'Reilly, Brysse, Oppenheimer, and Oreskes, 'Characterizing uncertainty in expert assessments', 737.

[76] Grubler, Ermoliev, and Kryazhimskiy, 'Coping with uncertainties: examples of modeling approaches at IIASA', 215.

[77] Brown, 'Prospects for the open treatment of uncertainty in environmental research', 79.

vii Linguistic Uncertainty

This type of uncertainty arises from the often ambiguous, vague or under-specific scientific vocabulary.[78] Besides these, certain terms carry different meanings in natural and social science, which gives rise to additional linguistic uncertainty.[79] Interestingly, the terms 'cause' and 'causal inference' have divergent meanings in legal and natural sciences. Causes in natural sciences are naturally occurring factors that lead to the same outcome, whereas causes for purposes of law are of a narrower scope, hence, not all causes in science will be legally appreciable.[80] For instance, through the lens of science a weather condition leading to a slippery road is a 'cause' of a resulting car accident, however, in terms of establishing legal responsibility for that accident, weather is seen as a causal factor that is not necessarily legally relevant (as it would much rather be for example the failure of the relevant authority to maintain the road or repair road conditions).

viii Unknown Unknowns

Last but not least, there are parameters, relevant relationships, and feedbacks that the scientific community is not even aware of.[81] In surprisingly many fields of science, we are simply unaware of the fine-grained nature of the underlying processes,[82] which prevents us to be able to meaningfully describe the system's behaviour. This is the terrain of scientific surprises, which presents another persistent form of scientific uncertainty.

2.4.2 UNCERTAINTY IN LAW. The existence of inherent ambiguity in scientific results often frustrates science-based legal decision-making. It is common knowledge among scientists that scientific uncertainty is inherent to some degree in all scientific results and can never be fully eliminated.[83] Lawyers, however, often do not have a proper understanding of the true nature of scientific uncertainty. As one commentator warns, courts tend to subscribe to the 'positivist' philosophy of science, which assumes a constant expansion of scientific knowledge,[84] and to hold associated belief to a view that uncertainty can be fully eliminated.

The apparent uneasiness of judges with accepting irreducible uncertainty in science is quite surprising considering that uncertainty is not at all alien to law. Quite the contrary, one of the prime functions of law is to regulate 'uncertainty in

---

[78] Regan, Colyvan, and Burgman, 'A taxonomy and treatment of uncertainty for ecology and conservation biology', 618.

[79] Grubler, Ermoliev, and Kryazhimskiy, 'Coping with uncertainties: examples of modeling approaches at IIASA', 215.

[80] Hart and Honoré, *Causation in the Law*, pp. 112–13.

[81] Grubler, Ermoliev, and Kryazhimskiy, 'Coping with uncertainties: examples of modeling approaches at IIASA', 214.

[82] Keith Beven, 'Facets of uncertainty: epistemic uncertainty, non-stationarity, likelihood, hypothesis testing, and communication' (2016) 61(9) *Hydrological Sciences Journal* 1652.

[83] R. A. Carpenter, 'Uncertainty in managing ecosystems sustainably' in J. Lemons (ed.), *Scientific Uncertainty and Environmental Problem Solving* (Blackwell Science, 1996), pp. 118–59.

[84] Brennan, 'Causal chains and statistical links', 478–9.

social relations'.[85] Importantly, law resembles science inasmuch as neither requires absolute certainty,[86] and in fact, law itself is also inherently uncertain.[87] At the same time, law is similarly not comfortable with accepting the possibility of error and that of erroneous factual claims.[88] Jörg Kammerhoffer provides a detailed account of the many respects in which international law will always remain uncertain.[89] He distinguishes four levels of epistemological uncertainty: uncertainty of the law-making rules, uncertainty as to what constitutes a valid source of international law, uncertainty as to the normative content of substantive rules, and uncertainty due to the conflict of competing norms.[90] Even though these uncertainties fall into the category of normative uncertainty in contrast to science's uncertainty as to the facts, nevertheless, the pervasive presence of ambiguity in law arguably prompts a heightened tolerance towards factual uncertainty as well. At the end of the day, law and legal processes actively influence how uncertainty is framed,[91] and hence what implications it may have for the judicial process.

The fact remains that the uncertain nature of science is often cited among the most daunting challenges of both regulating environmental risks[92] and adjudicating environmental claims.[93] Adjudicatory solutions are slowly evolving to treat the presence of scientific uncertainty in an adequate way. Judicial attitude towards probabilistic scientific proof is consequential not only for shaping environmental claims' prospects for success, but also for influencing the extent to which judges are willing to expand the boundaries of their inquiry into the scientific dimensions of disputes. For all these reasons scientific uncertainty appears to be one of the defining underlying factors shaping the process and dynamics of environmental adjudication.

---

[85] A. Garrido-Munoz, 'Managing uncertainty: the International Court of Justice, "objective reasonableness" and the judicial function' (2017) 30 *Leiden Journal of International Law* 457–74 at 473.

[86] A. R. Klein, 'Causation and uncertainty: making connections in a time of change' (2008) 49 *Jurimetrics* 5–50 at 6.

[87] E. W. Thomas, *The Judicial Process: Realism, Pragmatism, Practical Reasoning and Principles* (Cambridge University Press, 2005), pp. 115–25.

[88] Klein, 'Causation and uncertainty: making connections in a time of change', 6.

[89] J. Kammerhofer, *Uncertainty in International Law: A Kelsenien Perspective* (Routledge, 2011).

[90] Kammerhofer, *Uncertainty in International Law*, pp. 3–4.

[91] M. Ambrus, R. Rayfuse, and W. Werner, 'Risk and international law' in M. Ambrus, R. Rayfuse, and W. Werner (eds.), *Risk and the Regulation of Uncertainty in International Law* (Cambridge University Press, 2017), pp. 3–9 p. 5.

[92] Peel, *Science and Risk Regulation in International Law*, pp. 98–102; D. Bodansky, J. Brunnée, and E. Hey, 'International environmental law mapping the field' in D. M. Bodansky, J. Brunnée, and E. Hey (eds.), *The Oxford Handbook of International Environmental Law* (Oxford University Press, 2008), pp. 6–25 p. 7; M. Ambrus, R. Rayfuse, and W. Werner, *Risk and the Regulation of Uncertainty in International Law* (Cambridge University Press, 2017).

[93] Viñuales, 'Legal techniques for dealing with scientific uncertainty in environmental law', 439; D'Aspremont and Mbengue, 'Strategies of engagement with scientific fact-finding in international adjudication', 240–72; Cranor, 'The challenge of developing science for the law of torts', p. 261.

3 *Legitimacy Challenges of Relying on Science by Legal Adjudicators*

Besides epistemic and doctrinal challenges addressed above, invoking scientific authority in a legal dispute gives rise to a set of legitimacy challenges rooted in the fact that judges need external epistemic support in making their factual determinations. Using scientific expertise has been long recognized as a prerequisite to making legitimate decisions.[94] The role of expertise in buttressing legitimacy of decisions has been traditionally evaluated through the concepts of input and output legitimacy.[95] The former means that expert involvement entails more participatory, and hence, more legitimate decision-making processes. Output legitimacy, in turn, refers to the expectation that decisions based on expertise are of higher quality. In the context of adjudication, requesting scientific input has been seen a prerequisite to making rational decisions,[96] which are seen as equivalent to non-arbitrary and therefore legitimate judgments.

The relationship between scientific expertise and legitimate judicial decisions is, in fact, not unidirectional, but a more complex one. Having recourse to scientific input in a litigious context not only scaffolds the legitimacy of decisions, but also raises peculiar legitimacy concerns. On the one hand, involving experts in a case threatens inadvertent delegation of the adjudicatory function and causes challenges for judges to preserve their monopoly over the resolution of the dispute (Subsection 3.1). On the other hand, the extra-legal cognitive authority of scientific arguments, which is hierarchically juxtaposed to legal authority, raises questions as to selecting the appropriate rationality to justify adjudicatory findings in scientific matters in an epistemically legitimate way (Subsection 3.2).

3.1 Inadvertent Delegation of the Judicial Power

As it may be clear by now from the foregoing discussion, science as an extra-legal cognitive authority may challenge the discretionary monopoly of judges over resolving science-intensive disputes. This leads to debates about the appropriate division of competence between adjudicators and scientific experts. The main concern in this respect relates to the possibility of inadvertent delegation of adjudicatory power to unelected experts, which is examined here in greater detail.

Ever since the Enlightenment, the rationalist tradition of adjudication proclaimed that the function of a court of law is to apply law to the facts.[97] In this vein, the traditional cornerstone of judicial fact-finding holds that it is for adjudicators to assess the significance and legal relevance of the facts of the case, while

---

[94] Peel, *Science and Risk Regulation in International Law*, p. 58; Viñuales, 'Legal techniques for dealing with scientific uncertainty in environmental law', 479.

[95] Ambrus, Arts, Hey, and Raulus, *The Role of 'Experts' in International and European Decision-Making Processes*, p. 6.

[96] Werner, 'The politics of expertise', p. 47.

[97] Foster, *Science and the Precautionary Principle in International Courts and Tribunals*, p. 5.

experts ought only to assist judges by elucidating the facts.[98] The ostensible simplicity of drawing a clear distinction between establishing facts and applying law proves to be deceptive. Complying with such a judicial mandate becomes particularly difficult in environmental disputes that are based on rules, which routinely incorporate scientific notions. Interpreting them frequently drags scientific arguments into the legal discourse. As observed by Hersch Lauterpacht, legally relevant facts have always mixed fact and law to some extent, and international courts have long been accustomed to that.[99] Yet in science-based disputes, where law and facts are inextricably linked, judges often experience difficulties in properly allocating powers between experts (to reveal facts) and judges (to apply rules to those facts) in a court proceeding. These challenges are aptly reflected in an impressive body of scholarship on the theory of using expert evidence.[100]

A particular danger is engendered by experts, who may inevitably 'be drawn into questions of legal interpretations through their involvement in the application of legal terms',[101] as scientific facts are inextricably linked to the content of legal definitions.[102] This generates frustration among judges and fears of losing their decision-making competence by delegating too much of the judicial function to experts, and thereby eroding the judicial authority.[103] Yet science-intensive claims ought not to prevent judges from discharging their adjudicatory function. Judge Yusuf in his declaration in *Pulp Mills* aptly summarized the arguments dissolving concerns over inadvertent delegation of adjudicatory power:

> [T]he question arises as to whether there is a risk that the recourse to an expert opinion may take away the role of the judge as the arbiter of fact and therefore undermine the Court's judicial function. My answer is in the negative. First, it is not for the expert to weigh the probative value of the facts, but to elucidate them and to clarify the scientific validity of the methods used to establish certain facts or to collect data. Secondly, the elucidation of facts by the experts is always subject to the assessment of such expertise and the determination of the facts underlying it by the Court. Thirdly, the Court need not entrust the clarification of all the facts submitted to it to experts in a wholesale manner. Rather, it should, in the first instance, identify

[98] Foster, 'New clothes for the emperor?', 152.
[99] H. Lauterpacht, *The Development of International Law by the International Court* (Stevens, 1958), p. 35.
[100] Boisson de Chazournes, Mbengue, Das, and Gros, 'One size does not fit all – uses of experts before international courts and tribunals'; Boisson de Chazournes, Ruiz Fabri, Mbengue, Das, and Gros, 'The expert in the international adjudicative process'; Foster, *Science and the Precautionary Principle in International Courts and Tribunals*; Mbengue, 'Scientific fact-finding at the International Court of Justice: an appraisal in the aftermath of the *Whaling* case'; Mbengue, 'International courts and tribunals as fact-finders'; Foster, 'New clothes for the emperor?'; Foster, 'The consultation of independent experts by international court and tribunals in health and environmental cases'; Alvarez, 'Are international judges afraid of science?'; Payne, 'Mastering the evidence'.
[101] *Pulp Mills*, Joint Dissenting Opinion of Judges Al-Khasawneh and Simma, para. 17.
[102] Foster, *Science and the Precautionary Principle in International Courts and Tribunals*, p. 77.
[103] D. Peat, 'The use of court-appointed experts by the International Court of Justice' (2014) 84 *British Yearbook of International Law* 271–303 at 289; Payne, 'Mastering the evidence', 1195.

the areas in which further fact-finding or elucidation of facts is necessary before resorting to the assistance of experts.[104]

In light of the above, we can safely establish that 'it certainly remains for the Court to discharge the exclusively judicial functions, such as the interpretation of legal terms, the legal categorization of factual issues'.[105] Despite this now quasi consensual view among adjudicators, the practicalities of scientific fact-finding of international courts and tribunals show a varied picture. We shall see in the comparative analysis that international adjudicators tend to assign different roles to experts and are willing to rely on their advice to markedly differing extent.

3.2 Risking Epistemic Trespassing

Another danger threatening the legitimacy of judgments arises when adjudicators feel confident enough to evaluate scientific knowledge claims according to their own (legal or everyday) logic paying no regard to the aims and methods of the underlying science. Such a reasoning is epistemically arbitrary, which undermines the epistemic legitimacy of a decision.[106] Simply put, epistemic non-arbitrariness stands for a requirement that a given knowledge claim ought not to be judged 'based on standards alien to it'.[107] Arbitrary reasoning in this sense conflates different cognitive authorities and endorses findings that do not do justice to the epistemic realm to which a given knowledge claim belongs.

Science-intensive legal disputes are loaded with interdisciplinary questions. What does constitute significant environmental harm or reasonable risks warranting regulation? What projects could be regarded as pursuing scientific research? These questions can only be answered based on evidence from both the scientific and the legal realm, and hence, are essentially interdisciplinary in nature. Solving interdisciplinary dilemmas often invites epistemic trespassing. Epistemic trespassers violate norms of rational decision-making when they judge questions outside their field of expertise.[108] They may commit trespassing either because they lack cross-disciplinary evidence or the skills necessary to answer a question shared by several disciplines.[109]

In the context of scientific adjudication, epistemic trespassing manifests in epistemically arbitrary adjudicatory reasoning. This occurs for instance when adjudicators decide about the *scientific validity* of a scientific evidence, or if a judicial decision about the scientific dimensions of a dispute (e.g. whether a certain toxic

---

[104] *Pulp Mills*, Declaration of Judge Yusuf, para. 10.
[105] *Pulp Mills*, Joint Dissenting Opinion of Judges Al-Khasawneh and Simma, para. 12.
[106] For a more detailed analysis of epistemic legitimacy see Section III, Subsection 2 in this chapter.
[107] D'Aspremont and Mbengue, 'Strategies of engagement with scientific fact-finding in international adjudication', 268.
[108] N. Ballantyne, 'Epistemic trespassing' (2019) 128 *MIND* 367–95.
[109] Ballantyne, 'Epistemic trespassing', 369.

emission was in fact the cause of an injury) is rendered irrespective of the scientific evidence, by solely relying on common-sense appreciation of the substance's assumed toxicity (e.g. with reference to the distance between the victim and the source of pollution). Such a reasoning is problematic from the perspective of legitimacy as epistemic non-arbitrariness is often seen as one of the many factors that confer legitimacy on a judicial decision.[110] It may be clear by now from the foregoing examples that an epistemically arbitrary finding would be vulnerable to criticism of other litigants and third parties relying on the cognitive authority of science to challenge the legitimacy of such findings. In other words, the legitimating power of scientific knowledge can effectively undermine the legally constructed legitimacy of an epistemically arbitrary judicial decision.

To guard against such challenges, judges may give two reasonable answers to the risk of epistemic trespassing. They either stop trespassing and develop a basic understanding of the underlying scientific dilemma or confine their decision to a narrower issue that safely falls in their competence.[111] The first scenario squares well with basic requirements of the intellectual due process theory, which posits that in order to avoid making epistemically arbitrary acceptance or refusal of science-based claims, judges must understand 'the cognitive aims and methods of science'.[112] This means that in order not to craft epistemically arbitrary judicial reasoning, judges must grasp the core of the scientific basis of the parties' arguments. The second scenario calls for an approach where judges remain in a terrain of legalistic analysis and reasoning that at the same time reflects on the scientific aspects of disputes to the greatest extent possible. As we shall analyse later in greater detail, both judicial pathways are reflected in the environmental case-practice of international fora.[113]

4 Implications for Judicial Engagement with Science

The three-fold challenge of engaging with science in the courtroom bears some important messages for adjudicators, which are worth summarizing before delving into the more in-depth assessment of scientific techniques of international fora.

To begin with, contrary to laymen's hopes, scientific knowledge always remains ambiguous and inherently uncertain, and similarly to its subject, the natural world, it is in constant change and flux. Scientific facts are volatile and can only partially describe the infinite complexity they form part of. And this will not get any better. Our rapidly growing understanding of the natural processes will only drag further, previously unknown uncertain details into the scope of judicial inquiry, instead of

---

[110] S. Brewer, 'Scientific expert testimony and intellectual due process' (1998) 107 *Yale Law Journal* 1535–681 at 1680; D'Aspremont and Mbengue, 'Strategies of engagement with scientific fact-finding in international adjudication', 270.

[111] Ballantyne, 'Epistemic trespassing', 376.

[112] Brewer, 'Scientific expert testimony and intellectual due process', 1539.

[113] See specifically the discussion in Chapter 10 Section II, Subsections 2 and 3.

providing clear-cut answers to judicial queries. One could not escape this reality by insisting on getting the impossible. Policymakers and adjudicators alike therefore ought to devise appropriate tools, which correspond to scientific realities and provide effective answers to the needs of society, even if those are backed by, or cloaked in, uncertain facts. Complexity is inextricably and inescapably linked to modern human life and now it must also be incorporated in social institutions, inter alia adjudication.

Undoubtedly, when adjudicators decide to take scientific input into due account, the ambiguity of scientific results may cause hurdles in their assessment. Scientific data are often incomplete and are burdened with uncertainty and paucity, which as has been shown cannot be fully eliminated from scientific results despite constant progress of scientific research. This is at odds with a frequently held myth that courts could or should actually 'find the truth' in scientific disputes.[114] Attributing science the capability of uncovering the ultimate factual truth in a given case may often be a sign of misplaced respect for science. Moreover, entrenched differences in the methods, approaches, and fundamental notions of law and science also entail specific problems, when scientific facts need to be squeezed into traditional frames of legal doctrines and concepts, such as causation or proof.

Lastly, the extra-legal cognitive authority of science often seems to intimidate adjudicators, which has direct repercussions on the extent to which they are willing to consider science in their deliberations. The existence of diverse judicial techniques adjusting the level of science in adjudication suggests that the extent to which science is allowed to enter the legally relevant aspects of disputes is a matter of adjudicatory choice. It is certainly possible to accommodate science in the adjudicatory process if judges are willing to do so. Still, one sees that scientific questions are often either handled with excessive deference precluding any in-depth adjudicatory assessment of science-intensive aspects of disputes or are downplayed in the judicial inquiry. Undoubtedly, science may lend considerable persuasive force to arguments appealing to its authority, yet this need not intimidate adjudicators. Judicial inquiry ought not to be paralysed by waiting for science's final and certain say. Judges need to realize that scientific uncertainty does not prevent them from announcing legal findings of adequate legal certainty.[115] Just as uncertainty plays a distinct role in science and in law, certainty also has autonomous meaning in the two realms. Yet scientific uncertainty is still too often regarded as an insurmountable obstacle to conducting meaningful judicial inquiry in environmental disputes.

Overall, acknowledging the limits of scientific knowledge may boost a more direct judicial engagement with science in the courtroom. As will be argued later in more

---

[114]   Alvarez, 'Are international judges afraid of science? A comment on Mbengue'.

[115]   Judge Donoghue suggests that 'the legal dispute to be decided by the adjudicators does not require resolution of the underlying scientific uncertainty'. See J. E. Donoghue, 'Expert scientific evidence in a broader context' (2018) 9 *Journal of International Dispute Settlement* 379–87 at 382.

detail in Chapter 9, due and justified respect for science ought not to result in the judicial avoidance or downplaying of scientific arguments in the process of adjudication. Quite the opposite, thorough and adequate engagement with the scientific aspects of disputes can buttress the persuasive force of adjudicatory reasoning. At this point it may be apt to stress that proactive judicial engagement with science should not be read as an endorsement or encouragement for any attempt at replacing scientific authority with clearer, more accessible non-scientific authority in pursuit of 'post-truth' agendas. While certain legitimate argumentative practices may be grounded in legal or intuitive rationality, it will be argued that those should only be deployed in exceptional cases to complement scientific rationality, but not as automatic replacement for scientific authority.

As we shall see in Chapter 9, scientific arguments are often downplayed in contemporary adjudicatory practice. This not only results in gloomy prospects for claims supported by scientific evidence, but on a more abstract level, it also causes challenges for adjudicators in crafting a persuasive and legitimate reasoning. Reasoning where scientific aspects and evidence left unaddressed becomes vulnerable to criticism. Those armed with scientific facts will have a convincing case picturing the decision as biased and factually incorrect and hence altogether illegitimate. Viewed from this perspective, overlooked, neglected or marginalized scientific dimensions of disputes can easily become the Achilles heel of the authority of an adjudicatory finding. These implications for the legitimacy and persuasiveness of adjudicatory reasoning will be further detailed in Chapter 10.

These theoretical foundations sought to lay the groundwork for one of the key proposition of this study; namely, that the use of science in environmental dispute resolution should not be conceived as a judicial quest for the final investigation of factual reality implicated in a case, but as a more complex process in which judges should aim to accommodate probabilistic and volatile scientific facts to reach their legal determination. Adjudicators thus need to become 'sophisticated consumers'[116] of scientific insights inasmuch as they ought to appraise the extent to which science can actually contribute to judicial deliberation and reasoning. The deeper understanding of the structural differences between law and natural sciences, canvassed above, seeks to foster this by facilitating a better incorporation of scientific input in the adjudicatory process.

II ADJUDICATORY TECHNIQUES FOR SCIENTIFIC ENGAGEMENT: THE FRAMEWORK OF THIS STUDY

This analysis will focus on the techniques with which legal adjudicators handle scientific arguments and thereby adjust the level of science that is allowed to enter the sphere of judicial deliberation. The inquiry also appraises the extent and ways in

---

[116] Faigman, 'Where law and science (and religion) meet', 1679.

which the presence of science impacts traditional judicial doctrines and practices, especially adjudicatory reasoning.

A closer look at the case law reveals numerous and divergent methods with which judges seek to engage with the scientific aspects of disputes, which are examined here under the term of 'judicial engagement with science'. On an abstract level, this concept serves to describe the ways in which adjudicators interact with the scientific aspects of disputes, more specifically, the extent to which they assess, interpret, and investigate scientific arguments and expert evidence. Scientific engagement of international adjudicators will be used in this book as an analytical framework to evaluate various judicial techniques adjusting the level of science that is allowed to enter the process of adjudication. In order to allow for a more fine-grained assessment, strategies for scientific engagement will be examined with respect to the following adjudicatory stages:

   (i)   with respect to the framing of the legal dispute, the study will assess the extent to which scientific arguments are deemed as having a decisive force with respect to reaching a decision in the dispute;
   (ii) with respect to methods of fact-finding, the study will scrutinize the extent to which scientific experts are appointed and heard by adjudicators, and the types of experts they are inclined to use;
   (iii) with respect to causal inquiry, the inquiry will address the causal tests and standards with which causal nexus are assessed by adjudicators between the alleged harm and its consequences based on scientific evidence; and
   (iv) with respect to the standard and extent of judicial review, the study will evaluate the ways in which adjudicators scrutinize the scientific evidence received. More specifically, the extent to which deference is afforded to claims of science will be appraised, together with methods of reviewing scientific claims in depth.

As an important caveat, the above categories are not mutually exclusive in the sense that certain judicial techniques may operate on more than one stage of the adjudicatory process (e.g. one may speak of the framing of causal inquiry, in which case the first and the third stage of the framework would be merged into one). Also, occasionally, certain aspects appear to run so closely together that their analytic separation may seem to be an artificial or even strained exercise. Yet defining distinct stages allows for a more systematic and consistent assessment on the functioning of the different adjudicatory tools, and hence, appears necessary for purposes of the present comparative analysis.

In the context of science-based policy-making, it has been suggested that expert knowledge may be utilized in three distinct ways: for instrumental, symbolic, and strategic purposes.[117] Adjudicators also use scientific arguments for various ends.

---

[117]   L. Schrefler, 'Reflections on the different roles of expertise in regulatory policy making' in M. Ambrus, K. Arts, E. Hey, and H. Raulus (eds.), *The Role of 'Experts' in International and European Decision-Making Processes* (Cambridge University Press, 2011), pp. 63–81 pp. 69–71.

Sometimes science is relied upon directly to reconstruct the relevant facts of the case, while in other instances, scientific references provide an avenue for expanding or narrowing the adjudicatory purview, or the parties' room for manoeuvre. Concrete examples for such strategic and instrumental usage of science will be examined in the forthcoming chapters with regard to each relevant jurisdiction.

1 *Framing of Disputes: Adjusting the Level of Science Entering the Judicial Inquiry*

The reach of scientific arguments, that is, the extent to which they are deemed legally relevant and occasionally even decisive to the legal claim at hand, for a significant part depends on how adjudicators frame the underlying dispute. In fact, tailoring the legally relevant dimensions of a dispute in a certain way is perhaps the single most influential tool in the hands of adjudicators with respect to adjusting the science intensity of their inquiry.[118] Its central role in adjudication justifies addressing framing as a separate category from questions of scientific fact-finding, causation, and the standard of review.

Courts may easily reason their way into being able to decide science-intensive cases irrespective of their scientific dimensions, by focusing only purely legal issues. This aptly illustrates that the framing of disputes primarily hinges on the willingness and ability of adjudicators to engage with science and expert opinions. Identifying the legally relevant aspects of a case is always a matter of judicial choice, given the many competing legal configuration that are possible to grasp the relevance of the facts of a given dispute. As one commentator puts it, '[w]hether a particular fact has legal relevance is a product of interpreting some text'.[119] And it comes as no surprise that any legal text may give rise to rival interpretations. Considering the variations of selecting the legally relevant aspects of the same set of contested facts, the extent to which science-based concepts and arguments are placed in the centre or on the periphery of the adjudicatory assessment depends on the choice of the bench. This research therefore views international judges as gatekeepers, who set the level of science that may enter the judicial inquiry.

It will be argued that the framing of disputes is a highly strategic choice on the part of adjudicators, which has a decisive impact on the outcome of the case. Most saliently, adjudicatory attitude towards framing science-intensive disputes fundamentally impacts science-backed environmental claims' chances for success. As also noted by the report of the UN Secretary General concerning the gaps in international environmental law, international fora's fragmented and limited application of

---

[118] The strategic importance of framing in fulfilling the judicial mandate in science-intensive cases is also flagged by Judge Donoghue, see Donoghue, 'Expert scientific evidence in a broader context', 382–3.

[119] Faigman, 'Where law and science (and religion) meet', 1665.

scientific data is among the most typical challenges of effective enforcement of international environmental law.[120]

It is also to be noted at the outset that framing is closely related, though not equal, to judicial economy. Framing, as understood here, also encompasses other judicial tailoring techniques whereby less science-intensive aspects of legal obligations merit more attention in rendering a final decision. In a wider sense, judicial economy requires international judges to use their adjudicatory powers rationally and most efficiently.[121] More concretely, it stands for judicial choices narrowing the scope of a decision[122] by not addressing particular issues raised by the parties. Theoretically speaking, there is a significant limit to exercising such powers, namely, that the judicial tailoring of disputes must not compromise the factual realities of a case.[123] As will be argued, however, the exercise of judicial economy in environmental disputes sometimes comes close to what threatens with deciding disputes irrespective of the underlying facts and, thus, with exceeding the above mentioned limits.

The role of substantive legal principles must also be addressed as an important aspect of framing. Applicable principles of international environmental law have considerable impact on the depth of appraising the scientific aspects of a given dispute. The extent to which adjudicators are permitted to rely in their assessment on concepts such as the precautionary principle has a transformative influence on their engagement with science. The principle may have important implications for how adjudicators integrate scientific evidence in their judgments, and the types of evidence they deem legally relevant.[124] Also, as obligations stipulated in the body of international environmental law gain more precise shape and 'bite', adjudicative bodies may have a larger room for manoeuvre in their scientific engagement, thereby facilitating a more meaningful resolution of environmental disputes. The reasoning of the Trail Smelter Tribunal well-illustrates how justice considerations could assist adjudicators in bridging the gap between uncertain scientific facts and 'certain' judicial findings. The award reiterates that where an illegal conduct 'itself is of such a nature as to preclude the ascertainment of the amount of damages with certainty, it would be a perversion of fundamental principles of justice to deny all relief to the injured person',[125] and accordingly, it awards compensation to victims of

---

[120] Secretary-General of the United Nations, 'Gaps in international environmental law and environment-related instruments: towards a global pact for the environment, Report of the Secretary-General' (2018) UN Doc. A/73/419, para. 90.

[121] F. M. Palombino, 'Judicial economy and limitation of the scope of the decision in international adjudication' (2010) 23 *Leiden Journal of International Law* 909–32 at 909.

[122] Palombino, 'Judicial economy and limitation of the scope of the decision in international adjudication', 910.

[123] Palombino, 'Judicial economy and limitation of the scope of the decision in international adjudication', 910.

[124] Boisson de Chazournes, Mbengue, Das, and Gros, 'One size does not fit all – uses of experts before international courts and tribunals', 489–90.

[125] The Trail Smelter Award cited the judgment of the United States Supreme Court in *Story Parchment Company* v. *Paterson Parchment Paper Company*, US Supreme Court, 24 February 1931, 282 U.S. 555,

air pollution. The role and impact of substantive principles will thus be analysed in each substantive chapter as part of discussing the framing of disputes.

The forthcoming chapters will address different judicial approaches to selecting the legally relevant aspects of environmental disputes. One may note, at the outset, that in many cases the 'configuration of the disputes to date has not ultimately required a closer involvement with the scientific evidence'.[126] While the marginalization of science is often apparent in international case law, this research will also point to emerging techniques that facilitate reflecting on the scientific dimensions of legal disputes.

As a further caveat, framing of environmental disputes will be seen as a closely connected, though analytically distinct issue, from scientific fact-finding, and thus, will be discussed separately. Once disputes are framed in a way that scientific aspects are encompassed in the ambit of legally relevant aspects, adjudicators need to translate scientific facts into legal findings, the first step of which will trigger the process of fact-finding.

2 *Scientific Fact-Finding: The Use of Experts and Expert Opinions*

Fact-finding,[127] that is, the 'reconstruction of the reality that is supposed to have existed at the moment the dispute arose'[128] confers a highly complex task on judges even in cases not involving scientific facts. When the facts of a case are science-heavy, science inevitably becomes part of fact-finding in the form of scientific evidence.

The process of scientific fact-finding is the main tool with which adjudicators garner scientific advice. The modalities and procedural avenues of fact-finding therefore influence the extent to which judges can control the entering of science into the litigious discourse. Some procedures and institutional arrangements allow for in-depth discussion of the scientific dimensions of legal controversies, whereas others may offer a more limited judicial interaction with science. The extent to which adjudicators are willing to get involved in appraising the evidence determines the degree of control they exercise over scientific expertise.

Moreover, the procedure in which experts are selected and examined by judges has direct bearing on the legitimacy of the outcome, that is, the adjudicatory

---

see *Trail Smelter* Arbitration *(United States, Canada)* Award, 16 April 1938 and 11 March 1941, 3 RIAA 1905, at 1920.

[126] Foster, 'The consultation of independent experts by international court and tribunals in health and environmental cases', 406.

[127] This inquiry uses the term 'fact-finding' as the evidentiary practice of international courts and tribunals. Fact-finding in other contexts is used as a synonym for inquiry, a means of non-judicial peaceful dispute settlement, see *UN Handbook on Peaceful Settlement of Disputes between States*, 1992, para. 77, available at legal.un.org/cod/books/HandbookOnPSD.pdf (last accessed on 10 January 2020).

[128] D'Aspremont and Mbengue, 'Strategies of engagement with scientific fact-finding in international adjudication', 245.

decision itself. Thorough scientific fact-finding is essentially a procedural prerequisite of crafting persuasive science-intensive adjudicatory reasoning and in this sense constitutes an important aspect of the present inquiry. Procedural scientific fact-finding powers of international courts and tribunals have already been subject to extensive scholarly commentary, with respect to specific regimes and jurisdictions[129] and also with a more general scope in cross-cutting, comparative assessments.[130] Not duplicating these efforts, the focus of this book will be on the implications the different avenues of garnering expert advice have for the legitimacy of adjudicatory reasoning.

2.1 Free Assessment of the Evidence

The fact-finding of international courts and tribunals, as a general rule, is governed by the principle of free assessment of the evidence.[131] Normally the obligation to provide the court with evidence rests with the parties. Due to the principle of free admission of evidence, parties have discretion to submit whatever proof they deem most relevant to prove or disprove the facts of their case.[132] However, international litigation procedures are not entirely adversarial in nature, given that international judicial fora usually have the power to ask for the advice of independent bodies or experts and hence to establish the facts of the case by themselves.

2.2 Different Methods and Procedures for Taking Expert Evidence

Evidence, understood as 'something [which] tends to prove or disprove the existence of an alleged fact',[133] may take diverse forms ranging from documents to expert testimonies. As a general rule, there is no hierarchy between different types of

---

[129] Gruszczynski, *Regulating Health and Environmental Risks under WTO Law*; M. Fitzmaurice, *Whaling and International Law* (Cambridge University Press, 2016); Orellana, 'The role of science in investment arbitrations concerning public health and the environment'; D. P. Ratliff, 'The PCA optional rules for arbitration of disputes relating to natural resources and/or the environment' (2001) 14 *Leiden Journal of International Law* 887–96; Payne, 'Mastering the evidence'; Peat, 'The use of court-appointed experts by the International Court of Justice'; Ridell and Plant, *Evidence before the International Court of Justice.*

[130] Boisson de Chazournes, Mbengue, Das, and Gros, 'One size does not fit all – uses of experts before international courts and tribunals'; Foster, *Science and the Precautionary Principle in International Courts and Tribunals*; Foster, 'The consultation of independent experts by international court and tribunals in health and environmental cases'; M. M. Mbengue, 'International courts and tribunals as fact-finders: the case of scientific fact-finding in international adjudication' (2011) 34 *Loyola International & Comparative Law Review* 53; Alvarez, 'Are international judges afraid of science'.

[131] R. Wolfrum, 'Taking and assessing evidence in international adjudication' in *Law of the Sea, Environmental Law and Settlement of Disputes: Liber Amicorum Judge Thomas A. Mensah* (Martinus Nijhoff Publishers, 2007), pp. 341–56 p. 142.

[132] Wolfrum, 'Taking and assessing evidence in international adjudication', p. 348.

[133] *Russia – Pigs (EU)*, Report of the Appellate Body, WT/DS475/AB/R (23 February 2017), para. 5.63.

evidence.[134] Expert opinions may be garnered in different institutional arrangements.[135] Scientists who appear as experts may be cross-examined by the other party and questioned by the bench as well. Nonetheless, it is also possible to include scientists in the team of counsels in the capacity of an advocate, in which case cross-examination is not possible. Although in such a case parties have greater command over what science actually 'speaks' to the court,[136] the persuasive force of such scientific position, in turn, may be compromised owing to scientists' apparent involvement in partisan advocacy.

In most cases, scientific evidence is brought before courts by party-appointed experts. More often than not, such party-appointed experts provide the courts with conflicting scientific evidence, thus, judges easily get entangled in a 'battle of experts' as they lack requisite scientific training to readily choose between competing scientific claims. Allowing the parties to appoint independent experts[137] may abate such concerns as *ex tribunal* and *ex curia* experts are usually tasked with reviewing the evidence submitted by the parties. Accordingly, parties often seek to enhance the evidentiary value of their experts' opinions by arguing that they are, in fact, present in the capacity of an independent expert. In the *Whaling in the Antarctic* case, for instance, one of the experts called by Australia stressed that the counsels did not familiarize him with their legal strategy and thus, argued to be appearing in an independent capacity.[138] Yet despite the fact that party-appointed experts often do not receive compensation for their services,[139] and irrespective of the fact that their testimony may well be driven by a desire to share results of years-long pursuit of scientific knowledge, the independence of party-appointed experts will always be questionable in the eye of the other party. This remains the case even though such experts are indeed scientists with an international reputation to protect,[140] which may provide an effective incentive not to supply the court with biased results.

A better solution for the problem of partisan evidence might be to have recourse to court-appointed experts,[141] and thereby gaining impartial expert opinions. Faced

[134] Wolfrum, 'Taking and assessing evidence in international adjudication', p. 354.
[135] Boisson de Chazournes, Mbengue, Das, and Gros, 'One size does not fit all – uses of experts before international courts and tribunals'.
[136] Foster, *Science and the Precautionary Principle in International Courts and Tribunals*, p. 89.
[137] Foster, 'The consultation of independent experts by international court and tribunals in health and environmental cases'.
[138] M. Mangel, 'Whales, science, and scientific whaling in the International Court of Justice' (2016) 113 *Proceedings of the National Academy of Sciences* 14523–7 at 14523.
[139] This was the position of Canada in the *Asbestos* case decided by a WTO panel, *European Communities – Measures Affecting Asbestos-Containing Products*, Complaint by Canada, WT/DS135 (11 April 2011), cited by Foster, *Science and the Precautionary Principle in International Courts and Tribunals*, p. 100.
[140] This was the argument of Argentina to argue for the independence of the experts included in its team of counsels in the *Pulp Mills* case. See *Pulp Mills*, Verbatim Record, Tuesday 29 September 2009, para. 21.
[141] Foster, 'The consultation of independent experts by international court and tribunals in health and environmental cases'; Peat, 'The use of court-appointed experts by the International Court of Justice'.

with saliently little use of this particular way of fact-finding in international practice, some scholars advocate for a more frequent appointment of *ex curia* experts.[142] In their joint dissenting opinion Judges Simma and Al-Khasawneh also urged the ICJ to use such powers.[143] The Court notably had recourse to court-appointed experts only three times,[144] but it has never used such powers in environmental disputes. The apparent defects of such a practice is illustrated by the fact that three out of seven instances, when dissenting judges voiced concerns for not appointing *ex curia* experts, occurred in environmental disputes.[145] At the same time, The trade-off of using court-appointed experts is that it deprives the parties of the opportunity to cross-examine the scientists. This induces some commentators to oppose the use of *ex curia* experts out of concerns for transparency and due process, given that such a procedure would effectively decrease the parties' control over scientific fact-finding.[146]

There would be other avenues for international courts and tribunals to garner scientific information independently from the parties' submission and to guard against dangers of partisan evidence. Despite their apparent reluctance to avail themselves of the possibility, many international judicial fora have the power to request information from, and even to consult with, international organizations having requisite expertise.[147] Moreover, there are novel ways of scientific fact-finding, too. An example is called expert witness conferencing, and can be seen in the practice of certain investment tribunals. The procedure allows experts of both sides to present their views in the presence of the other side, where experts may ask questions from one another while answering questions of adjudicators.[148] Another increasingly used fact-finding technique is to incorporate necessary technical knowledge within the judicial panel itself, by appointing expert adjudicators and expert assessors. Expert assessors[149] sit with a bench without having a right to vote, while expert adjudicators have the full power of an arbitrator even though they are not lawyers but experts of scientific fields relevant to the dispute. Such a solution is most embraced in the practice of the Permanent

---

[142]   Foster, 'New clothes for the emperor?'; Orellana, 'The role of science in investment arbitrations concerning public health and the environment', 64.

[143]   *Pulp Mills*, Joint Dissenting Opinion of Judges Al-Khasawneh and Simma, para. 8.

[144]   Peat, 'The use of court-appointed experts by the International Court of Justice', 277–9. For more details see Chapter 3 Section III, Subsection 2.3.

[145]   For the dissenting opinions see the *Temple of Preah Vihear, Kasikili/Sedudu Island, Qatar* v. *Bahrain, Nicaragua* v. *U.S., Gabcikovo-Nagymaros, Pulp Mills* and the *Whaling in the Antarctic* cases as cited by Peat, 'The use of court-appointed experts by the International Court of Justice', 280–8.

[146]   Mbengue, 'Scientific fact-finding at the International Court of Justice: an appraisal in the aftermath of the *Whaling case*', 549.

[147]   See for example Statute of the International Court of Justice, San Francisco, 26 June 1945, in force 24 October 1945 (1945) 39 AJIL Supp 215 Article 34(2), and the WTO panel also sought the advice of the WHO in the Continued Suspension of Obligations dispute, *Canada – Continued Suspension of Obligations in the EC – Hormones Dispute*, Panel Report, WT/DS321/R (31 March 2008), Annex E.

[148]   Foster, *Science and the Precautionary Principle in International Courts and Tribunals*, p. 123.

[149]   See for example the practice of ITLOS (see Chapter 8 Section III, Subsection 2.2) and more generally: Peat, 'The use of court-appointed experts by the International Court of Justice', 298.

Court of Arbitration, the procedural rules of which expressly allow the appointment of an expert on the panel.

There are many tools with which restoring or at best scaffolding judicial control over scientific expertise is possible for judges. These all require an active adjudicatory involvement in the assessment of scientific evidence. For instance, experts may be asked to comment on their expert opinions on a more general context, without prejudice to the given case, or judges may instruct party-appointed experts to prepare a joint report setting out their points of agreement or disagreement.[150]

Despite all the complexities of judicial fact-finding, there is an emerging scholarly consensus that courts and tribunals ought to assume an active role in grasping the scientific dimension of disputes and in seeking expert opinions when needed.[151] Commentators also suggest that a greater involvement in scientific fact-finding fits neatly within the capabilities of international adjudicators.[152] No less an insider than Judge Bruno Simma, writing extra-judicially, encourages international judges 'not to remain passive, rather to display greater readiness to use, indeed exhaust'[153] their various fact-finding powers.

2.3 Related Evidentiary Issues: The Standard and Burden of Proof

The chosen standard of proof signals the level of probative evidence that is required by the given forum to deem a certain claim established.[154] The standard of proof may vary between a more lenient 'more likely than not' standard, also referred to as the preponderance of the evidence, and much higher standards of proof. The most well-known among the latter is the 'beyond reasonable doubt' standard. International judicial fora rarely announce their applicable standard of proof, though generally it appears to correspond to the 'preponderance of the evidence' standard.[155] Finding a standard of proof established is an inherently subjective exercise.[156] As addressed later in greater detail, this subjectivity works against uncertain scientific facts before fora comprising only legally trained judges. One may even suggest that the

---

[150]   Foster, *Science and the Precautionary Principle in International Courts and Tribunals*, p. 79.

[151]   F. R. Jacur, 'Remarks on the role of *ex curia* scientific experts in international environmental disputes' in N. Broschiero (ed.), *International Court and the Development of International Law: Essays in Honour of Tullio Treves* (T. M. C. Asser Press, 2013), pp. 441–55 p. 453; Foster, *Science and the Precautionary Principle in International Courts and Tribunals*, pp. 131–2; Payne, 'Mastering the evidence', 1218.

[152]   Foster, 'The consultation of independent experts by international court and tribunals in health and environmental cases', 392; D. Shelton, 'Complexities and uncertainties in matters of human rights and the environment: identifying the judicial role' in J. H. Knox and R. Pejan (eds.), *The Human Right to a Healthy Environment* (Cambridge University Press, 2018), pp. 97–121 p. 119.

[153]   B. Simma, 'The International Court of Justice and scientific expertise' (2012) 106 *Proceedings of the Annual Meeting (ASIL)* 230–3 at 232.

[154]   Foster, *Science and the Precautionary Principle in International Courts and Tribunals*, p. 223.

[155]   Wolfrum, 'Taking and assessing evidence in international adjudication', p. 354.

[156]   Wolfrum, 'Taking and assessing evidence in international adjudication', p. 355.

subjectivity inherent in finding uncertain scientific claims persuasive constitutes the Achilles heel of proving science-intensive environmental claims.

Rules of burden of proof are devised by courts to allocate the risks of possible errors in fact-finding on one of the parties.[157] Generally, the *actori incumbit probatio* principle applies.[158] This generates particular repercussions for those applicants' chances for success, who bring environmental claims based on uncertain or incomplete scientific data.[159] For this reason scholarly suggestions have been put forward favouring a reversal of the burden of proof,[160] yet international courts have remained dismissive towards this idea.

3 *Causal Inquiry*

Scientific evidence features a central role in causal claims in a variety of legal contexts, from liability claims for causing environmental harm, through alleged human rights violation caused by environmental pollution or destruction, to environmental counterclaims filed in investment disputes. Science-based causal inquiry also gains legal relevance indirectly in assessing the extent of states' prevention obligations existing under human rights law and the due diligence obligation under customary international environmental law. Under the human rights law doctrine of positive obligations, states are required to take active measures to prevent third parties encroaching upon human rights of the individual. Similarly, due diligence obligations of states mandate enacting appropriate regulatory and enforcement measures to prevent private actors from causing harm to the environment.[161] Both such inquiries involve an implicit causal element though it is rarely recognized and discussed in the literature. In the human rights regime, the causal inquiry informs the types of environmentally harmful activities the territorial state ought to regulate and the corresponding extent of environmental harm that ought to be prevented.

With respect to environmental due diligence obligation, causality forms part of the assessment whether the state's measure was appropriate in light of its prevention obligation. According to the formulation of the International Law Commission (ILC), states do 'not bear the risk of unforeseeable consequences'[162] imposed upon neighbouring states by their harmful activity. It follows that due diligence obligation only extends to preventing or mitigating such foreseeable harm. Whether a certain

---

[157] Faigman, 'Where law and science (and religion) meet', 1676.

[158] Wolfrum, 'Taking and assessing evidence in international adjudication', pp. 344–45.

[159] Foster, *Science and the Precautionary Principle in International Courts and Tribunals*, p. 187.

[160] One of the most elaborate accounts was provided by Caroline Foster, who advocated for a reversal in order to give effect to the precautionary principle, see Foster, *Science and the Precautionary Principle in International Courts and Tribunals*, pp. 240–77.

[161] ILC, 'Draft Articles on Prevention of Transboundary Harm from Hazardous Activities (with Commentaries)' (2001) *Yearbook of the International Law Commission* (vol II, part 2) 153, Article 3, for more details see L.-A. Duvic-Paoli, *The Prevention Principle in International Environmental Law* (Cambridge University Press, 2018), pp. 179–98.

[162] ILC, 'Draft Articles on Prevention of Transboundary Harm', Commentary to Article 3, para 5, at 153.

environmental harm was foreseeable is informed by an implicit causal inquiry. By virtue of common-sense logic, only those injuries are foreseeable that, causally speaking, are conceivable outcomes of the alleged cause, that is, the state's act or omission complained of.

Scientific facts generate idiosyncratic problems with respect to establishing causation. This gives rise to unique judicial techniques adjusting the extent to which scientific evidence may be relevant for the causal inquiry. Methods of establishing causation are particularly suitable to showcase the intricacies of judicial engagement with science for a host of reasons. First, science-heavy causal links are a prerequisite for establishing international liability for environmental harm, therefore they often become subject to international litigation. Second, causality is among the very few questions of law, where adjudicators inescapably need to confront with and be ascertained about relevant scientific facts.[163] Therefore, one may expect that judges would inevitably confront this science-intensive element in their assessments. Third, causality well displays the frictions between legal and scientific concepts given that the term carries fundamentally different attributes and requirements in law and in natural sciences, as discussed earlier in this chapter. For all these reasons, causation will in this study serve as a litmus test for the thoroughness of adjudicators' engagement with science.

3.1 Causality in International Law

Scholarly literature is virtually silent on causal requirements and causal tests applicable in international law. The rare exceptions[164] are dedicated to general questions of causality in international law and do not address the specific intricacies of conducting a causal inquiry based on uncertain scientific facts common to environmental disputes. International judicial bodies also address the issue of causation in broad brushstrokes, often leading to inconsistent causal requirements or implicit causal inquiry. The disturbing absence of clarity in jurisprudence generates considerable frustration in those who seek to discern consistent rules and causal requirements in the practice of international courts. One may share the impression of Tony Honoré and H. L. A. Hart, who concluded that 'causation in the law is less a concept to be analysed than a ghost to be exorcized'.[165] Though they were writing this in the context of causation in the law generally, the metaphor holds all the more true for causation problems peculiar to international environmental law.

---

[163] Donoghue, 'Expert scientific evidence in a broader context', 382.
[164] Plakokefalos, 'Causation in the law of state responsibility and the problem of overdetermination', 471–92; M. Straus, 'Causation as an element of state responsibility' (1984) 16 *Law & Policy in International Business* 893 at 893; A. Gattini, 'Breach of the obligation to prevent and reparation thereof in the ICJ's genocide judgment' (2007) 18 *European Journal of International Law* 695–713; A. Gattini, 'Breach of international obligations' in A. Nollkaemper and I. Plakokefalos (eds.), *Principles of Shared Responsibility in International Law: An Appraisal of the State of the Art* (Cambridge University Press, 2014), p. 25.
[165] Hart and Honoré, *Causation in the Law*, p. 3.

Causal requirements are not addressed explicitly either among the rules of state responsibility. Article 31(1) of Articles on Responsibility of States for Internationally Wrongful Acts (ARSIWA) only provides that full reparation is due for the injury 'caused'. The ILC has been repeatedly criticized for such brevity.[166] As will be seen later in Chapter 3, similarly opaque are the causal requirements of the no-harm rule, which imposes a due diligence obligation on states under customary international law[167] not to cause significant transboundary environmental harm.

Given the absence of explicit international law rules, it comes as no surprise that causal discussions in international law much rely on national tort law concepts. Building on common-law tort rules, international law also conceives the causal inquiry as a two-step analysis.[168] First, factual causation needs to be established, which aims to ascertain a causal link between the causes and its consequences. Common-law torts apply the *sine qua non* or 'but-for' test for the factual causation inquiry.[169] The but-for test regards a conduct as a 'cause' if absent the conduct, the harm would not have occurred. With a view to the blind spots of this but-for test, the 'substantial factor' test is used as an alternative in some domestic laws, which corresponds to the so-called NESS test (Necessary Element of a Sufficient Set test) that was developed by tort law scholars.[170] These alternative tests are useful for identifying factual causes when no 'but-for' cause can be identified. An apposite, everyday example for causes that fall short of the but-for test, but nevertheless have appreciable causal role, can be illustrated through a simple majority vote. Out of the five participants, four cast an affirmative vote, therefore, the vote is successful with a simple majority. However, none of the votes alone would be a but-for cause of the action they have just decided. In contrast, under the substantial factor test the affirmative votes would qualify as a cause of the action voted for.

Having established the factual causes of an injury, in the second step of causal inquiry courts delineate the scope of responsibility by identifying the proximate cause of an effect. For one may not be held liable for every material consequence flowing from its acts, certain factors limiting the scope of liability are necessary. When international courts specify their requirements, they usually employ concepts of remoteness, foreseeability or proximity to that end.[171]

---

[166] J. Crawford, *State Responsibility: The General Part* (Cambridge University Press, 2013), pp. 492–3.
[167] For an in-depth assessment on the customary nature of the no-harm rule see Duvic-Paoli, *The Prevention Principle in International Environmental Law*, pp. 91–136.
[168] Plakokefalos, 'Causation in the law of state responsibility and the problem of overdetermination', 475.
[169] The American Law Institute, *Third Restatement of the Law of Torts for Physical and Emotional Harm*, §26.
[170] R. W. Wright, 'Causation, responsibility, risk, probability, naked statistics, and proof: pruning the bramble bush by clarifying the concepts' (1987) 73 *Iowa Law Review* 1001 at 1019. Wright explains that under the NESS test 'a particular condition is a cause of (contributed to) a specific result if and only if it was a necessary element of a set of antecedent actual conditions that was sufficient for the occurrence of the result'.
[171] Plakokefalos, 'Causation in the law of state responsibility and the problem of overdetermination', 475.

3.2 Causal Links Based on Uncertain Scientific Facts: Uncertain Causation

Whether a certain conduct can be regarded as the cause of a harmful outcome is, thus, not a simple scientific or factual question. Law on causation sets forth different causal tests, as causal requirements are not necessarily the same in relation to every breach but may vary among fields of international law.[172] Causality therefore in the view of this study should be conceived more as a mixture of factual inquiry and policy considerations. Policy in this sense marks a wide variety of considerations that courts do weigh when deciding about the limits of responsibility.[173] Such considerations become all the more understandable in view of the ultimate 'blaming' function[174] of causal inquiry, that is, to attribute a harmful result to some of the actors involved. Any analysis appraising causality should be mindful of the fact that causation is a legal construct, which describes more than a mere approximation of the factual realities of the case. As Sheila Jasanoff puts it, causation is designed 'to integrate expert judgments about the plausibility of a particular causal story with law's normative interest in deciding which kinds of stories are best for society'.[175] Such an understanding of causality opens the door to critically appraising the causal inquiry of international fora. In doing so, inconsistent or hidden causal analyses will be seen as a conscious choice of adjudicators rather than inevitable corollary of underlying factual complexities.

Causation theories are often disrupted by uncertain causation (also referred to as 'causal uncertainty',[176] 'indeterminate causation',[177] and 'causal indeterminacy'[178]); that is, our incomplete knowledge about 'the empirical causal truth' in a given case.[179] The occurrence of environmental harm often raises the question whether the injury can be traced back to actions of multiple actors[180] or whether it was caused by an amalgam of human actions and natural forces. Nevertheless, such uncertainty is ubiquitous in all situations involving harm and is in no way unique to environmental cases. Causal uncertainty typically arises from the multiplicity and similarity of possible causes; the passage of time, which impedes gathering relevant evidence;

---

[172] J. Crawford, *The International Law Commission's Articles on State Responsibility* (Cambridge University Press, 2002), pp. 204–5; D. Shelton, 'Righting wrongs: reparations in the articles on state responsibility' (2002) 96 *American Journal of International Law* 833–56 at 846.

[173] Hart and Honoré, *Causation in the Law*, p. 103.

[174] B. M. Zupančič, 'Causation in cases of environmental degradation: the missing link in adjudicating human rights' (2011) 3 *The Yearbook of Polar Law Online* 113–28 at 113.

[175] Jasanoff, *Science at the Bar*, p. 119.

[176] Steel, *Proof of Causation in Tort Law*, p. 5.

[177] J. Paterson, 'Law's approach to harm under uncertainty' in R. Goldberg (ed.), *Perspectives on Causation* (Hart Publishing, 2011), pp. 383–408 p. 385.

[178] D. Rosenberg, 'The causal connection in mass exposure cases: a "public law" vision of the tort system' (1984) 97 *Harvard Law Review* 849 at 866.

[179] Steel, *Proof of Causation in Tort Law*, p. 15.

[180] Such a scenario can give rise to claims of shared responsibility for the harm. In more detail see A. Nollkaemper and I. Plakokefalos (eds.), *Principles of Shared Responsibility in International Law* (Cambridge University Press, 2017).

the unobservability of causation; the incomplete knowledge of causal mechanisms; the counterfactual nature of causation; human error, especially that of experts; and the costs of obtaining causal knowledge in a given legal proceedings.[181] This list of difficulties in itself illustrates the considerable challenges posed for science-intensive causal inquiry of adjudicators.

Overall, causal inquiries of international courts and tribunals vary greatly, just like their tendencies to find a causal claim established. The judicial handling of causation involving uncertain science will in the forthcoming chapters serve as indicium of international judicial fora's willingness to interact with the scientific aspects of environmental cases.

4 *Standard and Extent of Judicial Review*

The fourth aspect of judicial engagement with science that will be examined in this study is the standard and extent of review. The standard of review describes the intrusiveness of the chosen scrutiny; and relying on more intrusive standards yields more extensive judicial reviews. As shown below, more extensive judicial review will ultimately extend the scope of the adjudicatory purview. Building on the rather extensive scholarly commentary[182] regarding general standard of review issues in environmental and health-related disputes, this book will survey the extent to which international fora are willing to replace their traditionally deferential review with more intrusive standards. It will also interrogate the trade-offs between the intrusiveness of the chosen standard and adjudicators' ability to craft a persuasive reasoning justifying their review of science-based claims.

---

[181] Steel provides a detailed analysis of these sources. Steel, *Proof of Causation in Tort Law*, pp. 7–10.

[182] Gruszczynski and Werner, *Deference in International Courts and Tribunals*; Gruszczynski, *Regulating Health and Environmental Risks under WTO Law*; L. Gruszczynski, 'Science and the settlement of trade disputes in the World Trade Organization' in B. Mercurio and N. Kuei-Jung (eds.), *Science and Technology in International Economic Law: Balancing Competing Interests* (Routledge, 2014), pp. 11–29; Gruszczynski, 'Standard of review and scientific evidence in WTO law and international investment arbitration'; L. Gruszczynski, 'How deep should we go? Searching for an appropriate standard of review in the SPS cases' (2011) 2 *European Journal of Risk Regulation* 111–14; Ioannidis, 'Beyond the standard of review: deference criteria in WTO law and the case for a procedural approach'; C. E. Foster, 'Adjudication, arbitration and the turn to public law "standards of review": putting the precautionary principle in the crucible' (2012) 3 *Journal of International Dispute Settlement* 525–58; S. W. Schill, 'Deference in investment treaty arbitration: re-conceptualizing the standard of review' (2012) 3 *Journal of International Dispute Settlement* 577–607; S. Hamamoto, 'From the requirement of reasonableness to a "comply and explain" rule: the standard of review in the *Whaling* judgment' in M. Fitzmaurice and D. Tamada (eds.), *Whaling in the Antarctic: The Significance and Implications of the ICJ Judgment* (Brill Nijhoff, 2016), pp. 38–52; C. E. Foster, 'International adjudication – standards of review and burden of proof: Australia-apples and whaling in the Antarctic' (2012) *Review of European Community and International Environmental Law* 80–91; Y. Fukunaga, 'Standard of review and "scientific truths" in the WTO dispute settlement system and investment arbitration' (2012) 3 *Journal of International Dispute Settlement* 559–76.

4.1 Quest for an Appropriate Standard of Review: How Much Deference Courts Ought to Grant Scientific Expertise?

In international law standard of review[183] is seen as a procedural mechanism, which determines the depth and intensity of judicial scrutiny and, ultimately, the extent to which national decision-makers can exercise discretion insulated by judicial review. The standard of review also functions as a mechanism for distributing powers between supranational judicial organs and states, by striking a balance between the competence of sovereign states and international bodies respectively.[184]

In the context of cases examined in the upcoming chapters, judicial scrutiny, and the corresponding standard of review, typically concern factual determinations, that is, whether a national measure is adequately supported or warranted by scientific evidence. This is most typical in the judicial scrutiny of scientific risk regulatory decisions and other science-backed factual claims of sovereign states. In these contexts, specific challenges arise when a court of law is asked to distinguish valid scientific claims from non-scientific ones, where science serves only as a pretext and, therefore, should be considered invalid.

The applicable standard of review may spread across a theoretical spectrum between two extremes: *de novo* review and total deference. Between the two, there are many possible formulations ranging from more intrusive tests to less intrusive ones. The *de novo* standard of review entrusts an additional actor, typically a judicial organ, with reviewing the initial determinations of national level decision-making authorities.[185] While more deferential standards would grant states certain latitude or discretion in making their own determinations. The upcoming chapters will detail the varying degrees of deference that international courts and tribunals grant states in making scientific claims.

Deference as a matter of international law, which is subject to appraisal here, should be distinguished from deference afforded to competent authorities and agencies under domestic law in making scientific conclusions.[186] Also, one may speak of deference granted to policy choices as well as to factual findings. International jurisdictions justify their deferential review by a number of

---

[183] L. Gruszczynski and W. Werner, 'Introduction' in L. Gruszczynski and W. Werner (eds.), *Deference in International Courts and Tribunals: Standard of Review and Margin of Appreciation* (Oxford University Press, 2014), pp. 1–15 p. 4.

[184] L. Gruszczynski, 'Standard of review of health and environmental regulations by WTO panels' in G. Van Calster and D. Prévost (eds.), *Research Handbook on Environment, Health and the WTO* (Edward Elgar, 2014), pp. 731–57 p. 734.

[185] Gruszczynski, 'Standard of review of health and environmental regulations by WTO panels', p. 733.

[186] See for example the investor-state dispute settlement tribunal's award in the *Glamis Gold Ltd.* v. *US* case, *Glamis Gold Ltd.* v. *US*, UNCITRAL, Award (8 June 2009), para 617. The tribunal rejected the respondent's argument that a deferential standard of review is readily transferable from US and Canadian law to international investment arbitration.

factors, for example, democratic legitimacy of primary decision-makers, or the allocation of powers between sovereigns and international courts. In an environmental law context, the apparent 'push for deference'[187] is normally explained with the absence of scientific expertise on the bench, which makes the judicial review of science-based decisions problematic from a legitimacy point of view.

Critics of a too-deferential review point out that granting wide margin of appreciation to states in certain contexts would in fact enlarge sovereignty of a particular state at the expense of others.[188] The dangers of a deferential judicial review is particularly relevant in the present inquiry as appealing to the authority of science may be used in certain cases to mask states' political interests.[189] In such cases, if adjudicators demonstrate self-restraint and adopt a lenient approach to reviewing science-based claims they, in fact, would rubber stamp states' political motivations disguised as science. Such fears appear to be justified if one considers either environmental risk regulatory decisions, the often politicized nature of which have now become well-known,[190] or the appeal to scientific research seeking to insulate a state-funded whaling programme from judicial review.[191] Similar efforts of states to refer to scientific research in order to back up the taking of protected species may easily resurface in the future under a number of environmental conventions.[192]

4.2 Extent of Review and Corresponding Scope of the Judicial Purview

Different standards of review entail different boundaries for the judicial review and, therefore, endorse different scope for the judicial purview. Adjudicators' approach to the boundaries of their inquiry will impact the ways and extent to which scientific arguments will be included in the judicial assessment and reasoning. As will be seen later in the analysis of the practice of each court and tribunal, certain judges are more inclined to perceive the boundary between law and science as an impermeable

---

[187] Foster, *Science and the Precautionary Principle in International Courts and Tribunals*, p. 14.

[188] E. Bjorge, 'Been there, done that: the margin of appreciation and international law' (2015) 4 *CJICL* 181–90 at 190.

[189] For a similar argument made in the context of WTO law see A. Orford, 'Trade, human rights and the economy of sacrifice' in A. Orford (ed.), *International Law and its Others* (Cambridge University Press, 2006), pp. 156–96 pp. 166–73.

[190] Foster, *Science and the Precautionary Principle in International Courts and Tribunals*, p. 15.

[191] *Whaling in the Antarctic (Australia v. Japan: New Zealand intervening)* (Judgment) (2014) ICJ Rep, 226.

[192] Several multilateral environmental agreements (MEA) incorporate the notion of scientific research, for example the Convention on the Conservation of Migratory Species of Wild Animals, Bonn, 6 November 1979, in force 1 November 1983, (1979) 1651 UNTS 333, Article III (5) (a) allows taking of endangered species for 'scientific purposes', and the Agreement on the Conservation of Polar Bears, Oslo, 15 November 1973, in force 26 May 1976, (1973) 2898 UNTS 243, Article III (1)(a) permits taking of polar bears for 'bona fide scientific purposes'.

wall, while others are more willing to identify some benchmarks based on which they can engage with the underlying scientific facts while exercising their judicial function.

In this vein, the cognitive authority of science is often referred to as a reason for narrowing the scope of judicial task. In the extreme, litigants and some international judges argue for the non-justiciability of science-intensive concepts. On the contrary, there is a growing trend in the practice of international fora to evaluate 'amalgam-concepts' in which law and science are blended together. Judge Keith, who endorses a more proactive approach towards the judicial task explained that scientific concepts can be appraised from the law's perspective. For instance, courts can evaluate scientific evidence meaningfully by scrutinizing 'whether it demonstrates coherent scientific reasoning'.[193]

At the end of the day, the purview of adjudication is a matter of judicial choice and it depends on judges' willingness 'to apply judicial mind to scientific data'[194] in order to grasp and evaluate the complexity of interlinked issues of law and science. The overview of international adjudication will reveal that the scope of judicial purview in interpreting intertwined concepts is far from being settled, as adjudicatory bodies develop divergent practices and tests to delineate the boundaries of their inquiry.

III THE IMPACT OF SCIENCE ON JUDICIAL REASONING

The extent to which science is allowed to enter the adjudicative process will be examined in this book from the perspective of adjudicatory reasoning. More specifically, it will be argued that if adjudicators decide to marginalize science and carve it out from their sphere of investigation, as will be shown is often the case in contemporary environmental adjudication, specific challenges arise with respect to crafting a persuasive reasoning in science-heavy disputes. In such cases, adjudicators would need substitutes for scientific references in order to justify their choices between competing and often conflicting science-based claims. At the same time, using scientific standards in the reasoning is an equally intricate task for judges in light of the many epistemic and doctrinal complexities as well as legitimacy challenges addressed above. Direct judicial interaction with and appraisal of scientific input therefore warrants specific reasoning techniques to preserve the epistemic legitimacy of the judicial decision.

Before introducing the various types of argumentative practices that can be discerned from international case-law, a brief overview is due on the standing scientific arguments enjoy in current environmental dispute resolution.

---

[193] *Whaling in the Antarctic*, Declaration of Judge Keith, para. 8.
[194] Mbengue, 'Scientific fact-finding at the International Court of Justice: an appraisal in the aftermath of the *Whaling* case', 533.

1 *Low Level of Science Allowed to Enter Adjudicatory Deliberations in Environmental Disputes*

The ubiquitous nature of scientific facts and components in environmental disputes[195] would intuitively warrant a significant role for science in international environmental adjudication. Simultaneously with a surge in the number of such disputes, one commentator voiced a reasonable expectation that 'the relative merits of the rival scientific views advanced by the parties will likely be a major point to be decided'[196] by courts and tribunals. Yet the practice of international adjudication shows quite the opposite, as thoroughly entertaining the parties' scientific arguments is still far from being the norm in the current adjudicatory landscape.

Science altogether does not enjoy a privileged position in the analysis of international adjudicators. Generally speaking, environmental adjudication manifests various attempts at marginalizing or circumventing the underlying scientific facts, thus, environmental case-law has been largely characterized by 'the low profile accorded to scientific input'.[197] This may come as little surprise considering that scientific expertise does not carry a decisive role in shaping environmental policy-making processes either. Indeed, policy-making practice shows that scientific warnings can in no way be considered a sufficient condition for enacting a given environmental policy that would abate the very risks experts have identified.[198] In light of this, the often-marginal role of science in adjudication may seem reasonable or even justifiable. Yet one may also argue that policymaking and adjudication are not entirely analogous contexts in respect of decision-makers' interaction with science. Policymaking admittedly, and legitimately, serves to form a subjective value judgment on behalf of a wider constituency, which decision is only 'informed'[199] by the underlying science. Whereas in an adjudicatory context, allowing such avowedly subjective considerations to shape the judicial outcome seems to be more problematic. Parties in a litigation seek a neutral arbiter for their dispute, which arguably warrants against embracing subjective value judgments to an excessive extent as it can undermine the legitimacy of the dispute resolution process. Viewing from this perspective, science as a somewhat objective source of authority justifiably claims a more privileged position in unbiased judicial adjudication.

---

[195] Bodansky, 'The legitimacy of international governance', 620.

[196] Viñuales, 'Legal techniques for dealing with scientific uncertainty in environmental law', 478.

[197] Foster, 'The consultation of independent experts by international court and tribunals in health and environmental cases', 407.

[198] S. Andersen, 'The role of scientific expertise in multilateral environmental agreements: influence and effectiveness' in M. Ambrus, K. Arts, E. Hey, and H. Raulus (eds.), *The Role of 'Experts' in International and European Decision-Making Processes* (Cambridge University Press, 2014), pp. 105–25 pp. 117–19; S. Andersen and J. B. Skjærseth, 'Science and technology from agenda setting to implementation' in D. Bodansky, J. Brunnée, and E. Hey (eds.), *The Oxford Handbook of International Environmental Law* (Oxford University Press, 2008), pp. 183–202 pp. 191–2.

[199] Richard Lazarus dubs environmental policy-making 'scientifically-informed value judgments', see Lazarus, *The Making of Environmental Law*, p. 22.

Nevertheless, the current adjudicatory landscape suggests that international judges still have an ambivalent relationship with scientific input. Scholarly commentary points to the minimization of the role of science[200] in judicial evaluation, or writes about salient reluctance of international judges to appraise scientific proof,[201] and their tendency to hide their evidentiary assessments of complex factual circumstances.[202] D'Aspremont and Mbengue argue that international adjudicators may adopt a 'nihilist', a 'protectionist', or a 'minimalistic' approach towards engaging with scientific evidence.[203] These commentaries have featured a handful of decisions to illustrate said tendencies in the case law. This study adopts a more comprehensive scope and appraises the judicial attitudes towards science across all major international jurisdictions, showing a variety of adjudicatory choices along the stages of the judicial process that adjust the science-intensity of environmental dispute settlement.

2 Science and the Legitimacy of Adjudicatory Reasoning

Throughout this book, judicial engagement with science will be analysed with a view to securing the legitimacy of judgments in environmental disputes. More particularly, this study will explore how different methods for scientific engagement affect the array of available legitimate reasoning styles. This research posits that the extent to which adjudicators choose to engage with the scientific dimensions of disputes will have repercussions on the ways in which they can craft persuasive decisions.

Simply put, legitimacy means 'the right to rule',[204] due to which a given community regards the authority of a decision justified. Commentators usually distinguish between normative legitimacy, defined by legal or political standards, and sociological legitimacy, measured by the perception of legitimacy of international courts among relevant audiences.[205] Within these categories one may speak of source, process, and outcome legitimacy of international courts.[206] Among the traditional

---

[200] Viñuales, 'Observations sur le traitement des motifs scientifiques dans le contentieux environnemental international', pp. 104–5.

[201] Mbengue, 'International courts and tribunals as fact-finders', 61.

[202] Wolfrum, 'Taking and assessing evidence in international adjudication', p. 342.

[203] D'Aspremont and Mbengue, 'Strategies of engagement with scientific fact-finding in international adjudication', 252–8.

[204] A. Buchanan, 'The legitimacy of international law' in S. Besson and J. Tasioulas (eds.), *The Philosophy of International Law* (Oxford University Press, 2010), pp. 79–96 p. 79.

[205] H. G. Cohen, A. Føllesdal, N. Grossman, and G. Ulfstein, 'Legitimacy and international courts: a framework' in H. G. Cohen, A. Føllesdal, N. Grossman, and G. Ulfstein (eds.), *Legitimacy and International Courts* (Cambridge University Press, 2018), pp. 1–40; Y. Shany, *Assessing the Effectiveness of International Courts* (Oxford University Press, 2014), pp. 137–58.

[206] Y. Shany, 'Stronger together? Legitimacy and effectiveness of international courts as mutually reinforcing or undermining notions' in N. Grossman, H. G. Cohen, A. Føllesdal, and G. Ulfstein (eds.), *Legitimacy and International Courts* (Cambridge University Press, 2018), pp. 354–71 pp. 355–60.

factors supporting the legitimacy capital of adjudicative bodies, the source of courts' legal power, the circumstances of their establishment, the perceived fairness and just nature of their judgments, the independence of judges, as well as their expertise are all relevant factors.[207] Besides these, the quality of the judgment also impacts legitimacy. Providing well-reasoned judgments is a requirement for the legitimacy of judicial bodies.[208] This is underpinned by empirical studies conducted among lawyers acting as counsels before international jurisdictions, which shows that this audience unequivocally regards clearly visible judicial reasoning as a prerequisite to the legitimacy of judgments.[209]

Typically, the legitimacy of a judicial reasoning is mostly assessed in light of how adjudicators apply and interpret the *law*.[210] Yet the specific aspect of how the presence of scientific *factual arguments* as a source of epistemic authority may impact the legitimacy of adjudicatory authority and reasoning, a quality that will be called here epistemic legitimacy, has remained largely under-theorized in scholarly literature. Epistemic legitimacy stands for various requirements posed by the presence of scientific knowledge claims for adjudicatory reasoning.[211] Inadequate ways of reflecting on the scientific aspects of disputes can easily result in 'inaccurate, opaque' and altogether 'unconvincing'[212] decisions and thereby erode the epistemic legitimacy capital of individual judgments and that of the adjudicative body, too.

This book therefore places epistemic legitimacy at its centre to raise judicial and scholarly awareness of the challenges and importance of the concept. It investigates points of conflict and modes of interaction between scientific and legal authority in an adjudicatory setting. The adjudicative process often becomes a battleground of competing or even conflicting claims, where legal and scientific knowledge may offer different narratives of the state of factual affairs. Producing epistemically legitimate decisions thus is among the defining challenges of science-intensive litigation, which shapes the dynamics of adjudication as a hidden or even an invisible force. As it will be argued, the legitimacy of judicial reasoning is inextricably linked to whether and if so, how science is appreciated at specific stages of adjudication. Specifically, the extent to which disputes are framed in a way so that science is incorporated in the legal assessment, the modalities of expert involvement in the fact-finding process, the extent to which scientific facts on causal nexus are acknowledged in the assessment, as well as adjudicators' willingness to scrutinize

---

[207]   Shany, 'Stronger together? Legitimacy and effectiveness of international courts as mutually reinforcing or undermining notions', pp. 357–9.

[208]   Shany, *Assessing the Effectiveness of International Courts*, p. 37.

[209]   Boisson de Chazournes, Mbengue, Das, and Gros, 'One size does not fit all – uses of experts before international courts and tribunals', 487.

[210]   Grossman, 'Solomonic judgments and the legitimacy of the International Court of Justice', p. 61.

[211]   For a similar inquiry in the context of WTO law see C. A. Thomas, 'Of facts and phantoms: economics, epistemic legitimacy, and WTO dispute settlement' (2011) 14 *Journal of International Economic Law* 295–328.

[212]   Thomas, 'Of facts and phantoms', 288.

scientific claims will ultimately determine the extent to which the judicial reasoning can reflect on and accommodate scientific authority. In this vein, this study on the interrelations between the presence of science in a dispute and the legitimacy of the resulting judgment will be built upon a comparative analysis of the judicial tools applied along the abovementioned four stages of the adjudicatory process.

2.1 Science as a Prerequisite to Making Legitimate Decisions

Against this backdrop, this book concentrates on reasoning styles with which international courts and tribunals can persuasively deal with scientific arguments in a legal dispute. The chosen justification method has direct implications for the legitimacy of adjudicatory decisions. Traditionally, a decision will not be deemed legitimate if it is poorly reasoned, or invokes irrelevant or contradictory considerations.[213] Apparent scientific dimensions of a case complicate matters further as in this case, proper interaction with science in the judicial reasoning becomes a crucial factor in securing legitimacy for the judgment. To begin with, an almost truism of fact-finding holds that 'it is not possible to make sound legal judgments if they are not based upon a proper appreciation of the facts',[214] in our case, scientific facts. For this reason, due to the intertwined nature of scientific facts and legal concepts in science-based disputes, meaningful judgments can only be delivered if adjudicators adequately manage the law-science interface. Accordingly, courts may face reputational risks[215] when they render decisions in scientific disputes with marginalizing expert evidence.[216]

Furthermore, a reasoning which excludes saliently relevant aspects from the judicial deliberation, as it is often the case in science-intensive disputes when adjudicators downplay the role of scientific arguments, depreciates the legitimacy capital of a judgment. To illustrate this problem, this book will offer a re-contextualized reading of King Solomon's anecdote to articulate the point that what could have been rightfully regarded as a legitimate way of deciding science-intensive disputes in the past would not suffice today.[217] The analogy rests on deeming Solomon's biblical judgment essentially similar to science-intensive

[213] C. Gerstetter, 'Substance and style: how the WTO adjudicators legitimize their decisions' in A. Føllesdal and G. Ulfstein (eds.), *The Judicialization of International Law: A Mixed Blessing?* (Oxford University Press, 2018), pp. 64–85 p. 65.

[214] Ridell makes this argument in a wider context relating to fact-finding of the International Court of Justice. Ridell, 'Scientific evidence in the International Court of Justice: problems and possibilities', 257.

[215] For a similar argument in the context of regulatory policymaking see Schrefler, 'Reflections on the different roles of expertise in regulatory policy making', p. 78.

[216] See the abundant scholarly and judicial criticism aimed at the majority's findings in the *Pulp Mills* judgment of the International Court of Justice, which did not evaluate in-depth the scientific evidence submitted.

[217] For further elaboration on the implications of the Solomonic metaphor for the legitimacy of science-intensive adjudication see Chapter 9 Section II, Subsection 1.2.

disputes inasmuch as the dispute brought before him concerned contested biological motherhood. This study will argue that rendering Solomonic judgments based on common-sense wisdom instead of considering scientific evidence revealing the scientific aspects of cases would constitute epistemically illegitimate argumentation in contemporary adjudication.

Proper engagement with the scientific dimensions of environmental disputes is crucial also because striking down sensitive domestic policy decisions, such as environmental or health regulations, in an unjustified way can easily spark public protest.[218] It is for this reason vital in the context of international adjudication not to issue arbitrary judgments in scientific disputes. Transparent and well-reasoned engagement with science ultimately supports the legitimacy of adjudicatory fora that are facing heightened scrutiny and expectations for impartial and unbiased treatment of cases. As a related aspect, engaging with the scientific dimensions of disputes and not to make poor scientific findings hiding adjudicators' position statements[219] is also vital for preserving legitimacy in the face of rising suspicion and backlash against globalization,[220] and globalized institutions such as international adjudicatory bodies.[221]

The extent to which adjudicators account for the underlying scientific facts is also consequential due to the increasing competition between international courts and tribunals. The proliferation of international fora entails an 'interpretative fragmentation',[222] marking conflicting interpretations of law by various jurisdictions. Analogously to that, one may also speak of conflicting approaches to interrogating the factual background of disputes. Omitting or marginalizing apparent scientific facts upon which legal controversies rest would not only run the risk of undermining the legitimacy of judgments, but ultimately would challenge the confidence placed in the given judicial body. This could, in turn, drive away potential claimants towards other jurisdictions. As more fora become available, litigants will have recourse to those, where they can trust that all aspects of their case 'will be fully and duly appreciated'.[223]

---

[218]   R. Howse, 'The World Trade Organization 20 years on: global governance by judiciary' (2016) 27 *European Journal of International Law* 9–77 at 30.

[219]   Viñuales, 'Observations sur le traitement des motifs scientifiques dans le contentieux environnemental international', p. 114.

[220]   D. Caron and E. Shirlow, 'Dissecting backlash' in A. Føllesdal and G. Ulfstein (eds.), *The Judicialization of International Law: A Mixed Blessing?* (Oxford University Press, 2018), pp. 159–82 p. 163.

[221]   L. B. de Chazournes, 'Plurality in the fabric of international courts and tribunals: the threads of a managerial approach: a rejoinder – fears and anxieties' (2017) 28 *European Journal of International Law* 1275–81 at 1280–1.

[222]   A. Pellet, 'Should we (still) worry about fragmentation?' in A. Føllesdal and G. Ulfstein (eds.), *The Judicialization of International Law: A Mixed Blessing?* (Oxford University Press, 2018), pp. 228–42 pp. 229–30.

[223]   D'Aspremont and Mbengue, 'Strategies of engagement with scientific fact-finding in international adjudication', 270.

Proper adjudicatory treatment of science is also warranted for a reason stemming from the 'public' function of adjudication. In contrast to the private function, which only necessitates resolving the parties' dispute, the public function of courts focuses on securing values and objectives of a wider community. One commentator explicitly suggests that the 'establishment of scientific facts ... and the resolution of disputes over contradictory facts should be seen as a public function of relevance to the international community as a whole rather than simply part of a private dispute'.[224] Such third-party effects of adjudication[225] are particularly salient with respect to environmental claims, which constitute a peculiar set of community interest in international law, and as such, do not easily fit within the frames of bilateral dispute settlement mechanisms.[226]

Finally, if scientific references go unchecked in the courtroom, scientific knowledge can be abused to legitimize environmentally harmful practices.[227] This aptly illustrates that judicial control over scientific evidence is consequential with regard to the efficient enforcement of environmental law obligations. The ways in which adjudicators engage with science ultimately determine the extent to which environmental law obligations could have a real 'bite'. In order for international environmental adjudication to reach maturity, a more thorough engagement with scientific arguments of litigants is therefore warranted.

2.2 Convincing and Legitimate Reasoning Styles

Let us now sharpen our focus on the modalities of crafting epistemically legitimate judgments. Without going into the details of drawing the appropriate contours of judicial purview, which will be discussed later,[228] suffice it to highlight at this point that securing epistemic legitimacy does not compel judges to resolve scientific debates or to actually find the scientifically correct answer to the scientific dilemma underlying the legal controversy at hand. Rather, epistemic legitimacy requires the judicial reasoning conform to both the logic of law and science.[229] In order to fulfil this requirement, judicial argumentation must in all cases respect the cognitive authority of science. This imperative compels not to disregard the scientific profiles of disputes, not to make epistemically arbitrary judgments about scientific

---

[224] N. A. Craik, 'Recalcitrant reality and chosen ideals: the public function of dispute settlement in international environmental law' (1998) 10 *The Georgetown International Environmental Law Review* 551–80 at 572.

[225] C. Guarnieri and P. Pederzoli, *The Power of Judges* (Oxford University Press, 2002), p. 9.

[226] J. Brunnée, 'International environmental law and community interests: procedural aspects' in E. Benvenisti and G. Nolte (eds.), *Community Interests Across International Law* (Oxford University Press, 2018), pp. 151–75 p. 170.

[227] Craik, 'Recalcitrant reality and chosen ideals', 572.

[228] See Chapter 10.

[229] J. Lawrence, 'The structural logic of expert participation in WTO decision-making process' in M. Ambrus, K. Arts, E. Hey, and H. Raulus (eds.), *The Role of 'Experts' in International and European Decision-Making Processes* (Cambridge University Press, 2014), pp. 173–93 p. 174.

arguments by substituting legalistic logic for scientific appraisal, while equally not to attempt resolving scientific debates in a court proceeding.

The presence of cognitively authoritative scientific arguments may boost or, if not properly accounted for, may hinder the persuasiveness of the legal judgments delivered in science-intensive cases. A main proposition of this study is that adjudicators have to engage with science in a proper way in order to harness the cognitive authority of science in crafting persuasive and legitimate reasoning. The central yardstick in this respect is not that using *more* science would necessarily result in better-reasoned judgments. Rather, the crucial question on which the legitimacy of a science-intensive judgment hinges is *how* adjudicators reflect on the scientific aspects of disputes in their reasoning.

As we shall see, judicial reasoning may be built upon diverse benchmarks and standards to justify the acceptance or rejection of a particular science-heavy claim or argument. The typology of this study will distinguish four different types of reasoning styles dependent upon the rationality judges appeal to. These will be dubbed intuitive, scientific, legal, and hybrid reasoning styles. In view of the present book, intuitive reasoning techniques are used, when adjudicators rely on yardsticks borrowed from conventional, everyday wisdom to validate science-backed arguments. In turn, scientific benchmarks are applied when experts' findings are weighed against the standards set by the scientific community in the respective field of expertise. This rationality implies that adjudicators defer completely to the epistemic standards and methodological rigor of the scientific community. In contrast, with legal reasoning style adjudicators judge scientific arguments according to legalistic logic, for example with reference to notions amenable to legal evaluation. Hybrid standards signal a specific set of standards that are akin to legal benchmarks inasmuch as they lend themselves to judicial evaluation, the application of which, however, always necessitates a close interaction with scientific facts. These reasoning techniques will be further elaborated on and illustrated with numerous examples from environmental case law in Chapter 10 accompanied by a discussion of the advantages and disadvantages of each of them under specific factual circumstances.

PART II

Techniques for Judicial Engagement with Science
in the Practice of International Courts and Tribunals

3

Judicial Engagement with Science in the Environmental Case Law of the International Court of Justice

The Court is unable to accept the position that in order to decide this case, it must first make a determination upon a disagreement between scientists of distinction as to the more plausibly correct interpretation of apparently incomplete scientific data.[1]

Continental Shelf (*Libya* v. *Malta*), 1985

The conclusions of scientific experts might be indispensable in distilling the essence of what legal concepts such as 'significance' of damage, 'sufficiency', 'reasonable threshold' or 'necessity' come to mean in a given case.[2]

Dissenting Opinion of Judges Al-Khasawneh and Simma, 2010

This chapter investigates the ways in which questions of natural sciences appear before the International Court of Justice (ICJ) and analyses the judicial techniques of the Court aiming to deal with scientific arguments in international environmental disputes. States on both sides increasingly rely on highly technical arguments backed up by expert analysis to offer interpretation of the scientific aspects of cases. The chapter will identify an evolving trend in the ICJ's engagement with science, which has started with the marginalization of scientific evidence, continued with making only superficial evidentiary assessments, but more recently has seen an increasing willingness to engage with science in a more meaningful way.

Science has been shaping the adjudicatory analysis in many respects since the Court has begun to hear environmental disputes, the brief history of which will be overviewed in Section I. The chapter will then analyse different engagement techniques with science along the four stages of the adjudicatory process, such as framing (Section II), scientific fact-finding (Section III), causal inquiry (Section IV), as well as the extent and standard of review (Section V).

---

[1]   *Continental Shelf (Libya v. Malta)* (Judgment) (1985) ICJ Rep 13, para. 41.
[2]   *Pulp Mills on the River Uruguay (Argentina v. Uruguay)* (2010) ICJ Rep 14, Joint Dissenting Opinion of Judges Al-Khasawneh and Simma, para. 17.

I ENVIRONMENTAL DISPUTES APPEAR ON THE COURT'S DOCKET

By including the predecessor of the ICJ, the Permanent Court of International Justice (PCIJ) in the scope of this inquiry, the appropriate point of departure to study the international environmental jurisprudence lies in the dispute concerning the *Diversion of Water from the Meuse*,[3] decided by the PCIJ in 1937. The Netherlands initiated this proceeding against Belgium for the unilateral diversion of the river. In its counterclaim, Belgium alleged that the Netherlands committed an earlier breach by building locks. The PCIJ provided a narrow reading of the case and found that neither party was in breach of their obligations under the bilateral treaty regime of 1863. The noteworthy aspect of the case for purposes of the present analysis is that the PCIJ, for the first time in its history, arranged for a site visit to the locks in question.[4]

Despite the fact that even early decisions[5] of the ICJ contributed to the development of environmental law norms, the first strict sense environmental dispute was only referred to the Court in 1993 in the *Certain Phosphate Lands in Nauru* case, which was settled out of court.[6] It was followed by the *Nuclear Tests* case, which involved claims of harm caused to Australian territory by the nuclear fallout of French atmospheric nuclear tests.[7] This case did not reach the merits phase, since the Court found that the claim had no longer any object. The Court refrained from 'expressing any views'[8] on opposing scientific positions of the parties concerning the harmful consequences of nuclear testing. It nevertheless noted that the UN Scientific Committee on the Effects of Atomic Radiation has recorded measurable quantities of radioactive matter throughout the world on account of nuclear testing. Yet when the Court was facing France's opposite allegation that her own tests had generated only 'infinitesimal' quantities of radioactive matter, the Court deferred these science-intensive questions to the merits phase.[9] One may only guess how the Court would have handled these scientific dimensions had it reached discussing them in a substantive manner.

---

[3] *Diversion of Water from the Meuse (Netherlands v. Belgium)* (Judgment) (1927) PCIJ Series A/B, No. 70, 9.

[4] Romano, *The Peaceful Settlement of International Environmental Disputes A Pragmatic Approach*, pp. 237–8.

[5] The *Corfu Channel case (U.K. v. Albania)* (1949) ICJ Rep 4, and the *Barcelona Traction, Light and Power Company, Limited case (Belgium v. Spain)* (Judgment) (1970) ICJ Rep 3, 32 were relevant for the purposes of subsequent development of international environmental law norms. The former declared due diligence obligations of states, while the latter announced the existence of *erga omnes* obligations, both of which are important normative development for international environmental law. For a more detailed discussion on the relevance of these early decisions see J. E. Viñuales, 'The contribution of the International Court of Justice to the development of international environmental law: a contemporary assessment' (2008) 32 *Fordham International Law Journal* 236–44, at 232.

[6] *Certain Phosphate Lands in Nauru (Nauru v. Australia)*, (Discontinuance) Order of 13 September 1993, (1993) ICJ Rep 322, the case was settled by the parties.

[7] *Nuclear Tests (New Zealand v. France)* (Judgment) (1974) ICJ Rep 253, para. 18.

[8] *Nuclear Tests*, Judgment, para. 18.

[9] *Nuclear Tests*, Judgment, para. 18.

In the aftermath of the *Nuclear Tests* case, the proceedings initiated by New Zealand's *Request for an Examination of the Situation* would have equally provided an apt opportunity for the Court to elaborate on its approach to scientific facts. Facing the risks of France's underground nuclear tests run on the Mururoa atoll, New Zealand filed an application requesting the ICJ to examine, pursuant to paragraph 63 of the *Nuclear Tests* judgment, whether France had complied with its earlier commitment to cease the nuclear weapons tests. New Zealand essentially based the application on a growing body of scientific evidence pointing to the direction that French underground nuclear explosions were compromising the atoll's structure and threatening with long-term leakage.[10] However, all these aspects were again not entertained by the Court as it ruled that these matters were outside the scope of paragraph 63 of its earlier judgment, and for this reason it dismissed the request.[11] Yet again, the ICJ manoeuvred its reasoning in a way that it did not need to touch upon contested scientific arguments. The Advisory Opinion on the *Legality of the Threat or Use of Nuclear Weapons* discussed some important concepts relating to international environmental law though not in a contentious context.[12] The *Kasikili/Sedudu Island* case[13] also discussed questions of environmental law, however, its subject matter concerned maritime delimitation; therefore, it falls out of the narrow scope of this analysis.

The turning point in the Court's practice in resolving environmental disputes arrived with the *Gabcikovo-Nagymaros Project* case (*Gabcikovo-Nagymaros*) in 1997,[14] which was the first environmental dispute decided on the merits. Since then, we have witnessed a steady increase in the number of environmental disputes referred to the Court, such as the *Pulp Mills case* (2010),[15] the *Aerial Herbicide Spraying* case[16] (referred to the Court in 2008 and settled by the parties in 2013[17]), the *Whaling in the Antarctic* case (2014),[18] the *Certain Activities Carried out by Nicaragua in the Boarder Area* and *Construction of a Road along the San Juan River* joined cases (2015),[19] where the Court also issued interim measures

---

[10] *Request for an Examination of the Situation in Accordance with the Court's Judgment of December 1974 in the Nuclear Tests Case (New Zealand v. France)* (Provisional Measures) Order of 22 September 1995, (1995) ICJ Rep 288, paras. 33–5.

[11] *Request for an Examination of the Situation*, Provisional Measures, para. 65, See in greater detail: C. E. Foster, *Science and the Precautionary Principle in International Courts and Tribunals* (Cambridge University Press, 2011), pp. 56–8

[12] *Legality of the Threat or Use of Nuclear Weapons* (Advisory Opinion) (1996) ICJ Rep 266, para. 29.

[13] *Kasikili/Sedudu Island (Botswana v. Namibia)* (Judgment) (1999) ICJ Rep 1045, 1153.

[14] *Gabcikovo-Nagymaros (Hungary/Slovakia)* (Judgment) (1997) ICJ Rep 7.

[15] *Pulp Mills on the River Uruguay (Argentina v. Uruguay)* (Judgment) (2010) ICJ Rep 14.

[16] *Aerial Herbicide Spraying (Ecuador v. Colombia)* (Discontinuance) Order of 13 September, (2013) ICJ Rep 278.

[17] *Aerial Herbicide Spraying* (Discontinuance) Order of 13 September 2013.

[18] *Whaling in the Antarctic (Australia v. Japan: New Zealand intervening)* (Judgment) (2014) ICJ Rep 226.

[19] *Certain Activities Carried out by Nicaragua in the Border Area (Costa Rica v. Nicaragua)* and *Construction of a Road in Costa Rica along the San Juan River (Nicaragua v. Costa Rica)* (Judgment) (2015) ICJ Rep 665.

(2011),[20] and a compensation judgment (2018).[21] At the writing of this book, the *Dispute over the Status and Use of the Waters of the Silala* is pending before the ICJ (referred to the Court in 2016).[22] The initial eagerness of the Court to deal with environmental disputes is signalled by the creation of a Special Environmental Chamber in 1993,[23] which, however, has never been used given the lack of cases referred to it. In 2006 the ICJ decided not to hold elections for the bench of that chamber.[24]

1 Science Becomes Legally Relevant before the Court

Perhaps the most salient way in which scientific dimensions of environmental disputes become legally relevant lies in the context of invoking international responsibility for environmental harm. In such a context, factual issues of harm and causation are necessary though not sufficient prerequisites of finding a breach of the substantive aspect of the no-harm rule. Furthermore, scientific arguments can also emerge in describing environmental risks that may become legally relevant either in the context of states' environmental impact assessment (EIA) obligations[25] or as possible grounds for invoking circumstances precluding wrongfulness, that is, invoking the state of ecological necessity or distress.[26]

Rights and obligations enshrined in multilateral environmental agreements (MEAs) may also become subjects of legal disputes, where scientific arguments are of relevance for interpreting certain provisions. The most well-known treaty-based environmental claim with significant scientific aspect was filed in the *Whaling in the Antarctic* case, where the dispute zeroed in on the criteria due to which a state-funded whaling programme can be regarded as being conducted 'for purposes of scientific research'.

Lastly, science is also present in environmental disputes in more subtle ways. Given that the growing scientific understanding is an important factor in triggering the formation of new international environmental law norms, science to a certain

---

[20] *Certain Activities*, (Provisional Measures) Order of 8 March 2011, (2011) ICJ Rep 6.

[21] *Certain Activities Carried out by Nicaragua in the Border Area (Costa Rica v. Nicaragua)*, (Judgment on compensation) (2018) ICJ Rep 15.

[22] *Dispute over the Status and Use of the Waters of the Silala (Chile v. Bolivia)* filed with the Registry of the Court on 6 June 2016. The latest development in the case was the authorization of the submission of an additional pleading by the Republic of Chile on 21 June 2019.

[23] Press Release No. 1993/20, Constitution of a Chamber of the Court for the Environmental Matters (July 19, 1993), available at www.icj-cij.org/files/press-releases/3/10373.pdf (last accessed 10 January 2020).

[24] See the website of the ICJ overviewing the standing committees and chambers, available at www.icj-cij.org/en/chambers-and-committees (last accessed 10 January 2020).

[25] The threshold of environmental risks triggering an EIA obligation was discussed in the *Pulp Mills* as well as the *Certain Activities/Construction of a Road* cases. These will be addressed in more detail later in this chapter, see Section II, Subsection 2.3.

[26] The legal and scientific standards for invoking ecological necessity lay at the heart of the *Gabcikovo-Nagymaros* case, see *Gabcikovo-Nagymaros*, Judgment, paras. 49–58.

extent underlies all disputes relating to the environment. In *Gabcikovo-Nagymaros*, the Court expressly noted that 'new scientific insights' gave rise to 'new norms and standards'.[27] These science-induced norms necessitated, in the Court's view, that the parties 'look afresh at the effects on the environment'[28] and seek a reinterpretation of the original text of the 1977 Treaty in order to allow environmental objectives to be duly accounted for.[29] This suggests that the growing scientific understanding of anthropogenic impact on the environment influences the ways in which the ICJ interprets existing legal obligations.

Yet the various scientific references entering international disputes through the above mentioned entry points may only carry legal weight if disputes are framed in a way that regard scientific dimensions as part of the judicial analysis. This brings us to the decisive role of framing techniques, which will be discussed in the section that follows.

II FRAMING SCIENCE-INTENSIVE DISPUTES: CARVING OUT SCIENCE FROM LEGALLY RELEVANT ASPECTS OF DISPUTES

Given the myriads of different ways in which legally relevant questions can be identified and reconstructed from the facts of a case, it comes as no surprise that competing framings of the same legal conflict are not only possible but may also be inevitable. The environmental case law of the ICJ aptly illustrates that the presence of scientific facts and arguments fundamentally impacts the ways in which judicially relevant issues are selected and the judicial inquiry is framed. As Judge Donoghue points out writing extra-judicially, adjudicatory framing adjusts the science-intensity of a dispute by delineating the areas of expertise deemed relevant in a case.[30] As will be seen below, more subtle ways of judicial framing can also be detected in the ICJ's case law. In addition, the epistemic authority of science impacts not only the Court's framing, but also the ways in which the parties themselves approach and frame their science-intensive conflicts.

It is argued here that science's strong appeal to neutrality and authority triggers three types of reactions from litigants and adjudicators. The autonomous and objective nature of scientific arguments seem to deter the parties from having recourse to adjudication, where such arguments would deprive them of influencing judges' perception of the key aspects of the dispute. Sometimes the parties themselves try to avoid the adjudication of science-heavy conflicts, as evidenced by a relative frequency of out-of-court settlements in such cases (Subsection 1).

---

[27] *Gabcikovo-Nagymaros*, Judgment, para. 140.
[28] *Gabcikovo-Nagymaros*, Judgment, para. 140.
[29] *Gabcikovo-Nagymaros*, Judgment, para. 142. With the wording of the judgment: '[w]hat is required in the present case by the rule of pacta sunt servanda, as reflected in Article 26 of the Vienna Convention of 1969 on the Law of Treaties, is that the Parties find an agreed solution within the cooperative context of the Treaty'.
[30] Donoghue, 'Expert scientific evidence in a broader context', 386.

Similarly, the same attributes of science arguably impact judges as well by inducing them to frame their inquiry in a way as to carve out scientific issues from their analysis. This results in framing techniques downplaying the role of science in the Court's inquiry (Subsection 2). Among such judicial framing techniques, mandating the parties' negotiations in science-intensive questions (Subsection 2.1), the prevalence of finding procedural breaches (Subsection 2.2), as well as decoupling the notion of 'risk' from its scientific criteria (Subsection 2.3) will be discussed. Yet at the same time, scientific justifications can also appear as a convenient source of authority, which judges cite as a final and neutral arbiter of intricate and highly sensitive aspects of disputes. This manifests in decisions where scientific aspects are assessed meaningfully, for which examples will be addressed in the final sections of this chapter (Sections III–V).

1 *The Parties' Approach Towards Science: Settling Science-Heavy Claims Out of Court*

As mentioned above, the specificities of science-intensive disputes appear to influence the parties' litigation strategy as well. Saliently, all international claims only featuring alleged substantive breaches of the no-harm obligation were settled; and only those environmental claims reached the Court that, alongside damage claims, also included alleged violations of procedural obligations, as evidenced by *Pulp Mills* and *Construction of a Road* cases. Given the diversity of factors that may motivate out-of-court settlements, attributing a given outcome to a single cause may be impossible or misleading. One should also be mindful of the diplomatic and political sensitivities[31] usually involved in liability claims. Nevertheless, with the above caveat, many reasons are inherent in science-heavy claims that may induce the parties to reach a settlement and hence may explain this peculiar pattern in environmental disputes settlement.

First, the absence of universally accepted definition of actionable 'environmental damage'[32] entails that there is no settled scope for compensable harm in international environmental lawsuits. Second, not only is there a considerable difference in the possible coverage of the notion 'environmental harm', but the scientific methods for valuing environmental harm also vary to a great extent.[33] These taken together engender a great deal of uncertainty surrounding ecological damage valuation. Certain methods that seek to capture the entirety of the loss of ecosystem services may suggest astronomical amounts of damages.[34] These inherent ambiguities in

---

[31] See for example with regard to the *Aerial Herbicide Spraying* case, analysed later in this section.

[32] Fitzmaurice, 'Principle 13 liability and compensation', p. 352.

[33] M. T. Huguenin, M. C. Donlan, A. E. van Geel, and R. W. Paterson, 'Assessment and valuation of damage to the environment' in C. Payne and P. H. Sand (eds.), *Gulf War Reparations and the UN Compensation Commission: Environmental Liability* (Oxford University Press, 2015), pp. 1–41 p. 91.

[34] *Certain Activities*, Judgment on compensation, 2018, para. 57.

ecological damage quantification may create an additional incentive for respondent states to settle claims of ecological damage.

Considerations of uncontrollable scientific complexities do appear to play a significant role in motivating settlements. Commentators have earlier noted with respect to the *Gut Dam* Arbitration between the United States and Canada that the fear of adjudicating causal issues was the main motivation behind out-of-court settlement in the case.[35] Similar impetus has arguably been at play in the environmental disputes that were settled before they could have reached the ICJ. Chronologically first in line, Australia settled claims with Nauru that were filed for irreparable damage caused to Nauruan territory by phosphate mining activities of Australia, the then trustee of these lands. Nauru claimed that the failure of Australia to enact any measure to rehabilitate mined-out lands breached its international law obligations.[36] Upon settlement, Australia paid AUD 107 million for compensation[37] for the vast environmental damage that left 80 per cent of Nauru's territory barren.[38]

The second instance when the parties opted for settling their claims of environmental damage, right before they could have been assessed by the Court on the merits, was in the *Aerial Herbicide Spraying* case. Ecuador filed treaty-based claims against Colombia for aerial spraying of toxic herbicides across their shared borders. The spraying had allegedly 'already caused serious damage to the environment' and to the health of affected populations, and 'pose[d] a grave risk of future damage' on the territory of Ecuador.[39] Commentators held high hopes that the ICJ would finally seize the opportunity to resolve an inter-state environmental liability claim, and in so doing would clarify the content of key environmental law norms.[40] The facts of the case would have also warranted an elaborate scientific fact-finding process, as they raised highly technical questions of different deposition rates of chemicals under varying weather conditions and the changing altitudes of spraying flights.[41] Judging by the application, which contained numerous references[42] to scientific evidence of harm already occurred and pointed out the carcinogenic potential of herbicide use, the case indeed provided a strong call for close judicial interaction with the scientific

---

[35] Lefeber, *Transboundary Environmental Interference and the Origin of State Liability*, pp. 90–1. The dispute concerned an unexpected increase in water levels along the St Lawrence River on US territory, which US citizens who suffered extensive property damage attributed to an upstream dam built by Canada decades ago. See more on the dispute in Romano, *The Peaceful Settlement of International Environmental Disputes: A Pragmatic Approach*, p. 31.

[36] *Certain Phosphate Lands in Nauru*, Application instituting proceedings, filed on 19 May 1989, paras. 42–8.

[37] Louka, *International Environmental Law Fairness, Effectiveness, and World Order*, p. 472.

[38] Louka, *International Environmental Law Fairness, Effectiveness, and World Order*, p. 471.

[39] *Aerial Herbicide Spraying*, Application instituting proceedings, filed on 31 March 2008, para 2.

[40] Viñuales, 'Contribution of the International Court of Justice to the development of international environmental law', 255; Foster, 'New clothes for the emperor?', 151.

[41] A. B. Loewenstein, 'Adjudication of environmental impact assessment claims before international courts and tribunals' in C. Voigt (ed.), *International Judicial Practice on the Environment: Questions of Legitimacy* (Cambridge University Press, 2019), pp. 288–310 p. 309.

[42] *Aerial Herbicide Spraying*, Application instituting proceedings, paras. 13–23.

dimensions. The parties however decided at a later stage to settle the claims. In a bilateral agreement, they set up an exclusion zone free from spraying to prevent any contamination from drifting to Ecuadorian territory.[43] Yet again, one should bear in mind the sensitive political questions involved in *Aerial Herbicide Spraying*. Ecuador alleged that Colombia's spraying programme targeted illicit coca and poppy plantations and Colombia refused to disclose relevant data including the chemical composition of the herbicide used.[44] Avoiding heightened international attention surrounding court proceedings could have been an equally strong motivation for Colombia to settle.

2   *Judicial Framing Techniques Downplaying Science*

There have been a number of occasions when the Court effectively avoided deciding scientific aspects of legal disputes put before it. Three major ways readily emerge from the Court's case law carving out scientific aspects from the judicial inquiry. The ICJ sometimes refers science-heavy issues back to the parties' negotiations (Subsection 2.1). It also often evaluates risk assessment criteria of EIA obligations based on solely non-scientific factors (Subsection 2.2). The Court may also prioritize procedural obligations over substantive ones in reconstructing the legally relevant aspects of disputes (Subsection 2.3).

2.1   Mandating the Negotiation of the Parties

It is not at all newsworthy that the ICJ remains cautious in evaluating highly politicized and sensitive claims of sovereign states. Judicial economy has long characterized the Court's practice, that is, a tendency to narrow the scope of its judgment to the extent possible, and thereby to avoid elaborating on contested issues that are not deemed essential to decide the dispute at hand.[45]

The exercise of judicial economy is an established practice of the Court in various types of claims,[46] though the presence of science-heavy arguments does appear to provide a considerable impetus for the narrow framing of disputes. Commentators have also noted the apparent efforts made by judges in the *Gabcikovo-Nagymaros* case to 'acrobatically avoid'[47] the substantive, ecological aspect of the dispute. While it decided about issues of state succession, treaty law, and state responsibility, the

---

[43]   *Aerial Herbicide Spraying*, Order of 13 September.

[44]   *Aerial Herbicide Spraying*, Application instituting proceedings, para. 3.

[45]   Palombino, 'Judicial economy and limitation of the scope of the decision in international adjudication', 922.

[46]   C. Gray, 'The 2016 judicial activity of the International Court of Justice' (2017) 111 *American Journal of International Law* 415–36 at 415–36.

[47]   S. Stec and G. Eckstein, 'Of solemn oaths and obligations: the environmental impact of the ICJ's decision in the case concerning the Gabcikovo-Nagymaros project' (1997) 8 *Yearbook of International Environmental Law* 41–57 at 42.

Court saliently stopped short of specifying the requirements of reasonable and equitable allocation of the waters of the Danube,[48] just as it did not concretize the scope of environmental damage to be compensated by Slovakia.[49] All in all, with respect to virtually all science-heavy aspects, the Court recurrently urged the parties to find 'an agreed solution'.[50] Judge Bedjaoui stressed that despite the extreme difficulties involved in such a fact-intensive dispute, the Court 'ought ... to have the final say'.[51] Yet the majority took a different path and 'basically threw the dispute back into the lap of the parties'.[52]

In the Court's reading, it has only been asked to determine the basis of compensation but not the quantum of damages.[53] Yet such a conceptualization of the judicial task does not strictly follow from Article 2(2) of the Compromis, which provides that 'the Court is also requested to determine the legal consequences, including the rights and obligations for the Parties, arising from its Judgment'. It is argued here that even if the Court's task was indeed confined to ruling only on the basis but not the quantum of compensation, it still should have had to determine the basis and scope of compensation with enough clarity. It appears that the Court had considerable room for manoeuvre in interpreting its task established by the Compromis and it made a strategic choice not to touch upon the science-intensive question of determining the quantum of compensation. The Court's preference for entrusting the parties with determining the quantum of compensation also surfaced later in *Certain Activities/Construction of a Road*. Yet, in that case, the Court was willing to announce the quantum of damages in a separate judgment on compensation, having the parties been unable to come up with an agreed solution within the fixed time limit.[54]

2.2 Giving Precedence to Procedural Obligations over Science-Heavy Substantive Ones

It is noteworthy that in *Pulp Mills* the Court found that Uruguay has breached a procedural obligation to inform and notify affected parties about its activities' potential environmental impact, whereas all claims concerning substantive breaches have been dismissed.[55] Similarly, in *Certain Activities* and *Construction*

---

48 *Gabcikovo-Nagymaros*, Judgment, para. 140. The parties 'must find a satisfactory solution for the volume of water to be released into the old bed of the Danube'.
49 *Gabcikovo-Nagymaros*, Judgment, para. 155, section (2) D.
50 *Gabcikovo-Nagymaros*, Judgment, para. 142, and the same was mandated in para. 140: The parties 'must find a satisfactory solution for the volume of water to be released into the old bed of the Danube'.
51 *Gabcikovo-Nagymaros*, Separate Opinion of Judge Bedjaoui, para. 60.
52 Romano, *The Peaceful Settlement of International Environmental Disputes: A Pragmatic Approach*, p. 256.
53 *Gabcikovo-Nagymaros*, Judgment, para. 152.
54 *Certain Activities/Construction of a Road*, Judgment, para. 229.
55 *Pulp Mills*, Judgment, para. 282.

of a Road claims concerning significant transboundary harm were dismissed, and only a procedural violation has been found on the part of Costa Rica, namely, a failure to conduct a proper EIA.[56] These suggest that the bench is inclined to prioritize procedural requirements over substantive obligations.[57] Some ICJ judges argue that this is because procedural obligations are more concrete compared to abstract substantive obligations.[58] While this position undoubtedly holds true, the avowedly fact-intensive nature[59] of issues of harm and causation seems also to play a major role in framing the judicial inquiry in this peculiar way. The apparent reluctance of the ICJ to engage in meaningful scientific fact-finding and causal inquiry in relation to environmental liability claims appears to be attributable to the fact that judges can rule on procedural obligations more comfortably, as these normally constitute considerably less science-heavy aspects of disputes at hand.

2.3 Decoupling the Legal Appraisal of Risks from Science: Judicial Review of EIA Obligations

Environmental impact assessment obligations are frequently featured in international litigation, which is partly connected to the fact that states in these proceedings can escape proving causality with environmental harm.[60] Given that EIA obligations arise before any environmental damage occurs, both the parties and the bench are saved from complications that arise in connection with proving a violation of a substantive obligation, as addressed above.

States have a customary law obligation to prepare an EIA regarding activities carried out within their jurisdiction risking to cause significant environmental harm to other states.[61] Yet the threshold of risk that triggers such an obligation and the minimum requirements as to the content of a valid EIA are not settled either in terms of law,[62] or as to the facts. The ICJ thus far has refrained from distilling any objective, scientific criteria, leaving states with broad discretion in this respect. This section will first address the criteria triggering EIA obligations as set out in the practice of the Court. Then it will offer some grounds for criticism with respect to the ICJ's approach to the scientific aspects of risk assessments.

---

[56] *Certain Activities/Construction of a Road*, Judgment, para. 229.
[57] O. McIntyre, 'The contribution of procedural rules to the environmental protection of transboundary rivers in light of recent ICJ case law' in L Boisson de Chazournes (ed.), *International Law and Freshwater* (Edward Elgar, 2013), pp. 239–66 pp. 239–40.
[58] *Pulp Mills*, Joint Dissenting Opinion of Judges Al-Khasawneh and Simma, para. 26.
[59] Donoghue, 'Expert scientific evidence in a broader context', 382.
[60] Loewenstein, 'Adjudication of environmental impact assessment claims before international courts and tribunals', p. 289.
[61] *Pulp Mills*, Judgment, para. 204.
[62] This was explicitly suggested by Judge Bhandari in his Separate Opinion in *Certain Activities/Construction of a Road*, para. 6: 'public international law presently offers almost no guidance as to the specific circumstances giving rise to the need for an EIA, nor the requisite content of any such assessment'.

2.3.1 CRITERIA FOR ASSESSING THE THRESHOLD OF RISK TRIGGERING AN EIA. EIA
obligations lay at the heart of the *Pulp Mills* and the *Certain Activities/
Construction of a Road* cases. The Court avoided using scientific benchmarks on
both occasions, which suggests that the ICJ is only ready to use non-scientific
benchmarks for assessing the significance of risks that triggers this obligation. In
Construction of a Road the Court evaluated whether Costa Rica lawfully omitted
preparing an EIA prior to constructing a road along the San Juan River. The
reasoning shows that the Court appraised the significance of risks solely in light of
the territorial state's own preliminary risk assessment.[63] Although the Court stressed
that the risks are to be judged by the magnitude, location, and geographic conditions
of the project,[64] the ambiguous reference to domestic law raises concerns for
decoupling risk assessments from the underlying science. The reasoning altogether
begs the question 'how much – if any – actual empirical or scientific approaches are
actually relied upon by the Court'[65] when it assesses whether there have been
significant risks of transboundary harm triggering the duty to prepare an EIA?

The ICJ sets similarly vague criteria as to the minimum requirements for the
content of an EIA. Disputing states routinely refer to the failure of the other party to
sufficiently study the potential impacts of the activity complained of.[66] The Court
hitherto has not given any objective, let alone scientific, standards to define the
validity criteria of an EIA from an international law point of view. In *Pulp Mills*, the
ICJ expressly mandated that 'it is for each State to determine . . . the specific content
of the environmental impact assessment required in each case, having regard to the
nature and magnitude of the proposed development and its likely adverse impact'.[67]
Arguably, this rule is not a simple *renvoi* to domestic law with respect to the content
of an EIA,[68] as the need for taking the nature and magnitude of the project into
account calls for an objective assessment. Nevertheless, having such a formulation,
any international law requirements on the minimum content of an EIA are deprived
of a real bite. This is well depicted by the fact that thus far the ICJ has found no

---

[63] *Certain Activities/Construction of a Road*, Judgment, para. 154.
[64] *Certain Activities/Construction of a Road*, Judgment, para. 155.
[65] D. Desierto, 'Evidence but not empiricism? Environmental impact assessments at the International
Court of Justice in certain activities carried out by Nicaragua in the border area (*Costa Rica
v. Nicaragua*) and construction of a road in Costa Rica along the San Juan River (*Nicaragua
v. Costa Rica*), EJIL Talk! (Feb. 26, 2016)'. Available at https://bit.ly/2zQmzDa (last accessed
10 January 2020).
[66] See for example the arguments raised by Uruguay in the Pulp Mills dispute, *Pulp Mills*, Judgment,
para. 203.
[67] *Pulp Mills*, Judgment, para. 205.
[68] The *renvoi* argument was raised by Costa Rica in the *Certain Activities/Construction of a Road* (see
Judgment, para. 148), but it was implicitly refuted by the Court in its reasoning as to the finding of
a violation regarding Costa Rica's conduct (Judgment, paras. 153–6). Several judges support the view
that the judgment negates the *renvoi* argument (Separate Opinion of Judge Donoghue, para. 15, and
Separate Opinion of Judge ad hoc Dugard, para. 18). However, Judge Bhandari is of the opinion that
the Pulp Mills decision allows such a *renvoi* (Separate Opinion of Judge Bhandari, para. 29).

breach on account of preparing an insufficient EIA. Violations were declared only for the failure to prepare a timely assessment, prior the authorization of the project.[69]

2.3.2 CRITICAL ASSESSMENT OF DECOUPLING EIA FROM THE SCIENCE OF RISK ASSESSMENT. The Court's current not so empiricist[70] approach to EIA can be critiqued on many grounds. First, one may argue that it fails to meet requirements for epistemic non-arbitrariness, that is, not to evaluate scientific notions according to standards alien to scientific logic,[71] in this case, by purely legal standards. Tying the obligation of EIA to 'the presence of significant risk of harm', as was announced by the Court,[72] is no more than an empty rhetoric, when in fact the Court decouples the meaning of 'risk' from the science of environmental risk assessment. The notion of 'significant environmental risk' constitutes an essentially extra-legal concept,[73] which is elevated to a normative framework by the legal rules governing EIA obligations, nevertheless, it remains a scientific concept. Against this background, the Court's reasoning that treats scientific concepts as if they were purely legal constructs commits epistemic trespassing.

Second, constructing the notion of risk as an empty shell also runs against the approach of the ILC, which regards risk as an objective concept.[74] The commentaries to the 2001 Draft Articles on Prevention of Transboundary Harm from Hazardous Activities explicitly mention 'developments in scientific knowledge' within the ambit of requisite risk assessment procedures.[75] Therefore, referring the threshold criterion essentially back to states' discretion is problematic also from that perspective.

Third, states may too easily abuse their room for manoeuvre. In the face of such attempts, Judge Bhandari proposed taking respective international agreements and soft law documents into account to limit states' discretion. For instance, the Espoo Convention mandates compulsory EIA with regard to certain types of industries that are harmful enough to warrant a presumption of potential for significant harm,[76] and the UNEP Principles also stipulate certain minimum requirements

---

[69] *Certain Activities/Construction of a Road*, Judgment, paras. 161–73. Similarly, international arbitral tribunals only found a breach for the complete absence of an EIA. See discussion on the *South China Sea* arbitral award in Chapter 4.

[70] Desierto, 'Evidence but not empiricism?'.

[71] D'Aspremont and Mbengue, 'Strategies of engagement with scientific fact-finding in international adjudication', 269, 271.

[72] *Certain Activities/Construction of a Road*, Judgment, para. 156.

[73] On the notion of extra-legal concepts that exist outside the law's sphere but are used in the process of legal reasoning, see V. Lowe, *International Law* (Oxford University Press, 2007), pp. 98–9.

[74] See more on that line of criticism: Desierto, 'Evidence but not empiricism?'.

[75] ILC, 'Draft articles on prevention of transboundary harm', Commentaries to Article 1, para. 15.

[76] Convention on Environmental Impact Assessment in a Transboundary Context, Espoo, 25 February 1991, in force 10 September 1997, 1989 UNTS 309. Although the Espoo Convention is not yet regarded as reflecting customary international law, Judge Bhandari sets it as a progressive guideline for future law-making developments in the field of EIA obligations, see *Certain Activities/Construction of a Road*, Separate Opinion of Judge Bhandari, para. 42.

for the content of EIAs.[77] Indeed, discerning similar scientifically relevant requirements would be most useful in better defining substantive EIA criteria under
international law.

Finally, decoupling minimum standards of EIA procedures from any sort of
scientific standards threatens inconsistent judgments, that is, delivering different
decisions in factually comparable situations. The Court arrived at an opposite
conclusion in the *Certain Activities/Construction of a Road* cases regarding the
obligation to prepare an EIA with respect to two activities that were equally threatening wetlands designated under the Ramsar Convention. While the ICJ found that
Nicaragua had no obligation to prepare an EIA regarding its dredging activity,[78] it
ruled that Costa Rica was under such an obligation with respect to its construction of
a road.[79] Not only the outcome but also the legal analyses leading to these opposite
findings were strikingly different. With respect to Costa Rica's construction, the
Court made a detailed factual assessment of the relevant factors of the project, in
which the fact that the works impacted a Ramsar wetland was held decisive in
mandating an EIA.[80] In contrast, regarding Nicaragua's dredging that impacted
another Ramsar site, the Court concluded without any detailed factual assessment[81]
that there were no significant risks warranting an EIA.[82] It is submitted here that by
manifestly avoiding substantive benchmarks, including objective, empirical, and
scientific parameters, the ICJ is susceptible to making inconsistent decisions concerning environmental risks.

III SCIENTIFIC FACT-FINDING TECHNIQUES OF THE ICJ

The extent to which the Court evaluates scientific evidence is the most indicative of
the role and weight attached to scientific arguments in deciding environmental
disputes. Despite some 'cautious' improvements in this respect,[83] the Court's scientific fact-finding methods are still vulnerable to criticism. Compared to the paths
taken by other international judicial fora in cases involving scientific aspects, most
notably the PCA, the WTO, the ITLOS, and investment arbitration tribunals; the
ICJ appears to be the most unwilling to engage with scientific expertise. This may

---

[77]   UNEP Governing Council, 'Goals and Principles of Environmental Impact Assessment', GC Dec.
        14/25 (II) (1987), endorsed by 'International co-operation in the field of the environment', UNGA Res.
        42/184 (XLII) (11 December 1987), Principle 4.
[78]   *Certain Activities/Construction of a Road*, Judgment, para. 105.
[79]   *Certain Activities/Construction of a Road*, Judgment, para. 155.
[80]   *Certain Activities/Construction of a Road*, Judgment, para. 155.
[81]   *Certain Activities/Construction of a Road*, Judgment, para. 105.
[82]   Judge ad hoc Dugard comments on this aspect in his Separate Opinion, *Certain Activities/
        Construction of a Road*, Separate Opinion of Judge ad hoc Dugard, para. 34.
[83]   Ridell, 'Scientific evidence in the International Court of Justice: problems and possibilities', 229–58;
        Desierto, 'Evidence but not empiricism?' ; J. G. S. Coustasse and E. Sweeney-Samuelson,
        'Adjudicating conflicts over resources: the ICJ's treatment of technical evidence in the *Pulp Mills*
        case' (2011) 3 *Goettingen Journal of International Law* 447–71 at 447–71.

have repercussions on the significance of the Court vis-à-vis other judicial bodies in resolving science-heavy conflicts. As Ridell warns: 'the International Court of Justice can retain its importance in international dispute resolution, if it sufficiently addresses the easily rectifiable deficiencies in the area of scientific evidence'.[84]

The following analysis will first discuss the evolution of the ICJ's scientific fact-finding during its more than twenty year-long environmental jurisprudence (Subsection 1), then it will review the changing procedural avenues in which expert advice has been garnered (Subsection 2), and the Court's approach to handling complex scientific expert evidence (Subsection 3). It will conclude with a general discussion on applicable standard and burden of proof (Subsection 4), and listing recurrent proposals urging a more active judicial engagement with scientific evidence (Subsection 5).

1 *The Beginnings: Declining to Consider Scientific Evidence*

The first environmental contentious case decided by the Court, the *Gabcikovo-Nagymaros* dispute, has seen a rather poor evidentiary assessment. In fact the Court chose not to consider the abundant expert evidence submitted by the parties, and found the absence of an imminent environmental risk without evaluating any scientific data describing such peril.[85] This path has already generated harsh criticism in contemporaneous scholarship.[86] The present study points out additional concerns regarding the Court's reasoning from the perspective of legitimacy. Importantly, this criticism does not relate to the actual outcome of the judicial assessment but questions the legitimacy of their reasoning and that of the procedure in which judges formed their opinions. As will be argued, solid and legitimate conclusions can hardly be drawn regarding matters of ecological risks without considering the weight of relevant scientific reports submitted by the parties.[87]

First of all, Hungary and Slovakia both regarded the issue of environmental risks as a scientific question, which is clearly evidenced by the sheer number of expert reports adduced. The Hungarian Reply alone included a 100-page long 'scientific rebuttal' in which it analysed the Slovakian scientific claims in detail.[88] Also, the scientific aspect of the conflict was thoroughly investigated by a fact-finding

---

[84]   Ridell, 'Scientific evidence in the International Court of Justice: problems and possibilities', 229.
[85]   A. Koe, 'Damming the Danube: the International Court of Justice and the Gabcikovo-Nagymaros project (Hungary v. Slovakia)' (1998) 20 *Sydney Law Review*, 612 at 616.
[86]   Koe, 'Damming the Danube', 616; Stec and Eckstein, 'Of solemn oaths and obligations: the environmental impact of the ICJ's decision in the case concerning the Gabcikovo-Nagymaros project', 41–57; Romano, *The Peaceful Settlement of International Environmental Disputes A Pragmatic Approach*, pp. 259–60.
[87]   For a similar proposition see Ridell and Plant, *Evidence before the International Court of Justice*, p. 348.
[88]   *Gabcikovo-Nagymaros*, Reply of the Republic of Hungary, Volume 2, Scientific Rebuttal, 20 June 1995, 1–108.

mission of the European Communities,[89] which also made express recommendations as to the amount of water to be discharged to the Danube's old riverbed in order
to prevent irreversible adverse impact. Hence procedural fairness considerations
alone would have warranted an open evaluation of the party-adduced expert evidence. Yet the Court chose to circumvent evaluating the evidence regarding environmental risks. One commentator rightly dubbed this judicial strategy as
'minimizing science'[90] in adjudication. Despite the many challenges posed for
scientific fact-finding relating to alleged situations of ecological necessity,[91] marginalizing substantive scientific arguments of the parties is problematic especially in
light of the apparent inconsistency between 'the strong environmentally friendly
language'[92] of the judgment and the conclusion reached.

Judges' aversion to evaluate scientific evidence is normally defended based on two
grounds. First, that the bench lacks technical expertise, and second, that a clear
distinction must be drawn between disputed legal claims and scientific controversies
underlying these claims. Proponents of a 'de-scientized' judicial inquiry stress that
courts of law cannot decide about the latter aspect. However, Judge Herczegh
dissenting aptly pointed out the limited reach of such arguments: 'As a judicial
organ, the Court was admittedly not empowered to decide scientific questions touching on biology, hydrology, and so on, or questions of a technical type which arose out
of the G/N [Gabcikovo-Nagymaros] Project; but it could – and even should – have
ruled on the legal consequences of certain facts alleged by one Party.'[93]

This criticism goes to the crux of the weakness of the Court's scientific fact-
finding, namely, that the ICJ often draws conclusions about scientific arguments
without making a transparent evaluation of the underlying facts. In the material
case, the Court dismissed Hungary's plea of ecological necessity by distinguishing
'possible peril', described by uncertain scientific claims, from the 'objective existence of a peril', which was to be supported by foreseeable future damage.[94] A slight
majority found that the several hundred pages long scientific evidence only sufficed
to suggest 'serious uncertainties',[95] but could not establish an objective peril

---

[89]   Mission report of the Commission of the European Communities Czech and Slovak Federal
       Republic and Republic of Hungary, 31 October 1992, Bratislava (Annex 13 to the Memorial of
       Republic of Hungary); Commission of the European Communities Republic of Hungary,
       Slovak Republic, Working Group of Monitoring and water management experts for the Gabcikovo
       system of locks. Report on Temporary water management regime, 1 December 1993, Bratislava
       (Annex 19 to the Memorial of Republic of Hungary).
[90]   Viñuales, 'Observations sur le traitement des motifs scientifiques dans le contentieux environmental
       international', pp. 114–16.
[91]   ILC, 'Second report of the Special Rapporteur, James Crawford, on state responsibility' (1999) UN
       Doc. A/CN.4/498/Add.2, para 288.
[92]   J. Crawford, '*In Dubio Pro Natura*: The Dissent of Judge Herczegh' in Péter Kovács (ed.),
       International Law: A Quiet Strength (Pázmány Press, 2011), pp. 251–69 p. 268.
[93]   *Gabcikovo-Nagymaros*, Dissenting Opinion of Judge Herczegh, p. 177.
[94]   *Gabcikovo-Nagymaros*, Judgment, para. 54.
[95]   *Gabcikovo-Nagymaros*, Judgment, para. 54.

justifying a state of necessity. Choosing between these two legal scenarios the factual bases of which run so closely together, without touching upon the scientific evidence submitted, let alone providing any justification supported by the evaluation of the evidence, seriously undermines the legitimacy of the reasoning.

2 *Using Expertise: From Counsels to Witnesses and Beyond*

The avenue in which the Court gathers expert advice impacts the extent to which it can exercise control over expertise, and hence, is highly relevant in terms of the legitimacy of its engagement with scientific arguments. The evolving fact-finding techniques of the ICJ are addressed below.

2.1 Expert Counsels

Compared to saliently missing evidentiary assessment in *Gabcikovo-Nagymaros*, the *Pulp Mills* decision has marked a slight improvement in the scientific fact-finding of the Court. All judges acknowledged the importance of expert opinions, though the bench was divided on the exact procedure in which these opinions ought to be presented. The parties chose to include scientific experts in their team of counsels.[96] Under Article 43 of the statute, these 'expert counsels' were only allowed to be questioned by the bench. The majority found such a procedural solution less helpful compared to having scientists acting as expert witnesses.[97] Importantly, expert witnesses could be subject to cross-examination.[98] Judge Greenwood notes a further disadvantage of using scientists as counsels, namely, that it may seed some distrust in the bench, since the party offering such expert opinion may be seen as 'unacceptably blur[ring] the distinction between evidence and advocacy'.[99] This practice was, therefore, later abandoned by the parties.

2.2 Expert Witnesses: And Ways of Scrutinizing Party-Adduced Evidence

After *Pulp Mills*, party-adduced evidence has been presented by expert witnesses.[100] This option opened up a range of possibilities for the Court to scrutinize the evidence in order to choose between rival scientific claims offered by the experts. The most typical solution is to allow cross-examination, and increasingly, the questioning of the experts by the judges themselves (Subsection 2.2.1). Nevertheless, the

---

[96] *Pulp Mills*, Judgment, paras. 22–5. In the Gabcikovo-Nagymaros dispute, the parties also had recourse to such an approach, and included hydrologist experts in their team of counsels and advocates. *Gabcikovo-Nagymaros*, Judgment, paras 9–10.

[97] *Pulp Mills*, Judgment, para. 167.

[98] Rules of Court, 14 April 1978, in force 1 July 1978, (1978), Article 65.

[99] *Pulp Mills*, Separate Opinion of Judge Greenwood, para. 27.

[100] Rules of Court, Articles 57, 63.

ICJ apparently continues to rely on certain 'second-order indicators'[101] to interpret conflicting or scarce scientific evidence (Subsection 2.2.2).

2.2.1 CROSS-EXAMINATION AND QUESTIONING BY THE BENCH.

Cross-examination could assist the Court in testing the credibility and consistency of scientific data submitted by the parties. In the *Certain Activities/Construction of a Road* cases, the Court allowed the counsels to cross-examine the experts of the other side.[102] As has been discussed above, however, the expert evidence was still insufficient for the Court to find a breach of the no-harm rule established.

Arguably, the *Whaling in the Antarctic* case marks thus far the most effective judicial use of scientific expertise. Expert witnesses of the parties[103] were cross-examined by the parties and were also questioned by the bench. Importantly, judges did not give '*carte blanche* acceptance of expert opinions',[104] nor did they use opposing scientific views as an excuse for disregarding the expert advice. The *Whaling in the Antarctic* judgment can be viewed as the first occasion when the Court engaged with conflicting scientific claims in a meaningful way.[105] Australia's expert, Professor Mangel, later formed a very optimistic opinion concerning the ICJ's use of expert advice and its success in bridging the law–science divide inherent in the factual intricacies of the dispute. His words are worthy of being reproduced in full here:

> Judges demonstrated understanding of the need for testable questions, appropriate sample size (e.g. paras. 160–198), how models and data are connected, adjusting field work according to circumstances (e.g. paras. 201, 206–212), and peer review broadly defined (e.g., paras. 84, 155, 156, 219). That is, it is clear that the Judges understood the links between objectives of a scientific study, methods to achieve those objectives, and the importance of appropriate sample size.[106]

According to an empirical survey conducted among scientists acting before international courts, experts usually doubt the Court's ability to assess conflicting evidence on its own, and regard cross-examination as a necessary vehicle to assist judges in identifying the significant issues.[107] Yet cross-examination holds strikingly different value in the eye of scientists and lawyers. While counsels view it as the 'best mean

---

[101] Donoghue, 'Expert scientific evidence in a broader context', 381.

[102] *Certain Activities/Construction of a Road*, Judgment, para. 34.

[103] Australia brought Dr Nick Gale, the Chief Scientist of the Australian Antarctic Program and Professor Marc Mangel, a mathematician and a renowned expert in the field of providing scientific advice to environmental policy-making, and Japan called Professor Lars Walloe from the University of Oslo.

[104] Mangel, 'Whales, science, and scientific whaling in the International Court of Justice', 14526.

[105] P. Sands, 'Climate change and the rule of law: adjudicating the future of international law' (2016) 28 *Journal of Environmental Law* 19–35 at 29.

[106] Mangel, 'Whales, science, and scientific whaling in the International Court of Justice', 14526.

[107] Boisson de Chazournes, Mbengue, Das, and Gros, 'One size does not fit all – uses of experts before international courts and tribunals', 484.

possible"[108] to make legal sense of scientific claims, experts generally do not conceive cross-examination as a self-sufficient technique to scrutinize scientific evidence.[109]

2.2.2 SECOND-ORDER INDICATORS. Judge Donoghue expressly points to the importance of so-called second-order indicators in the ICJ's practice to scrutinize party-adduced evidence.[110] She explains that the Court tends to regard those facts established that are consensual among the parties. Even greater weight is attached to unfavourable facts that are not contested, or even conceded, by the respective party. The bench may also find a respective fact established by drawing adverse inferences from a party's unexplained omission to adduce a piece of evidence that is otherwise expected from it.[111] Lastly, scrutinizing the independence and impartiality of experts is purported to be an important second-order indicator for the Court whether to accept a certain scientific claim as valid.[112]

2.3 *Ex Curia* Experts

A recurrent dilemma is whether the Court ought to avail itself of its procedural power to appoint *ex curia* experts under Article 50 of its Statute. Notably, the ICJ has never used such a power in environmental disputes, and altogether only in three cases it appointed its own experts.[113] An empirical survey suggests that the majority of judges are contended with the present scheme of gathering expert advice solely from the parties' submissions and only a handful of judges would support a greater reliance on *ex curia* experts.[114] Some members of the bench already voiced concerns about the prevailing fact-finding practice of the Court. Most eminently, dissenting Judge Simma and Judge Al-Khasawneh in *Pulp Mills* stressed that traditional fact-finding methods would not suffice in cases involving highly complex and technical scientific evidence,[115] and argued that the Court should have had recourse to *ex curia* experts. Judge Yusuf also emphasized that it would 'serve the Court well in the future to make better use of the powers granted to it by its Statute'[116] in science-intensive cases. In contrast, Judge Donoghue, writing extra-judicially, cautioned against

---

[108] Boisson de Chazournes, Mbengue, Das, and Gros, 'One size does not fit all – uses of experts before international courts and tribunals', 487.
[109] Boisson de Chazournes, Mbengue, Das, and Gros, 'One size does not fit all – uses of experts before international courts and tribunals', 484.
[110] Donoghue, 'Expert scientific evidence in a broader context', 384–5.
[111] Donoghue, 'Expert scientific evidence in a broader context', 384–5.
[112] Donoghue, 'Expert scientific evidence in a broader context', 385.
[113] *Corfu Channel*; *Delimitation of the Maritime Boundary in the Gulf of Maine Area (Canada v. US)* (Judgment) (1984) ICJ Rep 246; *Maritime Delimitation in the Caribbean Sea and the Pacific Ocean (Costa Rica v. Nicaragua)* Order of 31 May 2016, (2016) ICJ Rep 235.
[114] Boisson de Chazournes, Mbengue, Das, and Gros, 'One size does not fit all – uses of experts before international courts and tribunals', 480–2.
[115] *Pulp Mills*, Joint Dissenting Opinion of Judges Al-Khasawneh and Simma, para. 12.
[116] *Pulp Mills*, Judgment, Declaration of Judge Yusuf, para. 14.

relying on court-appointed experts out of fear that the Court would be less likely to admit that its own expert committed a methodological error, leaving the bench dependent on the advice received.[117] Some scholars deem court-appointed experts as a panacea to the inefficiencies of the Court's scientific fact-finding,[118] while others see a greater reliance on court-appointed experts threatening inadvertent delegation of the judicial task.[119]

Notably, the Court also has the power of appointing assessors, who sit with the bench without the right to vote.[120] Yet, this avenue of gathering expert advice has not been used in the Court's practice either. The Court does seem to benefit, however, from independent expert reviews commissioned by the parties for purposes not directly relating to the court proceedings. In *Pulp Mills*, Uruguay presented the ICJ with an expert report prepared by the International Finance Corporation regarding the financing assessment of the underlying pulp mills project.[121]

2.4 Shadow Experts

In contrast to court-appointed experts, the ICJ has been willing to consult experts on an informal basis, who are routinely called 'phantom experts' given that their identity is not revealed to the parties.[122] Sir Robert Jennings, former President of the Court, has alluded to the veiled use of such informal experts on many occasions in the Court's practice. These shadow experts are functioning as temporary registry staff members, tasked with giving scientific insights to judges on a confidential basis.[123] The use of such secret experts drew substantial criticism in the literature,[124] mainly out of transparency concerns. Interestingly, ICJ judges reportedly do not share these concerns in connection with the *'expert fantômes'*.[125] Supporting this technique it may also be appreciated that to some extent informal consultations are inevitable and that relying on shadow experts enhances the parties' confidence in the Court's ability to grasp the technical aspects of the case.[126] An empirical survey shows that

---

[117] Donoghue, 'Expert scientific evidence in a broader context', 386.
[118] Foster, 'New clothes for the emperor?'; L. Malintoppi, 'Fact finding and evidence before the International Court of Justice (notably in scientific-related disputes)' (2016) 7 *Journal of International Dispute Settlement* 421–44 at 444.
[119] Peat, 'The use of court-appointed experts by the International Court of Justice', 289.
[120] Rules of Court, Article 9.
[121] *Pulp Mills*, Judgment, para. 166, see also in more detail: Loewenstein, 'Adjudication of environmental impact assessment claims before international courts and tribunals', p. 309.
[122] Peat, 'The use of court-appointed experts by the International Court of Justice', 288.
[123] Simma, 'The international court of justice and scientific expertise', 231.
[124] Peat, 'The use of court-appointed experts by the International Court of Justice', 288; Ridell and Plant, *Evidence before the International Court of Justice*; Viñuales, 'Observations sur le traitement des motifs scientifiques dans le contentieux environnemental international', p. 120.
[125] Boisson de Chazournes, Mbengue, Das, and Gros, 'One size does not fit all – uses of experts before international courts and tribunals', 482.
[126] Foster, 'New clothes for the emperor?', 171.

this fact-finding technique has nevertheless been adamantly opposed by a sample of counsels and experts acting before the Court.[127]

2.5 International Organizations

The Court also has the power to request relevant information from international organizations, which can be a useful addition to its fact-finding toolkit. The ICJ may, either on its own motion or at the request of a party, ask a public international organization to furnish information relevant to a case before it and may also receive information presented by such organizations on their own initiative.[128] Yet this fact-finding avenue is also under-utilized in environmental disputes. Reports of competent international organizations can also reach the bench indirectly, if the Court calls upon the parties to produce such evidence.[129] In the *Certain Activities/ Construction of a Road* cases, the ICJ requested from Nicaragua the report of the Ramsar Advisory Mission concerning one of the Ramsar sites relevant to the dispute.[130]

3 *Expert Evidence: Mathematical Models, Ecological Damage Valuation, and the Use of New Technologies*

Scientific evidence may appear in highly technical forms including maps, graphs, aerial photography, model calculations, and satellite imagery. The types of evidence that are deemed legally appreciable by the Court are also indicative of its scientific engagement.

3.1 Mathematical Models

The Court's uneasy relationship with highly specialized models has been manifest ever since the scarce evidentiary findings crafted in *Gabcikovo-Nagymaros* and *Pulp Mills*. *Certain Activities/Construction of a Road* showcased similar difficulties in evaluating highly technical model calculations. Nicaragua claimed that Costa Rica's construction of a road along the San Juan River increased sediment levels and allegedly changed the morphology and navigability of the river by accumulating and forming deltas in the riverbed.[131] The ICJ did not find those model calculations persuasive enough that described the deposition of the sediment from the construction site and it concluded that models were insufficient to preclude the natural

---

[127]   Boisson de Chazournes, Mbengue, Das, and Gros, 'One size does not fit all – uses of experts before international courts and tribunals', 487.
[128]   Statute of the International Court of Justice, Article 34; Rules of Court, Article 69.
[129]   Rules of Court, Article 62.
[130]   *Certain Activities/Construction of a Road*, Judgment, para. 41.
[131]   *Certain Activities/Construction of a Road*, Judgment, paras. 197–202.

formation of the deltas.[132] Model calculations have been similarly dismissed in the *Territorial and Maritime Dispute* case.[133]

3.2 Ecological Damage Valuation

A particularly science-intensive question concerns the valuation of ecological damage, which raises complex question of causality and damage quantification. The compensation judgment in the *Certain Activities* case was hoped to bring a revolutionary turn in the ICJ's scientific fact-finding. Although such expectations for a large part proved to be excessive, given that the Court neither questioned the experts nor appointed independent experts or consulted with international organizations, the judgment did signal a considerable improvement in terms of commenting on the scientific aspects of disputes. In the material case, the ICJ awarded compensation to Costa Rica for direct injuries resulting from the wrongful conduct of Nicaragua, that is, breaching Costa Rica's territorial sovereignty.

This was the first time that the Court adjudicated a claim for compensation for environmental damage.[134] Notably, the ICJ adopted an ecosystem services approach,[135] which in itself amounts to an innovative step, marked by embracing the concept of ecosystem services. It further announced that any 'consequent impairment or loss of the ability of the environment to provide goods and services, is compensable under international law'.[136] It was in this context that the Court had to monetize the loss of ecosystem services provided by the wetland demolished by Nicaragua on the disputed territory that was found to be belonging to Costa Rica.[137] The parties could not agree on the quantum of reparation, and therefore Costa Rica requested the Court's judgment to declare the amount of compensation. The parties fundamentally disagreed over the scientific methods for environmental damage calculations.[138] Costa Rica put forward a 'value transfer approach' to valuation, which would account for 'direct use value' of tradeable services (such as timber), and also for 'indirect use value' for non-tradeable ecosystem services (e.g. climate regulation services).[139] In contrast, Nicaragua would have preferred a valuation based on 'ecosystem service replacement costs'. This approach was used by the UN Compensation Commission in administering the Gulf War reparation

---

[132] *Certain Activities/Construction of a Road*, Judgment, paras. 203–4.
[133] *Territorial and Maritime Dispute (Nicaragua v. Colombia)* (Judgment) (2012) ICJ Rep 624, para. 36.
[134] *Certain Activities*, Judgment on compensation, para. 41.
[135] *Certain Activities*, Judgment on compensation, para. 46.
[136] *Certain Activities*, Judgment on compensation, para. 42.
[137] *Certain Activities*, Judgment on compensation, paras. 22–3, 27.
[138] The Court noted the differences between the parties' preferred methodologies and their contrasting scientific views relating to the valuation of the environmental harm as set forth in the Memorial and the Counter-Memorial. See *Certain Activities*, Order 18 July 2017, (2017) ICJ Rep 285.
[139] *Certain Activities*, Judgment on compensation, para. 47.

claims,[140] which stands as an eminent international precedent for ecological damage valuation.[141] The ICJ ultimately embarked upon conducting its own assessment regarding the valuation of various ecosystem services and did not accept either of the calculations offered by the parties in their entirety.[142]

The Court itself declared its methodology to be an 'overall valuation'[143] providing only a rather 'opaque'[144] scientific reasoning. The bench took issue with the calculations offered by the parties as it 'ha[d] doubts regarding the reliability of certain aspects of [the parties'] methodology'.[145] The Court decided to make adjustments to 'account for the shortcomings'[146] in their methodologies, though without setting out the details of its own corrected analysis. It summarily concluded that only a few percentages of the total amount claimed by Costa Rica would be deemed reasonable.[147]

From the perspective of scientific engagement, the scientific inquiry and the corresponding reasoning of the Court can be critiqued on several grounds. The most problematic aspect is that the ICJ chose between scientific methodologies without asking for any expert assistance in a transparent way, nor did it assess in detail the reasons for refuting the quantification methods offered by the experts of Costa Rica. The Court firmly declared that 'an overall valuation c[ould] account for the correlation between the removal of the trees and the harm caused to other environmental goods and services (such as raw materials, gas regulation and air quality services, biodiversity …)'.[148] This finding was not, however, supported with any scientific reasoning and, hence, its well-foundedness remains questionable.

Furthermore, many important details from the Court's calculations were not revealed. Although the Court did engage with science when it cherry-picked bits and pieces from the diverse quantifications offered by the experts, it did so in secret. With the words of Judge ad hoc Dugard, 'we simply do not know' how the trees are valued by the Court, whether the average price of standing timber has been calculated for the eliminated stock and the growth potential of that stock over a fifty-year period, or only the trees felled have been valued together with the loss of such trees over a fifty-year recovery.[149] The ICJ obviously opted for one of these methods but it concealed the details of its calculation. This is a particularly salient gap in the reasoning, especially because the Court itself noted that the removal of trees was 'the most significant damage to the area'.[150] Lastly, the Court did not indicate any

---

[140] Nicaragua referred to the practice of the UN Compensation Commission in its submissions, which is noted by the Court in *Certain Activities*, Judgment on compensation, para. 50.
[141] The practice of the UN Compensation Commission will be detailed in Chapter 9.
[142] *Certain Activities*, Judgment on compensation, para. 52.
[143] *Certain Activities*, Judgment on compensation, paras. 80, 81, 83.
[144] *Certain Activities*, Judgment on compensation, Dissenting Opinion of Judge ad hoc Dugard, para. 22.
[145] *Certain Activities*, Judgment on compensation, para. 79.
[146] *Certain Activities*, Judgment on compensation, para. 86.
[147] *Certain Activities*, Judgment on compensation, para. 157.
[148] *Certain Activities*, Judgment on compensation, para. 76.
[149] *Certain Activities*, Judgment on compensation, Dissenting Opinion of Judge ad hoc Dugard, para. 16.
[150] *Certain Activities*, Judgment on compensation, para. 79.

explanation for rejecting the 'well-reasoned report by Professor Thorne',[151] an expert in soil science. Instead, it simply did not attach any monetary value for the impediment to soil formation. There were apparent gaps in the Court's assessment also relating to environmental baseline conditions, the estimated recovery period, and the cost of remediation measures estimated during such period.[152]

In sum, the Court's reasoning as to the scientific justifications for its choices remains quite poor, where scientific concepts are expounded without openly requesting for expert advice or indicating any explanation for accepting or rejecting certain scientific data. The precise quantification of ecological damage may well prove a highly technical and difficult task, but what the Court awards seems only to be an 'inflated sum' for the damage caused.[153] Yet, notwithstanding the many indications of the Court's still 'unsatisfactory fact-finding',[154] the ICJ this time at least saliently tried to devote attention to the scientific aspects of environmental damage valuation. These efforts should be viewed, despite all deficiencies in the technicalities of execution, as a step towards a laudable direction, as it marks a cautious divergence from earlier attempts at marginalizing or even wiping out science from the judicial reasoning. However, there is still considerable room for improvement for the Court in terms of the transparency, and hence the legitimacy, of its reasoning.

3.3 Earth Observation Technologies

Another noteworthy aspect of decisions issued in the *Certain Activities/ Construction of a Road* saga is the use of geospatial information as scientific proof. Costa Rica submitted satellite images to prove the presence of Nicaraguan troops on its territory and to provide persuasive evidence on the extent of environmental damage caused to Costa Rican territory. The Court found the imagery as persuasive evidence on the presence of Nicaraguan military groups on the territory, which led to the issuance of provisional measures.[155] Later, the ICJ found that the high-resolution satellite imagery also showed that the tree removal 'likely' occurred during the presence of Nicaraguan troops in the area.[156] The Court was also ready to find that a UNOSAT report based on remote sensing data was 'strong evidence to suggest' that the respective channels were also constructed

---

[151]   *Certain Activities*, Judgment on compensation, Dissenting Opinion of Judge ad hoc Dugard, para. 27.

[152]   D. Desierto, 'Environmental damages, environmental reparations, and the right to a healthy environment: the ICJ Compensation Judgment in *Costa Rica* v. *Nicaragua* and the IACtHR Advisory Opinion on marine protection for the greater Caribbean, EJIL Talk! (Feb 14, 2018)' available at https://bit.ly/2Bj6SEY (last accessed 30 January 2020).

[153]   *Certain Activities*, Judgment on compensation, Dissenting Opinion of Judge ad hoc Dugard, para. 47.

[154]   *Certain Activities*, Judgment on compensation, Dissenting Opinion of Judge ad hoc Dugard, para. 22.

[155]   *Certain Activities/Construction of a Road*, (Provisional Measures) Order of 22 November 2013, (2013) ICJ Rep 354, para. 46.

[156]   *Certain Activities*, Judgment on compensation, para. 98.

during the relevant period.[157] States are now also incentivized to submit relevant satellite imagery to the Court as the costs of producing the report was found to be compensable.

The use of earth observation data in this case well illustrates the increasing intrusion of geospatial information technologies into the sphere of international adjudication – a trend which will most likely to continue in the future. These imaging techniques can yield particularly powerful scientific proofs. Satellite images are easily intelligible to laymen judges and provide an intuitively appealing and objective account of the factual circumstances also allowing tracking any changes over time. The rapid development and sophistication of remote sensing technology[158] can equip future litigants with scientific proofs for even more nuanced environmental processes such as gradually emerging or protracted pollution. Using geospatial information as scientific evidence fosters ensuring equal opportunities for litigants, as save for commercial providers, a vast amount of imagery can be derived from major international and national satellites free of charge. Furthermore, geospatial technologies can also provide high resolution real-time data that may in some cases even substitute for site visits of the Court, mimicking domestic environmental law developments, where national courts increasingly use such evidence as inspection tools.[159]

4 *The Standard and Burden of Proof*

The applicable standard of proof relating to scientific evidence became first relevant in the *Pulp Mills* judgment. The ICJ however only dealt expressly with the burden of proof and omitted any discussion on the standard of proof.[160] Coupled with the lack of detailed reasoning on the probative value attached to each of the evidence adduced, one cannot infer to the precise standard the Court employed. Judge Greenwood put forth a proposition that in environmental cases a balance of probabilities standard was preferable, though he was of the opinion that the facts of the case would not have met even this lower standard.[161] Neither was the applicable standard expressly announced in the subsequent *Certain Activities/Construction of a Road* cases. Here again, only the Separate Opinion of Judge ad hoc Dugard touched upon the issue of standard of proof by proposing to use the preponderance

---

[157] *Certain Activities*, Judgment on compensation, para. 98.
[158] For a recent report released by the Group on Earth Observations detailing the recent application of remote sensing in environmental policymaking see https://bit.ly/36UeLfH (last accessed 6 January 2020).
[159] K. Sulyok, F. Bögös, T. Paloniitty, and M. Eliantonio, 'Summary report of the European Forum of Judges for the Environment – Answers to the questionnaire concerning the role of science in environmental adjudication', 2019, pp. 8–9, available at https://bit.ly/2U1YXCt (last accessed 6 January 2020).
[160] *Pulp Mills*, Judgment, paras. 160–8.
[161] *Pulp Mills*, Separate Opinion of Judge Greenwood, para. 26.

of the evidence standard.[162] As to the burden of proof, the Court firmly rejected[163] the possibility of reversing the burden of proof in the face of uncertain science. Hence, such a strong reading of the precautionary principle has not been embraced by the Court.

Judges may react to the uncertainties inherent in scientific proof in an asymmetric way. Not being familiar with the conventions and processes of scientific knowledge production, lawyers sometimes may be sceptical about the reliable and unbiased nature of scientific arguments or be induced to assume political considerations behind environmental arguments that are based on uncertain science. The Dissenting Opinion of Judge Oda in *Gabcikovo-Nagymaros* appears to provide an example of that. Judge Oda first asserts that 'it cannot be said that the drafters of either the Treaty or of the Joint Contractual Plan failed to take due account of the environment'.[164] This language suggests that Judge Oda did not question the credibility and scientific soundness of decisions made by leaders of the contracting Communist Parties, which negated all scientific concerns pertaining to the project when concluded the treaty in 1977, despite having no detailed prior EIA.[165] In the following sentence, Judge Oda voices a 'firm conviction' that concerns about environmental risks raised by environmental opposition groups in Hungary were without merit. A judicial reasoning suspecting political bias with regard to certain scientific claims but refuting those in relation to other scientific assumptions without any in-depth assessment of the scientific evidence might be vulnerable to criticism, as it appears to be arbitrary from an epistemic point of view.

5 *Proposals for Future Developments in Scientific Fact-Finding*

Commentators altogether agree that it is necessary to increase the ICJ's scientific fact-finding capacities,[166] and they only differ as to the exact modalities of desirable fact-finding the Court ought to embrace. Suggestions range from appointing so-called special masters[167] to creating a pre-trial procedure where *ex curia* experts, chosen from a list provided by competent international organizations, would draft a report answering scientific questions of the judges.[168] Besides these specific suggestions as to preferred avenues for gathering expert advice, proposals with a more general scope can also be found. Many scholars and practitioners would favour if judges were more active in delineating the factual questions they deem relevant to decide the dispute

---

[162] *Certain Activities/Construction of a Road*, Separate Opinion of Judge ad hoc Dugard, para. 33.
[163] *Pulp Mills*, Judgment, para. 164.
[164] *Gabcikovo-Nagymaros*, Dissenting Opinion of Judge Oda, para. 12.
[165] *Gabcikovo-Nagymaros*, Judgment, para. 57.
[166] Peat, 'The use of court-appointed experts by the International Court of Justice', 299; Ridell and Plant, *Evidence before the International Court of Justice*, p. 353; Malintoppi, 'Fact finding and evidence before the International Court of Justice (notably in scientific-related disputes)', 421.
[167] Payne, 'Mastering the evidence', 1201.
[168] Peat, 'The use of court-appointed experts by the International Court of Justice', 300–301.

and would give advice as to the desirable or expected content of expert reports.[169] This would indeed spare the Court from facing divergent and, therefore, partly irrelevant expert submissions and also would reduce the amount of expert documentation.

As noted above, the sheer amount of evidence filed with the Court proved to impede the Court's ability to grasp the scientifically relevant aspects of the case, and hence was rather counterproductive in many instances. Room for improvement therefore exists in this respect as well. Furthermore, an empirical research calls for enhanced co-operation between party-appointed experts to narrow down their points of agreement.[170] This would allow the ICJ to develop a more thorough understanding of the scientific dimensions of the dispute. Another suggestion calls for a more flexible and less formalized interaction between the bench and the parties throughout the process of fact-finding.[171] Finally, the Court could also more frequently avail itself of the opportunity to draw negative inferences from a party's failure to submit scientific evidence.[172]

The next opportunity for the Court to engage with science-heavy claims presents itself in the *Silala* case currently pending.[173] This water dispute revolves around the question whether the Silala River system constitutes an international watercourse. Chile submits that it does, because it flows naturally into Chile from the springs located in Bolivia due to the inclination of the terrain. Whereas Bolivia claims that the waters had been artificially diverted to Chile by works of the Chilean railroad company almost a hundred years ago; and therefore, asserts sovereign rights over it. Besides the right to equitable and reasonable utilization of the waters, Chile also claims Bolivia's responsibility for causing transboundary harm originating from several projects affecting the quality and quantity of the water, including the construction of a military post on Bolivian territory.[174]

The *Silala* dispute is likely to turn on scientific facts, which are pertinent not only to the obligation to prevent transboundary harm, but also to the categorization of the waters' status. The high profile of science in this respect is signalled by the fact that before initiating the legal proceeding, the parties have established a bilateral technical commission to jointly collect information on the hydrological system of the waters.[175] Yet there is only limited data available on the hydrological connections between

---

[169]   Boisson de Chazournes, Mbengue, Das, and Gros, 'One size does not fit all – uses of experts before international courts and tribunals', 486.

[170]   Boisson de Chazournes, Mbengue, Das, and Gros, 'One size does not fit all – uses of experts before international courts and tribunals', 486.

[171]   Malintoppi, 'Fact finding and evidence before the International Court of Justice (notably in scientific-related disputes)', 441.

[172]   Malintoppi, 'Fact finding and evidence before the International Court of Justice (notably in scientific-related disputes)', 425.

[173]   The Application was filed with the Court on 6 June 2016.

[174]   *Dispute over the Status and Use of the Waters of the Silala (Chile v. Bolivia)*, Application instituting proceedings, paras. 35–6, 49–50.

[175]   *Dispute over the Status and Use of the Waters of the Silala*, Application instituting proceedings, para. 27.

surface and groundwater in the region, which could closely speak to the legal dilemma put before the ICJ.

This case undoubtedly provides an opportunity for the Court to expand on its interaction with science. In light of the argumentation of Chile, which reportedly strongly builds on scientific arguments,[176] and considering the direct bearing of hydrological evidence on the characterization of the waters, the facts of the case strongly call for substantive evaluation of the scientific narratives from an epistemic point of view. The *Silala* dispute, thus, is most likely putting the Court at a crossroads: it may either return to its formerly dominant practice and marginalize apparent scientific aspects in its judicial inquiry, or it may choose to face scientific controversies and engage with the scientific evidence in a thorough and open manner. In the latter scenario, science can actually assist the Court by providing a neutral basis for settling the highly sensitive political conflict, which lies in the background to the court proceeding. Notably, the UN Environmental Programme classified the Silala region as 'one of the most hydro-politically vulnerable basins in the world'.[177] The *Silala* case therefore no doubt features a high-profile dispute – both scientifically and geopolitically. The usual sensitivities of ruling on causality and international responsibility for environmental harm – which are problems the Court is all too familiar with – in this case are exacerbated by increasing water scarcity and severe climate change impacts threatening the entire region.

IV CAUSAL INQUIRY

Disputes concerning the responsibility of states for causing transboundary environmental damage are of special relevance for this study, given that the heart of these cases revolves around questions of scientific proof and alleged causal links between the states' conduct and environmental harm,[178] which are all extremely science-heavy issues. The ways in which the Court handles scientific proof of causation has significant practical relevance as it directly impacts the prospects of environmental claims. Before delving into analysing the ICJ's causal assessments (Subsection 2), an overview is due on the manifold role of causality in the Court's inquiry in environmental cases (Subsection 1).

---

[176] At the time of writing this manuscript, the Memorial has not yet been disclosed by the Court. However, Chile has reportedly submitted a six-volume Memorial, in which it discusses inter alia its scientific argument for the characterization of the Silala River system. Ronald Bruce St John, 'Andean water wars: the *Silala* case' (5 August 2019) available at: www.coha.org/andean-water-wars-the-silala-case/ (last accessed 12 January 2020).

[177] United Nations Environment Programme, *Hydropolitical Vulnerability and Resilience along International Waters: Latin America and the Caribbean*, Nairobi: UNEP Publications (2007), 65, available at: http://wedocs.unep.org/handle/20.500.11822/7803 (last accessed 12 January 2020).

[178] Craik, 'Recalcitrant reality and chosen ideals: the public function of dispute settlement in international environmental law', 571–2; Donoghue, 'Expert scientific evidence in a broader context', 382.

1 *Relevance of Causal Links in Environmental Responsibility*

In cases entertaining international responsibility for environmental harm, causality is relevant at three separate stages of the judicial inquiry.[179] First, to decide whether the obligation not to cause significant transboundary harm has been breached. Environmental damage causal upon wrongful state conduct is a necessary element of violating the primary norm of the no-harm rule. Second, the causal nexus becomes relevant when the harm at hand is of a nature that it potentially might have been caused by several possible sources, and the respondent state is only one of the potential causes (instances of 'causal uncertainty'). And finally, causation may be relevant for purposes of calculating the quantum of compensation. In such cases causality plays an important role on the level of secondary norms of state responsibility. A more detailed discussion of these three phases follows below.

1.1 Causal Requirements on the Level of Primary Norms: The No-Harm Rule

The *sic utere tuo* principle, or the no-harm rule, which was first articulated in the *Trail Smelter* Arbitration,[180] has been repeatedly regarded by the Court as an established part of customary international law.[181] This rule confers an obligation on states to prevent significant transboundary environmental harm from occurring. Causing damage to the global commons, areas beyond national jurisdictions or the territory of another state are equally prohibited.[182] The no-harm rule emphatically creates a due diligence obligation,[183] and not that of result. Therefore, the occurrence of severe environmental harm in itself would not establish the origin state's liability, unless a failure to fulfil a duty of care with respect to prevention is also established. The precise content of such due diligence standard has remained thus far somewhat unclear[184] and is subject to clarification by the Court.

Establishing a causal link between a state's action or omission and the harmful consequences suffered is arguably the Achilles' heel of international environmental

---

[179] Plakokefalos, 'Causation in the law of state responsibility and the problem of overdetermination', 474.

[180] For a more detailed discussion of the case see Chapter 4 Section III, Subsection 1.

[181] *Gabcikovo-Nagymaros*, Judgment, para. 53; *Certain Activities/Construction of a Road*, Judgment, para. 104; *Pulp Mills*, Judgment, para. 101.

[182] A. Douhan, 'Liability for Environmental Damage' in R. Wolfrum (ed.), *Max Planck Encyclopedia of Public International Law* (2013 ed.). See also Principle 21 of Stockholm Declaration.

[183] *Pulp Mills*, Judgment, para. 101; C. Redgwell, 'International environmental law' in M. Evans (ed.), *International Law* (Oxford University Press, 2014), pp. 688–726 p. 697; M. Fitzmaurice, 'International responsibility and liability' in D. M. Bodansky, E. Hey, and J. Brunnée (eds.), *The Oxford Handbook of International Environmental Law* (Oxford University Press, 2008), pp. 1011–35 p. 1014.

[184] Louka, *International Environmental Law Fairness, Effectiveness, and World Order*, p. 475; Duvic-Paoli, *The Prevention Principle in International Environmental Law*, p. 208.

liability.[185] The challenges of proving causality lie at the heart of deficient enforcement of environmental responsibility of states. Difficulties in gathering sufficient causal proofs may deter prospective applicants from initiating burdensome and lengthy proceedings against wrongdoing states; and in cases where they do, evaluating scientific proofs poses a major challenge for international judges.

In this vein, some attribute the apparent lack of initiating international legal proceedings by injured states against the USSR for the Chernobyl incident to the inherent difficulties of establishing causality for transboundary harm.[186] Indeed, when respondents face international nuclear damage claims, they eagerly use the causality requirement as a shield, which places the burden of proof on the applicant. Such strategic reliance on the causal requirement has been most evident in the *Nuclear Tests* case initiated by Australia against France. The position of France well reflects that the heart of the problem of state responsibility for environmental harm lies in the fact that 'in the absence of ascertained damage attributable to its nuclear experiments'[187] no violation of international law can be established.

1.2 Multiple Possible Wrongdoers: Problems of Uncertain Causation in Establishing Environmental Responsibility

More complex causal scenarios may also arise,[188] complicating matters even further for proving an environmental damage. The most frequent obstacle to finding a causal link established between an environmental harm and the industrial activity on a neighbouring state is the presence of possible competing causes. Competing causes may contribute to the same harm or one of them may cause the entire damage alone. As significant transboundary harm must be causal upon a human cause; states may exonerate themselves by demonstrating that natural factors triggered the harmful consequences.[189] Accordingly, respondent states routinely argue with the presence of competing natural causes unrelated to their conduct, and claim that those have caused, wholly or partly, the injury. For instance, Costa Rica in *Certain Activities/Construction of a Road* argued that 'the aggradation of the Lower San Juan River [was] an inevitable natural phenomenon that is unrelated to the construction of the road'.[190] The Court agreed and found that it was not proven 'that

[185] A. Kiss, 'Present limits to the enforcement of state responsibility for environmental damage' in F. Francioni and T. Scovazzi (eds.), *International Responsibility for Environmental Harm* (Graham and Trotman, 1991), pp. 3–14 p. 5; C. Négre, 'Responsibility and international environmental law' in J. Crawford, A. Pellet, and S. Olleson (eds.), *The Law of International Responsibility* (Oxford University Press, 2010), pp. 803–13 p. 805.

[186] Négre, 'Responsibility and international environmental law', p. 805.

[187] *Nuclear Tests*, (Interim Measures), Order of 22 June 1973, (1973) ICJ Rep 135, para 28 (emphasis added).

[188] Some of these difficulties are illustrated by Dupuy and Viñuales, see Dupuy and Viñuales, *International Environmental Law*, pp. 315–16.

[189] H. Xue, *Transboundary Damage in International Law* (Cambridge University Press, 2003), pp. 6–7.

[190] *Certain Activities/Construction of a Road*, Judgment, para. 201.

any morphological changes in the Lower San Juan have been caused by the construction of a road in particular'.[191] Such difficulties in establishing a causal link are illustrative consequences of scientific uncertainty burdening causal proofs.

1.3 Causal Requirements on the Level of Secondary Norms of State Responsibility

Provided that all required elements of an internationally wrongful act have been established, the injured state may ask for full reparation of the injury caused under Articles 31 and 34 of Articles on Responsibility of States for Internationally Wrongful Acts (ARSIWA).[192] Hence, the territorial state to which environmental harm was caused may only receive monetary compensation for the portion of the harm that was in fact caused by the state breaching the no-harm rule.

The compensation judgment in *Certain Activities* provides an apposite example of the causal problems arising on the level of secondary norms. As noted above, here the Court had to rule on the quantum of compensation payable for ecological damage caused by Nicaragua in breach of Costa Rica's sovereignty.[193] The ICJ emphasized that environmental damage 'may be due to several concurrent causes, or the state of science regarding the causal link between the wrongful act and the damage may be uncertain'.[194] Against this background, the Court's causal test requiring 'direct and certain causal link'[195] between the ecological damage and the unlawful acts strikes as a rather restrictive causal test.

In the material case, the Court ultimately found that all heads of damages claimed by Costa Rica (i.e. the trees cut, loss of raw materials, gas regulation and air quality services, and loss of biodiversity) were direct consequences of Nicaragua's wrongful activities.[196] Importantly, however, causality between the unlawful dredging and the felling of trees was not debated by Nicaragua. This may also signal that the Court is only comfortable with finding causality established where the requisite link is not contested among the parties.

2 *The Court's Approach to Assessing Uncertain Causal Links: Reluctance to Deal with Science*

The ICJ has been famously evasive in conducting meaningful causal inquiries even in cases that do not entertain scientific uncertainties.[197] Suffice it to refer to the

[191]   *Certain Activities/Construction of a Road*, Judgment, para. 204.
[192]   International Law Commission, Responsibility of States for Internationally Wrongful Acts, adopted by the UN General Assembly resolution 56/83 of 12 December 2001, and corrected by document A/56/49(Vol. I)/Corr.4.
[193]   *Certain Activities/Construction of a Road*, Judgment, para. 139.
[194]   *Certain Activities*, Judgment on compensation, para. 34.
[195]   *Certain Activities*, Judgment on compensation, para. 72.
[196]   *Certain Activities*, Judgment on compensation, para. 75.
[197]   Plakokefalos, 'Causation in the law of state responsibility and the problem of overdetermination', 483–6.

opaque and inconsistent causal assessments conducted in *Corfu Channel* and in *Bosnian Genocide*. Both cases concerned a concomitant causes scenario, where the same loss could be potentially attributed to more than one cause. In *Corfu Channel*, the Court did not expressly discuss the applicable causal test.[198] Nevertheless the United Kingdom was allowed to recover the full amount of its claim against Albania, irrespective of the fact that it was not proven that Albania had laid down the mines causing the injury complained of.[199] As opposed to this, in *Bosnian Genocide* the Court found, on the apparent basis of a *sine qua non* (or but-for) test of causation,[200] that since Serbia's failure to prevent genocide was not a *sine qua non* cause of the violation, its conduct was no cause at all.[201] The Court's analysis as to the requisite causal link was as follows: 'Such a nexus could be considered established only if the Court were able to conclude from the case as a whole and with a sufficient degree of certainty that the genocide at Srebrenica would in fact have been averted if the Respondent had acted in compliance with its legal obligations. However, the Court clearly cannot do so.'[202] The weakness of the *sine qua non* causal test was pointed out by James Crawford who stressed that in complex cases, where the damage is brought about by a combination of factors, often none of the causal factors alone can be regarded as a *sine qua non* cause.[203] In a similar vein, the Court has been criticized for this causal approach, since in such a reading Serbia's omission, which was not the only cause of the genocide in Bosnia was conceived to be '*no cause at all*'.[204]

For all these reasons, when causal claims are based on uncertain and contested scientific facts, establishing causality confers a highly intricate task on judges. In *Pulp Mills*, for instance, the judges were asked inter alia to evaluate 'the effects of the breakdown of nonylphenol ethoxylates, the binding of sediments to phosphorus, the possible chain of causation which can lead to an algal bloom'.[205] In light of these complexities, it may come as no surprise that the Court often frames its causal inquiry to emphasize uncertainty inherent in the underlying evidence and finds it as an insurmountable obstacle to establish causality. The Court's haphazard assessment of the scientific aspect of causal claims resulted in many instances in the rejection of such links with brief explanations lacking meaningful references to the

---

[198] The lack of causal inquiry was criticized by Judge Ecer, see *Corfu Channel (Albania v. UK)* (Compensation) (1949) ICJ Rep 244, Dissenting Opinion of Judge Ecer, para. 254.

[199] *Corfu Channel*, para. 250; ILC, 'Second Report of the Special Rapporteur, James Crawford, on State Responsibility', para. 34.

[200] Crawford, *State Responsibility: The General Part*, p. 499.

[201] *Application of the Convention on the Prevention and Punishment of the Crime of Genocide (Bosnia and Herzegovina v. Serbia and Montenegro)* (Judgment) (2007) ICJ Rep 43.

[202] Bosnian Genocide, Judgment, para. 462.

[203] Crawford, *State Responsibility: The General Part*, p. 499.

[204] Gattini, 'Breach of the obligation to prevent and reparation thereof in the ICJ's Genocide judgment', 710.

[205] The most troubling scientific aspects of the case were listed in *Pulp Mills*, Joint Dissenting Opinion of Judges Al-Khasawneh and Simma, para. 4.

scientific evidence adduced. Notably, the lack of requisite causation precluded finding a breach of substantive obligation not to cause environmental harm in every liability claim states have presented to the Court.

In the material case, Argentina alleged that Uruguay had caused significant harm to the Uruguay River's ecosystem by authorizing the operation of two pulp mills along the shared watercourse and submitted ample scientific evidence to that effect. The Court however remained dismissive of finding causal links established based on uncertain scientific evidence reflecting mere statistical probabilities. It chose to take a rather 'passive approach'[206] and missed the opportunity to interpret and legally appreciate the probative force of the expert evidence. The judgment emphasized that the Court saw 'no need' to go into a detailed assessment of the diverse technical evidence submitted.[207] As a result, the lengthy discussion of the party-adduced scientific evidence[208] essentially boiled down to a variation on expressing the insufficiency of the scientific causal proofs.[209] The Court referred to diverse reasons for ruling that Argentina failed to prove its allegations: the lack of 'significant difference between the sets of data' describing the amount of dissolved oxygen before and after the commissioning of the mills,[210] the lack of 'clear' attribution between the presence of polluting agents and the operation of the mill,[211] the lack of 'clear evidence' of causality,[212] the absence of a 'clear relationship',[213] and the absence of 'conclusive evidence'[214] was pointed out by the majority.

These elusive findings triggered especially harsh criticism from judges and commentators,[215] most eminently put forward by dissenting members of the bench.[216] They all claimed that the highly complex nature of the science involved should not have necessarily led to such limited evaluation of the underlying facts. Dissenting Judge Al-Khasawneh and Judge Simma asserted the judgment was 'flawed methodologically',[217] and even dubbed it a 'wasted opportunity' for the Court to demonstrate 'its ability, and preparedness, to approach scientifically complex disputes in a state-of-the-art manner'.[218] Rather, the majority has clung to its old habits, which has proven to be deficient in science-intensive cases.[219] The core of

[206] *Pulp Mills*, Joint Dissenting Opinion of Judges Al-Khasawneh and Simma, para. 6.
[207] *Pulp Mills*, Judgment, para. 213.
[208] *Pulp Mills*, Judgment, paras. 229–65.
[209] *Pulp Mills*, Judgment, paras. 229–65.
[210] *Pulp Mills*, Judgment, para. 239.
[211] *Pulp Mills*, Judgment, paras. 240, 250, 254.
[212] *Pulp Mills*, Judgment, paras. 257, 259.
[213] *Pulp Mills*, Judgment, para. 262.
[214] *Pulp Mills*, Judgment, para. 265.
[215] Ridell, 'Scientific evidence in the International Court of Justice: problems and possibilities', 242.
[216] See the Joint Dissenting Opinion of Judges Al-Khasawneh and Simma, Declaration of Judge Yusuf, Dissenting Opinion of Judge Vinuesa.
[217] *Pulp Mills*, Joint Dissenting Opinion of Judges Al-Khasawneh and Simma, para. 2.
[218] *Pulp Mills*, Joint Dissenting Opinion of Judges Al-Khasawneh and Simma, para. 28.
[219] *Pulp Mills*, Joint Dissenting Opinion of Judges Al-Khasawneh and Simma, para. 3.

various criticisms lies in the fact that the underlying scientific evidence at hand has been 'as scientifically certain as is possible in a judicial proceeding'.[220] And indeed, to demonstrate the feasibility of evaluating the legal relevance of the given scientific data, Judge Vinuesa in his dissent provided a detailed judicial assessment of all fact-intensive allegations of Argentina. He also pointed out the inconsistencies and gaps in the scientific findings of the judgment.[221]

In the *Certain Activities/Construction of a Road* joint cases, causal uncertainty arose in the form of potential parallel causes. In the face of intricate causal complexities, the Court again refused to find a legally appreciable causal link. It did not establish any harm to the macro-invertebrate richness in the San Juan River, as it 'found it difficult to attribute any difference in macro-invertebrate . . . abundance . . . to the construction of the road alone, as opposed to other factors such as the size of the catchment area and the nutrient levels therein'.[222]

In the compensation judgment issued in *Certain Activities*, the Court indicated its willingness to address the factual difficulties arising in its causal inquiry, and confirmed that '[u]ltimately, it [was] for the Court to decide whether there [was] a sufficient causal nexus between the wrongful act and the injury suffered'.[223] In the material case, the Court was ready to find a 'direct and certain' causal nexus between some of the monitoring expenses incurred by Costa Rica and the internationally wrongful conduct of Nicaragua.[224] Yet establishing this link did not require assessing technical scientific evidence, as conflicting expert evidence was only at play in the environmental damage calculations, addressed above.

V STANDARD AND EXTENT OF JUDICIAL REVIEW

The ICJ used the term 'standard of review'[225] for the first time in its *Whaling in the Antarctic* judgment. The dispute revolved around the interpretation of the exemption provided under the 1946 International Convention on the Regulation of Whaling (ICRW) from the general moratorium for whaling. Article VIII ICRW allows for Special Permit Whaling that is conducted 'for purposes of scientific research'. Japan essentially claimed that its whaling programme, the Second Phase of the Japanese Whale Research Program under Special Permit in the Antarctic (JARPA II), pursued 'scientific objectives' and therefore fell under Article VIII of ICRW. In contrast, Australia argued that Japan relied on science only as a pretext, because JARPA II led to the killing of several thousands of whales without producing

---

[220] *Pulp Mills*, Joint Dissenting Opinion of Judges Al-Khasawneh and Simma, para. 2.

[221] *Pulp Mills*, Dissenting Opinion of Judge Vinuesa, paras. 74–98, at 79, Judge Vinuesa expressly claims that some of the majority's determinations were 'made without a coherent scientific basis'.

[222] *Certain Activities/Construction of a Road*, Judgment, para. 212.

[223] *Certain Activities*, Judgment on compensation, para. 34.

[224] *Certain Activities*, Judgment on compensation, para. 112.

[225] Hamamoto, 'From the requirement of reasonableness to a "comply and explain" rule: the standard of review in the *Whaling* judgment', p. 39.

any peer-reviewed scientific publication,[226] while it generated huge volumes of whale meat that was lucratively sold on the Japanese market. In light of this Australia purported that JARPA II was, in fact, economic whaling conducted under the 'guise' of scientific research.[227]

At the heart of the dispute lay the requisite standard of review. In order to decide this controversy, the Court had to find a judicial pathway for singling out claims of 'real' science from non-science among the bulky expert evidence offered by the parties. As a preliminary matter, the ICJ first had to face the question whether and if so in what respects such an issue could be subject to legal determination. As a second step, the Court had to devise a standard of review with which it could scrutinize the scientific arguments of both parties, who submitted diametrically opposing views as to what counted as a whaling programme conducted 'for purposes of scientific research', and as 'science' more generally.

The following analysis regarding the ICJ's standard of review is structured into three main parts. Subsection 1 discusses the divergent adjudicatory views on the justiciability of the term 'scientific research'. Subsection 2 evaluates the ICJ's chosen standard of review in light of divergent criticism, defending it in many respects based on insights from the philosophy of science. Subsection 3 concludes with mapping the implications of the standard of review for the extent of the ICJ's judicial purview in science-intensive cases.

1 The Extent of Review: Justiciability of the Term Scientific Research

Taking an official position on the boundary between valid and spurious claims of science, and such appeals to scientific research, is a rather delicate and sensitive exercise for a court of law. As has been repeatedly argued in this study, 'science' is an independent epistemic realm, hierarchically juxtaposed to that of law, therefore, judges often, by default, feel the absence of necessary expertise, and even that of legitimacy, to provide a definition on science. Against this backdrop it comes as no surprise that the bench did not reach a unanimous position on this question.

1.1 The Majority View on Scientific Research: A Justiciable Issue

The majority did not find it necessary to provide a general definition on scientific research for purposes of international law.[228] Neither did the Court 'pass judgment on the scientific merit'[229] of the stated objectives of JARPA II. Without commenting

---

[226] During the course of JARPA II Japan produced only two peer-reviewed scientific studies but those did not relate to the stated research objectives. Mangel, 'Whales, science, and scientific whaling in the International Court of Justice', 14525.

[227] *Whaling in the Antarctic*, Judgment, para. 101.

[228] *Whaling in the Antarctic*, Judgment, para. 86.

[229] *Whaling in the Antarctic*, Judgment, para. 88.

on the abstract or concrete meaning of scientific research, the Court immediately proceeded to the second stage of its inquiry, to interpret the meaning of the phrase 'for purposes of'. For this interpretative exercise, the ICJ construed an 'objective'[230] standard of review with which it ultimately ruled that JARPA II failed to satisfy requirements of the ICRW.

In reaching such a conclusion, the Court purposefully did not rely on any of the criteria offered by Australia and New Zealand as constituents of conducting scientific research. New Zealand suggested defining science by relying on the 'methodology, design and characteristics' of scientific research.[231] Australia's expert, Professor Marc Mangel, submitted four 'essential characteristics of science' to be used for distinguishing science from non-science. According to these, scientific research has (i) achievable objectives (research hypothesis), (ii) appropriate methods that are likely to achieve the stated objectives, (iii) is subject to peer review, and (iv) ensures avoidance of adverse effects on stocks.[232]

What the Court ultimately did to approach the concept of scientific research from a legal perspective was to devise a 'reasonableness' test to assess whether the programme's 'design and implementation are reasonable in relation to its stated scientific objectives'.[233] If JARPA II failed this reasonableness assessment, the Court held that it could not be regarded as being 'for purposes of' scientific research. The judgment listed several factors that were relevant to decide whether the use of lethal methods was reasonable, among others, the scale of lethal sampling, the methodology to select such sample sizes, the programme's scientific output, and the extent of scientific co-operation in relation to the programme.[234] Notably, these considerations do reflect several of the objective criteria advanced by Australia but which the Court did not directly rely on.

JARPA II, which replaced the first special permit whaling programme, JARPA, with refined objectives, had four stated research objectives[235]: (i) monitoring the Antarctic ecosystem (inter alia, monitoring the habitat and the feeding ecology of whales), (ii) constructing a multi-species model on competition among whale species, (iii) elucidating temporal and spatial changes in stock structure, and (iv) improving the management procedure for Antarctic minke whale stocks.[236] Lethal methods were central to the design of JARPA II, since the ICRW allows for selling the meat incidental to programmes granted with special permits.[237] The special permit provided Japan with catch limits of 850 minke whales, 50 fin whales and 50

---

230 *Whaling in the Antarctic*, Judgment, para. 67.
231 *Whaling in the Antarctic*, Judgment, para. 64.
232 *Whaling in the Antarctic*, Judgment, para. 74.
233 *Whaling in the Antarctic*, Judgment, para. 88.
234 *Whaling in the Antarctic*, Judgment, para. 88.
235 *Whaling in the Antarctic*, Judgment, paras. 113–18.
236 *Whaling in the Antarctic*, Judgment, para. 113.
237 *Whaling in the Antarctic*, Judgment, paras. 83 and 94.

humpback whales per season.[238] The Court did not find lethal sampling per se unreasonable,[239] however, it ruled that special permits ought not to 'use lethal sampling on a greater scale than is otherwise *reasonable* in relation to achieving the program's stated objectives'.[240]

Therefore, the key aspect of JARPA's legal evaluation considered whether lethal sample sizes were reasonable for achieving its stated objectives. To answer that question, the Court compared the sample sizes and the research objectives of JARPA and JARPA II respectively, and found that while sample sizes approximately doubled,[241] the objectives and methods used 'appear[ed] to have much in common'.[242] Therefore, the Court concluded that the substantially increased target sample sizes were not reasonable.[243] Also, the fact that no humpback whales have been taken despite a pre-set sample size was found to be indicia of unreasonable design of the programme, since neither the research objective nor the methods were adapted to the actual numbers of the whales taken.[244]

1.2 Dissents: Variations on Non-Justiciability of Scientific Concepts

The majority's position on how to interpret scientific research in the context of international law has met with a large number of dissenting and separate opinions. The different judicial views as to how to approach science in the dispute are highly consequential for the ICJ's purview, given that the Court could not legitimately decide on matters deemed purely scientific in nature. Expanding the boundaries of science would, thus, narrow down the corresponding sphere of judicial competence in a science-intensive dispute. In the material case, doing so would have conveniently carved out a great deal of scientific controversy from the Court's adjudicatory power.

Such a more restricted judicial task was endorsed by Judge Xue, who argued that 'determination of scientific research is primarily a matter of fact subject to scientific scrutiny'.[245] A similar approach was furthered by Japan, who wanted to persuade the Court that the entire matter at hand falls out of the ICJ's purview. Vaughan Lowe, acting on behalf of Japan, argued during the oral hearing that the Court 'can no more impose a line separating science from non-science than it could decide what is and what is not "Art"'.[246] Judge Owada even argued that 'this Court, as a court of law, [was] not professionally qualified to give a scientifically

---

[238]   *Whaling in the Antarctic*, Judgment, para. 231.
[239]   *Whaling in the Antarctic*, Judgment, para. 135.
[240]   *Whaling in the Antarctic*, Judgment, para. 94, emphasis added.
[241]   *Whaling in the Antarctic*, Judgment, paras. 146–51.
[242]   *Whaling in the Antarctic*, Judgment, paras. 153–5.
[243]   *Whaling in the Antarctic*, Judgment, para. 224.
[244]   *Whaling in the Antarctic*, Judgment, para. 226.
[245]   *Whaling in the Antarctic*, Judgment, Separate Opinion of Judge Xue, para. 15.
[246]   Statement of Mr. Vaughan Lowe, QC, verbatim record, public sitting on Monday 15 July 2013, at 3 pm, at the Peace Palace, CR/2013/22, p. 60, paras. 19–20.

meaningful answer [to the question of what science is], and should not try to pretend that it can'.[247]

Similarly, Judge Abraham would have preferred a more narrowly construed judicial review in such cases, where 'nothing [was] truly solid'[248] due to competing scientific claims. In his view, methodological flaws in the research design and doubts about the proper nature of implementation were not sufficient to cast doubt on Japan's claim regarding the scientific nature of its whaling programme.[249] Judge Sebutinde regarded such a definitional task 'more suited to scientists rather than lawyers', but later she concluded that the concept was perfectly amenable to means of treaty interpretation, first and foremost by having recourse to the ordinary meaning of the term scientific research as provided by the Oxford English Dictionary.[250] The need for such a literal interpretation was advanced by Judge Bennouna as well.[251] The reasonableness standard was altogether challenged by members of the bench for not being 'grounded in law or in the practice of the Court',[252] for being a 'magic formula' used 'out of [its] context',[253] or a concept that simply fell out of the judicial purview.[254]

On a more abstract level, the *Whaling in the Antarctic* judgment and the divergent dissenting and separate opinions showcase a wide array of potential approaches to interpreting science-intensive legal concepts. It aptly points out that depending on the approach and interpretative paths judges take, the legal significance of science can be construed very differently. The Court may hold that it is beyond the judicial task to interrogate the deeper meaning of a scientific concept and to make evaluations about the essential characteristics of scientific research. In such a case, a number of dilemmas arise. First and foremost, who should have the power to define the meaning of scientific research as enshrined in the ICRW? Is it to be entrusted to the scientific community, or should that interpretation be reserved for the contracting parties? If so, what is the appropriate extent of latitude that is to be given to contracting states? Should a party have the discretion of giving a special permit for 'what it considers to be'[255] scientific research? Or should the judicial scrutiny be limited to a bad faith assessment, as was put forward by Japan?[256] The ICJ ultimately declined the possibility in *Whaling in the Antarctic* to open the gates for such a subjective interpretation, by holding that 'whether the killing of whales ... is for the purposes of scientific research cannot depend simply on that State's perception'.[257]

[247] *Whaling in the Antarctic*, Judgment, Dissenting Opinion of Judge Owada, para. 24.
[248] *Whaling in the Antarctic*, Judgment, Dissenting Opinion of Judge Abraham, para. 40.
[249] *Whaling in the Antarctic*, Judgment, Dissenting Opinion of Judge Abraham, paras. 41–6.
[250] *Whaling in the Antarctic*, Judgment, Separate Opinion of Judge Sebutinde, para. 9.
[251] *Whaling in the Antarctic*, Judgment, Dissenting Opinion of Judge Bennouna, para. 120.
[252] *Whaling in the Antarctic*, Dissenting Opinion of Judge Yusuf, para. 15.
[253] *Whaling in the Antarctic*, Dissenting Opinion of Judge Owada, para. 34.
[254] *Whaling in the Antarctic*, Separate Opinion of Judge Xue, para. 15.
[255] *Whaling in the Antarctic*, Judgment, Declaration of Judge Keith, para. 7.
[256] *Whaling in the Antarctic*, Judgment, para. 65.
[257] *Whaling in the Antarctic*, Judgment, para. 61.

Alternatively, judges may regard the notion of scientific research as a matter of ordinary treaty interpretation falling under the scope of VCLT,[258] and hence could find it falling in their purview but confine their assessment to the legalistic issues implicated in the case. As a last possible argumentative pathway, the Court may also devise a legal test with which it can venture into expounding interlinked issues of law and fact inherent in the term scientific research.

The majority in *Whaling in the Antarctic* ultimately regarded this issue as a matter for judicial interpretation neatly fitting within the ICJ's judicial purview. A central tenet of this study is that they rightly did so. The Court crafted an objective standard of review to limit states' discretion with respect to invoking scientific research. This is all the more remarkable considering that Article VIII of ICRW on Special Permit Whaling provides that 'any Contracting Government may grant to any of its nationals a special permit authorizing that national to kill, take and treat whales for purposes of scientific research subject to such restrictions as to number and subject to such other conditions as the Contracting Government thinks fit'.[259] Yet science, perceived as a source of objective cognitive authority, was seen as posing considerable limits to the discretion enshrined in that provision.

2 *Standard of Review: The Reasonableness Test*

As has been discussed above, the Court refused to accept the definition of science as provided by Australia's expert and was equally reluctant to come up with its own definition on the defining characteristics of science. Instead, it decided to scrutinize the conformity of JARPA II with ICRW by examining whether 'the programme's design and implementation are reasonable in relation to achieving its stated objectives'.[260]

The following analysis will interrogate more deeply the arguments in favour of and against the reasonableness test (Subsection 2.1). First, it will defend the ICJ's standard of review based on insights from the philosophy of science (Subsection 2.1.1), by arguing that not attempting to provide an essentialist definition on scientific research seems to be a justifiable choice, even though some grounds for criticism remain (Subsection 2.1.2). It will further posit that the reasonableness standard of review yields an intrusive scrutiny (Subsection 2.2), and it has a distinctive epistemic nature, which facilitates a more direct judicial engagement with science (Subsection 2.3).

---

[258] *Whaling in the Antarctic*, Judgment, Separate Opinion of Judge Sebutinde, para. 9. For a similar proposition see M. M. Mbengue and R. Das, 'The ICJ's engagement with science: to interpret or not to interpret?' (2015) 6 *Journal of International Dispute Settlement* 568–77 at 573.

[259] International Convention for the Regulation of Whaling, Washington DC, 2 September 1946, in force 10 November 1948, (1948), Article VIII (1).

[260] *Whaling in the Antarctic*, Judgment, para. 67.

2.1 Define or Not to Define Science?

The majority of ICJ judges preferred not to offer a general legal definition on scientific research. This interpretative solution triggered extensive debate among scholars of the field. Some commentators have criticized the Court for not crafting a legal definition on science, and for adopting a circular test[261] instead, which is based on an 'arbitrary'[262] selection of certain criteria of scientific research that, in fact, 'have been plucked from the ether'.[263] Yet, the decision not to *define* science is not equivalent to not *interpreting* science. Clearly, the Court has 'assigned a certain meaning to this term'[264] to proceed with its analysis. The majority even geared its interpretation towards establishing an objective legal benchmark, that of reasonableness, which the Court assessed in light of an extensive body of expert evidence produced in the written submissions, and by a vigorous questioning of experts.[265]

Commentators often see the reasonable test as a failure 'to provide a coherent explanation for a term crucial to resolving the dispute at hand'.[266] Mbengue and Das draw an intuitively appealing parallel from the ICJ's case law, where in the *Navigational and Related Rights* case[267] the Court found no difficulty in interpreting the term 'commerce' as appearing in a text of an international treaty.[268] Yet it will be argued here that, from a theoretical and analytical point of view, science is to be distinguished from other terms embedded in treaties that gain their substantive meaning from practices of everyday life, such as commerce.

To further counter criticism aimed at the unfoundedness of the reasonableness standard, it is to be argued that reasonableness is in fact nothing more than an appeal to rationality.[269] In this sense reasonableness is an objective criterion flowing from states' general obligation of good faith,[270] for one cannot rely on an argument in good faith unless its position is reasonable. The test has also been praised for being a 'loose limit' not excessively curtailing the sovereign powers of states.[271] Moreover, the standard of reasonableness is no way alien to the ICJ jurisprudence. The ICJ has

---

[261]   B. Gogarty and P. Lawrence, 'The ICJ *Whaling* case: missed opportunity to advance the rule of law in resolving science-related disputes in global commons?' (2016) 77 *ZaöRV* 161–97 at 181.

[262]   B. Gogarty and P. Lawrence, 'The ICJ *Whaling* case: science, transparency and the rule of law' (2014) 23 *Journal of Law, Information and Science* 134–160 at 157.

[263]   Gogarty and Lawrence, 'The ICJ *Whaling* case: science, transparency and the rule of law', 154.

[264]   Mbengue and Das, 'The ICJ's engagement with science', 573.

[265]   Mangel, 'Whales, science, and scientific whaling in the International Court of Justice', 14526.

[266]   Mbengue and Das, 'The ICJ's engagement with science', 574.

[267]   Dispute regarding Navigational and Related Rights (*Costa Rica* v. *Nicaragua*), Judgment, 2009, ICJ Rep 213, paras. 57–71.

[268]   Mbengue and Das, 'The ICJ's engagement with science', 575.

[269]   Garrido-Munoz, 'Managing uncertainty: the International Court of Justice, "objective reasonableness" and the judicial function', 461.

[270]   Garrido-Munoz, 'Managing uncertainty: the International Court of Justice, "objective reasonableness" and the judicial function ', 467.

[271]   E. Cannizzaro, 'Proportionality and margin of appreciation in the *Whaling* case: reconciling antithetical doctrines?' (2016) 27 *European Journal of International Law* 1061–9 at 1068.

previously applied the notion of reasonableness on three prior occasions.[272] Further to these precedents, the reasonableness test has also been applied for similar science-intensive inquiry in international arbitration practice.[273]

Interestingly, the scientist appearing before the Court on behalf of Australia was less critical about the Court's solution and acknowledged that 'defin[ing] science was beyond the realm of this case'[274] and applauded the judges for 'demonstrating understanding of the need for testable questions, appropriate sample size, [and] how models and data are connected'.[275] Indeed, as will be argued in the forthcoming section, the Court was right when it refrained from defining science and instead crafted the reasonableness test, which allowed it to conduct the most extensive review possible by a court of law in a controversy deeply permeated with science.

On top of the above-mentioned arguments in favour of the Court's chosen standard of review, this book offers an additional perspective from which this argumentative path of the majority can be justified in the sections that follow.

2.1.1 DEFENDING THE COURT'S APPROACH TOWARDS SCIENTIFIC RESEARCH. Critiques of the reasonable test seem to be oblivious to the epistemic dimension of the question whether, and if so, how, concepts of science can be evaluated from a legal point of view. This issue, in fact, has strong and direct ties with the realm of philosophy of science, more specifically, Science and Technology Studies (STS), where ample scholarly literature has been dedicated to the epistemic complexities of defining science and to draw its boundaries. These insights can present an important additional perspective in appraising the reasonableness test of the ICJ.

For decades, philosophers of science attempted to identify some deterministic characteristics of science, along which science can be delineated from non-science.[276] Philosophers have therefore long attempted to draw boundaries between known and unknown, as well as facts and subjective values.[277] Chronologically first in line essentialists views were formed, contending the 'possibility and analytic desirability of identifying unique, necessary and invariant qualities that set science

---

272 Garrido-Munoz cites *Gabcikovo-Nagymaros*, *Pulp Mills*, and *Gulf of Maine* cases as examples for the application of the 'reasonableness' standard in previous ICJ decisions. See Garrido-Munoz, 'Managing uncertainty: the International Court of Justice, "objective reasonableness" and the judicial function', 463.

273 *Abyei* Arbitration (*Sudan v. The Sudan People's Liberation Movement/Army*) (Permanent Court of Arbitration) Final Award, 22 July 2009, para. 537.

274 A. Press, 'Science in the court! The role of science in "Whaling in the Antarctic"' in M. Fitzmaurice and D. Tamada (eds.), *Whaling in the Antarctic* (Brill Nijhoff, 2016), pp. 346–86 p. 383.

275 Mangel, 'Whales, science, and scientific whaling in the International Court of Justice', 14526.

276 Irwin, 'STS perspectives on scientific governance', p. 588.

277 B. E. Singleton and R. Lidskog, 'Science, red in tooth and claw: whaling, purity, pollution and institutions in marine mammal scientists' boundary work' (2018) 1 *Environment and Planning E: Nature and Space* 165–85 at 167.

apart from other cultural practices'.[278] In contrast, the later prevailing constructivist views questioned the possibility of selecting any particular demarcation criteria that can distinguish science from non-science universally in every context, where this demarcation may be relevant.[279]

Hence, to the question concerning 'what science is', a range of evolving views and conceptualizations have already been offered in the philosophy of science. An early eminent proposition came from Karl Popper, who placed falsifiability in the centre of his definition on science. He demarcated scientific claims from non-scientific ones by asking whether they are potentially falsifiable through empirical evidence.[280] Yet under such definition, non-empirical practices, such as pure mathematics, would fail to count as science, therefore it is not a workable definition according to our modern understanding of science.

Later, Robert K. Merton discerned some social norms to distinguish scientific claims from non-scientific ideology. He suggested that the requirement of falsifiability be replaced with an institutionalized 'ethos of science', which takes form in four specific social norms of science. According to Merton, those endeavours can be called science that conform to the following social norms: universalism, communism (i.e. the results of scientific research is common property of humankind as a common achievement and shared heritage), disinterestedness (where the institutional goal of science prevails over private interests of scientists), and organized scepticism (as opposed to dogma-driven acceptance of claims in absence of evidence).[281] Yet, the inherent weakness of Merton's definition is that these social norms of science do not necessarily translate into behaviour patterns of actual scientists and, therefore, often fail to provide an accurate account of science.

While Popper and Merton were subscribed to essentialism, Thomas Kuhn was one of the early scholars, who questioned the feasibility of drawing sharp demarcation lines. Nevertheless in his seminal book entitled *The Structure of Scientific Revolutions*[282] he proposed that the presence of a paradigmatic consensus among scientists could be used to distinguish science from non-science. And indeed, the progress of scientific research, although at least in natural sciences, can be described and explained through patterns of paradigm shifts. From this perspective, beliefs that later prove to be errors or unfounded myths ought not to be dismissed as non-scientific, if they conform to the paradigm prevailing at the time.[283] Kuhn's definition on science is thus 'working under the paradigm',[284] for deserting the paradigm is equated with ceasing to practice science. The blind spot of such a definition lies in the fact that social sciences, including law, are usually

---

[278]   T. Gieryn, 'Boundaries of science', p. 393.
[279]   T. Gieryn, 'Boundaries of science', p. 393.
[280]   Popper, *The Logic of Scientific Discovery*, p. 18.
[281]   Merton, 'The normative structure of science', pp. 270–8.
[282]   T. Kuhn, *The Structure of Scientific Revolutions*, 1962, 1970 ed. (The University of Chicago), p. 34.
[283]   Thomas Gieryn, 'Boundaries of science', p. 402.
[284]   Kuhn, *The Structure of Scientific Revolutions*, p. 34.

not driven by or do not conform to any organizing consensus and, therefore, would not qualify as science.

Acknowledging the repeated failed attempts to find inherent and universal characteristics of science, instead of demarcation, constructivists focus on 'boundary-work', which is essentially 'an attribution of selected characteristics to the institution of science ... for the purposes of constructing a social boundary that distinguishes some intellectual activity as non-science'.[285] Being mindful of the apparent limitations of any essentialist attempts to provide an a priori definition of science, scientific claims can be better recognized on a case-by-case basis, through the boundary-work of various actors involved in the specific context of a given case. As constructivists put it, the boundaries of science are 'negotiated' epistemically by scientists and society, since 'nothing of [science's] borders and territories is fixed ... in a deterministic way'.[286]

The above discussion has important implications for the matter of interest here in as much as it suggests that any attempts on part of a court of law to define science a priori and universally would be susceptible to analytical challenges. Therefore, the judicial task ought to be conceived more as engaging in boundary-work rather than being entangled in a hopeless exercise of defining science that is understood as a 'pure' category of objective authority. Insights from STS suggest that adjudicators should in fact decide whether *for purposes of* a given legal debate, a certain knowledge claim could legitimately appeal to the epistemic authority of science in the social setting of legal dispute resolution. If so, then judges may legitimately allocate persuasive force to a given scientific claim. It is proposed here that the *Whaling in the Antarctic* case has seen a legitimate and persuasive judicial solution, when the Court did not define scientific research but developed the reasonableness test in order to choose between the parties' science-based positions.

2.1.2 ROOM FOR CRITICISM. Criticism nevertheless seems to be warranted for the Court's overly cautious and hesitant approach in pinpointing to the essential (though not deterministic) characteristics of a whaling programme that is deemed to be conducted for purposes of scientific research. The often elusive reasoning concerning the application of the standard of review may be read as undermining the firm operative part as it somewhat blurs relevant characteristics of scientific research that can be discerned from the judgment. Not only does the decision announce that JARPA II 'can broadly be characterized as "scientific research"',[287] but it also stops short of attaching significant enough legal relevance to several discrepancies revealed by expert statements as to the implementation of JARPA II. Notably, even Japan's own expert, Professor Valloe, admitted that neither did he

[285] T. Gieryn, 'Boundaries of science', p. 405.
[286] T. Gieryn, 'Boundaries of science', p. 406.
[287] *Whaling in the Antarctic*, Judgment, para. 127.

'understand how they [Japan] have calculated their sample sizes'.[288] Yet the Court merely noted that 'the lack of transparency in the ... sample size d[id] not necessarily demonstrate that the decisions made with regard to particular research times lack[ed] scientific justification'.[289]

Also, the judgment appears to be too lenient with respect to the open-ended time frame and the scientific output of the programme. The ICJ solely hinted that 'it would have been more appropriate'[290] to establish at least some intermediary targets rather than designing an infinite research programme, and later only stated that the 'scientific output to date appear[ed] limited'.[291] These additional remarks can easily be read as not bearing relevance as to the scientific nature of a whaling programme, which further weakens the applicability and reach of the Court's findings in future cases.

The usefulness and workability of the reasonableness assessment with respect to future whaling disputes was also called into question.[292] Critics note that the standard of review is unclear and leaves too much room for manoeuvre for state parties to 'redefine the scope of their own obligations' under the ICRW.[293] They also assert that since the test fails to mandate a retrospective evaluation of the scientific research at hand, such a reasonableness criterion would only allow scrutiny to any 'scientific whaling' after the lapse of several years,[294] when significant volume of data have been generated through the lethal taking of thousands of whales. This casts considerable doubts on the efficacy of the reasonableness test with respect to ensuring compliance with the ICRW regime.

Japan's take on the reasonableness requirement also raises queries about the efficiency of the announced standard of review. As one of the counsels for respondent has put it, the Court crafted the requirement of reasonableness 'as an obligation to state reasons',[295] according to which '[e]ach time, in each situation and with respect to each action, States would need to publicly provide detailed reasons in a timely manner, otherwise, they might be held internationally responsible for the failure to do so'.[296] Such a narrow reading of the reasonableness criterion would be

---

[288] International Court of Justice, Court Record, CR/2013/14 p. 41.
[289] *Whaling in the Antarctic*, Judgment, para. 195.
[290] *Whaling in the Antarctic*, Judgment, para. 216
[291] *Whaling in the Antarctic*, Judgment, para. 219.
[292] Cymie Payne's contribution to the panel discussion entitled 'Adjudicating international environmental disputes: lessons from recent jurisprudence', American Society of International Law 2017 Annual Meeting, Washington DC.
[293] Gogarty and Lawrence, 'The ICJ *Whaling* case: missed opportunity to advance the rule of law in resolving science-related disputes in global commons?', 182.
[294] Gogarty and Lawrence, 'The ICJ Whaling case: missed opportunity to advance the rule of law in resolving science-related disputes in global commons?', 183.
[295] Hamamoto, 'From the requirement of reasonableness to a "comply and explain" rule: the standard of review in the Whaling judgment', p. 50.
[296] Hamamoto, 'From the requirement of reasonableness to a "comply and explain" rule: the standard of review in the Whaling judgment', p. 52.

indeed of limited reach in future disputes. Whether the Court would be willing to conceive the reasonableness review as a more substantive test depends on its willingness to engage in a more nuanced and even more detailed boundary-work between science and non-science in any subsequent proceedings.

Having said that, the effectiveness of the chosen standard of review would be best measured against future conflicts arising from the aftermath of the decision. Japan has announced that it would abide by the ICJ's judgment. Yet shortly thereafter Japan launched a new whaling programme under the special permit provision of the ICRW (called New Scientific Whale Research Program in the Antarctic Ocean, NEWREP-A), which includes lethal take of 333 minke whales per annum, during a twelve-year period, while pursuing broadly similar goals to JARPA.[297] Japan also resumed whaling operations in its territorial waters and exclusive economic zone as of July 2019. The question of reasonableness between research objectives and implementation could be in principle relevant with respect to the legal evaluation of NEWREP-A. However, the material chances of a subsequent proceeding focusing on the compliance of Japan with the Court's requirements have become ever weaker. Japan first amended its declaration under Article 36(2) of the Court's Statute to exclude 'any dispute arising out of, concerning, or relating to research on, or conservation, management or exploitation of, living resources of the sea'.[298] This eliminates the possibility to bring new claims against Japan on this jurisdictional basis either under customary international law or under applicable treaty provisions. With an even more marked turn, Japan formally notified the International Whaling Commission (IWC) of its withdrawal from the commission's work.[299] This is particularly relevant because this body has the power of passing binding decisions upon its members.[300]

2.2 Conducting an Intrusive Judicial Review

The practical significance of the reasonableness assessment is that it enabled the Court to scrutinize the science-backed claims of the parties to a considerable extent. The Court's ambitious standard of review is all the more striking in light of the alternative interpretations that were promoted by the parties and certain members of the bench. Notably, Japan offered a much narrower reading, according to which reasonableness was only relevant in examining whether 'a State [could] reasonably regard this [JARPA II] as scientific research'[301] but refuted the possibility of being an

---

[297] Press, 'Science in the court! The role of science in "Whaling in the Antarctic"', pp. 384–5.
[298] Declaration recognizing the jurisdiction of the Court as compulsory, submitted by Japan on 6 October 2015, section (3), available at www.icj-cij.org/en/declarations/jp (last accessed 11 January 2020).
[299] See the website of the International Whaling Commission, available at https://iwc.int/statement-on-government-of-japan-withdrawal-from-t (last accessed 11 January 2020).
[300] International Convention for the Regulation of Whaling, Article V(1).
[301] Statement of Mr Vaughan Lowe, QC, verbatim record, public sitting on Monday 15 July 2013, at 3 pm, at the Peace Palace, CR 2013/22, p. 60. para. 20,

objective benchmark. In contrast, Australia submitted a broader notion of reasonableness, grounded in the obligation of good faith, a general principle of international law.[302] Australia argued that good faith implementation required Japan in the material case to 'have due regard to and respond to the views of the IWC, particularly those urging the cessation of the lethal elements of any program'.[303] New Zealand proposed a slightly different third reading on reasonableness. It referred to the *Gabcikovo-Nagymaros* judgment, which compelled states 'to apply a treaty provision in a reasonable way and in such a manner that its purpose can be realised'.[304] The dissenting Judge Owada would have preferred yet another reading, according to which reasonableness is conceived as a 'yardstick for ascertaining whether a decision or an action is or is not "arbitrary" or patently "out of bounds"'.[305]

The reasonableness standard, as constructed by the ICJ, yields a rather intrusive standard of review. Japan would have preferred[306] the standard used by the WTO Appellate Body, which does not examine whether the science-based decision was correct, but only interrogates whether 'the assessment is supported by coherent reasoning and respectable scientific evidence and is, in this sense, objectively justifiable'.[307] This standard of review is a rather intrusive one, however, it does not allow WTO panels to conduct a *de novo* assessment of the scientific facts by substituting its own scientific conclusions for the member state's risk assessment. The Court ultimately decided not to borrow this test,[308] and applied the reasonableness assessment instead, which arguably came close to a *de novo* appraisal,[309] and, thus, was slightly even more intrusive than the one mandated by the WTO. Importantly, the ICJ's standard of review also avoided a strictly deferential approach, according to which the bench should have blindly followed one of the experts' definitions on scientific research.

At the end of the day, the lack of providing a general definition on scientific research did not bar the Court from conducting an in-depth and substantive review of the research items of JARPA II. The roughly eighty-paragraph long elaborate judicial evaluation of the elements of the design, methodologies, and implementation of the alleged research programme[310] depicts an intrusive judicial scrutiny.

[302] *Whaling in the Antarctic*, Memorial of Australia, para. 4.61.
[303] *Whaling in the Antarctic*, Memorial of Australia, para. 5.126.
[304] *Whaling in the Antarctic*, Written observations of New Zealand, para. 12.
[305] *Whaling in the Antarctic*, Dissenting Opinion of Judge Owada, para. 39.
[306] Japan's position was reiterated in the judgment, *Whaling in the Antarctic*, Judgment, para. 66.
[307] *Continued Suspension of Obligations in the EC – Hormones dispute*, Appellate Body Report, WT/DS320/AB/R (16 October 2018), p. 246, para. 590.
[308] The dissenting opinion of Judge Owada referred to the report of the WTO Appellate Body in the *Continued Suspension of Obligations in the EC – Hormones Dispute*, WT/DS320/AB/R.
[309] Judge Owada described the Court's approach as 'making a de novo assessment', and he criticized the Court for this, see *Whaling in the Antarctic*, Dissenting Opinion of Judge Owada, para. 38; Eyal Benvenisti regards the standard as a means of conducting strict scrutiny. E. Benvenisti, 'Community interests in international law' in E. Benvenisti and G. Nolte (eds.), *Community Interests Across International Law* (Oxford University Press, 2018), pp. 70–85 p. 82.
[310] *Whaling in the Antarctic*, Judgment, paras. 147–222.

2.3 The Reasonableness Test: A Hybrid Standard of Review

This study claims that the biggest advantage of the reasonableness standard lies in the fact that it allows adjudicators to engage with scientific concepts in an in-depth and meaningful way while still speaking in the language of a legal assessment. The reasonableness review allows legal adjudicators to adequately interpret concepts that are situated on the border of the legal and the scientific realm, and in this sense, are 'hybrid' notions. The term scientific research provides an apposite example for such a concept, given that it is embedded in a legal text, the ICRW, though in order to discern its meaning, legal adjudicators need to rely on scientific expertise.

The reasonableness criterion in itself is also a hybrid standard. Judge Owada was perplexed by its peculiar nature, when posed a rhetorical question whether '[i]s it the legal context or is it the scientific context that the Court claims to be engaged in?'[311] The answer, it is submitted here, is 'both', because in order to provide a meaningful, in-depth *legal* interpretation of the term scientific research, which does justice to the complexities of modern scientific realities, the interpreter's task cannot be confined solely to the ordinary meaning of this term. Adjudicators should consult with *scientific* experts to be able to grasp the substantive characteristics of scientific research conducted in the relevant field and then appraise the reasonable nature of the research scheme. Yet, appraising the reasonableness of any conduct falls neatly within the epistemic competence of judges and the traditional scope of the judicial task alike.

Throughout this study, legal tests and benchmarks underlying certain judicial reasoning techniques that are similar to 'reasonableness' will be dubbed as hybrid standards.[312] The hybrid nature of such benchmarks refers to the fact that they bridge the legal and the scientific epistemic realms inasmuch as they require adjudicators to develop a thorough understanding of the underlying *science*, while they are still amenable to *judicial* appraisal. Emphatically, reasonableness is not a purely scientific standard, as it presupposes an act of balancing, which is alien to scientific judgment. Therefore, forming an opinion on the reasonableness of JARPA II, does not in strict sense entail an evaluation of the scientific nature of the programme. Reasonableness is, in fact, a key feature of legal reasoning[313] and, thus, allows international judges to assume a more active role in appraising the legally relevant characteristics of scientific research, without however making epistemically arbitrary judgments about the scientific truth of the evidence submitted. The epistemic

---

[311] *Whaling in the Antarctic*, Judgment, Dissenting Opinion of Judge Owada, para. 25.

[312] The terminology of this study draws on literature from the philosophy of science. The term 'hybrid' has been used by Bruno Latour in STS literature to describe hybrid constructs in which the scientific and the social aspects are inextricably entangled with each other. Also, Peter M. Haas distinguished 'hybrid' facts from brute and social facts. Just like hybrid reasoning techniques, hybrid facts also 'stretch the reach' of a given expert community. See B. Latour, *We have Never Been Modern* (Harvester Wheatsheaf, 1993), p. 3; Haas, 'Ideas, experts and governance', p. 25.

[313] S. Bertea, 'Certainty, reasonableness and argumentation in law' (2004) 18 *Argumentation* 465–78 at 474.

nature and the practical feasibility of such hybrid standards will be elaborated in more detail in Chapter 10.[314]

Support for applying such a hybrid approach in science-intensive cases is also suggested by Judge Keith, who explained that scientific concepts can be appraised from the law's perspective to select what 'demonstrates coherent scientific reasoning supporting central features of the programme'.[315] And indeed, the majority should be praised for taking up this job and conducting such a science-intensive legalistic assessment. In contrast to that, Judge Owada, dissenting, would have preferred a more restricted approach, where the judicial purview does not include expounding science-based concepts. He argues that 'even though there may be certain elements in the concept that the Court may legitimately and usefully offer as salient from the viewpoint of legal analysis',[316] the ICJ should not do so, as it 'should focus purely and simply on the issue of the scope of what constitutes activities "for purposes of scientific research" according to the plain and ordinary meaning of the phrase'.[317] The ordinary meaning of scientific research, as provided by the Oxford English Dictionary is as follows: 'systematic pursuit of knowledge concerning the structure and behaviour of the physical and natural word through observation and experiment'. As it may be apparent by now, subscribing to such a formalistic and vague definition of science would have deprived the Court from conducting a substantive review of elements of JARPA II. In such a scenario, the programme in all likelihood would have survived judicial scrutiny.

It is argued here that the majority's two-step analysis, which focused more on the first part of the definition ('for purposes of') that is more amenable to legal analysis compared to the second part ('scientific research') was a necessary, if not the most appropriate, judicial tool, which enabled the Court to provide a persuasive reasoning still speaking in a legalistic language. Considering the complexity of sorting out claims of science and non-science, the reasonableness standard ought to be praised for it enables international adjudicators to balance competing values that are impossible to quantify.[318] As was noted by Australia's scientific expert, 'even though the Court did not define science, the process of science is interwoven in the standard of review for comparing the objectives, design and implementation of JARPA II'.[319] This 'interwoven' nature of science and the legal assessment will be seen throughout this study as giving rise to a distinctive judicial argumentative technique, that is, the use of hybrid epistemic benchmarks. Similar benchmarks from the practice of

---

[314] See Chapter 10 Section II, Subsection 4.
[315] *Whaling in the Antarctic*, Declaration of Judge Keith, para. 8.
[316] *Whaling in the Antarctic*, Judgment, Dissenting Opinion of Judge Owada, para. 24.
[317] *Whaling in the Antarctic*, Judgment, Dissenting Opinion of Judge Owada, para. 23.
[318] Garrido-Munoz, 'Managing uncertainty: the International Court of Justice, "objective reasonableness" and the judicial function', 462.
[319] Mangel, 'Whales, science, and scientific whaling in the International Court of Justice', 14524.

international adjudicative bodies will be examined later in more detail in Chapters 9[320] and 10.[321]

3 Doctrinal Implications of the Reasonableness Test for the Judicial Purview

The reasonableness assessment has wider implications reaching far beyond the issue of standard of review. It informs doctrinal debates concerning the proper scope of judicial task in dealing with fact-intensive cases. Setting such an intrusive standard of review broadens the extent of the Court's review and therefore allows for expanding the scope of the judicial purview. This issue bears significance considering that there still appears to be no consensus among ICJ judges about the appropriate scope of the Court's judicial function. Despite the fact that the joint dissenters and Judge Vinuesa[322] both dismissed the majority's 'flawed'[323] methodology in *Pulp Mills* and criticized the judgment for the lack of finding substantive breaches due to the poor evaluation of the evidence, they were in no agreement as to the appropriate scope of the judicial task.

The two opinions in fact canvass entirely different pictures on the appropriate judicial purview in science-intensive cases. Judge Vinuesa emphasizes the Court's apparent incapability to evaluate the 'scientific integrity of the scientific methodologies applied',[324] and 'the credibility of the scientific submissions',[325] which altogether suggest that the Court ought not to aspire to make conclusions as it clearly lacks 'proper expertise of knowledge'.[326] In contrast to that, the joint dissenters saw this case as an opportunity for the Court to discharge 'exclusive judicial functions' in 'the interpretation of legal terms and the legal categorization of factual issues'.[327] They also emphasized that 'the task of a court of justice is not to give a scientific assessment'[328] regarding the scientific submissions' credibility, validity or viability. Scholarly opinions also suggest that the international judicial function does not create a need for resolving scientific debates.[329]

The *Whaling in the Antarctic* case provided an apt opportunity for ICJ judges to revisit the limits and essence of the judicial task. Judge Sebutinde regarded such a definitional task 'more suited to scientists rather than lawyers'.[330] This view was shared by Judge Owada, according to whom 'this Court, as a court of law, is not professionally qualified to give a scientifically meaningful answer [to the question of

---

[320] See Chapter 9 Section V, Subsection 2.3.
[321] See Chapter 10 Section II, Subsection 4.
[322] *Pulp Mills*, Dissenting Opinion of Judge Vinuesa, para. 69.
[323] *Pulp Mills*, Joint Dissenting Opinion of Judges Al-Khasawneh and Simma, para. 2.
[324] *Pulp Mills*, Dissenting Opinion of Judge Vinuesa, para. 72.
[325] *Pulp Mills*, Dissenting Opinion of Judge Vinuesa, para. 72.
[326] *Pulp Mills*, Dissenting Opinion of Judge Vinuesa, para. 72.
[327] *Pulp Mills*, Joint Dissenting Opinion of Judges Al-Khasawneh and Simma, para. 12.
[328] *Pulp Mills*, Joint Dissenting Opinion of Judges Al-Khasawneh and Simma, para. 4.
[329] Mbengue, 'International courts and tribunals as fact-finders', 76.
[330] *Whaling in the Antarctic*, Separate Opinion of Judge Sebutinde, para. 9.

what science is], and should not try to pretend that it can'.[331] This has been, however, countered by the majority, which declared the controversy falling within the Court's purview.

By conducting the reasonableness review, the ICJ altogether took a step towards an active role in supervising science-based disputes without, however, requiring judges to decide about scientific truth. In this respect, the *Whaling in the Antarctic* judgment seems to be highly consequential for future cases as it provides a valuable precedent for a broader conception of the ICJ's judicial function that is not confined to strictly non-scientific considerations, such as good faith assessments. Overall as to the extent of judicial engagement with science, the *Whaling in the Antarctic* judgment seems to strike the most appropriate balance between epistemic non-arbitrariness that warns against judges acting as super-experts and judicial inaction that would undermine the Court's authority.

---

[331]   *Whaling in the Antarctic*, Dissenting Opinion of Judge Owada, para. 24.

4

Science in the Practice of Inter-State Arbitral Tribunals

The Tribunal is of the opinion that these [fumigations] are due to the existence for a considerable period of a sufficient velocity of the gas-carrying air current to cause a mixing of this with the surface atmosphere.[1]

Trail Smelter Arbitral Award, 1938

This chapter deals with inter-state environmental arbitral disputes, which are brought before ad hoc arbitral panels, or tribunals constituted under the aegis of the Permanent Court of Arbitration (PCA). Among ad hoc international arbitral awards, the *Trail Smelter* and the *Lake Lanoux* Arbitrations will be examined in detail. From PCA practice, the *Iron Rhine Railway* and the *Indus Waters Kishenganga* arbitral decisions will be scrutinized.[2] A peculiar set of environmental arbitrations are commenced under Annex VII of the United Nations Convention on the Law of the Sea (UNCLOS), among which those disputes will be elaborated on that bespeak the scientific engagement of arbitrators, namely, the *Southern Bluefin Tuna*, the *MOX Plant*, the *MOX Plant OSPAR* Arbitration, the *Chagos Marine Protected Area*, and the *South China Sea* arbitral proceedings.[3] As an important caveat, it must be emphasized at the outset that any assessment as to the trends in international arbitration could only provide a piecemeal picture considering the ad hoc constitution of tribunals with different arbitrators appointed for each and every case. As a result, adjudicatory practice in arbitration is much more fragmented

---

[1] *Trail Smelter* Arbitration *(United States, Canada)*, Award, 16 April 1938, 3 RIAA 1905, at 1924.

[2] The *Rhine Chlorides* case, *Rhine Chlorides Arbitration concerning the Auditing of Accounts (Netherlands v. France)* (Permanent Court of Arbitration), Award, 13 May 2014, will not be discussed here, as it did not entertain scientific arguments in the merits phase.

[3] The *Land Reclamation by Singapore in an around the Straits of Johor (Malaysia v. Singapore)* dispute, which was instituted under Annex VII of UNCLOS, will not be detailed as it was settled by the parties, therefore it falls outside the scope of this inquiry. See *Land Reclamation by Singapore in an around the Straits of Johor (Malaysia v. Singapore)* (Permanent Court of Arbitration), Award on Agreed Terms, 1 September 2005, 27 RIAA 133, recital 25. The same dispute has reached the ITLOS as well, which will be discussed in Chapter 9.

compared to permanent judicial fora rendering the reach of any generalized analytic remarks somewhat limited.

I   SCIENCE ENTERS ENVIRONMENTAL ADJUDICATION

Inter-state arbitration holds important potential for resolving environmental conflicts. Several international environmental treaties contain dispute settlement clauses referring to the PCA,[4] which may provide the basis for a number of environmental disputes in the future. One commentator explicitly suggests the superiority of arbitration over the ICJ to settle international environmental disputes,[5] given that arbitral tribunals conduct a more thorough review of scientific facts. Although it is true that disputed scientific facts are not construed as precluding the performance of adjudicatory function in inter-state arbitration, a closer look reveals that some panels do have a controversial relationship with science-intensive claims. The panels' varying tolerance towards science is reflected in the ways in which they frame and reconstruct relevant legal issues in a dispute. In some cases, arbitrators are willing to regard scientific arguments as relevant, or even decisive, to the case at hand, while on other occasions they eliminate the scientific dimension of the dispute. These varying framing techniques will be examined in Section II. Tribunals also differ in their approaches to evaluating scientific evidence signalled by differing fact-finding procedures, as addressed in Section III. Some decisions touch upon issues of causation, which will be discussed in Section IV. The applicable standard of review vis-à-vis scientific claims of litigants has not been explicitly raised in relevant international arbitrations; hence it will not be elaborated on in this chapter.

II   FRAMING OF DISPUTES: CARVING OUT SCIENCE OR HARNESSING ITS AUTHORITY

Although a good number of disputes with scientific profile are referred to inter-state arbitration, not every decision reaches the depth of the underlying science. The status of scientific arguments largely depends on how adjudicators frame the dispute.

---

[4] For example, Convention on International Trade in Endangered Species of Wild Flora and Fauna, Washington DC, 3 March 1973, in force 1 July 1975, 993 UNTS 243; Convention of Migratory Species of Wild Animals, Bonn, 23 June 1979, in force 1 November 1983, (1980) 19 ILM 15; Convention on the Protection for the Alps, Salzburg, 7 November 1991, in force 6 March 1995, 1917 UNTS 137; Convention on the Protection and Use of Transboundary Watercourses and International Lakes, Helsinki, 17 March 1992, in force 6 October 1996, (1992) 31 ILM 1312; and the Convention on the Transboundary Effects of Industrial Accidents, Helsinki, 17 March 1992, in force 19 April 2000, (1992) 31 ILM 1330, cited by A. C. Kiss, 'Environmental disputes and the Permanent Court of Arbitration' (2003) 16 *Hague Yearbook of International Law* 41–6 at 45.

[5] Romano, *The Peaceful Settlement of International Environmental Disputes a Pragmatic Approach*, p. 328.

Arbitral tribunals have consistently regarded science-intensive disputes justiciable. The non-justiciability of such cases was most clearly advanced by Japan in the *Southern Bluefin Tuna* Arbitration.[6] 'At the core of the dispute'[7] lay the parties' disagreement as to whether the tuna stock had in fact begun to recover due to restrictions instituted for total allowable catch. Japan argued that the claims at hand were 'questions of scientific judgments'[8] and, hence, non-justiciable. Whereas Australia maintained that the treaty was devoid of meaning if disputes concerning questions of scientific fact and opinion were not justiciable. The Annex VII arbitral tribunal observed that the dispute at hand was 'not confined to matters of scientific judgment only',[9] and remained seized of the matter. Hence these early attempts at carving out scientific disputes from adjudicatory competence proved to be futile.

Yet, the fact that arbitral tribunals do intend to adjudicate science-intensive claims does not mean that they are equally willing to closely consider the scientific dimension of such disputes. In the majority of environmental disputes, tribunals adopted various techniques to carve out scientific evidence from the legally decisive aspects of disputes. The divergent framing techniques that will be discussed below aptly illustrate that the extent to which science plays a decisive role in environmental adjudication is not set a priori. In fact, it varies greatly depending upon the approach of adjudicators and sometimes on the parties' litigation strategy. Subsection 1 will list the most characteristic adjudicatory framing techniques that downplay the role of science. Subsection 2 will then describe arbitrations, where scientific aspects were not considered due to the parties' choices. Subsection 3 will conclude with framing techniques that include science in the adjudicatory assessment and utilize the authority of scientific claims for a strategic reason.

1 *Marginalizing Science by Adjudicators*

Arbitrators can reason their way into escaping science-intensive evaluation in many ways. Some choose not to comment in the award on the scientific questions forming the crux of the parties' disagreement (Subsection 1.1), others explicitly disregard the science-intensive arguments and evidence in their legal assessment (Subsection 1.2). Interestingly, these avoidance techniques are not confined to the early phase of environmental arbitration but are spread across the history of inter-state disputes, shown by the examples that follow.

---

[6] *Southern Bluefin Tuna (New Zealand – Japan, Australia – Japan)* (Permanent Court of Arbitration), Award, 4 August 2000, 28 RIAA 1.

[7] *Southern Bluefin Tuna* Arbitration, para. 22.

[8] *Southern Bluefin Tuna* Arbitration, para. 40.

[9] *Southern Bluefin Tuna* Arbitration, para. 65.

1.1 Not Commenting on Scientific Issues Underlying the Legal Dispute

The first international arbitration arising out of a conflict over natural resources was the 1893 *Bering Sea Fur Seals* Arbitration[10] between Great Britain, administering Canada, and the United States, which at the material time had just acquired the territory of Alaska from Russia. A rapid decline in the population of migratory fur seals ignited this legal dispute between the two leading fur sealer nations, as shrinking herds began to jeopardize the viability of the industry. This historic dispute provides an early example of how international environmental cases have often been decided without touching upon the scientific aspects, even though such questions usually lay at the core of the conflict.

The heart of the inter-state controversy at hand concerned a scientific issue, that is, the cause of the decreasing number of seals. The United States claimed that the decline was due to the increased pelagic sealing on the high seas from where the seals were migrating to the Pribilof Islands on US territory. The US government even presented the arbitral tribunal with opinions of leading naturalists from several countries to substantiate that the sole cause of the decreasing herds was sealing on the seas.[11] Whereas the United Kingdom claimed that the real cause was over-exploitation of the seals on the island.[12] Contrasting scientific views notwithstanding, the legal dispute as set forth in the Arbitration Agreement was strictly confined to the legal question as to whether the United States was entitled to enforce a protective legislation outside of its territorial seas on the basis of the right to property.[13] The panel concluded that domestic legislation could not lawfully restrict another sovereign's hunting rights on international waters,[14] and thus, found in favour of Great Britain. As a corollary of such framing of the dispute, it is understandable that the judgment did not comment on the scientific causes of the declining seal population.

Similar science-evasive framing techniques are applied in more recent decisions as well. To take one example, the *Chagos Marine Protected Area* case can be mentioned. This arbitration proceedings concerned the creation of a no-take Marine Protected Area (MPA) in the Exclusive Economic Zone (EEZ) belonging to the Chagos Archipelago, over which Mauritius had claims of sovereignty and fishing rights.[15] The United Kingdom, to which the area belonged in colonial times, unilaterally declared the MPA in order to prohibit all fisheries activities therein. The United Kingdom sought

---

[10]   *Bering Sea Fur Seals* Arbitration *(United States v. UK)*, Award, 15 August 1893, 28 RIAA 263.
[11]   *Fur Seal* Arbitration, *Proceedings of the Tribunal of Arbitration, Bering Fur Seal Arbitration, 1892, The Case of the United States of America*, Volume II, Washington, DC: Government Printing Office, pp.165–86, 414–33.
[12]   Romano, *The Peaceful Settlement of International Environmental Disputes: A Pragmatic Approach*, p. 134.
[13]   *Bering Sea Fur Seals* Arbitration, Question 5, 28 RIAA 263, at 267.
[14]   *Bering Sea Fur Seals* Arbitration, 28 RIAA 263, at 269.
[15]   For a general overview of the historical background to the dispute and the main legal issues entertained in the arbitration see D. A. Colson and B. J. Vohrer, 'In Re Chagos Marine Protected Area *(Mauritius v. UK)*' (2015) 109 *American Journal of International Law* 845–51; M. J. N. Meetarbhan, 'Re-examining the Chagos Marine Protected Area arbitration: the Lancaster House undertakings' (2015) 45 *Environmental Policy and Law* 248–55.

to justify its measure by reference to environmental protection goals, which it underpinned by repeated appeals to scientific studies.[16] Prior to designation, the United Kingdom held a domestic public consultation process, which concluded that there was 'sufficient scientific information to make a convincing case'[17] for creating the MPA. Mauritius challenged the designation under UNCLOS and altogether contested the environmental motivations of the United Kingdom. It argued that even if environmental concerns were the prime purpose of the MPA, it failed to meet such objectives due to 'the insufficiency of scientific justification'[18] provided.

Yet, the adjudicatory analysis in the award did not reach the level of such scientific argumentation. The panel found severe shortcomings in the procedure in which the MPA had been established, and it emphatically 'has taken no view on the substantive quality or nature of the MPA or on the importance of environmental protection'.[19] This saved the tribunal from entertaining scientific considerations. The panel instead invited the parties to enter into negotiation 'with a view to achieving a mutually satisfactory arrangement for protecting the marine environment'.[20] The previously discussed scientific arguments may now only resurface in the out-of-court settlement phase of the *Chagos* saga.

1.2 Disregarding Science-Intensive Arguments of the Parties

Certain tribunals go even further and decline to engage with the scientific subject-matter of disputes even where the parties' submissions expressly cover scientific issues. Awards rendered in the *MOX Plant* controversy illustrate such an approach. The *MOX Plant* dispute generated several legal proceedings before different international adjudicatory fora, providing a 'poster child'[21] for the fragmented nature of international environmental dispute resolution systems.[22] Complaints were filed with ITLOS, an Annex VII Arbitral Tribunal, and an arbitral tribunal set up under the 1992 Convention for the Protection of the Marine Environment of the North-East Atlantic (OSPAR Convention). Later, the European Court of Justice also issued a judgment in an infringement proceeding launched against Ireland for violating its exclusive jurisdiction by bringing the dispute

---

[16] *Chagos Marine Protected Area* Arbitration (*Mauritius* v. *UK*) (Permanent Court of Arbitration) Award, 18 March 2015, para. 289.

[17] *Chagos Marine Protected Area* Arbitration, para. 286, citing the conclusion of the public consultation.

[18] *Chagos Marine Protected Area* Arbitration, para. 495.

[19] *Chagos Marine Protected Area* Arbitration, para. 544.

[20] *Chagos Marine Protected Area* Arbitration, para. 544.

[21] D. M. Bodansky, 'OSPAR arbitration of the MOX Plant dispute' (2008) 08–002 *University of Georgia School of Law Research Paper Series* 1–20 at 2.

[22] For a more detailed discussion on the fragmentation of environmental dispute settlement system see Y. Shany, 'The first MOX Plant award: the need to harmonize competing environmental regimes and dispute settlement procedures' (2004) 17 *Leiden Journal of International Law* 815–27.

before the UNCLOS arbitral tribunal.[23] The diverse legal claims all concerned a mixed-oxide (MOX) nuclear fuel plant commissioned by the United Kingdom in Sellafield.

The first award of the *MOX Plant* saga, referred to as the *MOX Plant OSPAR* Arbitration,[24] was issued by a tribunal constituted under the OSPAR Convention. The claim centred on the United Kingdom's refusal to provide Ireland with unredacted versions of two reports concerning the economic justifications for commissioning the plant. The United Kingdom omitted certain data and figures with reference to business confidentiality. Ireland argued that the redactions in the reports precluded a meaningful assessment whether expected economic benefits were capable of outweighing and, thus, justifying the negative environmental consequences of the MOX plant under a cost-benefit analysis.

Ireland based its claims on Article 9 of the OSPAR Convention, which ensures a right to access to information 'on the state of the maritime area, on activities or measures adversely affecting or likely to affect' the environment. Ireland claimed a broad definition of information comprising all data relevant to the cost-benefit analysis of the plant. In Ireland's view every piece of information was relating to the state of the environment that led to allowing nuclear discharge into the sea.

The tribunal disagreed and construed a more restrictive definition of environmental information.[25] The reasoning of the panel for the narrow reading speaks directly to the issues relevant in this study. The majority opined that the request for redacted information was outside the scope of Article 9, because it did not relate to an activity likely to affect the marine environment. Notably, it did so without hearing any expert evidence assessing the likelihood of the plant's adverse impact.[26]

The award therefore provides an example for adjudicatory framing, which conveniently circumvents complex factual questions. Arbitrator Griffith also points out in his dissent that the majority's finding against the likelihood of adverse effects to the environment was made 'without any assessment and identification of its factual basis, and in an apparent disregard of the admitted environmental damage'.[27] The dissent also lends support to the proposition that such a framing went quite against the parties' submissions. Litigants extensively dealt with the likelihood of future environmental damage in their written as well as oral pleadings.[28] Yet the adjudicatory analysis effectively disregarded the parties' substantive and science-heavy arguments regarding the possibility of adverse effects. Instead, the majority deemed those

[23] *Commission of the European Communities v. Ireland*, Judgment of the Court, C-459/03, European Court of Justice, Grand Chamber (30 May 2006).
[24] *Dispute Concerning Access to Information Under Article 9 of the OSPAR Convention (Ireland v. UK)* (Permanent Court of Arbitration), Award, 2 July 2003, 42 ILM 1118.
[25] *Dispute Concerning Access to Information Under Article 9 of the OSPAR Convention (Ireland v. UK)*, para. 170.
[26] *MOX Plant OSPAR Arbitration (Ireland v. UK)* (Permanent Court of Arbitration), Award, 2 July 2003, para. 179.
[27] *MOX Plant OSPAR Arbitration*, Dissenting Opinion of Gavan Griffith, para. 89.
[28] *MOX Plant OSPAR Arbitration*, para. 88.

aspects decisive that 'received only a passing reference and attention' in the parties' submissions.[29]

Similar adjudicatory framing can be seen in the second arbitral award in the *MOX Plant* saga, rendered by an UNCLOS Annex VII Arbitral Tribunal.[30] Ireland claimed that the United Kingdom was acting contrary to Article 194 of UNCLOS prescribing an obligation to prevent pollution of the marine environment by discharging certain radioactive substances ancillary to the functioning of the MOX Plant into the Irish Sea.[31] The application was ultimately withdrawn,[32] following the European Court of Justice's judgment finding a violation of its exclusive jurisdiction between member states' disputes,[33] thus the arbitral tribunal only decided about a request of Ireland for interim measures sought to prevent serious harm to the marine environment. In the interim measures award the tribunal briefly touched upon issues of environmental harm in dismissing the request[34] in a surprisingly short, all together three-paragraphs long, assessment. After having noted the United Kingdom's position, according to which the quantities of radioactive substances with extremely long half-life were 'infinitesimally small',[35] the tribunal quickly found that Ireland failed to establish any serious harm that may be causal upon the operation of the MOX Plant without any meaningful scientific inquiry or justification for its finding.[36]

2 *Marginalizing Science by the Plaintiff*

Scientific arguments are sometimes missing from the analysis due to the parties' own litigation strategy. The *Lake Lanoux* Arbitration[37] provides an example for the marginalization of science by the plaintiff's reluctance to bring any techno-scientific argument into the debate. As will be demonstrated below the factual details might have been decisive for reaching a different outcome in the dispute.

This arbitration zeroed in on water usage rights over a shared freshwater resource. In order to create opportunities for an electricity generator dam, France intended to unilaterally divert a tributary stemming from Lake Lanoux and providing 25 per cent of the waters of the river Carol, which later enters Spanish territory. The French scheme proposed that the diverted waters would be returned to the Carol through a tunnel above the Spanish border. The parties disagreed about the lawfulness of this proposal.[38] The legal basis of the dispute was a series of bilateral treaties concluded among Spain

---

[29] MOX Plant OSPAR Arbitration, para. 65.
[30] MOX Plant (Ireland v. UK) (Permanent Court of Arbitration) 6 June 2008.
[31] MOX Plant Arbitration, Order No 3, 24 June 2003, para. 9.
[32] MOX Plant Arbitration, Order No 6.
[33] C-459/03 *Commission of the European Communities* v. *Ireland*, Judgment (30 May 2006).
[34] MOX Plan Arbitration, Order No 3, 24 June 2003.
[35] MOX Plan Arbitration, Order No 3, 24 June 2003, para. 46.
[36] MOX Plant Arbitration, Order No 3, 24 June 2003, para. 55.
[37] Lake Lanoux Arbitration *(France* v. *Spain)* (1957) Award, 16 November 1957, 12 RIAA 281.
[38] Spain insisted that any project involving diversion of the waters is only lawful to the extent that it consented to it, but it emphatically refused to do so. Spain further claimed that the French proposal is

and France, the Treaty of Bayonne and its supplement, the Additional Act. These provided that works by any one party aiming to change the course or the volume of watercourse were subject to notification and consultation with the affected state.[39] The Additional Act also stipulated a prohibition to building dams or any other obstacle that was 'capable of harming'[40] the neighbouring country.

Surprisingly, the parties almost couched their arguments as if the dispute were a battle of competing abstract conceptualizations of the scheme's effects on the distribution of water. They did not even address the techno-scientific feasibility or the consequences of the project. For instance, Spain failed to argue with the possibility that the works would pollute or change the chemical composition or the temperature of the waters, and only argued that the diversion of the water would change 'the order of Nature'.[41] Yet it did not provide any scientific explanation for this concept nor did it list scientific objections to the project.[42] Spain's failure to employ techno-scientific arguments may be owed to the fact that no engineers were included in its delegation, as opposed to France, which had three engineer experts on its team.[43]

The panel itself noted that the lack of 'sufficient factual evidence' on the alleged difference between the volume of the diverted and returned waters prevented adjudicators from assessing the factual basis of the conflict.[44] In many instances the arbitrators explicitly alluded to claims that 'could have been argued' for discussing the scientific and technological aspects of the project, but which were missing from the pleadings.[45] In lack of any techno-scientific arguments regarding the potential harmful consequences of this novel technology, the panel regarded the diversion of water as a corollary of exercising sovereign power on a state's own territory and ruled in favour of France. Ironically, in making its final conclusion the tribunal explicitly referred to the 'state of modern technology' as providing justification for permanently diverting waters for purposes of electricity generation.[46] Overall, the reasoning of the tribunal gives the impression that had Spain been more willing to cite scientific findings and address the technical weaknesses and risks of the project, it might have had a better chance to win the case.

a prohibited modification of the natural flow of the waters under the Treaties of Bayonne, since the proposed re-channelling would change the 'order of Nature' and would make the restoration of waters into the Carol dependent on the will of France, which upsets the equality of the parties in breach of Article 12 of the treaties. France argued that the treaties do not restrict sovereign actions confined within a state's territory and the scheme would respect the rights and interest of Spain. The tribunal found that France did not breach its treaty obligations.

39 Additional Act of 26 May 1866, Article 11.
40 Additional Act of 26 May 1866, Article 12.
41 *Lac Lanoux* Arbitration, Award, Section 7 of the Reasoning pertaining to Question A.
42 *Lake Lanoux* Arbitration, Award, Section 7 of the Reasoning pertaining to Question A.
43 Romano, *The Peaceful Settlement of International Environmental Disputes: A Pragmatic Approach*, p. 232.
44 *Lake Lanoux* Arbitration, Award, Section 5 of the Reasoning pertaining to Question A.
45 *Lake Lanoux* Arbitration, Award, Section 6 of the Reasoning pertaining to Question A.
46 See *Lake Lanoux* Arbitration, Award, Section 8 of the Reasoning pertaining to Question A, '[t]he state of modern technology leads to more and more frequent justifications of the fact that waters used for the production of electric energy should not be returned to their natural course'.

3 *Including Science in the Legally Relevant Aspects of Disputes*

Some arbitral tribunals have been willing to entertain scientific arguments and incorporate them in the judicial inquiry. Such framing of disputes enables adjudicators to harness the cognitive authority of science for various strategic purposes.

3.1 Science as a Gentle Neutralizer of Disputes

Arbitrators may appeal to science in searching for a neutral arbiter of disputes. They may harness the perceived objectivity of science by ultimately deferring the resolution of disputed scientific aspects to scientists. An early example of such a strategic reliance on scientific expertise is reflected in the *Trail Smelter* Arbitration,[47] which featured a conflict between the United States and Canada triggered by massive air pollution caused by the Consolidated Mining and Smelting Company operating in the town of Trail, Canada.[48] The arbitration sought justice for agricultural producers in the State of Washington, whose orchards, property, and livestock have been damaged due to sulphur dioxide emission of the smelter's smokestacks. The experts of the two sides agreed on the existence of the injury, but adamantly disagreed as to its cause.[49] Due to the elaborate fact-finding commissioned by scientific experts, it took more than ten years to resolve the dispute.[50] The tribunal ultimately concluded that the Trail smelter caused the damage and hence it ordered Canada to pay USD 78,000 in indemnity for the injury caused.[51]

The conflict was highly politicized by both sides partly due to vested industrial interests[52] and hence was overshadowed by the 'clash of sovereignties'.[53] Yet, this did not bar the tribunal from giving due consideration to the underlying scientific facts. Quite the opposite, the lengthy scientific reasoning[54] of the panel gives the

---

[47]   *Trail Smelter* Arbitration (United States, Canada) Awards, 16 April 1938 and 11 March 1941, 3 RIAA 1905.

[48]   It may be less well known that the historical arbitration was followed by another inter-state dispute between the United States and Canada regarding the remediation of the contaminated site of the Trail smelter. In 2003, the US Environmental Protection Agency issued an order seeking to enforce extraterritorially its domestic rules of remediation set out in CERCLA legislation. For more details, see N. Craik, 'Transboundary Pollution, Unilateralism, and the Limits of Extraterritorial Jurisdiction: The Second Trail Smelter Dispute' in R. Bratspies and R. A. Miller (eds.), *Transboundary Harm in International Law* (Cambridge University Press, 2006), pp. 109–24 p. 109.

[49]   *Trail Smelter* Arbitration, Award, 16 April 1938, Part Two (4) 3 RIAA 1905, at 1921.

[50]   The conflict lasted from 1928 to 1941, when the tribunal handed down its award. J. E. Read, 'The Trail Smelter dispute (abridged)' in R. Bratspies and R. A. Miller (eds.), *Transboundary Harm in International Law* (Cambridge University Press, 2006), pp. 27–33 p. 27.

[51]   *Trail Smelter* Arbitration, Award, 16 April 1938.

[52]   J. R. Allum, '"An outcrop of hell": history, environment, and the politics of the Trail Smelter dispute' in R. Bratspies and R. A. Miller (eds.), *Transboundary Harm in International Law* (Cambridge University Press, 2006), pp. 13–26 pp. 21–2.

[53]   S. C. McCaffrey, 'Of paradoxes, precedents, and progeny: the *Trail Smelter* arbitration 65 years later' in R. Bratspies and R. A. Miller (eds.), *Transboundary Harm in International Law* (Cambridge University Press, 2006), pp. 34–45 p. 40.

[54]   For more details see Section III, Subsection 1 in this chapter.

impression that the objective, technical details of the case appeared to the arbitrators as a convenient way of neutralizing the political core of the dispute.

The panel's satisfaction with having science as the main arbiter of the dispute is also suggested by the clause of the final award concerning the amendment or the suspension of the regime, which provided for a mechanism to refer such initiatives in the future before a commission comprising three eminent scientists.[55] The tribunal regarded the emission limitations set out in the award as a test regime, which could be altered if 'scientific advance in the control of fumes should make it possible and desirable'.[56]

The *Iron Rhine Railway* decision[57] reflects a similar framing technique, where arbitrators delegated the final resolution of scientific aspects of an inter-state conflict to a committee of independent experts. The dispute concerned Belgium's intended reactivation of the historic Iron Rhine railway on the territory of the Netherlands. The dispute focused on the scope of obligations the Netherlands could reasonably impose on Belgium under the 1839 Separation Treaty with respect to the reactivation. The environmental aspect of the case flowed from the fact that the Netherlands designated some parts of the route as a nature reserve under domestic and EU law. The Netherlands required Belgium to take costly noise protection measures to abate the freight transport's adverse environmental effects, which the latter regarded as a disproportionate burden under rules of the bilateral treaty.

The tribunal defined the scope of its task as excluding the investigation of 'questions of considerable scientific complexity as to which measures will be sufficient to achieve compliance with the required levels of environmental protection'.[58] The panel emphasized that such issues ought to be left to scientific experts and thus, ordered the parties to appoint a commission of independent experts to establish the exact quantum of the costs payable for these measures.[59] By such a framing, the *Iron Rhine* Tribunal ensured that scientific expertise would govern the resolution of the controversy. This solution not only accommodates science's cognitive authority in the adjudicatory process, but also bestows the appearance of objectivity and neutrality on the award itself, which are the preconditions for a just and legitimate decision.

3.2 Establishing a Breach of Substantive Obligations with Reference to Exceptionally Grave Facts

The *South China Sea* award marks one of the rare occasions when an international tribunal established a breach of substantive environmental law obligations.

---

[55] *Trail Smelter* Arbitration, Award, 11 March 1941, 3 RIAA 1905, at 1978.
[56] *Trail Smelter* Arbitration, Award, 11 March 1941, 3 RIAA 1905, at 1973.
[57] *Iron Rhine Railway* Arbitration *(Belgium v. Netherlands)* (Permanent Court of Arbitration), Final Award, 24 May 2005.
[58] *Iron Rhine Railway* Arbitration, para. 235.
[59] *Iron Rhine Railway* Arbitration, para. 235.

Arguably, the exceptional gravity of the scientific facts canvassing the environmental destruction entailed by the Chinese artificial island-building activity played a significant role in establishing responsibility for causing environmental harm.

The Philippines alleged that besides engaging in artificial-island construction activities on several coral reefs,[60] China also tolerated and actively supported environmentally harmful fishing techniques,[61] the harvesting of endangered species, and the damaging of coral reefs by propeller chopping.[62] Furthermore, the absence of preparing an adequate environmental impact assessment (EIA) and that of notification and consultation were also among the applicant's claims.[63] The tribunal found a series of breaches and ruled that China violated its duty to protect and preserve the marine environment under Article 192, and also condemned it for polluting the marine environment, for failing to preserve rare or fragile ecosystems and habitats of endangered species under Article 194(5), and for not co-operating and co-ordinating with other states under Articles 123 and 197 of UNCLOS.

What is relevant for the purposes of the present analysis is the adjudicatory reasoning establishing a substantive violation for the obligation not to cause harm to the marine environment. Instead of focusing only on procedural breaches, which is the norm in international environmental adjudication, the *South China Sea* Tribunal was willing to entertain substantive environmental law obligations, which inevitably dragged relevant scientific aspects into the legal analysis. It is argued here that the straight-forward scientific evidence attesting an exceptionally grave destruction provided a convenient basis, if not an impetus, for the panel to make such a finding.

Notably, both the island construction activities and the resulting ecological destruction at hand were of extraordinary scale and gravity. The Chinese state policy on massive island-building activity created 12.8 million km^2 of new land on the top of submerged lands and reefs during less than three years.[64] China deployed a large fleet of vessels with ship-borne drill extending from the dredging vessels into the seabed to extract the soil, rock, and reef necessary on the reclamation sites. The overall damage caused to coral reef was estimated to affect a vast area of 124 km^2,[65] a magnitude that was justifiably dubbed 'ecocide' by an article cited by the award.[66] The tribunal also found that fishermen were harvesting endangered giant clams with

[60] Coral reefs at Cuarteron Reef, Fiery Cross Reef, Gaven Reef, Johnson Reef, Hughes Reef, Mischief Reef, and Subi Reef. See *South China Sea Arbitration (The Republic of the Philippines* v. *The People's Republic of China)* (Permanent Court of Arbitration), Award, 12 July 2016, para. 979.
[61] The tribunal found a lack of violation with respect to the use of cyanide and explosives for illegal fishing, since there was not enough evidence to establish that China failed to meet its due diligence obligations in this regard (*South China Sea* Arbitration, para. 975).
[62] *South China Sea* Arbitration, para. 848.
[63] *South China Sea* Arbitration, para. 911.
[64] *South China Sea* Arbitration, para. 854.
[65] *South China Sea* Arbitration, para. 850, citing the McManus Report.
[66] *South China Sea* Arbitration, footnote 917 referred to the article V. R. Lee, 'Satellite imagery shows ecocide in South China Sea', *The Diplomat* (15 January 2016).

a propeller-chopping method, that is, by using propellers to break up coral and release giant clams, leaving affected coral reefs in 'complete devastation'.[67]

Yet, the panel's peculiar framing not stopping short of analysing substantive obligations in depth, cannot be disentangled from the heavy power politics lurking behind the dispute. One should also be cognizant of the many non-scientific factors that might have also influenced the panel's firm conclusion concerning the series of breaches. For one, China's absence from the proceedings also rendered it easier to make conclusive findings based on scientific reports. Otherwise, the respondent might have challenged the expert findings or could have made clarifications on relevant public statements of Chinese officials the tribunal relied on. Furthermore, the South China Sea region has recently become a hotspot of geopolitical rivalry, creating a political climate where China's territorial ambitions in the region[68] meet with strong resentment of the Global North. The United States is increasingly worried that China's actions would jeopardize the regional status quo and stability,[69] and threaten the United States' unhindered access to waters with exceptional trade significance.[70] The EU, though declaring its neutral position in the conflict, reinforced its commitment to closely collaborating its policy towards the Asia-Pacific region with the United States.[71] As China appointed no arbitrator on the bench[72] out of protest against the illegitimate nature of the proceeding, the panel included no arbitrator to be sensitive to China's perspective. Perhaps it is not far from truth to say that a Western-oriented panel[73] judged the conduct of an ever-dominant Eastern power, whose territorial and global ambitions have met with considerable suspicion.

III SCIENTIFIC FACT-FINDING IN INTERNATIONAL ARBITRATION

With regard to their elaborate procedural rules for scientific fact-finding, international arbitral tribunals appear to be a most promising fora for resolving science-heavy legal disputes. The Optional Rules for Arbitration of Disputes

---

[67] *South China Sea* Arbitration, para. 847.

[68] E. Fels and T.-M. Vu, 'Introduction: understanding the importance of the disputes in the South China Sea' in E. Fels and T.-M. Vu (eds.), *Power Politics in Asia's Contested Waters* (Springer, 2016), pp. 3–23 p. 5; S. L. Kheng, 'China's nationalist narrative of the South China Sea: a preliminary analysis' in E. Fels, and T.-M. Vu (eds.) *Power Politics in Asia's Contested Waters* (Springer, 2016), pp. 159–72 p. 159.

[69] Fels and Vu, 'Introduction: understanding the importance of the disputes in the South China Sea', p. 11. Notably, not only China and the Philippines but Vietnam and Malaysia have also laid claims to the territory.

[70] T. Fravel, 'U.S. policy towards the disputes in the South China Sea since 1995' in E. Fels and T.-M. Vu (eds.), *Power Politics in Asia's Contested Waters* (Springer, 2016), pp. 389–402 pp. 390–1.

[71] G. Will, 'Distant partners: Europe and the South China Sea' in E. Fels and T.-M. Vu (eds.) *Power Politics in Asia's Contested Waters* (Springer, 2016), pp. 469–92 pp. 477–8.

[72] *South China Sea* Arbitration, para. 30.

[73] Members of the panel were Judge Rüdiger Wolfrum, Judge Stanislaw Pawlak, Judge Jean-Pierre Cot, Professor Alfred H. A. Soons, and Judge Thomas A. Mensah serving as president, all of whom were appointed by the President of ITLOS. See *South China Sea* Arbitration, para. 30.

Relating to Natural Resources and/or the Environment adopted in 2001[74] furnish the PCA with extensive fact-finding powers, including the possibility to appoint the panel's own experts[75] and to request from the parties a non-technical summary indicating the scientific background to the case they agree on.[76] One also finds the arguably most thorough evidentiary assessments in arbitral proceedings as well as the most innovative fact-finding techniques allowing a close incorporation of scientific expertise in the panels. Albeit these innovative procedures are rarely used in practice, save for some notable proceedings that are addressed in the sections that follow.

1 *Setting a High Bar: Surprisingly Thorough Fact-Finding*

The historic *Trail Smelter* decision sets the high-water mark for engaging with the scientific evidence in international arbitration. The panel's legal assessment almost bordered a scientific evaluation when it interpreted conflicting scientific explanations offered by the scientists. A thorough adjudicatory interaction with uncertain scientific evidence on a comparable scale was only reproduced decades later in the *Kishenganga* dispute.

The scientifically most heavy aspect of the *Trail Smelter* dispute concerned how American farmers could prove that the smelter's toxic emissions were able to cause severe damage in the long run, even though the adverse effects might remain invisible for years to the layman's eye. United States scientists were only furnished with experimental data in this respect, which did not prove to be convincing enough in the first place to justify an injunctive relief. Canadian government-funded scientists purposefully built on this weakness of the US argumentation to use it as a leverage; they sought to triumph by submitting convincing and straightforward data describing the economic loss the industry would suffer from the relief sought.[77]

The award elaborated on the persuasive force of each scientific study submitted by the parties; it even identified their methodological errors and inconsistencies.[78]

---

[74] A similar procedure is provided for science-intensive conciliation under the aegis of PCA, see Optional Rules for Conciliation of Disputes Relating to Natural Resources and/or the Environment. For more details on the Optional Rules see Ratliff, 'The PCA optional rules for arbitration of disputes relating to natural resources and/or the environment'.

[75] Optional Rules for Arbitration of Disputes Relating to Natural Resources and/or the Environment Article, 19 June 2001, Article 27(1).

[76] Optional Rules, Article 24(4).

[77] Allum, '"An outcrop of hell": history, environment, and the politics of the Trail Smelter dispute', p. 25.

[78] The tribunal criticized that the total number of experiments was large, but the number of tests devoted to establishing each type of result was rather small; that none of the experiments lasted for an entire growing season; that the two expert teams worked separately and did not compare their results; and that experimental results did not square with injuries observed in the field, etc., see *Trail Smelter* Arbitration, Award, 16 April 1938, 3 RIAA 1905, at 1921.

Surprisingly, the tribunal even dismissed a scientific theory that was endorsed by witnesses of both sides, and formulated what it calls to be a more adequate interpretation of the scientific facts:

> The witnesses for both Governments appeared to be definitely of the opinion that the gas was carried from the Smelter by means of surface winds, and they based their views on this theory of the mechanism of gas distribution. The Tribunal finds itself unable to accept this theory. It has, therefore, looked for a more probable theory, and has adopted the following as permitting a more adequate correlation and interpretation of the facts which have been placed before it.[79]

The reasoning of the tribunal remains equally science-heavy later on as well. It imposes limits on fumigations after studying a wide range of relevant scientific factors including 'wind directions and velocity, atmospheric temperatures, lapse rates, turbulence, geostrophic winds, barometric pressures, sunlight and humidity, along with atmospheric sulphur dioxide concentrations'.[80] The tribunal was very well aware of the merits of its thorough assessment of scientific issues. It explicitly noted that '[t]his is probably the most thorough study ever made of any area to atmospheric pollution by industrial smoke'.[81]

The evidentiary assessment of the tribunal is also noteworthy, especially if one considers the material time of the proceedings. During a three-year-long investigation, the panel, which was assisted by two scientists designated by respective governments, observed three complete growing seasons and the behaviour of smoke clouds.[82] Taken together the monitoring carried out by a pre-trial International Joint Commission, the tribunal and the parties' experts, one may find that the harmful processes were studied for altogether more than a decade, which is unprecedented in international environmental dispute resolution.[83]

The tribunal required the injury be established 'with clear and convincing evidence'.[84] This is a much higher threshold compared to standards usually set in contemporary environmental disputes. The historical context and the sensitive political issues at stake might well explain announcing such a standard.[85] The high threshold may even be a mere rhetorical tool, which in fact served to reassure sovereign powers that their interests were duly considered.[86] Despite the emphasized commitment towards a high standard of proof, the tribunal was mindful of the evidentiary difficulties of the injured state. This is signalled by the fact that the

---

[79] *Trail Smelter* Arbitration, Award, 16 April 1938, 3 RIAA 1905, at 1922.
[80] *Trail Smelter* Arbitration, Award, 11 March 1941, 3 RIAA 1905, at 1974.
[81] *Trail Smelter* Arbitration, Award, 11 March 1941, 3 RIAA 1905, at 1973.
[82] Read, 'The Trail Smelter Dispute (Abridged)', p. 30.
[83] Romano, *The Peaceful Settlement of International Environmental Disputes: A Pragmatic Approach*, p. 277.
[84] *Trail Smelter* Arbitration, Award, 11 March 1941, 3 RIAA 1905, at 1965.
[85] McCaffrey, 'Of paradoxes, precedents, and progeny: the Trail Smelter arbitration 65 years later', pp. 39–40.
[86] McCaffrey, 'Of paradoxes, precedents, and progeny: the Trail Smelter arbitration 65 years later', p. 40.

award[87] cites decisions of US courts[88] emphasizing the unjust nature of letting the wrongdoer escape liability in cases, where the nature of the harm makes it impossible to substantiate the full extent of harm. These considerations suggest that the panel was, in fact, much more open to accept lower standards of proof with a view to the peculiarities of scientific evidence. Thus, arguably, the restrictive, high standard of proof was only announced for diplomatic reasons as a rhetorical gesture.

The *Trail Smelter* decision can rightly be labelled as 'courageous'[89] and 'path-breaking'.[90] The panel relied heavily on technical scientific evidence and did not refrain from critically singling out the input that it deemed methodologically flawed. Also, the award contained review mechanisms to ensure that the regime would keep pace with developing scientific understanding of the underlying harmful processes; a method that has subsequently been forgone for quite some time only to be rediscovered in recent decisions in the practice of the WTO[91] and international arbitration.[92]

For all these reasons, the *Trail Smelter* award appears to be well ahead of its time, compared to which more recent international environmental judicial decisions are generally lagging behind. Subsequent arbitral decisions rarely produced scientific investigations comparable either in terms of the depth of the scientific inquiry or the length of legal appraisal of the scientific results.[93] Judge ad hoc Dugard even set the *Trail Smelter* decision as an example for the ICJ to follow[94] which appears to be well justified. One may nevertheless note that scientific evidence at that time was perhaps less abstract, technical, and therefore less cryptic to non-expert adjudicators compared to the highly complex, computer-based modelling results that are often presented to courts in contemporary proceedings.

2 *Appointing Expert Arbitrators*

The PCA Optional Rules allow for appointing arbitrators, who are not members of the PCA but have special expertise in the subject-matters of the disputes.[95] The *Kishenganga* Arbitration[96] featured this rare and innovative fact-finding technique,

---

[87] *Trail Smelter* Arbitration, Award, 16 April 1938, Part Two 3 RIAA 1905, at 1920.
[88] *Story Parchment Company v. Paterson Parchment Paper Company.*
[89] McCaffrey, 'Of paradoxes, precedents, and progeny: the Trail Smelter arbitration 65 years later', p. 45.
[90] McCaffrey, 'Of paradoxes, precedents, and progeny: the Trail Smelter arbitration 65 years later', p. 39.
[91] See for example *Japan – Apples and Australia – Salmon* cases; for more details on reassessment proceedings in WTO jurisprudence see Peel, *Science and Risk Regulation in International Law*, pp. 321–30.
[92] See for example *Kishenganga* Arbitration, discussed in Subsection 2.
[93] Romano, *The Peaceful Settlement of International Environmental Disputes: A Pragmatic Approach*, p. 277.
[94] *Certain Activities*, Judgment on compensation, Dissenting Opinion of Judge Dugard, 2018, para. 47.
[95] Optional Rules, Article 8(3).
[96] *Indus Waters Kishenganga* Arbitration *(Pakistan v. India)* Partial Award, 18 February 2013, and *Indus Waters Kishenganga* Arbitration *(Pakistan v. India)* Final Award, 20 December 2013.

namely, the use of expert arbitrators. Expert arbitrators are scientists acting as adjudicators with full voting powers. In the material case, the panel also included a highly qualified engineer and professor in hydrology besides eminent jurists. As we shall see below, the fact that scientific expertise was closely incorporated within the panel enabled the tribunal to engage actively with the science implicated in the conflict. More specifically, adjudicators conducted two site visits, and did not shy away from openly evaluating challenges levelled against the methodologies of party-adduced evidence.[97]

The facts of the case involved India's new hydro-electric plant, called Kishenganga Hydro-Electric Project (KHEP), for which waters of the river Kishenganga/Neelum had to be diverted via tunnels.[98] Pakistan claimed that the diversion would decrease the water it received downstream, which would reduce the electricity generating capacity of its own hydropower project called Neelum-Jhelum Hydro-Electric Project, which was planned to be situated on the Kishenganga upstream to the point where the diverted water is returned to the river bed.[99]

The dispute entertained three basic legal issues.[100] First, whether India is entitled to use a so-called drawdown flushing method under the 1960 Indus Water Treaty. Second, whether inter-tributary diversion is allowed under the treaty, in which respect the panel found that as long as a certain minimum flow of water is ensured by India, the diversion is in conformity with the Indus Water Treaty. Lastly, the dispute concerned the quantity of minimum flow that India ought to ensure at the KHEP with regard to environmental considerations and pre-existing agricultural water uses of Pakistan. This latter question entailed the most science-intensive inquiry concerning the potential adverse environmental impacts associated with different minimum flows.

The parties submitted divergent data on the required minimum flows and associated environmental impacts.[101] Pakistan's preferred minimum flow levels fell in the range of 10–100 cubic meters per second (cumecs),[102] while India submitted levels below ten cumecs.[103] The parties put forth extremely technical challenges vis-à-vis the evidence of their counterparts in terms of the accuracy of the statistical regression analysis, the appropriate span of data set,[104] and of the methodology of

---

[97]   *Indus Waters Kishenganga* Arbitration, Partial Award, para. 252, *Kishenganga*, Final Award, paras. 31–2.
[98]   *Indus Waters Kishenganga* Arbitration, Partial Award, para. 155.
[99]   *Indus Waters Kishenganga* Arbitration, Partial Award, para. 158.
[100] For a more detailed discussion on the environmental relevance of the Kishenganga Award see J. Moussa, 'Implications of the Indus Waters Kishenganga Arbitration for the International Law of Watercourses and the Environment' (2015) 64 *International & Comparative Law Quarterly* 697–715; J. Ahmad, 'Indus Waters Kishenganga Arbitration and state-to-state disputes' (2013) 29 *Arbitration International* 507–38.
[101] *Indus Waters Kishenganga* Arbitration, Final Award, para. 97.
[102] *Indus Waters Kishenganga* Arbitration, Final Award, para. 55.
[103] *Indus Waters Kishenganga* Arbitration, Final Award, para. 44.
[104] *Indus Waters Kishenganga* Arbitration, Partial Award, para. 252, *Kishenganga*, Final Award, paras. 31–2.

gathering relevant hydrological data.[105] Yet these did not bar the panel from making its own factual and legal determination. Appointing an expert arbitrator apparently enhanced legal adjudicators' ability and willingness to thoroughly reflect on party-adduced evidence and even to resolve contradictions between them.[106] The award therefore features detailed discussion of divergent expert positions on hydrology, statistics, and hydrological engineering.

The panel found in the first place that environmental considerations alone would have compelled a minimum flow of at least 12 cumecs.[107] Yet, ultimately, the required level was lowered to 9 cumecs to account for India's economic interests.[108] This specific minimum flow was mentioned by the parties only once, when India's agent pointed this out as the highest acceptable flow level for India.[109] Hence, the dispute also showcases that thorough judicial engagement with science does not necessarily go hand-in-hand with accommodating environmental interests, as the scientifically informed inquiry ultimately yielded to economic policy considerations. The ultimate decision of the panel appears to be less informed by the scientific inquiry into potential environmental consequences and be more of a rule-of-thumb balancing, which adjusted the required flow to the prevailing economic interests. Put differently, despite the panel's rigorous scientific assessment, it still set 'a relatively severe criterion'[110] for the environment, which can be criticized on normative grounds.[111]

Yet as far as the arbitrators' interaction with the mass of scientific evidence is concerned, the tribunal can be deemed as adopting an ambitious and meticulous approach. Incorporating scientific competence in the panel altogether yielded an adjudicatory reasoning confidently touching upon complex scientific issues. For this reason, from an epistemic point of view, the *Kishenganga* Tribunal can be regarded as an ideal panel for deciding science-heavy disputes, since it was equipped with adequate scientific expertise that is crucial for being comfortable with assessing the technical details of the case.

The award also mandates a review mechanism for reconsidering the amount of minimum flow in the future. It may be possible on the request of any of the parties from seven years after the diversion took place to account for unforeseen effects of

---

[105]   *Indus Waters Kishenganga* Arbitration, Final Award, paras. 90–1, of special importance is footnote 148.
[106]   For a similar position see J. R. Cook, 'In re Indus Waters Kishenganga Arbitration (*Pakistan v. India*)' (2014) 108 *American Journal of International Law* 308–14 at 314.
[107]   *Indus Waters Kishenganga* Arbitration, Final Award, para. 104.
[108]   *Indus Waters Kishenganga* Arbitration, Final Award, para. 116.
[109]   'It is impossible to justify a 10 cumecs minimum release, let alone higher releases', *Indus Waters Kishenganga* Arbitration, Final Award, para. 47.
[110]   *Indus Waters Kishenganga* Arbitration, Final Award, para. 113.
[111]   The *Kishenganga* Tribunal was the first international tribunal to ever replace the equality of riparian states with granting 'significant rights' to the upstream state over the downstream neighbour. Thereby it disregarded the customary law obligation of respecting downstream states' equitable use of freshwater resources. For more details on this line of criticism see Moussa, 'Implications of the Indus Waters Kishenganga Arbitration for the International Law of Watercourses and the Environment'.

climate change.[112] This again provides an example of duly reflecting on the volatile nature of scientific facts in the process of adjudication, which seeks to resolve disputes in a final manner. Devising such solutions requires a close engagement with science by legal adjudicators; it is therefore no coincidence that one finds such clauses in disputes, where adjudicators adopt a hands-on approach to the scientific dimensions.[113]

3 *Appointing Ex Tribunal Experts*

The use of tribunal-appointed experts is another rarely applied procedural tool with which arbitrators can effectively buttress their epistemic competence. The *South China Sea* dispute has thus far seen the only attempt in international arbitration practice to use such a fact-finding technique extensively. Adjudicators were facing highly technical evidence in the form of, inter alia, satellite imagery, nautical surveying, and hydrographical data,[114] the evaluation of which posed unexpectedly complex challenges. The tribunal adopted an unusually sophisticated procedure for taking expert evidence.[115] It amended its Rules of Procedure to provide for detailed procedural rules for appointing *ex tribunal* experts.[116] Even though the PCA Optional Rules explicitly provide for the possibility to utilize such experts, they are, in fact, rarely appointed in practice. Hence the *South China Sea* Tribunal's reliance on several independent experts may even be regarded as 'drawing new contours'[117] for scientific fact-finding in international arbitration.

Given that China stayed away from the proceeding, the tribunal had to consider potential factual and legal arguments that might have supported the lawfulness of China's activities.[118] Also, it needed to make sure that the scientific information was unbiased on which several of the breaches were based. In doing so it was assisted not only by tribunal-appointed experts, but arbitrators also garnered scientific advice more informally, by addressing questions to scientists who were not formally appointed as *ex parte* or *ex curia* experts, though whose scientific study was cited by one of the experts.[119] The tribunal engaged in an unconventionally extensive

---

[112] *Indus Waters Kishenganga* Arbitration, Final Award, paras. 117–19.

[113] For further examples of scientific review procedures in the practice of other judicial bodies see Chapter 9 Section II, Subsection 2.3.

[114] J.-H. Paik, 'South China Sea Arbitral Awards: Main Findings and Assessment' (2017) 20 *Max Planck Yearbook of United Nations Law Online* 367–407 at 406.

[115] M. M. Mbengue, 'The South China Sea Arbitration: innovations in marine environmental fact-finding and due diligence obligations' (2016) 110 *ASIL Unbound* 285–9 at 287.

[116] See Rules of Procedure of the South China Sea Arbitral Tribunal, Rule 24.

[117] Mbengue, 'The South China Sea Arbitration: innovations in marine environmental fact-finding and due diligence obligations', 288.

[118] China's position was reconstructed by the panel from public statement of Chinese officials in *South China Sea* Arbitration, paras. 912–24.

[119] The tribunal also asked one expert to seek clarifications from Professor McManus. See also: Mbengue, 'The South China Sea Arbitration: innovations in marine environmental fact-finding and due diligence obligations', 288.

dialogue with both the parties' experts and with its own experts, and even facilitated communication between party-appointed and tribunal-appointed scientists.[120] The panel's procedural rules also allowed for the cross-examination of both types of experts.

The Philippines appointed one coral reef ecologist expert[121] and submitted two experts' reports to the panel.[122] The tribunal sought the views of three additional coral reef specialists in the capacity of independent *ex curia* experts to fully investigate the harmful effects of the dredging activity[123] and to review the scientific findings of party-adduced evidence. With the assistance of *ex curia* experts, the tribunal took a position on contested science-based submissions of both parties and rejected those it viewed as unsupported by the evidence.[124] In this vein, one of the *ex tribunal* experts found that the Philippines' party-appointed expert over- and understated some aspects of the damage.[125]

Both the tribunal-appointed and the party-appointed experts' findings were in stark contrast with the public statement of Chinese officials and reports prepared by the Chinese State Oceanic Administration (SOA).[126] While the expert reports described large-scale ecological damage and confirmed that the degradation of coral reefs was caused by propeller chopping, Chinese statements maintained that the coral reef had a sub-healthy status even before the construction.[127] The SOA report further alleged that the construction mimicked natural island formation and, therefore, produced only natural ecological effects.[128] Independent experts claimed that these allegations were 'in disagreement with the available information'.[129] The tribunal hence firmly went on to base its findings solely on *ex curia* expert evidence it found 'compelling'.[130] Yet whenever experts could not provide clear-cut evidence on certain harmful conducts, the tribunal inferred that China complied with its obligations.[131]

[120]   N. Oral, 'The South China Sea Arbitral Award, Part XII of UNCLOS, and the protection and preservation of the marine environment' in S. Jayakumar, T. Koh, R. Beckman, T. Davenport, and H. Phan (eds.), *The South China Sea Arbitration: The Legal Dimension* (Edward Elgar, 2018), pp. 223–46 p. 234.

[121]   *South China Sea* Arbitration, para. 818.

[122]   *South China Sea* Arbitration, para. 89, section (b).

[123]   *South China Sea* Arbitration, para. 821.

[124]   L. Reed and K. Wong, 'Marine entitlements in the South China Sea: the arbitration between the Philippines and China' (2016) 110 *American Journal of International Law* 746–60 at 760.

[125]   The Ferse report, see *South China Sea* Arbitration, para. 980.

[126]   *South China Sea* Arbitration, para. 982.

[127]   *South China Sea* Arbitration, para. 982, section (f).

[128]   *South China Sea* Arbitration, para. 922.

[129]   *South China Sea* Arbitration, para. 982.

[130]   *South China Sea* Arbitration, para. 983, '[b]ased on the compelling evidence, expert reports, and critical assessment of Chinese claims described above, the Tribunal has no doubt that China's artificial island-building activities on the seven reefs in the Spratly Islands have caused devastating and long-lasting damage to the marine environment'.

[131]   Mbengue, 'The South China Sea Arbitration: innovations in marine environmental fact-finding and due diligence obligations', 289.

Even though the tribunal did not expressly voice an opinion on the scientific merits of the Chinese claims, the wholesale rejection of these arguments implies that the panel regarded them as having no scientific credibility. Such an open and critical evaluation of contradicting scientific evidence remains a rarity in international adjudication. This arguably cannot be severed from China's non-participation in the proceedings as the tribunal might have felt more comfortable to dismiss Chinese scientific arguments under such circumstances.

Be that as it may, relying on *ex curia* experts is an undoubtedly positive fact-finding innovation, which helps legal adjudicators assess complex data submitted by the parties, and saves them from the difficulties of sorting out reliable evidence on their own in a sound and legitimate way. Scholars often urge courts and tribunals to assume an active role in grasping the scientific dimension of the disputes and to seeking independent expert opinions when needed.[132] Practitioners alike often call for appointing *ex tribunal* experts.[133] Having recourse to independent experts supports the objectivity and impartiality of the dispute resolution process, which is often a much needed asset in settling politically sensitive disputes.

IV CAUSAL INQUIRY

International adjudicators rarely discuss their causal tests openly, and they tend to set quite restrictive causal requirements for scientific causal proof. In inter-state arbitral practice causal arguments were featured in the *MOX Plant OSPAR* Arbitration, as Article 9 of the OSPAR Convention on which Ireland based its claim creates an implicit causality requirement. The relevant provision ensures a right to access to any information 'on the state of the maritime area, on activities or measures adversely affecting or likely to affect' the environment. In Ireland's view every piece of information fell under Article 9 that had led to the decision of allowing nuclear discharge into the sea, including the relevant UK report on the plant's cost-benefit analysis. The arbitrators rejected the causal argumentation of Ireland, labelling it an 'inclusive causality' doctrine, under which 'anything, no matter how remote, which facilitated the performance of an activity is to be deemed part of that activity'.[134] By doing so, the award set a quite high threshold for establishing causality.

Dissenting Arbitrator Griffith harshly criticized the restrictive causal test of the majority. In his reading, Article 9 did not require relevant causal nexus to be 'direct and proximate, or even sufficiently proximate', instead, 'any relationship between future negative effects of the MOX Plant operation and the information'[135] requested

---

[132]   Jacur, 'Remarks on the role of *ex curia* scientific experts in international environmental disputes', p. 453.
[133]   See the contribution of Mr Andrew Loewenstein (Foley Hoag LLP) as speaker of the panel discussion entitled 'Adjudicating environmental disputes' at ASIL Annual Meeting 2017, Washington DC.
[134]   *MOX Plant OSPAR* Arbitration, para. 164.
[135]   *MOX Plant OSPAR* Arbitration, Dissenting Opinion of Gavan Griffith, para. 97.

should have sufficed for the panel to establish causation. This account illustrates well some of the more lenient, alternative causal tests that could have been more favourable to scientific evidence.

As was seen in Chapter 3, there are remarkably few occasions when a causal link between a state conduct and a given environmental harm is found established in international environmental litigation. Two notable exceptions are the *Trail Smelter* and the *South China Sea* Arbitrations. In *Trail Smelter*, the tribunal was furnished with expert evidence that it found unhelpful. The panel opined that the parties' experts adopted a 'mental attitude'[136] of attributing the entirety of the injury principally to the one causal factor that was advantageous for their respective sides. Adjudicators therefore took matters in their own hands and did not refrain from conducting their own investigation into atmospheric science to reveal the causal role of sulphur fumigations of the smelter in bringing about the damage.

The *South China Sea* Tribunal was willing to find requisite causal link between the Chinese actions and omissions as well as the resulting widespread environmental harm. Even though the Chinese position maintained that any coral reef degradation was not causal upon the dredging activity but was a result of competing natural and man-made causes, such as overfishing, tourism, and climate change,[137] the tribunal regarded scientific evidence leaving 'no doubt' that the ecological damage could be attributed to Chinese island-building activity.[138] Both arbitral proceedings therefore have seen science-based causal claims established, where arbitrators confidently navigated among scientific assessments to reconstruct relevant causal processes.

---

[136] *Trail Smelter* Arbitration, Award, 16 April 1938, 3 RIAA 1905, at 1922, citing Judge Johnson in the United States District Court, *Anderson v. American Smelting & Refining Co.*, US District Court, 1919, 265 Federal Reporter 928.
[137] *South China Sea* Arbitration, para. 923.
[138] *South China Sea* Arbitration, para. 983.

5

Science in the Environmental Jurisprudence of Regional Human Rights Courts

The Court considers, however, that in the present case scientific uncertainty is not accompanied by sufficient and convincing statistical evidence. ... The Court therefore notes that the applicants had failed to prove the existence of a sufficiently established causal link.

Tătar v. Romania, 2009[1]

This chapter reviews the weight regional human rights courts attach to scientific evidence and arguments in establishing violations of human rights standards in case of environmental destruction and pollution. The close link between human rights guarantees and environmental protection has now become widely acknowledged in the adjudicatory practice of the three major regional human rights systems. Therefore, the following analysis is dedicated to the jurisprudence of the European Court of Human Rights (ECtHR), the Inter-American Court of Human Rights (IACtHR), the African Court of Human and Peoples' Rights (ACtHPR), as well as the Economic Community of West African States Court of Justice (ECOWAS Court). More and more claims before these fora rest on scientific evidence, and the presence of scientific arguments shape their judicial inquiry (Section I). In deciding about alleged violations of human rights safeguards, these courts face intricate questions on how to frame the judicial inquiry (Section II), appraise causal links between health injuries and toxic exposure (Section III), gather and evaluate expert evidence (Section IV), and set the appropriate standard of review (Section V). This chapter will examine these aspects of the ever-expanding environmental jurisprudence of regional human rights courts.

---

[1] *Tătar* v. *Romania*, Application No. 67021/01, Judgment (27 January 2009), para. 106. Original in French, translation by the author.

I SCIENCE BEFORE HUMAN RIGHTS COURTS IN ENVIRONMENTAL
COMPLAINTS

A growing number of cases are filed with regional human rights courts, in which applicants refer to scientific studies to support their claim on human rights violations occurring due to adverse environmental impacts. The majority of such claims concern environmental destruction and exposure to various toxic agents released by a variety of industrial activities, ranging from oil wells to nuclear facilities. Such toxic exposure claims trigger filing science-intensive arguments by the victim and invite scientific considerations from (the often-reluctant) international courts.

1 *Environmental Claims in the European System*

The European human rights system played a pioneering role in utilizing human rights guarantees for environmental protection on the international level. The court's practice significantly evolved over time to ultimately discern environmental safeguards from the European Convention on Human Rights (ECHR),[2] which has been famously silent on environmental rights. The first lines of cases concerning environmental nuisance were either settled,[3] found inadmissible[4] or concluded with finding of no violation.[5] The first violation on account of environmental pollution was declared in 1994 in *López Ostra* v. *Spain*, which opened the door for an increasing number of environmental complaints.

In the absence of an explicit right to a safe, clean or balanced environment enshrined in the ECHR, toxic exposure claims are adjudicated under other provisions, such as Article 2 (right to life),[6] Article 8 (right to private and family life), Article 10 (right to information), Article 1 of Additional Protocol No. 1 (right to property), as well as Article 6 (right to fair trial). This chapter will focus on the jurisprudence pertaining to Article 8 and Article 2 of the ECHR, as the ECtHR predominantly deals with environmental claims under these provisions.

---

[2] Council of Europe, *European Convention for the Protection of Human Rights and Fundamental Freedoms, as amended by Protocols Nos. 11 and 14*, 4 November 1950, ETS 5.

[3] *Arrondelle* v. *UK*, Application No. 7889/77, Decision (15 July 1980); *Baggs* v. *UK*, Application No. 9310/81, Decision (14 October 1985).

[4] *G. and E.* v. *Norway*, Application No. 9278/81, Decision (3 October 1983).

[5] *Powell and Rayner* v. *UK*, Application No. 9310/81, Judgment (21 February 1990).

[6] To date there have been six environmental nuisance cases that were found admissible under Article 2: *Öneryildiz* v. *Turkey*, Application No. 48939/99, Judgment (30 November 2004); *Budayeva and Others* v. *Russia*, Application Nos. 15339/02, 21166/02, 20058/02, 11673/02 and 15343/02, Judgment (29 September 2008); *Kolyadenko and Others* v. *Russia*, Application Nos. 17423/05, 20534/05, 20678/05, 23263/05, 24283/05, and 35673/05, Judgment (28 February 2012); *Vilnes and Others* v. *Norway*, Application Nos. 52806/09, 22703/10, Judgment (5 December 2023); *L. C. B.* v. *UK*, Application No. 23413/94, Judgment (9 June 1998); and *Brincat and Others* v. *Malta*, Application Nos. 60908/11, 62110/11, 62129/11, 62312/11, and 62338/11, Judgment (24 July 2014).

Article 8 was applied, among others, to toxic industrial air pollution,[7] risks entailed by gold mines using cyanide leaching technology,[8] heavy metal pollution of drinking water,[9] groundwater contamination,[10] destruction of a swamp area near the applicant's home,[11] excessive noise of night clubs[12] and that of public transportation,[13] as well as severe vibration caused by heavy traffic.[14] In the context of dangerous activities, there is a significant overlap between the scope of obligations arising under Article 2 and Article 8.[15] Principally, it is the magnitude of risks involved that determines the applicable provision; Article 2 applies only to life-threatening circumstances,[16] whereas risks that fail to meet this relatively high threshold will be assessed under Article 8 provided that they clearly affect the private life of the applicant.[17] As a result, the majority of cases with environmental relevance are usually assessed under Article 8. Table 5.1 provides a brief overview of the doctrinal framework of the judicial inquiry under Article 2 and Article 8 in toxic exposure cases.

2 *Environmental Claims in the Inter-American System*

The Inter-American system has quickly become an active contributor to the progressive development of the human rights protection of the environment. Respective guarantees are currently provided under the American Convention on Human Rights (ACHR) and its Additional Protocol on Human Rights in the area of economic, social, and cultural rights (San Salvador Protocol). Prior to these instruments, the non-binding OAS Declaration of the Rights and Duties of Man has listed human rights

---

[7] *Ledyayeva and Others* v. *Russia*, Application Nos. 53157/99, 53247/99, 53695/00, and 56850/00, Judgment (26 October 2006); *Fadeyeva* v. *Russia*, Application No. 55723/00, Judgment (9 June 2005); *Cordella and Others* v. *Italy*, Application Nos. 54414/13, 54264/15, Judgment (24 January 2019).

[8] *Taşkın and Others* v. *Turkey*, Application No. 46117/99, Judgment (10 November 2004); *Öckan* v. *Turkey*, Application No. 46771/99, Judgment (28 March 2006); *Tătar* v. *Romania*; *Lemke* v. *Turkey*, Application No. 17381/02, Judgment (5 June 2007).

[9] *Bacila* v. *Romania*, Application No. 19234/04, Judgment (30 March 2010).

[10] *Dzemyuk* v. *Ukraine*, Application No. 42488/02, Judgment (4 September 2014).

[11] *Kyrtatos* v. *Greece*, Application No. 41666/98, Judgment (22 May 2003).

[12] *Moreno Gómez* v. *Spain*, Application No. 4143/02, Judgment (16 November 2004).

[13] *Bor* v. *Hungary*, Application No. 50474/08, Judgment (18 June 2013).

[14] *Grimkovskaya* v. *Ukraine*, Application No. 38182/03, Judgment (20 July 2011); *Deés* v. *Hungary*, Application No. 2345/06, Judgment (9 November 2010).

[15] *Brincat and Others* v. *Malta*, para. 85.

[16] The right to life encompasses situations, where there is an imminent risk to life of the victim. The mere fact that the victim survives has no bearing on the applicability of Article 2. The provision is not only applicable to deaths caused directly by state action, but also extends to situations, when the state has a positive obligation *vis-à-vis* private parties, whose conduct might threaten the life of persons. Accordingly, the ECtHR emphasized that Article 2 encompasses cases where 'the physical integrity of an applicant was threatened by the action of a third party'. Article 2 typically applies to natural disasters and dangerous activities, such as nuclear tests, operation of landfills, and deep-sea oil drilling.

[17] *Brincat and Others* v. *Malta*, paras. 84–85.

TABLE 5.1 *Doctrinal framework of Article 2 and Article 8 of the ECHR in toxic exposure cases*

	Article 2 (right to life)	Article 8 (right to respect for private and family life)
Triggering conditions for application	The physical integrity of an applicant was threatened (i) by the action of the state (or state agent) or (ii) by a third party's action[18] when the state had regulatory obligations vis-à-vis a third party.[19]	(i) Pollution exceeding a minimum level of severity,[20] (ii) which is caused by a state directly or indirectly (in a failure to regulate private industry), and (iii) which has a 'direct adverse effect'[21] on the individuals' private or family life or well-being.
Obligation of state	(i) Negative: refrain from unlawful killing[22] (ii) Positive: to take appropriate measures to safeguard lives/prevent avoidable loss of lives in case of dangerous activities and natural disasters[23] by putting in place a legislative and administrative framework[24] and enact regulations for practical measures.[25] Procedural (positive): in case of loss of lives on account of an infringement of the right, the state should provide adequate response (by investigating and providing civil, administrative or disciplinary remedies[26]).	(i) Positive: to adopt measures vis-à-vis private actors causing environmental harm to guarantee the right to private life.[27] A 'failure to regulate private industry' can raise the state's responsibility.[28] (ii) Negative: to refrain from undue interference with private life (when polluting entity is owned, operated or controlled by the state[29]).

(continued)

[18] *Brincat and Others* v. *Malta*, para. 82.
[19] Council of Europe, *Manual on Human Rights and the Environment*, 2nd ed. (Council of Europe Publishing, 2012), p. 18.
[20] *Fadeyeva* v. *Russia*, para. 69.
[21] Council of Europe, *Manual on Human Rights and the Environment*, p. 20, *Guerra and Others* v. *Italy*, Application No. 14967/89, Judgment (19 February 1988), para. 57.
[22] B. Rainey, E. Wicks, and C. Ovey (eds.), *Jacobs, White and Ovey: The European Convention on Human Rights*, 6th ed. (Oxford University Press, 2014), p. 143.
[23] Council of Europe, *Manual on Human Rights and the Environment*, 37.
[24] *Öneryildiz* v. *Turkey*, paras. 129–132.
[25] *Brincat and Others* v. *Malta*, paras. 109,112.
[26] Council of Europe, *Manual on Human Rights and the Environment*, p. 19.
[27] Council of Europe, *Manual on Human Rights and the Environment*, p. 53. *Moreno Gómez* v. *Spain*, para. 61. See also *Fadeyeva* v. *Russia*, in which the ECtHR explicitly stated that state's responsibility 'may arise from a failure to regulate private industry' (para. 89).
[28] *Fadeyeva* v. *Russia*, para. 89.
[29] *Fadeyeva* v. *Russia*, para. 89.

TABLE 5.1 *(continued)*

	Article 2 (right to life)	Article 8 (right to respect for private and family life)
Cases when the state can be held liable for injuries caused by third parties	States' positive obligations arise also when human lives are at 'real and immediate risk' due to private companies' activity in case the state had known or ought to have known about the risks.	If there is a 'sufficient nexus' between the polluter and the state[30] (in such a case the 'state could reasonably be expected to act so as to prevent and to put an end to the alleged infringements'[31]).
Actionable damage	(i) Death, or (ii) Real and imminent risk to life.	Direct interference with private and family life.[32]
Causation should be established between	The conduct and the applicant's death or imminent threat to her life	Pollution and 'direct adverse effect' on private life.
Causal test	No specific test has been announced.	No causal test, the case is decided by assessing proxies.
Deference afforded to states	states have a wide margin of appreciation, thus impossible or disproportionate burden must not be imposed on them without considering their choices and resources.[33]	(i) Negative obligations: emissions exceeding domestic safety levels from a state-owned source is automatically unlawful (ii) Positive obligations: states have a wide margin of appreciation (deferential review). The test is whether national authorities have struck a fair balance between the individual's right and the interest of the community in furthering economic development.
Burden of proof	On the applicant	On the applicant
Standard of proof	Beyond reasonable doubt (met by 'the coexistence of sufficiently strong, clear and concordant inferences or of similar unrebutted presumptions of fact'[34]). It allows flexibility with a view to the evidentiary difficulties.[35]	
Remedy (under Article 41)	(i) Obligation to put an end to the breach (ii) Just satisfaction: pecuniary and non-pecuniary damages or finding of a violation[36] (damages are not automatic consequences) and costs and expenses[37]	

[30] *Fadeyeva v. Russia*, para. 92.
[31] *Fadeyeva v. Russia*, para. 89.
[32] K. Oliphant and K. Ludwichowska, 'Damage' in A. Fenyves, E. Karner, H. Koziol, E. Steiner (eds.), *Tort Law in the Jurisprudence of the European Court of Human Rights* (De Gruyter, 2011), pp. 397–448 pp. 430–1.
[33] *Budayeva and Others v. Russia*, para. 135.
[34] *Fadeyeva v. Russia*, para. 79.
[35] *Fadeyeva v. Russia*, para. 79.
[36] E. Steiner, 'Just satisfaction under Art. 41 of ECHR: a compromise in 1950 – problematic now' in A. Fenyves, E. Karner, H. Koziol, and E. Steiner (eds.), *Tort Law in the Jurisprudence of the European Court of Human Rights* (De Gruyter, 2011), pp. 3–26 p. 16.
[37] Steiner, 'Just satisfaction under Art. 41 of ECHR: a compromise in 1950 – problematic now', p. 14.

safeguards. After the entry into force of the ACHR, the OAS Declaration is still legally relevant as it complements the binding provisions of the former.[38] For purposes of the present analysis, the following provisions are relevant from these catalogues: Article 4 (right to life), Article 5 (right to physical, mental, and moral integrity), Article 26 (full realization of the rights implicit in the economic, social, educational, scientific, and cultural standards enshrined in the OAS Charter) of ACHR, Article XI of OAS Declaration (right to the preservation of health and to well-being), as well as Article 11 of the San Salvador Protocol, providing for a standalone right to a healthy environment. These are the provisions in relation to which alleged violations are most frequently supported by scientific evidence and scientific arguments and, therefore, form the subject matter of this study. Notably, in environmental cases a host of other provisions are invoked as well, such as the right of access to information or public participation (Article 23 of ACHR), as well as the right to property (Article 21 of ACHR). These rights are especially important in the context of protecting indigenous communities.[39]

The enforcement mechanism of the Inter-American system consists of the Inter-American Commission of Human Rights and the IACtHR. The commission decides about the admissibility of claims. In the case of a positive decision, the commission or the state party may refer the case to the IACtHR provided that the state in question accepted the jurisdiction of the court. Affected individuals will have again standing before the court to plead their case. The IACtHR also has the power of issuing Advisory Opinions upon the request of a state party.

From a doctrinal point of view, the Inter-American system handles the harm, and the risk of harm to human life or health, quite similarly to the Strasbourg regime. The commission stressed the relevance of environmental pollution for human rights guarantees with words echoing the famous *López Ostra* test of the Strasbourg Court: '[s]evere environmental pollution may pose a threat to human life and health, and in the appropriate case give rise to an obligation on the part of a state to take reasonable measures to prevent such risk, or the necessary measures to respond when persons have suffered injury'.[40]

---

[38]   Interpretation of the American Declaration of the Rights and Duties of Man, Advisory Opinion OC-10/89, 14 July 1989, InterAmCtHR Series A No. 10.

[39]   *Mayanga (Sumo) Awas Tingni Community* v. *Nicaragua*, Judgment of 31 August 2001, IACtHR Series C No. 79; *Case of the Saramaka People* v. *Suriname*, Judgment of 28 November 2007, IACtHR Series C No. 172; *Case of the Indigenous Community Yakye Axa* v. *Paraguay*, Judgment of 17 June 2005, IACtHR Series C No. 125; *Case of the Sawhoyamaxa Indigenous Community* v. *Paraguay*, Judgment of 29 March 2006, IACtHR Series C No. 146; *Case of the Xákmok Kásek Indigeneous Community* v. *Paraguay*, Judgment of 24 August 2010, IACtHR Series C No. 21.

[40]   Inter-American Commission on Human Rights, *Report on the Situation of Human Rights in Ecuador*, OEA/Ser.L/V/II.96, doc. 10 rev. 1, 92 (1997), Chapter VIII.

3 *Environmental Claims in the African System*

Environmental rights occupy a particularly important position in the human rights protection system of Africa.[41] The chief human rights document, the African Charter on Human and Peoples' Rights (Banjul Charter), guarantees a standalone right to a general satisfactory environment (Article 24), which is couched as a collective right of the peoples, and the right to natural wealth and resources (Article 21). In toxic exposure cases, the right to life (Article 4) also bears importance.

Individual and interstate petitions may be filed with the African Commission on Human and Peoples' Rights, a quasi-judicial body having the power of making recommendations.[42] The adjudicatory enforcement mechanism comprises two main courts endowed with the power of accepting human rights claims: the ACtHPR and the ECOWAS Court. Both fora have a peculiar mandate to hear cases not only the basis of the Banjul Charter but on any other international human rights conventions, which both parties have ratified.[43]

II FRAMING THE JUDICIAL INQUIRY

Adjudicators may avail themselves of certain substantive rules and principles of international environmental law in order to adjust the extent to which they reflect on the scientific aspects of disputes. The invocation of the precautionary principle is a stark example of that, as it enables judges to circumvent problems posed by uncertain science for making conclusive judicial findings. For this reason, the invocation of this principle will be viewed here as a specific framing technique. Precautionary reasoning allows adjudicators to frame their inquiry so as to reflect on scientific input in a way that does not preclude basing substantive findings on uncertain scientific facts.

The precautionary principle functions across several stages of the adjudicatory process. Most typically, it is applied as a powerful reasoning technique in weighing contradicting policy choices, but it can also justify employing evidentiary presumptions or alleviating the burden of proof.[44] It can also serve strategic

---

[41] For a general overview of the legal bases and case law see L. Chenwi, 'The right to a satisfactory, healthy, and sustainable environment in the African regional human rights system' in J. H. Knox and R. Pejan (eds.), *The Human Right to a Healthy Environment* (Cambridge University Press, 2018), pp. 59–85.

[42] T. Buergenthal, 'The evolving international human rights system centennial essays: in honor of the 100th anniversary of the AJIL and the ASIL' (2006) 100 *American Journal of International Law* 783–807 at 798.

[43] Buergenthal, 'The evolving international human rights system centennial essays: in honor of the 100th anniversary of the AJIL and the ASIL', 800.

[44] Viñuales, 'Legal techniques for dealing with scientific uncertainty in environmental law', 450; D. Bodansky, 'Scientific uncertainty and the precautionary principle' (1991) 33 *Environment* 4 at 43; Foster, *Science and the Precautionary Principle in International Courts and Tribunals*, pp. 241–5.

purposes in the reasoning, namely, to exclude certain justifications for inaction, to justify mandating proactive measures,[45] or to establish a prima facie case of a violation.[46]

The jurisprudence of the ECtHR showcases an apposite example for such a strategic application of the principle. The Strasbourg Court has been famously more open towards this principle than the majority of international courts. This is not very surprising considering the salient embrace of the principle in the risk regulatory paradigm of European states and the European Union. In *Tătar* v. *Romania*, the ECtHR openly adopted a precautionary stance.[47] The facts of the case concerned a cyanide spill occurring in a gold mine due to a combination of extreme weather conditions and relaxed domestic permitting requirements, especially with respect to environmental impact assessment (EIA) proceedings. Basing its reasoning on the precautionary principle allowed the court to firmly conclude that domestic EIA measures were insufficient for the purposes of Article 8, as the respondent state failed in its obligation to satisfactorily assess the potential risks of the mining activity.[48] In other words, in this case the precautionary reasoning served as a tool to bridge the gap between uncertain scientific risks and the causal complexities underlying the cyanide spill on the one hand, and the breach of human rights standards on the other hand.

Nevertheless, the reach of the precautionary justification was in fact limited even in *Tătar*, which is otherwise regarded as 'the high-water mark'[49] of the ECtHR's precautionary approach. As will be seen later, *Tătar* featured another set of uncertain factual allegations regarding the causal role of the toxic spill in aggravating the asthma of the victim at hand. In this respect, however, the ECtHR did not rely on precautionary argumentation, and hence it dismissed the probabilistic, uncertain medical evidence suggesting a causal link between the presence of cyanide and the respiratory disease.

III CAUSAL INQUIRIES TO HANDLE SCIENCE IN HUMAN RIGHTS CLAIMS

Causality has a two-fold role in environmental human rights adjudication. On the one hand, the causal nexus between a state's measure or omission and its

[45] D. Bodansky, 'Deconstructing the precautionary principle' in D. Caron and H. N. Scheiber (eds.), *Bringing New Law to Ocean Waters* (Martinus Nijhoff, 2004), pp. 381–91 pp. 383–6.

[46] Shelton, 'Complexities and uncertainties in matters of human rights and the environment: identifying the judicial role', p. 117.

[47] *Tătar* v. *Romania*, para. 120. For scholarly commentary on the role of precautionary reasoning in the judgment see O. W. Pedersen, 'The European Court of Human Rights and international environmental law' in J. H. Knox and R. Pejan (eds.), *The Human Right to a Healthy Environment* (Cambridge University Press, 2018), pp. 86–98 pp. 89–90; Shelton, 'Complexities and uncertainties in matters of human rights and the environment: identifying the judicial role', pp. 113–17.

[48] *Tătar* v. *Romania*, para. 112.

[49] Pedersen, 'The European Court of Human Rights and International Environmental Law', p. 90.

harmful effects on the environment and/or human health is relevant to establish a violation of state parties' negative obligations (i.e. not to violate the protected sphere of rights) as well as their positive obligations (i.e. to prevent private actors from infringing the rights of individuals). On the other hand, human rights courts may award pecuniary and non-pecuniary damages for human rights violations caused by environmental pollution. Causal inquiries (would) therefore also play a key role in determining the quantum of compensation.

As will be seen, establishing causality is an especially problematic part of the judicial inquiry in human rights adjudication. A common challenge is rooted in the underlying science. Before addressing the methods developed by respective courts for conducting science-based causal inquiry, a short overview is due on the difficulties in establishing causal links based on uncertain and ambiguous science in cases of toxic exposure.

1 *Sources of Causal Uncertainty Inherent in Cases of Toxic Exposure*

Applicants must establish a causal link between the harm and the allegedly wrongful conduct in order to prove a violation and to receive compensation. This requirement often triggers adducing pieces of scientific evidence concerning the victim's health condition and the extent of environmental pollution that allegedly caused the injury. As a result of peculiar challenges present in these cases, judges face a specific set of evidentiary problems in establishing causality. Throughout this chapter, uncertain causation is understood as referring to the following specific problems common to toxic exposure cases:

(i) The most typical difficulty is illustrated by the accident metaphor.[50] In a car accident the cause of physical injuries is readily discernible and can rarely be attributed to anything else other than the collision. However, in toxic exposure cases identifying the 'cause' of injury can be particularly complicated, as there might be numerous possible sources of exposure, as in occupational-disease cases.[51] Moreover, in case of an accident, the cause and effect relations between the collision and the injuries are plausibly justified in our everyday experiences.[52] However, in toxic exposure cases the mechanism of disease development is usually not well understood and not directly observable.[53]

---

[50] A. F. Foerster and C. Gregorski Rolph (eds.), *Toxic Tort Litigation* (American Bar Association Publishing, 2013), p. 139.

[51] The American Law Institute, *Third Restatement of the Law of Torts for Physical and Emotional Harm*, §28, Comment on Subsection (a) c. (2).

[52] The American Law Institute, *Third Restatement of the Law of Torts for Physical and Emotional Harm*, §28 Comment on Subsection (a) c. (1).

[53] The American Law Institute, *Third Restatement of the Law of Torts for Physical and Emotional Harm*, §28 Comment on Subsection (a) c. (1).

(ii)   An injury may have a long latency period,[54] even trans-generational,[55] that may render the identification of a causal link especially challenging. Latency periods complicate the finding of general causation and the lapse of time impedes identifying past exposures.[56]

(iii) Though human epidemiological studies provide the most precise and certain proof of causal links surrounding human health impairment, such studies are often not conducted for ethical reasons.[57] Observational data on human exposure might be available; however, they can easily fall short of statistical significance due to the infrequency of the outcome of interest.[58] In the absence of human studies, experimental animal studies may be relied on, but the need to extrapolate from such results weakens their probative value,[59] not to mention the ethical objection against animal experimentation to study toxic effects.

(iv)   Epidemiological studies are resource intensive; therefore, research results concerning a particular toxin are often not readily available. The costs are compounded if one faces a rare disease, which requires studies involving larger samples.[60]

(v)   Toxins rarely have signature effects that allow fingerprinting the causal agent. It is far more common that several disease factors contribute to a symptom common to all of them.[61] Additionally, the same causal agent might cause numerous health impairments, while only a few of them are unique enough to be regarded as signature diseases. For instance, while asbestos might cause asbestosis, mesothelioma, lung cancer, and fibrosis, only asbestosis and mesothelioma are regarded as signature diseases.[62]

(vi)   Uncertainty may surround the diagnosis of injury. Certain diseases can only be fully recognized after death has occurred, and there may be possible biases on the experts' side if they are aware of the dose of exposure when making the diagnosis.[63]

---

[54] C. F. Cranor, *Toxic Torts Science, Law and the Possibility of Justice* (Cambridge University Press, 2006), p. 173.

[55] For instance, the DES litigation concerned a drug containing diethylstilbestrol, the harmful effects of which manifested in the offspring of the women who took the miscarriage prevention drug during their pregnancy.

[56] M. D. Green, 'The future of proportional liability: the lessons of toxic substances causation' in M. S. Madden (ed.), *Exploring Tort Law* (Cambridge University Press, 2005), pp. 352–99 p. 373.

[57] Cranor, *Toxic Torts Science, Law and the Possibility of Justice*, p. 9.

[58] This obstacle arose in the *In re Neurontin* case where causal factor leading to suicide was disputed. The court noted that the infrequency of suicide diminishes the probative value of the small number of such occasions. *In re Neurontin Mktg., Sales Practices & Prods. Liab. Litig.*, US District Court of Massachusetts, 5 May 2009, 612 F.Supp.2d 116.

[59] Cranor, *Toxic Torts Science, Law and the Possibility of Justice*, p. 10.

[60] Cranor, *Toxic Torts Science, Law and the Possibility of Justice*, pp. 173–4.

[61] Cranor, *Toxic Torts Science, Law and the Possibility of Justice*, p. 175.

[62] R. Kundis Craig, A. R. Klein, and J. Sanders, *Toxic and Environmental Torts Cases and Materials* (West, 2010), p. 159.

[63] Green, 'The future of proportional liability: the lessons of toxic substances causation', p. 379.

(vii)   The level of exposure is often uncertain,[64] yet in the case of certain diseases, exposure that occurred at a specific time can be of particular relevance.[65] Quantifying the latter can be difficult.

(viii) Epidemiological studies are group-based,[66] meaning that they can only describe the incidence of a disease in a group, and not the cause of a given individual's disease within that group. Specific problems arise in the context of determining whether the association of data indicates a causal connection.[67] In group-based studies, selection bias and random error are particularly relevant.[68] Even if the sample data are correct, attributing the group-based epidemiological findings to individual cases inevitably involves uncertainty.[69]

> To avoid such problems of group-based data, it might be advisable to supplement them with particularized evidence describing the individual plaintiff's characteristics.[70] However, the individualized approach does not preclude other types of uncertainty, since the role that toxic exposure and individual background risks play in developing a given disease may be in doubt. And even if science can substantiate the existence of genetic background risks, it remains uncertain whether the exposure and the genetic risk factor have additive, antagonistic, or synergetic effects.[71]

(ix)   Finally, multiple competing causal agents may be present,[72] among which some have only 'weak' causal effects, that is, they create only a small incremental increase in disease risk, while others are of 'strong' casual effects, conferring a substantial increase of risk.[73]

The following sections analyse the practice of human rights courts to address such factual complexities in their legal analysis. Given that the ECtHR conducts the most elaborate, and as will be argued, most controversial causal inquiry among regional human rights courts, this will be subject to detailed scrutiny. The Inter-American and African commissions and courts have just started to hear cases featuring disputed or ambiguous causal links, therefore only basic causal requirements have been announced so far.

---

[64] Kundis Craig, Klein, and Sanders, *Toxic and Environmental Torts Cases and Materials*, p. 159.

[65] Green, 'The future of proportional liability: the lessons of toxic substances causation', p. 378. In certain cases, early or peak doses can be relevant while in others, the total length of the exposure.

[66] Green, 'The future of proportional liability: the lessons of toxic substances causation', p. 352.

[67] A. B. Hill, 'The environment and disease: association or causation?' (2015) 108 *Journal of the Royal Society of Medicine* 32–37.

[68] Green, 'The future of proportional liability: the lessons of toxic substances causation', pp. 380–1.

[69] Brennan, 'Causal chains and statistical links', 512.

[70] S. C. Gold, 'The more we know, the less intelligent we are? How genomic information should, and should not, change toxic tort causation doctrine' (2010) 34 *Harvard Environmental Law Review* 369 at 392.

[71] Gold, 'The more we know, the less intelligent we are?', 394.

[72] S. H. Knudsen, 'The long-term tort: in search of a new causation framework for natural resource damages' (2014) 108 *Northwestern University Law Review* 475–542 at 530.

[73] Cranor, *Toxic Torts Science, Law and the Possibility of Justice*, p. 176.

2 *Role of Science-Based Causality in the European System*

Science-based causality engenders a set of notorious difficulties for the court's inquiry.[74] A former judge at the Strasbourg Court even dubbed causation the 'missing link in adjudicating human rights',[75] and criticized the court for subscribing to an 'archaic perception of causation'.[76] The following analysis conducts an in-depth review of the ECtHR's causal requirements. Although causal analyses remain hidden or at best marginal in the ECtHR's judgments, some causal criteria have been cursorily flagged in the reasoning confirming the legal relevance of causal links between environmental pollution and its impact on human health and well-being. These causal links impact the applicability of Articles 2 and 8, the finding of a violation of these provisions, and the awarding of damages under Article 41.

2.1 Relevance of Causation under Article 2 of the ECHR

In cases decided under the right to life, the causal link between the alleged violation and the applicant's death or imminent threat to their life lies at the core of the inquiry.[77] The *L. C. B.* v. *UK* case illustrates that a state's positive obligations are triggered by a probable causal link between the injury and the state measure. This case featured claims by an applicant who had suffered from leukaemia since her early childhood, allegedly due to her father's exposure to radiation during his service at a UK nuclear military base before the applicant was born. The judgment clearly articulates that 'the State could only have been required of its own motion to take steps in relation to the applicant if it had appeared likely at that time that any such exposure of her father to radiation might have engendered a real risk to her health'.[78] A failure to demonstrate such causal link, thus, is fatal to a claim under Article 2.

This wording indicates that scientific proof of a causal nexus between a toxic agent and the death of individuals informs the scope of states' positive obligations to protect the right to life. If the evidence suggests the lack of a legally appreciable causal role of a given pollutant in endangering human life, the court finds that its release should not have been prevented by the state and, therefore, such complaints are inadmissible.[79] Notably, as stressed in *Smaltini*, the court takes the scientific

---

[74] Shelton, 'Complexities and uncertainties in matters of human rights and the environment: identifying the judicial role', 109; D. L. Shelton, 'Developing substantive environmental rights' (2010) 1 *Journal of Human Rights and the Environment* 89–120 at 114–16; P. Sands, 'Human rights, environment and the *Lopez-Ostra* case' (1996) *European Human Rights Law Review* 597–618 at 615; Boyle and Harrison, 'Judicial settlement of international environmental disputes', 270.

[75] Zupančič, 'Causation in cases of environmental degradation'.

[76] Zupančič, 'Causation in cases of environmental degradation', 118.

[77] Council of Europe, *Manual on Human Rights and the Environment*, p. 37, *Budayeva and Others v. Russia*, para. 158.

[78] *L. C. B.* v. *UK*, para. 38.

[79] *Smaltini* v. *Italy*, Application No. 43961/09, Decision (24 March 2015).

knowledge available for the authorities at the time of exposure as its point of reference in assessing the causal role of the polluting agents.[80]

2.2 Causation under Article 8 of the ECHR

In claims brought under the right to private and family life, causality is relevant at three stages of the inquiry; first in deciding the applicability of the provision, and subsequently, as to the finding of a breach. In cases of violation, causality will be relevant at the stage of awarding compensation.

2.2.1 POLLUTION THAT TRIGGERS APPLICATION. According to the ECtHR's case law, which is consistent on this point, Article 8 is applicable when there is pollution caused by the state directly or indirectly in a failure to regulate private industry;[81] when the pollution exceeds a certain minimum level of severity[82]; and when the pollution or environmental degradation has a 'direct adverse effect'[83] on the individual's private and family life or well-being. There is no arguable claim if the detriment is 'negligible in comparison to the environmental hazards inherent to life in a modern city'.[84]

In the case of toxic emissions, the ECtHR may find a 'direct effect' even when the pollution did not seriously impair the victim's health. In *Brânduşe* v. *Romania*, a prisoner suffering from noxious odours from a nearby rubbish tip succeeded with his claim in the clear absence of any health injury. The court found that well-being can be affected even in such cases.[85] The test of applicability focuses on whether the interference was capable of causing the harm at hand (whether it was 'potentially harmful'[86]). In practical terms this requirement means that proving a causal link between the pollution and the health impairment is a sufficient, but not necessary, requirement for applying Article 8.

2.2.2 THE NECESSARY CAUSAL LINK FOR FINDING OF A VIOLATION – WHICH REMAINS HIDDEN IN THE ANALYSIS. As addressed above, states have a negative obligation to refrain from interference with private life by engaging in severely polluting activity. Furthermore, with a view to their power to regulate potentially harmful industrial activities, states have a positive duty to prevent others from

---

[80] *Smaltini* v. *Italy*, para. 60.
[81] *Fadeyeva* v. *Russia*, para. 89, where the ECtHR explicitly stated that state's responsibility 'may arise from a failure to regulate private industry'.
[82] *Fadeyeva* v. *Russia*, para. 69.
[83] Council of Europe, *Manual on Human Rights and the Environment*, p. 20, *Guerra and Others* v. *Italy*, para. 57.
[84] *Fadeyeva* v. *Russia*, para. 69.
[85] *Brânduşe* v. *Romania*, Application No. 6586/03, Judgment (7 April 2009), para. 67. It was reinforced in *Dzemyuk* v. *Ukraine*, para. 82.
[86] *Dzemyuk* v. *Ukraine*, para. 84.

interfering with the enjoyment of the amenities of one's home and family life.[87] In terms of assessing the fulfilment of positive obligations, the ECtHR grants a wide margin of appreciation to states in striking a fair balance between environmental rights of individuals and the economic interests of the larger community.[88] Only in case the court finds a manifest error in such balancing, would it declare a violation.

Causal inquiries are implicated in establishing violations of both the positive and the negative obligations, even though the court rarely discusses requisite causal links in an open and consistent manner. Certain judgments do, however, allude to the significance of causal nexus in finding a breach. First, in order to decide whether severe pollution, either caused by a public or a private actor, constitutes a breach of Article 8, the ECtHR requires 'the existence of proven and serious consequences for the health of the applicant',[89] as this triggers states' positive obligation 'to adopt and implement reasonable and appropriate measures that protect [the applicant's] well-being'.[90] Accordingly, a state cannot be held liable for a failure to regulate private industry, if the harm complained of is a result of pre-existing conditions and not that of the emission at hand. In other words, causality is relevant in the reasonableness inquiry as it informs determining the scope of states' positive obligations by identifying the harmful effects states ought to prevent.

Furthermore, problems engendered by pre-existing conditions, which appear as competing possible causes (also referred to as plurality of causes[91]), are pervasive in toxic exposure cases. The ECtHR makes clear in *Ledyayeva and Others* v. *Russia* that even though 'severe pollution adversely affects public health in general, [. . .] it is often impossible to quantify its effects in each individual case, and distinguish them from the influence of other relevant factors, such as age, profession, etc.'.[92] Such statements, however, are never followed by a thorough inquiry to decide about causal processes at play in the given case. In the material case, the ECtHR 'refrain[ed] from making any conclusive findings as to whether or not the industrial pollution was the cause of the applicants' specific diseases'.[93]

It is notable that almost none of the applicants has been able to successfully prove causation based on uncertain evidence when the causal link was disputed by the other party. Instead, violations are declared, when the defendant government does not contest the causal link surrounding the harmful effects.[94] This provides

---

[87] *Hatton and Others* v. *UK*, Application No. 36022/97, Judgment (8 July 2003), para. 98.
[88] For a more detailed discussion on the margin of appreciation doctrine see Section V, Subsection 1 in this chapter.
[89] *Bacila* v. *Romania*, para. 71. The judgment is available in French only, translation by the author.
[90] *Bacila* v. *Romania*, para. 71
[91] *Tătar* v. *Romania*, para. 105. Translation by the author.
[92] *Ledyayeva and Others* v. *Russia*, para. 90.
[93] *Ledyayeva and Others* v. *Russia*, para. 100.
[94] *Bacila* v. *Romania*, para. 63; *Dubetska and Others* v. *Ukraine*, Application No. 30499/03, Judgment (10 February 2011), see M. Fitzmaurice, 'The European Court of Human Rights, environmental damage and the applicability of Article 8 of the European Convention on Human Rights and Fundamental Freedoms *Dubetska and Others* v. *Ukraine*, European Court of Human Rights

a convenient factual basis for the ECtHR to find a violation without assessing the probative value of scientific evidence. In exceptional cases, when the ECtHR has found a violation, it has not elaborated on the reasons for accepting the evidence submitted; rather, it has simply concluded that it 'has accepted the link between the medical conditions ... and the exposure'.[95]

Finally, the relevance of causal links is demonstrated also by the *Leon and Agnieszka Kania* judgment, where the ECtHR dismissed the application with reference to the applicant's failure to submit 'a valid claim supported by medical record' demonstrating adverse health effects caused by the lawful noise pollution.[96] This statement implies that the ECtHR might consider finding a violation even if the pollution did not exceed domestic safety standards, provided that its adverse health effects and the respective causal link are established.

2.2.3 SCIENCE-BASED CAUSATION IN AWARDING COMPENSATION: LATENCY PERIODS.
A causal connection between the violation and the damage sustained is relevant also to awarding compensation.[97] The lack of causality precludes awarding damages. Latency periods are an additional source of uncertain causation that burdens the applicant in toxic exposure cases. The problem of latency periods is well illustrated by the judgment in which the ECtHR denied pecuniary damages for loss of earnings associated with the health impairment caused by the violation. Among the reasons for awarding no pecuniary damages, the ECtHR explicitly referred to the 'prevailing perceptions and lack of precise knowledge at the material time about the possible long-term effects'.[98]

3 *Causal Inquiry in the European System: A Proxy-Based Assessment*

The ECtHR has never expressly articulated its methodology for finding a violation of positive obligations under Article 8. The present survey of case law suggests that the ECtHR frames its causal inquiry in a peculiar way as to carving out science from the legally relevant factors and instead, it has recourse to certain non-scientific proxies when it decides about violations. By virtue of this approach, which I will call here proxy-based methodology, the ECtHR can adjudicate environmental cases without re-examining complex scientific evidence. This proxy-based judicial approach undoubtedly eases and accelerates

---

(Application No. 30499/03), Judgment of 10 February 2011, Not Yet Reported' (2011) 13 *Environmental Law Review* 107–114 at 114.
[95] *Brincat and Others* v. *Malta*, para. 150.
[96] *Leon and Agnieszka Kania* v. *Poland*, Application No. 12605/03, Judgment (21 July 2009), paras. 102–3.
[97] M. Kellner and I. C. Durant, 'Causation' in A. Fenyves, E. Karner, H. Koziol, and E. Steiner (eds.), *Tort Law in the Jurisprudence of the European Court of Human Rights* (De Gruyter, 2011), pp. 449–92 p. 455.
[98] *Vilnes and Others* v. *Norway*, para. 270.

the court's procedure, albeit it also has serious shortcomings, which will be discussed below.

3.1 Decoupling Article 8 Obligations from Uncertain Causal Links

The proxy-based approach is a corollary of the test announced in the *López Ostra* case, where the ECtHR decoupled Article 8 obligations from the requirement of causing health impairment to the plaintiff. In the material case, the first occasion when the ECtHR found a violation regarding pollution, the court awarded damages to the applicant, who suffered from excessive toxic air pollution emanating from a neighbouring plant.

The court formulated its test governing its Article 8 inquiry as follows: 'severe pollution may affect individuals' well-being and affect their private life adversely without seriously endangering their health'.[99] As a consequence, the applicant does not need to prove causation between the environmental pollution and its harmful physical or mental consequences to support their claim. The test, in fact, circumvents problems arising from uncertain causation by requiring a 'sufficiently close link'[100] between the state's measure – or omission – and the sphere of private life, and not the actual health injury itself. Under the judicially protected sphere of Article 8, the scope of the right to private life is thus broader than health. It encompasses not only protection against health injuries but other aspects of 'well-being' as well. Nevertheless, health injuries caused by a state's action or omission remain relevant under Article 8 as being the most direct form of interference that is prohibited by the provision.

The *López Ostra* test indicates a conscious turn away from assessing scientific evidence relevant to adjudicating causes of toxic exposure. Tellingly, the European Commission of Human Rights, which examined the case as to admissibility at a quasi-preliminary stage of the ECtHR's proceeding, concluded that the plant at hand 'could endanger the health of those living nearby and that there could be a causal link between those emissions and the applicant's daughter's ailments'.[101] Given that the judgment itself cites this finding, it is difficult to escape the conclusion that the ECtHR purposefully formulated the *López Ostra* test so as to circumvent the issue of causation by not requiring proof of a causal link involving the health injury.

The *López Ostra* decision is usually praised by human rights scholars,[102] since it has brought considerable benefits in terms of enforcing environmental claims,

---

[99] *López Ostra* v. *Spain*, Application No. 16798/90, Judgment (9 December 1994), para. 51.
[100] *Dzemyuk* v. *Ukraine*, para. 81; *Hardy and Maile* v. *UK*, Application No. 31965/07, Judgment (14 February 2012), para. 189.
[101] *López Ostra* v. *Spain*, para. 49.
[102] R. Desgagné, 'International decisions' (1995) 89 *American Journal of International Law* 788–91 at 789–90.

especially in light of the ECtHR's previous prevailing practice to dismiss environmental pollution claims.[103] Indeed, relying on the abstract and less tangible concept of 'private life' alleviates the evidentiary burden that rests with the applicant, as it enables the ECtHR to find violations even when the causal link between the pollution and the harm cannot be substantiated.[104] As a consequence of this approach, one might expect that human rights-based environmental protection would entail 'a slight easing of the requirements for scientific proof of causation'.[105] However, in the practice of the ECtHR, plaintiffs rarely win toxic exposure cases, for reasons that will be explored later in the analysis.

3.2 The Proxies that Substitute for a Science-Based Causal Inquiry: Identification and Assessment

The ECtHR evaluates whether defendants' conduct amounted to a breach of their positive obligation based on certain criteria that intuitively seem to be reliable factors for estimating the harmful nature of the pollution at hand. Although the court has never articulated its proxy-based methodology as a doctrinal approach to evaluating states' conduct, it in fact justifies its findings of a violation with reference to a set of non-causal criteria that are dubbed here as proxies.

The ECtHR uses the assessment by proxies as a substitute for a cause-and-effect inquiry. Instead of providing an elaborate causal assessment seeking to reconstruct the elements of the causal scenario that led to the injurious interference, the court relies on the overall impression of the case. This approach enables the court to circumvent assessing the uncertain causal link between the pollution and the injury and eliminates the technical aspects of the case in order to avoid confrontation with its scientific (and uncertain) details. Even when the causal link could be established based on scientific evidence, the ECtHR apparently justifies its finding of a breach with reference to other criteria. This approach, however, can only result in rough justice. As will be seen shortly, the majority of the proxies cannot be justified scientifically and therefore do not yield persuasive judicial reasoning for distinguishing cases concerning factually comparable pollution.

This study identifies six such proxies in the court's environmental jurisprudence that are:

(i)   the distance between the polluter and the applicant's home;
(ii) whether the pollution was on-going or only a by-product of previous industrial activity;
(iii) the occurrence of prior accidents producing large-scale pollution;

---

[103] *Powell and Rayner* v. *UK*.
[104] Indeed, judgments declaring a violation often note that the causal link with the injury claimed was dubious. *Fadeyeva* v. *Russia*, para. 80; *Ledyayeva and Others* v. *Russia*, para. 37; *Grimkovskaya* v. *Ukraine*, para. 60.
[105] Boyle and Harrison, 'Judicial settlement of international environmental disputes', 270.

(iv) the lawfulness of the toxic emission under domestic law;

(v) exceptional facts bearing on the case/the egregiousness of the circumstances;

(vi) whether the state's decision-making process failed to comply with rule of law/procedural guarantees.

In some instances, the court examines several of the proxies, while in others it only considers one of them. These proxies have not been articulated as exclusive criteria for applying Article 8 or for finding a breach under the provision. Moreover, the court did not announce the proxies a priori, rather, it developed them gradually in response to particular circumstances. However, the fact that the ECtHR dismissed a claim expressly because it did not meet its proxies[106] suggests that it tends to regard them as exclusive criteria. Nevertheless, the court is certainly free to add new proxies. What follows is a discussion of each of the proxies thus far applied by the court.

(i) The ECtHR tends to attach particular relevance to the distance between the polluter's location and the applicant's home,[107] which is used as a proxy for assessing the 'direct effect' of the toxic pollutant, a criterion for applying Article 8.[108] As a reason for refusing to apply Article 8 in *Ivan Atanasov* v. *Bulgaria*, the ECtHR referred to the fact that the applicant's home was 'a considerable distance' from the tailings pond of a former copper mine, the source of the pollution.[109] In this case, justifying the claim's dismissal by the distance proxy was problematic in light of the risk assessment report of the national authority, which showed heavy metal concentration in the pond's sludge in excess of statutory levels, and estimated a risk of contamination within a radius of ten kilometres around the pond.[110] Given that the applicant lived only one kilometre away from the pond (and thus, within the zone of possible contamination), the facts of the case would have enabled the ECtHR to find a direct effect, had it engaged in proper evidentiary inquiry instead of relying solely on the formalistic distance proxy.

This proxy is also objectionable from a scientific point of view, as the toxicity and the associated health risks of pollution cannot be examined merely with reference to the distance between the source and the exposed individual. Further, this proxy-based decision is also inconsistent with *Guerra and Others* v. *Italy*, where the polluting factory was similarly one kilometre away from the applicants' home,[111] yet the distance did not prevent the ECtHR from finding a violation under Article 8.

---

[106]   *Ivan Atanasov* v. *Bulgaria*, para. 76.

[107]   Sands, 'Human rights, environment and the *Lopez-Ostra* case', 615. Sands noted that the ECtHR was 'particularly impressed by the fact that the applicant lived just 12 metres from the offending plant'.

[108]   See *Ivan Atanasov* v. *Bulgaria*, para. 76.

[109]   *Ivan Atanasov* v. *Bulgaria*, para. 76.

[110]   *Ivan Atanasov* v. *Bulgaria*, paras. 31–4.

[111]   *Guerra and Others* v. *Italy*, para. 12.

(ii) When it comes to assessing the conformity of a state conduct with the Convention, the ECtHR also weighs whether the pollution is a 'result of an active production' that 'can lead to the sudden release of large amounts of' toxins.[112] This proxy, however, cannot be justified from a scientific point of view either. Hazardous substances released from a former industrial site can well remain dangerous for many decades; thus, the fact that the factory ceased to operate has, in fact, no bearing on the toxic nature of the site.

(iii) In terms of Article 8 obligations, the ECtHR also considers whether prior incidents occurred involving the industrial activity under consideration.[113] Prior industrial accidents were an explicit ground for finding a violation of Article 8 in *Guerra and Others v. Italy*.[114] However, this proxy is clearly too permissive, as it identifies only the most egregious instances of pollution. As discussed above, the protected sphere of private life under the *López Ostra* test is much broader than prohibiting interference caused by severe industrial accidents.

(iv) The lawfulness of an emission under domestic law is another important proxy for assessing the facts of a case, although it plays a different role in terms of assessing compliance with positive and negative obligations. A state-owned entity's unlawful emission automatically triggers a violation, while a private industrial actor's unlawful emission is only one relevant factor out of many for deciding whether a state has fulfilled its positive obligations.

The ECtHR attaches a causal presumption to this proxy, by holding that where pollution exceeds domestic safety levels it 'becomes potentially harmful to the health and well-being of those exposed to it. This is a presumption, which may not be true in a particular case.'[115] Applying the presumption, the ECtHR may find that 'the applicant's health deteriorated *as a result of* her prolonged exposure to the industrial emissions'.[116] The presumption is evoked with two caveats. First, it is only triggered by pollution 'significantly above statutory levels'.[117] Thus, pollution that only slightly exceeds statutory limits, which is often the case, falls short.[118] Second, the applicant needs to establish a 'very strong combination of indirect evidence',[119] which is contingent upon the ECtHR's approach to appraising scientific evidence. As will be seen shortly, the court applies a rather strict approach to scientific evidence and tends not to rely on statistical probabilities. Third, the presumption

---

[112] *Ivan Atanasov v. Bulgaria*, para. 76.
[113] *Ivan Atanasov v. Bulgaria*, para. 76.
[114] The ECtHR distinguished *Ivan Atanasov* from *Guerra* on the grounds of lack of prior incidents, *Ivan Atanasov v. Bulgaria*, para. 76.
[115] *Fadeyeva v. Russia*, para. 87.
[116] *Fadeyeva v. Russia*, para. 88, emphasis added.
[117] *Bor v. Hungary*, para. 24; *Moreno Gómez v. Spain*, paras. 57–63; *Deés v. Hungary*, para. 23.
[118] See, for example, *Martínez Martínez and Pino Manzano v. Spain*, Application No. 61654/08, Judgment (3 July 2012).
[119] *Fadeyeva v. Russia*, para. 88.

is only applicable, when available causal proof does not yield a conclusive answer. In this vein, in the *Cordella* case, where more than a hundred applicants have been exposed to carcinogen toxic emissions in excess of domestic statutory levels, the court did not even consider applying the presumption, instead it investigated the causal nexus based on epidemiological reports.[120] These factors altogether suggest a narrow scope for applying this causal presumption in the Strasbourg case law.

Overall, the domestic legality proxy seems to play a significant role in the ECtHR's assessment, inasmuch as it is most willing to find a breach when the respondent state breached its own domestic regulations. This approach serves as a 'restricting feature'[121] in the court's case law, and it may signal a 'slight retreat'[122] in the ECtHR's formerly ambitious jurisprudence by narrowing the scope of inquiry to violations of domestic environmental quality standards.

Nevertheless, the domestic legality proxy is the only one that can be justified on scientific grounds. In cases when pollution exceeds health-based standards, this proxy directly relates to the toxic nature of the pollution and, thus, approximates the causal link between the exposure and the injury. Accordingly, when invoking this presumption, the ECtHR itself also noted that the applicable domestic safety levels were health-based standards.[123] Yet, domestic safety levels may sometimes be established irrespective of the pollution's health effects in the case of technology-based standards. In these instances, the domestic legality proxy can be over-inclusive, namely, it can result in violation even if the adverse health effects were not in fact caused by the toxic pollution. Overall, this proxy leads to mixed results, since it provides a less precise outcome than a causal assessment based on the evidence of the particular case.

(v) The egregiousness of the circumstances serves as an additional proxy. The gravity of environmental destruction has been assessed by the court on the basis of, for instance, the death toll among exposed individuals,[124] the duration of pollution,[125] the obsolete nature of industrial technology involved,[126] and the government's failure to meet applicable EU environmental laws as evidenced by a judgment of EU courts in an infringement proceeding.[127] As noted by one commentator regarding the *López Ostra* case, 'it is difficult to escape the conclusion that the exceptional facts of this case provided the principal bases for the Court's

---

[120] *Cordella and Others* v. *Italy*, discussed in Section IV, Subsection 1.2.
[121] Pedersen, 'The European Court of Human Rights and international environmental law', p. 87.
[122] Pedersen, 'The European Court of Human Rights and international environmental law', p. 96.
[123] *Fadeyeva* v. *Russia*, para. 87.
[124] *Guerra and Others* v. *Italy*, para. 61.
[125] *Bor* v. *Hungary*, para. 26, noting that it took sixteen years for the state to respond adequately and abate excessive noise pollution.
[126] *Ledyayeva and Others* v. *Russia*, para. 10; *Fadeyeva* v. *Russia*, para. 11.
[127] *Cordella and Others* v. *Italy*.

finding'.[128] This stance holds true for subsequent decisions as well. Although this proxy can undoubtedly be useful for finding a violation where the dirtiest polluters are involved; state-of-the art technology that is equally destructive to the individual's well-being would escape scrutiny under this assessment. Similarly, the duration of unabated pollution would certainly work well as a proxy for finding a breach in cases of long-standing emissions; however, it falls short of catching transient though injurious emissions. Yet, based on the track record of the Strasbourg Court in finding violations in cases of environmental pollution, this proxy seems to be the most decisive. One is left with the impression that the legal reasoning, including the causal assessment, is tailored by the court *ex post facto*, according to the judges' overall impression of the gravity of the circumstances.

(vi) Finally, compliance with the rule of law in states' regulatory obligations also seems to play a major role in the ECtHR's analysis. This proxy was relied on in *Taşkın and Others v. Turkey*, which concerned environmental and health risks imposed by a gold mine using cyanide technology. The authorities first refused to give a permit to the mine, however, after the prime minister intervened, they ultimately issued authorization. The ECtHR noted that when state organs fail to comply with require-ments for the proper administration of justice, the procedural guarantees that the state should ensure under Article 8 are 'rendered devoid of purpose'.[129] Thus, it declared a violation.

3.3 Drawbacks of the Proxy-Based Method

Although the use of proxies might appear to be suitable for determining the vague scope of private life, and in many cases, it would provide a remedy against the most severe forms of environmental pollution, this method can be critiqued on grounds of epistemic legitimacy and consistency.

Since proxies disregard the science underlying causal links, their use allows certain kinds of pollution to escape judicial scrutiny, even when the injury was, scientifically speaking, *caused* by the toxic agent released. This application of the *López Ostra* test runs afoul of its grammatical meaning, according to which Article 8 prohibits even less severe interferences than actual health injuries. In avoiding complex causal inquires and scientific evidentiary assessments, the ECtHR sacrifices predictable and nuanced judicial decision-making based on an objective and consistent approach to the scientific evidence available in the case file. Moreover, the use of proxies can only provide rough justice, as the decision results from an overall, rule-of-thumb assessment of the facts rather than from a thorough causal analysis of the harm and the alleged violation, and therefore risks being over or under-inclusive.

---

[128] Sands, 'Human rights, environment and the *Lopez-Ostra* case', 616.
[129] *Taşkin and Others v. Turkey*, paras. 124–5.

Without considering scientific evidence of causation, the Strasbourg jurisprudence inevitably leads to highly controversial results by not remedying the very core of the interference with private and family life, namely, causing physical injury to the applicant. Equally disturbing outcomes are the findings of a violation where the actual harm was not a result of the defendant state's action or omission, even though that action satisfied many proxies. Overall, diminishing the role science and causation play in the court's assessment narrows the scope of environmental harm against which the ECHR provides protection.

Furthermore, the proxy-based approach yields inconsistent results by leaving certain victims uncompensated. This shortcoming is flagged by sets of cases where, despite similar facts and scientifically comparable harm, the ECtHR has reached different outcomes as to whether they constitute a violation. One of these sets is *Giacomelli* v. *Italy* and *Ivan Atanasov* v. *Bulgaria*. The former complaint addressed a waste treatment plant, while the latter focused on a restoration of the tailings pond of a former copper mine that contained heavy metals. Both cases concerned situations where the authorities failed to prepare a proper EIA prior to the industrial activity.[130] In *Ivan Atanasov*, robust expert evidence suggested the existence of considerable risks of heavy metal pollution; in *Giacomelli*, there was a risk of toxic waste leakage.[131] In *Giacomelli*, the applicant did not prove that any harm was sustained, nor did the ECtHR require actual harm for finding a violation. In *Ivan Atanasov*, the applicant did not claim harm either,[132] as his application concerned pervasive risks of a reclamation scheme that were left unabated by the state.[133]

However, while in *Giacomelli*, the ECtHR found a violation, in *Ivan Atanasov* it reached the opposite outcome. It listed five reasons, corresponding to certain proxies, for not finding a violation: (1) the distance between the pond and the applicant's home, (2) the lack of active production on the site, (3) the lack of prior accidents, (4) the absence of proof of an increased morbidity rate, and (5) the lack of a showing of actual harm to the applicant's health.[134] The only proxy whereby *Giacomelli* produced a different result was the presence of active operation. However, this is hardly a scientifically sound reason for treating these cases differently, if one considers the grave health risks posed by non-restored former industrial sites. Hence, this proxy cannot justify the different judicial outcome.

Another set concerns the different awarding of pecuniary damages under Article 41 for adverse health consequences. In *Tătar*, the 'plurality of causes' problem barred the ECtHR from deciding whether the cyanide leakage was the cause of the

---

[130]   *Giacomelli* v. *Italy*, Application No. 59909/00, Judgment (2 November 2006), para. 86; *Ivan Atanasov* v. *Bulgaria*, para. 22.

[131]   *Giacomelli* v. *Italy*, para. 55.

[132]   *Ivan Atanasov* v. *Bulgaria*, para. 78.

[133]   *Ivan Atanasov* v. *Bulgaria*, para. 3.

[134]   *Ivan Atanasov* v. *Bulgaria*, para. 76.

applicant's aggravated asthma. As a result, the court did not award damages to the applicant.[135]

In contrast, in *Vilnes*, competing causes were not an obstacle to the finding of a violation and the awarding of non-pecuniary damages. This complaint concerned health damages incurred by seven former divers who worked for oil drilling companies in the North Sea and sustained damage to their central nervous systems after their employment.[136] To prevent divers from getting decompression sickness, domestic authorities were responsible for enforcing safety standards set out in decompression tables for governing the length of time for decompression. In this case, the ECtHR concluded that the diving company's overly rapid decompression tables 'had probably been a strong contributory cause of the applicants' health deteriorations'.[137] Possible competing causes, thus, did not preclude the finding of a causal link.

Still another inconsistency emerges from a comparison of the *L. C. B.* and *Brincat* cases. The judgments in these cases took different directions on whether the defendant state ought to have known about the existence of health risks associated with toxic exposures caused by the state. In the first case, the underlying hazardous activity consisted of nuclear tests run by the United Kingdom between 1952 and 1967, to which the applicant's father was exposed.[138] The second case featured Malta's ship repair industry, which from the 1950s exposed to asbestos unprotected workers, who later either died of mesothelioma or sustained various types of cancer.[139]

In both cases, the states submitted that they were not aware of the risks imposed on their citizens. They also contested the causal link between the exposures and the health injuries claimed.[140] A further similarity is that scientific discourse had begun to raise awareness about the pervasive health risks of both types of exposure at the time of the states' conduct.[141] The applicant in *L. C. B.* relied on research that was conducted prior to his exposure, right after the Hiroshima and Nagasaki bombings, which showed a statistical association between the incidence of leukaemia and radiation exposure. In *Brincat*, the ECtHR acknowledged that WHO and ILO started to raise awareness about the dangers of asbestos already in the 1950s. Therefore, the extent of uncertainty surrounding the harmful effects of both exposures was arguably comparable at the time of states' injurious conduct; and thus, respective states ought equally to have known about the health hazards. In spite of these similarities, the ECtHR reached different outcomes. In *L. C. B.*, the court subscribed to the view that the United Kingdom should not have known about the

---

[135] *Tătar* v. *Romania*, para. 105.
[136] *Vilnes and Others* v. *Norway*, paras. 9, 14, 20.
[137] *Vilnes and Others* v. *Norway*, paras. 233, 273.
[138] *L. C. B.* v. *UK*, para. 13.
[139] *Brincat and Others* v. *Malta*, para. 12.
[140] *L. C. B.* v. *UK*, para. 31. and *Brincat and Others* v. *Malta*, para. 75.
[141] *L. C. B.* v. *UK*, paras. 17., 28; *Brincat and Others* v. *Malta*, para. 9.

risks of nuclear radiation,[142] whereas in *Brincat*, Malta was held liable for violating the workers' right to life because, in the ECtHR's view, Malta ought to have known about the health hazards of asbestos.[143]

Finally, due to the lack of a clear causal inquiry, the court's reasons for finding or not finding a violation remain obscure and, thus, future plaintiffs are left with little guidance as to the evidentiary requirements of the ECtHR.

For all these reasons, this peculiar judicial framing of causal assessments yields decisions that may run against the factual realities of the case and therefore are vulnerable to challenges based on factual scientific data. As will be argued later, the ECtHR could hardly justify its isolation from scientific facts in times where scientific fact-finding techniques could in fact offer legally relevant insights into the actual causal relations leading to the harmful injury complained of in human rights claims. The price of using such a proxy-based assessment is therefore weakening the persuasiveness and (epistemic) legitimacy of the judicial decision.

3.4 The Status of Science in the Causal Inquiry of the Strasbourg Court

As demonstrated above, the inquiry of the ECtHR in science-intensive cases is governed by assessing non-scientific proxies. This approach grants the court considerable latitude in crafting its legal reasoning detached from uncertain and highly technical scientific facts. It appears that the proxies altogether leave the court with a more or less accurate picture of the factual background of the case, allowing judges to cursorily appraise the egregiousness of state omissions to prevent private actors from damaging the environment and human health. In many cases this approach would not yield wholly inaccurate results, as rule-of-thumb assessments, rooted in intuitive rationality may in some cases overlap with scientifically informed decisions. Yet this fact does not entirely blunt criticism based on concerns for epistemic legitimacy.[144] When scientific evidence is available on the case file but does not inform the legal inquiry out of conscious adjudicatory choice, the persuasive force of the judgment is easily compromised.

In light of the ECtHR's prevailing practice during the first two decades of hearing environmental complaints, scientific realities have not been decisive for the court in appraising violations of private life caused by environmental pollution. This is clearly visible in the judicial assessment of causal processes leading to individual health injuries. Even though the Strasbourg Court may award pecuniary and non-pecuniary damages for victims of environmental pollution, due to which some commentators regard its jurisprudence as 'a system of tort law',[145] its inquiry is much more loosely linked to the underlying scientific facts than that of tort law

---

[142] *L. C. B.* v. *UK*, para. 38.
[143] *Brincat and Others* v. *Malta*, para. 105.
[144] For more details see discussion in Chapter 10 Section II, Subsection 3.1.1.
[145] Oliphant and Ludwichowska, 'Damage', p. 447.

courts.[146] Furthermore, as will be discussed in Section V of this chapter, human rights courts grant a wide margin of appreciation to respondent states, which is again alien to tort law jurisprudence.

Interestingly, in recent cases a more articulate role has been accorded to scientific reports, which may indicate some hesitant signs of judicial awareness on the inescapable relevance of scientific facts underlying environmental applications. Applicants and third parties increasingly file scientific studies providing the ECtHR with epidemiological data on the health injuries claimed.[147] While even in such cases the court still exerts visible efforts to escape explicit science-based assessments, judges nevertheless often end up commenting on these scientific reports at considerable length.[148] The court's reasoning in *Cordella* and in *Smaltini* suggests that respective scientific evidence on the causal role of toxic emissions in engendering health injuries, even though may not be decisive on its own as to finding a violation, is nevertheless informative for the court in appraising the respondent state's failure to address environmental and health risks. As the ECtHR grows accustomed to the inevitable confrontation with scientific evidence, it may in the long run adopt a more thorough and empirical approach towards assessing environmental claims.

The fact remains that avoiding the scientific aspects of cases generates a good number of inconsistencies in the ECtHR's environmental case law. To remedy these, this book ultimately argues that the court ought to consider the scientific evidence in causal claims involving health injuries. The ECtHR should aim, to the extent possible, to base its decision whether a violation has taken place on the causal assessment of the scientific aspects of the case. By revisiting the scientific evidence submitted to it, the court may preserve the epistemic legitimacy of its reasoning.

It remains to be emphasized that conducting a thorough causal analysis in toxic exposure cases does not mean that the ECtHR should disregard its proxies entirely. Proxies can be suitable tools for determining unlawful conduct that encroaches upon the broader sphere of private life, that is, those adverse effects on well-being that do not cause health injuries (e.g. grave health risks imposed on the individual). Violations of the procedural aspects of states' environmental obligations (such as conducting an EIA or providing access to environmental information) can also be assessed through proxies.

However, once health injuries emerge in the context of a toxic exposure, consistent and predictable jurisprudence can only be achieved if the court considers causation and evaluates the scientific evidence submitted when it decides whether the *López Ostra* test has been fulfilled. Basing decisions on causal inquiry would produce more accurate results, would result in a procedurally fairer jurisprudence by revealing the evidentiary standards parties need to meet and which the court

---

[146] K. Sulyok, 'Managing uncertain causation: lessons for the Strasbourg Court from US toxic tort litigation?' (2017) 18 *Vermont Journal of Environmental Law* 521–69.
[147] *Cordella* and Others v. *Italy*, *Smaltini* v. *Italy*.
[148] *Cordella* and Others v. *Italy*, paras. 150–6; *Smaltini* v. *Italy*, paras. 26–35.

would be expected to follow in future cases. Overall it is argued here that engaging with the underlying science would further buttress the persuasive force of the ECtHR's argumentation.

4 Science-Intensive Causal Links in the Inter-American System

From an analytical point of view, causal links can be legally relevant in the Inter-American system in two respects: for establishing extra-territorial application of human rights standards (Subsection 4.1) and for substantiating violations of certain guarantees (Subsection 4.2).

4.1 Extraterritorial Application of Human Rights Guarantees

The idea of extraterritorial application of human rights has long been discussed in scholarly commentary with a general scope[149] and also specifically in the context of environmental protection.[150] The doctrinal and practical significance of causality implicated in such a context has come to the forefront in the Environment and Human Rights Advisory Opinion of the IACtHR.[151] In this proceeding, Colombia requested the court to define the scope of state obligations in relation to the environment under the rights to life and to personal integrity recognized in Articles 4 and 5 of ACHR. Specifically, it asked whether a person, even if they are not within the territory of a state party, should be considered subject to the jurisdiction of that state if, as a result of damage to the environment or risk of environmental damage caused in the area protected by an international environmental convention, which can be attributed to the state – that is a party both to the given convention and to the ACHR – their human rights have been violated or are threatened.[152]

---

[149] M. Milanovic, *Extraterritorial Application of Human Rights Treaties* (Oxford University Press, 2011); A. Reinisch, 'Human rights extraterritoriality: controlling companies abroad' in E. Benvenisti and G. Nolte (eds.), *Community Interests Across International Law* (Oxford University Press, 2018), pp. 396–413; R. Wilde, 'Socioeconomic rights, extraterritorially' in E. Benvenisti and G. Nolte (eds.), *Community Interests Across International Law* (Oxford University Press, 2018), pp. 381–95.

[150] A. Boyle, 'Human rights and the environment: where next?' (2012) 23 *European Journal of International Law* 613–42 at 638; J. E. Viñuales, 'A human rights approach to extraterritorial environmental protection? An assessment' in N. Bhuta (ed.), *The Frontiers of Human Rights* (Oxford University Press, 2016), pp. 177–221; L.-A. Duvic-Paoli and J. E. Viñuales, 'Prevention' in J. E. Viñuales (ed.), *The Rio Declaration on Environment and Development: A Commentary* (Oxford University Press, 2015), pp. 107–38 pp. 107–38.

[151] Environment and Human Rights Advisory Opinion OC-23/17, 15 November 2017, InterAmCtHR Series A No. 23/17.

[152] An almost identical hypothetical question provides the main thread of scholarly assessment of J. E. Viñuales published less than a month after the request for the Advisory Opinion was filed on 14 March 2016. Many of his findings anticipate what the court later announced in the Advisory Opinion. See Viñuales, 'A human rights approach to extraterritorial environmental protection? An assessment', p. 192.

In a remarkable opinion, the IACtHR answered this question in the affirmative by holding that extraterritorially affected victims are subject to the jurisdiction of the state of origin if there is a causal link between the activities present on that state's territory and the adverse effects on human rights outside of its territory. Causality, therefore, has just been placed at the heart of human rights adjudication in the Inter-American regime. Causal nexus between a state's due diligence obligation to prevent transboundary environmental harm to occur and violations of human rights is now crucial for establishing extraterritorial jurisdiction of a state within the Inter-American regime. The IACtHR stressed that 'there must always be a causal link between the damage caused and the act or omission of the State of origin in relation to activities in its territory or under its jurisdiction or control'.[153] As one commentator observed, causality plays a dual rule in this inquiry inasmuch as the court should establish 'the link between, firstly, state action or inaction and environmental degradation and, secondly, between such degradation and an impairment of human rights abroad'.[154]

This new, causality-based jurisdictional link extends the traditional,[155] effective control-based scope of jurisdiction. This extension goes one step further along the imaginary causal chain of events tracing the consequences of the state's exercise of effective control over its territory. It is rooted in the understanding 'that it is the State in whose territory or under whose jurisdiction the activities were carried out that has the effective control over them and is in a position to prevent them from causing transboundary harm that impacts the enjoyment of human rights of persons outside its territory'.[156] From the obligation to prevent transboundary harm, it follows that '[t]he exercise of jurisdiction arises when the State of origin exercises effective control over the activities that caused the damage and the consequent human rights violation'.[157]

For limiting the scope of extraterritorial jurisdiction, the Advisory Opinion requires the harm caused to be significant.[158] It rules that any damage qualifies as such 'that may involve a violation of the rights to life and to personal integrity'.[159] The court reminds, in line with previous observations of Viñuales,[160] that the duty to prevent human rights violations is an obligation of conduct and not that of result; hence, the key aspect of the IACtHR's inquiry will focus on the state's efforts to prevent significant damage to occur under its effective control. Accordingly, non-compliance of a state

---

[153] Environment and Human Rights Advisory Opinion, para. 103.
[154] Viñuales, 'A human rights approach to extraterritorial environmental protection? An assessment', p. 219.
[155] Boyle, 'Human rights and the environment', 637.
[156] Environment and Human Rights, Advisory Opinion, para. 102.
[157] Environment and Human Rights, Advisory Opinion, para. 104 (h).
[158] Environment and Human Rights, Advisory Opinion, para. 104 (f).
[159] Environment and Human Rights, Advisory Opinion, para. 140.
[160] Viñuales, 'A human rights approach to extraterritorial environmental protection? An assessment', p. 198.

would not necessarily flow from the mere fact of violating certain human rights.[161] The
IACtHR does not specify the limits any further, but refers the question of delimiting
the scope of extraterritorial jurisdiction to a case-by-case analysis.[162] What clearly
emerges even from these vaguely described contours is that extraterritorial jurisdiction
is tied only to severe forms of environmental destruction that are capable of infringing
upon the protected spheres of human rights. This confirms the trends anticipated by
Viñuales, namely, that 'spatial expansion [of jurisdiction] may potentially come at the
price of a contraction of the scope for environmental protection *per se*'.[163]

For purposes of the present analysis the most noteworthy aspect of the
Advisory Opinion is the strategic role causal inquiry will play in establishing
extraterritorial human rights claims. With an unprecedented move in international human rights law, the IACtHR takes causality as 'a standalone basis'[164] to
establish a state's extraterritorial jurisdiction. From a doctrinal point of view,
however, this innovative ruling has a problematic aspect, inasmuch as it
remains silent on the actual causal test. As has been repeatedly emphasized
throughout also in this study, '"causality" might be an oversimplification to
describe the often complex factual link between the State's omission and its
extraterritorial consequences'.[165]

The causal nexus, which – depending on the actual test, may either be 'direct',
'clear', 'plausible' or even 'indirect' or 'contributory' – will govern the applicability of
human rights obligations of a state for violations triggered by transboundary environmental harm or the threat of such harm. As causal claims are inextricably tied to
underlying scientific facts, human rights claims will in all likelihood entertain
disputed causal chains and conflicting scientific views on the actual cause of alleged
human rights violations. At the time of writing this book, it is yet to be seen how the
IACtHR would frame its causal assessments and to what extent it will engage with
scientific evidence in its inquiries.

4.2 Causality in Proving Violation in Individual Cases

Similarly to the Strasbourg regime, for establishing a violation of the right to physical
integrity no actual health injury needs to be substantiated in the Inter-American
human rights protection system. The Inter-American Commission on Human
Rights has emphasized that 'severe environmental pollution which may cause

---

[161]   Environment and Human Rights, Advisory Opinion, para. 143.
[162]   Environment and Human Rights, Advisory Opinion, para. 140.
[163]   Viñuales, 'A human rights approach to extraterritorial environmental protection? An assessment',
        p. 194.
[164]   For a detailed assessment on possible doctrinal and pragmatic problems arising from the wide scope
        of causality and jurisdiction see A. Berkes, 'A new extraterritorial jurisdictional link recognised by the
        IACtHR', EJIL Talk! (28 March 2018). Available at https://bit.ly/36W99BJ (last accessed
        11 January 2020).
[165]   A. Berkes, 'A New extraterritorial jurisdictional link recognised by the IACtHR'.

serious physical illness, impairment and suffering on the part of the local populace, are inconsistent with the right to be respected as a human being'.[166] Causal link is, in contrast, an expressly necessary element in the context of awarding compensation under Article 63 of ACHR. In the *Saramaka People* case, the IACtHR emphasized that people must be compensated for the material damage 'directly caused' by the violation.[167]

A good number of toxic exposure claims are yet to reach the IACtHR. Such claims have thus far been heard by the commission in the admissibility phase. The claims were virtually always rendered admissible based on the review of underlying facts. The petitions will later be heard on the merits first by the commission. If the state failed to meet the recommendations addressed to it, the commission could refer the case to the IACtHR provided that all procedural prerequisites are met. These are particularly science-intensive claims alleging violations on account of severe health injuries caused by toxic exposure. Chronologically first in line, the petition of the Community of San Mateo was filed against Peru, claiming that the authorities permitted a toxic waste dump near the community causing serious contamination and negative health effects.[168] The commission also issued precautionary measures calling for immediate governmental action.[169] Later in 2009, the Community of La Oroya lodged a complaint for authorizing the operation of a metallurgic plant causing serious pollution resulting in illness and death of local residents.[170] A noteworthy aspect of the commission's scientific fact-finding is that it relied on a WHO guideline[171] to find that the claim was admissible under Article 4 and 5 of ACHR.

In 2010, the commission declared admissible a petition concerning the infamous 'cancer alley' of Louisiana in the *Mossville* v. *US* case. Residents of Mossville alleged various health problems caused by toxic pollution released from fourteen chemical-producing industrial facilities that have been granted permits in and around the city. Petitioners submitted a report prepared by the University of Texas showing widespread injuries, attesting that '84% of the Mossville residents surveyed present nervous system problems; 71% cardiovascular problems; 57% skin problems', and adverse mental health impacts.[172] Residents were found to have dioxin in their blood

---

[166] Inter-American Commission on Human Rights: *Report on the Situation of Human Rights in Ecuador*, Chapter VIII.

[167] *Saramaka People v. Suriname*, Judgment, para. 199.

[168] Inter-American Commission on Human Rights: *Community of San Mateo de Huanchor v. Peru*, Admissibility Decision, Report No. 69/04.

[169] For more details see D. L. Shelton, 'Environmental rights and Brazil's obligations in the Inter-American human rights system' (2009) 40 *George Washington International Law Review* at 733–77.

[170] Inter-American Commission on Human Rights, the *Community of La Oroya v. Peru*, Admissibility Decision, Report No. 76/09.

[171] In more detail see D. Shelton, 'Developing substantive environmental rights' (2010) 1 *Journal of Human Rights and the Environment* 89–120 at 117.

[172] Inter-American Commission on Human Rights: *Mossville Environmental Action Now v. US*, Admissibility Decision, Report No. 43/10, para. 10.

three times higher than the national average. Documents were also filed showing that the facilities emitted substances that were 'scientifically known to cause cancer'[173] and various health impairments. Bearing in mind 'the complex questions of fact and law',[174] the commission for the first time declared a case admissible under the right to privacy while referring to the established practice of the Strasbourg Court.

In *People of Quishque-Tapayrihua* v. *Peru*[175] and in *Communities of the Sipakepense and Mam Mayan People* v. *Guatemala* petitions against pollution originating from mines were found admissible under Article 5.[176] Eventual merits discussions and final decisions in these cases may answer, from a doctrinal point of view, many crucial questions as to the prospects and technical requirements of proving toxic exposure claims and could reveal how the IACtHR frames its causal assessment in science-heavy claims.

5 Causal Links in the African System

In the African regime, toxic exposure claims usually concern large-scale and egregious pollution, where the excessive health risks caused by apparent absence of state policies are evident, and sometimes even openly acknowledged by the state.[177] For this reason scientific evidence demonstrating causal nexus between severe health consequences and respective state measures or omissions thus far has not played a crucial role in substantiating a violation.

In the African system, the tort law function of human rights adjudication is less articulated compared to that of the ECtHR. African courts usually take an action-forcing approach towards pollution claims requiring effective policies and regulations from respective governments rather than awarding monetary compensation for victims of toxic pollution. A large-scale oil spill in the Niger Delta caused by poor maintenance of infrastructure, human error, and lack of effective clean-up was entertained in *SERAP* v. *Nigeria*. The decade-long unabated oil pollution has vastly destroyed crops, damaged the productivity of soil, contaminated water on which communities depended, and reportedly caused various illnesses. The ECOWAS Court noted that the core problem in tackling environmental degradation 'resides in lack of enforcement of the legislation and regulation in

[173] *Mossville Environmental Action Now* v. *U.S.*, para. 11.
[174] *Mossville Environmental Action Now* v. *U.S.*, para. 43.
[175] Inter-American Commission on Human Rights: *People of Quishque-Tapayrihua* v. *Peru*, Admissibility Decision, Report No. 62/14, OEA/Ser.L/V/II.151 Doc. 27 24 July 2014; *Communities of the Sipakepense and Mam Mayan People* v. *Guatemala*, Report No. 20/14, OEA/Ser.L/V/II.150 Doc. 24 3 April 2014.
[176] Inter-American Commission on Human Rights: *Communities of the Sipakepense and Mam Mayan People* v. *Guatemala*, Admissibility Decision, Report No. 20/14.
[177] *Socio-Economic Rights and Accountability Project (SERAP)* v. *Republic of Nigeria*, Judgment No. ECW/CCJ/JUD/18/12, General List No. ECW/CCJ/APP/08/09, Judgment, para. 95. Further referred to as *SERAP* case.

force',[178] and did not award monetary compensation for the victims, even though acknowledged that the devastating pollution 'may have even caused health problems to many'.[179] The reasoning of the judgment alludes to the fact that the lack of awarding compensation was due to the applicants' failure to specify the individual victims among whom the astronomical amount of damages claimed (USD 1 billion) could have been distributed.[180]

The ACtHPR has only recently started to hear cases involving environmental destruction. The *Ogiek* case[181] was decided in 2017 and concerned the eviction of the Ogiek people from their ancestral land by Kenyan authorities.[182] Causality became relevant in the context of proving a violation of the right to life. Due to the lack of sufficient evidence, the commission ultimately did not establish a causal connection between the evictions of the Ogieks and the violation ensuing from the alleged death of some members of the community.[183]

IV SCIENTIFIC FACT-FINDING TECHNIQUES

Scientific evidence and factual allegations are filed with every regional human rights court though they differ in terms of the depth and the level of detail in which they comment on such expert reports. What appears to be a common feature nevertheless is the reluctance to engage with probabilistic and contested scientific evidence.

1 *The Fact-Finding Powers of the Strasbourg Court*

The ECtHR primarily relies on the fact-finding of domestic courts and competent authorities by reviewing the evidence that is already on the case file.[184] It entails that the level of science infiltrating the ECtHR's inquiry is largely dependent on the scientific engagement of domestic authorities. In addition to that, applicants increasingly cite the findings of competent national and international institutions[185] as well as submit scientific and medical reports[186] with domestic authorities and courts in underlying proceedings. These scientific reports ultimately reach the ECtHR, as

---

[178]   *SERAP* v. *Nigeria*, Judgment, para. 108.
[179]   *SERAP* v. *Nigeria*, Judgment, paras. 114.
[180]   *SERAP* v. *Nigeria*, Judgment, paras. 114–115.
[181]   *African Commission on Human and Peoples' Rights* v. *Republic of Kenya*, Application No. 006/2012, Judgment, 26 May 2017, further referred to as *Ogiek* case.
[182]   For a general analysis see R. Roesch, 'The *Ogiek* case of the African Court on human and peoples' rights: not so much news after all?' EJIL Talk! (16 June 2017). Available at https://bit.ly/3gJS7eK (last accessed 11 January 2020).
[183]   *Ogiek*, Judgment, para. 155.
[184]   *Cordella and Others* v. *Italy*, para. 160.
[185]   For instance, in *Smaltini*, applicants refer to both WHO studies and reports of the Italian Association against Leukemia, Lymphoma, and Melanoma.
[186]   *Fadeyeva* v. *Russia*, para. 46, *Cordella and Others* v. *Italy*.

applicants refer to them as evidence of health injuries caused by unabated pollution violating protected spheres of private life.

The procedural rules of the ECtHR allow for gathering independent expert advice. To surmount its lack of scientific expertise, the court has the power to appoint experts.[187] Pursuant to the Rules of Court, the ECtHR may 'ask any person or institution of its choice to obtain information, express an opinion or make a report, upon any specific point'.[188] Yet, the Strasbourg Court, like other international fora, has not been utilizing this power, which is usually explained by the court's overwhelming caseload.[189] By the time the ECtHR started to decide environmental cases on the merits, scholars expected the court to use its evidentiary powers in environmental cases.[190] However, judicial practice evolved in quite the opposite direction, as detailed in the following sections.

1.1 Too High a Level of Certainty Is Required

The ECtHR's standard of proof is generally high as it uses the beyond reasonable doubt standard,[191] which is met by 'the coexistence of sufficiently strong, clear and concordant inferences or of similar unrebutted presumptions of fact'.[192] While the court emphasized that it allows flexibility in this respect with regard to the evidentiary difficulties involved,[193] in its practice, it rarely accepts probabilistic proof of causation.

The court's approach to statistical evidence was at the core of the decision reached in *Tătar v. Romania*. Several pieces of evidence were not refuted by the ECtHR, yet it still refused to accept them as adequate proof of causation. A report jointly issued by the UN Environmental Programme and the Romanian authorities established the existence of excessive cyanide pollution near the applicant's home,[194] the city hospital reported an increased number of respiratory diseases among local children,[195] and many experts agreed that cyanide might cause irritation to the respiratory tract. However, the court found that these pieces of evidence were insufficient 'to create a causal probability'[196] between the cyanide leaching and

---

[187]   D. Harris, M. O'Boyle, E. Bates, and C. Buckley, *Law of the European Convention on Human Rights* (Oxford University Press, 2014), p. 144.
[188]   Rules of Court 'A' (entry into force February 1, 1994), Rules 41 (2); see also Harris, O'Boyle, Bates, and Buckley, *Law of the European Convention on Human Rights*, p. 144.
[189]   S. T. Ebobrah, 'International human rights courts' in C. Romano, K. J. Alter, and Y. Shany (eds.), *The Oxford Handbook of International Adjudication* (Oxford University Press, 2014), pp. 225–49 p. 231.
[190]   Sands, 'Human rights, environment and the *Lopez-Ostra* case', 615.
[191]   Harris, O'Boyle, Bates, and Buckley, *Law of the European Convention on Human Rights*, p. 148.
[192]   *Fadeyeva v. Russia*, para. 79.
[193]   *Fadeyeva v. Russia*, para. 79.
[194]   *Tătar v. Romania*, para. 95.
[195]   *Tătar v. Romania*, para. 105.
[196]   *Tătar v. Romania*, para. 105.

the aggravated asthma. The court refused to engage in 'probabilistic reasoning'[197] as in its view, this would only be acceptable if the claim is 'accompanied by sufficient and convincing statistics'.[198]

In his dissent, Judge Zupančič heavily criticized the ECtHR for embracing an overly formalistic 'classical causal approach', which 'does not know the concept of uncertainty'. Later writing extra-judicially, he also emphasized that: '[i]t is disappointing that the European Court of Human Rights remains [. . .] in the [. . .] not so enlightened perception of what cause and effect in law is – in a situation in which the environmental pollution is at least one of the major contributing factors to problems that led the plaintiff to the Court'.[199]

As is demonstrated by the case of *Brincat and Others* v. *Malta*, even when the ECtHR finds a breach, it avoids evaluating uncertain scientific proof of causation. This case concerned liability for a state's omission that resulted in health injuries. The ECtHR 'accepted the link between the medical conditions affecting the relevant applicants and their exposure to asbestos',[200] but did not provide any reasoning for its causal findings. This stance is interesting because the underlying facts were far from being entirely clear and the court has a high threshold for accepting scientific claims. Thus, the finding of a causal link would certainly have deserved a more in-depth discussion.

The medical certificate of the deceased worker only indicated that the death was '*likely* to be a result of asbestos exposure'.[201] Also, the National Cancer Institute held that whether asbestos-related diseases develop depends on a number of factors, among others, smoking.[202] This is especially important, given that some of the applicants were smokers.[203] However, instead of weighing the contradictory evidence, the ECtHR found Malta liable for endangering the lives of the applicants on the grounds that, on account of its ILO membership, the government knew or ought to have known about the dangers of asbestos.[204] This statement implies that the court was convinced that the asbestos *was the cause* of the harm sustained, even if not primarily on the basis of the expert evidence, but on account of widely held views on the toxic nature of asbestos.

Such ad hoc weighing of non-scientific evidence may be objectionable from a doctrinal point of view, as it obfuscates the evidentiary requirements of the ECtHR. Liability for a state's omission that allegedly resulted in health injuries simply cannot be decided without considering the scientific evidence on causality. This is not to say that the outcome of the judgment could not have been justified

---

[197] *Tătar* v. *Romania*, para. 105 ('*raisonnement probabiliste*' – translation from French by the author).
[198] *Tătar* v. *Romania*, para. 105.
[199] Zupančič, 'Causation in cases of environmental degradation', 122.
[200] *Brincat and Others* v. *Malta*, para. 150.
[201] *Brincat and Others* v. *Malta*, para. 75, emphasis added.
[202] *Brincat and Others* v. *Malta*, para. 76.
[203] *Brincat and Others* v. *Malta*, para. 12.
[204] *Brincat and Others* v. *Malta*, paras. 105–6.

from a moral and even from a scientific point of view; nevertheless, it illustrates well the court's ambivalent approach towards scientific evidence.

1.2 Probabilistic Evidence: Rare and Exceptional Acceptance

The ECtHR famously considered the possibility to 'engage in probabilistic reasoning' in *Tătar*; though ultimately it decided not to find a causal link based on the statistical evidence submitted to it.[205] In contrast, two more recent decisions suggest that the court is moving in the laudable direction of assessing probabilistic scientific evidence.

The court accepted a probabilistic proof of causation in *Vilnes and Others v. Norway*. Despite the lapse of time between the applicants' diving and the manifestation of their health impairments, during which many possible competing causes could have emerged, the court found 'a *strong* likelihood that the applicant's health had significantly deteriorated as a result of decompression sickness'.[206] This time, the likelihood provided a sufficient basis for the court to find a violation. It should be noted, however, that much of the credit for the ECtHR's turn in this instance belongs to the domestic court. The court only reiterated the relatively straightforward statement of the Norwegian High Court, which acknowledged the existence of a causal link between the too-rapid decompression tables and the victims' health injuries.[207]

Later, in *Cordella and Others v. Italy*, the court referred to a number of epidemiological studies examining the prevalence of certain diseases and the mortality rate in the population affected by a major steel plant's emission. These pieces of scientific evidence showed 10 per cent higher rate of birth defects as well as 20 per cent higher rate of child mortality in the affected region compared to the national average, which the court found conclusive enough to establish a causal link between the pollution and the health injuries.[208] Having accepted that the steel plant endangered the health of the applicants, it found that the government failed to regulate the industry so as to ensure effective protection of the rights, and hence, declared a violation. These cases might be an indication of the ECtHR's growing understanding of the true nature of probabilistic scientific evidence and readiness to base legal findings on such expert evidence.

2 Fact-Finding of the Inter-American Court in Cases Involving Environmental Damage and Pollution

In the Inter-American system, scientific facts underlying petitions are first considered by the Inter-American Commission for Human Rights. Some of the commission's inquiries are highly empirical. In its 1997 country report

---

[205] *Tătar* v. Romania, paras. 105–6.
[206] *Vilnes and Others* v. Norway, para. 233, emphasis added.
[207] *Vilnes and Others* v. Norway, para. 139.
[208] *Cordella and Others* v. Italy, paras. 163–6.

concerning Ecuador[209] the commission investigated alleged violations on account of oil exploitation. Local people alleged that they suffered from skin diseases and chronic infection due to groundwater contamination. A striking feature of the commission's report is that it cites several studies conducted by NGOs and expert bodies measuring the level of contamination and the extent of adverse health impacts among the population.[210]

Yet the commission usually does not venture into detailed factual assessment of the scientific studies that it is inclined to accept. In the Ecuador report, it summarily concluded that: '[t]he information received and analysed by the Commission, as well as the data and insights gathered during its on-site observation, have largely substantiated' the grievances of the petitioners. Also, in the very early *Yanomami* case, the commission found a violation by noting in passing that there was 'sufficient background information and evidence to conclude that . . . the failure of the Government of Brazil . . . has resulted in . . . injury to them [Yanomami People]'.[211] Similarly brief fact-finding occurs when the commission decides about the admissibility, since it conducts only a prima facie investigation.[212]

As to the scientific fact-finding of the IACtHR, its Procedural Rules allow for hearing expert evidence offered by the parties and requesting additional documents either from them or from any entity.[213] It can also summon on its own motion any experts whose opinion it deems relevant.[214] The court extensively uses such powers, although so far only experts in the social sciences were called. In *Awas Tingni v. Nicaragua*,[215] the IACtHR allocated three days[216] for hearing extensive testimonies from four expert witnesses in the field of ethnography, anthropology, and sociology, and summoned one expert witness on its own motion. The IACtHR notably sets a more flexible standard of proof than the Strasbourg Court.[217]

---

[209]   Inter-American Commission on Human Rights, *Report on the Situation of Human Rights in Ecuador*, Chapter VIII.

[210]   It explicitly states that 'the study concluded that Oriente residents are exposed to levels of oil-related contaminants far in excess of internationally recognized guidelines, and that human ingestion of water or fish from the waters sampled poses a significantly increased risk of serious health effects including cancer, neurological and reproductive problems'.

[211]   *Yanomami v. Brazil*, Resolution No. 12/85, Case No. 7615, Brazil, 5 March 1985.

[212]   Inter-American Commission on Human Rights: *Mossville Environmental Action Now v. U.S.*, Admissibility Decision, Report No. 43/10, para. 41.

[213]   Rules of Court of the Inter-American Court of Human Rights, approved by the Court at its Forty-Ninth Regular Session held from November 16 to 25, 2000, Article 44.

[214]   Rules of Court of the Inter-American Court of Human Rights, Articles 44(1), 46.

[215]   *Awas Tingni*, Judgment on merits, reparations, and costs.

[216]   J. A. Amiott, 'Environment, equality, and indigenous peoples' land rights in the Inter-American human rights system: *Mayagna (Sumo) Indigenous Community of Awas Tingni v. Nicaragua*' 32 *Environmental Law* 873–904 at 899.

[217]   Shelton, 'Complexities and uncertainties in matters of human rights and the environment: identifying the judicial role', p. 113.

From a scientific fact-finding point of view, the most interesting judgment was handed down in the *Saramaka People* case,[218] where the IACtHR was confronting the issue of ecological damage valuation. Having heard expert opinions on the logging habits of the Saramakas, the court found a causal link between the logging concessions awarded by the state and significant property damage to ancient Saramaka land.[219] In this vein, the IACtHR awarded USD 75,000,000 as material damages, which was criticized[220] for being of a too low quantum in light of the expert evidence attesting the 'traumatic'[221] environmental impact of the logging. Indeed, the judgment saliently failed to provide a detailed analysis on valuation.[222]

Recently the IACtHR has performed a more thorough fact-finding in *Lhaka Honhat* v. *Argentina*, although this case did not feature complex science-based allegations contested by the parties. The claim has been submitted by indigenous communities for Argentina's failure inter alia to provide them with effective access to the property title over their ancestral territory and to take effective action against illegal logging on their land. Moreover, authorities also did not prevent cattle farming in the area from inflicting environmental damage through overgrazing and contamination of water bodies. In appraising state responsibility for not preventing environmental harm, the court cited several expert reports[223] confirming the role of uncontrolled livestock grazing in ecosystem degradation.

What is even more significant in this case in terms of the IACtHR's interaction with scientific expertise is the hands-on approach taken towards awarding remedies for violating the right to a healthy environment, adequate food, water, and cultural identity of the indigenous community. The court ordered Argentina to devise an action plan with the help of specialists having the requisite technical knowledge, setting forth necessary measures to conserve clean drinking water, to remedy existing contamination and to prevent further deforestation. The court expressly withheld the power to compel the specialists to complete or expand the study should it find the actions foreseen deficient and undertook to supervise the implementation process until it is satisfied that the reparation measure has been complied with.[224] This provides a particularly efficient judicial guarantee for securing effective implementation of the environmental action plan.

---

[218] *Saramaka People v. Suriname*, Preliminary objections, merits, reparations, and costs, in general see L. Brunner, 'The rise of peoples' rights in the Americas: the *Saramaka People* decision of the Inter-American Court of Human Rights' (2008) 7 *Chinese Journal of International Law* 699–711.

[219] *Saramaka People v. Suriname*, Preliminary objections, merits, reparations, and costs, para. 199.

[220] M. A. Orellana, '*Saramaka People* v. *Suriname*' (2008) 102 *American Journal of International Law* 841–7 at 847.

[221] *Saramaka People v. Suriname*, Judgment, para. 151.

[222] Orellana, '*Saramaka People* v. *Suriname*', 847.

[223] Case of *Indigenous Communities Members of the Lhaka Honhat (Our Land) Association v. Argentina*, Judgment of 6 February 2020, Series C No. 400, paras. 280–5 (only in Spanish).

[224] *Lhaka Honhat v. Argentina*, Judgment, paras. 333–5.

3 Fact-Finding Powers of African Human Rights Courts

The *SERAP* case is perhaps the most illustrative of the ECOWAS Court's scientific fact-finding. The reasoning reveals that the court extensively relies on second-order justifications in the evaluation of scientific evidence. The court expressly noted that it was inclined to uphold facts as decisive that are subject to agreement among the parties.[225] The court also found a report of Amnesty International admissible. Though it ruled that the report alone could not be regarded as conclusive evidence for the harmful impacts of oil pollution, given that its findings were corroborated by well-known facts, the court accepted them as established.[226]

Similarly, the ACtHPR hears expert evidence, albeit its jurisprudence also shows that it is only inclined to rely on uncontested facts.[227] This raises doubts as to the efficiency of African human rights courts in deciding cases involving more subtle pollution, where conflicting evidence may arise. In the *Ogiek* case, the petition sought monetary compensation for all the damage suffered, including the Ogiek's loss of property and natural resources. The ACtHPR deferred deciding on compensation to a separate judgment, which at the writing of this manuscript is still pending. Hence, we shall see how natural resource damage valuation, a particularly science-intensive aspect of the dispute, will be handled by the court.

Lastly, it is to be noted that *locus standi* criteria appear to be decisive for accurate scientific fact-finding in human rights adjudication. The African regime is known for its permissive rules allowing various NGOs to bring claims before the ECOWAS Court or the African Commission on Human and Peoples' Rights, which may later refer them to the ACtHPR. Given that victims of environmental human rights violations often belong to the most vulnerable and marginalized groups, affected petitioners themselves would be in complete lack of resources to produce meaningful scientific evidence. In contrast, NGOs can effectively plead their cases while also revealing the scientific dimensions of environmental destruction, as proven by a successful track record in environmental pollution cases.[228]

V STANDARD OF REVIEW IN HUMAN RIGHTS ADJUDICATION

In human rights adjudication, the standard of review has a specific manifestation in the margin of appreciation doctrine,[229] developed by the ECtHR. While human

---

[225] *SERAP* v. *Nigeria*, Judgment, para. 94.

[226] *SERAP* v. *Nigeria*, Judgment, para. 94.

[227] *Ogiek*, Judgment, para. 183.

[228] For cases brought by NGOs see for instance the *Ogoniland* case before the African Commission on Human and Peoples' Rights, *The Social and Economic Rights Action Centre and the Center for Economic and Social Rights* v. *Nigeria*, Communication 155/96, October 2001; the *SERAP* case, and the *Ogiek* case, where the Centre for Minority Rights Development (CEMIRIDE) and Minority Rights Group International (MRGI) brought the original complaint to the commission.

[229] Legg, *The Margin of Appreciation in International Human Rights Law*.

rights courts outside Europe have not adopted this doctrine, they also afford deference to states.

1 The Strasbourg System: The Margin of Appreciation Doctrine

Any discussion on the European system of human rights protection would be incomplete without addressing the margin of appreciation doctrine, which markedly shapes the jurisprudence of the Strasbourg Court. The ECtHR famously grants a wide margin of appreciation to states in terms of formulating their environmental policies and balancing conflicting environmental and economic interests. In terms of negative obligations[230] of states, a breach of domestic law necessarily leads to a finding of a violation.[231] In contrast, domestic legality of a regulatory measure complained of is not a conclusive test for complying with positive obligations, as a breach of a given domestic law in this respect does not automatically trigger a violation of the convention.[232] By granting deference to states' policy choices, the ECtHR reviews state action or omission by using the test whether national authorities have struck a fair balance between the individual's right to life free from undue interference with their private and family life, and the interest of the community as a whole in furthering economic development.

As a consequence, the ECtHR's role in reviewing environmental policies is emphatically subsidiary and is only exercised in exceptional circumstances, when national authorities commit a 'manifest error' in balancing competing interests.[233] A manifest error is generally found in cases of gross negligence by national authorities, when they fail to address or mitigate significant pollution exceeding domestic safety standards. For instance, persistent air pollution almost five times higher than domestic safety standards[234] and an enduring noise pollution 15 per cent above the safety standards[235] met this high threshold of finding a violation.

One of the conceptual justifications for granting wide latitude to states lies in the expertise and competence of national authorities.[236] The same grounds give rise to a deferential approach towards making scientific claims as well. In other words, the margin of appreciation doctrine – which traditionally applies vis-à-vis making policy choices – corresponds to a deferential standard review in the ECtHR's practice, which manifests in the superficial review of the scientific positions offered by respondent governments in furthering said policy objectives. This is quite surprising

---

[230] Article 8(2) of the ECHR provides that 'there shall be no interference by a public authority with the exercise of this right except such as is in accordance with the law and is necessary in a democratic society in the interests of ... the economic well-being of the country'.

[231] *Fadeyeva* v. *Russia*, para. 95.

[232] *Fadeyeva* v. *Russia*, para. 98.

[233] *Fadeyeva* v. *Russia*, para. 105.

[234] *Fadeyeva* v. *Russia*, para. 32.

[235] *Deés* v. *Hungary*, para. 23.

[236] Legg, *The Margin of Appreciation in International Human Rights Law*, p. 145.

if one considers that the court has been inclined to re-assess expert evaluations submitted by respondents in cases concerning the lawfulness of an incarceration or valuation of a land.[237] Yet, in its environmental jurisprudence it has been consistently deferential towards the scientific assessments of national authorities. What is more, the court's own scientific fact-finding avowedly relies on opinions and assessments conducted by competent authorities on the national level. The deferential standard of review towards the scientific justifications for state measures appears as a necessary corollary to the superficial evidentiary assessment of the ECtHR.

2 *The Inter-American and African Systems: Measure of Deference*

The margin of appreciation doctrine was famously not accepted overseas in terms of allowing wide latitude for states in balancing competing rights and interests in realizing human rights guarantees.[238] This does not mean, however, that deference towards the factual findings of states is not present in the African and Inter-American regional human rights regimes. Deferential standard of review is predicated upon the fact-finding techniques of the ECOWAS Court and the ACtHPR, which are, as discussed above, both unwilling to base findings on scientific evidence that is contested by the state party in question.

---

[237] Legg, *The Margin of Appreciation in International Human Rights Law*, pp. 148–50.
[238] J. Contesse, 'Contestation and deference in the Inter-American human rights system subsidiarity in global governance' (2016) 79 *Law and Contemporary Problems* 123–46 at 133.

6

Scientific Claims before the WTO

It was not the Panel's task ... to determine whether there is an appreciable risk of cancer arising from the consumption of meat from cattle treated with oestradiol–17β. Instead, the Panel was called upon to review the European Communities' risk assessment.[1]

WTO Appellate Body, 2008

This chapter reviews the quasi-judicial case practice of the WTO dispute settlement system, consisting of WTO panels and the Appellate Body (AB). The analysis will centre on decisions where assessing the consistency of trade measures with provisions of WTO law necessitated a close interaction with science by panellists. This assessment therefore focuses on a portion of WTO law, which entails scrutiny of scientific legality criteria[2] that are enshrined in Article XX of General Agreement on Tariffs and Trade (GATT), in the Agreement on the Application of Sanitary and Phytosanitary Measures (SPS Agreement) as well as the Agreement on Technical Barriers to Trade (TBT Agreement). As a corollary of the narrow scope of this study, not every WTO decision with relevance for the protection of the environmental or public health will be addressed here,[3] only those where scientific arguments influenced the adjudicatory inquiry.

Due to the large number of sophisticated scientific references contained throughout WTO law, coupled with the various types of expert evidence that are heard by

---

[1] *US – Continued Suspension of Obligations* case, Report of the AB, WT/DS320/AB/R (16 October 2008), para. 614.

[2] J. Pauwelyn, 'Expert advice in WTO dispute settlement' in G. A. Bermann and P. C. Mavroidis (eds.), *Trade and Human Health and Safety* (Cambridge University Press, 2006), pp. 235–56 p. 235.

[3] Environmental considerations were alien to WTO law from its inception and only started to permeate it through dispute settlement entertaining environmental measures of states. Significant decisions in this regard, which however will not be addressed here on account of lack of significant scientific aspects are inter alia the *US – Reformulated Gasoline, US – Tuna, EC – Seal Products* cases. For more details on the intersection of environmental protection and WTO law see J. Gomula, 'Environmental disputes in the WTO' in M. Fitzmaurice, D. M. Ong, and P. Merkouris (eds.), *Research Handbook on International Environmental Law* (Edward Elgar, 2010), pp. 401–25 pp. 401–25; K. Kulovesi, 'Fragmented landscapes, troubled relationships: the WTO dispute settlement system and international environmental law' (2008) 19 *Finnish Yearbook of International Law* 29–62 at 29–62.

panels, WTO jurisprudence can justifiably be portrayed as the most science-intensive practice in the international arena. Facing the 'extraordinarily wide range of factual, scientific and legal issues'[4] raised in WTO proceedings, dispute settlement bodies developed perhaps the most elaborate standards of review with respect to scientific claims as well as the most diverse fact-finding procedures to engage with scientific expertise. For all these reasons, it is not uncommon that other international tribunals and judges refer to fact-finding methods of WTO panels as judicial 'best practice'.[5] Scholars also frequently cite WTO solutions as potential remedies to the apparent deficiencies in the scientific engagement of international adjudicatory bodies.[6]

The reports of WTO panels and the AB indeed bespeak a wide variety of adjudicatory engagement techniques with science, which will be put in the centre of analysis of this chapter. It will first enumerate the ways in which scientific arguments may become legally relevant in WTO disputes (Section I). Then this chapter will elaborate on the numerous ways in which scientific evidence is taken and evaluated by panels and will discuss the standards of review applicable to scrutinizing scientific claims (Section II). The changing canons of deference afforded by WTO dispute settlement bodies have yielded to diverse argumentative techniques for providing persuasive science-based analyses underpinning adjudicatory findings. These reasoning techniques will be addressed in Section III. As science-based causal links per se have not been placed in the centre of WTO disputes, causal inquiry of panels and the AB will not be examined in a separate section.

I SCIENCE IN THE CONTEXT OF WTO LAW

Various provisions invite scientific arguments and evidence in the corpus of WTO law. There are several express legality criteria enshrined in WTO agreements that embody scientific concepts or standards. With regard to these, panellists are often

---

[4]   *EC – Biotech*, Report of the Panel, WT/DS291/R, WT/DS292/R, WT/DS293/R (29 September 2006), para. 5.15.

[5]   Judges Al-Khasawneh and Simma in their Joint Dissenting Opinion in the *Pulp Mills* case, para. 16. state that '[i]t is perhaps the World Trade Organization, ... which has most contributed to the development of a best practice of readily consulting outside sources in order better to evaluate the evidence submitted to it'; Judge Owada in his Dissenting Opinion in *Whaling* referred to the WTO jurisprudence as a 'useful point of reference for this Court in the present case'. *Whaling in the Antarctic*, Dissenting Opinion of Judge Owada, para. 37; For scholarly positions favouring WTO solutions see J. Harrison, 'Addressing the procedural challenges of environmental litigation in the context of investor-state arbitration' in Y. Levashova, T. Lambooy, and I. Dekker (eds.), *Bridging the Gap between International Investment Law and the Environment* (Eleven Publishing, 2015), pp. 87–113 p. 96.

[6]   Mbengue, 'Scientific fact-finding at the International Court of Justice: an appraisal in the aftermath of the *Whaling* case', 549; Peat, 'The use of court-appointed experts by the International Court of Justice', 290.

simply prevented from framing the adjudicatory inquiry in a way to circumvent science. As a result, even though panellists may still exercise judicial economy to avoid making controversial findings,[7] this cannot result in a complete neglect or marginalization of underlying scientific legality criteria. Relevant audiences also deem appropriate reconstruction of the scientific factual background of disputes as a prerequisite to preserving the neutrality of adjudicatory decisions.[8] For this reason, science functions both as a *legality* and *legitimacy* criterion in the context of WTO law. Put it differently, science has a strategic role in establishing the legality of certain trade measures on the one hand, and in preserving the legitimacy of the entire adjudicatory process, on the other hand. Science is also necessary for establishing the 'internal legitimacy'[9] of states' measures, by demonstrating their adequate scientific basis, which in turn dissolves concerns about disguised protectionism.

This section will briefly review the various references to science that are built in WTO law, due to which panels and the AB could not escape engaging with interlinked scientific and legal determinations while framing their inquiry. There are essentially four different legal contexts in which science and scientific evidence become legally relevant for the adjudicatory assessment and the outcome of a WTO dispute.

First, scientific arguments can be raised in the 'likeness' assessment conducted under the provisions of GATT. Importing states must not discriminate against 'like' products of other members and shall accord such products all advantages that are granted to domestic products (requirement of National Treatment)[10]; and all privileges accorded to products of one member must also be given to products of all other members (the so-called Most-Favoured-Nation treatment)[11]. In *EC – Asbestos*, the AB ruled that it is appropriate to take into consideration the health risks of a given product in the likeness assessment.[12] Hence, it is in this context in which scientific arguments may enter a WTO dispute in the first place. Yet health risks are no way the sole or the decisive factor in the likeness assessment given that the end-use of respective products, and consumers' willingness to treat the products as interchangeable, are also relevant.[13]

Second, scientific arguments may be weighed in the necessity analysis under Article XX of GATT. Article XX (b) provides for an exemption, under which restricting international trade of like products is deemed justifiable if the measure in question is 'necessary to protect human, animal or plan life or health'. Furthermore, Article XX (g) allows trade restrictive measures that are necessary to

---

[7]   Gerstetter, 'Substance and style: how the WTO adjudicators legitimize their decisions', pp. 80–1.
[8]   Boisson de Chazournes, Mbengue, Das, and Gros, 'One size does not fit all – uses of experts before international courts and tribunals', 500.
[9]   Gruszczynski, 'Science and the settlement of trade disputes in the World Trade Organization', p. 12.
[10] GATT, Article III (2), (4).
[11] GATT, Article I (1).
[12] *EC – Asbestos*, Report of the AB, WT/DS135/AB/R (12 March 2001), para. 192 b).
[13] *EC – Asbestos*, Report of the AB, para. 117.

protect exhaustible natural resources. Importantly, lawful measures under paragraphs b) and g) must also satisfy the chapeau of Article XX, which requires measures not to constitute arbitrary or unjustifiable discrimination, or a disguised restriction on international trade.

Under this provision, scientific information may be relevant for evidencing that a measure falls within the scope of Article XX, that is, that it relates to the protection of human, animal or plant life or health. Taking an early example, the GATT panel in *Thailand – Cigarettes* noted based on WHO expert evidence that 'smoking constituted a serious risk to human health and that consequently measures designed to reduce the consumption of cigarettes fell within the scope of Article XX(b)'.[14] In a similar vein, in *US – Shrimp* 'modern biological sciences' served as proof that 'living resources are just as "finite" as petroleum'[15] and therefore measures affecting endangered species also fell under the scope of Article XX (g).

Importantly, the test of necessity under Article XX is only met if no reasonably available alternative measures exist that would be less trade restrictive.[16] Assessing the availability of such solutions also often invites expert evaluation. In *EC – Asbestos*, the AB approved the panel's finding, based on the scientific evidence submitted,[17] contending that the 'controlled use' of asbestos-containing products did not qualify as an alternative for France to achieve its chosen level of health protection against asbestos-related health risks.[18] Similarly, in *Brazil – Retreaded Tyres*, the panel evaluated expert evidence to examine alternative measures to the landfill disposal of waste tyres, the adverse health risks of which have been adequately demonstrated by scientific evidence.[19]

Third, scientific engagement of adjudicators becomes directly relevant, when panels determine their standard of review. Parties may challenge the objectivity of the panel's assessment under Article 11 of the WTO's Understanding on Rules and Procedures Governing the Settlement of Disputes (DSU), which requires a panel to make an 'objective assessment of the matter before it, including an objective assessment of the facts'. Obviously, what makes an assessment 'objective' is subject to legal interpretation. The AB discerned some exact procedural and substantive requirements in this respect.[20] However, it afforded quite extensive discretion to panels in their evidentiary assessments by pronouncing that as long as a panel does not '"deliberately disregard", "refuse to consider", "wilfully distort", or

---

[14] *Thailand – Cigarettes*, Report of the Panel, DS10/R – 37S/200 (5 October 1990), para. 73.
[15] *US – Shrimp*, Report of the AB WT/DS58/AB/R (12 October 1998), para. 128.
[16] *EC – Asbestos*, Report of the AB, para. 172.
[17] *EC – Asbestos*, Report of the Panel, WT/DS135/R (18 September 2000), para. 8.209.
[18] *EC – Asbestos*, Report of the AB, para. 174; *US – Standards for Reformulated and Conventional Gasoline*, Report of the Panel, WT/DS2/R (29 January 1996), para. 6.24.
[19] *Brazil – Measures Affecting Imports of Retreaded Tyres*, Report of the Panel, WT/DS332/R (12 June 2007), para. 7.183.
[20] D. Palmeter, 'The WTO standard of review in health and safety disputes' in G. A. Bermann and P. C. Mavroidis (eds.), *Trade and Human Health and Safety* (Cambridge University Press, 2006), pp. 224–34 p. 225.

"misinterpret" the evidence',[21] the objectivity of its assessment cannot be successfully called into question. Nevertheless, scientific evidence may become legally relevant when the panel's assessment is challenged with reference to scientific evidence that has been misinterpreted or marginalized in the process.

A fourth, and perhaps most elaborate way in which scientific arguments are raised in WTO disputes is related to the SPS Agreement. This agreement sets out the detailed rules of introducing specific SPS measures that sought to protect human, animal, and plant life.[22] Scientific requirements in the SPS Agreement function as an express mechanism guarding against SPS measures serving disguised protectionism. Members therefore shall demonstrate that contested SPS measures were backed up by adequate scientific evidence. As a matter of principle, members have a right to set their appropriate level of protection (ALOP) and indicate a maximum level of risk they are willing to tolerate.[23] The SPS Agreement nevertheless urges members to harmonize their SPS measures by basing them on international standards, guidelines, and recommendations (SGR).[24] Nevertheless, Article 3.3 allows Members to aim for a higher level of protection compared to what is ensured by international SGR provided that 'there is scientific justification' for divergence from international standards. Scientific evidence and reasoning abound in applying these elaborate rules to a given SPS measure.

Furthermore, the SPS Agreement contains the most stringent scientific evidentiary requirements for assessing the conformity of risk assessments with WTO law.[25] It sets several scientific criteria with the objective of limiting the impact of such measures on international trade.[26] Article 5.1 of the SPS Agreement requires SPS measures 'be based on' a risk assessment that, according to Article 5.2, shall take into account 'available scientific evidence'. Article 5.1 mandates that such measures are to be applied only to the extent that (i) they are necessary to protect human, animal or plant life, (ii) are based on 'scientific principles', and (iii) are not maintained without 'sufficient scientific evidence'. Moreover, Article 5.7 creates a possibility for members to act even in cases where relevant scientific evidence is insufficient to perform a risk assessment, in which case they may adopt provisional SPS measures on the basis of 'available pertinent information'. This provision may also be read as

---

[21] *Australia – Measures Affecting Importation of Salmon*, Report of the AB, WT/DS18/AB/R (20 October 1998), para. 266.

[22] For the exact definition on SPS measures see Annex A (1) of the SPS Agreement.

[23] The 6th recital of the SPS Agreement confirms this by adding that nothing in the agreement would require 'Members to change their appropriate level of protection of human, animal or plant life or health'. For more details see Gruszczynski, 'Standard of review of health and environmental regulations by WTO panels', p. 738.

[24] SPS Agreement, Article 3.1.

[25] A. O. Sykes, 'Domestic regulation, sovereignty and scientific evidence requirements: a pessimistic view' in G. A. Bermann and P. C. Mavroidis (eds.), *Trade and Human Health and Safety* (Cambridge University Press, 2006), pp. 257–70 p. 258; Gruszczynski, 'Standard of review of health and environmental regulations by WTO panels', p. 739.

[26] Gruszczynski, 'Standard of review of health and environmental regulations by WTO panels', p. 737.

the application of the precautionary principle in a WTO law context.[27] More recently, Article 6 of the SPS Agreement has also become contested in disputes. The provision requires SPS measures be adapted to the sanitary or phytosanitary characteristics of the area, from where the product is originated and to which it is destined. Members shall also recognize disease-free areas and areas of low pest or disease prevalence, the determination of which shall be based on relevant scientific factors, such as that of geography and epidemiology.

It may come as no surprise that the interpretation of these provisions invites science-intensive arguments from parties and panels alike. In order to guard against vague appeals to science and scientific research in general, the agreement narrows down the scope of acceptable forms of scientific references. One may even have the impression that the SPS Agreement aims to 'domesticate' science, when it provides exact definitions under which scientific claims are permissible in an SPS dispute and may justify a given SPS measure. For instance, the SPS Agreement stresses that only those 'scientific justifications' are relevant under the Agreement that are formed 'on the basis of examination and evaluation of available scientific evidence *in conformity with the relevant provisions* of this Agreement'.[28] Such a definition arguably serves to preclude vague references to science from having decisive force in a WTO dispute.

Similarly, the SPS Agreement also provides criteria for a valid scientific risk assessment. The notion of risk assessment is key as Article 5.1 mandates SPS measures be based on risk assessment. The AB requires that risk assessments must also be based on scientific principles and not to be maintained without sufficient scientific evidence, on account of Article 2.2.[29] The AB also mandates a substantive criterion, namely, that 'a rational relationship' must exist 'between the measure and the risk assessment'.[30] Later a WTO panel clarified this criterion by requiring that valid SPS measures 'be "sufficiently warranted" or "reasonably supported" by a risk assessment'.[31] The AB also stresses that such a rational relationship presupposes a 'situation that persists and is observable between an SPS measure and a risk assessment'.[32]

Moreover, Annex A, section 4 of the SPS Agreement also explicitly specifies the obligatory elements of a risk assessment: the identification of the disease targeted, and the evaluation of the likelihood of entry, establishment or spread of that disease together with its potential adverse effects. The actual content of the 'evaluation of likelihood' has also been subject to legal dispute. In *Australia – Salmon* the AB

---

[27] J. Zander, *The Application of the Precautionary Principle in Practice* (Cambridge University Press, 2010), p. 62.
[28] Note 2 attached to Article 3.3 SPS Agreement, emphasis added.
[29] *EC – Hormones*, Report of the AB, WT/DS26/AB/R, WT/DS48/AB/R (16 January 1998), para. 180.
[30] *EC – Hormones*, Report of the AB, para. 193.
[31] *EC – Biotech*, Report of the Panel, WT/DS291/R, WT/DS292/R, WT/DS293/R (29 September 2006), para.7.3030.
[32] *EC – Hormones*, Report of the AB, para. 189.

stressed that it is 'not sufficient that a risk assessment conclude[d] that there [was] a possibility of entry', as it had to 'evaluate the "likelihood"',[33] either 'quantitatively or qualitatively'.[34] Such evaluations again drag scientific arguments into the dispute.

Additionally, there are certain procedural requirements for conducting risk assessments. SPS measures that were based on scientific principles and various scientific studies, without conducting a risk assessment, would be found inconsistent with Article 5 of SPS Agreement. In *US – Poultry*, the United States imposed a ban on poultry imported from China with reference to various academic studies and evidences on China's food safety crisis. Among others, the United States cited statements of the Chinese Ministry of Health addressing 'high risks' regarding food security in China.[35] By finding the measure inconsistent with the SPS Agreement, the panel signalled that the scientific requirements built in the text function as legal and procedural criteria, which cannot be swept away by wholesale reference to scientific studies.

Importantly, an SPS measure does not necessarily have to square with majority scientific opinions. As explained in the *EC – Hormones* case, responsible governments 'may act in good faith on the basis of what, at a given time, may be a divergent opinion coming from qualified and respected sources'.[36] Hence, minority scientific opinions may legitimately form the basis of SPS measures, if respective expert inputs are regarded as originating from qualified and respected scientific sources.

The above criteria undoubtedly set elaborate requirements for acceptable scientific basis of SPS measures. An important caveat is due, however, regarding the role of science in this respect. First, despite repeated references to science in the text, 'science would be a necessary, rather than decisive, input into SPS risk assessment',[37] given that additional socio-economic considerations are also mandated by the agreement.[38] Also, on a more general level, it would be misleading to perceive risk assessments as a purely scientific exercise for they include normative value choices of the risk assessors in determining the level of risk they deem acceptable.[39] Scientific results therefore need to be referenced to other legitimate factors.[40] Indeed, states do consider a wider range of issues than solely scientific information in their risk assessments. The level of acceptable risk is determined through deliberative procedures of policy-making, the process of which though 'scientifically

---

[33] *Australia – Salmon*, Report of the AB, para. 123.

[34] *Australia – Salmon*, Report of the AB, para. 124.

[35] *US – Poultry*, Report of the Panel, WT/DS392/R (29 September 2010), paras. 7.188–7.190.

[36] *EC – Hormones*, Report of the AB, para. 194.

[37] Peel, *Science and Risk Regulation in International Law*, p. 184.

[38] Articles 5.4–5.6 of the SPS Agreement stipulate further requirements to account for technical and economic feasibility in designing an SPS measure.

[39] E. Reid, 'Risk assessment, science and deliberation: managing regulatory diversity under the SPS Agreement' (2012) 4 *European Journal of Risk Regulation* 535–44 at 542.

[40] Reid, 'Risk assessment, science and deliberation: managing regulatory diversity under the SPS Agreement', 542.

informed',[41] is not compelled by science.[42] These important limitations as to the reach of scientific references in SPS disputes have to be borne in mind in appraising panellists' engagement with science.

Similarly to the scientific legality criteria built in the SPS Agreement, scientific information could carry legal weight also under the TBT Agreement. Article 2.2 stipulates that technical regulations of members shall not be more trade-restrictive than necessary to fulfil a legitimate objective, taking into account the risks non-fulfilment would create. Among such legitimate objectives, protection of human health and animal or plant life or health, as provided under Article 2.1, is explicitly listed. Article 2.2 further provides that in assessing such risks, relevant considerations include, inter alia, available scientific and technical information, processing technology and intended end-uses of respective products. For instance, in the *US – Tuna II (Mexico)* dispute, both parties set forth several scientific publications and studies attempting to prove or disprove the harmful impacts of using purse seine netting on dolphins, a tuna fishing method with considerable marine mammal bycatch, which was targeted by a US labelling scheme for tuna products.[43] In the *Australia – Tobacco Plain Packaging* dispute[44] the panel again reviewed scientific studies at length concerning the effects of tobacco plain packaging measures on the smoking behaviour of affected population.

Lastly, Article 2.5 of the TBT Agreement attaches great evidentiary value to standards issued by international organizations, which are therefore of special relevance in proving science-based claims, and hence, will be discussed later.[45]

II SCIENTIFIC FACT-FINDING IN THE WTO: PRACTICES OF USING SCIENTIFIC EXPERTISE

World Trade Organization dispute settlement bodies are known for extensively using scientific expertise.[46] Panellists and members of the AB are traditionally

---

[41] See this argument in the context of environmental policy-making with a general scope and not only with respect to environmental risk assessment procedures in Lazarus, *The Making of Environmental Law*, p. 22.

[42] Andersen, 'The role of scientific expertise in multilateral environmental agreements: influence and effectiveness'.

[43] *US – Tuna II* (Mexico), Report of the Panel, WT/DS381/R (15 September 2011), paras. 7.495–7.503 citing and analysing several scientific publications and studies from the parties' submissions.

[44] *Australia – Certain Measures Concerning Trademarks, Geographical Indications and Other Plain Packaging Requirements Applicable to Tobacco Products and Packaging*, Report of the Panel, WT/DS435/R (Honduras), WT/DS441/R (Dominican Republic), WT/DS458/R (Cuba), and WT/DS467/R (Indonesia) (28 June 2018).

[45] See Section II, Subsection 4 in this chapter.

[46] For a detailed analysis on the use of experts by WTO panels and AB see L. Gruszczynski, 'The role of experts in environmental and health related trade disputes in the WTO: deconstructing decision-making processes' in M. Ambrus, K. Arts, E. Hey, and H. Raulus (eds.), *Irrelevant, Advisors or Decision-Makers? The Role of 'Experts' in International Decision-Making* (Cambridge University Press, 2014), pp. 216–37.

trade law specialists having a governmental background,[47] who therefore need epistemic support from scientists to legitimately decide about the above-mentioned scientific legality criteria. Adjudicators have several ways at their disposal to garner external expertise. World Trade Organization panels and the AB are not only assisted by party-appointed experts, but they also often rely on independent experts and appeal to the expertise of relevant international organizations. Moreover, highly technical disputes brought before the WTO prompted adjudicators to develop novel procedures for expert consultations,[48] for which they gained reputation as front runners of adjudicatory scientific fact-finding.

A brief discussion shall now follow first on the types of experts allowed in the WTO system (Subsections 1–3), and second, on the evidentiary practice of WTO panels relying on scientific standards of international organizations (Subsection 4).

1 Party-Appointed Experts

Parties have a de facto possibility to have recourse to their own experts, despite the fact that the DSU makes no mention of party-appointed experts. Scientists are usually included in the party's delegation, though they may be called to file expert evidence and answer questions of the panels in the capacity of an expert.[49]

An empirical survey suggests that even though panellists have the possibility to ask questions from party-appointed experts, they generally adopt a rather passive approach to expert evidence,[50] and their questions seem to focus more on the legal issues.[51] Cross-examination is not allowed under the DSU, as relevant actors find this formalized mechanism alien to the quasi-judicial nature of the dispute settlement mechanism.[52] Closer adjudicatory interaction with expert opinions is further impeded by the parties' apparent tendency not to engage in a dialogue with one another, up to a point that certain parties reportedly have even refused to answer questions of their counterpart.[53] There also seems to be a shared view among panellists and the WTO Secretariat that the parties' experts are inherently partial.[54]

---

[47]   Pauwelyn, 'The WTO 20 years on: "global governance by judiciary" or, rather, member-driven settlement of (some) trade disputes between (some) WTO members?', 1125.

[48]   Foster, *Science and the Precautionary Principle in International Courts and Tribunals*, p. 114.

[49]   Boisson de Chazournes, Mbengue, Das, and Gros, 'One size does not fit all – uses of experts before international courts and tribunals', 499.

[50]   Boisson de Chazournes, Mbengue, Das, and Gros, 'One size does not fit all – uses of experts before international courts and tribunals, 499.

[51]   C. Valles, 'Different forms of expert involvement in WTO dispute settlement proceedings' (2018) 9 *Journal of International Dispute Settlement* 367–78 at 375.

[52]   Boisson de Chazournes, Mbengue, Das, and Gros, 'One size does not fit all – uses of experts before international courts and tribunals', 502.

[53]   Boisson de Chazournes, Mbengue, Das, and Gros, 'One size does not fit all – uses of experts before international courts and tribunals', 502.

[54]   Boisson de Chazournes, Mbengue, Das, and Gros, 'One size does not fit all – uses of experts before international courts and tribunals', 499, 501.

2 *Independent Experts: Panel-Appointed Experts and In-House Expertise*

The most typical form of gathering expert advice is through appointing the panel's own experts. Under the SPS Agreement, consulting with experts chosen by the panel is even mandatory.[55] Panel-appointed experts are perceived as impartial and hence can duly fulfil their task of helping panellists get better acquainted with the scientific background to disputes.[56] Appointing the panel's own experts does not hollow out the ordinary allocation of the burden of proof. The AB reminds that WTO panels have 'significant investigative powers', however, they are not entitled 'to rule in favour of a complaining party which has not established a *prima facie* inconsistency based on specific legal claims asserted by it'.[57] In this vein, the powers of panels are limited inasmuch as they cannot establish a violation solely on the basis of expert evidence with respect to a claim that had not been proved by the respective party.[58]

With respect to disputes relating to agreements covered by the DSU,[59] panels are explicitly encouraged by Article 13 of the DSU to rely on expert evidence. Panels may either appoint an expert review group under Appendix 4 of the DSU or consult with individual experts. The task of panel-appointed experts is usually not to 'make their own conclusions but to evaluate' the scientific evidence put forward by the parties.[60] The panel may ask for an agreed list of experts from the parties[61] or the panel may seek assistance of a competent international organization in selecting the most appropriate experts in the relevant fields. To take an example, in *Russia – Pigs* the panel chose individual experts from the list provided by the World Organization for Animal Health and the FAO.[62]

Save for cases where securing advice from panel-appointed experts is mandatory, the panel determines the need for consulting an expert based on seeking the parties' views regarding the matter. Hence the parties normally retain considerable control over the selection of experts as they may express their views on the profiles of experts relevant to the case,[63] and can object to scientists suggested by the other party,[64] and even to those recommended by an international organization.[65] They do so usually on the basis of conflict of interest. Perhaps unsurprisingly, parties on many occasions

---

[55] SPS Agreement, Article 11(2).
[56] Boisson de Chazournes, Mbengue, Das, and Gros, 'One size does not fit all – uses of experts before international courts and tribunals', 497, 502.
[57] *Japan – Measures Affecting Agricultural Products (Varietals)*, Report of the AB, WT/DS76/AB/R (22 February 2009), para. 129.
[58] Pauwelyn, 'Expert advice in WTO dispute settlement', p. 249.
[59] For the list of WTO agreements covered by the DSU see Appendix 1 of DSU.
[60] *US – Continued Suspension of Obligations*, Report of the Panel, WT/DS320/R (31 March 2008), para. 7.555.
[61] *Russia – Pigs*, Report of the Panel, WT/DS475/R (19 August 2016), para. 1.21.
[62] *Russia – Pigs*, Report of the Panel, para. 1.23.
[63] *Russia – Pigs*, Report of the Panel, para. 1.19.
[64] *Russia – Pigs*, Report of the Panel, para. 1.26.
[65] *US – Animals*, Report of the Panel, WT/DS447/R (24 July 2015), para. 1.16.

have discouraged panels from seeking independent experts' advice. Parties in *US – Animals*, and the EU[66] in *Russia – Pigs* suggested that 'they did not consider it necessary for the panel to consult with individual experts',[67] and the United States also contested the usefulness for the panel to consult with international organizations regarding the scientific aspects.[68] Yet, since WTO panels are not bound by the parties' views, in both above mentioned cases they had nevertheless recourse to expert advice from both individual experts and international organizations.

Whenever scientific expertise has been requested, WTO panels adopt their working procedures for the expert consultation on a case-by-case basis,[69] in which regard they enjoy a large measure of discretion in tailoring procedural rules to the circumstances of the particular case.[70] The expert consultation process normally comprises a written and an oral phase, and it begins with the selection of experts. The parties are invited to comment on the questionnaire submitted to the experts and to suggest further questions.[71] They are also asked to submit written observations to the replies of experts.[72] During the oral phase of taking expert evidence, the panel holds a joint meeting among the parties, their experts, and its own experts, which is usually held between the two rounds of substantive oral hearings, aiming to answer further questions of the panel.[73] Transcripts of joint meetings, along with the written responses of experts, are annexed to the panel's report. In highly technical cases, expert statements not infrequently amount to several hundreds of pages. To take the *EC – Biotech* case as an example, the written replies of experts alone amounted to 256 pages and taken together with the transcript of the meeting and the parties' observations as to the expert replies, the discussion of strict sense scientific factual issues totalled slightly more than 600 pages, excluding the extremely fact-intensive legal evaluation contained in the report itself.[74]

World Trade Organization panels also have the option to benefit from in-house expertise provided by the WTO Secretariat. While it is normally confined to furnishing panels with economist expertise,[75] special subject-matter experts may also be available regarding SPS cases.[76] Their function extends to reviewing the evidence received from the parties' experts or the panel's own experts.[77]

---

[66] *Russia – Pigs*, Report of the Panel, para. 1.18.
[67] *US – Animals*, Report of the Panel, para. 1.13.
[68] *US – Animals*, Report of the Panel, para. 1.13.
[69] *US – Animals*, Report of the Panel, para. 1.13.
[70] Foster, *Science and the Precautionary Principle in International Courts and Tribunals*, p. 114.
[71] *Australia – Apples*, Report of the Panel, WT/DS367/R (9 August 2010), para. 1.34.
[72] *US – Animals*, Report of the Panel, para. 1.21.
[73] Foster, *Science and the Precautionary Principle in International Courts and Tribunals*, pp. 115–17.
[74] See Annex H, I and J of the panel report in *EC – Biotech*.
[75] Valles, 'Different forms of expert involvement in WTO dispute settlement proceedings', 376–7.
[76] I. Van Damme, 'The assessment of expert evidence in international adjudication' (2018) 9 *Journal of International Dispute Settlement* 401–10 at 404.
[77] Van Damme, 'The assessment of expert evidence in international adjudication', 405.

3 *Novel Ways of Expert Consultation*

Lastly, some novel developments aiming to ensure transparency in expert consultation shall be mentioned. Procedural rules of the DSU only require confidentiality as to the panels' deliberations,[78] but are silent as to other phases of the procedure. As scientific issues implicated in cases concerning scientific risk assessments have begun to gain importance not only in the parties' eyes, but also to the wider international community, WTO panels are confronted with a need for opening up the procedure of scientific fact-finding to the public. For the first time in GATT/WTO history, the panel hearing the *Continued Suspension of Obligations* cases decided to open its hearings to the public through a closed-circuit broadcast.[79] This possibility extended only to sessions with the parties and to the joint meeting with experts as not all third parties had agreed to open their session to the public, which therefore remained confidential.[80]

A number of innovative and flexible techniques have been employed to facilitate interaction with and among experts, including the so-called hot-tubbing, expert teaming, pre-hearing conferences, and the preparation of joint expert reports. Yet an empirical survey among counsels suggests that this audience sees little value in these novel techniques.[81]

4 *Standards Issued by International Organizations*

The WTO's dispute settlement bodies often refer to standards of international organizations to support its position on scientific claims. They even have an express legal mandate to do so. Article 3.2 of the SPS Agreement creates a presumption of consistency with the agreement for measures that 'conform to' standards of certain international organizations.[82] This, however, is constructed as a rebuttable presumption.[83] Article 2.5 of the TBT Agreement also contains a rebuttable presumption of consistency with international trade for technical regulations that are in accordance with relevant international standards.

Besides giving rise to specific presumptions, international standards may also carry evidential value for WTO panels. One of the decisive reasons for which such standards are deemed legally relevant proof lies in their evidence-based nature. The panel in *US – Clove Cigarettes* relied on the WHO Framework Convention on

---

[78] See Article 14 DSU.

[79] *US – Continued Suspension of Obligations*, Report of the Panel, para. 7.43.

[80] *US – Continued Suspension of Obligations*, Report of the Panel, para. 7.40.

[81] Boisson de Chazournes, Mbengue, Das, and Gros, 'One size does not fit all – uses of experts before international courts and tribunals', 500.

[82] Annex 3 lists three such standard-setting international organizations: Codex Alimentarius Commission for food safety measures; World Organization for Animal Health (OIE), and International Plant Protection Convention.

[83] *EC – Hormones*, Report of the Panel, WT/DS26/R/USA (18 August 1997), para. 170.

Tobacco Control (FCTC) as persuasive evidence with an explicit reference to the fact that the convention has been based on 'the best available scientific evidence'.[84]

One may find a host of similar references to standards of expert international institutions in WTO case practice. As early as in 1990 in *Thailand – Cigarettes*, the GATT panel consulted with the WHO regarding the adverse health risks of cigarettes.[85] Later, in *EC – Asbestos*, the AB cited opinions of the WHO and other international bodies to the effect of acknowledging the carcinogenic risks associated with asbestos.[86] There is a continuing trend with respect to reliance on international scientific standards evidenced by for instance the more recent *US – Animals*, which featured consultation with the World Organization for Animal Health.[87]

As a general rule, the more complex the factual background of a case is the more diverse sources of expertise are garnered by WTO panels. For instance, in *Continued Suspension of Obligations* alongside six individual experts, the panel asked for written advice from the Codex Alimentarius Commission, the Joint FAO/WHO Expert Committee on Food Additives, and the International Agency for Research on Cancer.[88]

III CHANGING CANONS OF DEFERENCE: STANDARD OF REVIEW OF SCIENTIFIC CLAIMS

The preceding sections have dealt with the various ways in which WTO panels request and make use of scientific evidence. Another major issue in the scientific engagement of WTO panellists is the degree of deference they afford to states in reviewing their scientific claims.

There is no specific statutory standard of review mandated for the scrutiny of health or environmental regulations of WTO members.[89] There is only one specific standard enshrined in Article 17.6 of the Agreement of Anti-Dumping. Apart from that, the general standard of review under Article 11 of the DSU applies, requiring an 'objective assessment of the facts'. This simple-sounding task generated highly complex and oscillating interpretations as to the content of this mandate.

The forthcoming analysis is structured into five main parts. The first concerns the theoretical underpinnings of policy dilemmas concerning setting various standards of review (Subsection 1). The second focuses on the evolving standards of review applicable to members' scientific determinations under the SPS Agreement, which attracted the most in-depth scientific considerations by adjudicators. Ever since the first impression decision concerning the SPS Agreement issued in *EC – Hormones*,

[84] *US – Clove Cigarettes*, Report of the Panel, WT/DS406/R (2 September 2011), para 7.230.
[85] *Thailand – Cigarettes*, Report of the Panel, para. 27.
[86] *EC – Asbestos*, Report of the AB, para. 162.
[87] *US – Animals*, Report of the Panel, para. 1.11.
[88] *US – Continued Suspension of Obligations*, Report of the Panel, para. 1.7.
[89] P. C. Mavroidis, 'The gang that couldn't shoot straight: the not so magnificent seven of the WTO appellate body' (2017) 27 *European Journal of International Law* 1107–18 at 1108.

the AB has been consistent in reiterating that the appropriate standard of review is 'neither de novo review, nor "total deference", but rather the "objective assessment of facts"'.[90] A case-by-case review shall further elucidate the exact requirements flowing from this objective assessment obligation. As will be seen below, the application of the standard, and indeed the standard itself, has undergone significant evolution over time. The mandated review has started off as bordering a *de novo* review (Subsection 2) and later on has become more deferential (Subsection 3). A much-debated aspect of the WTO jurisprudence is whether panels are deferential enough towards members' science-based claims. Subsection 4 thus evaluates the changing canons of deference from this perspective. Finally, Subsection 5 discusses the different reasoning methods with which panels have striven for crafting persuasive justifications for their legal determinations heavily affected by scientific evidence.

1 *Policy Dilemmas in Setting the Standard of Review*

The question whether WTO panellists' task involves deciding about scientific controversies was settled relatively early compared to other international fora. In 2000 a WTO panel ruled in *EC – Asbestos* that 'it is not the function of the panel to settle a scientific debate'.[91] Having said that, the scope of possible adjudicatory intervention may still vary to a great extent, as is duly reflected in the different standards of review under SPS case practice. A more deferential review would entail less intrusion to the scientific bases of measures, while less deference necessitates more in-depth engagement with science – both in terms of the evidentiary assessment and the adjudicatory reasoning.

A fundamental tension in the WTO jurisprudence stems from the need to reconcile two opposing interests: respect for members' sovereign regulatory powers on the one hand, and the prevention of disguised protectionism, on the other hand. While the former calls for a deferential approach towards members' scientific risk assessments, the latter necessitates meaningful scrutiny of scientific claims. The applicable standard of review used by panels and the AB is, thus, determined by the sum of these opposing forces. These tensions pose a fundamental challenge for setting scientific evidentiary criteria, inasmuch as WTO panels must choose between either 'eviscerat[ing]' those criteria by deferring to scientific assessments of members, or affording them a 'real bite'[92] at the expense of domestic authorities' capacity to regulate risks as they deem fit. These policy considerations lay behind the varying degrees of deference WTO panels afford governments in making scientific claims.

---

90 *EC – Hormones*, Report of the AB, para. 117.
91 *EC – Asbestos*, Report of the Panel, WT/DS135/R (18 September 2000), para. 8.181
92 Sykes, 'Domestic regulation, sovereignty and scientific evidence requirements: a pessimistic view', p. 258.

Discretion and the corresponding standard of review may be defined in three different contexts within WTO jurisprudence.[93] First, dispute settlement bodies apply a certain standard for reviewing factual determinations of members in scientific matters. In this context, the possible intensity of the review ranges between *de novo* scrutiny and total deference.[94] Second, the extent of discretion is also applicable to the relationship between panels and the AB, which both have latitude in their legal interpretation as not being bound by the parties' legal determinations.

Third, panels enjoy a wide discretion in their evidentiary assessments, given that the AB's review is rather limited in this respect.[95] This latter discretion finds its roots in Article 11 of the DSU, which mandates that panels shall make an 'objective assessment of the facts'. Apart from that the AB allows a large room for manoeuvre for panels in their fact-finding. This means that only egregious 'disregard', 'distortion', or 'misinterpretation'[96] of the evidence would amount to a 'bad faith'[97] evaluation – marking that the panel exceeded the limits of its discretion. Importantly, in the practice of the AB, mistakes on part of the panels in the accuracy of interpreting expert evidence do not constitute 'deliberate disregard of evidence'.[98]

What counts as objective assessment of the facts, however, proved to be susceptible to remarkably divergent interpretations in the practice of WTO panels. Moreover, the AB has substantially changed the requirements flowing from this mandate, turning an almost *de novo* review into a more deferential standard. The evolving scrutiny of the panels, together with the changing requirements of the AB, will be addressed in the sections that follow.

2 *Bordering* De Novo *Review in Early SPS Cases: From* Hormones *to the Panel Report in* Continued Suspension of Obligations

As discussed above, the critical requirement for introducing valid SPS measures is the existence of a rational relationship between the risk assessment and the respective measure. It follows that the legality of an SPS measure will ultimately hinge on the extent of scrutiny with which panels review the rationality of its linkage with the risk assessment. The key question concerns whether the panel may revisit the underlying scientific evidence and formulate its own appreciation of relevant scientific determinations, or instead, it is precluded from substituting its own assessment for members' scientific conclusions.

---

[93] Gruszczynski, 'Standard of review of health and environmental regulations by WTO panels', pp. 734–5.
[94] For more details see Chapter 2.
[95] *EC – Asbestos*, Report of the AB, para. 161.
[96] *EC – Hormones*, Report of the AB, para. 133.
[97] *EC – Hormones*, Report of the AB, para. 138.
[98] *EC – Hormones*, Report of the AB, paras. 138–9.

In its initial decisions, the AB answered this question by allowing panels to 'put risk assessments under a microscope'[99] and to evaluate them quite closely. This question arose for the first time in the *EC – Hormones* case, where the contested measure was an import ban instituted by the European Communities (EC) on meat and meat products derived from cattle to which certain natural hormones were administered for growth promoter purposes. The EC took action with reference to an alleged risk of conferring carcinogenic effects on consumers of hormone-treated beef meat.

In the material case, the panel and the AB both found that the scientific research cited by the EC was too general, and therefore the measure was inconsistent with the SPS Agreement.[100] The AB itself acknowledged that risk assessment decisions could have a rational relationship with divergent (even minority) scholarly opinions that are at odds with mainstream scientific opinions prevailing at the time,[101] and, thus, such a measure could, in principle, be in conformity with the SPS Agreement. It, however, ruled that the facts of the material case did not fulfil this theoretical possibility.

The scientific reports relied on by the EC all concluded that the consumption of meat to which growth hormones were administered was safe, albeit studies indeed 'show[ed] the existence of a general risk of cancer'[102] in the case of using large doses of growth hormones. Importantly, these studies did not specifically address the risks imposed by hormone residues found in meet to which hormones had been administered.[103] The AB stressed that a measure banning the use of certain hormones used as growth promoters would not have a requisite 'rational relationship'[104] with scientific opinions describing carcinogenic risks of growth promoters, if the latter were not 'sufficiently specific to the case at hand'.[105] The fundamental problem with the EC's reports might be that they identified carcinogenic risks only with respect to cases involving much higher dosages of hormones than what were likely to be present in the meat as residues.[106]

As to the standard of review, the panel and the AB did not accept the deferential reasonableness standard set forth by the EC.[107] Instead, the AB approved the panel's approach to 'examine the scientific conclusions implicit in the SPS measure . . . and the scientific conclusions yielded by a risk assessment'.[108] This language implies that the AB encouraged panels to conduct in-depth scientific assessments. In the material

99   Howse, 'The World Trade Organization 20 years on: global governance by judiciary', 59.
100   *EC – Hormones*, Report of the AB, paras. 199–200.
101   *EC – Hormones*, Report of the AB, para. 194.
102   *EC – Hormones*, Report of the AB, para. 200.
103   *EC – Hormones*, Report of the AB, paras. 199–200.
104   *EC – Hormones*, Report of the AB, para. 192.
105   *EC – Hormones*, Report of the AB, para. 200.
106   Peel, *Science and Risk Regulation in International Law*, p. 206.
107   *EC – Hormones*, Report of the AB, para. 15.
108   *EC – Hormones*, Report of the AB, para. 193.

case, the scrutiny of scientific evidence allowed the panel to develop the specificity requirement, which proved to be a device for conducting an intrusive review based on which SPS measures can be invalidated.

It is also true, however, that the language of the AB made some significant gestures towards sovereign regulatory power.[109] For instance, it indisputably allowed taking minority scientific views into account, and acknowledged that apart from risks that can be measured by laboratory experiments, there are 'real world' risks, generated by the practice of administering the hormones, which also had to be considered by prudent governments.[110] This, however, can well be read as the AB simply 'tipped its hat'[111] towards WTO members' sovereignty. Judging by the outcome of the case, where the EC measure was found to be inconsistent with the SPS Agreement, it is argued here that the lasting legacy of the *Hormones* decision lies in paving the way for setting an intrusive standard of review towards scientific claims.

In the same year, the decision in the *Australia – Salmon* case followed. Australia instituted a ban on importing ocean-caught Pacific salmon with reference to the risk of introducing new diseases into the domestic fish population. In face of the Canadian challenge, Australia sought to defend its import ban by claiming 'due deference' for its findings in matters of fact.[112] The AB again rejected to automatically accept factual allegations of members,[113] and emphasized that panels 'are not required to accord to factual evidence of the parties the meaning and weight as do the parties'.[114] This again confirmed the rather intrusive approach of the AB towards scientific determinations of members.

A similar approach is reflected in the *Japan – Apples* decision, where a Japanese prohibition on importation of apples from the United States was subject to review. Japan introduced this ban as an SPS measure to counter the risks of transmitting the fire blight disease, which was absent from its territories but was present in the United States. Having reviewed the scientific evidence, the panel concluded that it suggested 'a negligible risk of possible transmission through apple fruit',[115] and ruled that the importation ban was 'clearly disproportionate'[116] to that risk, and therefore lacked a rational relationship with the evidence. In its appeal, Japan argued for granting 'a certain degree of discretion' towards the ways in which it weighed and evaluated scientific evidence.[117] Yet again, the AB rejected to deviate from the

---

[109]   Gruszczynski, 'Standard of review of health and environmental regulations by WTO panels', pp. 740–1.
[110]   *EC – Hormones*, Report of the AB, para. 187.
[111]   Sykes, 'Domestic regulation, sovereignty and scientific evidence requirements: a pessimistic view', p. 262.
[112]   *Australia – Salmon*, Report of the AB, para. 267.
[113]   *Australia – Salmon*, Report of the AB, para. 267.
[114]   *Australia – Salmon*, Report of the AB, para. 267.
[115]   Cited by the AB Report, *Japan – Apples*, Report of the AB, WT/DS245/B/R (26 November 2003), para. 146.
[116]   Cited by the AB Report, *Japan – Apples*, Report of the AB, para. 147.
[117]   *Japan – Apples*, Report of the AB, para. 150.

objective assessment requirement it has been advocating for ever since the *Hormones* dispute.[118]

In the *EC – Biotech* dispute, the United States and Canada challenged two pieces of EC secondary legislation[119] regarding the approval procedures for deliberate release of biotech products into the environment and concerning novel food ingredients. The complainants also challenged some EC member states' safeguard measures that were adopted on the basis of the contested EC secondary legislation prohibiting the import of biotech products. According to the submission, these were measures incompatible with the SPS Agreement.

The more than 2,400-page long panel report[120] deals with extremely science-intensive questions, where the panel had to evaluate among others, the (in)sufficiency of the available scientific information regarding the adverse risks of GMO products. This was necessary to assess whether EC member states could legitimately adopt their safeguard measures under Article 5.7 of the SPS Agreement. The panel consulted six individual experts who, unsurprisingly, did not arrive at a consensus on all respective scientific questions,[121] leaving the panellists with competing scientific narratives. Occasionally, the panels formed an opinion against what seemed to be a majority view among the experts. For instance, to the question whether the evidence was sufficient for France to carry out a risk assessment concerning seed production of a GMO oilseed rape, all three experts seemed to agree that between 1998 and 2002, there was no sufficient information available.[122] This position was strengthened by the report of the French Biomolecular Engineering Committee as well.[123] Still, the panel firmly concluded that it agreed with the position of the complainants that 'the body of available scientific evidence permitted the performance of a risk assessment'[124] for France without providing any detailed evidentiary explanations.[125]

As a sequel to the *EC – Hormones* dispute, the United States and Canada imposed duties on imports from EC member states. The EC brought a WTO complaint challenging the continued suspension of concessions, resulting in a case commonly referred to as the *Continued Suspension of Obligations* dispute. The dispute had another prong in which the United States and Canada claimed the inconsistency of the EC's revised SPS measure. The EC adopted these measures upon funding several

---

[118] *Japan – Apples*, Report of the AB, para. 165.

[119] EC Directive 2001/18 governing the 'deliberate release into the environment of genetically modified organisms' and EC Regulation 258/96 regulating novel foods and food ingredients.

[120] Including all the addenda.

[121] Gruszczynski, *Regulating Health and Environmental Risks under WTO Law: A Critical Analysis of the SPS Agreement*, pp. 195–6.

[122] See the written answers of experts (Dr Snow, Dr Squire, and Dr Andow) *EC – Biotech*, Report of the Panel, Addendum no. 7 (Annex I), WT/DS293/R/Add.7. (29 September 2006), paras. 99–101.

[123] See the written answers of experts (Dr Snow, Dr Squire, and Dr Andow) *EC – Biotech*, Report of the Panel, Addendum no. 7, para. 104.

[124] *EC – Biotech*, Report of the Panel, para. 7.3300.

[125] Gruszczynski, 'Standard of review of health and environmental regulations by WTO panels', p. 742.

research projects and seeking seventeen scientific opinions.[126] The new EC directive equally excluded US and Canadian hormone-treated meat products from the EC market on a provisional basis, claiming that the available pertinent scientific information was insufficient to conduct a risk assessment.

In terms of intrusiveness of the adjudicatory scrutiny, the high-water mark was undoubtedly the panel's decision in *US – Continued Suspension of Obligations*, where the panel explicitly acknowledged that it would effectively substitute its own view for the EC's risk assessment:

> While, on some occasions, we followed the majority of experts expressing concurrent views, in some others the divergence of views were such that we could not follow that approach and decided to accept the position(s) which appeared, *in our view, to be the most specific in relation to the question at issue and to be best supported by arguments and evidence.*[127]

Even though the panel repeated the mantra according to which it is not well-suited to conduct a *de novo* review, what it did came, in fact, very close to a *de novo* appraisal of the risks. The main scientific question of the case lay in whether there was sufficient scientific evidence proving the genotoxic potential of oestradiol, one of the hormones used as feed additives, in concentrations that were designed for use as growth promoters. The EC submitted evidence demonstrating that the hormone did have carcinogenic effects, but these results related to much higher concentrations.[128] However, if administered properly, the hormone would be present in the meat fit for human consumption only as residues, and with respect to such concentrations, the EC could not provide evidence as to carcinogenic effects.[129] On a more pragmatic level, the EC argued with 'real life' risks stemming from the possibility that farmers might use the growth hormone in excess amounts.[130]

The panel defined its task as assessing whether 'the scientific evidence supports the conclusions' of the EC expert body's risk assessment.[131] The experts gave divergent views as to the oestradiol's *in vivo* genotoxic potential when administered in small concentrations. The panel provided a survey of expert advice to find out whether 'the majority of the experts ... agreed with the conclusion' of the EC's risk assessment.[132] Panellists seemingly remained perplexed by the conflicting opinions received and arrived at a rather contradicting conclusion, namely, that 'the link, if any, between cancer and consumption of hormone-treated meat [could not], at

---

[126] Peel, *Science and Risk Regulation in International Law*, p. 191.

[127] *US – Continued Suspension of Obligations*, Report of the Panel, para. 7.420, emphasis added.

[128] *US – Continued Suspension of Obligations*, Report of the Panel, para. 7.543.

[129] *US – Continued Suspension of Obligations*, Report of the Panel, para. 7.541–45.

[130] *US – Continued Suspension of Obligations*, Report of the Panel, para. 7.546.

[131] *US – Continued Suspension of Obligations*, Report of the Panel, para. 7.552.

[132] For the AB's assessment on the panel's inquiry see *US – Continued Suspension of Obligations*, Report of the AB, para. 598.

present, be confirmed *nor refuted*', but nevertheless concluded that 'the science [did] not support the conclusions in the [EC] Opinions'.[133]

The logic behind the panel's finding is quite problematic if one considers that the panel itself acknowledged that scientific evidence was too ambiguous and incomplete to support a finding of the absence of health risks. Still the panel effectively imposed the burden of ambiguity on importing states. This choice not only appears to be arbitrary, but it also goes against the ordinary burden of proof under the SPS Agreement, where by default, the complaining party shall prove the incompatibility of an SPS measure.[134] By finding that the evidence did not support the conclusions reached in the risk assessment (i.e. the existence of an increased risk of cancer), the panel ruled that measures of the EC were inconsistent with Article 5.1 of the SPS Agreement for it failed to prepare an adequate risk assessment.[135]

The above review of the case practice served to demonstrate that despite that the AB has constantly stressed that the appropriate standard was neither *de novo* nor total deference, one cannot escape but notice that the scrutiny of WTO panels and the AB effectively came close to a *de novo* review in the initial line of decisions.

3 *Turning Towards a More Deferential and Nuanced Approach: A Two-Stage Standard of Review*

3.1 A Deferential Turn in the Mandated Scrutiny

The mandated standard of review was changed by the AB when the EC filed an appeal against the panel report in *Continued Suspension of Obligations* exactly for challenging the *de novo* standard of review. Borrowing the words of the appellant's submission, the panel 'decided to become the jury on the correct science ... by picking and choosing between conflicting and contradictory opinions of the experts in an arbitrary manner'.[136] The EC also emphasized that there was 'reputable support within the relevant scientific community'[137] for its position in the face of 'genuine and legitimate scientific controversy'.[138] In this vein, it submitted that the appropriate standard of review had to assess whether there was 'reasonable scientific basis for the SPS measure'.[139]

---

[133] *US – Continued Suspension of Obligations*, Report of the Panel, para. 7.570, emphasis added.
[134] Pauwelyn, 'Expert advice in WTO dispute settlement', p. 255.
[135] *US – Continued Suspension of Obligations*, Report of the Panel, para. 7.573.
[136] EC appellant's submission, cited by the AB in *US – Continued Suspension of Obligations*, Report of the AB, para. 585.
[137] EC appellant's submission, cited by the AB in *US – Continued Suspension of Obligations*, Report of the AB, para. 585.
[138] EC appellant's submission, cited by the AB in *US – Continued Suspension of Obligations*, Report of the AB, para. 585.
[139] EC appellant's submission, cited by the AB in *US – Continued Suspension of Obligations*, Report of the AB, para. 587.

Considering the apparent contradiction in the panel's reasoning addressed above, it is not very surprising that the AB on appeal declared the panel's fact-finding erroneous for not conducting an objective assessment of the facts,[140] and it also reversed the allocation of the burden of proof.[141] What is unprecedented, however, is the fact that the AB also substantially modified the applicable standard in SPS cases turning towards a more deferential standard of review. The AB though reiterated its first SPS decision where it declined to accept the deferential 'reasonableness' standard as then put forward by the EC,[142] this time it proved to be more open to relax the standard of review and to slightly approximate the scrutiny that the EC advocated for.

The position of the AB is worthy of being reconstructed in full here, given that it has become the new rule governing standard of review:

> Where a panel goes beyond this limited mandate and acts as a risk assessor it would be substituting its own scientific judgment for that of the risk assessor and making a de novo review and, consequently, would exceed its functions under Article 11 of DSU. Therefore, the review power of a panel is not to determine whether the risk assessment undertaken by a WTO Member is correct, but rather to determine whether that risk assessment is supported by coherent reasoning and respectable scientific evidence and is, in this sense, objectively justifiable.[143]

The AB also provided some benchmarks for assessing whether a certain scientific position came from a 'respected and qualified' source. It reiterated that the 'correct-ness of the views need not have been accepted by the broader scientific community' but the given scientific position 'must nevertheless have the necessary scientific and methodological rigor to be considered reputable science', and it must be considered 'legitimate science according to the standards of the relevant scientific community'.[144]

As is clear from the above, the AB first read the 'objective assessment of the facts' requirement of Article 11 of the DSU as mandating a 'rational relationship' between the evidence and the SPS measure, where science supported the conclusions of the risk assessment. Whereas subsequently, the AB modified its interpretation and emphasized instead that the legally decisive aspect was whether the risk assessor provided a 'coherent reasoning' based on 'respectable scientific evidence'. To put it simply, under this revised scrutiny, in order for an SPS measure to be consistent with the agreement, the underlying risk assessment need not be *supported* by science (and therefore qualifies as 'the' single scientifically correct answer), it is enough if it is *objectively justifiable* in light of scientific evidence (and therefore constitutes 'a' legitimate answer to the scientific controversy).

---

[140]   *US – Continued Suspension of Obligations*, Report of the AB, para. 537.
[141]   *US – Continued Suspension of Obligations*, Report of the AB, para. 580.
[142]   *US – Continued Suspension of Obligations*, Report of the AB, para. 587.
[143]   *US – Continued Suspension of Obligations*, Report of the AB, para. 590.
[144]   *US – Continued Suspension of Obligations*, Report of the AB, para. 591.

It may seem that these changing descriptions of the standard are merely a play with words. Yet the differently couched standards are consequential as they would entail markedly different outcomes in an SPS dispute. If a panel adhered to the rather intrusive standard of review the AB had set in its initial decisions, it would find an SPS measure inconsistent where scientific facts cannot *clearly* support the conclusions reached in the importing state's risk assessment. In contrast to that, should a panel take a more deferential approach, it would only investigate whether the particular conclusion reached can be seen as justifiable in light of the evidence. Importantly, several competing and even contradicting scientific conclusions may seem to be justifiable at the same time, especially, in the case of 'hard cases' involving persistent scientific uncertainties in the respective science.

In the material dispute, the AB emphasized that the panel should have determined whether scientific evidence came from a respected and qualified source and should have assessed whether the reasoning of the EC was 'objective and coherent so that the conclusions reached in the risk assessment sufficiently warrant the SPS measure'.[145] This language conforms to the more deferential approach described above. The AB itself was not able to complete the analysis regarding the compatibility of EC measures with the SPS Agreement, because of the numerous flaws in the panel's factual findings.[146] Hence, the more deferential turn in the AB's approach resulted in reversing the panel's finding of inconsistency.

In sum, under the contemporary stance of SPS law, panels are required not to discuss the expert evidence on a general level to discern scientific opinions that are unanimously supported. Instead, they ought to discuss the concrete evidence relied upon by the importing member and interrogate whether the particular piece of evidence came from a respected and qualified source.[147] With this radical shift in its approach to the applicable standard of review, the AB now mandates a two-fold requirement. As stressed already in *Continued Suspension of Obligations*, risk assessments (i) ought to be supported by coherent reasoning on the one hand, and (ii) should be justifiable in light of respectable scientific evidence, on the other hand.

This test has been further developed in later decisions of the AB, most eminently in the *Australia – Apples* dispute.[148] The case concerned a ban instituted by Australia on apples imported from New Zealand with reference to the risk of the spread of three pests. The AB not only reiterated its deferential standard introduced in *Continued Suspension of Obligations*, but at the same time it appeared to reclaim power to conduct intrusive reviews with regard to the less science-intensive part of risk assessments, that is, the reasoning provided by the risk assessors. Such a nuanced

[145] *US – Continued Suspension of Obligations*, Report of the AB, para. 598.
[146] *US – Continued Suspension of Obligations*, Report of the AB, para. 620.
[147] *US – Continued Suspension of Obligations*, Report of the AB, para. 603.
[148] For more details on the decision see Gruszczynski, 'How deep should we go? searching for an appropriate standard of review in the SPS cases'.

approach seems to strike a fair balance between affording deference to members' scientific determinations, while also maintaining the panels' possibility to meaningfully scrutinize risk assessment measures.

In the material case, the intrusive review into the coherency of the reasoning entailed that the panel could not only review the *final conclusion* of the risk assessment, but could also assess whether *intermediate conclusions* 'found sufficient support in the evidence'.[149] The panel dismissed Australia's submission, which advocated for a more relaxed standard. Australia would have preferred a standard of review only scrutinizing the intermediate conclusions as to whether they were within a range of what could be considered legitimate science.[150] The panel introduced some important transparency requirements, too, which were confirmed by the AB. According to this, a panel is entitled to scrutinize whether the 'use of expert judgment' has been 'sufficiently document[ed]' in the risk assessment procedure.[151] Most importantly, a risk assessment is also expected to 'explain how it arrived at the expert judgments it made at intermediate steps'.[152]

More recent WTO jurisprudence confirms that panels adhere to the facially limited mandate the AB announced in *Continued Suspension of Obligations*. In 2015, the *US – Animals* panel reiterated the confines of its mandate, which are worthy of being reproduced in full here:

> we bear in mind that the Panel's role is not to conduct its own risk assessment based on scientific evidence gathered by the Panel or submitted by the parties during the Panel proceedings. Similarly, the Panel will not impose its own scientific opinion on the United States. Our task is not to substitute our judgment for that of the United States or determine whether the science relied upon was actually 'correct'. Instead, our task … is to determine the following: (i) whether there is a risk assessment; (ii) if that risk assessment is 'appropriate to the circumstances'; (iii) whether the science supports the conclusions in the risk assessment; (iv) whether the importing Member's measures are based on that risk assessment.[153]

The deferential scrutiny applicable to SPS measures was also upheld in *Russia – Pigs*, in which the AB issued its report in 2017 concerning Russia's ban on importing pork products. Russia banned import of pork from EU member states with reference to risks of spreading African swine fever. The dispute revolved around interpreting Article 6.3 of the SPS Agreement, which requires exporting members to provide necessary evidence to importing states in order to demonstrate their territories being disease-free areas. On appeal, Russia claimed that the panel had to consider the importing member's 'assessment and findings of the quality and credibility of the scientific and technical evidence relied upon by the importing

---

[149] *Australia – Apples*, Report of the AB, WT/DS367/AB/R (29 November 2010), para. 230.
[150] *Australia – Apples*, Report of the AB, paras. 230–1.
[151] *Australia – Apples*, Report of the AB, para. 248.
[152] *Australia – Apples*, Report of the AB, para. 248.
[153] *US – Animals*, Report of the Panel, para. 7.321.

Member'.[154] The AB rejected such an explicit plea for a more intensive scientific scrutiny by the panel. It stressed that a WTO panel is not 'called upon to determine *for itself*, based on the evidence provided by the exporting Member, whether the relevant areas are, and are likely to remain, pest-free',[155] given that 'a panel's review under Article 6.3 is limited to assessing whether the evidence provided by the exporting Member … is of a nature, quantity and quality sufficient to enable the importing Member's authorities ultimately to make a determination as to the pest or disease status of the areas'.[156] The AB hence emphasized that the evaluation of the evidence is a task reserved for importing states.

To sum up, the AB in more recent disputes has consistently applied the two-prong test of the standard of review, which includes checking the evidentiary bases of SPS measures, and scrutinizing the consistency of risk assessors' reasoning. This approach has been applied also in the context of the TBT Agreement by the panel in the *Australia – Tobacco Plain Packaging* case.[157]

3.2 Two-Stage Standard of Review: Combining Deference with Intrusive Scrutiny

The revised applicable standard of review in SPS cases ensures a deferential adjudicatory attitude towards the evidentiary basis of SPS measures, while it also preserves room for intrusive scrutiny as to the reasoning provided by WTO members. Through this two-stage analysis, the AB aims to analytically dissect the process of a scientific risk assessment in which law and science are closely interlocked. In so doing, the AB seeks to avoid getting entangled in futile efforts to investigate the scientific correctness of an SPS measure in assessing whether the measure was 'supported' by or 'based on' scientific evidence. The reasoning is more amenable to judicial scrutiny, since in the AB's words 'it is through the reasoning of the risk assessor that it should be possible to understand whether the risk assessment is based on the scientific evidence and whether in turn the proposed measures are based on the scientific evidence and on the risk assessment'.[158]

Moreover, due to this new standard of review, panels need not focus only on whether intermediate conclusions are 'legitimate according to the standards of the scientific community'.[159] Instead, panellists can move away from applying strictly speaking scientific justifications, and can expand their inquiry into analysing the coherence and objectivity of the reasoning. This will have important ramification as to the epistemic rationality on the basis of which the AB justifies its findings. These implications will be addressed later in Subsection 5.

---

[154] *Russia – Pigs*, Report of the AB, WT/DS475/AB/R (23 February 2017), para. 5.67.
[155] *Russia – Pigs*, Report of the AB, para. 5.72.
[156] *Russia – Pigs*, Report of the AB, para. 5.87.
[157] *Australia – Tobacco Plain Packaging*, Report of the Panel, para. 7.516.
[158] *Australia – Apples*, Report of the AB, para. 227.
[159] *Australia – Apples*, Report of the AB, para. 231.

Despite these important epistemic differences, a closer examination suggests that in terms of its practical consequences, this new test much resembles the old intrusive review mandated to panels prior to the AB report in *Continued Suspension of Obligations*. At the end of the day, the AB made clear in *Australia – Apples* that a risk assessment reasoning will not be seen as coherent and objective if it 'did not rely on adequate scientific evidence'.[160] It is argued here that this interpretation re-opens the door for panels to scrutinize the evidentiary bases of risk assessments, which was their main concern in the initial SPS cases under the formerly applicable intrusive review.

In sum, the newly mandated scrutiny of the risk assessor's reasoning seems to enable adjudicators to closely engage with scientific evidence underlying risk assessments and it creates opportunities for panels to 'make [their] own evaluation and enquiry into the substance of evidence'.[161] Doing so arguably comes close once more to an intrusive,[162] if not a *de novo*, review.[163]

4 Appraisal of the Changing Standards of Review

The SPS Agreement may very well showcase the most technical and science-intensive legal mandate among WTO provisions, hence it is no wonder adjudicators of SPS disputes could not escape the perplexing task of scrutinizing scientific justifications provided by importing states. The AB's oscillating practice in applying varying levels of scrutiny triggers queries as to the existence of any consistent underlying rationale guiding adjudicatory review. Some commentators claim that the AB is more deferential to members where matters of public health are at stake,[164] in contrast to measures protecting plant health, where the standard tends to be more intrusive.[165] Such a differential application of scrutiny may be justified with a view to the drastic consequences of erroneously outlawing national health policies.[166] Yet inconsistent practice in this respect gives the impression that WTO dispute settlement bodies base their decision on a 'smell test',[167] that is on a rough assessment, if not gut feeling, as to whether the respective WTO member

[160] *Australia – Apples*, Report of the AB, para. 254.
[161] Gruszczynski, 'How deep should we go? searching for an appropriate standard of review in the SPS cases', 114.
[162] Reid, 'Risk assessment, science and deliberation: managing regulatory diversity under the SPS agreement', 540.
[163] Gruszczynski, 'How deep should we go? searching for an appropriate standard of review in the SPS cases', 114.
[164] Gruszczynski, 'Standard of review and scientific evidence in WTO law and international investment arbitration', p. 172; Mavroidis, 'The gang that couldn't shoot straight: the not so magnificent seven of the WTO appellate body', 1116–17.
[165] Gruszczynski, 'Standard of review of health and environmental regulations by WTO panels', p. 757.
[166] Mavroidis, 'The gang that couldn't shoot straight: the not so magnificent seven of the WTO appellate body', 1117.
[167] Palmeter, 'The WTO standard of review in health and safety disputes', p. 234.

has behaved correctly or incorrectly, in which realities of risks and actual scientific evidence play little role.

Scholarly opinions differ in terms of the preferred standard of review. One commentator argues that domestic measures should deserve less deference if they were 'taken behind closed doors',[168] as opposed to decisions where foreign and public interests were adequately considered. Whereas others call for a wholesale deferential approach by the WTO,[169] or quite the opposite, warn against a too-lenient standard.[170] The two-stage standard of review allowing for an intrusive review of the consistency of the risk assessor's reasoning also triggered criticism.[171]

The preceding analysis has sought to argue that the two-stage standard of review, which provides room for both deference towards and scrutiny of science-based claims appears to strike a necessary, and appropriate, compromise. The explicitly intrusive standard has led panels to get entangled in strained speculations in an effort to garner sufficient scientific evidence in support of one of the competing scientific narratives. This is illustrated by the panel's report in *Continued Suspension of Obligations*, where it ended up deciding about the correctness of the parties' scientific claims. Such an approach is also deficient from an epistemic legitimacy point of view, to which point we shall return later. At the same time, shifting to an entirely deferential standard would be equally problematic given that panels have a 'duty to engage with [the] evidence',[172] which would be rendered devoid of meaning if members had unlimited discretion in offering scientific explanations for their measures.

In levelling this analysis, it remains to be pointed out that the main difference between the varying degrees of scrutiny WTO dispute settlement bodies have adopted lies in their methods of reasoning. As will be argued in the coming section, the applicable standard of review determines the epistemic character of the adjudicatory reasoning and, thus, the ways in which panels can craft convincing justifications for their stance adopted vis-à-vis scientific evidence. Simply put, a *de novo* standard of review entails a reasoning that is based on scientific rationality. Whereas the two-stage review invokes a peculiar amalgam of scientific and legal rationality when takes its focus on the coherence of the reasoning provided by the primary risk assessor. These two types of standard of review embody entirely

---

[168] Ioannidis, 'Beyond the standard of review: deference criteria in WTO law and the case for a procedural approach', p. 96.
[169] Fukunaga, 'Standard of review and "scientific truths" in the WTO dispute settlement system and investment arbitration', 576.
[170] Foster, 'International adjudication – standards of review and burden of proof: *Australia–Apples* and *Whaling in the Antarctic*', 83.
[171] Reid, 'Risk assessment, science and deliberation: managing regulatory diversity under the SPS Agreement', 539–40; Gruszczynski, 'Standard of review of health and environmental regulations by WTO panels', p. 755.
[172] *US – Continued Suspension of Obligations*, Report of the AB, para. 553.

different approaches towards scientific knowledge in a legal dispute. While one of them avowedly reasons *only with science* as reflected in the expert input, the other form of the judicial review preserves some room for the autonomous evaluation of legally trained adjudicators.

This brings us to Subsection 5, which expands on how different epistemic rationalities appear in the assessments of WTO dispute settlement bodies.

5 *Reasoning Techniques: With or Without Scientific Rationality*

The closeness of scientific facts and legal concepts is invariably present in WTO law as well. We have seen above how express provisions of WTO law compel panels to evaluate and reflect on ample and often contradicting scientific evidence in accepting or rejecting the parties' claims. The AB has most succinctly pointed out this interlinkage, if not dialectic relationship, between the factual and legal assessment: '[d]etermination of the credibility and weight properly to be ascribed to ... a given piece of evidence is part and parcel of the fact finding process ... The consistency or inconsistency of a given fact ... with the requirements of a given treaty provision is, however, a *legal characterization* issue.'[173]

This simple sounding task engenders a number of intricate questions on a closer analysis. First and foremost, how, that is on what epistemic bases, could WTO adjudicators justify their legal conclusions drawn with respect to science-based factual issues? What is the proper role of scientific rationality in making such a legal characterization? Should adjudicators be confined to assess the same attributes of scientific knowledge as the experts? If so, can they appropriately do so from an epistemic point of view? If not, where are the boundaries of their argumentative space, what qualities of science-based positions should they scrutinize?

It will be argued here that WTO adjudicators gave divergent responses to the above queries. They have either referred to scientific standards, and thus, appealed to the epistemic authority of science, or they have developed non-scientific criteria to justify their inferences and legal determinations about the scientific aspects of disputes. This has given rise to different adjudicatory reasoning styles in WTO jurisprudence, which will be examined and classified in the coming sections. It will be shown that certain adjudicatory justification methods directly draw on the cognitive authority of science (Subsection 5.1), while other reasoning techniques either rely on legalistic logic (Subsection 5.2) or intuitive rationality (Subsection 5.3). Finally, more complex benchmarks, dubbed as 'hybrid' standards, will also be identified among reasoning styles of WTO dispute settlement bodies (Subsection 5.4).

---

[173] *EC – Hormones*, Report of the AB, para. 132, emphasis added.

5.1 Reasoning with Scientific Knowledge: Epistemic Deference to Science

Certain reasoning techniques directly appeal to scientific authority to justify adjudicatory findings. In such decisions, choices among competing claims are directly justified by *scientific* references.[174] The WTO AB has been praised for such an epistemically deferential approach to science, when it relies on scientific standards in scrutinizing expert opinions underlying SPS risk assessments.[175] The most illustrative example of such reasoning style can be found in the AB report in *Continued Suspension of Obligations*. Here the AB required panels to scrutinize the scientific basis of the risk assessment as to whether it could be regarded as legitimate science 'according to the standards of the relevant scientific community'.[176] A similar reference to scientific authority was made when the AB relied on scientific criteria to examine whether scientific bases of SPS measures had 'the necessary scientific and methodological rigor'.[177] This argumentation clearly uses scientific benchmarks to evaluate whether the scientific evidentiary basis of an SPS measure is acceptable for purposes of WTO law.

It is argued here that such epistemically deferential reasoning towards scientific experts is a corollary to setting intrusive standards of review. Interrogating the 'correctness' of the scientific basis of SPS measures inevitably necessitates reference to scientific standards to preserve the epistemic non-arbitrariness of the adjudicatory analysis. Exercising epistemic deference to science helps adjudicators remedy concerns about their lack of epistemic competence in scientific matters.

Yet, applying such a scientific reasoning is not immune to weaknesses and corresponding criticism. First of all, epistemic deference to science subscribes to a myth of objective scientific validation.[178] Furthermore, relying on such a rationality does not wipe out concerns about inadvertent delegation of adjudicatory power to non-elected experts. When utilizing scientific standards, adjudicators need to completely rely on expert opinions, leaving them susceptible to experts' good faith erroneous scientific evaluation, or even biased opinions. Nevertheless, on a practical level, the free assessment of evidence principle may guard adjudicators against such fears of 'eroding'[179] the judicial function. The fact remains that such a reasoning method has its limits as to feasibility with regard to available expert evidence and the capability of the scientific community to form a conclusive view on the pertinent technical question. Further details and implications of such

---

[174] D'Aspremont and Mbengue, 'Strategies of engagement with scientific fact-finding in international adjudication', 268.
[175] D'Aspremont and Mbengue, 'Strategies of engagement with scientific fact-finding in international adjudication', 268.
[176] *US – Continued Suspension of Obligations*, Report of the AB, para. 591.
[177] *US – Continued Suspension of Obligations*, Report of the AB, para. 591.
[178] D'Aspremont and Mbengue, 'Strategies of engagement with scientific fact-finding in international adjudication', 269.
[179] Payne, 'Mastering the evidence', 1195.

scientifically deferential reasoning on the legitimacy of adjudicatory decisions will be addressed in Chapter 10.

5.2 Developing Legal Benchmarks: Relying on Standards of International Organizations

Besides justification practices stemming from scientific rationality, WTO dispute resolution bodies also reason with legal benchmarks that are easily amenable to judicial appraisal. Legal argumentative benchmarks rest on legalistic rationality and authority, and therefore fit neatly within the epistemic competence of judges. A quite frequently used legal benchmark in the context of WTO law lies in making reference to standards of international organizations.[180] As has been shown above, panels and the AB often cite standards of international organizations to support their positions regarding scientific allegations.[181]

Reference to such standards has the epistemic benefit of conferring persuasiveness and thus legitimacy on a certain scientific knowledge claim on account of the reputation and perceived expertise of the issuing organization. The carefully negotiated nature of such scientific standards also seems to be a relevant factor in establishing their persuasive force.[182] Notably, WTO panels do not interrogate the actual standard-setting process, that is whether the standard in question was accepted unanimously or only with a majority.[183] International standards for this reason provide a quite convenient method of reasoning for adjudicators to single out respected and legitimate scientific knowledge.

However, from a pragmatic point of view, the practical effectiveness of such reasoning is limited given the finite number of accepted international guidelines concerning the causes of suspected health risks. Also, the ever-expanding scope of potentially toxic materials and food additives limit the potential of using such standards as a frequent point of reference in adjudication. Moreover, the often time-consuming nature of procedures leading to accepting such scientific guideline may hinder their practical benefits for supporting legitimate reasoning. The need for timely decision-making in trade disputes may preclude waiting for the issuance of such standards in a given dispute.[184]

---

[180] For a detailed assessment of the relevant international organizations and their standard setting processes see Gruszczynski, *Regulating Health and Environmental Risks under WTO Law: A Critical Analysis of the SPS Agreement*, pp. 79–90.

[181] See Section II, Subsection 4 in this chapter.

[182] L. Gruszczynski, 'WHO Framework Convention on Tobacco Control as an international standard under the TBT Agreement?' (2012) 9 *Transnational Dispute Management* 1–14 at 9.

[183] Gruszczynski, *Regulating Health and Environmental Risks under WTO Law: A Critical Analysis of the SPS Agreement*, p. 88.

[184] S. J. Smyth, W. A. Kerr, and P. W. B. Phillips, 'Recent trends in the scientific basis of sanitary and phytosanitary trade rules and their potential impact on investment' (2011) 12 *The Journal of World Investment & Trade* 5–26 at 16.

On a separate note, the specificity of the scientific information included in such guidelines and standards can cause further complications, when they do not exactly match that of the contested measure. In such cases, WTO adjudicators first have to examine whether respective scientific guidelines can be regarded as a 'standard of international organization' that may carry special evidentiary value, as addressed above in Section II, Subsection 4. This was exactly among the litigated issues in the *Australia – Tobacco Plain Packaging* case, where the panel first had to determine whether the FCTC Guidelines could be regarded as international standards for purposes of Article 2.5 of the TBT Agreement. The panel was unable to find that the FCTC Guidelines was amounting to a 'relevant international standard', because it was

> not clear [to the panel] which elements or components within the Article 11 and Article 13 FCTC Guidelines would form a 'document' encapsulating the totality of the 'rules, guidelines or characteristics', that a WTO Member would be required to follow if it decides to adopt a measure providing for tobacco plain packaging 'in accordance with' an international standard.[185]

Even though in the material case the FCTC Guidelines were not sufficiently specific to enable the panel to presume that the Australian tobacco plain packaging measure was in accordance with such standards, and therefore, consistent with WTO law, the panel nevertheless repeatedly cited the guideline as persuasive evidence for several factual findings, albeit it always did so together with some other pieces of evidence. This suggests that the FCTC Guidelines did carry probative force in the eyes of WTO adjudicators.

Despite the above limitations, legal benchmarks do enable adjudicators to transform scientific information into legal evaluation in a persuasive manner. They carry considerable advantages for the epistemic legitimacy of reasoning inasmuch as they save adjudicators from navigating into unchartered waters of scientific assessments. Instead, legal benchmarks provide for an essentially legalistic reasoning, in which adjudicators can reach a legitimate conclusion in a comfortable way.

Theoretically, there would be another argumentative choice available to adjudicators, that is to weigh scientific facts similarly to ordinary fact-finding. Such an approach has triggered scholarly criticism for 'hiding behind legal reasoning',[186] while trying to 'shield itself from scientific controversies'.[187] Yet, the AB expressly declined the possibility of walking down this path in *EC – Asbestos*, where it stressed that a panel should not weigh rival scientific opinions according to ordinary legal rules of standard of proof, which would mandate the 'preponderant' expert position

---

[185] *Australia – Tobacco Plain Packaging*, Reports of the Panel, para. 7.330.
[186] D'Aspremont and Mbengue, 'Strategies of engagement with scientific fact-finding in international adjudication', 253.
[187] D'Aspremont and Mbengue, 'Strategies of engagement with scientific fact-finding in international adjudication', 253.

to prevail.[188] The WTO's reluctance to equate scientific and legal fact-finding is therefore indicated by the fact that members need not necessarily place their risk assessments on the majority view of competing scientific theories in order to pass an SPS measure fully consistent with WTO law. Importantly, in WTO law as long as the evidence relied on by a state 'comes from a qualified and respected source',[189] it can lawfully form the basis of an SPS measure even if it constitutes, at the material time, a minority scientific view.[190]

The benefits and trade-offs of using similar legal benchmarks in judicial reasoning will be elaborated on in greater detail in Chapter 10.[191]

5.3 Intuitive Rationality: Semantic Analysis

One may also find reasoning methods that are backed by everyday knowledge and, thus, are based on intuitive rationality. Crafting justifications in this way does not require neither scientific nor legal training, as these methods appeal to common-sense grammatical interpretation of non-technical terms. Accordingly, they are, in fact, grounded in intuitive rationality available to every reasoner.

A stark example of such techniques is provided by cases revolving around the interpretation of Article 3 of the SPS Agreement, which encourages members to 'base' their SPS measures as far as possible on 'international standards, guidelines and recommendations'. A number of WTO disputes concerned the question whether a given SPS measure was indeed based on a relevant international standard. In their reasoning, panels were usually preoccupied with the grammatical inter-pretation of Article 3. This triggered an essentially semantic analysis, in which the scientific merits of the underlying evidence played little or no role.

The *US – Animals* can be taken as an apposite example of WTO panels' semantic analysis. Argentina challenged a US ban on importation of fresh beef and swine products from regions of Argentina that had failed to be categorized as free from foot-and-mouth disease. Argentina claimed that the measure was not based on the relevant international standard, the Terrestrial Code of the World Organization for Animal Health.[192] The United States on the contrary argued that its measure was based on the Terrestrial Code, and the import ban was necessitated by a higher level of its desired protection. The panel found that the protocols of the Terrestrial Code did not mandate a ban, quite the opposite, allowed the trade with beef alongside with mitigating measures.[193] The panel ruled that if a measure is contradictory to a standard, it could not be regarded as being based on that standard.[194]

---

[188]   *EC – Asbestos*, Report of the AB, para. 178.
[189]   *EC – Asbestos*, Report of the AB, para. 178.
[190]   *EC – Asbestos*, Report of the AB, para. 178.
[191]   Chapter 10 Section II, Subsection 2.
[192]   *US – Animals*, Report of the Panel, para. 7.199.
[193]   *US – Animals*, Report of the Panel, paras. 7.235–6.
[194]   *US – Animals*, Report of the Panel, para. 7.237.

To mention a few further examples of semantic reasoning, in *EC – Sardines*, the AB remarked that 'there must be a very strong and very close relationship between two things in order to be able to say that one is "the basis for" the other'.[195] Similarly, in *EC – Hormones*, the AB was also concerned with the grammatical meaning of the terms involved, when it stated that '[a] thing is commonly said to be "based on" another thing when the former "stands" or is "founded" or "built" upon or "is supported by" the latter'.[196] The AB also considered that, to be based on an international standard, a measure 'may adopt some, not necessarily all, of the elements of the international standard'.[197] With such a reasoning, the AB could conveniently decide the contested issue whether the EC was entitled to institute a ban on hormone-treated meat, while the relevant international standard, the Codex Alimentarius,[198] only mandated maximum acceptable daily intakes and maximum residue limits for hormones in the meat.[199] This decision also shows how semantic reasoning yields relatively straightforward legal argumentation even in cases with factually complex scientific background.

In sum, relying on grammatical analysis enables WTO panels to reach their decisions through a purely logical reasoning, which circumvents cumbersome direct engagement with the scientific aspects of risks and risk assessment decisions. Adjudicators in such cases do not need to appeal to scientific rationality to rule on the consistency of an SPS measure but can discern requirements and interpretative guides from the legal rule embedding the respective scientific term. Similar reasoning techniques from the practice of other international adjudicative fora will be examined more in depth in Chapter 9,[200] whereas general remarks on the advantages and disadvantages of such a reasoning style will be discussed in Chapter 10.[201]

5.4 Developing a Hybrid Benchmark: Scrutinizing the Coherency of Reasoning

There is a yet another argumentative technique, the coherency test, which emerged simultaneously with the currently applicable two-stage standard of review combining a rather deferential scrutiny as to the scientific basis of SPS measures with a more intrusive review as to the coherence and objectivity of the risk assessor's reasoning. One encounters serious difficulties in trying to fit the coherence analysis strictly within either among legal or scientific reasoning techniques. Indeed, the coherency of a science-based reasoning is not a purely scientific category or attribute, neither can it be decided by sole reference to legal logic. At the same time, this concept is

---

[195] *EC – Sardines*, Report of the AB, WT/DS231/AB/R (26 September 2002), para. 245.
[196] *EC – Hormones*, Report of the AB, para. 163.
[197] *EC – Hormones*, Report of the AB, para. 171.
[198] The Codex Alimentarius is a collection of internationally adopted food standards presented in a uniform manner.
[199] *EC – Hormones*, Report of the Panel, para. 8.59.
[200] Chapter 9 Section V, Subsection 2.4.
[201] Chapter 10 Section II, Subsection 3.1.2.

also more elusive than to be simply appraised based on common-sense knowledge. Consequently, this book argues that such concepts constitute a separate reasoning technique, namely hybrid reasoning, which relies on a combination of scientific and legalistic rationality.[202]

The coherence analysis enables panellists to couch their reasoning in legal terms, given that they should emphatically not address the correctness of the underlying science,[203] or resolve longstanding scientific controversies,[204] but to review whether intermediate steps in the assessment were revealed and adequately documented in a transparent and coherent manner in light of the scientific evidence. The scrutiny of the coherence and objectivity of reasoning yields an essentially legalistic assessment, which at the same time is closely related to the scientific aspects of the underlying facts.

Such a hybrid reasoning style yields two immediate benefits. First, it provides the best epistemic fit for legally trained adjudicators, since this argumentative technique does not call for substituting legal rationality for scientific rationality, and thus, it eliminates concerns relating to epistemic arbitrariness. Adjudicators can comfortably craft tests that are amenable to legalistic appraisal in order to form an opinion on the coherency of risk assessors' reasoning. To name a few, transparency and adequate documentation can be requirements that panellists may easily scrutinize. Moreover, incoherent reasoning can be detected, for instance, when inferences drawn are not logical, uncertainties are not revealed or neglected from the analysis, or where conclusions suffer from serious inconsistencies or gaps in the underlying facts. These qualities again can be comfortably assessed from a *legal point of view*, a terrain where lawyers may announce decisions in a legitimate way.

Furthermore, in fleshing out the content of the coherence analysis, the meaning accorded to the general standard of review under Article 11 of the DSU in the context of Article 4.2(a) of the Safeguards Agreement may be also informative. This provision is interpreted as requiring panels to review whether the authorities 'have provided a reasoned and adequate explanation of how the facts support their determination'.[205] In *US – Lambs*, the AB explained that this requirement carry the following meaning:

> a panel can assess whether the competent authorities' explanation for its determination is reasoned and adequate *only* if the panel critically examines that explanation, in depth, and in the light of the facts before the panel. Panels must, therefore, review

[202]   The epistemic nature and further attributes of hybrid concepts will be discussed more in depth in Chapter 10 Section II, Subsection 4.

[203]   Gruszczynski, 'How deep should we go? searching for an appropriate standard of review in the SPS cases', 114.

[204]   The EC raised such argument in favour of a least intrusive review before the panel in the *Continued Suspension of Obligations* cases. See *US – Continued Suspension of Obligations*, Report of the Panel, para. 4.377.

[205]   *US – Safeguard Measures on Imports of Fresh, Chilled or Frozen Lamb from New Zealand*, Report of the AB, WT/DS177/AB/R (1 May 2001), para. 108.

whether the competent authorities' explanation fully addresses the nature, and, especially, the complexities, of the data, and responds to other plausible interpretations of that data. A panel must find, in particular, that an explanation is not reasoned, or is not adequate, if some *alternative explanation* of the facts is plausible, and if the competent authorities' explanation does not seem adequate in the light of that alternative explanation.[206]

In SPS cases, which entertain measures based on complex scientific determinations, assessing the adequacy of an explanation would entail a highly science-intensive assessment. Judging whether a given reasoning 'responds to other plausible interpretations of the data' necessitates a close engagement with scientific controversies. This brings us to another major benefit of hybrid reasoning style, namely, that it does not preclude adjudicators from engaging with the scientific facts. On the contrary, it actively promotes adjudicatory interaction with science. For these reasons, building adjudicatory reasoning on hybrid standards enables panels to fulfil their mandate enshrined in the SPS Agreement and to enforce scientific legality criteria in a meaningful way. Engaging with the underlying science is not only a duty of panellists as trier of facts, but is also a necessary requisite of crafting a persuasive decision in science-heavy trade disputes.

5.5 Concluding Remarks on Reasoning Styles

The foregoing analysis sought to demonstrate the variety of ways in which legal adjudicators can evaluate and reflect on science-based arguments in WTO dispute resolution processes. The underlying substantive law provides a particularly science-intensive mandate, and the jurisprudence attests that WTO dispute settlement bodies do not shy away from thoroughly executing such a task. It is not the intention of this section, however, to single out the one and most suitable epistemic rationality for legally evaluating the scientific profile of trade disputes. In fact, the most appropriate reasoning style depends on the particularities of a given case. As the WTO case practice also evidences, intuitive, scientific, and legal rationality may all yield a credible and convincing adjudicatory narrative on the scientific questions implicated in the panellists' assessments. Yet, this is not to suggest that the different argumentation techniques are interchangeable; as some do appear to be more favourable than others in terms of securing the epistemic legitimacy of an adjudicatory reasoning under specific circumstances. The strengths and weaknesses of each reasoning style will be addressed in more detail in Chapter 10.

---

[206] *US – Safeguard Measures on Imports of Fresh, Chilled or Frozen Lamb from New Zealand*, Report of the AB, para. 106.

7

Science in the Practice of Investment Arbitral Tribunals

Because of the desirability of gaining a greater understanding of the particular area, the Tribunal agreed to . . . a visit to the site on December 21–22, 2010. Surely, none of us will forget the spectacle of Playa Grande Beach, lit by a full moon at about 1:00 A.M. on December 22, where a large female leatherback . . . finished digging her nest deposited some 50 soft eggs . . . and began to cover them.[1]

Unglaube Tribunal, 2012

This chapter addresses environmental investment disputes arising under Multilateral Investment Treaties (MIT), Bilateral Investment Treaties (BIT), investment contracts or domestic law provisions of host states, when an investor claims compensation either for discriminative treatment by the host state or for an alleged breach of specific investment rights guaranteed under the above agreements. The number of investment disputes has been steadily increasing since the 1990s,[2] generating almost a thousand disputes by early 2020,[3] among which a growing number of cases involve environmental components.[4]

This chapter maps the approach of investment tribunals to science-intensive legal questions and arguments in environmental disputes. Science penetrates investment arbitration to a considerable extent through at least six different entry points (Section I). Both the parties and arbitrators have recourse to scientific arguments for various

---

[1] *Marion Unglaube* v. *Costa Rica*, ICSID Case No. ARB/08/1, Award (May 16, 2012), para. 165.

[2] The number of investor-state disputes rose from only six registered cases to 568 ongoing cases between 1995 and 2013. Y. Levashova, 'Fair and equitable treatment and the protection of the environment: recent trends in investment treaties and investment cases' in Y. Levashova, T. Lambooy, and I. Dekker (eds.), *Bridging the Gap between International Investment Law and the Environment* (Eleven Publishing, 2015), pp. 53–84 p. 55.

[3] Investment Dispute Settlement Navigator of UN Conference on Trade and Development, available at https://investmentpolicy.unctad.org/investment-dispute-settlement (last accessed 22 January 2020).

[4] An empirical research identified forty-nine closed environmental investment disputes by the end of 2016. See D. Behn and M. Langford, 'Trumping the environment? An empirical perspective on the legitimacy of investment treaty arbitration' (2017) 18 *The Journal of World Investment & Trade* 14–61 at 18; J. E. Viñuales, *Foreign Investment and the Environment* (Cambridge University Press, 2012); Dupuy and Viñuales, *International Environmental Law*, p. 385.

strategic purposes in tailoring the scope of the legal dispute and managing the adjudicatory analysis (Section II). Although discerning general trends in the arbitral practice is impeded by the ad hoc constitution of investment tribunals and the fact that several proceedings are kept confidential, the presence of science seems to trigger similar solutions from panels in terms of their scientific engagement. Generally, arbitral tribunals are becoming gradually more open to consider science-based arguments and evidence in environmental disputes. Their fact-finding process is largely party-driven and panel-appointed experts are rarely used (Section III). Science-intensive causal claims are seldom investigated, with some notable exceptions (Section IV). Lastly, arbitral tribunals tend to afford a high measure of deference to host states' scientific claims, although they differ in the exact standard of review applied to scrutinize the soundness of science-backed measures (Section V).

I SCIENCE IN INVESTOR-STATE ENVIRONMENTAL ARBITRATION

This study is dedicated to a specific subset of the burgeoning field of investor-state dispute settlement, that is, arbitration featuring environmental policies of host states. After briefly describing the specificities of this particular type of disputes (Subsection 1), six entry points for science will be identified (Subsection 2). This will set the scene for analysing the methods used by arbitrators to engage with science in their assessments.

1 *Environmental Disputes Brought before Investment Arbitral Tribunals*

Foreign investments can be in line with environmental protection goals and may even promote such objectives;[5] albeit typically, investments create externalities for host states in the form of for example increased pollution, toxic waste disposal, or destruction of biodiversity.[6] Being cognizant of the potential conflict between the protection of investments and that of the environment, a growing number of international investment agreements (IIA) have started to contain express references to environmental concerns.[7] In parallel, host states' regulatory measures seeking to tackle ensuing adverse environmental impacts have given rise to an increasing number of 'investment v. environment' arbitrations.

Arbitrators have approached environmental justifications for regulatory actions that targeted foreign investments in markedly different ways. Initially, arbitral

---

[5] P.-M. Dupuy and J. E. Viñuales (eds.), *Harnessing Foreign Investment to Promote Environmental Protection* (Cambridge University Press, 2013).

[6] Dupuy and Viñuales, *International Environmental Law*, p. 379.

[7] J. E. Viñuales, 'Foreign investment and the environment in international law: current trends' in K. Miles (ed.), *Research Handbook on Environment and Investment Law* (Edward Elgar, 2019), pp. 12–37 p. 17.

tribunals were generally suspicious towards environmental regulation and suspected protectionism behind environmental reasoning.[8] In these disputes environmental objectives had to yield to investment protection, as the latter was deemed superior in times of conflict.[9] However, recent arbitral decisions have become more inclined to regard environmental measures as genuine exercise of police powers. Consequently, environmental or public health risks are increasingly deemed legitimate – and, thus, non-compensable – reasons for regulation.[10]

The ways in which investment tribunals approach environmental policies is particularly important, because unduly dismissive arbitral decisions towards sovereign regulatory power can have a considerable chilling effect on states' willingness to enact environmental regulations.[11] Being mindful of the intensifying criticism voicing legitimacy concerns in relation to environmental investment arbitration,[12] led a NAFTA tribunal to expressly stress that arbitrators 'must be sensitive to the need to avoid "regulatory chill", including with respect to protection of the environment'.[13] Even though some suggest that such concerns are unfounded[14] or that the extent of regulatory chill is, in fact, less marked in the environmental sector than in relation to other policies,[15] legitimate fears of regulatory chill remain part of both the public and the scholarly discourse. Especially in light of a prior occasion, when an investment dispute has been settled on condition that the host state lowered the water quality standard set for the investor's project.[16] Such alarming precedents fuel

[8]   Dupuy and Viñuales, *International Environmental Law*, p. 462; Viñuales, 'Foreign investment and the environment in international law: current trends', p. 27.
[9]   Viñuales, 'Foreign investment and the environment in international law: current trends', p. 27; Dupuy and Viñuales, *International Environmental Law*, p. 386; Sands, *Litigating Environmental Disputes: Courts, Tribunals and the Progressive Development of International Environmental Law*, p. 10. See for example *Compañía del Desarrollo de Santa Elena, S.A. v. Costa Rica*, ICSID Case No. ARB/96/1, Final Award (17 February 2000); *Metalclad Corporation v. United Mexican States*, ICSID Case No. ARB(AF)/97/1, Award (30 August 2000).
[10] For example *Glamis Gold Ltd. v. United States of America* (NAFTA) Award (8 June 2009); *Methanex v. United States of America* (NAFTA) Award (3 August 2005).
[11] For an empirical survey on the extent of regulatory chill see G. Van Harten and D. N. Scott, 'Investment treaties and the internal vetting of regulatory proposals: a case study from Canada' (2016) 12 *Osgoode Legal Studies Research Paper Series*.
[12] Behn and Langford distinguish five forms of legitimacy concerns specifically in relation to environmental ISDS, Behn and Langford, 'Trumping the environment?', 19–22.
[13] *William Ralph Clayton, William Richard Clayton, Douglas Clayton, Daniel Clayton and Bilcon of Delaware Inc. v. Canada*, PCA Case No. 2009–04, Award on jurisdiction and liability (17 March 2015), para. 737.
[14] C. Schreuer, 'Investment arbitration' in C. Romano, K. J. Alter, and Y. Shany (eds.), *The Oxford Handbook of International Adjudication* (Oxford University Press, 2014), pp. 295–315 p. 314.
[15] Behn and Langford, 'Trumping the environment?', 31.
[16] *Vattenfall AB, Vattenfall Europe AG, Vattenfall Europe Generation AG v. Federal Republic of Germany* (*Vattenfall v. Germany* (I)), ICSID Case No. ARB/09/6, for a detailed assessment of the settlement see N. Bernasconi-Osterwalder and R. T. Hoffmann, 'The German nuclear phase-out put to the test in international investment arbitration? Background to the new dispute *Vattenfall v. Germany* (II)', available at www.iisd.org/pdf/2012/german_nuclear_phase_out.pdf p. 4 (last accessed 11 January 2020).

a marked opposition against including investor-state arbitration clauses in major free trade agreements.[17]

Notwithstanding these legitimacy concerns surrounding investment arbitration, recent proceedings also suggest that investment disputes can be a vehicle to foster climate change mitigation measures[18] or to compel governments to thoroughly enforce their environmental legislation. Yet these instances seem to be insufficient to dissolve deep-seated concerns with which environmental lawyers observe the interaction between investment protection and environmental safeguards. Investment law and environmental law evolved as separate legal regimes,[19] and despite their increasing entanglement, they appear to share little, if any, common ground and conceptual basis,[20] while they protect different values and nurture fundamentally divergent attitudes[21] towards the natural environment.

2 *Entry Points for Science in Environmental Investment Disputes*

Science enters this tense relationship as an extrinsic factor, impacting the interaction of environmental protection and investment law in many ways. Environmental investment disputes feature complex questions of policy and science. This survey will focus on the role of scientific arguments in shaping the dynamic of resolving investment disputes. As a necessary initial step of the analysis, six different ways will be identified in which science may enter such disputes.

The first entry point through which science may become relevant in investment arbitration manifests when adjudicators appraise whether evidence of the host state substantiates the existence of genuine environmental risks, which may, in turn, justify enacting regulatory measures. For instance, in the *Methanex* case, discussed below, a central scientific issue was whether the use of methyl tertiary butyl ether (MTBE) as a fuel additive posed significant risk of drinking water contamination, calling for legitimate restrictions on foreign investment by the State of California.

Second, science may enter investment disputes at the stage of assessing whether a given regulation was a reasonable response to the risk identified. This is often measured by a proportionality analysis.[22] Scientific arguments may thus be

---

[17]   One hundred and twenty academics as well as the German parliament voiced concerns about the investor-state arbitration clause with respect to the draft Transatlantic Trade and Investment Partnership, see IISD blog, 13 August 2013, available at www.iisd.org/itn/2014/08/13/news-in-brief-16/ (last accessed 27 July 2017).

[18]   A. Asteriti, 'Climate change policies and foreign investment: some salient legal issues' in Y. Levashova, T. Lambooy, and I. Dekker (eds.), *Bridging the Gap between International Investment Law and the Environment* (Eleven Publishing, 2015), pp. 145–86 p. 158.

[19]   Viñuales, *Foreign Investment and the Environment*, p. 1.

[20]   For a more in-depth discussion on that see K. Miles, *The Origins of International Investment Law* (Cambridge University Press, 2013), pp. 125–211.

[21]   Miles, *The Origins of International Investment Law*, p. 8.

[22]   *Técnicas Medioambientales Tecmed SA v. United Mexican States*, ICSID Case No. ARB(AF)/00/2, Award (May 29, 2003), para. 122.

employed in distinguishing non-compensable genuine environmental regulation from indirect (regulatory) expropriation.[23] At this stage, host states may invoke the police powers doctrine[24] as a defence claiming that their measures otherwise tantamount to expropriation are nevertheless non-compensable. Also, a related invocation of scientific arguments occurs in cases where arbitrators scrutinize whether the host state acted in an arbitrary manner when imposed science-based measures, thereby infringing the fair and equitable treatment standard.

A third way of bringing scientific arguments into investment arbitration is by arguing that treating foreign investments differently is justifiable for scientific reasons.[25] An apt example for such a point of entry is the 'like circumstances' analysis under National Treatment clauses.[26]

A related fourth aspect can be distinguished, when science serves as a useful indicator to decide whether a BIT's stabilization clause is untenable with a view to new scientific knowledge regarding previously unforeseen risks.[27] New scientific information may warrant regulation despite stabilization clauses of BITs. If the regulation at hand failed this science-based inquiry, it would qualify as indirect, and therefore compensable, expropriation.[28]

Science may also become legally relevant when environmental liability claims are filed with investment tribunals. A fifth entry point of science into legal disputes thus occurs in the clothes of host states' counterclaims alleging environmental damage caused by the investor. Taking as an example, in *Perenco* Ecuador filed an environmental counterclaim against the investor, who was operating oil blocks in the Amazonian rainforest. The counterclaim centred on an oil spill originating from the blocks causing serious ecological damage.[29] Ecuador also filed liability counterclaims against Burlington Resources Inc., alleging that it is jointly and severally liable with Perenco for the severe ecological harm caused by abandoning the oil blocks. In *Burlington* v. *Ecuador*, the tribunal awarded nearly USD 40,000,000 for remediation of environmental damage caused in the Amazonian

---

[23] G. Bottini and M. Scheltema, 'Future Outlook: Bridging Gaps between Environment and International Investment Law or Juxtaposing Different Topics?' in Y. Levashova, T. Lambooy, I. Dekker (eds.), *Bridging the Gap between International Investment Law and the Environment* (Eleven Publishing, 2015), pp. 467–83 p. 482.

[24] Viñuales, *Foreign Investment and the Environment*, p. 366.

[25] Foster, *Science and the Precautionary Principle in International Courts and Tribunals*, p. 145.

[26] Lévesque, 'Science in the hands of international investment tribunals: a case for "scientific due process"', 264–5. Lévesque discusses the like circumstances analysis under NAFTA Chapter 11. In such cases, an investor may argue that a product ban instituted out of health or environmental considerations is arbitrary, if there are competing products that are not affected by the ban, and there are no scientifically valid reasons for treating the products differently.

[27] Orellana, 'The role of science in investment arbitrations concerning public health and the environment', 62.

[28] Orellana, 'The role of science in investment arbitrations concerning public health and the environment', 62.

[29] For example *Perenco Ecuador Limited* v. *The Republic of Ecuador*, ICSID Case No. ARB/08/6, Interim Decision on the Environmental Counterclaim (Aug 11, 2015), para. 34.

region.[30] Such environmental counterclaims are not yet common,[31] although their number is on the rise,[32] especially since states have started to incorporate clauses explicitly allowing environmental counterclaims in their BITs.[33]

A final, thus far, quite rare entry point for scientific arguments is manifest in claims brought for breaching an investment protection standard on account of the host state's failure to enforce its own environmental laws.[34] In *Peter Allard* v. *Barbados*,[35] a Canadian owner of a bird sanctuary alleged that inadequate actions of the host state caused or permitted environmental degradation to the swamp area, where his business was located. This allegedly has led to a decline in biodiversity, which in turn rendered his eco-resort unprofitable, thus it had to cease its operation. The claimant argued that Barbados' failure to enforce domestic environmental laws and to comply with international environmental legal obligations breached the Canadian-Barbados BIT.[36] The parties submitted ample scientific evidence on whether ecological degradation has indeed occurred, and if so, whether it was caused by omissions of governmental authorities.

Bilcon v. *Canada* featured a claim filed for the failure of the host state to enforce its environmental regulation in a non-arbitrary manner. Bilcon claimed that Canada violated the minimum standard of treatment under NAFTA when conducting an EIA regarding the investment concerning a quarry and a marine terminal development. The claimant explicitly complained that the risk assessor Joint Review Panel's 'conclusions were not based on science',[37] but referred to violating certain 'core community values', a standard that was not enshrined in Canadian law. The tribunal found a violation because it was of the view that Canada's environmental regulatory regime was applied to the project in an arbitrary, unfair, and discriminatory manner, depriving the investors of due process.[38] A similar question is featured in the pending

---

[30] *Burlington Resources Inc.* v. *Republic of Ecuador*, ICSID Case No. ARB/08/05, Decision on Counterclaims (Feb 6, 2017), para. 1075.

[31] Filing environmental counterclaims may not always be possible. Their feasibility largely depends on the wording of the dispute settlement clause. Besides, there must be a direct factual and legal connection between the claim and the environmental counterclaim. See generally A. Asteriti, 'Environmental law in investment arbitration: procedural means of incorporation' (2015) 16 *The Journal of World Investment and Trade* 248–73 at 257.

[32] For example *Marion Unglaube* v. *Costa Rica*, Award; *Marvin Roy Feldman Karpa* v. *Mexico*, ICSID Case No. ARB(AF)/99/1, Award (Dec 16, 2002). For more on the practice of filing counterclaims with investment tribunals see S. W. Schill and V. Djanic, 'International investment law and community interests' in E. Benvenisti and G. Nolte (eds.), *Community Interests Across International Law* (Oxford University Press, 2018), pp. 221–48 pp. 244–6.

[33] Asteriti, 'Environmental law in investment arbitration: procedural means of incorporation', 272.

[34] Viñuales, *Foreign Investment and the Environment*, p. 89.

[35] *Peter A. Allard* v. *The Government of Barbados*, PCA Case No. 2012–06, Award (June 27, 2016).

[36] Notice of Dispute, filed by Peter A. Allard, 8 September 2009, para. 14. Under the BIT, Barbados was obliged to 'provide full protection and security to investment of Canadian investors'.

[37] *Bilcon* v. *Canada*, Award on jurisdiction and liability (17 March 2015), para. 377.

[38] L. Létourneau-Tremblay and D. F. Behn, 'Judging the misapplication of a state's own environmental regulations' (2016) 17 *The Journal of World Investment & Trade* 823–32; M. Levine, 'Investor-state arbitration and domestic environmental governance: recent developments in Canada' in N. Craik,

Zelena v. *Serbia* case, where the investor claims that the government's failure to enforce legislation on the handling of hazardous animal by-products in an equal manner with respect to the claimant and its competitors made its operation unviable.[39]

A last example of arbitral proceedings featuring claims of governmental omission to enforce the host state's legal obligations is provided by *Renco* v. *Peru*,[40] where the investor operating the La Oroya mine filed a claim against Peru for breaching a provision of the investment treaty according to which the host state ought to remediate existing contamination and to assume full liability for environmental claims of third parties arising before and after the sale of the mine.[41] Since Peru refused to take responsibility for the lawsuits that were filed with US courts on behalf of 1,000 individuals against Renco for alleged personal injuries caused by toxic substances released from the mine,[42] Renco initiated an ICSID arbitration to show that these personal injury lawsuits fell under the scope of the investment treaty provision that retained Peru's full liability for environmental damage claims.

As the above six avenues for channelling science into the legal deliberation of arbitrators illustrate, science is entertained by arbitral tribunals in diverse legal contexts. The legal weight scientific arguments may carry varies across different entry points. In some cases, science appears to be a sufficient though not necessary criterion for making legal determinations. This occurs in proving the reasonable nature of scientific risk assessment procedures. Whereas in other scenarios, science constitutes a necessary condition to establish a legal claim, such as in the case of environmental counterclaims alleging environmental damage. There are also contexts where science serves as a 'proxy' informing the adjudicatory inquiry; for instance in assessing the host state's motivations behind environmental regulations.[43]

As it may be clear also from the above-cited *Bilcon* award, arbitrators do not necessarily confront with science in every case involving environmental components. In a number of environment vs. investment disputes, the legal inquiry does not reach the depth of the underlying science. Such a framing may be a direct corollary of the dispute's subject-matter, or sometimes science is carved out from the scope of analysis either because of the parties' argumentative strategy or on account of the choice of arbitrators. An overview shall now follow of the peculiar ways in which various actors in an arbitration strategically use scientific arguments to frame the dispute.

C. S. G. Jefferies, S. L. Seck, and T. Stephens (eds.), *Global Environmental Change and Innovation in International Law* (Cambridge University Press, 2018), pp. 296–314.

[39] *Zelena N.V. and Energo-Zelena d.o.o Indija* v. *Republic of Serbia*, ICSID Case No. ARB/14/27, Claimants' Press Release on Request for Arbitration (25 November 2014).

[40] *The Renco Group, Inc.* v. *The Republic of Peru*, ICSID Case No. UNCT/13/1.

[41] *Renco* v. *Peru*, Claimant's Memorial on Liability (20 February 2014), para. 3.

[42] *Renco* v. *Peru*, Claimant's Memorial on Liability (20 February 2014), para. 6.

[43] Foster, *Science and the Precautionary Principle in International Courts and Tribunals*, p. 144.

II FRAMING OF DISPUTES: STRATEGICALLY MANAGING THE SCIENCE-INTENSITY OF THE LEGAL INQUIRY

Scientific arguments may carry strategic value both in the hands of the claimant and the host state (Subsection 1), as well as in those of the arbitrators (Subsection 2). These actors aim for different epistemic gains from appealing to science, as will be detailed in the coming sections.

1 *Framing Techniques of Litigants*

Some initial investor-state disputes although featured alleged expropriation on account of environmental regulations, did not contain any meaningful scientific arguments. This was a result of host states' litigation strategy to claim their right to regulate without providing any scientific arguments in favour of respective environmental policies. In *Metalclad* v. *United Mexican States*,[44] Mexico barred a hazardous waste landfill from operation by enacting an ecological decree. Even though the town council referred to the 'environmental effect and impact on the site and surrounding communities' among the reasons for denying the permit, it submitted no evidence on this respect,[45] and thus the tribunal found it as an act of expropriation.[46] Also, in *Tecmed* v. *Mexico* the host state refused to renew the permit of a hazardous waste landfill with reference to environmental safety reasons,[47] although again, Mexican authorities found no 'evidence of any risk to health and the ecosystems' beforehand.[48]

In other instances, the claimants did not contest the ecological justifications for injurious state measures; in this way underlying scientific results were again not brought to the forefront of the dispute. *Santa Elena* v. *Costa Rica* and the later *Unglaube* v. *Costa Rica* Arbitration both concerned environmental regulations enacted to create national park reserves protecting host states' vulnerable ecosystems to the detriment of private real estate developments. The *Santa Elena* Tribunal did not consider the environmental – and ensuing scientific – justifications for the expropriation at hand.[49]

The *Unglaube* v. *Costa Rica* case has seen a more science-intensive inquiry. The dispute centred on a German national's ecotourist investment in Playa Grande, a picturesque beach on Costa Rica's Pacific coast and the nesting area of an endangered species, the leatherback turtle. The deduced number of females nesting at Playa Grande suggested a sharp decline in the leatherback population. The parties

44 *Metalclad Corporation* v. *United Mexican States*, ICSID Case No. ARB(AF)/97/1, Award (30 August 2000).
45 *Metalclad* v. *Mexico*, Award, paras. 92–3.
46 *Metalclad* v. *Mexico*, Award, para. 104.
47 *Tecmed* v. *Mexico*, Award, para. 36.
48 *Tecmed* v. *Mexico*, Award, para. 110.
49 *Santa Elena* v. *Costa Rica*, Award, para. 72.

debated the reasons for such a decline.[50] Bearing in mind Costa Rica's well-known reputation as an ecotourism destination, the government took steps to create a national park to protect this nesting habitat and thereby suspended the construction permits of the investor. The parties were in agreement concerning the worthiness of protecting the nesting area, however, they disagreed as to the scope of the government's right to regulate the use of investors' property under the Germany-Costa Rica BIT. The tribunal arranged for a site visit in Costa Rica, and arbitrators even witnessed a nesting process.[51] Yet, the award ultimately emphasized that '[w]hile the subject of the protection of endangered species is an important one, the Tribunal finds that the crucial elements of this dispute involve more mundane issues of fact and law as they relate to the legality of the actions in dispute between the Parties'.[52] It finally ruled that the Costa Rican actions amounted to a de facto expropriation.

In an attempt to better justify their environmentally induced measures, respondent governments have started to develop scientific arguments supporting their policies. The typical ways of raising scientific arguments are identified in the section that follows.

1.1 Emphasizing Due Process: Expanding Room for Exercising Police Powers

Host states may refer to the adequate nature of their procedure in which relevant science-based regulatory measures have been adopted. By advocating for such 'scientific due process'[53] criteria, such as using peer-reviewed scientific results, or the transparency and the participatory nature of the regulatory procedure, governments seek to expand their room for manoeuvre in enacting science-based policy decisions. In this vein, as long as the host state's scientific conclusions have been produced in a proper and transparent procedure, environmental regulations would withstand judicial scrutiny unless the results prove to be manifestly wrong. This position was clearly articulated in the *Methanex* Arbitration, where the United States appearing as respondent promoted a confined scope for the tribunal's review by stressing that '[t]he question is not whether the scientific conclusions were right or whether they were wrong. Instead, the question before this Tribunal is whether the scientific conclusions were so wrong that they could only be viewed as a pretext.'[54]

If such an argumentation prevails, science-based regulations are safe from adjudicatory challenge as long as investors could not substantiate a manifest error in the process of adopting relevant scientific measures. Conceptualizing states' regulatory space in such a manner also substantially simplifies the task of arbitrators as far as

---

50 *Unglaube* v. *Costa Rica*, Award, para. 164.
51 *Unglaube* v. *Costa Rica*, Award, para. 165.
52 *Unglaube* v. *Costa Rica*, Award, para. 167.
53 Lévesque, 'Science in the hands of international investment tribunals: a case for "scientific due process"'.
54 *Methanex.* v. *US*, Rejoinder of the Respondent United States of America (23 April 2004), para. 79.

their scientific engagement is concerned. It frees arbitrators from the need to investigate the scientific truth behind the regulation complained of by investors.

1.2 Emphasizing Uncertainties and Attacking Scientific Integrity

Claimants may try to undermine host states' scientific justifications by alluding to political motivations behind the scientific assessments to deprive scientific arguments from their persuasive nature. The *Methanex* case serves perhaps as the best illustration for this framing technique. Methanex, an MTBE producer, challenged the science behind a Californian regulation aiming to phase out MTBE based on alleged risks of drinking water contamination. Methanex argued that California's policy is nothing more than a politically motivated sham environmental protection measure.[55] It argued that the real cause of any possible water contamination is the poor enforcement of safety standards with regard to underground gasoline storage tanks; therefore, the ban was irrational and discriminatory against MTBE compared to other toxic fuel additives, which could also escape from the tanks though were not targeted by the regulation. Besides questioning the depth and consistency of the scientific report provided by the University of California in support of the ban, Methanex also appealed to political arguments claiming undue influence of the 'ethanol lobby' and 'political corruption'[56] behind the ban. These arguments ultimately did not suffice the panel to find a breach of NAFTA clauses, as will be discussed later.

Similarly, in *Chemtura* v. *Canada*, the claimant questioned the objectivity of the risk assessment, and claimed 'political pressures' on agency decision-making.[57] By doing so, Chemtura did not question the actual effects of lindane, the ban of which was the sanction complained of in the arbitration; rather, it aimed its criticism at the review procedure itself, seeking to prove that it 'was not a good faith scientific process'.[58]

In sum, this framing technique essentially seeks to offset host states' discretion in exercising their police powers. Such an argumentation is an effective tool for investors to restrict respondent governments' reference to scientific due process criteria, and thereby to narrow their regulatory space, or at a minimum, to render proving a claim of legitimate science-based regulation more cumbersome for respondents.

1.3 Precautionary Reasoning of States

Scientific uncertainties may be turned from a weakness of an argument to a virtue if host states could successfully invoke the precautionary principle. States sometimes

---

[55] *Methanex* v. *US*, Final Award, Part III. – Chapter A – 19, para. 41, citing Methanex's Reply, para. 147, Transcript Day 1.
[56] Allegations of Methanex as cited in the *Methanex* v. *US*, Final Award, Part III – Chapter B – Page 10, para. 21.
[57] *Chemtura* v. *Government of Canada*, Award, 2 Aug 2010, paras. 126, 153.
[58] Chemtura's position cited in *Chemtura* v. *Canada*, Award, para. 132.

seek to justify their measures imposed on foreign investments with reference to scientific uncertainty surrounding applicable risks. The success of appealing to a precautionary regulation, however, appears to be limited in investment arbitration. In *Windstream Energy* v. *Canada*, the panel did not accept the precautionary reasoning of the host state[59] with respect to risks of freshwater offshore wind power installations. Windstream Energy contested Canada's decision to halt the claimant's wind installation project on Lake Ontario following a public consultation that showed an overwhelming opposition against the development. Canada referred to limited knowledge available regarding the environmental impact of freshwater wind power stations and committed to carry out further research. However, the tribunal found that the government 'did relatively little to address the scientific uncertainty' surrounding environmental effects.[60] This reasoning suggests that the lack of pro-mised research played a major role in the panel's finding of a breach of the minimum standard of treatment of NAFTA.[61]

In a still pending fracking-related dispute, *Lone Pine* v. *Canada*,[62] the respondent withdrew the shale gas exploration licence of Lone Pine Ltd. based on a domestic legislation. Canada justified its ban on hydrocarbon developments in maritime estuary basins with a need for precaution.[63] It still remains to be seen whether the panel would allow the host state's precautionary measures to prevail.

1.4 Claiming Monopoly Over Fact-Finding

Parties may use the limited scientific competence of arbitrators as a leverage and claim monopoly over scientific fact-finding. This would translate into a narrow scope for judicial fact-finding in adjudicating science-based investment disputes. *Perenco* v. *Ecuador* evidences such an approach, where the investor submitted that the tribunal should not 'take as its task picking and choosing between the experts on each issue one by one, cafeteria-style, to arrive at some hybrid approach'.[64] In the material case, the two sides submitted diametrically opposing scientific evidence regarding the underlying environmental damage, which explains the strategic ben-efits of persuading the panel to reduce its evidentiary assessment to an either-or choice between the litigants' factual narratives.

---

[59] For Canada's position see *Windstream Energy LLC* v. *The Government of Canada*, PCA Case No. 2013–22, Award (27 September 2016), para. 207.
[60] *Windstream Energy*, Award, para. 378.
[61] *Windstream Energy*, Award, para. 380.
[62] *Lone Pine Resources Inc.* v. *The Government of Canada*, ICSID Case No. UNCT/15/2.
[63] *Lone Pine Resources Inc.* v. *Canada*, ICSID Case No. UNCT/15/2, Counter-Memorial (24 July 2015), para. 363. 'The decision to prohibit oil and gas exploration and development activities in the St. Lawrence River testifies to the level of precaution that the Quebec government has determined in the light of the lack of knowledge and the conclusions of the studies at its disposition' (original in French, English translation by the author).
[64] Perenco's Post-Hearing Brief, para. 50, cited by *Perenco* v. *Ecuador*, Interim Decision on the Environmental Counterclaim (11 August 2015), para. 584.

As will be seen in Section III, Subsection 1, a recurring difficulty in investment arbitration is that arbitrators are often left without necessary technical tools to find a middle ground between contrasting expert opinions.[65] Arbitral tribunals adopt no uniform approach to handle such difficulty and many of them struggle with finding an appropriate procedural solution. In the material case, the *Perenco* panel ultimately dismissed both sides' evidence and rather appointed an independent expert to re-sample the contaminated sites mentioned in the party-submitted expert reports.[66] This is not a common practice, however, as parties generally prefer to retain control over the fact-finding process.

2 *Adjudicatory Framing Techniques*

There are instances when the extent to which science plays a decisive role in the arbitral process hinges on the panel's approach towards the scientific dimension of the dispute. Initially, arbitral tribunals have tended to circumvent scientific considerations (Subsection 2.1), yet nowadays they are paying due regard to the scientific arguments of the parties to a growing extent. Particularly, they may use science as a benchmark for identifying arbitrary policies (Subsection 2.2) or use science to delineate the outer boundaries of their adjudicatory competence (Subsection 2.3).

2.1 Carving Out Scientific Aspects from the Scope of Inquiry

The first line of arbitral decisions gave outright precedence to investor's rights over environmental protection. In *Santa Elena* v. *Costa Rica* the panel ruled that expropriating private property is fully compensable under general international law irrespective of its environmental motive.[67] Notably, Costa Rica created a national park by expropriating the investor's environmentally unique Santa Elena beachside property, which was later even designated as a UNESCO World Heritage site. Costa Rica did not negate the fact of expropriation; the question put before the panel concerned the quantum of compensation due. The calculation method chosen by the tribunal excluded considering domestic environmental laws in place precluding the commercial development of the land, which could have reduced the property's fair market value, and hence, the amount of compensation. This inquiry entailed that the corresponding scientific evidence offered by Costa Rica to demonstrate the ecological value of the site[68] was also irrelevant for the

---

[65] Blackaby and Wilbraham, 'practical issues relating to the use of expert evidence in investment treaty arbitration', 656.

[66] *Perenco* v. *Ecuador*, Interim Decision on the Environmental Counterclaim, paras. 590–2.

[67] *Santa Elena* v. *Costa Rica*, Award, para. 71.

[68] Costa Rica had an expert witness, Professor Daniel Janzen, who provided evidence as to the ecological features of the Santa Elena property. *Santa Elena* v. *Costa Rica*, Award, para. 46.

tribunal. The award thus marks an adjudicatory framing technique eliminating the
scientific profile of disputes.

2.2 Using (the Absence of) Science as a Benchmark for Arbitrariness

Besides the occasions where tribunals regard scientific arguments irrelevant, arbitrators sometimes use the *absence* of scientific references as a basis for finding host
states' regulatory action arbitrary. The *Crystallex* case provides perhaps the clearest
example. The dispute concerned claims of Canadian investors arising from a denial
of permit to develop a gold mine in Venezuela. The claimant's mine operations
were terminated by the state authorities, which refused to issue an environmental
permit allowing the extraction.

As is apparent from the award and from the transcripts of the oral hearing, the
panel was actively searching for any proof of genuine scientific justifications for the
denial of the permit. The tribunal posed the expert witness an explicit question to
that effect,[69] signalling the decisive value of locating some objective, rational basis
for the denial. Yet domestic authorities apparently failed to produce scientific
studies and calculations to that effect. The tribunal regarded particularly relevant
that '[i]nstead of providing any scientific data to justify its conclusion',[70] Venezuela
denied the permit with vague references to 'environmental studies' and 'research'.

A similar dynamic can be discerned from the adjudicatory analysis in *Philip Morris*
v. *Uruguay*, although with a different outcome. In that case the presence of scientific
studies secured a positive outcome for the host state. The claimants contended that the
challenged measures mandating 80 per cent of the packaging of tobacco products be
covered with health warnings were arbitrary as they had been adopted 'without
a scientific evidence of their effectiveness'.[71] As Uruguay cited numerous scientific
studies to justify its measure, the panel was therefore convinced that:

> The connection between the objective pursued by the State and the utility of the
> two measures is recognized by the WHO and the PAHO Amicus Briefs ... At the
> time the measures were adopted, evidence was available at the international level
> regarding in particular consumers' misperception of the health risks attached to
> 'light' and 'lower tar' cigarettes ... Additional empirical evidence was offered,
> among other sources, by the Canada NGO Physicians for a Smoke-Free Canada
> and by the Brazilian experience. Numerous scientific studies had been published
> by that time in leading international journals cited by the U.S. Surgeon General
> and the U.S. National Cancer Institute.[72]

---

[69] *Crystallex International Corporation* v. *Bolivarian Republic of Venezuela*, ICSID Case No. ARB(AF)/
11/2, Award (4 April 2016), footnote 821 containing an excerpt from the oral hearing.

[70] *Crystallex* v. *Venezuela*, Award, para. 594.

[71] *Philip Morris Brands Sarl, Philip Morris Products SA and Abal Hermanos SA* v. *Oriental Republic of
Uruguay*, ICSID Case No. ARB/10/7, Award (8 July 2016), para. 392.

[72] *Philip Morris* v. *Uruguay*, Award, para. 392.

For all these reasons, the regulation was found to be in conformity with the fair and equitable treatment standard.[73]

2.3 No Second-Guessing of Scientific Truths

Several panels commented on the maximum extent to which they are inclined to engage with the scientific dilemma implicated in scientific risk assessments relevant in investment disputes. Tribunals in many arbitral proceedings stressed that it is beyond their task to investigate the factual scientific truth behind host states' regulatory decisions.

In *Chemtura* v. *Canada*, the tribunal famously stated that it would not 'second-guess the correctness'[74] of host states' science-based decision-making. The *Crystallex* v. *Venezuela* panel followed this example and made clear that '[i]t is not for an investor-state tribunal to second-guess the substantive correctness of the reasons which an administration were to put forward in its decisions'.[75] Instead, it defined its task as 'assess[ing] whether there have been serious procedural flaws which have resulted in the Permit being arbitrarily denied, or in the investor being treated non-transparently or inconsistently throughout the process'.[76] In the material case, such a framing led arbitrators to review the transparency of the domestic procedure, instead of evaluating the substantive outcome of the regulatory process.

Such an adjudicatory configuration of the legal inquiry decreases the science-intensity of the adjudicatory inquiry. As one commentator points out, it allows tribunals to 'downplay the need for an explicit decision on the scientific merits of each position',[77] and thereby saving adjudicators from being forced to decide the underlying scientific debate. Importantly, this conceptualization of the adjudicatory task spares arbitrators from a highly technical analysis, which in the majority of cases is a futile attempt at revealing the scientifically most correct answer to the underlying regulatory dilemma.

On other occasions arbitrators openly acknowledge the presence of uncertainties in relevant scientific data, without conceiving it as an obstacle to drawing legal conclusions. The tribunal in *Gold Reserve* v. *Venezuela* adopted a surprisingly managerial approach to scientific uncertainties involved in the facts of the case. To illustrate their firm and open approach towards ambiguities in scientific knowledge, their words are worthy of being reproduced in full here:

> the assessment of damages is often a *difficult exercise and it is seldom that damages in an investment situation will be able to be established with scientific certainty*. This is

[73] *Philip Morris* v. *Uruguay*, Award, para. 401.
[74] *Chemtura* v. *Canada*, Award, para. 134.
[75] *Crystallex* v. *Venezuela*, Award, para. 583.
[76] *Crystallex* v. *Venezuela*, Award, para. 585.
[77] J. E. Viñuales, 'Foreign investment and the environment in international law: an ambiguous relationship' (2010) 80 *British Yearbook of International Law* 244–332 at 278–9.

because such assessments will usually involve some degree of estimation and the weighing of competing (but equally legitimate) facts, valuation methods and opinions, which does not of itself mean that the burden of proof has not been satisfied. Because of this element of imprecision, it is accepted that tribunals retain a certain amount of discretion or a 'margin of appreciation' when assessing damages, which will necessarily involve some approximation. The use of this discretion should not be confused with acting on an *ex aequo et bono* basis, even if equitable considerations are taken into account in the exercise of such discretion. Rather, in such circumstances, the *tribunal exercises its judgment in a reasoned manner so as to discern an appropriate damages sum.*[78]

The noteworthy aspect of this reasoning lies in the arbitrators' position that exercising the judicial task and calculating appropriate damages is entirely feasible despite the inescapable uncertainties in the facts of the case. Such a This sincere acknowledgement of the limits of scientific knowledge, coupled with adjudicatory willingness to render a legal decision notwithstanding, makes this reasoning rather exceptional among science-based judicial decisions. This illustrates a peculiar adjudicatory attitude, where the impossibility to find the actual scientific truth does not create an insurmountable obstacle to exercising legal judgment. The *Gold Reserves* Tribunal thus felt confident enough to provide a judicial reasoning bridging uncertain facts and adjudicatory conclusions on the quantum of damages.

III SCIENTIFIC FACT-FINDING TECHNIQUES IN INVESTMENT ARBITRATION

Experts are commonly used in investment arbitration.[79] While party-appointed experts are commonplace (Subsection 1), the use of *ex tribunal* experts remains a rarity, and the desirability of using such a fact-finding technique is also debated (Subsection 2). Conflicting views on the most appropriate way of garnering expert advice seems to be stemming from competing ideals of legitimacy, which will be discussed in Subsection 3.

1 *Party-Appointed Experts*

The prevailing fact-finding method in investment arbitration is hearing evidence offered by party-appointed experts. This is often attributed to the influence of the common law litigation culture on investment arbitration, but insights into practice

---

[78] *Gold Reserve Inc. v. Bolivarian Republic of Venezuela*, ICSID Case No. ARB(AF)/09/1, Award (22 September 2014), para. 686. Internal footnotes omitted, emphasis added.

[79] The respective rules on experts are provided in the tribunal's specific rules of procedure, see for example ICSID Arbitration Rules, Rules 35, 36, UNCITRAL Arbitration Rules (2010), Article 28 (2). ICSID tribunals appoint experts even in the absence of express provisions in their procedural rules. Jacur, 'Remarks on the role of *ex curia* scientific experts in international environmental disputes', p. 444.

suggest that it is also a corollary of the arbitral procedure itself, where the parties are expected to fully argue their case, with the necessary expert reports included, before the first hearing on the merits.[80]

The dominance of party-adduced evidence has its drawbacks. Notably, the parties' evidentiary submissions sometimes can be biased to an extent that their evidentiary value is dubious and may even preclude any meaningful adjudicatory analysis. In the *Perenco* case, the tribunal rejected the scientific evidence presented by both party-appointed experts as they 'crossed the boundary between professional objective analysis and party representation'.[81] The panel deferred the decision on the extent of relevant oil contamination to a later stage after further fact-finding provided by an independent expert.[82] This shows that adjudicators expect good faith explanations from experts regarding divergent scientific claims, and the failure of a party to do so would result in serious deficit in the credibility, and thus, the weight of the evidence.

Active engagement with the scientific evidence may also be possible in the absence of tribunal-appointed experts. The most ambitious fact-finding assessment among arbitral tribunals has been perhaps conducted by the *Peter Allard* panel, which thoroughly reviewed party-adduced conflicting scientific evidence, and investigated the cause and extent of alleged ecological degradation without having recourse to an independent expert. The remarkably detailed factual analysis of the panel totalled in an almost twenty-page long assessment of the various party-adduced expert reports.[83] Quite unusually, the tribunal critically singled out the evidence it found to be 'speculative' or 'inapt' due to methodological inconsistencies.[84] The arbitrators found that the evidence did not prove that the claimant's property suffered ecological degradation in the relevant period. For reaching this conclusion, the panel did not shy away from evaluating whether seasonal variations were accounted for,[85] whether data were collected in a sufficiently long period,[86] whether alternative possible explanations for the same result were revealed,[87] and whether data patterns were satisfactorily explained[88] in the party-adduced scientific reports. Such questions are well beyond the scope of scientific issues that investment tribunals are normally willing to entertain.

---

[80]   Blackaby and Wilbraham, 'Practical issues relating to the use of expert evidence in investment treaty arbitration', 656.

[81]   *Perenco v. Ecuador*, Interim Decision on the Environmental Counterclaim (11 August 2015), para. 581.

[82]   *Perenco v. Ecuador*, Interim Decision on the Environmental Counterclaim, paras. 585, 587.

[83]   *Peter Allard v. Barbados*, Award, paras. 87–139.

[84]   *Peter Allard v. Barbados*, Award, paras. 94, 130.

[85]   *Peter Allard v. Barbados*, Award, para. 97, 99–102.

[86]   *Peter Allard v. Barbados*, Award, para. 109.

[87]   *Peter Allard v. Barbados*, Award, para. 163.

[88]   *Peter Allard v. Barbados*, Award, para. 125.

2 *Tribunal-Appointed Experts*

Investment arbitral tribunals normally have the power of appointing their own experts to assist them in revealing the scientific background of the case.[89] They are endowed with powers to seek information and technical advice from any expert or competent organization they deem appropriate.[90] Yet, appointing *ex tribunal* experts has thus far remained a rarity in the practice of investment arbitration. When panels opt for appointing their own experts, they typically do so after the final hearing took place, when they can formulate with enough precision the questions they need assistance with.[91] The role of tribunal-appointed experts is envisaged in helping adjudicators evaluate and choose between conflicting scientific claims by reviewing party-appointed evidence and responding to any adjudicatory queries.[92]

Arbitrators' reluctance to have recourse to such expertise can be contrasted with the manifold benefits relying on expertise confers on investment tribunals. Panel-appointed experts could guarantee to receive unbiased expert advice that is not seeking to blatantly support one of the parties. This may be of special concern with a view to the prevalence of such a problem. An empirical survey among arbitrators and counsels suggests that party-appointed experts may in certain cases be avowedly engaging in 'non-legal advocacy'.[93] Second, *ex tribunal* experts assist arbitrators in not being paralysed by contradicting partisan evidence, and therefore may foster a more active adjudicatory engagement with scientific evidence, which is actively promoted by many counsels.[94] As the *Perenco* Arbitration demonstrates, the assistance of independent experts makes the difficult task of selecting between competing scientific evidence a manageable task for arbitrators.

Moreover, reliance on tribunal-appointed experts is also called for by the considerable public interest involved in environmental investment arbitration.[95] This public interest element[96] entails that the contours of states' right to regulate environmental concerns should not be regarded as a strictly *inter*

---

[89] See ICC Arbitration Rules, Art. 25 (4); IVA Rules on the Taking of Evidence in International Arbitration, Art. 6 (29 May 2010); UNCITRAL Arbitration Rules, Article 29.
[90] NAFTA Articles 2014, 2015, IBA Rules on the Taking of Evidence in International Arbitration, Article 6, Article 27(1) of the UNCITRAL Arbitration Rules.
[91] Blackaby and Wilbraham, 'Practical issues relating to the use of expert evidence in investment treaty arbitration', 656.
[92] Blackaby and Wilbraham, 'Practical issues relating to the use of expert evidence in investment treaty arbitration', 664.
[93] Boisson de Chazournes, Mbengue, Das, and Gros, 'One size does not fit all – uses of experts before international courts and tribunals', 492.
[94] Blackaby and Wilbraham, 'Practical issues relating to the use of expert evidence in investment treaty arbitration', 655.
[95] Fukunaga, 'Standard of review and "scientific truths" in the WTO dispute settlement system and investment arbitration', 570.
[96] Harrison, 'Addressing the procedural challenges of environmental litigation in the context of investor-state arbitration', pp. 104–5.

partes matter.[97] Scrutinizing the extent to which states may impose environmental obligations on foreign investors has obvious repercussions on the well-being of the citizens of host states. Such considerable effects on community interests justify, or even call for, an adjudicatory approach to extensively seek independent expert opinions to ensure the well-foundedness of evidence describing likely environmental risks and impacts at hand.

One may argue that frequent reliance on tribunal-appointed experts runs against the deeply engrained party-driven nature of arbitration. Yet, a growing awareness among investment tribunals of the importance of duly accounting for the public interest is suggested by more recent arbitral proceedings. For instance, ICSID tribunals increasingly admit or explicitly ask for amicus briefs from NGOs.[98] In a similar fashion, the significant public interests involved in environmental disputes could and should be accounted for also by appointing independent experts.

3 *Engagement with Expertise: Appraisal from a Legitimacy Point of View*

Despite that practitioners are generally contented with the party-driven nature of scientific fact-finding, counsels also repeatedly emphasize the need for adjudicators to engage more actively with the fact-finding process.[99] Proposals specifically allude to the necessity of giving clearer instructions to experts about the issues of interest for the panel's inquiry, and interacting more closely with the experts.[100] Such a hands-on attitude is deemed beneficial by many, even though the parties often expect arbitrators to adopt a managerial approach only at later stages of the proceedings, granting enough flexibility for them in the initial phase of fact-finding.[101]

A growing array of novel fact-finding techniques could facilitate a more activist engagement with expert evidence. Witness conferencing, also known as hot-

---

[97] See Separate Opinion of Judge Weeramantry in *Gabcikovo-Nagymaros*, p. 118, stressing that '[w]e have entered an era of international law in which international law subserves not only the interests of individual States, but looks beyond them and their parochial concerns to the greater interests of humanity and planetary welfare. In addressing such problems, which transcend the individual rights and obligations of the litigating States, international law will need to look beyond procedural rules fashioned for purely *inter partes* litigation.'

[98] The first such occasion was in *Piero Foresti, Laura de Carli & Others* v. *South Africa* (ICSID Case No. ARB(AF)/07/1), where four NGOs specialized in the field of human rights and environmental protection were explicitly asked by the panel to submit amicus briefs on the public interest aspects despite the strong objection of the claimant. See more: Center for International Environmental Law publication entitled 'Tribunal in *Piero Foresti, Laura De Carli and Others* v. *the Republic of South Africa* grants CIEL and human rights organizations access to documents by the parties' (23 October 2009) available at https://bit.ly/3dBEKuU (last accessed 11 January 2020).

[99] Boisson de Chazournes, Mbengue, Das, and Gros, 'One size does not fit all – uses of experts before international courts and tribunals', 494; Blackaby and Wilbraham, 'Practical issues relating to the use of expert evidence in investment treaty arbitration', 655.

[100] Blackaby and Wilbraham, 'Practical issues relating to the use of expert evidence in investment treaty arbitration'.

[101] Boisson de Chazournes, Mbengue, Das, and Gros, 'One size does not fit all – uses of experts before international courts and tribunals', 493.

tubbing,[102] enables adjudicators to benefit from the simultaneous hearing of party-appointed experts, allowing them to reveal the weaknesses in the scientific argumentation of their counterparts. Expert teams may also be formed from scientists selected from the shortlist of the parties, and may be ordered to prepare a joint expert report for the panel.[103] Lastly, arbitrators may order for a pre-hearing meeting with party-appointed experts to delineate points of agreement and disagreement.[104] All these techniques enable arbitrators to develop their own appreciation of the scientific issues implicated in the legal controversy independently from the parties' submissions.

The fact remains that counsels generally prefer that *ex curia* experts remain exceptional in investment arbitration, if party-adduced evidence is insufficient.[105] The dilemma of which type of expertise investment tribunals ought to rely on is usually explained and answered with reference to the divergent litigious cultures of common law and civil law countries. *Ex tribunal* experts are more alien to common law traditions that appear to have a decisive impact on investor-state dispute settlement systems, so the argument goes. It will be argued here that revealing the different ideals of legitimacy that are fostered by *ex tribunal* and *ex parte* experts respectively puts this debate into a new perspective.

Notably, the parties and counsels generally favour allowing party-appointed experts to dominate the fact-finding process, as it allows them to maintain control over the evidentiary proceedings. As these actors take up a major part of investment tribunals' relevant audience, aligning the fact-finding procedure with such preferences and not having recourse to tribunal-appointed experts may seem a legitimate solution from the standpoint of sociological legitimacy. Yet, one should also be mindful of other conceptions of legitimacy while searching for the ideal contours of adjudicatory fact-finding. Specifically, the role of epistemic legitimacy needs to be underlined, which requires – as detailed elsewhere in this study[106] – that decision-makers be equipped with the necessary knowledge to assess every relevant aspect of disputes.

In the context of scientific fact-finding, epistemic legitimacy warrants for reinforcing the internal epistemic competence of tribunals by furnishing arbitrators with independent expert advice, which helps elucidate the technical aspects of the case without running the risk of producing evidence tainted with biased advocacy.

---

[102]   Blackaby and Wilbraham, 'Practical issues relating to the use of expert evidence in investment treaty arbitration', 667.

[103]   Boisson de Chazournes, Mbengue, Das, and Gros, 'One size does not fit all – uses of experts before international courts and tribunals', 496.

[104]   Blackaby and Wilbraham, 'Practical issues relating to the use of expert evidence in investment treaty arbitration', 665.

[105]   Boisson de Chazournes, Mbengue, Das, and Gros, 'One size does not fit all – uses of experts before international courts and tribunals', 492; Blackaby and Wilbraham, 'Practical issues relating to the use of expert evidence in investment treaty arbitration', 669.

[106]   See relevant discussion in Chapter 2 and Chapter 10.

Enhancing the scientific literacy of arbitral tribunals seems to be essential for equipping panels with the necessary knowledge and ability to deal with the scientific dimension of disputes. In other words, more frequent reliance on tribunal-appointed experts may be necessitated by concerns for epistemic legitimacy of investment decisions. From this perspective, therefore, adopting a peculiar amalgam of the two models of garnering expert evidence seems to be the optimal solution to scaffold the sociological and epistemic legitimacy of individual awards as well as science-intensive arbitration more generally.

IV CAUSAL INQUIRY

Investment arbitral tribunals rarely conduct a thorough causal inquiry into science-intensive claims. This is hardly surprising if one considers the rarity of discussing science-based causal claims in the context of environmental investment arbitration. Environmental counterclaims have provided thus far the most fertile ground for raising such science-intensive causal inquiries.

The *Peter Allard* award discussed the issue of competing causal claims. Surprisingly, the panel conducted a causal inquiry 'for the sake of completeness',[107] despite the fact that the investor failed to establish the harm, and therefore, deciding on causation was superfluous. The claimant argued that a decrease in water salinity triggered the loss of biodiversity in its eco-resort, which was due to Barbados' failure to maintain a sluice gate ensuring seawater connections with the swampy area, where the real estate development was situated. In contrast Barbados claimed that the sanctuary's salinity is maintained through subsurface seawater exchange and not primarily through the sluice gate. In terms of the causal investigation, the tribunal focused on whether the 'gate was a significant component in maintaining the salinity of the Sanctuary Lake',[108] instead of seeking for 'the' (but-for) cause of declining salinity.

This causal test can be seen as a laudable choice, since it pays due regard to the causal uncertainty inherent in causal mechanisms of ecosystem changes by not per se excluding the possibility to finding a causal link between Barbados' omission and the injury claimed. Nevertheless, in the material case the panel found no causal link established between the alleged mismanagement of the gate and the lake's changing salinity with a view to a more probable competing theory on subsurface seawater exchange.[109] Such science-intensive causal inquiry can nevertheless be applauded for investigating the scientific bases and evaluating the complex expert evidence from a legal point of view.

---

[107] *Peter Allard* v. *Barbados*, Award, para. 140.
[108] *Peter Allard* v. *Barbados*, Award, para. 157.
[109] *Peter Allard* v. *Barbados*, Award, paras. 158–64. The lack of causal link was supported by a widely held scientific theory on subsurface seawater exchange that was not disproved by the claimant. The tribunal also cited proof of several occasions when the gate permitted water connections.

V STANDARD AND EXTENT OF ADJUDICATORY REVIEW OF SCIENTIFIC CLAIMS

Arbitration practice showcases a relatively unified approach to deference in reviewing host states' science-backed claims (Subsection 1). Less homogenous are the actual legal tests with which arbitrators scrutinize the credibility of a scientific position put forth by host state governments. After discussing the various types of benchmarks used in this respect (Subsection 2), some analytic remarks are offered on the appropriate contours of reviewing the scientific bases of regulatory measures in the context of investment arbitration (Subsection 3).

1 *Affording Deference to Host States' Scientific Claims*

Investor-state arbitral tribunals generally favour setting a high bar for claims regarding alleged breaches of investment protection standards. As was highlighted in *Waste Management II* v. *Mexico*, breaches can be supported by a showing of 'complete lack of transparency and candour in an administrative process'.[110] The *Unglaube* Tribunal further clarified that in order to establish a breach of fair and equitable treatment standard, 'claimant must show more than mere legal error. Instead, as stated by the *Saluka* Tribunal, the evidence must establish actions or decisions which are "manifestly inconsistent, non-transparent, [or] unreasonable (i.e., unrelated to some rational policy)"'.[111]

The margin of appreciation doctrine therefore appears also in the practice of investment tribunals.[112] As the *Glamis Gold* Tribunal stressed, '[t]he idea of deference is found in the modifiers "manifest" and "gross" that make this standard a stringent one; it is found in the idea that a breach requires something greater than mere arbitrariness, something that is surprising, shocking, or exhibits a manifest lack of reasoning'.[113] In this vein, investment tribunals generally opt for granting a high degree of deference to states in terms of designing their environmental regulation.

The first occasion, when a panel expressly referred to deference was in the *S. D. Myers* v. *Canada* case, a dispute under NAFTA Chapter 11. Canada banned exporting polychlorinated biphenyl (PCB) waste, an environmentally hazardous chemical, with reference to its dangers to human health and the environment. The ban was instituted right after S. D. Myers obtained a licence to import PCB waste to the United States in order to destroy the hazardous compounds there. The tribunal concluded that the primary reason for the export ban was protecting the Canadian

---

[110] *Waste Management Inc* v. *United Mexican States*, ICSID Case No. ARB(AF)/00/3, Award (30 April 2004), para. 98.

[111] *Marion Unglaube* v. *Costa Rica*, Award, para. 246.

[112] Viñuales, *Foreign Investment and the Environment*, pp. 377–81.

[113] *Glamis Gold Ltd.* v. *The United States of America* (UNCITRAL) Award (8 June 2009), para. 617.

PCB disposal industry from competition,[114] since Canada merely asserted such risks but never investigated them.[115] Nevertheless, the panel emphasized that in the context of NAFTA's minimum standard of treatment clause a 'high measure of deference' had to be accorded to host states in designing their domestic public policies.[116]

Similarly, in *Chemtura* v. *Canada*, the tribunal emphasized that it is beyond its task to 'second-guess the correctness of the science-based decision-making of highly specialized national regulatory agencies'.[117] In the material case, Canada banned a pesticide called lindane after reviewing its environmental hazards. Such an adjudicatory approach in fact signals an implicit deference to the expertise and risk assessment of regulating host states.[118] The *Chemtura* Tribunal also rejected that a minimum standard of treatment clause would entail scrutinizing scientific legality criteria. The claimant argued that 'a lack of sufficient evidence to support a decision and/or basing a decision on irrelevant considerations, resulting in a decision that is clearly improper and discreditable'[119] would amount to a breach of that standard. However, the tribunal disagreed and emphasized that a regulatory procedure would only entail a breach of investment protection standards if it showed 'bad faith or disingenuous conduct' on the part of the host state.[120]

Though these criteria do raise a high bar for investors to establish a challenge against host state's scientific regulations, the *Chemtura* Tribunal also emphasizes that '[i]n assessing whether the treatment afforded to the Claimant's investment was in accordance with the international minimum standard, the Tribunal must take into account all the circumstances, including the fact that certain agencies manage highly specialized domains involving scientific and public policy determinations'.[121] This wording preserves the right to scrutinize to some extent the ways in which host states' regulatory agencies formulate their scientific opinions.

The deferential approach of investment tribunals is also reflected in the fact that host states are not required to base their regulations only on the prevailing position of the scientific community. The *Chemtura* Tribunal noted that 'scientific divergence to which the Claimant referred cannot in and of itself serve as a basis for a finding of breach of Article 1105 of NAFTA'.[122] This suggests that basing policy measures on minority scientific opinions can withstand scrutiny, at least in cases when – in the words of Canada's expert witness – the differences in scientific opinions 'are within

---

[114] S. D. Myers, Inc. v. Government of Canada (UNCITRAL) Partial Award (13 November 2000), para. 162.
[115] S. D. Myers v. Canada, Partial Award, para. 187.
[116] S. D. Myers v. Canada, Partial Award, para. 263.
[117] Chemtura v. Canada, Award, para. 134.
[118] Fukunaga, 'Standard of review and "scientific truths" in the WTO dispute settlement system and investment arbitration', 573.
[119] Chemtura v. Canada, Award, para. 112.
[120] Chemtura v. Canada, Award, para. 138.
[121] Chemtura v. Canada, Award, para. 123.
[122] Chemtura v. Canada, Award, para. 154.

the boundaries of acceptable sciences'.[123] Having ascertained that the risk assessment conclusions of Canada 'were within acceptable scientific parameters',[124] the tribunal found no breach of investment protection standards for the phasing out of lindane.

In sum, investment jurisprudence tends to afford a high measure of deference to host states' scientific claims.[125] Yet, such deference is not unlimited, as has been emphasized recurrently by tribunals.[126] This also implies that arbitrators do craft certain benchmarks to evaluate the acceptability of scientific claims. These will be discussed in the next section.

2 *Standards of Review: Indicia of Credible Scientific Positions*

Given that investment panels do not afford total deference to host states' scientific claims, a corresponding question immediately arises as to what benchmarks are available against which arbitrators can measure the soundness of host states' scientific claims. The applicable standard ought to enable tribunals to 'walk a fine line between adjudicating legal claims and deciding scientific disputes'.[127] Countering host states' argument that 'a high measure of deference to the facts and factual conclusions seems the only way to prevent investment tribunals from becoming science courts',[128] investment tribunals did in fact develop several tools to legally evaluate the ways in which respondent governments use regulatory science; without, however, becoming ensnared in evaluating the validity of scientific opinions.

The prevailing method seems to be to focus on the process in which regulatory science has been produced (Subsection 2.1). Another approach views international regulatory trends as a reliable proxy for assessing the credibility of scientific opinions on environmental risks (Subsection 2.2).

2.1 Using a Procedural Benchmark: Transparency of the Regulatory Process

Certain tribunals focus on the transparency and participatory nature of the process in which relevant regulatory science results have been produced. Others scrutinize the reasoning of the host state in accounting for scientific conclusions supporting policy measures.

---

[123] Quote from the testimony of Dr Costa, Canada's expert witness cited in the award, see *Chemtura* v. *Canada*, Award, para. 154.
[124] *Chemtura* v. *Canada*, Award, para. 154.
[125] Gruszczynski, 'Standard of review and scientific evidence in WTO law and international investment arbitration', p. 168.
[126] *Unglaube* v. *Costa Rica*, Award, para. 247; *Crystallex* v. *Venezuela*, Award, para. 584.
[127] Orellana, 'The role of science in investment arbitrations concerning public health and the environment', 49.
[128] *Glamis Gold* v. *US*, Award, para. 594, quoting the respondent's position.

2.1.1 TRANSPARENCY OF SCIENTIFIC KNOWLEDGE PRODUCTION. The *Chemtura* Tribunal stresses at the outset that 'it is not its task to determine whether certain uses of lindane are dangerous'.[129] Also, judging 'the correctness or adequacy of the scientific results' fell outside the tribunal's jurisdiction.[130] In order to assess the adequacy of the scientific basis of risk assessment procedures, panels increasingly examine whether host states used credible scientific evidence in the regulatory process.[131] This provides a convenient solution for scientifically lay adjudicators to form an opinion on rival scientific claims without, however, need to decide about the scientific merit of each claim.

In this vein, the *Chemtura* Tribunal conducted a detailed assessment focusing on the scientific review process leading to the ban on lindane. The award revisited minutes prepared on meetings, and examined testimonies of experts and witnesses involved in the policy-making procedure.[132] The inquiry was based on a two-prong test. The tribunal first determined 'whether the Special Review was conducted in such a manner as to reflect bad faith'[133] on the part of the respondent's expert agency. Second, it interrogated whether 'the review of lindane (even if in good faith), breached the due process rights of the Claimant. Such inquiry must take into account the review process as a whole'.[134]

A similar path has been taken by the *Glamis Gold* Tribunal. The *Glamis Gold v. US* case concerned a refusal of permitting a pit mine to prevent adverse effects on the environment and on indigenous communities. The tribunal opposed to make a definitive decision on the scientific truth claimed by the parties. Instead, it stressed that the panel 'may assess only whether there was reasonable evidence, and this, the government's reliance on such was not obviously and actionably misplaced'.[135] The panel's inquiry into the risk assessment procedure was practically narrowed down to an assessment of transparency and non-arbitrariness, partly due to the fact that the respondent itself framed the legal issues focusing on these two features of its risk assessment throughout the proceedings.[136]

Using procedural benchmarks to evaluate the soundness of scientific risk assessments leaves considerable room for host states to legitimately regulate uncertain environmental risks. The *Methanex* Tribunal found in favour of the host state even though there were pervasive uncertainties in the scientific conclusions supporting the measure complained of.[137] By doing so, the *Methanex* award has adopted

---

[129]   *Chemtura* v. *Canada*, Award, para. 134.
[130]   *Chemtura* v. *Canada*, Award, para. 153.
[131]   Orellana, 'The role of science in investment arbitrations concerning public health and the environment', 72.
[132]   *Chemtura* v. *Canada*, Award, para. 147 et seq.
[133]   *Chemtura* v. *Canada*, Award, para. 145.
[134]   *Chemtura* v. *Canada*, Award, para. 145.
[135]   *Glamis Gold* v. *US*, Award, para. 786.
[136]   *Glamis Gold* v. *US*, Award, para. 663.
[137]   *Methanex* v. *US*, Final Award, Part III – Chapter A, para. 54.

a surprisingly pro-regulatory approach compared to other investment decisions.[138] Despite numerous challenges set forth by the investor, the panel found that California's risk assessment on MTBE's public health risks was 'serious, objective and scientific'.[139] The tribunal arrived at this conclusion by reviewing the procedural attributes of the regulatory process, such as whether there was open and informed debate preceding the legislation and whether the data used had been subject to peer-review.[140] The *Methanex* Tribunal illustrates how the impartiality of the process of a risk assessment becomes an indicium of scientific credibility. The decision suggests that as long as all procedural attributes of a good faith regulatory procedure have been observed by the regulator, uncertainties in science are not fatal to environmental regulation reasonably targeting foreign investment.

The *Methanex* Tribunal also defined a rather deferential standard for judicial review. It stressed that it would only find a breach where scientific conclusions of the host state 'were so faulty that the Tribunal may reasonably infer that the science merely provided a convenient excuse for'[141] disguised protectionism. Accordingly, the arbitrators were investigating whether the scientific grounds for regulation were 'scientifically incorrect',[142] rather than ascertaining whether they were 'correct'. Framing the judicial inquiry in this way grants a certain measure of deference to sovereigns by reversing the burden of scientific uncertainty from regulators to investors.

The *Methanex* award garnered considerable applause for approaching science in a proper way.[143] Indeed, the decision manifests a close engagement with the scientific aspects of the controversy and a detailed fact-finding process, for which it can be praised. Specifically, it was acclaimed for requiring peer review from claims of regulatory science in order to be accepted as valid evidence.[144] Using peer review as a benchmark of acceptable scientific claims has nevertheless certain limitations due to which it cannot in and of itself solve all the problems adjudicators face in evaluating scientific input. The strengths and weaknesses of deeming peer review as the sole criterion of adjudicatory scrutiny will be examined in more detail in Chapter 10 Section II, Subsection 2.1.3.

---

[138] D. French, 'Environmental dispute settlement: the first (hesitant) signs of spring?' (2006) 19 *Hague Yearbook of International Law* 3–32 at 27.
[139] *Methanex* v. US, Final Award, Part III – Chapter A – 51, para. 101.
[140] *Methanex* v. US, Final Award, Part III – Chapter A – 51, para. 101.
[141] *Methanex* v. US, Final Award, Part IV – Chapter E para. 19.
[142] *Methanex* v. US, Final Award, Part III – Chapter A, para. 101.
[143] Orellana, 'The role of science in investment arbitrations concerning public health and the environment', 72; D'Aspremont and Mbengue, 'Strategies of engagement with scientific fact-finding in international adjudication', 261; Lévesque, 'Science in the hands of international investment tribunals: a case for "scientific due process"', 261.
[144] A. Alemanno, 'EU risk regulation and science: the role of experts in decision-making and judicial review' in E. Vos (ed.), *European Risk Governance: Its Science, Its Inclusiveness and Its Effectiveness*, Connex Report Series No. 6 (2008), pp. 37–88 pp. 65–7.

2.1.2 TRANSPARENT REASONING IN SCIENCE-BASED ENVIRONMENTAL PERMITTING.
Transparency requirements may also be enforced against the science-based reasoning provided by host states in their individual decisions. These criteria are
typically applied in scrutinizing the permitting process to which the investor's
project was subjected. When authorities disclose the scientific justifications of
their decisions, those are seen as indicia of a good faith and, hence, non-arbitrary
decision-making. Tribunals therefore impose on host states 'the burden to elucidate the reasons for' their decisions, preferably accompanied by 'some kind of
supporting data to explain why it was reaching the conclusion it reached'.[145]
Following this line or argumentation, the *Crystallex* Tribunal found that the
failure of the host state to demonstrate a 'precise and reasoned denial' amounted
to a breach of the fair and equitable treatment standard.[146] Vague and general
references by Venezuela to hydrological changes in the affected area, without
citing any supporting scientific authority, was an insufficient reason to deny a
permit in the tribunal's view.

2.2 Taking International Regulatory Trend as Evidence of Credible Scientific Positions

Another adjudicatory reasoning technique regards international regulatory trends as
a persuasive benchmark for the existence of genuine environmental risks, and
therefore as indicia of credible scientific positions. The *Chemtura* case evidences
such an adjudicatory reasoning. The fact that twenty states as well as the European
Union have banned or restricted the use of lindane seemed to be a decisive factor for
the tribunal to find the Canadian ban legitimate.[147] Similarly, multilateral environmental treaties, such as the Aarhus Protocol to the Long-Range Transboundary Air
Pollution Convention, the OSPAR Convention, and the Stockholm Convention on
Persistent Organic Pollutants, which all regarded lindane as a harmful substance,[148]
seemed to inform the tribunal's conviction that Canada acted in good faith while
banning the chemical with reference to its health hazards. The reasoning of the
tribunal explicitly refers to the practice of the international community, when it
points out: '[i]rrespective of the state of the science, however, the Tribunal cannot
ignore the fact that lindane has raised increasingly serious concerns both in other
countries and at the international level since the 1970s'.[149]

A more recent reference to the opinion of international expert organizations as
evidence of health risks was made in the *Philip Morris* v. *Uruguay* case. The dispute
featured a challenge against Uruguay's plain packaging measures for tobacco

---

[145] *Crystallex* v. *Venezuela*, Award, para. 593.
[146] *Crystallex* v. *Venezuela*, Award, paras. 593, 597.
[147] For the list of countries banning the lindane see *Chemtura* v. *Canada*, Award, para. 135.
[148] *Chemtura* v. *Canada* case, Award, paras. 135–7.
[149] *Chemtura* v. *Canada* case, Award, para. 135.

products, which was in the host state's view a legitimate regulation to protect public health. To evidence the reasonable nature of the regulation, and its necessity in light of genuine health risks, Uruguay relied on amicus briefs prepared by the WHO and the Pan American Health Organization. The tribunal attached evidentiary weight to these submissions as well as to the fact that Uruguay adhered to the evidence-based WHO Framework Convention on Tobacco Control.[150] These remarks have led the panel to deem the plain packaging measure as a non-arbitrary response to public health risks. As observed by one commentator, the *Philip Morris* Tribunal relied on these scientific opinions 'not because (or only because) it supplied "scientific" or technical data unfamiliar to lawyer-adjudicators', but mainly on account of the 'independent standing'[151] these scientific references had vis-à-vis the parties' submissions.

Invoking international regulatory trends has many advantages. The greatest strength of this reasoning style is that it can be seen as being relatively objective. Projecting such an image may have never been more important for arbitrators than nowadays, amidst fortifying legitimacy concerns surrounding environmental investment arbitration.[152] A further beneficial feature of such a reasoning lies in the fact that it implicitly appeals to common sense.[153] Invoking international regulatory tendencies provides a convincing scientific footing for adjudicatory conclusions, and a quick avenue to take a legal stance on the scientific controversy involved.

At the same time, attaching great significance to the practice of other states has its drawbacks. Such a standard of review is blind to newly emerging environmental risks. It is doubtful whether the ban on lindane that was featured in the *Chemtura* case could have equally been justified, had Canada been the first state regulating the chemical's environmental hazards. Further blind spots and weaknesses of building adjudicatory scrutiny of science-based regulations solely on international regulatory trends will be addressed in Chapter 10.[154]

2.3 Comment on the Appropriate Extent of Reviewing Scientific Regulations

There is no consensus as to the ideal way of handling scientific claims in investor-state disputes. Promoters of an explicit deferential review prefer if arbitrators reserved a wide room for police powers of host states. Indeed, persuasive arguments can be made to defend such a judicial attitude also from the perspectives of this study. A deferential attitude respects host states' police powers, especially by

---

[150] *Philip Morris* v. *Uruguay*, Award, paras. 391–4.
[151] J. E. Alvarez, 'The Search for objectivity: the use of experts in *Philip Morris* v. *Uruguay*' (2018) 9 *Journal of International Dispute Settlement* 411–22 at 422.
[152] Schill, 'Deference in investment treaty arbitration: re-conceptualizing the standard of review'.
[153] Jorge E. Viñuales, 'Observations sur le traitement des motifs scientifiques dans le contentieux environnemental international', p. 119.
[154] Chapter 10 Section II, Subsection 2.1.2.

allowing them to regulate uncertain environmental risks even on the basis of divergent, minority scientific opinions.

Albeit an overly deferential approach may also prove to be a double-edge sword. Host states may avail themselves of such a relaxed adjudicatory review to advance policies derogating from existing environmental legislation. In times when scientific scepticism is embraced by a growing number of populist political actors worldwide,[155] in extreme situations amounting to an outright 'war on science', one can readily think of circumstances where deference can be abused to serve de-regulatory purposes. Being mindful of the considerable adverse effects of environmental regulatory roll-back on the wider public, it appears advisable to argue for certain benchmarks that can limit host state's discretion in evaluating scientific claims.

Yet what shall be the guiding principle in defining the adjudicatory task in cases when the lawfulness of a science-based regulation is called into question? First of all, arbitral tribunals ought not to judge the scientific merits of the evidence,[156] but should investigate the credibility of science used in the regulatory process. As Viñuales puts it, investment tribunals 'must not focus on the science but on the process'.[157] Indeed, the focus of scrutiny should be on the ways in which the given scientific result had been produced.[158] Adjudicatory tests scrutinizing scientific due process criteria[159] or respect for scientific freedom,[160] for instance, may effectively guard against arbitrary decisions of host states.

Furthermore, in quite a good number of cases focusing on the regulatory procedure itself proves to be an adequate tool to single out disguised measures aiming to encroach upon investment protection guarantees. Several disputes featuring claims of denial or revocation of environmental permits are rooted in domestic procedures that suffer from serious rule of law deficiencies. These instances can be successfully identified through non-scientific benchmarks focusing on the conduct of authorities of the host state. In this way arbitrators can appraise and justify the non-conformity of said measures with investment protection standards in a way that is not only convenient, but also legitimate from an epistemic point of view.

Nevertheless, when questions of causality and environmental harm are featured in an investment dispute, a more in-depth engagement with scientific evidence ought not to be avoided. In such cases, assessing whether ambiguities in the data

---

[155] B. J. Preston, 'The end of enlightened environmental law?' (2019) 31 *Journal of Environmental Law* 399–411.

[156] Foster, *Science and the Precautionary Principle in International Courts and Tribunals*, p. 145.

[157] Viñuales, *Foreign Investment and the Environment*, p. 378.

[158] Orellana, 'The role of science in investment arbitrations concerning public health and the environment', 64–5.

[159] Lévesque, 'Science in the hands of international investment tribunals: a case for "scientific due process"'.

[160] Orellana, 'The role of science in investment arbitrations concerning public health and the environment', 72.

have been revealed, different possible interpretations have been adequately explained, as well as scrutinizing whether the chosen methodology was consistent with applicable data sets are of key importance for underpinning the legitimacy of the arbitral decision. Fortunately, arbitral practice shows promising developments in this respect, as one may find instances of adjudicatory reasoning closely reflecting on scientific questions.

8

Science Appears before the International Tribunal for the Law of the Sea

Considering that, although the Tribunal cannot conclusively assess the scientific evidence presented by the parties, it finds that measures should be taken as a matter of urgency to preserve the rights of the parties and to avert further deterioration of the southern bluefin tuna stock.[1]

ITLOS, 1999

The International Tribunal for the Law of the Sea (ITLOS) has jurisdiction over disputes arising under the UN Convention on the Law of the Sea (UNCLOS)[2] as well as related international conventions seeking to govern the use and protection of marine living resources.[3] Since 1996, ITLOS has been hearing a good number of cases where the parties relied on scientific concepts and expert evidence. Its diverse contentious case practice includes inter alia fisheries disputes,[4] boundary delimitation cases,[5] and prompt release cases,[6] many of which are relevant for marine environmental protection. Some advisory proceedings of the Tribunal also concern environmental rights and obligations and hence inform our analysis.[7] From among

---

[1]   *Southern Bluefin Tuna (New Zealand v. Japan; Australia v. Japan)* (Provisional Measures) ITLOS Nos. 3 and 4 (27 August 1999), para. 80.

[2]   United Nations Convention on the Law of the Sea, Montego Bay, 10 December 1982, in force 16 November 1994, 1833 UNTS 3.

[3]   In more detail see D. R. Rothwell, 'The contribution of ITLOS to oceans governance through marine environmental dispute resolution' in T. M. Ndiaye and R. Wolfrum (eds.), *Law of the Sea, Environmental Law and Settlement of Disputes: Liber Amicorum Judge Thomas A. Mensah* (Martinus Nijhoff, 2007), pp. 1007–24 p. 1022.

[4]   For example, *Southern Bluefin Tuna; Conservation and Sustainable Exploitation of Swordfish Stocks in the South-Eastern Pacific Ocean (Chile v. European Union)*, (Order) ITLOS No. 7 (20 December 2000); *Tomimaru (Japan v. Russian Federation)* (Judgment) ITLOS No. 15 (6 August 2007).

[5]   *Dispute Concerning Delimitation of the Maritime Boundary between Bangladesh and Myanmar in the Bay of Bengal (Bangladesh v. Myanmar)* (Judgment) ITLOS No. 16 (14 March 2012).

[6]   For example, *Camouco (Panama v. France)* (Judgment) ITLOS No. 5 (7 February 2000); *Monte Confurco (Seychelles v. France)* (Judgment) ITLOS No. 6 (18 December 2000); *Juno Trader (St Vincent and the Grenadines v. Guinea-Bissau)* (Judgment) ITLOS No. 13 (18 December 2004); and *Volga (Russian Federation v. Australia)* (Judgment) ITLOS No. 10 (3 December 2001).

[7]   *Request for an advisory opinion submitted by the Sub-Regional Fisheries Commission (SRFC)* (Advisory Opinion) ITLOS No. 21 (2 April 2015); Case No. 17 *Responsibilities and obligations of States sponsoring*

the disputes relating to the protection of the marine environment, those will be further examined here, where scientific arguments played (or could have played) a decisive role in the judicial inquiry. Section I will discuss entry points for science in the ITLOS case law, which is followed by enumerating various framing techniques of the Tribunal in Section II. Scientific fact-finding powers and evidentiary procedures will be discussed in Section III. As the standard of review has not been an articulate issue in the case law, this chapter will conclude with addressing the third stage of the relevant adjudicatory phases, namely, the causal inquiry of the Tribunal in Section IV.

I SCIENCE ENTERS ENVIRONMENTAL DISPUTES BROUGHT BEFORE ITLOS

The jurisprudence of ITLOS abounds with scientific arguments. In fact, respective disputes oftentimes can be traced back to 'an almost total lack of agreement on the scientific evidence'[8] between the parties in relation to possible adverse consequences of their conduct. The Tribunal nevertheless saliently seeks to perform a 'facilitative'[9] judicial function, prioritizing amicable settlement between the parties. This approach was heavily criticized by Judge ad hoc Shrearer, who powerfully argued against the Tribunal's tendency to 'shrink from the consequences of proven facts'.[10] Nevertheless, due to its willingness not to construe scientific uncertainty as an obstacle to judicial decision-making, ITLOS could certainly carry great relevance for resolving maritime disputes, where scientific aspects cannot be circumvented.

1 Remarks on the Institutional Set-Up

The Tribunal includes a separate judicial body, the Seabed Dispute Chamber, and it may also form special chambers to deal with particular categories of disputes.[11] When the Chamber for Marine Environmental Disputes was established in 2011, ITLOS was committed to 'respond to the special challenges'[12] of science-intensive environmental disputes.[13] The chamber, however, has not yet been used and hence it did not yield any practical benefits for litigants, despite the admitted motivation

---

persons and entities with respect to activities in the Area (Request for Advisory Opinion submitted to the Seabed Disputes Chamber) (Advisory Opinion) ITLOS No. 17 (1 February 2011).

[8] *MOX Plant (Ireland v. UK)* (Provisional Measures) ITLOS No. 10 (3 December 2000), Joint declaration of Judges Caminos, Yamamoto, Park, Akl, Marsit, Eiriksson, and Jesus.

[9] D. M. Johnston, 'Fishery diplomacy and science and the judicial function' (2000) 10 *Yearbook of International Environmental Law* 33–39 at 38.

[10] *Southern Bluefin Tuna*, Provisional Measures, Separate Opinion of Judge ad hoc Shrearer, p. 324.

[11] Statute of ITLOS, Article 15.

[12] Rothwell, 'The contribution of ITLOS to oceans governance through marine environmental dispute resolution', p. 1022.

[13] ITLOS, Resolution on the Chamber for Marine Environment Disputes, ITLOS Doc. ITLOS/2011/ Res. 2 (2011).

behind its creation to render the Tribunal more 'user-friendly'.[14] Other types of special chambers have been established. For instance, the *Swordfish* dispute was referred to an ad hoc special chamber consisting of five members.[15]

Parties to a dispute concerning UNCLOS provisions have the liberty to choose from four adjudicative bodies[16] to satisfy the compulsory dispute settlement requirement of UNCLOS.[17] Besides ITLOS, states may have recourse to the ICJ and international arbitration, the procedural rules of which are set out in Annex VII of UNCLOS.[18] They may also submit their disputes to a special expert-led arbitral tribunal constituted under Annex VIII of UNCLOS. Based on the track record of UNCLOS disputes, ITLOS seems to be more popular than Annex VII arbitration, while numerous disputes have been brought both to the Tribunal and arbitration,[19] hence their relationship can be better viewed as one of 'reciprocal complementation'.[20]

The Tribunal also has a reputation of being 'considerably more promising from an environmental perspective' than the ICJ.[21] Similar remarks can be made with respect to embracing the scientific aspects of disputes. Although the Tribunal is known for outsourcing the scientifically most loaded questions to the parties' negotiations, its jurisprudence equally reflects that scientific uncertainty did not to paralyse the judicial resolution of disputes. As will be argued below, ITLOS is willing to act on a precautionary basis to address scientific risks, and also invokes progressive developments in scientific knowledge to shape the content of state obligations.

Interestingly enough, states still saliently favour the ICJ over ITLOS, despite the latter's technical expertise in maritime disputes.[22] One commentator attributes this trend to states' fears that ITLOS would not observe sovereign interests with as close attention as the ICJ.[23] This reading suggests that state parties may prefer a dispute

---

[14] T. A. Mensah, 'The International Tribunal for the Law of the Sea and the protection and preservation of the marine environment' (1999) 8 *Review of European, Comparative and International Environmental Law* at 5.

[15] *Conservation and Sustainable Exploitation of Swordfish Stocks in the South-Eastern Pacific Ocean (Chile v. European Union)* (Order) ITLOS No. 7 (16 December 2009).

[16] UNCLOS, Article 287.

[17] Part XV of UNCLOS provides for a compulsory dispute settlement procedure entailing a binding decision.

[18] Annex VII arbitral tribunals were constituted to hear the *Chagos Marine Protected Area*, the *Southern Bluefin Tuna*, the *MOX Plant*, and *MOX Plant OSPAR Arbitration*, and the *South China Sea Arbitration*, which are addressed in Chapter 4.

[19] From among the cases considered in this chapter, the *Southern Bluefin Tuna*, the *MOX Plant*, and the *Straits of Johor* disputes were brought to both fora. Respective decisions of arbitral tribunals are addressed in Chapter 4.

[20] A. Proelss (ed.), *United Nations Convention on the Law of the Sea: A Commentary* (C. H. Beck Hart Nomos, 2017), p. 2466.

[21] Stephens, *International Courts and Environmental Protection*, p. 243.

[22] A. Telesetsky, 'The International Tribunal for the Law of the Sea: seeking the legitimacy of state consent' in N. Grossman, H. G. Cohen, A. Føllesdal, and G. Ulfstein (eds.), *Legitimacy and International Courts* (Cambridge University Press, 2018), pp. 174–215 pp. 180–4.

[23] Telesetsky, 'The International Tribunal for the Law of the Sea: seeking the legitimacy of state consent', p. 181.

settlement sensitive enough to their political considerations over one that focuses on the scientific dimensions of disputes. Such a pattern is particularly problematic if one considers the serious third-party effects of environmental dispute resolution, which challenges the strictly *inter partes* conception of environmental adjudication and the view that legitimate decisions can be brought without considering relevant scientific facts even if the litigants themselves may be satisfied with the Tribunal's 'descientized' approach. At the same time, the above trend may well explain why the ITLOS accords a low profile to scientific evidence in settling environmental disputes.

2 *Entry Points for Science in Legal Disputes*

Science may enter maritime disputes in a variety of ways. On the one hand, numerous provisions explicitly enshrine scientific concepts, giving legal terms a strong 'scientific flavour'[24] in the words of David Anderson, a former judge of the Tribunal. For instance, Part XII of UNCLOS sets out rules on protection and preservation of the marine environment and includes provisions on 'rare and fragile ecosystems',[25] 'alien species',[26] and the obligation not to 'transfer ... damage or hazards from one area to another'.[27] These provisions are increasingly litigated before various international fora[28] leading to science-heavy judicial assessments.

On the other hand, terms of art concerning scientific methodologies are also enshrined in Part XIII of UNCLOS dedicated to 'marine scientific research' (MSR), the interpretation of which requires techno-scientific considerations. The concept of MSR is not defined in the convention,[29] though is generally understood as describing activities undertaken in the ocean to expand scientific knowledge, covering a range of undertakings pursuing 'scientific purposes'.[30] Yet, technical experts disagree as to what exact methods of scientific data collection could be rightly labelled as MSR. The emergence of new technologies, primarily in satellite remote sensing, may also give rise to competing interpretations as to the precise scope of MSR.[31] The

---

[24]   D. Anderson, 'Scientific evidence in cases under Part XV of the LOSC' in M. H. Nordquist, R. Long, T. Heidar, and J. N. Moore (eds.), *Law, Science and Ocean Management* (Brill Nijhoff, 2007), pp. 503–18 p. 508.

[25]   UNCLOS, Article 194(5).

[26]   UNCLOS, Article 196.

[27]   UNCLOS, Article 195.

[28]   For an overview of the most important such decisions of international courts see M. Gavouneli, 'Protection standards for the marine environment: updating Part XII of the Law of the Sea Convention?' in S. Minas and J. Diamond (eds.), *Stress Testing the Law of the Sea* (Brill Nijhoff, 2018), pp. 254–66.

[29]   J. A. Roach, 'Marine scientific research and the new law of the sea' (1996) 27 *Ocean Development and International Law* 59–72 at 60.

[30]   J. A. Roach, 'Marine scientific research in the area' in M. Lodge and M. H. Nordquist (eds.), *Peaceful Order in the World's Oceans* (Brill Nijhoff, 2014), pp. 265–81 at 272.

[31]   A. Chircop, 'Advances in ocean knowledge and skill: implications for the MSR regime' in M. H. Nordquist, R. Long, H. Tomas Heidar, and J. N. Moore (eds.), *Law, Science and Ocean Management* (Martinus Nijhoff, 2007), pp. 575–618.

coverage of the term will be legally relevant for litigants as it impacts available methods of dispute settlement under UNCLOS.[32] Considering the hardship the ICJ faced in defining 'scientific research' in *Whaling in the Antarctic*, this provision would likely give rise to intricate interpretative exercise for ITLOS judges too, should this term become litigated.

To take a further example, Article 119 requires basing conservation measures on 'the best scientific evidence available' and the exchange of 'scientific information . . . relevant to the conservation of fish stocks'. Article 117 makes reference to 'the living resources of the high seas'[33] and rules governing the Exclusive Economic Zone (EEZ) include Article 67 on catadromous species, which is in itself a scientific category. Furthermore, Article 204 mandates analysis 'by recognized scientific methods' and Article 201 requires inter-state co-operation 'in establishing appropriate scientific criteria for the elaboration of rules'. The interpretation of all these terms would also draw on scientific insights.

A separate mention should also be made of the relevance of scientific information under Part XI of UNCLOS governing the regime relating to the area of deep seabed. Growing scientific understanding uncovers an expanding array of environmental risks associated with deep seabed mining, which warrant legal regulation.[34] Article 143 of UNCLOS governs MSR conducted in this area, entailing the same science-intensive dilemmas addressed above.[35] Also, sponsoring states have the obligation to conduct an environmental impact assessment (EIA),[36] discerning the exact content of which necessitates considering scientific evidence.[37] The Legal and Technical Commission of the International Seabed Authority (ISA) is also entangled in science-intensive assessments when formulate recommendations to the ISA Council on the implementation of regulations governing the exploitation of deep seabed minerals.[38] Specifically, the council has the power to disapprove areas for exploitation, where 'substantial evidence indicates the risk of serious harm to the marine environment'.[39]

---

[32]   A. Boyle, 'Forum shopping for UNCLOS disputes relating to marine scientific research' in M. H. Nordquist, R. Long, T. Heidar, and J. N. Moore (eds.), *Law, Science and Ocean Management* (Martinus Nijhoff, 2007), pp. 519–40.

[33]   UNCLOS, Article 117.

[34]   A. Jaeckel and R. Rayfuse, *Conceptions of Risk in an Institutional Context: Deep Seabed Mining and the International Seabed Authority* (Oxford University Press, 2017).

[35]   For more details on the regime governing MSR specifically in the area see Roach, 'Marine scientific research in the area'.

[36]   UNCLOS Article 206, Section 1(7) of 1994 Implementation Agreement. For a detailed assessment of the role and forms of expertise involved in an EIA process see J. M. Durden, L. E. Lallier, K. Murphy, A. Jaeckel, K. Gjerde, and D. O. B. Jones, 'Environmental Impact Assessment process for deep-sea mining in "the Area"' (2018) 87 *Marine Policy* 194–202.

[37]   For more details on the role of science in defining EIA obligations see T. Fukushima, 'The role of science for environmental impact evaluation resulting from ocean mining' (2018) 14 *The Marine Environment and United Nations Sustainable Development Goal* 251–62.

[38]   A. Jaeckel, 'An environmental management strategy for the international seabed authority: the legal basis' (2015) 30 *International Journal of Marine and Coastal Law* 93–119 at 100.

[39]   UNCLOS, Article 162(2) (x).

As this may result in the prohibition of a contractor's mining activity, scientific evidence in this context would in all likelihood be hotly debated by interested parties in a litigation. Advancements in techno-scientific knowledge also inform the stringency of environmental management plans the ISA may set for contractors with respect to their mining activities.[40]

Furthermore, Annex I of UNCLOS provides a list of 'highly migratory species' for purposes of Article 64 of UNCLOS. Since the negotiators failed to agree on a scientific definition of this category of species, an enumeration of applicable Latin names was adopted instead. Interestingly, including a certain species in the list has been a matter of politics and not of science.[41] There are a number of species that would qualify as highly migratory from a scientific point of view, though are still missing from the enumeration.[42] One may then suspect that the content of the annex is insulated from scientific arguments. Yet, science still makes its way into legal controversies surrounding the appendix. Hurdles arose, for instance, when taxonomists decided to divide the bluefin tuna, included in the annex, into two species (*Thunnus thynnus* and *Thunnus orientalis*).[43] The prevailing view holds that both species are to be regarded as highly migratory, because the drafters regarded them as identical at the time of adopting the annex.[44]

In addition, UNCLOS functions as a framework convention in the terrain of the protection of marine environment; hence it has been complemented by a number of multilateral environmental agreements (MEA).[45] These international treaties also contain scientific concepts and thereby provide a door for bringing scientific arguments into future litigation.

A peculiar entry point for scientific arguments lies in rules governing the provisional measure procedure of ITLOS,[46] according to which interim measures may not only be ordered to preserve the rights of the parties, but also to prevent serious harm to the marine environment.[47] Scientific insights are dragged into such disputes through questions of causation, environmental harm, and risk.[48]

---

[40] A. Jaeckel, 'Deep seabed mining and adaptive management: the procedural challenges for the International Seabed Authority' (2016) 70 *Marine Policy* 205–11 at 207–8.

[41] Proelss, *United Nations Convention on the Law of the Sea: A Commentary*, p. 2055.

[42] The commentary mentions some specific examples as well, see Proelss, *United Nations Convention on the Law of the Sea: A Commentary*, p. 2063.

[43] Proelss, *United Nations Convention on the Law of the Sea: A Commentary*, p. 2057.

[44] Proelss, *United Nations Convention on the Law of the Sea: A Commentary*, p. 2057.

[45] For a detailed list of such MEAs see Proelss, *United Nations Convention on the Law of the Sea: A Commentary*, pp. 1062–3.

[46] For an overview of such decisions see Y. Tanaka, 'Provisional Measures Prescribed by ITLOS and Marine Environmental Protection' (2014) 108 *Proceedings of the Annual Meeting, published by the American Society of International Law* 365–8; M. A. Waseem, 'ITLOS at 20: Provisional Measures and the Precautionary Approach' in S. Minas and J. Diamond (eds.), *Stress Testing the Law of the Sea* (Brill Nijhoff, 2018), pp. 150–69 at 156–7.

[47] UNCLOS, Article 290(1).

[48] T. Treves, 'Law and science in the interpretation of the law of the sea convention' (2012) 3 *Journal of International Dispute Settlement* 483–91 at 484.

Furthermore, science may enter disputes indirectly, by shaping the content of primary legal obligations. A stark example of that lies in how scientific and technological progress impacts the threshold of due diligence required by the law of the sea. It has been made clear by ITLOS that requirements flowing from states' due diligence obligations are not static over time, but are adjusted in light of new technologies.[49]

Lastly, science is also dragged into the judicially relevant spheres of disputes through questions of fact-finding. The scientific dimensions of cases are particularly articulate in fisheries disputes, where the core disagreement can often be traced back to differing views of the parties on whether overfishing is threatening with a collapse of a commercially important fish stock. Certain states in such cases impose conservation measures to prevent harmful impact on the stocks, the justifiability of which will depend on the well-founded nature of concerns for the stocks' viability. Scientific expertise therefore becomes crucial for the Tribunal in such scenarios to appraise the lawfulness of prohibitive measures in proceedings launched by adversely affected states.

The above enumeration canvasses only a selective illustration on provisions that 'contain elements of law and science' in the context of UNCLOS; the proper interpretation of which 'requires both legal and scientific expertise'.[50] Despite the impressively scientific language of applicable legal provisions and the diverse legal contexts that may invite scientific considerations, ITLOS hitherto has experienced only a limited number of disputes in which scientific notions have been relevant to the parties' arguments.

II FRAMING ENVIRONMENTAL DISPUTES

A number of framing techniques can be distinguished in ITLOS jurisprudence in relation to cases loaded with scientific controversies. The non-justiciability of science-heavy disputes was raised quite early on by the parties, however, ITLOS rejected such a narrow construction of its judicial function (Subsection 1).[51] Nevertheless, the weight and reach of scientific arguments have remained somewhat limited before ITLOS. Judge Tullio Treves, writing extra-judicially, revealed that 'scientific information was never used by ITLOS as the decisive argument in a case in favour of one party'.[52] Instead, scientific evidence regarding environmental threat

---

[49] *Responsibility of Sponsoring States* Advisory Opinion, para. 117; cited also by the SRFC Advisory Opinion, para. 132; For scholarly commentary see V. Schatz, 'Fishing for interpretation: the ITLOS Advisory Opinion on flag state responsibility for illegal fishing in the EEZ' (2016) 47 *Ocean Development and International Law* 327–45 at 335; D. Freestone, 'Responsibilities and obligations of states sponsoring persons and entities with respect to activities in the area' (2011) 105 *American Journal of International Law* 755–60 at 759.

[50] *Bay of Bengal*, Judgment, para. 411.

[51] For Japan's proposition that the 'disputes are scientific rather than legal' see *Southern Bluefin Tuna*, Provisional Measures, para. 42.

[52] Treves, 'Law and science in the interpretation of the law of the sea convention', 486.

or imminent harm has been considered as a justification to adopt interim measures on a precautionary basis (Subsection 2). Furthermore, the Tribunal tactically relies on progressive development of scientific knowledge to inform the content of due diligence obligation (Subsection 3). Lastly, the Tribunal saliently often refers the parties to expert-led consultations and settlements (Subsection 4). The role of the Tribunal can therefore be best characterized in science-intensive disputes as providing a 'curial supervision of the settlement process'.[53]

1 *Science-Intensive Disputes Are Deemed Justiciable*

The *Southern Bluefin Tuna* dispute revolved around the parties' markedly different interpretations on the scientific data describing trends in the population of a commercially highly important tuna.[54] In Japan's reading, the scientific evidence showed a recovery of the stocks, which supported a higher total allowable catch (TAC); while Australia and New Zealand maintained that the data did not show any such recovery and any further increase in the catch would threaten with the collapse of the southern bluefin tuna population. Legally speaking, the dispute before the Tribunal concerned the TAC of the tuna established under a regional regime of the Convention for the Conservation of Southern Bluefin Tuna. In an alleged effort to gather relevant data, Japan unilaterally launched an 'experimental fishing programme' to which the other two states objected, and applied for provisional measures to ITLOS.

It was in this context that Japan submitted the dispute being of a scientific, rather than of a legal nature, and argued that the case ought to be non-justiciable.[55] The Tribunal, however, was of the opposite view and held that 'the differences between the parties also concern[ed] points of law'.[56] This finding was highly consequential at the time as it could be read as encouragement to other fora 'to "intervene" in future fisheries conservations disputes that arise, at least in part, from disagreements within the scientific community'.[57] Indeed, the Tribunal summarily rejected Japan's attempt to carve out science-heavy claims from its purview, and such concerns have not surfaced since.

2 *Response to Uncertain Risks: Issuing Precautionary Measures*

Although the UNCLOS makes no explicit mention of the precautionary principle or approach, it has become a paradigmatic rule in fisheries management, and it

---

[53] Stephens, *International Courts and Environmental Protection*, p. 242.
[54] For more details see *Southern Bluefin Tuna*, Provisional Measures, Separate Opinion of Judge ad hoc Shrearer, p. 325.
[55] *Southern Bluefin Tuna*, Provisional Measures, para. 42.
[56] *Southern Bluefin Tuna*, Provisional Measures, para. 43.
[57] Johnston, 'Fishery diplomacy and science and the judicial function', 36.

permeates the regime of deep seabed mining and the protection of marine biodiversity.[58] Notably, ITLOS embraces the precautionary principle to the greatest extent among international fora.[59] The UNCLOS Commentary itself endorses a reading of Article 119 in line with the precautionary principle. This provision mandates using 'the best scientific evidence available', but the commentary emphasizes that 'measures may be taken even before scientific proof exists'[60] regarding overfishing. Such a reading of UNCLOS is also in line with other multilateral fisheries agreements, for example the 1995 UN Fish Stock Agreement, which explicitly incorporates the precautionary approach.[61]

Against this background it is perhaps more understandable why the Tribunal adopted a precautionary stance in the *Southern Bluefin Tuna* dispute. In its interim measures, the Tribunal ordered the parties to 'act with caution and urgency to ensure that effective conservation measures are taken to prevent serious harm to the stock'.[62] Judge Treves in his Separate Opinion emphasized that the urgency requirement should not:

> concern the danger of a collapse of the stock in the months which will elapse between the reading of the Order and the time when the arbitral tribunal will be in a position to prescribe provisional measures. This event, in light of scientific evidence, is uncertain and unlikely. The urgency concerns the stopping of a trend towards such collapse. The measures prescribed by the Tribunal aim at stopping the deterioration in the southern bluefin tuna stock. Each step in such deterioration can be seen as 'serious harm' because of its cumulative effect towards the collapse of the stock.[63]

The above wording clearly aligns with precautionary considerations, even though the Tribunal chose not to discuss the principle expressly in the order; only certain members of the bench alluded to its hidden relevance for shaping the judicial reasoning.[64] Nevertheless, the fact remains that ITLOS has kept using such language in later cases as well. In this vein in *Straits of Johor*, ITLOS again required in its provisional measures that Malaysia and Singapore acted with 'prudence and caution'.[65]

---

[58] R. Rayfuse, 'Precaution and the protection of marine biodiversity in areas beyond national jurisdiction' (2012) 27 *International Journal of Marine and Coastal Law* 773–81.

[59] Stephens, *International Courts and Environmental Protection*, p. 226.

[60] Proelss, *United Nations Convention on the Law of the Sea: A Commentary*, p. 840.

[61] Agreement for the Implementation of the Provisions of the UNCLOS 1982 Relating to the Conservation and Management of Straddling Fish Stocks and Highly Migratory Fish Stocks, New York, 4 August 1995, in force 11 December 2011, Article 5, 6.

[62] *Southern Bluefin Tuna*, Provisional Measures, para. 77.

[63] *Southern Bluefin Tuna*, Provisional Measures, Separate Opinion of Judge Treves, para. 8.

[64] *Southern Bluefin Tuna*, Provisional Measures, Separate Opinion of Judge Treves, para. 8; Separate Opinion of Judge ad hoc Shrearer, p. 327.

[65] *Land Reclamation by Singapore in and around the Straits of Johor (Malaysia v. Singapore)* (Provisional Measures) ITLOS No. 12 (8 October 2003), para. 99.

In *MOX Plant*, ITLOS was approached by Ireland for provisional measures seeking the suspension of the commissioning of the MOX plant. The Tribunal again reiterated its precautionary formula as a matter of principle,[66] however, the evidence was not found serious enough to establish the urgency of the situation and therefore, justifying the measures sought.[67] The Tribunal at this time seemed to reject the application of the precautionary principle,[68] as despite appealing to precautionary considerations, it allowed for continued commissioning of the plant.

Finally, the precautionary principle also applies in the context of conserving resources of the deep seabed. In the *Responsibilities and Obligations of States Sponsoring Persons and Entities with Respect to Activities in the Area Advisory Opinion*, ITLOS Seabed Disputes Chamber confirmed the direct obligations of sponsoring states 'to apply precautionary approach'.[69] The Advisory Opinion interprets the Nodules and Sulphides Regulations as transforming the 'non-binding statement of the precautionary approach in the Rio Declaration into a binding obligation'.[70]

3 Science as Both a 'Progressive Ceiling' and a 'Hard Floor' for State Obligations

As shown in the previous section, through adopting a precautionary approach, ITLOS does not conceive scientific uncertainty as an obstacle to mandating environmental protection measures. What is more, ITLOS even uses scientific knowledge to mandate progressively stricter environmental safeguards. Advancement in techno-scientific knowledge informs the content of the Tribunal's due diligence inquiry. As expressly stated in advisory opinions, the content of due diligence obligations is not static, but may change over time, requiring more stringent protection standards in light of 'new scientific or technological knowledge'.[71]

A noteworthy aspect of this conceptualization of science lies in the way in which the Tribunal manages to address both the weakness and the strength of scientific knowledge. With this formula, the Tribunal sets the most stringent protection standard possible for states by tying the content of due diligence to scientific developments and state-of-the-art technologies. By such a framing of the scientific aspect of disputes, ITLOS ensures that gaps in available scientific knowledge concerning environmental risks do not hollow out states' due diligence obligations.

---

[66] *MOX Plant*, Provisional Measures, para. 84.
[67] *MOX Plant*, Provisional Measures, para. 81.
[68] Stephens, *International Courts and Environmental Protection*, p. 236.
[69] *Responsibilities and Obligations of States*, Advisory Opinion, para. 122.
[70] *Responsibilities and Obligations of States*, Advisory Opinion, para. 127.
[71] *Responsibility of Sponsoring States*, Advisory Opinion, para. 117; SRFC, Advisory Opinion, para. 132.

Quite the contrary, new scientific information can even elevate the level of care and caution required from states.

By doing so, the Tribunal conceptualizes uncertain scientific knowledge, on the one hand, as a progressive and open 'ceiling', which mandates setting ever more ambitious protection standards. On the other hand, embracing the precautionary principle prevents states from using scientific uncertainty at their own advantage to delay timely action with reference to ambiguities in scientific knowledge. In other words, in the Tribunal's framing, science serves as a 'hard floor' requiring safety measures from states that cannot be lowered with reference to insufficient knowledge on applicable risks. Such a strategic management of scientific knowledge enables ITLOS to invoke scientific authority in mandating environment measures without the need to closely engage with scientific evidence.

4 *Referring Disputes to Expert-Led Consultation of the Parties*

The Tribunal's evasive approach to evaluating scientific evidence goes hand-in-hand with prioritizing procedural obligations. This is aptly reflected in prescribing the duty to co-operate, which is a common thread in the interim measures ordered in *Southern Bluefin Tuna*,[72] *MOX Plant*,[73] and *Straits of Johor*.[74] As Judge Treves points out extra-judicially, 'this approach seems to correspond to the degree to which courts and Tribunals, especially ITLOS, are ready to rely on scientific information submitted to them'.[75] Indeed, as we shall see below, the Tribunal is apparently uncomfortable with drawing definite legal conclusions from scientific evidence, while it often expects the parties to do exactly so.

The *Swordfish* case features a scientifically informed co-operative solution facilitated by an ITLOS Special Chamber for the final resolution of a fisheries dispute between Chile and the EU. Chile implemented conservation measures within its EEZ due to the declining stocks of swordfish in the South Pacific and unilaterally introduced a prohibition to unload in its ports the swordfish caught in waters beyond its jurisdiction. The EU challenged the prohibitory measures and their disagreement has led to a proceeding before the ITLOS Special Chamber.

The parties engaged in negotiations and adopted a mutually agreed understanding to settle their case. What is of significance here is that the ITLOS Special Chamber played an instrumental role in reaching an amicable settlement between the parties.[76] The bilateral understanding included setting up a Bilateral Scientific and Technical Committee. The main functions of this expert body were exchanging

---

[72] *Southern Bluefin Tuna*, Provisional Measures, Operative part, Section (e).
[73] *MOX Plant*, Interim Measures, Operative part, Section (1).
[74] *Straits of Johor*, Provisional Measures, para. 92 and Operative part, Section (1).
[75] Treves, 'Law and science in the interpretation of the law of the sea convention', 487.
[76] ITLOS Press release, ITLOS/Press 141, 17 December 2009, citing grateful acknowledgements of the agents of both sides for the Tribunal's role in ensuring the friendly settlement.

data on catch and stock status, providing science-based advice to fisheries stock managers, and advising the parties on the adoption of further conservation measures.[77] With regard to the understanding, the Tribunal ordered the discontinuance of the proceedings.

The role of ITLOS in securing the prompt resolution of the *Swordfish* dispute merits special attention, as it signals the importance of a hands-on adjudicatory supervision of co-operative regimes. The understanding established only a provisional regime.[78] Had this bilateral co-operation failed, the parties would have resumed their legal proceedings before the special chamber. In the material case, referring the resolution of debated scientific issues to an expert body ensured setting up a flexible joint management regime to secure the continuous evaluation of the threats imposed on fish stocks. It also secured scientific monitoring to guarantee that neither parties took excessive and unjustified measures with reference to scientific reasons. Science therefore was key in monitoring the parties' adherence to their agreement, and technological tools promoted effective implementation. In this vein, the fishing vessels were required to be monitored through a satellite-based system and had to carry scientific observers of the other party to supply the technical commission with reliable information as to the fishing operations.[79]

An even more articulate role has been assigned to scientific experts in forging a friendly settlement in *Straits of Johor*. The dispute concerned a land reclamation carried out by Singapore, which was, according to Malaysia, threatening with harm to the marine and coastal environment in the vicinity of territorial waters claimed by Malaysia.[80] The core of the disagreement between the parties was again the interpretation of scientific data on possible adverse effects of the infilling works. Singapore insisted that if 'the evidence were to prove compelling',[81] it would reconsider the suspension of works. The Tribunal was not willing to base its order on the technical and scientific evidence submitted by the parties,[82] and concluded that the urgency of the situation was 'less than self-evident'.[83] It did so, however,

---

[77]   *Swordfish*, Order, para. 12 including the text of the understanding, in which section 4 mandates establishing the Bilateral Scientific and Technical Committee.

[78]   Orellana, 'The *Swordfish* dispute between the EU and Chile at the ITLOS and the WTO' (2002) 71 *Nordic Journal of International Law* 55–81 at 69.

[79]   M. A. Orellana, 'The EU and Chile suspend the *Swordfish* case proceedings at the WTO and the International Tribunal of the Law of the Sea' (2001) 6(1) *ASIL Insights*.

[80]   The parties referred their dispute to an Annex VII arbitral tribunal, but later on applied for provisional measures to ITLOS.

[81]   Diplomatic note of Singapore of 2 September 2003, reiterated in *Straits of Johor*, Provisional Measures, para. 85.

[82]   Treves, 'Law and science in the interpretation of the law of the sea convention', 487.

[83]   *Straits of Johor*, Provisional Measures, Declaration of Judge Anderson, para. 3. For lack of any specific factual assessment substantiating the absence of urgent risks, see also the wording of the Order and Separate Opinion of Judge Cot in *Straits of Johor*, Provisional Measures, Separate Opinion of Judge Cot, para.1.

without conducting any specific factual assessment showing the reasons for this conclusion.

Yet, when the parties' negotiations reached a stalemate,[84] the ITLOS had a decisive role in compelling the parties' co-operation on the basis of an objective study commissioned by independent experts.[85] As a result, Singapore accepted Malaysia's proposal to 'jointly fund a scientific study by independent experts'.[86] The interim measures hence ordered the co-operation of the parties, specifically in establishing a jointly selected group of independent experts with the mandate of conducting a study within a year to determine the effects of the works and to propose measures to deal with any adverse effects found.[87]

The expert panel adopted its final report unanimously, which was considered a significant factor leading the parties to accept it as a solid basis for their settlement.[88] The Settlement Agreement was annexed to the Award on Agreed Terms issued by an international arbitral tribunal, which heard the dispute on the merits.[89] The agreement reiterates the recommendations of the group of experts, according to which Singapore among others had to 'modify the final design of its shoreline of its land reclamation'.[90] Put differently Accordingly, the parties' settlement essentially rests on the conditions laid down by the committee of experts, signalling that the effective resolution of the legal dispute has been backed up by a scientific consensus. The *Straits of Johor* decision therefore aptly illustrates how scientific input can catalyse finding mutually acceptable solutions for the parties, which allows adjudicators to resolve the legal dispute in a non-controversial and epistemically convenient way, escaping direct engagement with the scientific evidence themselves.

To sum up, the *Straits of Johor* case evidences a specific framing technique, namely, to refer scientific questions and the final resolution of the dispute to the parties' out-of-court consultation, which has to be guided by expert advice. This solution at a cursory glance may seem similar to the path taken by the ICJ in *Gabcikovo-Nagymaros*, where the court referred science-intensive questions back to the parties' negotiations.[91] Yet

---

[84] Parties clearly reached a deadlock in their negotiations, as noted by Judge Ndiaye in *Straits of Johor*, Provisional Measures, Separate Opinion of Judge Ndiaye, para. 9.

[85] B. N. Patel, *Law of the Sea International Tribunal for the Law of the Sea Jurisprudence: Case Commentary, Case-Law Digest and Reference Guide (1994–2014)* (Eastern Book Company, 2016), p. 34; T. Koh and J. Lin, 'The land reclamation case: thoughts and reflections speech' (2006) 10 *Singapore Year Book of International Law* 1–8 at 4.

[86] Diplomatic note of Singapore of 2 September 2003, reiterated in para. 85 of the *Straits of Johor*, Provisional Measures.

[87] *Straits of Johor*, Provisional Measures, Operative part, Section (a) paragraph (i).

[88] Koh and Lin, 'The land reclamation case', 5.

[89] *Land Reclamation by Singapore in and Around the Straits of Johor (Malaysia v. Singapore)* (Permanent Court of Arbitration) Award on Agreed Terms, 1 September 2005.

[90] *Straits of Johor*, Award on Agreed Terms, Annex: 2005 Settlement Agreement, Part A paragraph (i) section 1.

[91] For an assessment of the judgment see Chapter 3 Section II, Subsection 2.1.

a closer look reveals that the adjudicatory solution of ITLOS is much more efficient in ensuring an effective settlement between litigants, and also evidences a more meaningful exercise of the judicial function in the face of scientific controversies. The structural reason for that lies in the fact that ITLOS retained control over the consultation process by setting a short deadline and explicitly mandating scientific expertise to be the guideline driving the negotiation process.

With the close supervision of expert-led consultation of the parties, the ITLOS Chamber appears to strike a fair balance between carving out scientific controversies from the issues it is willing to address in its own legal inquiry on the one hand, and discharging the judicial function on the other hand. This peculiar way of framing the judicially relevant questions in a dispute showcases a strategic recourse to expert advice, which alleviates the epistemic burden of the Tribunal and, at the same time, preserves the ultimate control and oversight of ITLOS over resolving the legal dispute.

III SCIENTIFIC FACT-FINDING TECHNIQUES

Given the often highly specific subject matter of UNCLOS provisions, ITLOS proceedings frequently feature evidence that is of technical nature. In the oral hearings the parties may support their claims with inter alia 'maps, tables, graphs, photographs, digital video'[92] along with other types of documentary evidence.

1 Ex Parte Scientific Experts

Typically, ITLOS relies on the initiative of the parties to submit evidence.[93] Although it has the power to call upon them to submit any evidence on its own motion, the Tribunal has not made any order to that effect.[94] State parties frequently submit scientific expert evidence to the Tribunal. In *Straits of Johor*, for instance, scientists appeared in the capacity of experts, whom were cross-examined.[95] In the material case, hydraulic model calculations were found to be insufficient to substantiate the urgency of the situation regarding the risks claimed by Malaysia with respect to causing irreversible damage to the territorial sea by the land reclamation works.[96] Hence, ITLOS ultimately denied prescribing provisional measures on the basis of scientific evidence.

Reviewing the jurisprudence gives the impression that conflicting expert evidence seems to put the Tribunal into an uncomfortably difficult position. The Tribunal's preference for having 'uncontested scientific evidence' was alluded to in *Bay of*

---

92 *Straits of Johor*, Provisional Measures, para. 19.
93 Proelss, *United Nations Convention on the Law of the Sea: A Commentary*, p. 2411.
94 Proelss, *United Nations Convention on the Law of the Sea: A Commentary*, p. 2412.
95 *Straits of Johor*, Provisional Measures, paras. 20–1.
96 *Straits of Johor*, Provisional Measures, para. 72.

Bengal,[97] a maritime delimitation dispute, where science featured a central issue.[98] Interestingly enough, although the parties agreed on the scientific data describing the nature of the seabed, they differed on the interpretation of the term 'natural prolongation'.[99] The Tribunal openly acknowledged that 'it would have been hesitant to proceed with the delimitation … had it concluded that there was significant uncertainty as to the existence of a continental margin in the area'.[100] This statement is illustrative of the overall approach of ITLOS to scientific fact-finding. Namely, the Tribunal predominantly relies on party-adduced evidence, but it is only comfortable with relying on technical evidence not contested by the other party; hence one ought not to expect thorough evidentiary assessments from the Tribunal. This fact-finding approach has its obvious limitations in scientifically loaded disputes, where differing expert statements are the norm.

2 Enhancing the Tribunal's Internal Expertise

Although ITLOS has several procedural avenues for gathering independent expert advice or to incorporate scientific expertise in the bench, these powers are not applied in practice. Such noteworthy possibilities include appointing *ex curia* experts (Subsection 2.1), and expert assessors sitting with judges (Subsection 2.2), requesting an appropriate intergovernmental organization to furnish information relevant to a case before it,[101] and submitting disputes to a special arbitral panel consisting of scientific experts (Subsection 2.3). These scientific fact-finding procedures are unique from an international comparative point of view, yet the ITLOS has thus far not had recourse to any of such powers. It does rely, however, on shadow experts (Subsection 2.4).

2.1 Ex Curia Experts

The Tribunal does have the power to rely on its own experts, yet hitherto it has not appointed *ex tribunal* experts. This reluctance may arguably be rooted in the Tribunal's inclination to invoking the precautionary principle, which absolves ITLOS judges from in-depth evaluation of competing uncertain scientific evidence.[102] Yet, the Tribunal could benefit immensely from gathering *ex tribunal*

---

[97] *Bay of Bengal*, Judgment, paras. 411, 442–3.
[98] For a detailed assessment of the role of science in the *Bay of Bengal* judgment see T. Treves, 'Law and science in the jurisprudence of the International Tribunal for the Law of the Sea' in M. H. Nordquist, R. Long, T. Heidar, and J. N. Moore (eds.), *Law, Science and Ocean Management* (Brill Nijhoff, 2015), pp. 15–26.
[99] *Bay of Bengal*, Judgment, para. 412.
[100] *Bay of Bengal*, Judgment, para. 443.
[101] Article 84, Rules of the Tribunal, ITLOS/8 17 March 2009.
[102] Boisson de Chazournes, Mbengue, Das, and Gros, 'One size does not fit all – uses of experts before international courts and tribunals', 489.

expertise. As it has been explained above, independent expert advice on many occasions was seen as solid and trustworthy enough in the parties' eyes to form the basis of their mutually accepted settlement regimes. By the same token, states may be equally willing to deem adjudicatory conclusions legitimate if are based on *ex tribunal* expert evidence, should the Tribunal ever become less evasive about basing substantive findings on scientific facts.

2.2 Expert Assessors Sitting with Judges

Article 289 of UNCLOS provides for a peculiar and innovative procedure to buttress the epistemic competence of any court or tribunal that is asked to decide cases including 'scientific or technical matters' under UNCLOS. This provision allows for appointing 'in consultation with the parties, no fewer than two scientific or technical experts chosen preferably from the relevant list prepared in accordance with Annex VIII, Article 2, to sit with the court or tribunal but without a right to vote'. Reading this provision in conjunction with other applicable rules provides that such *ex curia* experts should also have legal expertise.[103] However, ITLOS has not yet availed itself of this procedural tool. Judge Treves openly attributes this to the possibility that the presence of experts equipped with both scientific and legal background may make the other judges feel 'uncomfortable'.[104]

2.3 Special Arbitration before a Panel of Scientists

Another noteworthy aspect of ITLOS proceedings is the option for submitting science-intensive disputes to special arbitration under Chapter VIII of UNCLOS. Any party to a dispute concerning the interpretation or application of provisions relating to fisheries, protection of the marine environment, marine scientific research or navigation, including issues of pollution or dumping, may refer the case to this special arbitral proceeding[105] as these types of disputes may be better suited to be decided by specialists.[106] A list of eligible experts is to be drawn up by competent international organizations, such as the IMO, FAO, or the UNEP.[107] Expert adjudicators would also need to be equipped with sufficient legal expertise.[108] Compared to Annex VII arbitration, the distinctive feature of Annex VIII proceedings is that parties could entrust the panel with conducting a factual inquiry to establish the relevant scientific facts of the case with a binding force.[109] Parties may

---

[103]   Treves, 'Law and science in the interpretation of the law of the sea convention', 485.
[104]   Treves, 'Law and science in the interpretation of the law of the sea convention', 485.
[105]   UNCLOS, Article 1 of Annex VIII.
[106]   Proelss, *United Nations Convention on the Law of the Sea: A Commentary*, p. 2492.
[107]   UNCLOS, Article 2(2) of Annex VIII.
[108]   UNCLOS, Article 2(3) of Annex VIII.
[109]   UNCLOS, Article 5(1)–(2) of Annex VIII.

also ask an Annex VIII tribunal to issue recommendations, which would form the basis for a review by the parties.[110]

This special arbitration also remains a mere theoretical possibility as it has never been applied in practice, and only eleven state parties to UNCLOS indicated Annex VIII arbitration as being among their preferred mechanisms for dispute settlement.[111] Annex VIII procedures is an innovative, though a 'more radical'[112] solution for integrating expert knowledge in adjudication. The reluctance of states to have recourse to such specialist-led arbitration squares well with the also hesitant approach of international tribunals, including ITLOS itself, to incorporate scientific expertise in the bench.

2.4 Shadow Experts

In contrast to the above forms of fact-finding powers that remain hypothetical possibilities, ITLOS has recourse to shadow experts, by occasionally hiring scientists as temporary registry staff members without consulting or even disclosing this fact to the parties.[113] As noted earlier in the context of the ICJ's similar practice,[114] such capacity-building method is objectionable from transparency and due process points of view.

3 *Standard of Proof*

The Tribunal has not elaborated on the burden of proof relating to uncertain scientific evidence in its orders or judgments. The most detailed account is provided by Judge Lucky in his Separate Opinion in *Straits of Johor*. He announced that in issuing binding provisional measures, the standard of proof is 'relatively high' before ITLOS.[115] He further adds that 'applicants must show a very strong probability upon the facts that serious harm will accrue in the future'.[116] The majority found no possible harm in the given case without, however, any evaluation of the probabilities substantiated by the evidence. In contrast to that, in the reading of Judge Lucky the possibility of 'serious harm to the environment and marine life has been sufficiently established'[117] even under this heightened standard of proof. This decision seems to be illustrative of the overall jurisprudence of ITLOS. The Tribunal appears to adopt a high standard for accepting scientific proof of risks and even when it is willing to

---

[110] UNCLOS, Article 5(3) of Annex VIII.
[111] Proelss, *United Nations Convention on the Law of the Sea: A Commentary*, p. 2492.
[112] Peat, 'The use of court-appointed experts by the International Court of Justice', 296.
[113] Proelss, *United Nations Convention on the Law of the Sea: A Commentary*, p. 1866.
[114] See Chapter 3 Section III, Subsection 2.4.
[115] *Straits of Johor*, Provisional Measures, Separate Opinion of Judge Lucky, para. 11.
[116] *Straits of Johor*, Provisional Measures, Separate Opinion of Judge Lucky, para. 13.
[117] *Straits of Johor*, Provisional Measures, Separate Opinion of Judge Lucky, para. 17.

find an urgent threat of harm established, it does not reveal its evidentiary assessment.

IV CAUSAL INQUIRY

The issue of causation typically arises in the context of liability for causing environmental damage to the marine environment. Two provisions on responsibility are provided by UNCLOS. Under Article 235 states are responsible for 'the fulfilment of their international obligations concerning the protection of the marine environment' in accordance with international law. Moreover, Article 139 enshrines a similar obligation with respect to the seabed and subsoil beyond national jurisdiction. In these areas states have to ensure that activities controlled by them comply with rules of UNCLOS. Article 139(2) prescribes liability rules governing cases where states are sponsoring private entities for conducting explorations in these areas.

The Tribunal elaborated on causal requirements only as a matter of principle in the *Responsibilities and Obligations of States Advisory Opinion*,[118] when it touched upon the issue of requisite causal links in the context of liability of sponsoring states. The opinion emphasizes that causality must be established at two separate stages in order to substantiate responsibility of the sponsoring state for the damage caused by a contractor. The first causal nexus must be shown between the activity of the contractor and the resulting damage,[119] and the second must be proven between the damage and the failure of the sponsoring state to carry out its own responsibilities,[120] that is, to exercise due diligence in securing compliance by the contractor.[121] The Advisory Opinion firmly states that 'there must be a causal link between the sponsoring state's failure and the damage, and such a link cannot be presumed'.[122] The opinion concludes its assessment at this point and provides no clarification as to the requisite test of causality. Apart from ruling out strict liability,[123] this brief reference to the causal nexus does not specify the causal requirement any further. The opinion can also be criticized for leaving gaps in the liability regime applicable to environmental damage that nevertheless occurs even if no causal link can be established.[124]

---

[118] *Responsibilities and Obligations of States*, Advisory Opinion.
[119] *Responsibilities and Obligations of States*, Advisory Opinion, para. 181.
[120] *Responsibilities and Obligations of States*, Advisory Opinion, para. 182.
[121] *Responsibilities and Obligations of States*, Advisory Opinion, para. 119.
[122] *Responsibilities and Obligations of States*, Advisory Opinion, para. 184.
[123] Y. Tanaka, 'Obligations and liability of sponsoring states concerning activities in the area: reflections on the ITLOS Advisory Opinion of 1 February 2011' (2013) 60 *Netherlands International Law Review* 205–30 at 220.
[124] E. Crawford, G. Hutton, and T. Stephens, 'Australian cases before international courts and tribunals involving questions of public international law 2011' (2013) 31 *Australian Yearbook of International Law* 173–8 at 177; I. Plakokefalos, 'Seabed Disputes Chamber of the International Tribunal for the

Contentious cases were all noticeably silent on issues of liability for environmental damage, which could have entailed a detailed causal inquiry.[125] The overall restrictive approach of the Tribunal to establishing causality resonates well, on a more abstract level, with its inclination to prioritize procedural obligations of states, for example that of co-operation and negotiation over investigating whether substantive obligations have been breached in light of the evidence.

Law of the Sea: responsibilities and obligations of states sponsoring persons and entities with respect to activities in the area', Advisory Opinion (2012) 24 *Journal of Environmental Law* 133–43 at 141; P. Vromman, 'Responsibilities and obligations of sponsoring states: ITLOS Advisory Opinion' (2012) 42 *Environmental Policy and Law* 90–6 at 93.

[125] A. Boyle, 'The environmental jurisprudence of the International Tribunal for the Law of the Sea symposium to mark the tenth anniversary ITLOS: the jurisprudence of the International Tribunal of the Law of the Sea: Assessment and Prospects' (2007) 22 *International Journal of Marine and Coastal Law* 369–82 at 370.

PART III

Engaging with Scientific Knowledge in the Judicial Reasoning

9

Trends in Judicial Engagement with Science: A Comparative Assessment

> Both Parties have placed on record an impressive amount of scientific material aimed at reinforcing their respective arguments. The Court ... concludes, however, that ... it is not necessary ... to determine which of those points of view is scientifically better founded.
>
> Gabcikovo-Nagymaros Project, 1997[1]

> [T]he assessment of damages is often a difficult exercise and it is seldom that damages in an investment situation will be able to be established with scientific certainty ... . in such circumstances, the tribunal exercises its judgment in a reasoned manner so as to discern an appropriate damages sum.
>
> Gold Reserve Tribunal, 2014[2]

This chapter sets out a comparative analysis of the various judicial tools that preceding chapters have identified in international adjudicative practice. The forthcoming assessment will centre on discerning some common patterns in the scientific engagement of judges; and will essentially argue for two parallel trends in international environmental case practice. Certain adjudicatory tools facilitate engaging with science and thereby accommodate scientific input in the adjudicatory analysis and reasoning; while a host of other methods help judges circumvent scientific insights and thereby downplay the role and weight of scientific arguments in resolving legal disputes. It is to be emphasized at the outset that major international judicial bodies cannot be neatly grouped into 'science-friendly' and 'science-evasive' jurisdictions. Instead, practically all of them apply methods both accommodating and downplaying science along the different stages of the adjudicative process. Depicting these divergent adjudicatory trends therefore necessitates an overview of the framing techniques, causal inquiry, scientific fact-finding, and standard of review applied by relevant jurisdictions. Accordingly, this analysis will be anchored to the four-stage framework of the judicial process that has been explored in previous chapters.

---

[1] *Gabcikovo-Nagymaros Project (Hungary/Slovakia)* (Judgment) (1997), ICJ Rep 1997, 7, para. 54.
[2] *Gold Reserve Inc. v. Bolivarian Republic of Venezuela*, ICSID Case No. ARB(AF)/09/1, Award (22 September 2014), para. 686.

The ultimate goal of this comparative exercise lies in identifying the limits to which science may penetrate contemporary adjudicatory inquiry. The catalogue of scientific engagement techniques of international fora will be viewed here from the prism of legitimacy. One of the main tenets of this study suggests that relying on scientific references in the judicial inquiry, or the lack thereof, impacts the ways in which adjudicators can legitimately justify their choices and conclusions in disputes with manifest scientific aspects. Simply put, adjudicators need to have recourse to different argumentative practices in cases, when they choose not to interact with scientific arguments compared to when they opt for incorporating scientific knowledge in the judicial analysis. The present chapter will enumerate the judicial tools that international courts and tribunals employ while taking one of these argumentative paths. This comparative overview lays ground to Chapter 10, which will discuss the question as to how the intrusion of science into the adjudicatory process affects the persuasive and legitimate nature of judicial reasoning.

I JUDICIAL TECHNIQUES ADJUSTING THE LEVEL OF SCIENCE IN ADJUDICATORY INQUIRY

To what extent and in what ways do international adjudicators engage with science when they reflect of scientific arguments raised in a dispute? Some answers have already been given to this query with respect to each of the relevant courts and tribunals in the previous chapters. In order to offer some more in-depth analytic remarks on the contemporary landscape of respective adjudicatory solutions, the ensuing analysis will identify and appraise, from a comparative standpoint, the similarities as well as divergences in the ways in which different fora treat scientific arguments. Instances where different jurisdictions display similar engagement with science are especially informative for present purposes, as they help single out judicial responses that manifest across several legal and adjudicatory contexts, and this way, may signal judicial reactions specifically triggered by the presence of science in a legal dispute.

Encounters with scientific knowledge in a judicial process prompt adjudicators to strike a delicate balance. They need to find the right compromise between neglecting expert advice and becoming dependent on it. Furthermore, they have to find the most appropriate extent and mode of using scientific references in their decisions. Some judges opt for decreasing the level of science allowed to enter their deliberation and reasoning, whereas others seek to 'scientize' the judicial process and their decisions to a certain extent. These adjudicatory responses run in parallel to each other forming two trends in international environmental case law marked by divergent judicial tools and argumentative techniques.

This analysis is structured in a bifurcated way. It will first review, with respect to each phase of the adjudicative process, the tools that serve to downplay science in the judicial inquiry and reasoning, followed by those methods that aim at incorporating it. Besides classifying and commenting on the common features of solutions applied by major international courts and tribunals, where it seems appropriate, the comparative analysis will also draw on potential judicial good practices from the case law of international claims commissions and domestic courts. These insights seek to demonstrate the wide array of judicial methods that would arguably be available also for international judges to secure a close(r) engagement with science.

Some caveats are due before delving into the comparative assessment. First, it is not the intention of this chapter to rehearse the content of the preceding ones, nor is it to squeeze each and every judicial decision mentioned earlier into one of the two trends. Rather, the comparative exercise will seek to reveal common patterns in the treatment of scientific arguments by the various jurisdictions. Second, nothing in this study purports that every judicial tool discussed herein has been deployed in the material case with a deliberate and specific judicial *intent* to marginalize or accommodate science. Instead, by scrutinizing the dynamics of the adjudicatory process, and by considering especially the outcome reached and the role attached to science in the reasoning, this study seeks to appraise the *effect* adjudicatory analysis has on the science-intensity of disputes. Surveying and understanding the impact that adjudicatory techniques exert on the reach of scientific arguments in the judicial process is informative, from an analytical point of view, for appraising the status and standing that science currently holds in environmental adjudication.

The forthcoming analysis will first theorize the two trends that can be discerned from environmental jurisprudence (Section I, Subsections 1 and 2). This will be followed by the bifurcated analysis identifying exact judicial tools enabling to downplay and to accommodate science respectively along the four stages of the adjudicative process (Sections II–V).

1 *Downplaying Science: And a Corresponding Need for Non-Scientific Justifications in the Reasoning*

As has been addressed in the preceding chapters, international judges act as gatekeepers determining the extent to which science is allowed to play a decisive role in their decision-making by devising different judicial tools at each phase of the judicial process. Certain adjudicatory techniques impede, or even preclude, the invasion of science into the legally relevant aspects of cases and thereby essentially downplay the weight attached to scientific knowledge in adjudication.

Emphatically, 'downplaying' in this context is not equal to situations when adjudicators rule against science-backed environmental claims. Instead, whether science is downplayed in the process of judicial decision-making is measured against the extent to which judges rely or reflect on scientific arguments in reaching their decisions. Downplaying, thus, refers to situations when science-based disputes are decided without commenting on the underlying science. Importantly, not every downplaying technique is detrimental to environmental claims. What is more, in certain occasions more favourable decisions to environmental interests can be reached even more easily, or more likely, through the application of certain non-scientific reasoning techniques, such as applying presumptions. Nevertheless, in the majority of cases, marginalizing scientific evidence hinders finding environmental claims established.

It is equally important to underline that not every downplaying technique endangers the epistemic legitimacy of adjudicatory decisions. In fact, in the words of Judge Donoghue, 'many cases involving disputed scientific assertions do not call for a finding on scientific facts'.[3] Indeed, in certain instances it may be entirely legitimate to craft a judicial reasoning that do not directly refer to the scientific authority of experts. Yet even in such cases, the cognitive authority of science necessitates a careful management of the scientific aspects implicated in the dispute. The forthcoming analysis will enumerate the various non-scientific authorities with which international adjudicators can justify their findings in a perfectly legitimate way from an epistemic point of view. The trade-offs and risks as well as benefits of using such non-scientific yardsticks in adjudicatory reasoning will be identified in Chapter 10.

2 *Integrating Science in the Judicial Inquiry: And Harnessing Its Cognitive Authority*

Besides various science-evasive judicial strategies an increasing number of tools can be found that allow international adjudicators to accommodate the peculiarities of uncertain scientific knowledge in applying legal doctrine to scientific facts. Incorporating science in the judicial assessment brings the important benefit of harnessing the cognitive authority of science for scaffolding the acceptability of adjudicatory findings. Specific examples of strategic appeals to scientific references have been addressed in the analytic chapters with respect to the practice of each relevant fora. However, doing so also poses special challenges for judges. It calls for enhancing their scientific competence through appropriate fact-finding techniques in order to retain their monopoly over the dispute resolution, and not to surrender the judicial function to scientific experts.

The fundamental trade-off here lies in the fact that science often appears as an appealing authority to turn to in deciding disputes, yet legal adjudicators rarely have adequate knowledge to interpret or use scientific data on their own. Judges are put in an even more difficult position when are faced with a choice among conflicting scientific narratives. To do so, they need to gather expert advice or otherwise increase the internal scientific capacities of the bench. Should judges be willing to frame the legally relevant issues in a way as to touch upon scientific facts, available fact-finding mechanisms would almost deterministically shape the prospects of science for getting appreciated in the judicial assessment. Finally, the different modalities of scrutinizing expert input also impact the depth of judicial engagement with science.

---

[3] Donoghue, 'Expert scientific evidence in a broader context', 381.

II FRAMING LEGAL DISPUTES: CHOOSING RELEVANT QUESTIONS TO DECIDE

The framing of legal disputes throughout this comparative study has referred to deliberate choices of adjudicators selecting aspects of a case that are deemed legally relevant in resolving a given environmental dispute. Judges may reason their way out of confronting with the scientific aspects of disputes, just as much they may also involve the technical aspects in the legally appreciable ambit of relevant facts – if they so decide. Framing embraces both procedural choices of adjudicators and the invocation of substantive principles, aptly illustrating the breadth and depth of framing techniques. Framing appears to be the single most consequential judicial tool for determining the reach of scientific arguments in adjudication. Such techniques are often more impactful for the status of science in a particular dispute than either the procedural powers of international courts or the body of substantive legal rules governing the conflict at hand. Put it at its most straightforward, framing signals what judges *actually do* in contrast to what they *could potentially do* in light of their procedural powers and argumentative possibilities. Hence, framing serves as a litmus test indicating the *willingness* of judges to engage with science – which appears to be the centre of gravity of the entire adjudicative process.

Obviously, the two opposing trends of judicial engagement with science are also manifest among the various framing techniques of international courts and tribunals. Some eliminate or diminish the scientific profile of disputes (Subsection 1), while others try to involve scientifically rooted questions in the scope of issues judges comment on in their decisions (Subsection 2). The coming sections will compare and analyse these framing methods.

1 *Adjudicatory Techniques Serving to Carve Out Science from the Judicial Inquiry*

This section reviews those framing practices that altogether aim to lower the science-intensity of the adjudicatory task by carving out science from the judicial inquiry. From a higher level of generality, a good number of adjudicatory argumentative solutions appear to ensure that scientific arguments do not have a decisive say in resolving legal disputes.

1.1 Extreme Solutions: Non-Justiciability and Out-of-Court Settlements

The most extreme avoidance strategies of international courts allow judges to either find science-intensive cases inadmissible[4] or to refer such questions to the

---

[4] For example the early practice of the ECtHR, for more details see Chapter 5. However, the major reason for the ECtHR's initial dismissive approach was arguably the fact that the ECHR did not provide an explicit protection against environmental nuisance.

merits phase that the dispute does not reach out of the court's decision.[5] Another framing technique would exclude scientific considerations from judicial competence by deeming them non-justiciable. Such a possibility has been raised but declined in *Southern Bluefin Tuna*,[6] and more recently, such views are mainly embraced by minority positions within international fora.[7]

Another framing technique leading to outright circumvention of science is offered by the parties when they settle their science-intensive claims out of court. As has been discussed in Chapter 3 with respect to disputes referred to the ICJ specifically, several cases featuring substantive issues of environmental harm and causation have been settled before the oral phase of the proceedings and, thus, ultimately were not decided by the Court. More subtle ways of downplaying science are, however, persistent in the case law, to which we now shall turn to.

1.2 Disregarding Science: Rendering Solomonic Decisions

An initial judicial reaction given to the presence of scientific questions in a legal dispute has been simply to carve these aspects out from the main thread of the judicial analysis. The most widely cited example bespeaking such a judicial strategy is the *Gabcikovo-Nagymaros* judgment, though such framing has been applied in inter-state arbitration[8] and investment disputes[9] as well. As two notable commentators of scientific fact-finding have put it, the ICJ decided this case based 'solely on the law, rather than making a full examination of the facts and the evidence'.[10] The judgment has become known for not resolving aspects of the dispute that were tainted with scientific complexities, namely, the allocation and sharing of freshwater resources and the extent of environmental risks and potential irreversible ecological damage. One commentator rightly observes that the Court actually minimized science in its inquiry when instead of taking a stand on the scientific facts openly, it 'camouflaged' its factual evaluation.[11] There are indeed good reasons for regarding

[5] For example *Nuclear Tests (New Zealand v. France)* (Judgment) (1974) ICJ Rep 253, Judgment, in more details see Chapter 3.
[6] *Southern Bluefin Tuna (New Zealand v. Japan; Australia v. Japan)* (Provisional Measures) ITLOS Nos. 3 and 4 (27 August 1999), Provisional Measures, addressed in more detail in Chapter 8 Section II, Subsection 1.
[7] See for instance *Whaling in the Antarctic (Australia v. Japan: New Zealand intervening)* (Judgment) (2014) ICJ Rep 226, Separate Opinion of Judge Sebutinde, para. 9, Dissenting Opinion of Judge Owada, para. 24, Separate Opinion of Judge Xue, para. 15.
[8] For example *Chagos Marine Protected Area* Arbitration (*Chagos Marine Protected Area* Arbitration *(Mauritius v. UK)* (Permanent Court of Arbitration) Award, 18 March 2015), and the *MOX Plant* case (*MOX Plant* Arbitration *(Ireland v. UK)* (Permanent Court of Arbitration) Award, 6 June 2008), for more details see Chapter 4 Section II, Subsections 1.1 and 1.2.
[9] For example *Compañía del Desarrollo de Santa Elena, S.A. v. Costa Rica*, ICSID Case No. ARB/96/1, Final Award (17 February 2000), para. 46. In more detail see Chapter 7 Section II, Subsection 1.
[10] Ridell and Plant, *Evidence before the International Court of Justice*, p. 353.
[11] Viñuales, 'Observations sur le traitement des motifs scientifiques dans le contentieux environnemental international', pp. 114–15.

the *Gabcikovo-Nagymaros* judgment as a proof of the Court's 'unwillingness or unsuitability'[12] at the time to deal with scientific aspects of disputes.

Such downplaying techniques have serious shortcomings for the acceptability of decisions. Hiding behind general reference to uncertainty and long-term risks, without however revisiting the evidence, adjudicators run the risk of acting in a rather 'suspicious'[13] manner. Indeed, there is an apparent discrepancy between judging the immediacy and gravity of an environmental peril without actually evaluating the scientific data submitted.[14]

Framing legal disputes in such a manifestly descientized way is especially problematic in cases when both litigants clearly regard scientific facts decisive and submit ample factual record in this respect. This was the case for instance in the *MOX Plant OSPAR* Arbitration,[15] where judicial reasoning was geared towards issues that the parties did not even elaborate on in their submissions or in their oral statements. In such cases, it may be especially problematic to remove science from the scope of judicial analysis and decision, as it could considerably erode the convincing force of the decision in the parties' eyes.

One may, however, argue that circumventing science in the judicial analysis and basing decisions on purely legal considerations is a perfectly legitimate solution to decide cases tainted with factual conundrum. Ever since the biblical anecdote, the judgment of King Solomon has been regarded as the archetypal example of rendering wise decisions in factually wicked cases, and after all, he also rendered justice on the basis of common-sense wisdom. The comparison is indeed relevant here given that the dispute settled by King Solomon featured competing claims of biological motherhood of two women and, as such, was also a science-intensive legal controversy in the sense understood in this book. Solomon obviously did not (and could not) comment on the nowadays apparent scientific dimensions of the case. Instead, he ordered the child cut in half, which moved the biological mother to immediately waive her claim just to spare her child's life; and from this gesture, Solomon could indirectly deduce the identity of the real mother. In this way, he rendered a 'wise' and factually correct decision based on purely non-scientific reasoning. If there was any science involved in Solomon's judicial decision, it was a basic understanding of human psychology.

In the narrative of this book, this biblical story carries an important message for adjudicators deciding science-heavy disputes in modern times. It can in no way be read as an endorsement for deciding such disputes based on purely non-scientific considerations. Quite the contrary, this analogy points out a major weakness of

[12] Ridell and Plant, *Evidence before the International Court of Justice*, p. 348.
[13] Viñuales, 'Observations sur le traitement des motifs scientifiques dans le contentieux environnemental international', p. 116.
[14] Ridell and Plant, *Evidence before the International Court of Justice*, p. 348.
[15] *MOX Plant OSPAR* Arbitration *(Ireland* v. *UK)* (Permanent Court of Arbitration), Award, 2 July 2003, in more details see Chapter 4 Section II, Subsection 1.2.

deciding scientific disputes without paying due regard to their undeniable scientific dimensions. Importantly, King Solomon justified his judgment based on common-sense wisdom, because he was understandably unable to benefit from scientific proof on biological motherhood, that is, DNA evidence. Under such circumstances, circumventing the underlying scientific aspects of the dispute was a perfectly legit-imate judicial solution. Yet, a similar a judicial attitude – subtle forms of which do appear in contemporary environmental adjudication – is insufficient for ensuring credibility and legitimacy for decisions rendered nowadays. Certainly, in the past when judges had no access to scientific evidence (note the biblical origin of Solomon's anecdote), wise and hence legitimate decisions could be successfully made with sole reference to non-scientific justifications such as legal, ethical, or common-sense principles. However, such Solomonic judgments would fail to con-fer legitimacy on adjudicatory decisions, when techno-scientific progress outpaces imagination and exerts a transformative impact on human societies.[16]

In this vein, when results of natural sciences can inform the judicial inquiry in many ways, deciding a dispute with apparent scientific profile in complete disregard of expert opinions is highly problematic from a legitimacy point of view. As will be argued later on in greater detail, reasoning on the basis of solely legalistic or intuitive logic is not always detrimental to the legitimacy of the decision. In fact, such reasoning styles may sometimes be the best available avenues to craft a convincing judicial argumentation in the face of uncertain science. Yet, non-scientific reasoning techniques are only prefer-able when they do not aim to replace scientific knowledge pertinent to the dispute.

1.3 Judicial Paralysis in the Face of Scientific Uncertainty

Through another strategic framing of disputes, judges may emphasize the infinite complexity and the inescapable uncertainty of scientific evidence to justify their choice not to decide a particularly fact-intensive aspect of a dispute. An apposite example of such judicial reasoning can be seen in the *Pulp Mills* judgment, where the ICJ summarily dismissed all eight accounts of lengthy scientific explanations offered by Argentina and found no violation of the no-harm rule with reference to the lack of 'sufficient'[17] and 'clear' evidence.[18] Similarly, in *Gabcikovo-Nagymaros*, the ICJ entirely omitted any consideration of the scientific evidence submitted, by famously holding that 'it is not necessary … to determine which of those points of view is scientifically better founded'.[19] Conceiving scientific controversies as

---

[16] The social effects of innovation were analytically assessed first by Ogburn right after World War II, when post-war industrial innovations triggered a globalized economy and society. W. F. Ogburn, 'How technology changes society' (1947) 249 *The Annals of the American Academy of Political and Social Science* 81–8.

[17] *Pulp Mills on the River Uruguay (Argentina v. Uruguay)* (Judgment) (2010) ICJ Rep 14, para. 254.

[18] *Pulp Mills*, Judgment, paras. 257, 259, 'clear relationship' is mentioned in para. 262; see in more detail in Chapter 3 Section IV, Subsection 2.

[19] *Gabcikovo-Nagymaros*, Judgment, para. 54. see in more detail in Chapter 3 Section III, Subsection 1.

a prohibitive obstacle to meaningfully consider the legal claims of the parties may undermine the legitimacy capital of the judicial decision.

1.4 Mandating the Parties' Negotiations Regarding Science-Heavy Aspects

International courts and tribunals saliently favour rendering solutions that are mutually acceptable for the parties. This leads to a recurrent judicial solution to prescribe co-operation and negotiation among litigants. Such an approach has its undoubted merits, although only if adequate safeguards are provided to promote, and even to secure, that the parties will in fact reach a mutually acceptable solution to their conflict. Respective case law suggests that such guarantees have not been provided in early environmental disputes.

Notably, the ICJ mandated the parties' negotiation to settle science-intensive aspects of their dispute in *Gabcikovo-Nagymaros*. This case illustrates how adjudicators may effectively circumvent science-intensive questions by referring those to consultation of the parties. Despite the fact that the protracted conflict showed that the parties have had irreconcilable views regarding the preferred water allocation scheme, the Court nevertheless repeatedly argued that Hungary and Slovakia had to find 'an agreed solution'[20] to all issues that could have been decided only by assessing bulky scientific evidence. In this vein, the question of compensation and the scheme of reasonable and equitable utilization of the water were all referred back to the parties. Such a narrow tailoring of the issues decided in the judgment conveniently distanced judges from scientific evidence.

The price of this effectively 'descientized' argumentation was, however, the salient inability of the judgment to resolve the underlying conflict. The parties failed even to begin a meaningful dialogue for more than a decade after the ICJ's judgment.[21] Subsequently, Slovakia filed a request for an additional judgment asking the Court to determine the modalities for executing the original judgment.[22] Ever since all attempts at engaging in meaningful negotiations have remained futile. Albeit in 2017, the parties agreed to the formal discontinuance of the proceedings before the Court,[23] their protracted bilateral consultation was unable to establish a mutually agreed solution for the pending scientifically loaded issues. Tellingly, the *Gabcikovo-Nagymaros* case has not been removed from the Court's list,[24] symbolizing the many questions the judgment left unanswered.

In more recent disputes, the ICJ is willing to apply a more hands-on approach to the judicial supervision of the parties' negotiations. In *Certain Activities/Construction of*

---

[20] *Gabcikovo-Nagymaros*, Judgment, paras. 140, 142.
[21] M. Szabó, 'The implementation of the judgment of the ICJ on the *Gabcikovo-Nagymaros* Dispute' (2009) V *Iustum Aequum Salutare* 15–25 at 22.
[22] Press release of the Court, No. 1998/28, 3 September 1998.
[23] Press release of the Court, No. 2017/31 21 July 2017.
[24] See the Court's list of pending cases, available at www.icj-cij.org/en/pending-cases (last accessed 21 January 2020).

a Road, the Court set a deadline for the parties to determine the amount of compensation payable by Nicaragua for the harmful environmental consequences of violating Costa Rica's territorial sovereignty; and the Court was ready to set the quantum of compensation when the parties failed to find a solution on their own.[25] Similar dilemmas have emerged in inter-state arbitration as well. It remains to be seen whether the negotiation mandated by the *Chagos Marine Protected Area* award will bring about an effective solution between the United Kingdom and Mauritius in terms of working out an environmental protection regime.[26] The tribunal, unlike the *Iron Rhine* panel or the ITLOS, did not take a managerial approach to mandating the participation of experts securing their decisive voice in working out the contours of an agreed solution. It only urged the parties to 'achieve a mutually satisfactory arrangement for protecting the marine environment'[27] without articulating any expectations for incorporating science and expertise in the process.

1.5 Emphasizing Procedural Requirements Over Substantive Obligations

The preference of international adjudicative fora to consider the procedural aspects of science-heavy environmental disputes manifests as another cross-jurisdictional framing strategy. The abundance of procedural obligations is quite salient as a matter of primary norms in international environmental law. Most eminently, the no-harm rule imposes an obligation of conduct and not that of result,[28] and requirements of notification,[29] consultation,[30] co-operation,[31] and conducting environmental impact assessments (EIA)[32] can all be perceived as primarily compelling states to be engaged in certain behaviour that may be defined in procedural terms. One may argue that the reason for the noticeable proceduralization of environmental litigation is a corollary of the underlying substantive law. In conflicts revolving around environmentally harmful projects and the absence of protective measures, judges may prefer procedural requirements because in this way they do not directly encroach upon substantive policy choices of sovereign actors.[33] While this may well explain the prevalence of procedural obligations among the primary

---

[25] *Certain Activities Carried Out by Nicaragua in the Border Area (Costa Rica v. Nicaragua)* (Judgment on compensation) (2018) ICJ Rep 15. For a more detailed analysis see Chapter 3 Section III, Subsection 3.2.

[26] *Chagos Marine Protected Area*, for further discussion on the scientific engagement displayed in the award see Chapter 4 Section II, Subsection 1.1.

[27] *Chagos Marine Protected Area*, Award, para. 544.

[28] For more details on the due diligence nature of prevention of transboundary harm see Duvic-Paoli, *The Prevention Principle in International Environmental Law*, p. 142.

[29] *Pulp Mills*, Judgment, para. 112.

[30] *Pulp Mills*, Judgment, para. 143.

[31] *Pulp Mills*, Judgment, para. 112.

[32] *Pulp Mills*, Judgment, para. 205.

[33] M. Koskenniemi, 'Peaceful settlement of environmental disputes' (1991) 60 *Nordic Journal of International Law* 73 at 74.

rules of international environmental law, it does not justify the adjudicatory practice of neglecting a meaningful (and science-intensive) investigation into alleged non-compliance with existing substantive obligations.

Nevertheless, such a trend spreads across the jurisprudence of several international fora. As for the ICJ, a breach of the substantive aspect of the no-harm rule has never been found established despite repeated claims of injured states;[34] whereas violations have been declared with respect to a wide array of procedural obligations in both *Pulp Mills*[35] and in *Certain Activities/Construction of a Road*.[36] Although the Permanent Court of Arbitration (PCA) found a breach of not to cause significant transboundary harm in the *South China Sea* Arbitration,[37] this ruling hitherto marks the sole occasion of an international adjudicative body announcing such a violation. The case practice of the International Tribunal for the Law of the Sea (ITLOS) also bespeaks a judicial attitude which evades ordering prohibiting measures on the basis of scientific evidence of environmental harm. Notably, in provisional measures the tribunal virtually always prescribed the co-operation of the parties.[38]

In sum, violations of procedural obligations can, no doubt, be established more easily in court proceedings,[39] and hence proceduralization in international environmental law can be seen as a promoter of holding states accountable for breaching their environmental obligations. Yet, downplaying substantive obligations not only contributes to descientizing environmental adjudication with all its repercussions on the legitimacy of the reasoning, but it is also unable to adequately remedy environmental harm that may nevertheless occur.

1.6 Decoupling the Concept of Risk from Science

The ICJ's reluctance to discern any scientific minimum criteria for EIA obligations of states[40] illustrates an adjudicatory tendency to hollow out scientific criteria of environmental law obligations. Tying the obligation of EIA to 'the presence of significant risk of harm', as announced by the Court,[41] is no more than an empty rhetoric, when the Court in fact decouples the meaning of risk

---

[34] *Pulp Mills*, Judgment, para. 169.; *Certain Activities/Construction of a Road*, Judgment, paras. 174, 113.
[35] *Pulp Mills*, Judgment, para. 282.
[36] *Certain Activities/Construction of a Road*, Judgment, para. 229 (6).
[37] *South China Sea* Arbitration *(The Republic of the Philippines v. The People's Republic of China)* (Permanent Court of Arbitration), Award, 12 July 2016, for a more detailed analysis see Chapter 4.
[38] *Southern Bluefin Tuna*, Provisional Measures, Operative part, Section (e); *MOX Plant (Ireland v. UK)* (Provisional Measures) ITLOS No. 10 (3 December 2000), Operative part, Section (1); *Land Reclamation by Singapore in and around the Straits of Johor (Malaysia v. Singapore)* (Provisional Measures) ITLOS No. 12 (8 October 2003), para. 92 and Operative part, Section (1).
[39] J. Brunnée, 'Procedure and substance in international environmental law: confused at a higher level?' (2016) 5(6) *ESIL Reflections*.
[40] *Certain Activities/Construction of a Road*, Judgment, para. 155.
[41] *Certain Activities/Construction of a Road*, Judgment, para. 156.

from the science of risk assessment. Although the notion of significant environmental risk is indeed essentially an extra-legal concept,[42] which is elevated to
a normative framework in the law governing EIA, it nevertheless remains
a scientific concept. Treating scientific concepts as if they were purely legal
constructs is problematic from the perspective of epistemic non-arbitrariness.[43]

1.7 Precautionary Reasoning: Bridging Gaps via Legal Principles

A common adjudicatory solution across jurisdictions is to rely on precautionary
reasoning in order to bridge the gap between uncertain scientific facts and judicial
findings. Relevant examples have been addressed earlier from the case law of the
European Court of Human Rights (ECtHR)[44] and ITLOS. Both of these fora
invoked the precautionary principle in order to be able to include uncertain
scientific risks in the scope of adjudicatory analysis. A particularly strong application
of the principle could be found in provisional measures and advisory opinions of
ITLOS.[45] The tribunal has set a threshold for states' vigilance that is progressively
elevating with technological innovations, which at the same time could not be
lowered with reference to the uncertain nature of scientific opinions describing
applicable environmental risks. But the embrace of the precautionary reasoning is
far from being uniform across relevant jurisdictions. Investment arbitral tribunals
have been markedly reluctant to use such a framing technique despite repeated
attempts by respondent states to rely on precautionary justifications.[46] Neither did
the ICJ conceive it as creating a standalone legal obligation or having the effect of
modifying the standard or the burden of proof.[47]

1.8 Decline to Second-Guess Scientific Truths

Another common pattern in judicial framing techniques, which results in decreasing the science-intensity of adjudicatory analyses, is to draw the boundary of the
judicially relevant questions in a way as to exclude the underlying scientific debate
itself. Such a framing enables adjudicators to smoothly escape from the need to

---

[42] Lowe, *International Law*, pp. 98–9. Lowe explicitly mentions sustainable development, equity, and
     fairness among those extra-legal concepts that in fact exist outside the law, and thus, they are not legal
     norms though are used in the process of legal reasoning.
[43] Further risks of non-scientific reasoning are discussed in Chapter 10.
[44] See Chapter 5 Section II.
[45] For example *Southern Bluefin Tuna*, Provisional Measures, *Responsibilities and obligations of States
     sponsoring persons and entities with respect to activities in the Area (Request for Advisory Opinion
     submitted to the Seabed Disputes Chamber)* (Advisory Opinion) ITLOS No. 17 (1 February 2011), para.
     117; *Request for an advisory opinion submitted by the Sub-Regional Fisheries Commission (SRFC)*
     (Advisory Opinion) ITLOS No. 21 (2 April 2015), para. 132; for more details see Chapter 8 Section II,
     Subsections 2 and 3.
[46] For more details see Chapter 7 Section II, Subsection 1.3.
[47] *Pulp Mills*, Judgment, para. 164.

scrutinize whether the sovereign risk assessor has actually arrived at the scientifically correct decision regarding scientific hazards. Judicial review of environmental risk assessment decisions takes place most frequently in the context of investment arbitration[48] and in WTO disputes.[49] Both regimes have seen adjudicatory framings emphasizing the limited scope of judicial review, thereby excluding second-guessing the scientifically solid nature of the underlying risk assessment decisions.

2 Incorporating Science in the Judicial Inquiry: Framing Disputes to Harness Science's Cognitive Authority

In parallel to the above-described avoidance strategies designed to circumvent science in the judicial analysis and reasoning, a growing body of case law attests that certain adjudicators seek to appreciate the scientific knowledge speaking to environmental controversies and to incorporate science in the legally relevant aspects of disputes. A major benefit of science-intensive judicial argumentation lies in various strategic purposes science may serve in the hands of adjudicators. Some typical strategic applications to which science may lend itself in the judicial process will be addressed below.

2.1 Mandating the Parties' Expert-Led Consultation

A strategic goal science may foster is appearing as a supplier of objective information for the parties in their quest for an agreed solution. International tribunals increasingly take a managerial approach towards out-of-court settlements in scientific disputes. In such cases by mandating expert-led consultation, adjudicators can rest assured that scientific dimensions will be duly accounted for in the final scheme, which they can easily rubberstamp in their orders.

The award of ITLOS Special Chamber in the *Swordfish* case is a stark example of how adjudicators can benefit from outsourcing science-intensive dispute resolution to experts. Chile and the EU crafted a mutually agreed regime, including the establishment of a Bilateral Scientific and Technical Committee,[50] with reference to which the tribunal could discontinue its proceedings without having to dive deep into the scientific aspects. In the *Straits of Johor* provisional measures order,[51] the

---

[48]   Relevant decisions are *Chemtura* v. *Government of Canada* (UNCITRAL) Award (2 August 2010), and *Crystallex International Corporation* v. *Bolivarian Republic of Venezuela*, ICSID Case No. ARB(AF)/11/2, Award (4 April 2016), see in more detail in Chapter 7.

[49]   See the WTO AB decision in *US – Continued Suspension of Obligations* case, Report of the AB, WT/DS320/AB/R (16 October 2008), analysed in more detail in Chapter 6.

[50]   *Conservation and Sustainable Exploitation of Swordfish Stocks in the South-Eastern Pacific Ocean Chile/European Union)* (Order) ITLOS No. 7 (16 December 2009), see in particular paras. 13–14. In more detail see discussion in Chapter 8 Section II, Subsection 4.

[51]   *Straits of Johor*, Provisional Measures, for more details see discussion in Chapter 8 Section II, Subsection 4.

Tribunal again kept science at its disposal, while still escaping a thorough scientific fact-finding procedure. The Tribunal compelled the parties to jointly set up a body of experts tasked with guiding their consultation process and proposing measures to deal with adverse effects of the land reclamation works. An arbitral tribunal hearing the dispute on the merits also ordered Singapore to ensure not to cause any harm to the area by taking into account the expert report.[52] The judgment of the Inter-American Court of Human Rights (IACtHR) resonates with these decisions inasmuch as it compelled the respondent to devise an action plan to remedy the environmental harm caused with the participation of relevant experts.[53] With such solutions, adjudicators in these cases effectively outsourced science-intensive questions to scientists, yet they were still able to secure the authority of science for their own decisions by ordering the final legal regime to be based on scientific facts.

Importantly, such a managerial approach to the parties' science-based negotiations ensures that the judicial body retains the ultimate control over the dispute by setting a deadline and a specific mandate for the expert panel, which guides their consultation. This solution is much more efficient than the path taken by the ICJ in the *Gabcikovo-Nagymaros* case, where the Court did not intend to have such a hands-on approach on the consultation process. Notably, the ICJ did not require the parties to pay due regard to the underlying science in finding a solution for disputed questions of water allocation. These marked differences in handling science-intensive issues in the legal dispute were arguably relevant factors in bringing strikingly different outcome in the two cases. In contrast to the failure of the *Gabcikovo* judgment to achieve meaningful negotiation and a final resolution to the conflict, both in *Straits of Johor* and in *Swordfish* the parties ultimately accepted the recommendations of the expert body, and reached a settlement to their dispute on these bases.[54]

2.2 Science as a 'Gentle Neutralizer' of Conflicts

The perceived objectivity of science can be a major asset for adjudicators in solving sensitive and entrenched disputes by using scientific experts as neutral arbiters. In this way adjudicators can harness the cognitive authority of science to buttress the legitimacy of their decision. The *Trail Smelter* Arbitration serves as an early example of neutralizing a harsh inter-state conflict through a decade-long and elaborate scientific fact-finding process, which ultimately uncovered the scientific cause of the injury.[55] A somewhat similar framing technique was followed by the *Iron Rhine* Tribunal.[56] In

---

[52] *Land Reclamation by Singapore in and Around the Straits of Johor (Malaysia v. Singapore)*, (Permanent Court of Arbitration), Award on Agreed Terms (1 September 2005), Operative part, Section 2.

[53] For more details see discussion on the *Lhaka Honhat* judgment in Chapter 5 Section IV, Subsection 2.

[54] For a more detailed analysis see Chapter 8 Section II, Subsection 4.

[55] For a more detailed analysis see Chapter 4 Section II, Subsection 3.1.

[56] For a more detailed analysis see Chapter 4 Section II, Subsection 3.1.

this case, adjudicators refrained from making any finding on the scientific subject matter of the dispute, that is, the extent of appropriate noise abatement measures and the costs thereof. Instead, the tribunal referred these issues to technical experts that the parties were supposed to appoint following the arbitration proceedings.

2.3 Scientific Review Procedures

The finality of judicial decisions in environmental disputes is a long-studied problem.[57] Any legal solution ordained by judges in such cases can only provide a temporary solution as it is inevitably conditioned on the rapidly changing environmental conditions. Some form of procedure therefore appears to be warranted in order to account for changes in the underlying environmental conditions and developments in scientific knowledge. Against this backdrop, judges may utilize scientific authority to review the obligations of the parties in order to keep pace with changes in natural processes and technological developments. Building scientific review mechanisms in adjudicatory decisions helps judges adequately reflect on the volatile nature of scientific knowledge, and therefore ensures that the balance struck between obligations of litigants in the judgment will be adjusted to changing factual realities. This fosters the acceptability of a given legal regime by affected parties, and also promotes accruing legitimacy for the decision both in the eyes of the litigants and the public.

Express utilization of science-based review procedures is still a rarity in the adjudicatory landscape compared to the number of disputes, where it can be potentially applicable. The most well-known examples are featured in the *Trail Smelter* Arbitration[58] and the *Kishenganga* dispute. In the latter case, the tribunal expressly laid out a review mechanism to account for uncertainties in predicting future flow conditions and effects of climate change.[59] On these bases, the award allows the reconsideration of the minimum flow requirement that was set by the panel on the basis of available scientific evidence.

2.4 Science as Indicium of Non-Arbitrariness

A closely related framing technique manifests in decisions where science is used as a benchmark for detecting arbitrary decisions. This is particularly relevant in the context of investment arbitration, where tribunals often have to scrutinize the motivation of host states behind contested measures.[60] In this context, panels regard the absence of actual scientific studies and data supporting the environmental

---

[57] C. E. Foster, *Science and the Precautionary Principle in International Courts and Tribunals* (Cambridge University Press, 2011), pp. 281–348.
[58] See in more detail in Chapter 4 Section II, Subsection 3.1.
[59] *Indus Waters Kishenganga* Arbitration (*Pakistan v. India*) (Permanent Court of Arbitration), Final Award, 20 December 2013, paras. 117–19. See also Chapter 4 Section III, Subsection 2.
[60] For a more detailed analysis see Chapter 7 Section II, Subsection 2.2.

measure at hand as a strong indicator of arbitrary policies that are inconsistent with investment protection regimes. This framing technique enables adjudicators to deem the lack of appropriate scientific bases for a given regulation as a legally decisive factor and find a breach accordingly.

Besides investment arbitration, the existence of appropriate scientific justifications is also regarded as indicia of unbiased, and thus lawful, measures in the context of WTO law. Under the scrutiny of the WTO Appellate Body (AB), those trade restrictions can be upheld that rest on a scientific risk assessment backed by sound and respectable scientific evidence and a coherent reasoning of the risk assessor. Measures that fail to meet these criteria are regarded as arbitrary and in contradiction with the Agreement on the Application of Sanitary and Phytosanitary Measures (SPS Agreement) and the Agreement on Technical Barriers to Trade (TBT Agreement). Yet again, requiring adequate scientific justifications for trade restrictive measures provides a legitimate way for WTO panels to decide sensitive and highly technical disputes.[61]

2.5 Performing the Judicial Task Despite Uncertainty

In contrast to paralysing the judicial task in the face of uncertain scientific results, one may also find disputes where international judges opt for exercising their judicial function despite these complexities and deem relevant questions amenable to judicial appraisal. From investment arbitration practice, the *Gold Reserve* v. *Venezuela* Tribunal particularly springs to mind when searching for examples for such an ambitious adjudicatory approach. Having noted the difficulties surrounding damage calculations involved in competing 'but equally legitimate'[62] facts and valuation methods, the tribunal firmly declared that it will nevertheless exercise its discretion and discern the sum of damages it deems appropriate.

More recently, the ICJ also uses a language that bespeaks a general willingness to adjudicate legal claims tainted with scientific uncertainty as to their factual bases. In the compensation judgment issued in *Certain Activities*, the Court noted the intricate issues ecological damage valuation entailed in terms of causal inquiry and fact-finding, but immediately added that such 'difficulties . . . must be addressed as and when they arise in light of the facts of the case' and declared that '[u]ltimately it is for the Court to decide'[63] these questions. Even though it is possible to read this particular sentence as a mere rhetorical gesture in an *obiter dictum*, it can still signal an important shift in how the Court approaches uncertain science as a matter of principle.

---

[61] For more details on the adjudicatory tests and solutions reviewing the legality of risk assessment decisions see discussion in Chapter 6 Section III, Subsection 3.

[62] *Gold Reserve Inc.* v. *Bolivarian Republic of Venezuela*, ICSID Case No. ARB(AF)/09/1, Award (22 September 2014), para. 686. For a more detailed discussion of the award see Chapter 7 Section II, Subsection 2.3.

[63] *Certain Activities*, Judgment on compensation, para. 34.

III COMPARATIVE ANALYSIS OF INTERNATIONAL SCIENTIFIC FACT-FINDING TECHNIQUES

Examining the evidentiary powers granted to adjudicative bodies is a necessary although not exhaustive step in appraising the current limits of scientific engagement of international courts and tribunals. A survey of evidentiary practices reveals an apparent gap between the usually broad procedural powers granted to international fora in terms of law, and the much narrower scope of methods that are actually utilized in practice. For this reason, the present overview shall not only address various fact-finding avenues that are available as hypothetical possibilities for different fora, but shall also identify the preferred methods that are prevalent in adjudicatory practice. Finally, while the idealized role of experts is to put 'scientific information into a form appropriate for legal application so that fair and well-reasoned decisions are the result',[64] the practice of scientific fact-finding reveals a more nuanced and varied picture of the extent of co-operation and interaction between judges and experts, which should also be discussed here.

Scientific fact-finding is a procedural prerequisite of forming legitimate science-based decisions.[65] Different fact-finding methods are thus of key importance for any attempt at better integrating science in the adjudicatory process. On the one hand, a more active engagement with the fact-finding process is a significant factor for supporting the sociological legitimacy of international fora. Counsels and advocates, who form a major part of relevant audience for international courts and tribunals, repeatedly emphasize their preference for international judges exercising a more hands-on approach with the fact-finding process.[66] On the other hand, closer interaction with scientific evidence is also beneficial for the epistemic legitimacy of judicial decisions.

1 *Adjudicators Distancing Themselves from Scientific Expertise*

Several approaches to scientific fact-finding actually impede, if not preclude, a meaningful adjudicatory engagement with science underlying the legal controversy at hand. This gives rise to varied examples for judges distancing themselves from the scientific evidence in several jurisdictions.

1.1 Disregarding Scientific Evidence

The most marked way of downplaying science in the fact-finding phase manifests in disputes, where adjudicators are reluctant to hear or evaluate expert evidence.

---

[64] Mangel, 'Whales, science, and scientific whaling in the International Court of Justice', 14526.
[65] Bodansky, 'The legitimacy of international governance', 288–90.
[66] Blackaby and Wilbraham, 'Practical issues relating to the use of expert evidence in investment treaty arbitration', 669; Boisson de Chazournes, Mbengue, Das, and Gros, 'One size does not fit all – uses of experts before international courts and tribunals', 483, 493–4.

Suffice it to refer to the only recently improving evidentiary practice of the ICJ. Notably, early environmental disputes were decided by the Court without reference to the underlying facts. The *Gabcikovo-Nagymaros* case has become famous for evidencing a 'factual anxiety',[67] which drove judges not even to enter into the process of scientific fact-finding.[68] In later cases, expert opinions were presented by 'counsels', which precluded conducting a cross-examination and, therefore, a meaningful judicial testing of the scientific opinions submitted.[69]

Deciding science-based legal issues without garnering expert evidence is also present in the ECtHR's jurisprudence regarding individuals' health injury claims caused by environmental pollution.[70] The Strasbourg Court has been consistently reluctant to use its existing evidentiary powers to ask for expert opinions in personal health injury claims, neither it considered pieces of expert evidence that have already been available on the case-file. Even in cases where the ECtHR was willing to rule in favour of a claim that has been supported by scientific input, the evidentiary analysis remained hidden and opaque. Such an evidentiary practice fails to integrate scientific input in judicial decision-making, and hence it does not benefit from the epistemic justification offered by science.

1.2 Expertise from Counsels and Partisan Evidence

Partisan evidence poses many challenges for tribunals in evaluating the scientific and evidentiary value of the proof submitted.[71] As was seen in *Perenco* investment arbitration, party-adduced expert evidence may be biased to such an extent that it is not suitable for providing basis for adjudicatory assessment.[72] In the material case, the tribunal dismissed all party-appointed expert evidence as both sides' experts 'crossed the boundary between professional objective analysis and party representation'.[73] Instead, the tribunal asked for independent expert advice.

In *Pulp Mills*, the ICJ has been put in a similar situation but took a different path. The Court heard scientists appearing as counsels who took part in the parties' delegations.[74] Such a scientific fact-finding method was expressly criticized in the judgment for it blurred the line between scientific advice and advocacy.[75] According to Judge Greenwood, presenting scientific evidence by counsels was 'unfair and

[67] M. M. Mbengue, 'Scientific fact-finding by international courts and tribunals' (2012) 3 *Journal of International Dispute Settlement* 509–24 at 517.
[68] Mbengue, 'Scientific fact-finding by international courts and tribunals', 517.
[69] *Pulp Mills*, Judgment, para. 167.
[70] For a detailed discussion see Chapter 5 Section IV, Subsection 1.
[71] Foster, *Science and the Precautionary Principle in International Courts and Tribunals*, p. 80.
[72] *Perenco Ecuador Ltd.* v. *Ecuador and Emprese Estatal Petróleos del Ecuador (Petroecuador)*, ISCID Case No. ARB/08/6, Interim Decision on the Environmental Counterclaim (11 August 2015), para. 581.
[73] *Perenco*, Interim Decision on the Environmental Counterclaim, para. 581.
[74] *Pulp Mills*, Judgment, para. 167.
[75] *Pulp Mills*, Judgment, para. 167.

unhelpful'.[76] Tainting expertise with advocacy indeed diminishes the authority of scientific input and jeopardizes the function expertise could (and should) have in the adjudicatory process.

There are procedural antidotes to such concerns. Having recourse to *ex curia* experts could hinder the dangers flowing from partisan evidence. Similarly, taking greater judicial control over evidentiary proceedings could also abate problems of party-controlled scientific fact-finding. Practitioners often call international adjudicators for specifying the task of experts by mandating clear terms of reference, or by holding mid-arbitration meetings.[77] Promoting close co-operation between party-appointed experts through for example witness-conferencing[78] can also enhance adjudicators' ability to identify questions on which the party-appointed experts genuinely disagree from a scientific point of view. These techniques can enable adjudicators to better retain epistemic control over the fact-finding process.

1.3 Reluctance to Require Independent Expert Advice

A quasi uniform trend in international adjudicatory practice is the salient hesitance to rely on independent experts. The ICJ has consistently declined initiatives to appoint *ex curia* experts in environmental cases. Even though in *Pulp Mills* as many as five dissenting judges would have preferred such a solution,[79] the Court has never used such powers in environmental disputes.[80] Several scholars promote the idea of using *ex curia* experts under Article 50 of the Statute of the Court.[81] Yet, the limited use of scientific evidence may not be easily changed, for it appears to be 'built in the Court's DNA'.[82] The same tendency appears in the practice of other international fora. The ECtHR and ITLOS, although both would have the power to garner court-appointed expert advice, have never availed themselves of such a possibility. As has been seen above, in investment arbitration their use has similarly been exceptional to date.

The hesitant application of this fact-finding technique may be traced back to a feeling of unease among judges over potentially delegating their judicial function to non-accountable experts.[83] Likewise, they may feel bound by such opinions, which

---

[76] *Pulp Mills*, Separate Opinion of Judge Greenwood, para. 27.
[77] Blackaby and Wilbraham, 'Practical issues relating to the use of expert evidence in investment treaty arbitration', 659, 666.
[78] Blackaby and Wilbraham, 'Practical issues relating to the use of expert evidence in investment treaty arbitration', 667.
[79] *Pulp Mills*, Joint Dissenting Opinion of Judge Al-Khasawneh and Simma, Declaration of Judge Yusuf, Separate Opinion of Judge Cançado Trindade, Dissenting Opinion of Judge ad hoc Vinuesa.
[80] Peat, 'The use of court-appointed experts by the International Court of Justice'.
[81] Ridell, 'Scientific evidence in the International Court of Justice: problems and possibilities', 253; Foster, 'New clothes for the emperor?', 142.
[82] Alvarez, 'Are international judges afraid of science? A comment on Mbengue', 83.
[83] Peat, 'The use of court-appointed experts by the International Court of Justice', 272.

may also explain the rarity of appointing independent experts in international adjudication.[84] Adjudicators may also be uncomfortable to dismiss a finding made by an expert they themselves appointed.[85] The reluctance of judges to rely on independent expertise is further exacerbated by the parties' desire to retain greater control over the fact-finding process through offering party-adduced evidence. Moreover, an empirical survey among international adjudicators and counsels suggests that there are still pending questions surrounding the exact functions of such experts; specifically whether their task is to give their own opinion or only to comment on party-adduced evidence.[86] These ambiguities may also hinder making practical use of such powers.

1.4 Missed Opportunities of Using Expert Arbitrators

Procedural powers of international courts to appoint expert judges or assessors are also left underutilized. Not only has the ICJ never appointed expert assessors,[87] nor did WTO panels include a scientist as called for by scholarly opinion.[88] The parties have a role in selecting ad hoc panellists for hearing their case, however, DSU sets qualification criteria for potential members, according to which they ought to have a background in trade law or in trade policy.[89] As of today, all the panellists appointed had a legal background.[90] Similarly, the WTO AB has a permanent membership,[91] consisting of international trade law experts.[92] These all suggest that the participation of scientists is very unlikely within WTO dispute resolution system.

The UNCLOS provides a special procedure under Annex VIII where arbitrators could be appointed from a list of scientific experts who are recommended by international organizations. Yet, disputes have never been referred to this type of arbitration. The ITLOS is also reluctant to avail itself of the possibility to appoint expert assessors, who are equipped with legal background as well to sit with the Tribunal without a right to vote.[93]

---

[84] Ridell and Plant, *Evidence before the International Court of Justice*, p. 334.

[85] Donoghue, 'Expert scientific evidence in a broader context', 386–7.

[86] Boisson de Chazournes, Mbengue, Das, and Gros, 'One size does not fit all – uses of experts before international courts and tribunals', 503–4.

[87] Discussed further in Chapter 3 Section III, Subsection 2.3.

[88] Pauwelyn, 'Expert advice in WTO dispute settlement', p. 256.

[89] Dispute Settlement Rules: Understanding on Rules and Procedures Governing the Settlement of Disputes, Marrakesh Agreement Establishing the World Trade Organization, Annex 2, 1869 UNTS 401 (1994), Article 8.1.

[90] P. V. den Bossche and W. Zdouc, *The Law and Policy of the World Trade Organization* (Cambridge University Press, 2013), p. 215.

[91] Kulovesi, 'Fragmented landscapes, troubled relationships: the WTO dispute settlement system and international environmental law', 37.

[92] G. Z. Marceau and J. K. Hawkins, 'Experts in WTO dispute settlement' (2012) 3 *Journal of International Dispute Settlement* 493–507 at 496.

[93] For more details on the evidentiary practice of ITLOS see Chapter 8 Section III, Subsection 2.

1.5 Second-Order Indicators

Relying on certain higher-order evidence has been suggested in cases when judges decide not to engage with scientific evidence directly, only through certain so-called second-order indicators,[94] which allow them to evaluate the merits of scientific evidence indirectly.[95] Such indicators may interrogate for instance whether a given scientific result has been subject to peer-review,[96] or the credentials a party-appointed expert holds.[97] The uncontested nature of certain scientific facts by litigants is also among the frequently applied higher-order evidence.

Judge Donoghue acknowledges the use of second-order indicators in the ICJ's evidentiary assessments,[98] and ITLOS also widely relies on such methods. The Tribunal may reportedly be impressed by the credentials of experts[99] and explicitly noted the significance of having uncontested scientific evidence.[100] The Economic Community of West African States Court of Justice and the African Court of Human and Peoples' Rights also highlighted its inclination to accept only those scientific facts established that are consensual among the parties.[101]

Against this background, the results of an empirical study conducted across judges of major international courts and tribunals are particularly alarming. This survey suggests that there is no consensus among judges on what independence and impartiality of experts actually mean, and what practical requirements should adjudicators measure against the scientific opinions submitted.[102] The absence of an agreed, clear, and elaborate set of factors to measure such qualities of experts questions the workability of second-order indicators, and suggests that using them as sole yardstick to evaluate scientific opinions may yield incoherent, ad hoc results and, therefore, cannot ensure proper judicial engagement with expert evidence.[103]

---

[94] R. Feldman, 'Evidentialism, higher-order evidence, and disagreement' (2009) 6 *Episteme* 294–312 at 304.

[95] O. Perez, 'Judicial strategies for reviewing conflicting expert evidence: biases, heuristics, and higher-order evidence' (2016) 64 *The American Journal of Comparative Law* 75–120 at 78–80.

[96] Donoghue, 'Expert scientific evidence in a broader context', 385.

[97] Perez, 'Judicial strategies for reviewing conflicting expert evidence', 79.

[98] Donoghue, 'Expert scientific evidence in a broader context', 384–5.

[99] Anderson, 'Scientific evidence in cases under Part XV of the LOSC', p. 518.

[100] *Dispute Concerning Delimitation of the Maritime Boundary between Bangladesh and Myanmar in the Bay of Bengal (Bangladesh v. Myanmar)* (Judgment) ITLOS No. 16 (14 March 2012) para. 411. For more details see Chapter 8 Section III, Subsection 1.

[101] For examples from the case law see Chapter 5 Section IV, Subsection 3.

[102] Boisson de Chazournes, Mbengue, Das, and Gros, 'One size does not fit all – uses of experts before international courts and tribunals', 504.

[103] For more details on the risks and disadvantages of using second-order evidence see Chapter 10 Section II, Subsection 3.1.3.

2 *Avenues of Engaging with Scientific Expertise*

Despite the above-listed gaps in thorough adjudicatory interaction with science, in more recent judicial practice there are signs of more 'rigorous'[104] assessment of the evidence submitted. As has been emphasized before, proper engagement with scientific evidence is directly relevant for crafting persuasive judicial decisions as '[a]sking for advice only confirms the professionalism and legitimacy of the tribunal concerned and the decision it finally takes'.[105] Accordingly, if adjudicators exert visible efforts in their reasoning to make sense of complex scientific facts, the decision reached may be seen as more legitimate and persuasive even if they ultimately make a policy decision against science-backed claims. The *Kishenganga* Arbitration may serve as an apt illustration for this. Although the arbitral tribunal first defined the 'minimum environmental flow' of the river at 12 cumecs, which would have been necessary for avoiding environmental harm to occur, it ultimately balanced this against India's industrial interests, and set the minimum flow requirement at 9 cumecs in its final decision.[106] Yet, the *Kishenganga* award did not met with scholarly criticism concerning its fact-finding comparable to the aftermath of the *Pulp Mills* or the *Gabcikovo-Nagymaros* judgments. The reason for that arguably lies in the more thorough fact-finding inquiry adopted by the *Kishenganga* Tribunal, which will be addressed below.

A variety of fact-finding techniques that seek to integrate science in the judicial process are addressed in the sections that follow. In particular, Subsection 2.1 examines fora that make use of *ex curia* experts, whereas Subsection 2.2 comments on the use of shadow experts and Subsection 2.3 on expert arbitrators.

2.1 Tribunal-Appointed Experts: PCA, WTO, and the UN Compensation Commission

Tribunal-appointed experts facilitate a deeper understanding of scientific input and correspondingly, a more active and direct judicial engagement with science. They are particularly appropriate solutions when adjudicators confront with contradicting expert evidence or suspect expert bias.[107] This procedural tool assists adjudicators in grasping the scientific dimensions of the underlying problem. As noted above, *ex tribunal* experts remain a rarity in international adjudication. Besides exceptional usage in investment arbitration,[108] only the WTO (Subsection 2.1.1) and the UN Compensation Commission (UNCC) (Subsection 2.1.2) have been appointing such

---

[104]   Paik, 'South China Sea arbitral awards', 406.
[105]   Pauwelyn, 'Expert advice in WTO dispute settlement', p. 252.
[106]   *Indus Waters Kishenganga* Arbitration, Final Award, para. 104. For more details see Chapter 4 Section III, Subsection 2.
[107]   Foster, 'New clothes for the emperor?', 143–4.
[108]   For example in *Perenco*, discussed in more detail in Chapter 7.

experts on a regular basis, and their use has been decisive for a particular dispute decided by the PCA (Subsection 2.1.3).

2.1.1 WTO. Any discussion on the use of independent experts would be incomplete without mentioning the expert consultation system of the WTO. In SPS cases, the use of experts is mandatory, and the experts are appointed by the panel after seeking the views of the parties on the persons to be consulted. Expert consultations are rather informal and are designed to maximize learning opportunities for panellists to familiarize themselves with the science behind the trade dispute.[109] During the joint meeting with experts, independent experts are invited to address any points of disagreement between them and are asked to answer questions of the panel and of the parties.[110] The AB nevertheless retains control over the fact-finding process as it appoints independent experts only for assessing the credibility of party-adduced scientific evidence;[111] and it explicitly excludes the possibility that independent expert opinions would serve as the sole basis of ruling in favour of a party.[112]

2.1.2 UNCC. Independent experts played a crucial role in the work of the UNCC hearing claims arising from the unlawful Iraqi invasion of Kuwait in the Gulf War (1990–1991). The UNCC was established by the UN Security Council and awarded the largest compensation in the history of international environmental damage claims.[113] Its evidentiary practice is for this reason highly relevant as a potential adjudicatory good practice. Before turning to presenting the ways in which independent experts were used by the so-called F4 Panel that administered environmental claims, a brief discussion shall follow to describe the mandate of the UNCC and the context in which it was operating.

The UNCC accepted various damage claims against Iraq on account of the harmful consequences of the Iraqi invasion of Kuwait. Security Council Resolution 687 (1991) affirmed Iraq's responsibility under international law for 'any direct loss, damage, including environmental damage and the depletion of natural resources, or injury to foreign Governments, nationals and corporations, as a result of Iraq's unlawful invasion and occupation of Kuwait'.[114] The application and interpretation of this seemingly clear jurisdictional basis resulted in a science-intensive claim procedure, which has set an important precedent for adjudicating environmental damage claims on the international level.

---

[109] Foster, *Science and the Precautionary Principle in International Courts and Tribunals*, p. 116.
[110] Foster, *Science and the Precautionary Principle in International Courts and Tribunals*, pp. 116–17.
[111] *Japan – Apples*, Report of the AB, WT/DS245/B/R (26 November 2003), paras. 129–30.
[112] *EC – Asbestos*, Report of the AB, WT/DS135/AB/R (12 March 2001), para. 8.81. For a more detailed discussion on the use of independent experts in the dispute resolution system of the WTO see Chapter 6 Section II, Subsection 2.
[113] P. H. Sand and J. K. Kammit, 'Public health claims' in C. Payne and P. H. Sand (eds.), *Gulf War Reparations and the UN Compensation Commission: Environmental Liability* (Oxford University Press, 2011), pp. 1–39 p. 26.
[114] UNSC Res. 687 (1991), para. 16.

The UNCC was a political body tasked with an essentially fact-finding function of 'examining claims, verifying their validity, evaluating losses, assessing payments and resolving disputed claims'.[115] Its principle organ, the Governing Council, consisted of representatives of members of the UN Security Council.[116] The Security Council appointed a separate panel of three international experts[117] (regularly referred to as the F4 Panel) to deal with specified claims regarding environmental damage and depletion of natural resources (so-called F4 claims). The panel was endowed with an administrative and quasi-judicial mandate to review the scientific evidence and to recommend compensation where it deemed appropriate. Overall, the F4 Panel reviewed 170 claims,[118] which were submitted by regional[119] and non-regional claimants[120] in a total amount of approximately USD 85 billion,[121] out of which USD 5.26 billion[122] was finally recommended for compensation. The claims submitted to the F4 Panel were dealt with in five instalments.[123]

[115]   Report of the UNSG dated 2 May 1991 to the Security Council, S/22559, para. 20.
[116]   M. Kazazi, 'Environmental damage in the practice of the UN Compensation Commission' in M. Bowman and A. Boyle (eds.), *Environmental Damage in International and Comparative Law* (Oxford University Press, 2002), pp. 111–31 pp. 111–12.
[117]   Thomas A. Mensah, as the chairman, and José R. Allen and Peter H. Sand as commissioners. M. Kazazi, 'The UNCC follow-up programme for environmental awards' in T. M. Ndiaye and R. Wolfrum (eds.), *Law of the Sea, Environmental Law and Settlement of Disputes: Liber Amicorum Judge Thomas A. Mensah* (Martinus Nijhoff, 2007), pp. 1109–29 p. 1109.
[118]   Kazazi, 'The UNCC follow-up programme for environmental awards', p. 1109.
[119]   Iran, Jordan, Kuwait, Saudi Arabia, Syria, and Turkey, see UN Compensation Commission Governing Council, 'Report and Recommendations made by the Panel of Commissioners Concerning the First Instalment of "F4" claims' S/AC.26/2001/16 (22 June 2001), para. 3.
[120]   Germany, the United States, the UK, the Netherlands, Canada, and Australia see UN Compensation Commission Governing Council, 'Report and Recommendations made by the Panel of Commissioners Concerning the Second Instalment of "F4" Claims' S/AC.26/2002/26 (3 October 2002), para. 2.
[121]   Kazazi, 'The UNCC follow-up programme for environmental awards', p. 1109.
[122]   P. H. Sand, 'Environmental dispute settlement and the experience of the UN Compensation Committee' (2011) 54 *Japanese Yearbook of International Law* 151 at 152.
[123]   The first instalment consisted of claims regarding expenses of monitoring and assessment of the damage allegedly resulting from air pollution, depletion of water resources, damage to groundwater resources and coastlines, oil pollution, damage to fisheries, forestry, wetlands and rangelands, agriculture and livestock triggered by actions of war. Altogether 107 such claims were submitted, out of which sixty-seven were deemed compensable. The second instalment concerned claims for costs of taking preventive measures against further environmental damage and those of providing assistance to injured states in abating that damage. Except for one, all such claims were accepted, though with reduced amounts. The third instalment featured claims on recovering the costs of remediation measures. All but one claim were accepted, though with reduced quantum. The fourth instalment also concerned expenses of remediation measures of environmental damage caused by damaged oil wells, oil spills into land and waters, oil well fires, mines, and movement of refugees. The fifth instalment dealt with compensation claims resulting from damage to or depletion of natural resources. Diverse heads of damages belong to this category. First, there were public health claims seeking compensation for costs of various medical treatments of refugees and the general public, reduced quality of life on account of pollution, and costs of monitoring public health risks. Second, there were claims for expenses of 'compensatory projects' aimed at replacing lost ecosystem services by establishing new habitats (e.g. creating new natural reserves that are capable of providing roughly equivalent services). Lastly, there were compensation claims for recovering the monetary value of ecosystem service loss due to massive oil pollution or remnants of war (which are

Given the science-intensive nature of the procedure, both the claimants and Iraq were assisted by a group of natural scientists to present, and to challenge respectively, the proofs supporting the claims.[124] The F4 Panel itself had recourse to scientific expert consultants of its own, representing an impressively diverse expertise, inter alia, desert ecology, botany, biology, agriculture, forestry, plant pathology, soil fauna, landscape ecology, terrestrial and marine remediation techniques, marine biology, coastal ecology, geology, hydrogeology, water quality, chemistry, civil engineering, veterinary toxicology, natural resource damage assessment, ecological and risk assessment, economics, statistics, remote sensing modelling of the transport of airborne pollutants, epidemiology, toxicology, demography, internal medicine, endocrinology, reproductive health, mental health, surgery, oncology, and psychiatry.[125] Moreover, the panel was further assisted by international organizations[126] such as the United Nations Environmental Programme.[127]

To sum up, the F4 Panel of the UNCC engaged with the scientific aspect of the claims to a noteworthy extent, by duly fulfilling its task to sort out acceptable scientific claims. Yet the F4 Panel's evidentiary proceeding is not immune to criticism. A major shortcoming relates to transparency concerns[128] as the claims themselves and all the supplemental information and evidence have been kept confidential.[129]

2.1.3 PCA. Arbitrations under the aegis of the PCA have the option to rely on tribunal-appointed experts. A tribunal in the *South China Sea* Arbitration availed itself of this power, where the panel appointed its own experts to scrutinize the

---

also called 'pure ecological damage' claims). These claims concerned inter alia reduced crop quality or decrease in catch of fisheries and were only deemed compensable if uncompensated losses remained following the compensatory projects. For a more detailed analysis see P. Gautier, 'Environmental damage and the United Nations Claim Commission: new directions for future international environmental cases?' in T. M. Ndiaye and R. Wolfrum (eds.), *Law of the Sea, Environmental Law and Settlement of Disputes: Liber Amicorum Judge Thomas A Mensah* (Martinus Nijhoff, 2007), pp. 177–214 p. 187.

[124] L. Wilde, 'Scientific and Technical Advice' in C. Payne, P. H. Sand (eds.), *Gulf War Reparations and the UN Compensation Commission: Environmental Liability* (Oxford University Press, 2015), pp. 1–11.

[125] S. 26/2005/10 UN Compensation Commission Governing Council, 'Report and Recommendations Made by the Panel of Commissioners Concerning the Fifth Instalment of "F4" Claims' (2005), para. 88.

[126] C. Payne, 'Environmental claims in context' in C. Payne and P. H. Sand (eds.), *Gulf War Reparations and the UN Compensation Commission: Environmental Liability* (Oxford University Press, 2015), pp. 1–31 p. 13.

[127] A UNEP Working Group of Experts on Liability and Compensation for Environmental Damage Arising from Military Activities was established soon after the UNCC to provide it with expert advice, UNEP, 'Report of the Working Group of Experts on Liability and Compensation for Environmental Damage Arising from Military Activities', Third Meeting, London 14–17 May 1996, section 4.

[128] Despite the F4 Panel's overall laudable approach to fact-finding, there were still quite a few occasions when the exact reasons for dismissing proofs on alleged causal links were not revealed, conflicting evidentiary statements were not contrasted, but dismissed or affirmed with vague statements. For example, 'evidence available from a variety of sources supports the conclusion that . . . ' without specifying the sources, see UN Compensation Commission Governing Council, 'Report and Recommendations made by the Panel of Commissioners Concerning the Third Instalment of "F4" Claims', S/AC.26/2003/31 (18 December 2003) para. 176.

[129] Huguenin, Donlan, van Geel, and Paterson, 'Assessment and valuation of damage to the environment', p. 30.

parties' scientific evidence concerning coral reef damage. *Ex tribunal* experts played
a fundamental role in reconstructing the extent of environmental damage causal
upon China's artificial island-building activities. The tribunal appears to be strikingly 'diligent'[130] in gathering scientific evidence to understand the 'hard facts' of the
case.[131] This all bespeaks the panel's intention to formulate its own understanding of
the scientific aspects of the case, which serves as a promising development in
international scientific fact-finding.

Ex curia experts in the material case were necessitated first and foremost by
China's non-participation in the proceedings. The independent experts were tasked
with investigating publicly available information on China's position as to the
scientific facts of the dispute, in particular with respect to the ecological impacts
of the dredging activity. It is also noteworthy, from the perspective of the legitimacy
of the tribunal's fact-finding, that whenever it found a relevant evidence insufficient
regarding the harmful impacts of alleged Chinese conducts, the tribunal inferred to
China's compliance with its obligations.

2.2 Shadow Experts

As has been demonstrated in previous chapters, in contrast to court-appointed
experts, both the ICJ and ITLOS regularly hire scientists as temporary staff members
to support their scientific competence. Although this fact-finding method may be
seen as a necessary compromise for supporting judges on an ad hoc basis in order to
reassure the parties that all aspects of their case will be duly considered, there are
serious transparency concerns pertaining to shadow experts. For this reason, their
use is arguably not the best possible solution for incorporating scientific knowledge
within international courts.

2.3 The Use of Expert Arbitrators

Appointing expert arbitrators ensures the closest incorporation of scientific expertise
within a bench or panel. Such a possibility is explicitly provided for in the Optional
Rules of Arbitration of Disputes Relating to Natural Resources and/or the
Environment, which has been utilized in the practice of the PCA, for instance in
the *Kishenganga* Arbitration.[132] Thus far the PCA is the only permanent international adjudicative body that uses such an option. Such fact-finding method seems
to strike a fair balance in disputes, where scientific facts go to the crux of the legal
controversy.

---

[130] Mbengue, 'The *South China Sea* arbitration: innovations in marine environmental fact-finding and
       due diligence obligations', 287.
[131] *South China Sea* Arbitration, Award, para. 847. For more details on the panel's scientific fact-finding
       see Chapter 4 Section II, Subsection 3.
[132] For a detailed assessment see Chapter 4 Section III, Subsection 2.

IV CAUSAL INQUIRY: THE ROLE OF SCIENCE IN THE CAUSAL ASSESSMENTS

The causal requirements of international adjudicators for finding a causal claim established based on scientific evidence serve perhaps the most illustrative litmus test for the doctrinal differences between law and natural sciences. As has been argued in Chapter 2, the legal notion of causation differs quite remarkably from factual mechanisms perceived as having causal role in the eyes of scientists. This is because causation in the law does not simply hinge on a factual causal inquiry,[133] but is informed by further causal tests defined in law. Various requirements compel a 'clear', 'direct', 'proximate', or at least 'not too remote' causal link in order to legally establish a causal claim. The application of these legal tests to scientific facts of a given case necessitates a judgment call and, therefore, at the end of the day establishing causal links is much influenced by the subjective decisions of adjudicators.

It is further to be emphasized that causal requirements are 'not necessarily the same in relation to every breach',[134] but may vary among the fields of international law. Yet, it is still somewhat striking that international adjudicative bodies impose quite different causal requirements within the same branch of law and even with respect to claims of scientifically and factually similar injuries.

The preceding chapters have canvassed the great variety of causal tests and causal inquiries of international courts and tribunals. The forthcoming comparative analysis will trace these divergent causal requirements to varying levels of judicial willingness to engage with the scientific aspects of legal claims. It will be argued that the prospect of science-based causal claims for success is ultimately dependent upon the causal policy of international adjudicators. Policy in this sense will refer to different levels of judicial willingness to engage with scientific causal evidence implicated in environmental cases. Setting the doctrinal and factual requirements for establishing causality is seen in this study as ultimately determined by the subjective policy choices of international judges. Support for this proposition can also be drawn from tort law scholars asserting that certain policy considerations do influence judicial causal analyses.[135]

The forthcoming sections shall provide an overview of the divergent causal standards set by international adjudicatory fora with respect to science-based causal claims. Subsection 1 reviews adjudicatory practices that deem the uncertain and

---

[133] Special Rapporteur Mr James Crawford makes such an argument in the context of state responsibility. See Third Report on State Responsibility, by Mr James Crawford, Special Rapporteur, Document A/CN.4/507 and Add. 1–4, para. 27.

[134] Draft articles on Responsibility of States for Internationally Wrongful Acts, with commentaries, Article 31, comment (10); Crawford, *The International Law Commission's Articles on State Responsibility*, pp. 204–5.

[135] Plakokefalos, 'Causation in the law of state responsibility and the problem of overdetermination', 478; W. Malone, 'Ruminations on cause-in-fact' (1955) 9 *Stanford Law Review* 60 at 60.

ambiguous nature of scientific facts as an insurmountable obstacle to establish a causal nexus. Subsection 2 will enumerate those attempting to integrate scientific input into the adjudicatory process by bridging the gap between law's constant strive for certainty and the ever-uncertain nature of scientific evidence. The analysis will include a brief outlook to potential judicial good practices of finding a causal link established. Relevant solutions of the UNCC will be discussed together with the fine-grained causal inquiry of US toxic tort litigation as well as innovative causal requirements used in domestic climate change litigation. Lastly, Subsection 3 will offer some analytical remarks on the contemporary contours of the causal policy of international adjudicators in science-intensive disputes.

1 Causal Inquiry that Downplays the Role of Science

There are many ways in which international adjudicators may reject science-backed causal claims without closely considering and interpreting the scientific evidence that describes the causal mechanisms leading to environmental harm or health injuries. The modalities are discussed in the sections that follow.

1.1 Circumventing Science in the Causal Inquiry: Proxy-Based Causality

Science disrupts the causal inquiry of the Strasbourg Court in an idiosyncratic way. The ECtHR refuses to consider scientific evidence adduced regarding the causal role of toxic exposure in engendering health injuries. Rather, it develops certain non-scientific proxies with which it conducts a rough assessment on whether the alleged pollution could be regarded as a cause of the injury, according to everyday knowledge. The ECtHR, as has been argued,[136] relies on proxies based on inter alia (i) the distance between the polluter and the applicant's home, (ii) the occurrence of prior accidents producing large scale pollution, (iii) the lawfulness of the toxic emission under domestic law, (iv) the on-going nature of the polluting activity, and (v) the egregiousness of the overall factual circumstances of the case. These causal proxies relate to non-scientific factors that do not necessarily have genuine causal role, scientifically speaking, in bringing about the injury complained of.

The assessment of the ECtHR as to whether to find of a causal link established between the pollution and the violation of the right to private and family life hinges on the above proxies. However, these proxies are often under-inclusive by allowing causally relevant pollution escape from legal scrutiny.[137] Also, in many cases they yield different results in factually comparable situations, which results in an inconsistent case-law with regard to the environmental aspect of Article 8 of the ECHR. For all these reasons, the tendency of the ECtHR not to look at the factual evidence

---

[136] For a more detailed discussion on the use of proxies see Chapter 5 Section III, Subsection 3.
[137] For a more detailed discussion on the use of proxies see Chapter 5 Section III, Subsection 3.

already on the case-file, from which real causal factors of injuries may be revealed with greater accuracy, generates a problematic result;[138] and removes the court from science to a conveniently great distance. As will be argued later on, however, this approach undermines the epistemic legitimacy of the judgments.[139]

1.2 Causal Tests Requiring Clear Science-Based Causal Links

Another technique with which international courts may disregard science in their causal assessment is imposing a restrictive causal test that scientific facts would almost never be able to meet, that is, to demonstrate 'clear' or 'certain' causal nexus. The preceding analytical chapters have seen various instances where adjudicators insisted on having clear causal links, for instance in the case law of the IACtHR in the context of compensation[140] or in the *Pulp Mills* judgment of the ICJ.[141] Likewise, international arbitration practice also features restrictive causal tests towards science-based claims.[142]

These tests intuitively seem to be justifiable in light of ensuring the imperative of procedural fairness, according to which the liability of a wrongdoer needs to be sufficiently established and not to be presumed lightly. However, equally valid is the point that, considering the ever-uncertain nature of scientific evidence, insistence on traditionally strict causal tests may be unduly dismissive towards science-based environmental claims. In order to level the playing field for science-backed claims, a more flexible causal policy seems to be warranted. Being mindful of the fact that certain sources of uncertainty can never be fully eliminated from scientific evidence as showed in Chapter 2, such a solution seems to pay due regard to applicable fairness considerations while also approximating scientific realities.

1.3 Restrictive Approach: High Standard of Proof and Refusal of Probabilistic Causal Proof

In environmental disputes parties often submit large amount of scientific evidence containing model results, estimations on probabilities of harm, risk assessments, and other technical details. The convincing force attached to such probability-based evidence varies in international jurisprudence. In certain jurisdictions, the threshold of proof is set so high that such probabilistic evidence could never meet it. While in others, the standard of proof is defined as a matter of law to be flexible enough to be responsive to scientific complexities; still, in the judicial practice scientific evidence

---

[138] Dissenting Opinion of Judge Zupančič in *Tătar v. Romania*, Application No. 67021/01, Judgment (27 January 2009); Zupančič, 'Causation in cases of environmental degradation', 118, 122.

[139] See Chapter 10 Section II, Subsection 3.1.1.

[140] *Case of the Saramaka People v. Suriname*, Judgment of 28 November 2007, IACtHR Series C No. 172, para. 199.

[141] *Pulp Mills*, Judgment, paras. 240, 250, 254.

[142] For example, *MOX Plant OSPAR* Arbitration, para. 164.

is rarely accepted. These solutions again result in a causal inquiry, where judges need not consider scientific proof of causation.

Probabilistic scientific evidence was filed with the ICJ in several cases, most importantly in *Gabcikovo-Nagymaros*, *Pulp Mills*, and in *Certain Activities/ Construction of a Road*, but the Court dismissed all pieces of probabilistic evidence for various reasons. These all bespeak a de facto high standard of proof with the Court in scientific disputes, even though in principle, the applicable standard of proof would be the balance of probabilities, that is, the preponderance of the evidence standard.[143] The crux of criticism for the ICJ's dominant approach towards probabilistic scientific evidence was most succinctly set forth by Judge ad hoc Vinuesa in his Dissenting Opinion in *Pulp Mills*:

> In various key passages, the Court reaches conclusions on alleged substantial violations while acknowledging the lack of scientific certainty underpinning those findings: 'Argentina has not convincingly demonstrated that Uruguay' (Judgment, para. 189); 'the Court is not in a position to conclude that Uruguay' (ibid., para. 228); it has 'not been established to the satisfaction of the Court' (ibid., para. 250); 'there is insufficient evidence' (ibid., para. 254); 'there is no clear evidence to link' (ibid., para. 259); 'a clear relationship has not been established' (ibid., para. 262); 'the record does not show any clear evidence' (ibid., para. 264).[144]

And indeed, the *Pulp Mills* judgment has revealed that the ICJ was not willing to accommodate science in its causal inquiry. The Court's adamant insistence on the need for certain and clear scientific proof has been attributed to judges' frustration of being left alone in a 'scientific vacuum'[145] in the case.

The practice of the ECtHR bears resemblance to the early evidentiary findings of the ICJ, addressed above. The Strasbourg Court generally uses a beyond reasonable doubt standard,[146] which is met by 'the coexistence of sufficiently strong, clear and concordant inferences or of similar unrebutted presumptions of fact'.[147] While the ECtHR emphasized in science-intensive cases that it allowed flexibility in this respect with regard to the evidentiary difficulties involved,[148] in its practice, it rarely accepted probabilistic evidence. Suffice it to refer to *Tătar v. Romania*, in which the court refused to engage in probabilistic reasoning,[149] and instead required causal claims that are 'accompanied by sufficient and convincing statistics'.[150]

Moreover, even when the Strasbourg Court is ready to find a science-based causal claim established, it does not expose its evidentiary assessment and reasoning. This

---

[143] Wolfrum, 'Taking and assessing evidence in international adjudication', p. 354.
[144] *Pulp Mills*, Dissenting Opinion of Judge ad hoc Vinuesa, para. 70.
[145] Mbengue, 'Scientific fact-finding by international courts and tribunals', 522.
[146] Harris, O'Boyle, Bates, and Buckley, *Law of the European Convention on Human Rights*, p. 148.
[147] *Fadeyeva v. Russia*, Application No. 55723/00, Judgment (9 June 2005); para. 79.
[148] *Fadeyeva v. Russia*, 79.
[149] *Tătar v. Romania*, para. 105. Translation from French by the author ('*raisonnement probabiliste*').
[150] *Tătar v. Romania*, para. 105.

hides the court's stance as to the persuasive force attributed to scientific evidence. Notably, both in *Brincat and Others* v. *Malta* and *Vilnes and Others* v. *Norway* judgments, the ECtHR deemed likely that there was a causal link between the applicant's health deterioration and the working conditions tolerated by respective states, however, the reasoning did not discuss the scientific evidence submitted.[151] The Strasbourg Court has altogether applied a rather strict approach to scientific evidence and proof of causation respectively and tended not to rely explicitly on statistical probabilities.

Judges of ITLOS seem to endorse a similar approach towards probabilistic evidence. The Tribunal did not base substantive findings on causal proofs in its contentious cases, hence, the causal proof requirements remain somewhat unclear. Nevertheless, Judge Lucky stressed that 'applicants must show a very strong probability upon the facts that serious harm will accrue in the future'.[152]

Overall, the success of environmental damage claims in the current landscape of international adjudication is particularly impeded by adjudicators' dismissive approach towards probabilistic evidence. Tellingly, compensation has only been awarded for environmental harm in international court proceedings when the facts of the case were exceptionally egregious, as it happened in the *South China Sea* Arbitration,[153] or when the parties did not dispute the occurrence of ecological harm.[154]

2 *Practices Facilitating Science-Based Causal Claims: Presumptions and Relaxed Causal Tests and Causal Proof Requirements*

International environmental adjudication also features some legal techniques that aim to facilitate finding a causal link established either by relaxing causal tests or by devising tools that allow establishing causality based on uncertain scientific facts. Examples for such techniques can also be drawn from the practice of international claims tribunals and domestic courts, specifically in climate change litigation and in toxic tort litigation. In the following sections, causal presumptions will be covered first (Subsection 2.1) from the practice of the US–Marshall Islands Nuclear Claims Tribunal (Subsection 2.1.1) and the ECtHR (Subsection 2.1.2). Second, causal tests of certain domestic courts will be addressed that facilitate finding science-based causal claims established (Subsection 2.2). In this respect, causal tests applied in US toxic tort case law will be addressed as this national jurisdiction is particularly well renowned for its innovative approach to assessing highly technical scientific evidence in adversarial proceedings (Subsection 2.2.1). Relaxed causal requirements

---

[151] *Vilnes and Others* v. *Norway*, Application Nos. 52806/09, 22703/10, Judgment (5 December 2023), para. 233.; *Brincat and Others* v. *Malta*, Application Nos. 60908/11, 62110/11, 62129/11, 62312/11 and 62338/11, Judgment (24 July 2014), para. 150.

[152] *Straits of Johor*, Separate Opinion of Judge Lucky, para. 13.

[153] For more details see Chapter 4 Section II, Subsection 3.2.

[154] *Certain Activities*, Judgment on compensation, see more detail in Chapter 3.

can also be found in the emerging field of domestic climate change litigation (Subsection 2.2.2). Then treatment of probabilistic proof of causation will be addressed in light of UNCC case-practice in connection with the Gulf War reparation claims (Subsection 2.3). Statistical evidence is also routinely accepted as causal evidence by US domestic courts in toxic tort litigation (Subsection 2.4).

2.1 Using Causal Presumptions to Allow Environmental Claims

Presumptions are regularly applied in the reasoning of international courts and tribunals.[155] Their major benefit lies in equipping adjudicators with an efficient legal device to render legal judgment under uncertainty.[156] Yet, employing presumptions is still exceptional in bridging gaps between ambiguous scientific evidence on the one hand, and establishing legal liability on the other hand. Causal presumptions can be found in the practice of two international fora, which will be detailed below. First, the case law of an international claims tribunal is to be addressed, which administered health injury claims arising out of nuclear tests. Second, a specific presumption will be discussed that has been established by the Strasbourg Court in claims involving massive air pollution.

2.1.1 US–MARSHALL ISLANDS NUCLEAR CLAIMS TRIBUNAL. Between 1946 and 1958 the United States used the territory of the Marshall Islands as detonation sites for its Nuclear Testing Program. The tests were of exceptional explosive power; the biggest equalled the force of one thousand Hiroshima bombs.[157] The detonations accordingly caused extensive damage to property, health, and the environment especially on the Bikini and Enewetak Atolls.[158] The United States assumed responsibility for the resulting damage, which led to the set-up of the Nuclear Claims Tribunal in 1988 to administer compensation claims procedures.[159] For purposes of the present analysis, the relevant aspect of the tribunal's practice is the way in which it awarded compensation for personal health injury claims.

   The tribunal employed an irrefutable presumption on the causal link between twenty-five medical conditions and the nuclear exposure[160] modelled after the

---

[155] Wolfrum, 'Taking and assessing evidence in international adjudication', p. 353.
[156] Viñuales, 'Observations sur le traitement des motifs scientifiques dans le contentieux environnemental international', pp. 122–3.
[157] J. C. Babione, 'Mission accomplished? Fifty-four years of suffering for the people of the Marshall Islands and the latest round of endless reconciliation' (2000) 11 *Indiana International and Comparative Law Review* 115–43 at 120.
[158] The Claims Tribunal awarded compensations in total USD 563,315,500 (to victims of Bikini Atoll) and USD 341,049,311 (for victims of Enewatak Atoll). For more on the proceedings see Louka, *International Environmental Law Fairness, Effectiveness, and World Order*, pp. 469–70.
[159] 1983 Compact of Free Associations between the United States and the Marshall Islands.
[160] D. Thornburgh, G. Reichardt, and J. Stanley, 'The nuclear claims tribunal of the Republic of the Marshall Islands: an independent examination and assessment of its decision-making processes' (2003) p. 27. Available at www.bikiniatoll.com/ThornburgReport.pdf (last accessed 30 January 2020).

technique used in a domestic nuclear exposure compensation programme of the United States.[161] The list of diseases triggering the presumption was provided in the tribunal's regulation. They were all conditions for which several pieces of expert evidence showed a 'significant statistical relationship' between exposure and disease development.[162] Victims manifesting these conditions did not need to prove specific causation regarding their health injuries. Diseases not included in the list were also compensable if claimants could adduce sufficient evidence on causality in their individual case.[163] The tribunal also established different compensation standards for smokers and non-smokers with respect to certain types of cancer that can be equally caused by the victim's lifestyle, that is, factors unrelated to the exposure.[164] The list was updated annually, and in fact was amended by ten diseases, in order to keep pace with increasing knowledge of medical sciences regarding the effects of nuclear radiation.[165]

The tribunal was particularly lenient in terms of establishing causation given that it has based its findings on statistical probabilities of general causation without any requirement of proof of specific causation. In so doing, it did not bar compensation in case of competing causal factors. The tribunal justified its approach with an overriding need for 'an efficient, simple, and cost-effective payment program', which alleviated the burden of 'difficulties of proof of causation' resting with victims.[166] These are seen here as explicit policy considerations alleviating the burden of causal requirements before the tribunal.

The case practice of the tribunal shows a much more generous approach than the jurisprudence of ECtHR, which applied stricter causal standards in nuclear exposure claims. The divergent judicial solutions in appraising the causal role of nuclear exposure in generating health injuries, notably carcinogenic effects, provide a most vivid example of the fragmentation of causal requirements in international law and concerning science-based claims more specifically. In contrast to the practice of the US–Marshall Islands Nuclear Claims Tribunal, the Strasbourg Court in the

---

[161] Thornburgh, Reichardt, and Stanley, 'The nuclear claims tribunal of the Republic of the Marshall Islands: an independent examination and assessment of its decision-making processes', p. 28. The procedure aimed to compensate victims of nuclear radiation in Nevada on account of atmospheric test detonations under the Radiation Exposure Compensation Act (1990).

[162] Thornburgh, Reichardt, and Stanley, 'The nuclear claims tribunal of the Republic of the Marshall Islands: an independent examination and assessment of its decision-making processes', p. 29.

[163] Thornburgh, Reichardt, and Stanley, 'The nuclear claims tribunal of the Republic of the Marshall Islands: an independent examination and assessment of its decision-making processes', p. 30.

[164] Thornburgh, Reichardt, and Stanley, 'The nuclear claims tribunal of the Republic of the Marshall Islands: an independent examination and assessment of its decision-making processes', p. 30. Thornburgh et al. cites the 2000 Annual Report of the Tribunal at 20.

[165] Thornburgh, Reichardt, and Stanley, 'The nuclear claims tribunal of the Republic of the Marshall Islands: an independent examination and assessment of its decision-making processes', pp. 29–30.

[166] *In the Matter of the People of Enewetak, et al.*, NCT No. 23–0902, Decision and Order, 23 September 1996, at 2, cited by Thornburgh, Reichardt, and Stanley, 'The nuclear claims tribunal of the Republic of the Marshall Islands: an independent examination and assessment of its decision-making processes', p. 27.

L. C. B. v. UK case refused to find a causal link established between a nuclear exposure and trans-generational carcinogenic effects. The applicant submitted a report commissioned by an Independent Advisory Board in the United Kingdom, which investigated the health effects of the Sellafield nuclear facility and found a 'statistical association between the incidence of leukaemia in children',[167] whose fathers were exposed to radiation prior to their conception. The ECtHR nonetheless concluded: '[h]aving examined the expert evidence submitted to it, the Court is not satisfied that there is a causal link between the exposure of a father to radiation and leukaemia in a child subsequently conceived'.[168] This proves to be a much more restrictive approach to causal proof than the evidentiary standards set by the Marshall Islands Nuclear Claims Tribunal.

These divergent solutions, on the one hand, tangibly support the proposition that the success of science-based health injury claims largely hinges on the policy considerations of judges, which manifest in the causal requirements they set for prospective applicants. On the other hand, the differing treatment of scientifically analogous injury claims also well illustrates the current state of play in the arena of international environmental liability claims. As the above set of examples also suggests, prevailing causal standards in international litigation tend to shield respondent states from liability claims save for cases they openly assume responsibility for a potentially injurious conduct.

2.1.2 CAUSAL PRESUMPTION USED BY THE ECTHR. There has been one extraordinary occasion in the practice of the ECtHR, which signalled the court's willingness to devise legal techniques to allow claims of health injuries to proceed even when are based on uncertain causal proof. In the famous *Fadeyeva* case, the Strasbourg Court has established a causal presumption in cases, where pollution significantly exceeded domestic safety levels. The court held that pollution 'becomes potentially harmful to the health and well-being of those exposed to it. This is a presumption, which may not be true in a particular case.'[169] Applying the presumption, the Strasbourg Court found that 'the applicant's health deteriorated *as a result of* her prolonged exposure to the industrial emissions'.[170]

Notably, the *Fadeyeva* case featured individuals' complaints of air pollution generated by one of the largest steel plants in Russia, with certain air pollutants being twenty to fifty times higher than maximum permissible limits under domestic law.[171] Medical reports confirmed a roughly three-fold increase in respiratory diseases among children and a decree noted the causal role of atmospheric pollution in the increase in various diseases.[172] It was against this background that the court was

---

[167]   *L. C. B. v. UK*, Application No. 23413/94, Judgment (9 June 1998), para. 17.
[168]   *L. C. B. v. UK*, para. 39.
[169]   *Fadeyeva v. Russia*, para. 87. For a more detailed discussion see Chapter 5 Section III, Subsection 3.2.
[170]   *Fadeyeva v. Russia*, para. 88, emphasis added.
[171]   *Fadeyeva v. Russia*, para. 15.
[172]   *Fadeyeva v. Russia*, para. 15.

inclined to find a causal link established between the functioning of the steel plant and the individual's claims of health injuries based on a 'strong combination of indirect evidence and presumptions'.[173]

The noteworthy aspect of this judgment is that the ECtHR, contrary to its prevailing approach to circumvent science in its assessment, this time was ready to find causality established. It relied on the causal presumption despite the fact that the applicant herself could only produce a medical report, which 'did not substantiate any causal link'[174] between her illness and the pollution. Yet Although in light of later case law, it is apparent that this causal presumption may only be triggered in cases of most severe pollution, and not by a slight excess of statutory limits of harmful substances, which is often the case.[175] Hence it is safe to say that the practical reach of this judicial tool is relatively limited in the ECtHR's case law.

Interestingly, presumptions are in a certain regard similar to the proxy-based method of the ECtHR mentioned in Subsection 1.1 above, inasmuch as both provide for courses of action when scientific assessment of causal relations seem to confer an exceedingly intricate task on adjudicators. However, these tools are different in an important respect. Simply put, proxies are used to relieve the ECtHR of considering scientific evidence *under all circumstances*, while evidentiary presumptions are normally only a *second-best option*, when scientific evidence directly describing causal mechanisms does not yield a conclusive answer.[176] In other words, the latter method does not relieve adjudicators of assessing scientific evidence as fully as possible to reconstruct the factual realities of the case. As will be shown in Chapter 10 in more detail, this structural difference between the above judicial tools is consequential for the epistemic legitimacy of respective methods of causal inquiry.[177]

2.2 Domestic Law Innovations: Causal Tests Facilitating Finding Causal Links Established

In contrast to international jurisdictions that tend to be restrictive in couching and applying causal tests, an increasing number of domestic court decisions have started to approximate causal standards to what scientific facts can actually deliver. A leading example of such domestic law innovation can be found in US toxic tort litigation, which developed several nuanced tests to accommodate uncertain scientific causal proofs. Another source of novel solutions is the emerging field of climate

---

[173] *Fadeyeva v. Russia*, para. 88.
[174] *Fadeyeva v. Russia*, para. 80.
[175] See for example, *Martínez Martínez and Pino Manzano v. Spain*, Application No. 61654/08, Judgment (3 July 2012).
[176] The ECtHR first reviewed causal evidence submitted by the applicant and only when it found it to be insufficient for purposes of establishing causation, did it apply the presumption of causality. See *Fadeyeva v. Russia*, paras. 80–8. This particular type of causal presumption is further discussed in Chapter 5 Section III, Subsection 3.2.
[177] See Chapter 10 Section II, Subsection 2.1.4.

change litigation, where domestic courts are more and more inclined to relax traditional causal requirements in order to find a causal claim established.

It has been previously argued in detail that causation in international law is relatively underdeveloped compared to domestic legal systems.[178] The latter have produced elaborate causal tests and scenarios comparable to the complexity of real-life causal processes; and these causal concepts of national laws often appear to impact the causal inquiry of international jurisdictions. It is for this reason apt and useful to examine some innovations of domestic legal systems in crafting causal tests in scientific disputes. In cases where international fora find them as persuasive decisions of domestic courts, they may inform the evolution of international adjudication as well.[179] Judicial dialogue between domestic and international fora can be particularly enriching with respect to the treatment of similar challenges, such as causation.[180] The brief overview on domestic law solutions serves putting international courts' causal inquiry into a wider context and in a different light. It is of course not suggested here that every domestic law solution could be readily transferred to the international level. However, these examples do underline that a more proactive judicial engagement with science can fit neatly within the judicial task and, thus, uncertain scientific facts ought not necessarily be construed as an insurmountable obstacle to establishing causal claims.

2.2.1 INNOVATIVE DOMESTIC LAW SOLUTIONS: CAUSAL TESTS IN US TOXIC TORT LAW. Toxic tort cases involve claims of personal injury, such as physical or psychological harm caused by exposure to a hazardous substance,[181] which can include a variety of causal agents, from pathogens and chemicals to radiation.[182] In order to keep pace with the advancement of science and technology, traditional US tort law theories adapted to the peculiarities of toxic exposure cases. They provide remedies for an expanding scope of 'harm' under the theory of trespass, negligence, public and private nuisance, strict liability, and product liability. In toxic tort cases US courts award damages for physical harm, increased risk of disease, medical monitoring, and also for psychological distress such as fear of future harm.[183]

Perhaps the most salient way in which scientific evidence modifies traditional causal inquiry[184] is the emergence of two distinct elements: general and specific

---

[178] See Chapter 2 Section II, Subsection 3.1 and Chapter 3 Section IV, Subsection 1 for more details on causal theories in international law.

[179] Decisions of domestic courts serve as subsidiary means for the determination of rules of international law, Statute of the International Court of Justice, Article 38(1)(d).

[180] J. Peel, 'Issues in climate change litigation' (2011) 1 *Carbon and Climate Law Review* 15–24 at 24.

[181] Foerster and Gregorski Rolph, *Toxic Tort Litigation*, p. 3.

[182] Foerster and Gregorski Rolph, *Toxic Tort Litigation*, p. 139.

[183] Foerster and Gregorski Rolph, *Toxic Tort Litigation*, p. 35.

[184] *Third Restatement of the Law of Torts for Physical and Emotional Harm* (The American Law Institute Publishers, 2010), §26 Comment g.

causation. Courts first assess general causation, that is, whether the causal agent at hand is capable of causing the harm complained of.[185] Normally, the inquiry only reaches the question of specific causation if the factfinder is satisfied that the test of general causation has been met.[186] An important caveat applies in the case of well-known signature diseases, where courts generally find causation if the exposure and the manifestation of the disease are both established.[187] If general causation is found to be established the court investigates specific causation, that is, whether the causal agent did actually cause the plaintiff's harm.[188] In this respect, courts should examine whether the plaintiff: (1) was indeed exposed to a dose at least comparable to that for which general causation is established; (2) was exposed to other potential causal agents; and (3) has individual genetic or behavioural characteristics that might present a background risk of the harm that occurred.[189]

The primary test of tort law causation is the but-for (*sine qua non* or factual) causal test.[190] However, all tort law systems acknowledge certain exceptions from this general causation theory.[191] The Third Restatement of Torts endorses the substantial factor test in case of multiple sufficient causal sets, namely, when none of the causal sets on its own would be a but-for cause.[192] The substantial factor test can also be used for ruling out causal agents that only have a *de minimis* causal contribution to the injury.[193] Moreover, US courts employ the substantial factor test in enhanced-injury cases, when only the extent of the harm that has been caused by a given defendant is uncertain. In such cases, the plaintiff needs only to establish that the tortfeasor's conduct was a substantial factor in the enhanced harm.[194]

United States toxic tort law had to accommodate several challenges to make legal sense of scientific facts. Perhaps the most pervasive problem in toxic exposure cases is that the same injury might have been caused by numerous possible causal agents. In some cases, it is virtually impossible to identify the actual cause, a situation that is called the defendant indeterminacy problem (Section A). In other instances, the tortfeasors are identifiable, but their contributions cannot be measured precisely, only estimated based on different disease development models (Section B). Further complications arise

---

[185] *Third Restatement of the Law of Torts for Physical and Emotional Harm* (The American Law Institute Publishers, 2010), vol. i §26 Comment g.

[186] Green, 'The future of proportional liability: the lessons of toxic substances causation', p. 371.

[187] Gold, 'The more we know, the less intelligent we are?', 401.

[188] *Third Restatement of the Law of Torts for Physical and Emotional Harm*, §26 Comment g.

[189] *Third Restatement of the Law of Torts for Physical and Emotional Harm*, §28 Comment on Subsection (a) c. (3).

[190] Steel, *Proof of Causation in Tort Law*, p. 16.

[191] Steel, *Proof of Causation in Tort Law*, p. 17. Steel surveys the tort law systems of Germany, France, and the United Kingdom.

[192] *Third Restatement of the Law of Torts for Physical and Emotional Harm*, §26, Comment j.

[193] Kundis Craig, Klein, and Sanders, *Toxic and Environmental Torts Cases and Materials*, p. 370.

[194] *Third Restatement of the Law of Torts for Physical and Emotional Harm* (The American Law Institute Publishers, 2010), §26, Comment j.

when multiple causal agents have synergistic effects (Section C). The innovative legal methods to cope with all these scenarios in toxic tort litigation are addressed below.

(A) Defendant Indeterminacy: Alternative Liability, Market-Share Liability

In cases where it is not possible to prove which one of the defendants' identical conducts was the actual cause of injury,[195] US tort law applies alternative liability.[196] This test has been recognized ever since the two hunters' dilemma entertained in *Summers* v. *Tice*.[197] In the toxic tort context, the textbook example of defendant indeterminacy is the flood of litigation related to a miscarriage prevention drug containing diethylstilbestrol (DES), the harmful effects of which were only manifested in the daughters of the women who took the drug during pregnancy.[198] The California Supreme Court applied alternative liability and reversed the burden of proof so that plaintiffs did not need to prove which specific defendant's drug they had taken, since adducing such evidence on specific causation would have been virtually impossible due to the lapse of time.[199] As there were hundreds of manufacturers who produced drugs containing DES, the California Supreme Court had to devise a new rule in order to allocate liability and not allow exculpation for the manufacturers. The method it used became known as 'market-share liability', since the court imposed liability on the defendants according to their respective market shares.[200]

(B) Multiple Exposures: Dose-Dependent (Threshold) Disease Development and One-Hit Exposure Theory   A ubiquitous challenge in toxic exposure cases is identifying which causal agent was 'the' cause of injury when the victim was exposed to many agents, each of which is known to have been capable of causing the injury.[201] The Third Restatement of Torts mandates the following solution for

---

[195] K. Oliphant, 'Uncertain factual causation in the Third Restatement: some comparative notes' (2010) 37 *William Mitchell Law. Review* 1599 at 1600.

[196] Steel, *Proof of Causation in Tort Law*, pp. 161–4.

[197] *Summers* v. *Tice*, 33 Cal.2d 80 (Cal. 1948). The Californian Supreme Court reversed the burden of proof so that the defendants had to bear the burden of the virtually impossible task of proving which one of them caused the actual health impairment to the plaintiff, given that both used the same type of gun and the same bullets.

[198] 'Note: market share liability: an answer to the DES causation problem' (1981) 94 *Harvard Law Review* 668 at 668.

[199] *Sindell* v. *Abbott Laboratories*, 607 P.2d 924, 937 (Cal.1980).

[200] For more details on the market-share liability see Steel, *Proof of Causation in Tort Law*, pp. 165–7. Even though market-share liability was an innovative and exceptionally useful tool to solve the specific problems posed by the DES cases, the Third Restatement warns that it will be of limited use in the future, since it is only applicable to cases where the manufacturers of the drug are unknown. This is exceptionally rare under present day circumstances, when pharmaceutical products are normally protected by patents, thus, the manufacturers are known. Moreover, market-share liability is only operational where all toxic products pose equivalent risks. *Third Restatement of the Law of Torts for Physical and Emotional Harm*, §28 Comment on Subsection (b)p.

[201] *Third Restatement of the Law of Torts for Physical and Emotional Harm*, §28 Comment on Subsection (a) c. (5).

US courts to tackle this problem in toxic torts cases.[202] First, courts need to distinguish among the evidentiary requirements for different models of disease development, following scientific differentiation between two main types of disease development: the threshold model, which describes dose-dependent diseases that manifest only above a certain threshold of exposure and whose severity is correlated with the exposure level (e.g. asbestosis), and the one-hit exposure model, applicable for non-dose-dependent illnesses (e.g. certain forms of cancer). Under the one-hit exposure theory, each exposure imposes distinct risks of developing the non-dose-dependent disease and, thus, each exposure is a separate cause of the disease. The threshold model implies that each dose of exposure creates a marginal additional harm.

For dose-dependent illnesses, the traditional rule of causation requires the plaintiff to show which of the multiple exposures was the actual cause of the disease (i.e. resulted in reaching the threshold).[203] However, to ease the evidentiary requirements for demonstrating the cause of such diseases, US courts started to apply the so-called Lohrmann test in asbestos litigation.[204] This test requires the plaintiff to adduce 'evidence of exposure to a specific product on a regular basis over some extended period of time in proximity to where the plaintiff actually worked'.[205] If the three-fold requirement of frequency, regularity, and proximity is met, courts are willing to regard the exposure as a 'substantial cause' of the harm.[206]

Similarly, in *Rutherford* v. *Owens-Illinois, Inc.*, the plaintiff had to demonstrate that the defendant's product was 'a substantial factor in causing or contributing to his risk of developing cancer' but he did not need to 'prove ... that fibers from a particular defendant's asbestos-containing products were those ... that actually began the cellular process of malignancy'.[207] This alternative causal test, thus, allows the plaintiff to prove that each of the multiple exposures was a cause-in-fact of the disease.[208] The Third Restatement promotes the adoption of this test in all cases when the exact disease development mechanism is unknown, as this is the best way of 'adapting proof requirements to the available scientific knowledge'.[209]

(C) Synergistic Effects of Multiple Causes   Causal agents may have synergistic effects in developing a harm. The Third Restatement provides that '[i]f the

---

[202]   *Third Restatement of the Law of Torts for Physical and Emotional Harm*, §28 Reporters' Note, Comment c. (5)

[203]   The American Law Institute, *Third Restatement of the Law of Torts for Physical and Emotional Harm*, p. §28, Comment on Subsection (a) c. (5).

[204]   M. A. Ceder, 'Dose of reality: the struggle with causation in toxic tort litigation, A' (2013) 51 *Houston Law Review* 1381 at 1165.

[205]   *Lohrmann* v. *Pittsburgh Corning Corp.*, 782 F.2d 1156, 1163 (4th Cir. 1986).

[206]   Foerster and Gregorski Rolph, *Toxic Tort Litigation*, pp. 148–9.

[207]   *Rutherford* v. *Owens-Illinois, Inc.*, 941 P.2d 1203, 1218 (Cal. 1997).

[208]   *Third Restatement of the Law of Torts for Physical and Emotional Harm*, p. §28 Comment on Subsection (a) c. (5).

[209]   *Third Restatement of the Law of Torts for Physical and Emotional Harm*, p. §28 Comment on Subsection (a) c. (5).

synergetic effect is sufficiently large, the excess incidence of disease due to synergetic effect will be greater than the excess incidence due to each of the agents separately'.[210] In such cases the factfinder is allowed to rule that the combined synergistic exposure was the cause of the harm.[211] United States courts usually allow harm to be apportioned in cases of synergetic effects between toxic exposure and causes inherent in lifestyle, such as smoking.[212] The plaintiff's genetic background risk of disease does not preclude the liability of a negligent actor if his conduct was a cause of the disease.[213]

The above innovative US toxic tort causal doctrines show that multiple causal agents can fit well into a judicial causal inquiry, when courts do not shy away from adjusting causal requirements to available scientific knowledge. Tort law causal tests bespeak a nuanced approach to causation seeking to approximate judicial expectations to scientific realities. Despite several differences between international and domestic adjudication in terms of the mandate and institutional structures of respective courts not to mention the underlying law, this judicial attitude towards scientific causal claims nevertheless can be informative to international adjudicators, even if not every doctrinal solution is readily transferable to the international level.

The above discussion sought to make a point that causal doctrine can be adjusted to scientific facts if judges conceive it as their task to appraise and investigate causal claims in a meaningful way. In the highly adversarial setting of tort law litigation, the parties' clear expectation is that the court thoroughly evaluates scientific causal proof, which lies at the heart of any tort law claim. Despite the fact that in some types of international environmental disputes the role of causal inquiry is less articulate, it will be argued here that the considerable third-party effects of environmental adjudication warrants for taking scientific causal evidence seriously, as the opposite would threaten with undermining the epistemic legitimacy and convincing force of judgments in the public eye.

2.2.2 RELAXING CAUSAL REQUIREMENTS IN CLIMATE CHANGE LITIGATION. One cannot escape noticing a new wave of successful climate change lawsuits filed with domestic courts in various jurisdictions.[214] Scholars have long discussed the prospects and

---

[210]   *Third Restatement of the Law of Torts for Physical and Emotional Harm*, p. §28 Comment on Subsection (a) c. (5).

[211]   *Third Restatement of the Law of Torts for Physical and Emotional Harm*, p. §28 Comment on Subsection (a) c. (5).

[212]   *Third Restatement of the Law of Torts for Physical and Emotional Harm*, p. §28 Reporters' Note, Comment c. (5).

[213]   *Third Restatement of the Law of Torts for Physical and Emotional Harm*, p. §28 Reporters' Note, Comment c. (5).

[214]   For example, *Asghar Leghari v. Federation of Pakistan* (W.P. No. 25501/2015), Lahore High Court Green Bench, *Kelsey Cascadia Rose Juliana, et al. v. US*, No. 6:15-cv-0157-TC. United States courts' jurisprudence has seen particularly abundant climate-related claims. For more details see David A. Grossman, 'Tort-Based Climate Litigation' in W. C. G. Burns and H. M. Osofsky (eds.),

desirability of climate change litigation claims,[215] but it is only recently that we witness a surge in actual court decisions, many finding in favour of climate change claims. Climate change litigation is an umbrella concept uniting claims filed against governments in an attempt to enforce the enaction and implementation of more ambitious climate mitigation policies as well as claims for climate change damages against sources of greenhouse gas (GHG) emission.[216] Courts face causal claims that focus on the causal relevance of a certain portion of emission, both from a scientific and a legal point of view. Besides intricate questions of proof and causation, climate change claims raise a plethora of difficulties in terms of establishing standing, delineating actionable types of damage,[217] setting the applicable threshold of harm,[218] or dealing with claims of contributory negligence.[219] It is well beyond the scope of this study to discuss all these intriguing legal questions, hence, it confines itself to the analysis of causal inquiries in climate change litigation claims.

Climate change claims are filed with domestic, regional, and international fora. International judicial fora have not yet rendered judgments concerning climate change damage claims, in which they could have expounded on the international legal requirements in relation to complex causal relations of GHG emissions and their adverse consequences. Yet it is most likely to be only a matter of time, as initiatives have already appeared on the international stage exploring the possibilities of international climate litigation cases. For instance, small island nation states are discussing the possibility to request the UN General Assembly to seek an Advisory Opinion of the ICJ on the legal responsibility of states to combat climate change.[220] Claims have also been filed under the international human rights

Adjudicating Climate Change: State, National, and International Approaches (Cambridge University Press, 2009), pp. 193–229; Brian J. Preston, *Climate Change Litigation* (Part 1), 1 Carbon and Climate Law Review (2011), 798–809, 798–809; For litigation in Australia and New Zealand see Jolene Lin, 'Climate change litigation in Asia and the Pacific', in G. Van Calster, W. Vandenberghe, and L. Reins (eds.), *Research Handbook on Climate Change Mitigation Law* (Edward Elgar, 2016), pp. 578–99. For a database of climate change litigation claims see Climate Change Litigation Databases of Sabin Center of Climate Change Law available at climatecasechart.com/ (last accessed 17 January 2020).

[215] A. Strauss, 'Climate change litigation: opening the door to the International Court of Justice' in W. C. G. Burns, H. M. Osofsky (eds.), *Adjudicating Climate Change* (Cambridge University Press, 2010), pp. 334–56 pp. 334–56; D. Hunter, 'The implications of climate change litigation: litigation for international environmental law-making' in W. C. G. Burns and H. M. Osofsky (eds.), *Adjudicating Climate Change* (Cambridge University Press, 2010).

[216] H. M. Osofsky, 'The intersection of scale, science, and law in *Massachusetts v. EPA*' in W. C. G. Burns and H. M. Osofsky (eds.), *Adjudicating Climate Change* (Cambridge University Press, 2010), pp. 129–44 p. 134.

[217] C. Voigt, 'Climate change and damages' in C. Carlarne, K. Gray, and R. Tarasofsky (eds.), *The Oxford Handbook of International Climate Change Law* (Oxford University Press, 2016), pp. 465–94 pp. 475–83.

[218] Voigt, 'Climate change and damages', pp. 471–3.

[219] Voigt, 'Climate change and damages', pp. 486–9.

[220] Voigt, 'Climate change and damages', p. 466.

regime. In 2005, the Inuit Circumpolar Conference filed a petition with the Inter-American Commission on Human Rights against the United States for its failure to address GHG emissions adequately and thereby violating rights enshrined in the American Declaration of the Rights and Duties of Man.[221] Although the commission declined to process the 167-page-long petition,[222] it signalled the possibility that climate change issues might be brought before international adjudicatory fora. Since 2004 petitions have also been filed with the World Heritage Convention in order to seek protection for World Heritage sites threatened by climate change impacts.[223] The possibility of an ITLOS Advisory Opinion in relation to the climate change obligations of states under UNCLOS is increasingly discussed, just as the potential international law bases of climate change damage claims. Even though the 2015 UN Paris Agreement on Climate Change[224] firmly rejects construing the 'loss and damage' concept as giving rise to liability or claims for reparation,[225] it is widely recognized that such claims could arise under customary international law.[226]

What is certain is that causal inquiry would pose a number of challenges for climate change lawsuits irrespective of the legal context and the exact adjudicative body before such claim may be brought. These problems would hinder not only climate change damage claims, but also claims seeking to enforce mitigation policies of states. In hearing both types of cases, national and international judges will inevitably experience a number of intricate causal problems.

First, climate science can only speak in probabilistic terms, even though the latest Synthesis Report of the International Panel on Climate Change has declared that 'it

---

[221] See in more detail H. M. Osofsky, 'The Inuit petition as a bridge? Beyond dialectics of climate change and indigenous peoples' rights' in W. C. G. Burns and H. M. Osofsky (eds.), *Adjudicating Climate Change* (Cambridge University Press, 2010), pp. 272–90.

[222] 'Inuit petition filed with the Inter-American Commission on Human Rights to oppose climate change caused by the United States of America', available at https://bit.ly/2yTTvKC (last accessed 21 January 2020).

[223] In more detail see E J. Thorson, 'The World Heritage Convention and climate change: the case for a climate-change mitigation strategy beyond the Kyoto Protocol' in W. C. G. Burns and H. M. Osofsky (eds.), *Adjudicating Climate Change* (Cambridge University Press, 2010), pp. 255–71; H. M. Osofsky, 'Climate change and dispute resolution processes' in R. Rayfuse and S. V. Scott (eds.), *International Law in the Era of Climate Change* (Edward Elgar, 2012), pp. 350–70 pp. 353–5.

[224] Paris Agreement to the United Nations Framework Convention on Climate Change, Paris, 12 December 2015, in force 4 November 2016, Doc. FCCC/CP/2015/10/Add.1.

[225] Article 8 of the Paris Agreement provides for the 'loss and damage' concept. For more details on its legal content see D. Bodansky, J. Brunnée, and L. Rajamani, *International Climate Change Law* (Oxford University Press, 2017), pp. 238–9.

[226] C. Voigt, 'State responsibility for climate change damages' (2008) *Nordic Journal of International Law* 1–22 at 7–9; M. G. Faure and A. Nollkaemper, 'International liability as an instrument to prevent and compensate for climate change' (2007) 123–79 at 144. See also the Declaration of Fiji, Kiribati, Nauru, Papua New Guinea, Tuvalu deposited to the UN Framework Convention on Climate Change, expressly reinforcing that the Convention '*shall in no way constitute a renunciation of any rights under international law concerning State responsibility for the adverse effects of Climate Change*' available at https://bit.ly/2MlIJ2W (last accessed 17 January 2020).

is extremely likely that more than half of the observed increase in global average surface temperature from 1951 to 2010 was caused by the anthropogenic increase in GHG concentrations and other anthropogenic forcings together'.[227] Notwithstanding this straightforward finding, international courts may still face difficulties in establishing causality between a specific human (corporate and/or state) action and the adverse effects of climate change. Second, metaphorically speaking, adverse climate change impacts arise like a 'death by a thousand cuts',[228] that is to say, out of the synergetic[229] and cumulative effects of myriads of GHG emitters. Third, causally attributing specific climate change damage to a particular emitter is often simply impossible,[230] as 'fingerprinting' is not feasible with regard to each GHG molecule. Nevertheless, apportioning the damage based on the gross GHG emission of the respondent is theoretically possible assuming the equal causal role of each ton of GHG emission in enhancing radiative forcing.[231] A further problem is posed by extremely long and complex causal 'chains', which could break quite easily. This begs the question as to what adverse impacts of climate change were foreseeable,[232] and therefore 'direct enough' consequences of a defendant's conduct to find causality established.

Against the backdrop of this causal conundrum, successful climate change lawsuits on the national level should all the more be appreciated. A landmark judgment of the US Supreme Court in *Massachusetts* v. *EPA*[233] was one of the first unanticipated victories in 2007. The Supreme Court found a causal link established amidst highly politicized debates surrounding uncertainty inherent in climate science. The case arose out of the claim of the State of Massachusetts complaining of losing its territory due to climate change induced sea-level rise. Massachusetts attributed the loss to the failure of the federal government to regulate carbon-dioxide emissions from new motor vehicles under the federal Clean Air Act, which mandated rule-making for the Environmental Protection Agency (EPA) regarding all air pollutants that may cause or contribute to air pollution that endangers public health. The EPA notably denied a rule-making petition to regulate GHG gases under said mandate. The petitioners challenged the denial, giving rise to the lawsuit, which ultimately reached the Supreme Court. The judges had to decide first whether Massachusetts satisfied the three-fold standing requirements under US constitutional law, which

---

[227] IPCC Climate Change 2014 Synthesis Report, Summary for Policymakers, 5, available at www.ipcc.ch/pdf/assessment-report/ar5/syr/AR5_SYR_FINAL_SPM.pdf (last accessed 17 January 2020).

[228] Peel, 'Issues in climate change litigation', 17–18.

[229] Voigt, 'State responsibility for climate change damages', 15.

[230] Voigt, 'State responsibility for climate change damages', 15.

[231] R. S. J. Tol and R. Verheyen, 'State responsibility and compensation for climate change damages: a legal and economic assessment' (2004) 32(9) *Energy Policy* 1109–30 at 1112.

[232] Voigt, 'State responsibility for climate change damages', 17.

[233] *Massachusetts* v. *Environmental Protection Agency*, US Supreme Court, 2 April 2007, 549 US 497 (2007). For a detailed analysis on the history, judicial dynamics, and consequence of the judgment see R. J. Lazarus, *The Rule of Five Making Climate History at the Supreme Court* (Harvard University Press, 2020).

are (i) a concrete and particularized injury, which is actual or imminent, (ii) that is traceable to the defendant, and (iii) that a favourable decision would redress the injury suffered.[234] To refute the causality criterion, the EPA referred to a report of the National Research Council, which was of the view that a causal link between anthropogenic emissions and the rise of surface temperature 'cannot be unequivocally established'.[235]

In the standing analysis, the US Supreme Court had to ultimately decide whether GHG emission of the new motor vehicle fleet of the United States was the 'cause' of climate change, which led to global warming entailing sea-level rise, which ultimately decreased the territory of the State of Massachusetts. The court has cut the Gordian knot of causation by providing an unexpected reasoning. It ruled that it is an 'erroneous assumption that a small incremental step, because it is incremental, can never be attacked'[236] in such a lawsuit. It does not diminish the remarkable nature of such a causal finding if one considers that the US transportation sector alone ranked as 'the third-largest emitter of carbon dioxide in the world'[237] at the time of rendering the judgment. As to the problem of too-long causal chains, the court firmly found that '[t]he risk of catastrophic harm, though remote, is nevertheless real'.[238] In other words, the Supreme Court did not allow any uncertainties in climate change science to prohibit the success of the science-based causal claim of Massachusetts.[239] As it may be clear from the foregoing, *Massachusetts* v. *EPA* serves as an apposite example of an innovative judicial decision recognizing the existence of a causal link *for purposes of the legal analysis* even if the nexus is based on uncertain science.

The judgment induced a flood of domestic climate change litigation not only within the United States,[240] but also worldwide, seeking to judicially enforce more ambitious climate actions from governments. In 2015, The Hague District Court ruled against the Dutch Government in the *Urgenda* case[241] and ordered the

---

[234] *Mass.* v. *EPA*, Judgment, 14.

[235] *Mass.* v. *EPA*, Judgment, 10.

[236] *Mass.* v. *EPA*, Judgment, 21.

[237] *Mass.* v. *EPA*, Judgment, 22.

[238] *Mass.* v. *EPA*, Judgment, 23.

[239] For a detailed assessment of the conceptions and usage of scientific uncertainty in the parties' submissions and the judges' reasoning see R. Von Burg, 'The Supreme Court cleans the air: legal and scientific standards for argument in *Massachusetts* v. *EPA*' (2017) 53 *Argumentation and Advocacy* 41–58.

[240] Similar lawsuits have been filed since then to federal courts. A recent example is a decision issued in November 2016 by a US District Court judge in Oregon, who allowed public trust claims to proceed that were brought by a group of children and James Hansen, a renowned climate scientist acting as a guardian for future generations. The lawsuit alleges that the US federal government, by permitting, authorizing, and subsidizing the exploitation, production, transport, and burning of fossil fuels played a significant role in creating the current climate crisis that would 'significantly endanger plaintiffs, with the damage persisting for millennia'. See *Kelsey Cascadia Rose Juliana et al.* v. *United States of America, et al.*, No. 6:15-cv-1517, No. 6:15-cv-01517-TC (D. Or. Nov. 10, 2016).

[241] *Urgenda Foundation* v. *The State of the Netherlands*, The Hague District Court, No. C/09/456689/HA ZA 13-1396.

government to curb its emissions by at least 25 per cent by the end of 2002 compared to 1990 levels. The court easily found a 'sufficient causal link' between Dutch emissions, global climate change, and the possibility of adverse impacts.[242] The Dutch Supreme Court, hearing the case on appeal in cassation in 2019, essentially argued that partial causation justifies partial responsibility and found that a relatively small emitter state can still be compelled to take its share in the reduction of GHG emissions.[243] Only a few months after the first *Urgenda* decision, the Pakistani Lahore High Court Green Bench judicially enforced the implementation of the national climate change policy framework in the *Leghari* case. In its reasoning, it repeatedly noted adverse climate change effects that were deemed causal upon expected changes in river flows and the shortening of growing seasons.[244]

Climate change damage claims, however, are far less successful, partly due to uncertainties in the requisite causal nexus. In 2016, the Essen District Court in *Lliuya v. RWE AG* dismissed damage claims filed by a Peruvian farmer for climate change-induced flood risks imposed by the melting of a nearby glacial lake. The home town of the claimant in the Andes, Huaraz, has already been flooded by the lake, which therefore had to take costly mitigation measures. The lawsuit was filed against RWE, the largest German electricity producer and a parent company of various local energy providers, which contributes to gross GHG emissions by 0.45 per cent. In the claimant's view, causality 'in the legal sense' exists between the emissions and the flood risk, and accordingly, sought to recover 0.45 per cent of the mitigation costs. Yet, the court found a lack of a linear causal chain and reasoned that among 'a myriad of causational contributions, it is impossible to attribute specific damages and impairments to their individual causers'.[245] Hence, the claim was dismissed. The appeal proceeding is currently pending before the Higher Regional Court Hamm, which ordered to enter the evidentiary phase.[246]

The above examples from climate change litigation show that policy considerations often do relax causal criteria in relation to certain claims, when traditional causal concepts of law would fail to identify the cause of an apparent injury. One may assume that the rapidly increasing number of climate change lawsuits, in the long run, will impact the causal doctrine of environmental adjudication as well.

---

[242] *Urgenda*, The Hague District Court, Judgment, para. 4.90.
[243] *Urgenda Foundation v. The State of the Netherlands*, Dutch Supreme Court, No. 19/00135, 20 December 2019, para. 5.7.5; see also: A. Nollkaemper and L. Burgers, *A New Classic in Climate Change Litigation: The Dutch Supreme Court Decision in the Urgenda Case*, EJIL Talk! (6 January 2020). Available at https://bit.ly/2yTtD1q (last accessed 17 January 2020).
[244] *Asghar Leghari v. Federation of Pakistan* (W.P. No. 25501/2015), Climate Change Order (14 September 2015), p. 9.
[245] *Lliuya v. RWE AG*, Case No. 2 O 285/15, Judgment (15 December 2016), Essen District Court, unofficial English translation of the judgment available at https://bit.ly/3eM4lSm (last accessed 17 January 2020).
[246] Updates on the case are available at https://germanwatch.org/en/huaraz (last accessed 22 January 2020)

Yet, the fact that climate change claims are even more 'wicked'[247] than claims arising from other types of environmental harm may, paradoxically, work against adopting similarly flexible causal tests in relation to non-climate-related environmental damage claims if judges deem climate-related claims exceptional. In any event, the abovementioned domestic law examples confirm that national law concepts of causation are currently undergoing a considerable change, which may eventually have an impact on international causal doctrine as well.

2.3 Accepting Mathematical Models as Causal Proof in the Gulf War Reparation Claims

Given that SC Resolution 687 (1991) formally declared the Iraqi government's responsibility under international law for the invasion of Kuwait and its direct harmful consequences,[248] the key question for the scope of Iraq's responsibility – that is, the amount of compensation due – was the existence of a direct causal link. Given that these claims therefore turned on scientific evidence,[249] the review procedure required a very high level of scientific literacy from UNCC Commissioners. Benefitting from expert advice, as detailed above, they were able to rely on and accept mathematical models and statistical evidence as proof of causality. Neither did they shy away from conducting a thorough causal analysis based on statistical scientific evidence and advanced computer-modelling techniques. One must appreciate the innovative and even bold approach taken by the F4 Panel, especially considering the immaturity of rules of international environmental responsibility at the time. Hence, many aspects of the UNCC's fact-finding can be regarded as a positive point of reference, even though these procedures formed a special regime derogating from rules of customary international law governing environmental responsibility in many respects.[250]

The F4 Panel has been applauded for taking a proactive approach to engaging with scientific evidence.[251] On numerous instances the panel openly evaluated

---

[247] R. J. Lazarus, 'Super wicked problems and climate change: restraining the present to liberate the future' (2008) 94 *Cornell Law Review* 1153.

[248] UNSC Res. 687 (1990), para. 16:

   Iraq, without prejudice to the debts and obligations of Iraq arising prior to 2 August 1990, which will be addressed through the normal mechanisms, is liable under international law for any direct loss, damage, including environmental damage and the depletion of natural resources, or injury to foreign Governments, nationals and corporations, as a result of Iraq's unlawful invasion and occupation of Kuwait.

[249] Sand and Kammit, 'Public health claims', p. 24.

[250] In contrast to the no-harm rule under customary international law, the UNCC panel did not need to show that the loss of resource directly resulting from the unlawful occupation exceeded the threshold of significant harm, or that the state in question has breached any standard of care applicable to the obligation of preventing such environmental harm in order to deem a claim compensable.

[251] Sand, 'Environmental dispute settlement and the experience of the UN Compensation Committee', 171.

pieces of evidence, criticized the underlying scientific methodology and sometimes proposed even modifications to models,[252] parameters of a model,[253] or remedial measures.[254] The panel accepted certain computer models as appropriate proofs[255] by stressing that despite all their inherent uncertainties, potential difficulties were not sufficient reasons for wholesale rejection of such evidence.[256] Similarly, the panel was open to accept statistical evidence, by refuting Iraq's assertion that such evidence should not be regarded as adequate proof.[257] Importantly, statistical evidence was not immune to scrutiny despite the fact that the panel consisted of lawyers. They confidently dismissed certain pieces of evidence when they were of the view that the scientific methodologies applied were flawed.[258]

2.4 Innovations of Domestic Courts: US Toxic Tort Litigation's Solutions for Accepting Statistical Evidence as Proof of Uncertain Causation

United States courts have also been struggling with establishing causation based on scientific expert evidence in toxic tort cases, albeit by now they widely accept and rely on probabilistic proof of causation. This appears to be a much more ambitious approach compared to international litigation where, as was shown above, statistical evidence is rarely deemed persuasive enough for purposes of the adjudicatory analysis. United States courts have developed a thorough approach to evaluating the probative force of expert evidence and have become quite successful in integrating uncertain scientific proof into legal theories of causation. These judicial good practices, thus, may again be a source of inspiration for international courts attesting that scientific causal proofs ought not to necessarily inhibit finding a causal nexus.

The Third Restatement of Torts acknowledges the need for adapting traditional tort rules of proof 'to a greater uncertainty inherent in agent-disease causation and

[252] For example, UN Compensation Commission Governing Council, 'Report and Recommendations Made by the Panel of Commissioners Concerning the Fifth Instalment of "F4" Claims', para. 115.
[253] For example, UN Compensation Commission Governing Council, 'Report and Recommendations Made by the Panel of Commissioners Concerning the Fifth Instalment of "F4" Claims', para. 426.
[254] For example, UN Compensation Commission Governing Council, 'Report and Recommendations made by the Panel of Commissioners Concerning the Third Instalment of "F4" Claims', para. 104.
[255] UN Compensation Commission Governing Council, 'Report and Recommendations Made by the Panel of Commissioners Concerning the Fifth Instalment of "F4" Claims', para. 439.
[256] UN Compensation Commission Governing Council, 'Report and Recommendations Made by the Panel of Commissioners Concerning the Fifth Instalment of "F4" Claims', paras 80–1. While doing so, the Panel cited the *Trail Smelter* arbitral award Arbitration (*United States, Canada*) Award (16 April 1938 3 RIAA 1905, at 1920), which reiterated that, where the wrongful act 'itself is of such a nature as to preclude the ascertainment of the amount of damages with certainty, it would be a perversion of fundamental principles of justice to deny all relief to the injured person'.
[257] UN Compensation Commission Governing Council, 'Report and Recommendations Made by the Panel of Commissioners Concerning the Fifth Instalment of "F4" Claims', para. 77.
[258] UN Compensation Commission Governing Council, 'Report and Recommendations Made by the Panel of Commissioners Concerning the Fifth Instalment of "F4" Claims', paras 696–7.

the specialized types of evidence'.[259] It is also mindful that all causal inquiries presuppose inferential reasoning, and it only allows reasonable inferences to be drawn.[260] Within these confines, US courts should make causal inferences on a case-by-case basis. The burden of proof is normally borne by the plaintiff; however, special rules accommodate the challenges of toxic tort cases. As one exception, in alternative-defendants situations, the burden of proof is reversed for the benefit of the plaintiff in certain jurisdictions.[261] There are no generally accepted rules on the burden of proof where pre-existing conditions contribute to the harm, as the nature of these conditions varies considerably and influences the imposition of the burden.[262] In this respect, courts generally consider whether the pre-existing condition was a result of innocent forces, such as the plaintiff's genetic heritage, or involved a conscious choice, for example, one of lifestyle, and whether the plaintiff was contributorily negligent.[263]

The following discussion showcases how US toxic tort litigation has successfully adapted to the various challenges posed by uncertain proof of causation. The preponderance standard and the acceptance of naked statistical evidence (Subsection 2.4.1) along with the doubling of relative risk standard (Subsection 2.4.2) are innovative tools enabling judicial reliance on uncertain scientific evidence, which will be discussed below.

2.4.1 ACCEPTING STATISTICAL DATA AS CAUSAL PROOF. The Third Restatement generally requires that the plaintiff prove the causal link with the preponderance of the evidence, meaning that the factor was more likely than not to be the cause of the injury.[264] The preponderance rule entails an 'all-or-nothing' type of liability.[265] If the plaintiff can prove the causal link on the balance of probability, the defendant is held liable for the entirety of the harm. The strong version of the preponderance rule allows for pure mathematical probabilities to meet this standard; while the weak version requires an actual belief on the part of the factfinder to meet that standard.[266]

United States courts increasingly accept naked statistical evidence produced by epidemiology when the circumstances of the case make it impossible to obtain particularized evidence. To use group-based, statistical epidemiological evidence

[259] *Third Restatement of the Law of Torts for Physical and Emotional Harm*, §28, Reporters' Note, Comment c. (1).
[260] *Third Restatement of the Law of Torts for Physical and Emotional Harm*, §28 Comment on Subsection (a) b.
[261] Oliphant, 'Uncertain factual causation in the Third Restatement', 1602.
[262] *Third Restatement of the Law of Torts for Physical and Emotional Harm*, §28 Comment on Subsection (a) d. (2).
[263] *Third Restatement of the Law of Torts for Physical and Emotional Harm*, §28 Comment on Subsection (a) d. (2).
[264] *Third Restatement of the Law of Torts for Physical and Emotional Harm*, §28.
[265] D. Rosenberg, 'The causal connection in mass exposure cases: a "public law" vision of the tort system' (1984) 97 *Harvard Law Review* 849 at 857.
[266] Rosenberg, 'The causal connection in mass exposure cases', 857.

for proving general causation, courts must ascertain whether the association of data indeed reflects causal connection and not just spurious association. For this purpose, US courts rely on the Bradford Hill criteria,[267] which were developed and originally used by scientists. A legion of case law demonstrates courts' willingness to accept epidemiological data as proof of general causation,[268] albeit statistical evidence alone is not always treated as adequate proof of specific causation.[269]

2.4.2 THE DOUBLING OF RELATIVE RISK AS PROOF OF CAUSATION. A certain type of statistical data gained special importance in US toxic torts, namely, epidemiological data showing the doubling of relative risk (often referred to by the shorthand reference of RR>2) as proof of causation.[270] The computation of the doubling of relative risk can be illustrated by the following example: 'if 5% of smokers get lung cancer, but only 1% of non-smokers do, the relative risk of smoker for lung cancer would be five, implying that smoking explains four of every five cases of lung cancer in smokers'.[271]

Toxic tort jurisprudence is split over whether courts should regard the doubling of relative risk as a proof of general[272] or specific causation.[273] Understandably, many courts find it troublesome to infer specific causation from group-based data that, in fact, provide no proof of an actual causal link to a specific individual's disease.[274] The Third Restatement nevertheless allows for the use of RR>2 as a proof of specific causation as well.[275] This shows US courts' willingness to accept naked statistical evidence to establish causation in toxic torts.[276]

Importantly, RR>2 is not a general panacea for every problem that arises in the 'black-box'[277] of uncertain causation. It is blind to the distinction of

---

[267] Hill, 'The environment and disease'.
[268] *Third Restatement of the Law of Torts for Physical and Emotional Harm*, §28 Reporters' Note, Comment c. (3).
[269] *Third Restatement of the Law of Torts for Physical and Emotional Harm*, §28 Reporters' Note, Comment c. (3). In such cases, case reports on instances of an individual's disease and biological mechanism evidence can serve as additional proof.
[270] Green, 'The future of proportional liability: the lessons of toxic substances causation', p. 391.
[271] Gold, 'The more we know, the less intelligent we are?', 373. Professor Gold suggests that the threshold of more than doubling the relative risk reflects the preponderance test, since a relative risk of two describes a case when the incidence of the disease in the exposed population is exactly the double than that in the exposed population, where the disease is attributable to background risks. In such a case, a randomly selected individual from the exposed group of the population who manifests the disease is equally likely to be either harmed *due to the exposure* or having developed the disease *due to background* causes. Gold, 'The more we know, the less intelligent we are?', 376.
[272] *Third Restatement of the Law of Torts for Physical and Emotional Harm*, §28 Reporters' Note, Comment c. (3).
[273] R. S. Carruth and B. D. Goldstein, 'Relative risk greater than two in proof of causation in toxic tort litigation' (2000) 41 *Jurimetrics* 195 at 204.
[274] Gold, 'The more we know, the less intelligent we are?', 374.
[275] *Third Restatement of the Law of Torts for Physical and Emotional Harm*, §28 comment c. (4).
[276] R. W. Wright, 'Proving causation: probability versus belief in R. Goldberg (ed.), *Perspectives on Causation* (Hart Publishing, 2011), pp. 195–220 p. 215.
[277] J. A. Grodsky, 'Genomics and toxic torts: dismantling the risk-injury divide' (2007) *Stanford Law Review* 1671–734 at 1688.

whether but-for the exposure, the disease would have not occurred at all or would have occurred only later in the plaintiff's life.[278] Hence, the RR>2 standard can be misused, as it systematically underestimates the probability of causation in cases when the exposure only accelerates the disease.[279] Another possible misinterpretation of the RR>2 standard is that relative risk might vary depending on the genetic heritage of a given individual.[280] Overall, the judicial use of the 'doubling of relative risk' standard stands as a laudable example of accepting irreducible uncertainty in scientific results. As the court noted in *Merrell Dow Pharmaceuticals Inc v. Havner*, '[t]he use of scientifically reliable epidemiological studies and the requirement of more than a doubling of the risk strikes a balance between the needs of our legal system and the limits of science'.[281] Indeed, the standard appears to be a useful tool for establishing causation when the evidence inevitably falls short of the traditional requirement of certainty.

3 Assessment: The Status of Science in the Causal Policy of International Courts

The above comparative overview reveals that the causal inquiries of international courts and tribunals vary greatly, just like their tendencies to find a science-based causal claim established. Two opposing trends emerge from this comparative assessment. Certain fora have been dismissive towards scientific facts and regard the uncertain nature of scientific evidence as an insurmountable obstacle to establish science-based causal links; whereas others have proven to be willing to modify traditional causal tests and standards of proof in order to integrate scientific knowledge in their causal inquiry.

A more fine-grained examination of the causal policy landscape of international adjudicators can offer some further analytic remarks. First of all, the science-intensity of international courts and tribunals' causal assessment vary to a great extent. In other words, adjudicators may justify their causal findings with or without reference to science. Certain jurisdictions tend to build their causal inquiry on scientific facts by accepting probabilistic evidence and lowering the threshold of required proof in order to find a legal claim established based on uncertain expert evidence. Yet numerous techniques exist that serve to circumvent the scientific basis of causal claims.

---

[278]   Greenland, 'Relation of probability of causation to relative risk and doubling dose', 1166.

[279]   S. Greenland and J. M. Robins, 'Epidemiology, justice, and the probability of causation' (2000) *Jurimetrics* 321–40 at 323.

[280]   Gold, 'The more we know, the less intelligent we are?', 390. He drew attention to some studies showing dramatic changes in relative risk of developing breast cancer among smoking women depending whether they carried the protective allele or not.

[281]   *Merrell Dow Pharmaceuticals Inc. v. Havner*, 953 SW 2d 706, 718 (Tex. 1997).

If we look more closely at decisions featuring science-intensive causal inquiry, it appears that they originate from fora that are adequately equipped with scientific fact-finding capabilities. It is no coincidence that every judicial body that accommodates science in its causal inquiry, notably, the UNCC, PCA, certain investment tribunals, and domestic courts have normally benefitted from independent expert advice or the presence of expert arbitrators in conducting their causal assessments. Presumptions are an exemption from this rule, as they appear also in the practice of judicial bodies that do not rely on the above fact-finding methods. Yet even in such cases, closing the gap between scientific and legal concepts of causation ultimately rests on adjudicators' awareness of what science can and cannot deliver in a legal dispute.

At the same time, certain adjudicators choose to downplay or circumvent scientific evidence and knowledge in appraising causal claims. In such cases, their causal assessment may either be built on traditional understanding of legal doctrines or on intuitive rule-of-thumb balancing of the causal role of scientific factors. However, the lesser the extent of judicial engagement with underlying facts is, the more vulnerable the reasoning is to criticism. Suffice it to refer to the various dissenting opinions in *Pulp Mills*, critiquing the majority's complete disregard for scientific realities in evaluating scientific causal proofs. Furthermore, if adjudicators are not willing to consider scientific knowledge in their causal analysis, they would need to rely on other types of rationality to justify their decisions. We shall return to some concrete examples in this regard in Chapter 10, including the epistemic risks this may induce.

On a separate note, international courts and tribunals generally tend to obfuscate their causal analysis. They often conflate the two distinct steps of causal inquiry,[282] namely, the stages of general and specific causation. This is aggravated by the fact that international adjudicative bodies normally do not even discuss the applicable causal test in an open manner. The Eritrea-Ethiopia Claims Commission, which administered claims arising out of an armed conflict, is a notable exception in this respect. It explicitly introduced a foreseeability criterion in its causal inquiry, when awarded compensation for losses to which Eritrea's invasion was a proximate cause.[283]

The UNCC also administered monetary compensation claims that were deemed directly arising from the unlawful invasion of Kuwait.[284] Yet, the UNCC Governing

[282] Plakokefalos, 'Causation in the law of state responsibility and the problem of overdetermination', 475.

[283] Eritrea–Ethiopia Claims Commission, Decision No. 7, Guidance Regarding *Jus ad Bellum* Liability, 27 July 2007, para. 13. See generally: M. J. Matheson, 'Eritrea-Ethiopia Claims Commission: damage awards' (2009) 13(13) *ASIL Insights*.

[284] UNSC Res. 687 (1990), para. 16:

Iraq, without prejudice to the debts and obligations of Iraq arising prior to 2 August 1990, which will be addressed through the normal mechanisms, is liable under international law for any direct loss, damage, including environmental damage and the depletion of natural resources, or

Council remained silent on the applicable causal test.[285] Similarly, the ICJ, the ITLOS as well as the ECtHR all refrained from announcing their causal nexus criterion in establishing environmental damage claims.[286] In this vein, it is often not clear whether courts require but-for or contributory causation to establish a legally relevant cause. The *Peter Allard* investment arbitration is a notable exception, where the tribunal expressly articulated that it deemed a factor to be a 'cause' even if it had only a 'significant component' in realizing the harmful effect.[287] The fact that causal reasoning remains opaque across several fora seems to be more than a coincidence; rather a strategic choice of adjudicators to retain control over inescapably uncertain facts and to preserve corresponding room for manoeuvre as to the outcome of each inquiry.

It is nevertheless to be appreciated that in more recent disputes several major fora conceive science-intensive causal inquiry to be a matter falling in judicial competence. In the compensation judgment rendered in *Certain Activities*, the ICJ stressed that 'it is for the Court to decide whether there is a sufficient causal nexus between the wrongful act and the injury suffered'.[288] It did not reveal, however, what would be seen as sufficient in a causal analysis, hence states (and scholars) were left again without any precise test or yardstick for making such a sufficiency determination. Overall, the fact remains that causality is an often overlooked and undertheorized aspect in the analysis of international courts and tribunals.

On the rare occasions when international jurisdictions do clarify their causal tests, another discernible trend points to the dominance of requiring clear and direct causal links. This demands a high level of certainty from underlying scientific facts, which would often be problematic if not outright impossible in light of the many forms of scientific uncertainty burdening expert evidence. The majority of jurisdictions tends to be dismissive towards probabilistic causal proofs, which can be partly explained by the salient difference between scientific and legal concepts of causation and that of adequate proof. Moreover, some international courts are reluctant to allow causal presumptions to close the gap triggered by inevitable uncertainties of causal evidence. Admittedly, there are certain notable exceptions, when national or international adjudicative bodies have been inclined to accept probability calculations as proof of a causal nexus. On the international level, the case-practice of the UNCC sets an important precedent, whereas on the national level, the practice of US courts in toxic tort litigation showcases some

---

injury to foreign Governments, nationals and corporations, as a result of Iraq's unlawful invasion and occupation of Kuwait.

[285] Plakokefalos, 'Causation in the law of state responsibility and the problem of overdetermination', 489.

[286] See for relevant examples in the practice of the ICJ in Chapter 3, regarding the ECtHR in Chapter 5, and regarding ITLOS in Chapter 8.

[287] *Peter A. Allard v. The Government of Barbados*, PCA Case No. 2012–06, Award (27 June 2016), Award, para. 157.

[288] *Certain Activities*, Judgment on compensation, para. 34.

innovative solutions in this respect. It is to be noted, however, that these judicial good practices may prove to be too confrontational and fact-intensive for more deferential international fora.

Among influential policy considerations we shall flag the role of substantive principles. Intuitive judgments, such as moral blaming, appear to play a decisive role in forming the causal policy of international fora. Scholars have long emphasized the role of judges' subjective judgments in setting their causal tests.[289] Contemporary international environmental case law also evidences this. Notably, causal claims leading to environmental damage were only found established on two occasions,[290] when the facts reflected particularly devastating environmental destruction, and respondent states, although for different reasons, did not contest the illegal nature of the harmful conduct in the legal proceedings.

The first occasion occurred in the practice of the UNCC, which assessed causality and the quantum of damages for the harmful consequences of the Iraqi invasion, for which the international responsibility of Iraq had already been established by the UN Security Council. The other instance of awarding environmental damage claims occurred in the *South China Sea* Arbitration, which concerned exceptionally extensive and grave environmental destruction caused by China's artificial island-building activity.[291] China stayed away from the proceedings and hence the tribunal delivered its award in absence of the respondent. It is submitted here that both of these science-based causal claims were not adjudicated in a vacuum. Quite the opposite, international political climate arguably was favourable towards both environmental damage claims, which might well have played a considerable role in the inclination of respective adjudicative bodies to find legal causality established.

Lastly, causal policy considerations of international adjudicators are also manifest in the divergent causal tests set by different fora in factually similar scenarios. One may find divergent evidentiary and causal standards with regard to scientifically (or medically) similar injury claims in the practice of the US–Marshall Islands Claims Tribunal as well as the ECtHR. As discussed above,[292] both fora heard health injury claims allegedly caused by nuclear exposure. While the Claims Tribunal adopted relaxed evidentiary and causal standards and awarded damages, the ECtHR has never found requisite causal nexus established between nuclear exposure and the diseases of the applicant.

The foregoing analysis demonstrates that the prevailing approach of international courts and tribunals towards causation could succinctly be described as

---

[289] Hart and Honoré, *Causation in the Law*, pp. 291–307.
[290] These relate only to cases where causality was disputed in the case. In the compensation judgment in *Certain Activities*, compensation was awarded for ecological damage, however, causation was not disputed by the respondent. See Chapter 3 Section IV, Subsection 1.3 for more details.
[291] See Chapter 4 Section II, Subsection 3.2 for more discussion.
[292] See Section IV, Subsection 2.1.1 in this chapter.

being a mixture of uncertain facts and opaque policy. The obscurity of causal reasoning gives the impression that causality, especially when based on scientific facts, is a neglected aspect of current jurisprudence and is very much still in its infancy. The inconsistent application of causal standards suggests that causation is almost treated as the second-class citizen of international adjudication. Causal requirements are either entirely omitted from the reasoning or treated in an arcane way. Furthermore, causal nexus is only found established if the wider context – such as formerly announced responsibility of the respondent state, or the overall egregiousness of factual circumstances – makes it a safe and relatively straightforward choice for adjudicators. Hence, there is still considerable room for improvement in international judicial practice both in terms of clarifying applicable causal tests and with respect to conducting thorough scientific fact-finding in relation to causal proofs.

Despite the unprivileged status of causal inquiry in contemporary international jurisprudence, causal claims are increasingly filed with international courts. Causality, in express or in more subtle ways, plays a relevant role before every international judicial body that hears environmental claims. In some jurisdictions, causality is just about to gain even more importance. Suffice it to refer to the IACtHR, which has recently put causality at the centre of its analysis in extraterritorial victims' claims regarding environmental pollution.[293]

One also witnesses a growing number of dissenting opinions[294] levelling criticism against hidden causal analysis of the majority. This is coupled with heightened academic interest in studying the causal requirements of specific regimes of international law in order to identify consistent and principled bases of judicial causal inquiry.[295] Whether these hesitant signs of change may gather momentum for a shift in judicial attitude towards causal inquiry may be too early to say. Nevertheless, these tendencies do suggest that international courts will be more frequently asked by litigants and the wider public to clarify and reveal their causal tests and analysis.

The outcome of this survey of the various causal policies of international adjudicators suggests that accommodating scientific input in the causal inquiry, despite all of its practical intricacies, appears to be warranted. At a time when growing scientific knowledge allows us to better understand scientific realities of complex natural processes, legal solutions that distance adjudicators from the scientific aspects of

---

[293]   For a more detailed discussion see Chapter 5 Section III, Subsection 4.1.

[294]   For example, Dissenting Opinion of Judge Zupančič in *Tătar* v. *Romania* (for more details see Chapter 5), and the Joint Dissenting Opinion of Judge Al-Khasawneh and Judge Simma as well as the Dissenting Opinion of Judge Vinuesa in the *Pulp Mills* case (for more details see Chapter 3).

[295]   Plakokefalos, 'Causation in the law of state responsibility and the problem of overdetermination'; Gattini, 'Breach of the obligation to prevent and reparation thereof in the ICJ's genocide judgment'; Straus, 'Causation as an element of state responsibility'; M. Jarret, *Contributory Fault and Investor Misconduct in Investment Arbitration* (Cambridge University Press, 2019), pp. 43–78; Gattini, 'Breach of international obligations'; Sulyok, 'Managing uncertain causation: lessons for the Strasbourg Court from US toxic tort litigation?'; J. Nedumpara, *Injury and Causation in Trade Remedy Law* (Springer, 2016).

causation run the risk of being detached from reality and, in turn, of losing legitimacy. Fortunately, international courts do have the power to close the gap between the law and the science of causation by embracing uncertain evidence to the extent possible. Given the absence of a universal causal principle that would 'relieve the courts of the burden of discretion or creative choice',[296] the task of (re)defining science-based causal requirements ultimately rests with judges.

V TRENDS IN SETTING THE STANDARD OF JUDICIAL REVIEW

The cognitive authority of science also appears to shape how far adjudicators are willing to go into the depth of underlying science in their judicial review. International jurisdictions face such a dilemma predominantly in reviewing the legality of scientific risk assessments typically before WTO dispute settlement bodies,[297] and in investment arbitration proceedings.[298] Scientific claims may also be legally relevant under certain environmental treaty regimes that contain direct references to scientific concepts, as illustrated by the *Whaling in the Antarctic* judgment.[299] In all these contexts, judges need to appraise scientific claims against different standards of review. The chosen standard will serve as a basis for justifying the outcome of the judicial review, that is, whether to uphold or reject a particular risk assessment or find an appeal to scientific authority acceptable or invalid from perspective of the law.

The remainder of this chapter is structured into two main parts. Subsection 1 maps current adjudicatory landscape regarding the extent of deference international fora tend to afford to sovereigns' scientific claims. Given that virtually every international court has by now become reluctant to grant total and automatic deference to such claims, adjudicators must select a benchmark against which scientific claims will be contrasted. Subsection 2 therefore reviews the variety of such yardsticks discerned from the practice of international fora.

1 *Balancing between Deferential and Intrusive Review*

International courts and tribunals have considerable room for manoeuvre in designing the boundaries and content of their judicial review. Some conduct a more intrusive review, while others are quite deferential towards states' scientific claims underlying environmental policies. On the whole we witness a surge in the number of tools fostering a judicial review, where scientific facts put constraints on states' political discretion. The particular standards of review have been previously discussed in detail with regard to WTO panels,[300]

---

[296]   Hart and Honoré, *Causation in the Law*, p. 130.
[297]   See Chapter 6 Section III.
[298]   See Chapter 7 Section V, Subsections 2.1–2.2.
[299]   See Chapter 3 Section V.
[300]   See Chapter 6 Section III.

investment arbitral tribunals,[301] and the ICJ;[302] hence the ensuing section will continue by pointing out common trends in granting regulatory autonomy to states over scientific matters.

The ICJ adopts a rather intrusive scrutiny towards states' appeals to science. It announced its standard of review in *Whaling in the Antarctic*, where it had to scrutinize whether Japan could legitimately claim that is was pursuing 'scientific whaling' under the special permit procedure of the ICRW. The Court had to devise a tool to distinguish claims of 'genuine science' from 'non-science'. The bench consciously avoided to provide a general definition of science, instead it announced an objective test of reasonableness to assess whether JARPA's 'design and implementation [were] reasonable in relation to its stated scientific objectives'.[303] The ICJ's substantive assessment, which amounted to an eighty-paragraph long inquiry, can surely be seen as an in-depth, substantive, and arguably even a '*de novo*',[304] review.

Interestingly, the standard of review has been geared to the opposite direction in the WTO jurisprudence. World Trade Organization panels first embarked on the intrusive task of scrutinizing whether a science-based measure was 'sufficiently supported or reasonably warranted'[305] by scientific evidence, which became highly problematic and controversial in cases tainted with irreducible scientific uncertainty. In such earlier cases, the intrusive review resulted in a finding of inconsistency regarding SPS measures in scientifically complicated cases. This occurred in the sequel to the *EC – Hormones* dispute, in the *Continued Suspension of Obligations* case, where the AB had to step in in order to mandate a more deferential approach towards WTO members' regulatory autonomy in cases of 'genuine and legitimate scientific controversy'.[306] The standard of review then became a two-stage analysis: (i) the first being a scrutiny as to the underlying scientific bases of SPS measures. This is a more deferential review as scientific evidence must only come from a legitimate scientific source, but positions representing a minority view within the scientific community become also acceptable. Whereas (ii) the second stage is a scrutiny as to the reasons provided by the risk assessor. This entails a scrutiny to whether the reasoning 'is objective and coherent in which the conclusions find sufficient support in the evidence'.[307] As is clear from the wording of this second arm of the review, WTO panels retain the possibility of conducting an intrusive review,

---

[301] See Chapter 7 Section V.

[302] See Chapter 3 Section V.

[303] *Whaling in the Antarctic*, Judgment, para. 88.

[304] Judge Owada described the Court's approach as 'making a de novo assessment', though he criticized the Court for this, see *Whaling in the Antarctic*, Dissenting Opinion of Judge Owada, para. 38.

[305] *EC – Hormones*, Report of the AB, para. 186.

[306] The EC's appellant submission, cited by the AB in *US – Continued Suspension of Obligations* case, Report of the AB, para. 585.

[307] *Australia – Measures Affecting the Importation of Apples from New Zealand*, Report of the AB, WT/DS367/AB/R (29 November 2010), para. 215.

even though the standard indeed became more deferential in nature compared to the initial practice.

Investment arbitration similarly manifests a deferential approach to reviewing host states' science-based regulations. The conceptual foundation of the relaxed review in this context can be traced back to the large extent arbitration may interfere with policy choices of sovereign states.[308] It is for this reason not very surprising that investment arbitration provides perhaps the most deferential approach to host states' scientific claims. The lenient review is perhaps best illustrated by the *Methanex* award, in which the tribunal stressed that a breach of investment protection standard was only possible where scientific conclusions claimed by host states 'were so faulty that the Tribunal may reasonably infer that the science merely provided a convenient excuse for'[309] disguised protectionism.

As a segue to the next topic of discussion, it is to be recalled that deference is not a monolithic concept as it may bring about considerably divergent reviews. Even though international adjudicators often use deference 'as a mantra',[310] they normally do not reveal the exact scheme of allocating competences between the state and the tribunal. Indeed, a deferential approach can, in fact, cover different content, that is, a host of legal and semi-legal yardsticks with which adjudicators review scientific claims of states. The coming section will detail the various tests international courts and tribunals employ in their scrutiny, and will show that they yield quite different extent of judicial review.

2 *Scrutinizing Scientific Claims: With or Without Reference to Scientific Rationality*

There are many possible ways of evaluating the acceptability of a scientific claim in a legal dispute. Adjudicators may either directly rely on scientific standards in their appraisals or decide not to engage with science and design some non-scientific benchmarks instead. To this extent, the parallel trends of downplaying and accommodating science in the judicial analysis are also manifest in choosing different epistemic benchmarks to underlie the standard of review. Some judges utilize standards of the scientific community to decide whether a scientific claim can withstand judicial review (Subsection 3.1). Others devise legal benchmarks to scrutinize science-based arguments (Subsection 3.2). Within this group, adjudicators may focus on the procedure in which respective scientific data have been produced and look for legal indicia of a transparent and inclusive scientific process (Subsection 3.2.1). Alternatively, judges may accept those scientific claims that are backed up by standards or guidelines of international organizations (Subsection

---

[308] Schill, 'Deference in investment treaty arbitration: re-conceptualizing the standard of review', 578.
[309] *Methanex v. The United States of America* (NAFTA) Final Award (3 August 2005), Part IV – Chapter E, para. 19.
[310] Schill, 'Deference in investment treaty arbitration: re-conceptualizing the standard of review', 579.

3.2.2) or square with established international regulatory trends (Subsection 3.2.3). A yet another option is to look at the substantive outcome of a risk assessment procedure and develop hybrid yardsticks for scrutinizing science-based reasoning (Subsection 3.3). A last possible judicial argumentative practice is to engage in a semantic analysis, which focuses on the textual and grammatical context of the scientific element embedded in the legal rule in question (Subsection 3.4).

2.1 Scrutiny with Science: Relying on Standards of the Scientific Community

The invocation of scientific methods and standards as means to select legally acceptable scientific claims has been most clearly applied in WTO jurisprudence. The WTO AB announced that the acceptability of a scientific opinion to serve as basis for an SPS measure would be assessed 'according to the standards of the relevant scientific community'.[311] Moreover, panels had to scrutinize whether a piece of evidence had 'the necessary scientific and methodological rigor'.[312] The AB initially even required panellists to determine whether a risk assessment 'is sufficiently supported or reasonably warranted'[313] by the scientific record of the case. In all these instances, for answering these questions adjudicators needed to explicitly refer to scientific standards, in other words, relied on scientific rationality to justify their adjudicatory conclusions.

2.2 Scrutiny without Science: Relying on Legal Standards to Judge Scientific Claims

Adjudicators may decide about the acceptability of scientific claims without engaging in depth with the scientific aspects of the case. One may witness an increasing reliance on non-scientific indications of legitimate scientific results in international courts' standards of review. Examples for such argumentative practices will be reviewed in the following sections. The epistemic advantages and perils of relying on such non-scientific benchmarks to evaluate scientific knowledge in an adjudicatory context will be further addressed in Chapter 10.

2.2.1 SCRUTINY OF THE PROCESS OF SCIENTIFIC KNOWLEDGE PRODUCTION. This comparative case law analysis revealed that several international fora employ procedural benchmarks to scrutinize the procedure in which respective scientific results have been produced. Focusing on the procedure of scientific research and science-based regulatory process, rather than the validity of its substantive, scientific outcome saves adjudicators from futile efforts to reveal the factual truth in scientific

---

[311] *US – Continued Suspension of Obligations*, Report of the AB, para. 591.
[312] *US – Continued Suspension of Obligations*, Report of the AB, para. 591.
[313] *EC – Hormones*, Report of the AB, para. 186.

debates.[314] Procedural benchmarks may interrogate whether international practices and scientific guidelines have been observed, whether public participation has been ensured in the process of producing the relevant scientific result, and whether the scientific opinion at hand was subject to peer-review.

One may find several examples of such yardsticks in investment arbitration. In *Chemtura* v. *Canada*, the tribunal made it clear that its appraisal centred on whether 'the review of lindane … breached the due process rights of the Claimant. Such inquiry must take into account the review process as a whole'.[315] The *Methanex* Tribunal added scientific peer-review to the procedural elements that may indicate credible scientific evidence. It explicitly reasoned that the scientific report at hand 'was subjected at the time to public hearings, testimony and peer-review; and its emergence as a serious scientific work from such an open and informed debate is the best evidence that it was not the product of a political sham',[316] and hence it was regarded as a credible scientific opinion in the arbitral proceedings.

For purposes of the present analysis the relevant feature of the above inquiry is that procedural benchmarks enable adjudicatory conclusions to rest on non-scientific rationality. The transparency of the scientific risk assessment procedure or the inclusive and open nature of the regulatory process are not scientific, but legalistic criteria. Accordingly, whether they have been adequately fulfilled in a given scientific process can be judged by scientifically lay adjudicators. Judges may comfortably assess the adequacy of public participation guarantees and transparency measures with reference to legal standards and according to legalistic logic.

Similarly, when adjudicators take peer-review as a yardstick of 'legitimate science', they rely on the authority of individual scientists, and not that of science as a system of rules, which again saves them from confronting the underlying scientific debate. Simply put, peer review is a conventional referee system, where reviewers scrutinize and evaluate the results of other scientists before accepting or rejecting them for publication in a scientific journal, and hence in a wider sense, as part of the scientific discourse. It has become a widely accepted practice since its first appearance in the seventeenth century.[317] When adjudicators use peer review as a rubberstamp of certified scientific knowledge,[318] they in fact defer to the judgment of a community of anonymous scientists. In this vein, when adjudicators rely on peer review to accept a certain scientific claim in a litigation, their reasoning draws on the reputation of renowned scientists and, even more so, on that of the respective

---

[314] Lévesque, 'Science in the hands of international investment tribunals: a case for "scientific due process"', 287; Orellana, 'The role of science in investment arbitrations concerning public health and the environment', 49.

[315] *Chemtura* v. *Canada*, Award, para. 145.

[316] *Methanex* v. *US*, Final Award, Part III – Chapter A – 51, para. 101.

[317] Royal Society: *Philosophical Transactions*: 350 years of publishing at the royal society (1665–2015), available at royalsociety.org/~/media/publishing350/publishing350-exhibition-catalogue.pdf (last accessed 20 January 2020).

[318] Jasanoff, *The Fifth Branch*, p. 61.

scientific journal. Notably, such a judicial reasoning functions as a checklist criterion, which can be utilized without scientific training. Whether the given evidence was subject to peer review or not is a binary question, which legal adjudicators could answer on their own without the need for actually understanding the subject-matter of the scientific debate itself.

2.2.2 STANDARDS ISSUED BY INTERNATIONAL EXPERT ORGANIZATIONS. Another possible argumentative practice that relies on non-scientific rationality to choose between scientific claims is to invoke standards issued by competent international organizations. The most articulate form of such a reasoning strategy is seen in WTO law and jurisprudence. Under Article 3.1 of the SPS Agreement, scientific risk assessments underlying SPS measures are presumed to be consistent with the agreement if they 'conform to' international standards, guidelines or recommendations. Similarly, Article 5 requires SPS measures to be 'based on' a risk assessment in which techniques developed by relevant international organizations should also be considered. World Trade Organization panels and the AB have therefore an express mandate to consider international standards as indicia of credible scientific opinions regarding environmental and health hazards.[319] Dispute settlement bodies refer to standards of international organization also outside the scope of the SPS Agreement. The GATT panel deciding the *Thailand – Cigarettes* dispute cited the opinion of the WHO as evidence of health hazards of smoking under Article XX of GATT.[320]

One may also find references to such standards in the jurisprudence of international courts that do not even have an express legal mandate to regard these standards decisive indicators of credible scientific positions. The ECtHR for instance cited opinions of the WHO and ILO in *Brincat and Others* v. *Malta*, as evidence of awareness of the health impacts of asbestos, which supported the applicant seeking redress to injuries suffered from asbestos exposure.[321] In *Fägerskiöld* v. *Sweden*, the ECtHR found an application inadmissible in relation to noise pollution, because it did not meet the threshold that the WTO classified as dangerous in its Guidelines for Community Noise.[322]

References to guidelines and reports issued by international organizations are ubiquitous in the case law of international adjudicatory bodies, ranging from detailed analysis to passing references in *obiter dicta* observations. As a survey among environmental judges of European national jurisdictions suggests, scientific standards of competent international and national institutions do inform domestic judicial inquiry as well. They are typically present as background elements in the courts' reasoning and assist judges in evaluating the scientific profile of disputes.[323]

---

[319] See inter alia *US – Animals*, Report of the Panel, WT/DS447/R (24 July 2015).
[320] *Thailand – Cigarettes*, Report of the Panel, DS10/R – 37S/200 (5 October 1990), para. 27.
[321] *Brincat and Others* v. *Malta*, paras. 38–40. For further examples see Chapter 5.
[322] *Fägerskiöld* v. *Sweden*, App. No.37664/04, Decision on admissibility (26 February 2008).
[323] K. Sulyok, F. Bögös, T. Paloniitty, and M. Eliantonio, Summary Report of the European Forum of Judges for the Environment – Answers to the questionnaire concerning the role of science in

A common thread in the above inquiries is that contrasting a given scientific evidence with such international standards does not necessitate scientific knowledge or literacy from adjudicators.

2.2.3 REGULATORY TRENDS OF OTHER STATES AS INDICIA OF LEGITIMATE SCIENTIFIC POSITION. One may also find subtle references to regulatory trends of other states as indicia of credible science. To take an example, the *Chemtura* Tribunal famously regarded the international regulatory trend banning lindane as persuasive indicia of genuine health risks posed by the chemical.[324] The tribunal was of the view that the host state's scientific evidence as to the seriousness of environmental risks was 'somewhat ambiguous'.[325] However, it concluded that 'irrespective of the state of the science'[326] the ban instituted with reference to scientific findings was nevertheless deemed legitimate because an increasing number of states enacted legislations regulating the chemical with a view to its risks on human health and the environment. This evaluation method is again rooted in legal logic attaching significance to the lawmaking of sovereign actors.

2.3 Hybrid Benchmarks: Bridging Scientific and Legal Reasoning

Among the standards of review set by international adjudicatory fora an idiosyncratic category can be discerned comprising judicial reviews that use benchmarks located on the border of scientific and legal analysis. Such adjudicatory reasoning techniques are termed here as relying on 'hybrid' yardsticks. This terminology may warrant further explanation. These standards of review are built on 'hybrid' concepts that can be appraised from a legal point of view, while are stemming from the science underlying the legal controversy. Notions such as reasonableness, consistency, or coherence are submitted to be 'boundary objects'[327] situated on the border the scientific and the legal realm.[328] Putting them in the centre of analysis allows adjudicators to reflect on scientific knowledge to some extent, while still speaking in the language of a legal assessment that fits in the epistemic competence of lawyer

environmental adjudication, 2019, p. 6, available at www.eufje.org/images/docConf/hel2019/Summary_report_Questionnaire_EUFJE2019.pdf (last accessed 17 January 2020).

[324] *Chemtura v. Canada*, Award, para. 135.

[325] *Chemtura v. Canada*, Award, para. 133.

[326] *Chemtura v. Canada*, Award, para. 135.

[327] S. L. Star and J. R. Griesemer, 'Institutional ecology, "translations" and boundary objects: amateurs and professionals in Berkeley's Museum of Vertebrate Zoology, 1907–39' (1989) 19 *Social Studies of Science* 397–420 at 393.

[328] The terminology of this study draws on literature from the philosophy of science. The term hybrid has been used by Bruno Latour in STS literature to describe hybrid constructs in which the scientific and the social aspects are inextricably entangled with each other. Also, Peter M. Haas distinguished hybrid facts from brute and social facts. Just like hybrid reasoning techniques, hybrid facts also 'stretch the reach' of a given expert community. See Latour, *We Have Never Been Modern*, p. 3; Haas, 'Ideas, experts and governance', p. 25.

adjudicators. Used in this sense, the hybrid nature of such reviews stands for bridging scientific and legal rationality in judicial reasoning. Importantly, this does not equal mixing different types of rationality, and hence, as will be argued, this reasoning style does not yield epistemically arbitrary decisions. Hybrid concepts form the basis of an essentially legalistic argumentation, and hence, can ultimately be traced back to legal rationality. The epistemic nature, possible application, as well as the benefits and trade-offs of using hybrid concepts in a judicial analysis will be explored more in depth in Chapter 10.

The forthcoming analysis focuses on 'hybrid' standards of reviews that have emerged in international environmental adjudication. As their shared feature, they all yield a more comprehensive review than the legalistic procedural benchmarks discussed above, as hybrid adjudicatory scrutiny may assess scientific claims from a substantive point of view. Relevant examples are the reasonableness assessment, which appeared in a decision of the ICJ and in the *Abyei* Arbitration (Subsection 3.3.1) and the coherence analysis of WTO dispute resolution bodies (Subsection 3.2.2). The discussion of these specific reviews will be followed by an overall assessment of the use of hybrid epistemic benchmarks in international adjudication (Subsection 3.2.3).

2.3.1 THE REASONABLENESS TEST. The ICJ coined the reasonableness test in the *Whaling in the Antarctic* judgment[329] as a standard of review for scrutinizing states' scientific claims, and Japan's appeal to the authoritative nature of scientific research more specifically. The reasonableness assessment is a stark example of using a hybrid standard of review to scrutinize scientific concepts. In the material case the Court reviewed whether there was a reasonable connection between the stated research objectives of Japan's whaling programme as well as its design and implementation.[330]

The judgment listed and examined several factors deemed relevant to decide whether the use of lethal methods could be 'reasonable' in a scientific whaling programme, such as the scale of lethal sampling, the methodology to select such sample sizes, the programme's scientific output, and the extent of international scientific co-operation in the programme.[331] The very fact that these factors largely overlap with the objective criteria of scientific research as advanced by Australia's scientific expert, confirms that the reasonableness test closely touches upon relevant scientific facts.

Emphatically, however, reasonableness is not a strict sense scientific concept, although as will be shown this quality is also relevant for crafting credible scientific reasoning.[332] As the notion of reasonableness is central to legal reasoning,[333] it is safely

[329]   *Whaling in the Antarctic*, Judgment, para. 67. For a more detailed discussion see in Chapter 3
        Section V.
[330]   *Whaling in the Antarctic*, Judgment, paras. 146–51.
[331]   *Whaling in the Antarctic*, Judgment, para. 88.
[332]   For a more detailed discussion see Chapter 10 Section II, Subsection 4.1.
[333]   Bertea, 'Certainty, reasonableness and argumentation in law'.

amenable to judicial evaluation. Judging the reasonableness of a scheme presupposes an act of balancing, which is at the heart of judicial decision-making. Judge Owada's rhetorical question seems to specifically point out, with a critical undertone, the hybrid nature of the reasonableness concept, when asks in his Dissenting Opinion: '[i]s it the legal context or is it the scientific context that the Court claims to be engaged in?'[334] In his reading, the two-faceted nature of the reasonableness test appears to be a sign of absurdity. However, as is argued here, hybrid reviews offer a persuasive argumentative technique enabling international judges to effectively adjudicate closely linked scientific and legal concepts. Viewing from this perspective, hybridity is to be seen as a virtue rather than a vice.

The *Abyei* Arbitration,[335] although concerns a boundary delimitation case and not an environmental dispute, also merits closer examination here as it applied the test of reasonableness too. The *Abyei* Tribunal conducted a highly technical assessment of evaluating whether scientific experts of the Abyei Boundaries Commission (ABC) exceeded their mandate. The ABC experts were tasked with defining and demarcating on map the boundaries of the relevant area of the nine Ngok Dinka chiefdoms transferred to Kordofan in 1905 'based on scientific analysis and research'.[336] Having delivered their report, the Government of Sudan were of the view that the ABC experts exceeded their mandate in delimiting the relevant area. The *Abyei* Tribunal thus had to define a standard of review towards assessing whether the experts correctly interpreted and implemented their mandate.

The panel approached this question in an essentially similar way as the ICJ did in the later *Whaling in the Antarctic*, and used the reasonableness test.[337] It opined that 'the articulation of reasons is the principal way by which reviewing bodies such as this Tribunal may ascertain reasonableness',[338] and hence focused its review on the reasoning of the experts. In appraising the appropriateness of the reasons provided, the tribunal ruled that the experts exceeded their mandate if their 'conclusions [were] unsupported by any reasons at all, if the reasoning [was] incoherent, or if the reasons provided [were] obviously contradictory or frivolous'.[339] Such a review shares the main epistemic characteristics of hybrid standards of review. At its core, the *Abyei* award interrogates how experts' scientific reasoning can be subjected to review by legal adjudicators, analogously to the legal dilemma entertained in *Whaling in the Antarctic*. The argumentation of the panel suggests that law's main expectation from scientific assessments lies in receiving coherent reasoning.

---

[334] *Whaling in the Antarctic*, Dissenting Opinion of Judge Owada, para. 25.
[335] *The Government of Sudan/The Sudan People's Liberation Movement/Army* (*Abyei* Arbitration) (Permanent Court of Arbitration), Final Award (22 July 2009).
[336] *Abyei* Arbitration, para. 521.
[337] *Abyei* Arbitration, paras. 486, 537.
[338] *Abyei* Arbitration, para. 534.
[339] *Abyei* Arbitration, para. 535.

2.3.2 THE COHERENCE REVIEW OF THE WTO DISPUTE SETTLEMENT BODIES. The WTO AB's prevailing standard of review shows some structural similarities to the reasonableness test. The AB mandated WTO panels to determine whether the risk assessment under scrutiny was supported by 'coherent reasoning and respectable scientific evidence and [was], in this sense, objectively justifiable'.[340] What is relevant for the present analysis is that reviewing the coherence of reasoning also functions as a hybrid standard of review. Argumentation theory, which interrogates how humans draw cognitive inferences in their reasoning has long studied the ways in which explanatory coherence is established in legal and scientific reasoning,[341] also attests the hybrid nature of this notion. This field of research suggests that coherence is an integral part of reasoning both in the scientific and the legal realm.[342] Consequently, by way of the coherency assessment, WTO panellists can set forth an essentially legalistic reasoning, which at the same time allows them to appreciate the scientific controversies involved in the underlying facts. Notably, incoherent reasoning can be detected from a *legal point of view*, in cases where the inferences drawn are not logical, the uncertainties are not revealed or neglected from the analysis, or where conclusions suffer from serious inconsistencies or gaps in the underlying facts. On balance, the 'coherence of the reasoning' review is a matter of legal judgment that is informed by scientific facts.

2.3.3 CONVERGENT SOLUTIONS FOR THE JUDICIAL REVIEW OF INTERTWINED SCIENTIFIC AND LEGAL ISSUES. The reasonableness and coherence tests appear to represent structurally similar answers to the dilemma of demarcating legal questions from the underlying scientific factual record for purposes of the judicial review. Their convergence is especially striking if one considers that another similar argumentative tool also appeared on the international stage in the practice of the judiciary of the European Union. The Court of First Instance (CFI) crafted a consistency assessment in *Pfizer* in the context of the judicial review of risk assessments carried out by EU institutions. The CFI announced that if risk assessors were to rely on an expert opinion, they had to 'assess the probative value of the [expert] opinion delivered' in which regard they had to ensure that 'the reasoning in the opinion [was] full, consistent and relevant'.[343] Later, in *Artegodan* the CFI reinforced that its review scrutinized 'the internal consistency of the opinion and the statement of reasons contained therein'.[344] The EU judiciary therefore construes

---

[340]　*US – Continued Suspension of Obligations*, AB Report, para. 590.

[341]　P. Thagard, 'Explanatory coherence' in J. E. Adler and L. J. Rips (eds.), *Reasoning: Studies of Human Inference and Its Foundations* (Cambridge University Press, 2008), pp. 471–513.

[342]　Thagard, 'Explanatory coherence', pp. 473–5.

[343]　*Pfizer Animal Health SA* v. *Council of the European Union*, Judgment of the Court, C T-13/99, Court of First Instance (Third Chamber) (11 September 2002), para. 198.

[344]　*Artegodan GmbH and Others* v. *Commission of the European Communities*, Judgment of the Court, Case T-74/00, Court of First Instance (Second Chamber, extended composition) (26 November 2002), para. 200.

its task as to examine whether an expert opinion accepted in a risk assessment decision 'contains a statement of reasons from which it is possible to ascertain the considerations on which the opinion is based, and whether it establishes a comprehensible link between the medical and/or scientific findings and its conclusions'[345] in the context of assessing the lawfulness of the decision.

Notably, this consistency review also functions as a hybrid scrutiny, as it mandates adjudicators to review the logical consistency of an expert report, which necessarily includes looking at the *scientific* subject matter of evaluation. At the same time, the test interrogates the *logical* consistency of the risk assessor's reasoning, the interpretation of which is commonplace in judicial argumentation. In conducting such an analysis, the CFI has also been carefully meandering on the border of legal and scientific appraisal, in order not to substitute the experts' assessment with its own view on the hazards involved, since such decision is emphatically reserved for primary risk assessors.

The reasonableness, coherence, and consistency tests though are couched slightly differently, bear resemblance to an extent that one may wonder whether they were modelled after each other, or are results of convergent evolution. Indeed, they represent essentially similar solutions for the cross-cutting challenge of science-intensive judicial review, only have been tailored to the specificities of each adjudicatory body's mandate and the applicable law. Chronologically first in line, the EU judiciary employed the consistency review in *Pfizer* in 2002, which was followed by the WTO AB's coherence review in 2008. The reasonableness test first appeared in the *Abyei* Arbitration in 2009 and was used later in the ICJ's judgment in 2014. The genesis of the reasonableness test in *Whaling in the Antarctic* is, however, unclear. The epistemic context in which the *Abyei* Tribunal conducted its reasonableness assessment was quite similar to the ICJ's dilemma in *Whaling* inasmuch as both cases ultimately concerned the way in which legal adjudicators could review the acceptability of a reasoning provided by scientific experts. In light of this, assuming cross-fertilization between the two judicial bodies may be a plausible assumption. Yet, Judge Owada in his Dissenting Opinion hinted that the reasonableness standard of review 'derive[d] its origin'[346] from the WTO jurisprudence.[347] Be that as it may, save for this occasion, there is no express indication in respective decisions of any co-ordination in terms of crafting similar hybrid standards of review.

Interestingly, investment arbitration tribunals remain more conservative in this respect and confine their inquiry solely to scrutinizing procedural aspects of scientific regulatory processes.[348] They normally choose to focus exclusively on the

---

[345] *Artegodan GmbH and Others v. Commission of the European Communities*, para. 200.

[346] *Whaling in the Antarctic*, Dissenting Opinion of Judge Owada, para. 33.

[347] Japan's position favouring a coherence review conducted by WTO panels has been reiterated in *Whaling in the Antarctic*, Judgment, para. 66. For more details see discussion in Chapter 3 Section V, Subsection 2.2.

[348] Gruszczynski, 'Standard of review and scientific evidence in WTO law and international investment arbitration', p. 170.

procedure in which scientific evidence was produced, and do not interrogate the coherence or consistency of risk assessments. This can be partly explained by the applicable law. Notably, no express scientific legality criteria are enshrined in investment treaties, whereas those are ubiquitous under WTO law. Also, legitimacy deficit of investment arbitration is undoubtedly relevant with respect to their evasive attitude towards conducting intrusive scrutiny of states' regulatory science and science-based decisions.

2.4 Standards of Review Based on Intuitive Rationality: Semantic Analysis

A fourth possible argumentative method for judging the acceptability of a scientific claim is to engage in a semantic analysis. In such cases adjudicators zero in on the contextual interpretation of the legal rule in which the relevant scientific notion is embedded. When adjudicators focus on the textual interpretation of phrases surrounding a scientific concept, their decisions are in fact justified by a purely grammatical-logical reasoning, which appeals to everyday, thus intuitive, rationality.

Two examples of semantic analysis are apparent in the standards of review of relevant international fora. The first can be derived from WTO jurisprudence, as panels are sometimes assessing whether a certain SPS measure 'conforms to' international standards or has been 'based on' a risk assessment.[349] This semantic reasoning flows from an explicit mandate enshrined in the SPS Agreement, which provides a convenient basis for panels to decide the acceptability of science-based SPS measures without interrogating their scientific bases. Adjudicators need only to scrutinize through grammatical interpretation whether the circumstances allow making an inference that respective measures were based on or conformed to a certain scientific standard.[350]

The second example is drawn from the ICJ's case law, particularly from the *Whaling in the Antarctic* judgment. Here the Court instead of focusing on the content and meaning of scientific research, took a different argumentative path and mainly expounded the context in which this notion was embedded, namely, Article VIII of the ICRW. The relevant provision reads as follows: 'any Contracting Government may grant to any of its nationals a special permit authorizing that national to kill, take and treat whales for purposes of scientific research'. The Court explicitly stressed that it did not need to 'pass judgment on the scientific merit or importance of those [research] objectives in order to assess the purpose of the killing of whales'.[351] As has been discussed earlier, while the parties focused primarily on competing definitions of scientific research, the ICJ mainly dealt with interpreting the 'for purposes of' part of the ICRW provision, and discerned the test of reasonableness from that phrase. This semantic analysis not only saved the Court from

---

[349] For more details see discussion in Chapter 6 Section III, Subsection 5.3.
[350] For relevant examples see Chapter 6 Section III, Subsection 5.3.
[351] *Whaling in the Antarctic*, Judgment, para. 88.

judging the scientific merits of a whaling programme, but also enabled judges to provide a reasoning still speaking in the language of a grammatical assessment, the persuasiveness of which is rooted in intuitive rationality. Further benefits of relying on similar intuitive styles of reasoning will be discussed in Chapter 10.

VI CONCLUDING REMARKS: WHERE DO INTERNATIONAL COURTS STAND WITH SCIENCE?

The above survey sought to lay out a cartography of varied judicial tools international fora employ to adjust the level of science that may enter their deliberations across different stages of adjudication. What can be discerned from this comparative exercise on the highest level of generality is that while certain methods serve to impede the intrusion of science into the legally relevant aspects of the judicial inquiry, others aim to integrate scientific knowledge in the adjudicatory process. This points to the existence of two opposite trends in the willingness of international courts and tribunals to engage with science in environmental disputes. The table below provides a summary of the various adjudicatory techniques yielding parallel trends in international adjudicative practice.

As Table 9.1 illustrates, adjudicatory tools leading to downplaying science in the judicial inquiry, as well as those that seek to integrate scientific knowledge are dispersed in the practice of international judicial fora. Scientific downplaying techniques are also scattered across the various stages of the adjudicatory process. To illustrate it with a hypothetical example, a certain court may apply framing techniques that regard science-heavy aspects be part of the legally relevant dimensions, while the same judicial body may choose to circumvent scientific facts in its causal inquiry.

Nevertheless, we may distinguish between more open and more reluctant fora towards appreciating and dealing with the scientific aspects of disputes. As a general rule, those adjudicative bodies seem to most readily engage with science that expound legal texts explicitly incorporating scientific legality criteria such as WTO dispute resolution bodies. Whereas those fora have been more reluctant to conduct in-depth scientific inquires, which were taken almost by surprise when respective parties started to submit science-heavy arguments and bulky, highly technical evidence. The most illustrative of such behaviour is perhaps the slowly evolving scientific engagement of the ICJ, which initially was highly reluctant to consider scientific evidence, yet it is gradually becoming more open towards science in its recent jurisprudence.

Moreover, usually those fora are more inclined to conduct a thorough engagement with science that have a broadly construed mandate, as opposed to courts and tribunals with a narrowly construed mandate. The latter seem to experience legitimacy deficit discouraging them from digging deep into highly technical scientific arguments of litigants. The case-practice of investment arbitral tribunals serves as an apposite example for such a judicial treatment of science.

TABLE 9.1 *Adjudicatory techniques that downplay or seek to integrate scientific knowledge in the judicial inquiry on the different stages of the adjudicatory process, with examples of relevant fora*

Different adjudicatory stages	Judicial techniques integrating science in the judicial inquiry/ reasoning	Judicial techniques downplaying science
Framing of disputes	treating science-intensive questions as justiciable issues	non-justiciability of scientific legal disputes
	treating scientific evidence as relevant to the legal controversy	deferring science-intensive aspects of disputes to the merits phase, which will not be reached out of a judicial choice (ICJ)
	giving proper weight to substantive obligations and willingness to find such breaches established (inter-state arbitration)	carving out science from the relevant aspects of adjudicatory decision (ICJ)
	mandating expert-led consultations (ICJ, ITLOS)	referring science-intensive questions back to the parties' negotiation (ICJ, inter-state arbitration)
	using science as a neutralizer of conflicts (inter-state arbitration)	prioritizing procedural obligations over substantive obligations (ICJ, ITLOS)
	scientific review mechanisms (inter-state arbitration)	decoupling 'risk' from science (ICJ)
	performing the judicial task despite uncertainty (investment arbitration, ICJ)	precautionary principle (ITLOS, ECtHR)
	science as an indicium of non-arbitrariness	declining to second-guess scientific truth (investment arbitration, WTO)
Scientific fact-finding	*ex curia* experts (PCA, WTO)	not evaluating expert evidence (ICJ, ECtHR)
	independent experts (UNCC)	experts as counsels (ICJ)
	expert arbitrators (PCA)	letting partisan evidence go unchecked (ICJ (initial), investment arbitration)
	shadow experts (ICJ, ITLOS)	not using existing powers to appoint independent experts (ITLOS, ICJ, ECtHR)

TABLE 9.1 *(continued)*

Different adjudicatory stages	Judicial techniques integrating science in the judicial inquiry/ reasoning	Judicial techniques downplaying science
		second-order indicators (ICJ, ITLOS, ECOWAS Court, ACtHPR)
Causal inquiry	causal presumption (Marshall Island Claims Tribunal, ECtHR)	too-high standard of proof, refuting probabilistic evidence (ECtHR, ICJ)
	relaxing causal tests (climate change litigation, US tort law)	causal proxies (ECtHR)
	accepting probabilistic causal proof, use of mathematical models (UNCC, US tort law)	
Standard of review	hybrid benchmarks: coherence (WTO), reasonableness (ICJ, PCA), consistency analysis (EU courts)	total deference
		international standards and regulatory trends as indicia of scientific credibility (ISDS, WTO)
		scientific due process (investment arbitration)
		semantic analysis (WTO, ICJ)

In levelling these comparative remarks, it remains to be emphasized once again that the underlying law or the procedural powers granted to international courts and tribunals, although important features, do not in themselves determine the extent to which scientific aspects of a legal dispute will be appreciated. The analytic chapters have offered numerous illustrations for instances, when courts opted for not utilizing their evidentiary powers or chose an argumentative path that marginalized science in the assessment. It follows that the overall extent to which the scientific profile of disputes will be appreciated is dependent upon the readiness of international adjudicators to 'get their hands dirty' with science. This comparative survey also demonstrates that adjudicators apply different argumentative techniques to build their reasoning in cases with substantial scientific dimensions, depending on the extent to which they are willing to engage with science. This segues into Chapter 10, which discusses systematically the benefits and trade-offs of each scientific as well as non-scientific argumentative technique with respect to preserving and promoting the legitimacy of judicial reasoning.

10

Science and the Legitimacy of Judicial Reasoning

Is it the legal context or is it the scientific context that the Court claims to be engaged in?[1]

Judge Owada, 2014

The preceding chapters demonstrated that the intrusion of scientific facts and arguments impacts the adjudicatory process in many ways. We have seen how international judges adjust the science-intensity of their assessments through traditional adjudicatory techniques, such as the framing of disputes, scientific fact-finding, causal inquiry, and setting the standard of review. The overall goal of canvassing the divergent roles judges assign to science in their inquiry is to map the argumentative space of judges by enumerating the possible styles of reasoning, which respect the epistemic authority of science and also fit in the competence of legal adjudicators.

Against this backdrop, the ultimate question this book seeks to answer is how environmental disputes, closely tied to scientific facts, can be legitimately and persuasively adjudicated – with or without directly relying on scientific rationality in the judicial reasoning. Do judges always have to be concerned with scientific methodologies and the soundness of opinions that underlie the parties' science-based arguments? Or can they turn away from scientific rationality and create presumptions under legal logic to accept or refuse a science-based claim, and if so, under what circumstances? And finally, when is it legitimate for judges to interrogate the reasonableness or the coherence of a science-based argument?

This chapter will show that the differing extent to which science is allowed to enter the judicial process warrants different reasoning techniques in order to preserve the legitimacy of the judgment. Section I will centre on revealing the interplay between science and the legitimacy of judicial reasoning. More specifically, it will contend that the extent to which science is incorporated in the judicial reasoning impacts the persuasiveness and legitimacy of the resulting judgment. Section II will examine the different rationalities on the basis of which adjudicators may justify

[1] *Whaling in the Antarctic (Australia v. Japan: New Zealand intervening)* (Judgment) (2014) ICJ Rep 226, Dissenting Opinion of Judge Owada, para. 25.

their findings concerning scientific facts and science-based arguments. This analysis will distinguish four main reasoning styles appealing to different types of rationality and will identify and discuss idiosyncratic risks and advantages of each of these argumentative techniques. In Section III, the chapter will conclude with offering some general recommendations for selecting the most appropriate reasoning style in order to ensure a solid approach to science under various factual circumstances and institutional arrangements.

I SCIENCE IN THE JUDICIAL REASONING: IMPLICATIONS FOR LEGITIMACY

Conforming to science in a judicial decision can be a basis for claiming legitimacy. Yet, in order for international courts to harness this opportunity, they not only need to gather expert evidence, but also have to reflect on scientific insights while drawing inferences in their decisions. Therefore, our focus henceforth will be on judicial reasoning, that is, explanations adjudicators provide for their findings. Reasoning, broadly defined, stands for 'a process of thought, where some beliefs (or thoughts) provide the ground or reason for coming to another'.[2] Judicial reasoning is a specific subset of practical reasoning with a peculiar purpose to resolve litigants' conflict in a final and authoritative manner.[3] The authority and persuasiveness of a judicial decision is therefore rooted in its reasoning, which serves to lay out sound justifications for the decision rendered.

Crafting judicial reasoning is both a prerogative and an obligation of courts. Drawing inferences from the law and facts as they deem fit is the essence of the power and discretion of judges with respect to a given controversy. At the same time, providing a reasoning is also warranted by the duty to give reasons for adjudicatory decisions, which aims to guard against arbitrary decision-making.[4] Requiring judges to reveal the grounds and *ratio* of their inferences renders the decision open to challenge and critique of the wider public, which ultimately fosters judicial accountability. Justifying judicial findings is therefore critical to the sociological legitimacy of respective fora, as the losing party and even the public[5] would not accept a decision as just and appropriate if the underlying reasons are not clearly and adequately explained therein.[6]

---

[2] J. E. Adler, 'Introduction: philosophical foundations' in J. E. Adler and L. J. Rips (eds.), *Reasoning: Studies of Human Inference and Its Foundations* (Cambridge University Press, 2008), pp. 1–34 p. 1.

[3] Dwyer, *The Judicial Assessment of Expert Evidence*, p. 71.

[4] Dwyer, *The Judicial Assessment of Expert Evidence*, p. 39; R. B. Stewart, 'Remedying disregard in global regulatory governance: accountability, Participation, and responsiveness' (2014) *American Journal of International Law* 211–70 at 252.

[5] T. Blackshield, 'Judicial reasoning' in T. Blackshield, M. Coper, and G. Williams (eds.), *The Oxford Companion to the High Court of Australia* (Oxford University Press, 2007), pp. 373–6.

[6] I. Griss, 'How judges think: judicial reasoning in tort cases from a comparative perspective' (2013) 4 *Journal of European Tort Law* 247–58 at 250.

It flows from the above that irrespective of the substance of a decision, the style of reasoning is in itself decisive for the legitimacy of the judgment. As has already been discussed,[7] the legitimacy of exercising judicial authority is closely tied to the quality of the reasoning.[8] Decisions that conform to ideals of neutrality, rationality, and clarity are normally seen as conferring legitimacy on the decision-maker.[9] The presence of scientific facts in a legal dispute, however, complicates matters for accruing such legitimacy. The volatile and non-conclusive nature of scientific knowledge renders appealing to ideals of legitimacy a more intricate task for judicial findings. Adjudicators can nonetheless benefit from referring to scientific arguments in their reasoning, for doing so can buttress the appearance of objectivity and rationality with respect to the decision.

Respecting and conforming to scientific knowledge can thus be an important basis for claiming legitimacy. Whether courts can successfully do so, ultimately depends on the modalities with which they incorporate science in the judicial assessment. In order to confer objectivity upon a judicial finding relating to the scientific profile of disputes, it must be based on a 'careful consideration of relevant facts'.[10] Consequently, automatically accepting a given scientific position or superficially examining scientific evidence do not suffice for securing legitimacy for the reasoning. As I shall argue later on, fulfilling the above mandate requires no less from adjudicators than developing a basic understanding of the scientific subject-matter underlying the legal controversy.

The aforementioned considerations point to a close dependency of the legitimacy of a decision on the adequate treatment of scientific arguments in the reasoning. The interplay between scientific expertise and the legitimacy of judgments has been traditionally approached through the lenses of input and output legitimacy. Input legitimacy posits that decisions made with reliance on expert advice are generally considered more rational and objective – therefore, more legitimate. Output legitimacy describes the view that expert involvement leads to better decisions, thus, it scaffolds the legitimacy of a judgment. Importantly, however, relying on expertise enhances the legitimacy of judicial decisions only if expert opinions are 'properly assessed and incorporated'[11] in the judgment. This specific aspect of legitimacy, namely, epistemic legitimacy, stands in the focus of this study, which requires that judgments properly account for the logic of scientific knowledge. Put it at its most straightforward, epistemic legitimacy of a decision is strengthened if adjudicators are able to harness, or at a minimum respect, the cognitive authority of science.

[7] See Chapter 2 Section III, Subsection 2.
[8] E. Voeten, 'International judicial behavior' in C. Romano, K. J. Alter, and Y. Shany (eds.), *The Oxford Handbook of International Adjudication* (Oxford University Press, 2014), pp. 550–68 p. 556.
[9] For this argument in the context of governance studies see D. C. Esty, 'Good governance at the World Trade Organization: building a foundation of administrative law' (2007) 10 *Journal of International Economic Law* 509–27 at 517–20.
[10] Esty, 'Good governance at the World Trade Organization', 517.
[11] Lawrence, 'The structural logic of expert participation in WTO decision-making process', p. 173.

Whereas if judges disregard or reflect on science in inadequate ways, their reasoning easily becomes inaccurate and unconvincing.

It flows from the above that the degree to which science is allowed to intrude the adjudicatory process will have implications for the array of (epistemically) legitimate reasoning styles that are available in the argumentative toolkit of courts and tribunals. It is proposed here that different scientific engagement techniques of courts invite differing methods of adjudicatory reasoning in order to give a persuasive account of the relevant facts and their legal implications. This book suggests that marginalizing science in the adjudicatory reasoning triggers a corresponding need for finding additional rationalities, that is, cognitively or intuitively appealing principles, which can underpin judges' final conclusions. In certain cases, providing non-scientific, that is, legalistic or intuitive justifications for science-based findings can be a legitimate reasoning technique. Yet the forthcoming analysis will also point out factual circumstances, when replacing scientific rationality erodes the factual accuracy of decisions and thereby decreases their legitimacy. As an alternative, judges may rely on scientific rationality by directly incorporating scientific knowledge in the judicial appraisal. As will be shown, both argumentative pathways entail idiosyncratic challenges for preserving the epistemic legitimacy of the decision.

It is important to emphasize at this point that using more science would not necessarily result in better reasoned and, hence, epistemically more legitimate judgments. The central issue in this respect is *how* adjudicators reflect on the scientific dimensions of disputes, and what type of rationality they appeal to under the given circumstances of specific cases. This guides our investigation into the field of epistemology, which is traditionally concerned with understanding how one knows or justifiably believes that a specific event occurred. In the context of judicial inquiry, this question formulates as how adjudicators can justifiably reason that X happened, as a result of which X is to be accepted as the factual basis of a legal claim.

In the narrower field of investigation of this book, that is, science-intensive adjudication, the key epistemological questions are the following: can one (justifiably, hence, legitimately) reason *against* scientific authority in a legal judgment? Can a non-scientist adjudicator (justifiably, hence, legitimately) reason *with* scientific knowledge, and if so, under what circumstances? And finally, based on what epistemic justifications can a legal adjudicator justifiably argue for accepting or rejecting a science-based claim? Our inquiry into the interrelation of science, legitimacy, and judicial reasoning shall now entertain these epistemological questions.

The ensuing analysis will in this vein offer an overview of the diverse argumentative practices with which adjudicators may justify their choices between science-intensive arguments while seeking to resolve disputes involving closely intertwined scientific and legal authority. These reasoning techniques are markedly different in terms of their underlying rationality; and the rationality available to judges in a given case is conditioned upon whether they integrated or downplayed the weight of science in their legal assessment.

II HOW CAN COURTS CRAFT LEGITIMATE REASONING IN SCIENCE-INTENSIVE CASES?

The comparative survey of environmental decisions set forth in Chapter 9 suggests that judges may give convincing reasons for their choices between competing science-based claims not only by appealing to scientific authority (and thereby trying to approximate their positions to 'the scientifically correct' answer to the underlying dilemma), but also via non-scientific rationality, typically legal and intuitive reasoning. The forthcoming analysis will analytically examine these reasoning styles built upon scientific, legal, hybrid, and intuitive epistemic authority.

Importantly, there is no abstract hierarchy between these modes of reasoning[12] and none of them is immune to epistemic challenges. In respect of relying on scientific rationality the challenge lies in ensuring that adjudicators are equipped with requisite internal epistemic capacities to understand the scientific points of contention. Otherwise, they would easily make epistemically arbitrary choices between two conflicting scientific claims, by judging the validity of scientific knowledge according to legal rationality. Invoking non-scientific rationality, either legal or intuitive benchmarks, may equally jeopardize the legitimacy of reasoning. Such a reasoning can in some cases contravene scientific knowledge concerning the factual realities of a dispute's scientific subject-matter. To guard against such a possibility, reasoners ought to be able to identify situations when relying on non-scientific yardsticks does not repudiate scientific logic. Making this judgment call equally necessitates that judges familiarize themselves with the scientific dimensions of disputes.

A more fine-grained analysis reveals further idiosyncratic benefits and trade-offs regarding each argumentative style in terms of ensuring factual accuracy, epistemic non-arbitrariness, practical feasibility, and preserving judicial control over the resolution of the dispute. The advantages and disadvantages associated with different reasoning techniques are addressed in the sections that follow.

1 *Appealing to Scientific Rationality*

Adjudicatory decisions may directly draw on the cognitive power of science to justify a particular choice between rival science-based arguments. In such cases, scientific authority directly supports the persuasiveness of adjudicatory assessment, as scientific standards and methods lie in the background to the judicial conclusions. These

---

[12] D'Aspremont and Mbengue, 'Strategies of engagement with scientific fact-finding in international adjudication', 271.

argumentative techniques are epistemically deferential to science, as science provides the ultimate benchmark against which the parties' claims are measured. A corollary of such an approach is a close reliance on experts, who speak to the court on behalf of the scientific community, when they evaluate the scientific veracity of competing scientific submissions.

'Outsourcing'[13] the scientific validity inquiry to experts has been an established practice both on the national and international level. On the international stage, the WTO has been known for embracing such an approach to the widest extent. In initial decisions, panels were required to review whether a given scientific evidence conformed to 'standards of the relevant scientific community' and was reflecting accepted 'methodological rigor'.[14] This attitude is consonant with prior domestic law solutions in the United States, where an admissibility test for scientific evidence was announced in 1923 in *Frye*, according to which a piece of scientific evidence had to be 'sufficiently established to have gained general acceptance in the particular field in which it belongs'.[15] Common to these reasoning methods is that they instruct adjudicators to blindly follow the opinion of relevant scientists on the acceptability of evidence.

Another argumentative appeal to scientific rationality, where judicial authority automatically adopts an expert position as its own without a meaningful scrutiny, occurs when international tribunals prescribe expert-led consultation for litigants in order to reach a mutually agreeable solution. Relevant case law demonstrates that international judges in such cases unconditionally give credit to solutions advised by scientists and simply reiterate their positions on scientific matters in concluding the legal proceedings.[16]

1.1 Benefits and Trade-Offs of Relying on Scientific Epistemic Standards

Invoking scientific authority in adjudicatory assessments brings a number of benefits. First of all, aligning judicial findings with state-of-the-art science is an important ground for claiming legitimacy for the decision. Reasoning with science-based arguments bestows an overall appearance of objectivity and neutrality on the legal

---

[13] D'Aspremont and Mbengue, 'Strategies of engagement with scientific fact-finding in international adjudication', 258–63.

[14] *US – Continued Suspension of Obligations* case, Report of the AB, WT/DS320/AB/R (16 October 2008), para. 591. For more details see Chapter 9 Section V, Subsection 2.1.

[15] *Frye v. United States*, 54 App. D.C. 46, 293 F. 1014 (1923). This approached was later abandoned by US courts, and has been replaced by the so-called Daubert standard, stipulating among others a peer review criterion for the admissibility of expert evidence, see *Daubert v. Merrell Dow Pharmaceuticals, Inc.*, 509 US 579 (1993).

[16] See for example, *Conservation and Sustainable Exploitation of Swordfish Stocks in the South-Eastern Pacific Ocean (Chile/European Union)* (Order) ITLOS No. 7 (16 December 2009); *Straits of Johor (Singapore v. Malaysia)* (Provisional Measures) ITLOS No. 12 (8 October 2003), for a more detailed analysis see Chapter 9 Section II, Subsection 2.1.

decision and allows judicial reasoners to harness the cognitive authority of science. The perceived objectivity of scientific knowledge translates into a number of strategic applications of science by courts and tribunals in framing their legal inquiry. Specific examples have already been addressed in detail.[17]

A more specific advantage of such a reasoning style is that it scores high in terms of factual accuracy. Judgments that draw on thorough evidentiary assessment are generally considered persuasive. Further to that, this argumentative practice observes the imperative of epistemic non-arbitrariness, that is, it does not mix legal and scientific rationality.[18] Indeed, relying on scientific benchmarks in judicial reasoning enables adjudicators to clearly delineate the questions, in which they epistemically defer to the assessment of scientific experts. In other words, adjudicators in such cases do not judge the validity of scientific standards according to their own logic and rationality, but rely on expert advice thereby observing the criterion of epistemic non-arbitrariness.

This virtue, however, may become a vice as it opens the door to concerns about inadvertent delegation, or even abdication[19] of adjudicatory power to non-elected experts, who are in possession of the epistemic competence necessary to evaluate the relevant scientific yardstick. A further downside relates to practical feasibility. Lengthy and costly evidentiary proceedings may not be available in a given dispute due to either financial constraints or because of the time pressure under which adjudicators operate. An additional challenge is posed by partisan evidence, that is, when the parties submit highly distorted data, and thereby abuse the cognitive authority of science. Such attempts have been flagged earlier in the practice of investment arbitration[20] and inter-state litigation[21] as well.

It is to be noted, that epistemically radically deferent rationality may not even yield a final legal answer. In many cases, '[d]eferring to science … cannot solve the relevant legal question, although it can produce a wealth of impressive sounding information'.[22] This is especially true for disputes concerning scientific risk assessments, which are in fact a composition of value judgments and scientific factual determinations. Moreover, in evidentiary procedures, it is ultimately the task of adjudicators to become ascertained about the facts of the case, even if they choose to

---

[17] For an overview of relevant decisions see Chapter 9 Section II, Subsection 2.

[18] D'Aspremont and Mbengue, 'Strategies of engagement with scientific fact-finding in international adjudication', 268.

[19] Mbengue, 'The South China Sea arbitration: innovations in marine environmental fact-finding and due diligence obligations', 289.

[20] See for example, the *Perenco* case, where the panel expressed its discontent with an expert, who 'crossed the boundary between professional objective analysis and party representation'. *Perenco Ecuador Ltd.* v. *The Republic of Ecuador and Empresa Estatal Petróleos del Ecuador (Petroecuador)*, ICSID Case No. ARB/08/6, Award (27 September 2019), para. 581.

[21] See for example the *Pulp Mills* case, where scientists appeared as counsels, which solution was criticized by the Court. *Pulp Mills on the River Uruguay (Argentina* v. *Uruguay)* (Judgment) (2010) ICJ Rep 14, para. 167.

[22] R. Feldman, *The Role of Science in Law* (Oxford University Press, 2009), p. 42.

defer to expert opinions. Hence, deference to scientific standards is usually not the end of a judicial inquiry and it cannot absolve adjudicators from their responsibility to engage with the substance of expert evidence.

Another possible problem emerges if adjudicators provide only poor evidentiary findings when dealing with expert evidence. International adjudicators all too often 'camouflage'[23] their opinions with rough assessments of the scientific information.[24] In such a case they are not able to harness the cognitive authority of science for their findings, as this reasoning technique altogether erodes the persuasiveness of adjudicatory decisions. This is typically the case when the judicial reasoning as to the weighing of evidence does not even remotely resemble the level of detail in which the experts submitted their opinions. Suffice it to refer to the *Pulp Mills* case, where lengthy evidence was dismissed summarily in merely one sentence not specifying the exact reasons for the dismissal. The ICJ merely kept repeating in slightly different textual variations that causality and adequate proof have not been 'established to the satisfaction of the Court'.[25]

In searching for an epistemically more legitimate way of appraising scientific evidence, the judiciary of the EU may provide a good judicial practice. In the judicial review of scientific risk assessment decisions, EU courts have explicitly ruled that should the primary risk assessor disregard an expert opinion in its assessment, it shall provide specific reasons that 'must be of a scientific level at least commensurate with that of the opinion'.[26] This requirement effectively guards against superficial evidentiary findings.

1.2 Possible Remedies to the Epistemic Risks of Scientific Reasoning Style

In the face of the above challenges, some remedies may still be offered for abating the risks of eroding the legitimacy of reasoning with scientific authority. First of all, epistemic capabilities of courts and tribunals could be buttressed through various procedural avenues. Increasing the internal scientific capacities of judges on the bench is therefore one of the applicable remedies. While some are sceptical about the capabilities of international judges to cope with the scientific dimension of disputes,[27] others are more optimistic and suggest that scientific training for judges in natural sciences may be an appropriate tool to improve their ability to engage with scientific evidence.[28] Judges hearing scientific disputes in European jurisdictions

---

[23] Viñuales, 'Observations sur le traitement des motifs scientifiques dans le contentieux environnemental international', p. 114.

[24] Viñuales, 'Observations sur le traitement des motifs scientifiques dans le contentieux environnemental international', p. 115.

[25] *Pulp Mills*, Judgment, para. 250.

[26] *Pfizer Animal Health SA* v. *Council of the European Union*, Judgment, T-13/99, Court of First Instance (Third Chamber) (11 September 2002), para. 199.

[27] Sands, 'International environmental litigation and its future', 1638.

[28] Bruce, 'The project for an international environmental court', p. 146.

are generally optimistic about the potential of organizing scientific training for judges and/or staff members for enhancing the scientific capacities of courts.[29]

Relying on *ex curia* experts, or expert arbitrators, could be a further avenue for strengthening the fact-finding capabilities of international courts. These practices can support courts in formulating their own understanding of the scientific dimensions of disputes and thereby save them from getting entangled in a battle of experts, which would compromise both the evidentiary credibility and the epistemic gains of the fact-finding process.[30] Yet, as we have seen in Chapter 9, the overwhelming majority of international adjudicative fora feel uncomfortable to utilize their existing powers of appointing *ex curia* experts, and there is still considerable uncertainty as to the desired role and tasks of independent experts in international court proceedings.

In certain scenarios, adjudicators can appeal to scientific authority without the need to develop heightened scientific capacities for in-depth fact-finding. This is possible when judges mandate expert-led negotiations for the litigants to solve their science-based controversy themselves. Such a scheme also effectively guards against expert bias as experts are appointed by the parties on a consensual basis, and any scientific disagreement can be adequately negotiated during the consultation process. Adjudicators hence will be put in a comfortable position to issue a decision that is built on mutually accepted scientific bases that are seen by litigants as legitimate and acceptable without the need to resolve any contradictions between expert submissions.

2 *Relying on Purely Legal Rationality in Judicial Reasoning*

When adjudicators do not directly rely on scientific knowledge to formulate findings relating to the scientific aspects of disputes, they need to appeal to non-scientific authority as a basis for justification. For one, they may rely on legal rationality. There is a wide array of possible tools to justify adjudicatory choices among competing scientific claims with reference to standards that are deemed authoritative by virtue of legal logic. The language of law yields an idiosyncratic reasoning technique that may not always be intelligible or persuasive to legally non-trained reasoners. Some even suggests that law speaks its own language creating a separate 'esoteric legal reality'.[31] The specificities of legal logic prompts distinguishing legalistic reasoning

[29] In a survey among environmental judges in European jurisdictions, the majority of respondents favoured training for judges and/or staff in environmental sciences in order to enhance courts' abilities to better adjudicate environmental cases. See K. Sulyok, F. Bögös, T. Paloniitty, and M. Eliantonio, Summary Report of the European Forum of Judges for the Environment, Answers to the questionnaire concerning the role of science in environmental adjudication, 2019, page 26, available at https://bit.ly/2TYpG2H (last accessed 18 January 2020).

[30] Perez, 'Judicial strategies for reviewing conflicting expert evidence', 107.

[31] P. Allott, 'Interpretation: an exact art' in A. Bianchi, D. Peat, and M. Windsor (eds.), *Interpretation in International Law* (Oxford University Press, 2015), pp. 373–92 p. 384.

style from other non-scientific argumentative practices, such as common-sense reasoning.

Applying legalistic reasoning typically warrants a legally trained reasoner, as these tools often operate according to peculiar rules that are alien and enigmatic for lay reasoners. For instance, presumptions are constructions that create a relevant connection between two facts (e.g. between a pollution and a health injury) for *purposes of the legal analysis*, even if relevant scientific facts, in fact, fall short of proving such a connection. Similarly, checking certain due process criteria in relation to the production of scientific knowledge operates as a quasi-presumption, because if requisite procedural benchmarks are met, adjudicators presume that the substantive scientific outcome of that process is credible, legitimate, and therefore acceptable in a litigation. What is noteworthy in this respect is that such an argumentation, which evaluates the substance of a scientific argument based solely on procedural qualities may prove unconvincing to layman reasoners.

Emphatically, yardsticks based on legal rationality ultimately could also be traced back to scientific knowledge, but building a reasoning on them does not necessitate scientific competence, and therefore, they function as non-scientific benchmarks. Specific illustrations for the scientific bases of legal argumentative tools will be addressed in Subsections 2.1.1–2.1.3.

2.1 Advantages and Disadvantages of Relying on Legal Benchmarks in the Judicial Assessment

Generally speaking, legalistic reasoning is deemed advantageous because it enables adjudicators to preserve their monopoly over the dispute resolution in an epistemically non-arbitrary way, as its use does not necessitate passing legal judgments about the veracity of scientific knowledge claims. Moreover, adjudicators can comfortably apply such reasoning style as they have the requisite tools under their full epistemic command. The downside of such an argumentation, on the other hand, is that legalistic reasoning may in certain cases avowedly substitute for scientific inquiry. Crafting purely legal reasoning in clear contradiction to available scientific knowledge or in lieu of scientific authority constitutes epistemic trespassing and erodes the factual accuracy of decisions. This is the case for instance when courts decouple the notion of environmental risk from the science of risk assessment,[32] construe scientific uncertainty as an insurmountable obstacle paralysing a meaningful judicial analysis,[33] or set aside expert reports and decide science-heavy issues without evaluating scientific evidence, a practice that has previously been labelled Solomonic decision-making.[34] These argumentative avenues run against the logic of science

---

[32] See Chapter 9 Section II, Subsection 1.6.
[33] See relevant examples from international case law and more details in Chapter 9 Section II, Subsection 1.3.
[34] See Chapter 9 Section II, Subsection 1.2 and Section III, Subsection 1.1.

and therefore do not respect its cognitive authority. This in turn generates risks for the convincing force of the reasoning. It follows from the above that purely legal argumentative tools appear to be appropriate only as complementary means of justification, when scientific benchmarks are not available.

Emphatically, not every legal argumentation style repudiates scientific knowledge. Certain legal reasoning techniques seek to accommodate the uncertain nature of science and to adjust traditional legal doctrines to the peculiarities of scientific input. For instance, certain normative principles may avowedly seek to render inevitably probabilistic and ambiguous scientific knowledge legally appreciable. Various applications of the precautionary principle[35] are a stark example of not replacing scientific knowledge but accommodating its uncertain nature in the judicial process. This solution is argued to constitute an epistemically legitimate effort to bridge law's need for certainty and irreducible forms of scientific uncertainty, because legal argumentation steps in only when relevant scientific knowledge is not available.

Whether having recourse to legal epistemic yardsticks in a specific case respects the authority of science should be decided on a case-by-case basis. If, for instance, in spite of a thorough scientific fact-finding process, respective scientific input remains too uncertain to provide a definitive answer to the question at hand, relying on legalistic reasoning can be the best available argumentative option. In this vein, when judges place emphasis on procedural environmental law obligations compared to substantive ones,[36] it can be seen as a legitimate recourse to legalistic reasoning, provided that they have attempted first to engage with science in their fact-finding to the extent possible in light of the institutional arrangement at hand. Overall, reasoning with purely legal rationality appears only to be legitimate in certain scenarios and not as a default argumentative practice.

In the ensuing sections those legal benchmarks will be elaborated on that raise specific advantages and trade-offs in terms of the legitimacy of reasoning, or where peculiar remedies are available for judges to safeguard the epistemic authority of their judgments.

2.1.1 STANDARDS AND GUIDELINES OF INTERNATIONAL ORGANIZATIONS. Adjudicators often have recourse to international organizations' standards to justify their choice whether to accept a scientific claim or evidence as representing legitimate science. Simply put, scientific guidelines and standards issued by international institutions can function as external references in making legal judgments about the soundness of scientific claims.[37] Such a mode of reasoning operates by virtue of legal rationality, because the authority of a scientific standard is detached from the epistemic

---

35   See Chapter 9 Section II, Subsection 1.7.
36   For more details see Chapter 9 Section II, Subsection 1.5.
37   Viñuales, 'Observations sur le traitement des motifs scientifiques dans le contentieux environnemental international', p. 117.

authority of the science included therein. In fact, the persuasive force attached to scientific knowledge reflected in such documents stems from the authority and international standing of the issuing organization. Adjudicators rely on the perceived competence and prestige of the respective institution, when they accept a piece of scientific evidence matching such standards as reflecting 'valid' science. Tellingly, international adjudicators normally cite guidelines issued by institutions with the highest international standing, which have a widely acknowledged expertise in the relevant scientific field.

That the epistemic character of this reasoning style is absolved from scientific rationality is clearly reflected in the fact that applying such benchmarks does not necessitate scientific competence from the reasoner. In other words, the scientific content and the correctness of the methodology represented in a given standard need not to be judged by adjudicators when they refer to such guidelines in their decisions. This confers a considerable benefit on judges as they can easily observe epistemic non-arbitrariness if they reason this way. Further to that, such an argumentative practice also minimizes the risk of expert bias inherent in party-adduced expert evidence, as only those scientific propositions would be accepted from among the submissions of the parties that correspond to such international guidelines.

The epistemic authority of international scientific standards and guidelines stems from the fact that they were not intended for a specific legal dispute,[38] but have been issued as general summaries of relevant scientific knowledge. Standards set by international organizations therefore benefit from being seen as 'agreed upon' by sovereign states prior to the given legal dispute. This bestows the appearance of objectivity also on judgments, which rely on international guidelines.

In the context of environmental policy-making, case studies have long suggested that consensual scientific knowledge enjoys a privileged position and are insulated from challenges of states in the context of negotiating multilateral environmental agreements (MEA).[39] Strategic usage of science-based MEAs by adjudicators has been addressed earlier in the context of tobacco control litigation before investment tribunals[40] and the WTO.[41] Notably, both fora adjudicated disputes by relying on the WHO Framework Convention on Tobacco Control, which was cited as a matter of fact and not that of law, which showcases the evidentiary value of such regulations.

It is of course not without drawbacks if courts and tribunals do not wish to venture beyond the comfortable fields of legalistic reasoning. For one, the finite number of environmental hazards and chemicals in relation to which international standards

---

[38] Viñuales, 'Observations sur le traitement des motifs scientifiques dans le contentieux environnemental international', p. 117; Alvarez, 'The search for objectivity', 422.

[39] Andersen, 'The role of scientific expertise in multilateral environmental agreements: influence and effectiveness', pp. 116–17.

[40] Alvarez, 'The search for objectivity'. See in more detail in Chapter 7 Section V, Subsection 2.2.

[41] Gruszczynski, 'WHO Framework Convention on Tobacco Control as an international standard under the TBT agreement?'. For more details see Chapter 6 Section II, Subsection 4.

have been previously issued limits the scope of cases in which they may be invoked. Even if there were international recommendations relevant to the environmental risks concerned in a given dispute, the applicable standard may still fall short of the required level of specificity to provide an answer to the legal dilemma at hand.

Notwithstanding the above, when relevant international guidelines are available and closely speak to the heart of the scientific controversy, accepting them as scientific proof strikes as an appropriate tool to assess science-based claims. Doing so also benefits litigants, who could this way overcome considerable hardship in producing persuasive scientific evidence. Building judicial findings on international standards may be most useful in climate change litigation, where reports of the International Panel on Climate Change (IPCC) can be regarded as a highly author- itative and elaborate scientific standard, which is also carefully negotiated between scientists and stakeholders.[42] Such a reasoning method hence should be encouraged whenever existing standards can inform the adjudicatory inquiry into the scientific controversies lying in the background to the legal dispute.

2.1.2 INTERNATIONAL REGULATORY TRENDS. International adjudicators some- times regard uniform regulatory decisions of sovereigns as a hallmark of legitimate and valid scientific knowledge.[43] As this reasoning style takes the lawmaking process of states as its benchmark, it is also essentially built on legalistic logic. Similarly to scientific standards of international bodies, the convincing force of regulatory trends also stems from the fact that it represents a scientific consensus that was reached irrespective of the parties' legal conflict. These all boost the credibility and the convincing nature of such references before adjudicators and the relevant public, as 'negotiated science' usually enjoys highly authoritative value in the eyes of non-scientist stakeholders.[44]

A blind spot of relying on international regulatory trends, however, is the 'first regulator' problem, meaning that this reasoning style is simply inadequate when a state faces emerging or newly discovered risks. A further drawback is that it can potentially be abused if reasoners were to regard the lack of regulatory action in certain jurisdictions as an indicator of scientifically valid opinions on the absence of applicable environmental hazards. Importantly, setting emission standards for cer- tain toxic chemicals in many states is adjusted to fit the industry's technology performance,[45] and does not directly rely on scientific knowledge on applicable health or environmental impacts. Just as much, rolling back previously more

---

[42] The main summary of IPCC reports is drafted together with IPCC member government representa- tives, see in more detail N. S. Ghaleigh, 'Science and climate change law: the role of the IPCC in international decision-making' in K. Gray, R. Tarasofsky, and C. Carlarne (eds.), *The Oxford Handbook of International Climate Change Law* (Oxford University Press, 2016), pp. 56–72 p. 66.

[43] Relevant examples have been addressed in Chapter 7 Section II, Subsection 2.2 and Chapter 9 Section V, Subsection 2.2.3.

[44] Jasanoff, 'Serviceable truths', 1741–3.

[45] A relevant example is the US Federal Clean Water Act (33 U.S.C. §1251 et seq. (1972)), which requires basing effluent discharge standards on technology-based standards.

stringent environmental regulations may have nothing to do with the extent of scientific risks imposed by the relevant polluting agent.[46] Given that environmental lawmaking notoriously involves balancing economic interests against scientific risks, the absence of relevant regulation or a deregulatory wave cannot be a legitimate indicator of the state of scientific knowledge concerning respective environmental risks. With this caveat, when discernible international regulatory trends point to the existence of acknowledged environmental risks, underpinning judicial reasoning with them strikes as a persuasive argumentative tool.

2.1.3 PROCEDURAL BENCHMARKS OF THE SCIENTIFIC PROCESS. Yet another legalistic reasoning focuses on 'scientific due process' criteria.[47] In this argumentative scenario, judges rely on procedural benchmarks to check whether certain attributes of an idealized process of scientific knowledge production have been fulfilled in the given case. A scientific due process-based argumentation accepts scientific results as credible and legitimate if they were produced in a transparent and participatory procedure, preferably also including peer review. An undoubted advantage of employing procedural yardsticks lies in relieving adjudicators from getting ensnared in substantive analysis of scientific evidence. Also, this method respects the imperative of epistemic non-arbitrariness.[48] Scholars for these reasons have been generally supportive of decisions where adjudicators focused their review on the procedure of scientific knowledge production.[49]

It is important to stress, however, that the objectivity of scientific research is established through a range of social practices and, thus, is a culturally embedded phenomenon, which may carry various meanings across different cultures.[50] Put differently, practices that are deemed ensuring objectivity of scientific research may vary among states. This should be borne in mind by international adjudicators, when they scrutinize the adequacy of a scientific risk assessment procedure conducted on the national level.

In particular, peer review requirement is often seen as a useful procedural benchmark for pinpointing valid and, hence, legitimate science.[51] Yet a closer look reveals

---

[46] See for instance the controversial new EPA rule of the Trump administration opening the door to loosening on mercury emissions of power plants, a toxic pollutant the health effects of which are long proven in scientific terms. Lisa Friedman and Coral Davenport: 'E.P.A. weakens controls on mercury', *New York Times*, 16 April 2020, available at www.nytimes.com/2020/04/16/climate/epa-mercury-coal.html (last accessed 28 May 2020).

[47] Lévesque, 'Science in the hands of international investment tribunals: a case for "scientific due process"'. See more details in Chapter 9 Section V, Subsection 2.2.1.

[48] D'Aspremont and Mbengue, 'Strategies of engagement with scientific fact-finding in international adjudication', 271.

[49] Orellana, 'The role of science in investment arbitrations concerning public health and the environment', 72; Lévesque, 'Science in the hands of international investment tribunals: a case for "scientific due process"', 20; Viñuales, *Foreign Investment and the Environment*, p. 378.

[50] Jasanoff, 'The practices of objectivity in regulatory science', pp. 312–17.

[51] Alemanno, 'EU risk regulation and science: the role of experts in decision-making and judicial review', pp. 65–7.

that requiring peer review is not a failsafe method either. The peer review process has its imperfections with ensuing limitations for using it as a single criterion to judge the credibility and legitimacy of scientific findings. Its pitfalls stem from various psycho-sociological factors, such as personal and systematic bias favouring accomplished scientists or methods in line with the reviewer's preference.[52] If one adds to the picture the rare, though significant, scandals involving intentional fraud and plagiarism in connection with the referee system of even prestigious scientific journals,[53] using peer review alone as the sole benchmark for evaluating the acceptability of scientific knowledge claims strikes one as a less than ideal solution. Scientists have a more realistic account of what peer review can actually deliver. They stress that 'peer review *per se* provides only a minimal assurance of quality, and that the public conception of peer review as a stamp of authentication is far from the truth'.[54] In light of this, it is more appropriate to consider peer review as a necessary, though not sufficient benchmark for scrutinizing the integrity and credibility of scientific results.

2.1.4 PRESUMPTIONS. Causal assessments feature the use of another legal benchmark that is to announce a causal nexus based on presumptions. Presumptions establish causality via legalistic rationality in the explicit acknowledgement that science is unable to provide a definite answer on the existence of a causal link. In other words, the authority of judicial reasoning in such cases is not created *because of* science, but rather *in spite of* it. It is the presumption itself, a genuine legal construction, which confers legitimacy on finding the causal nexus. Similarly, when traditional causal requirements are relaxed for the sake of establishing science-based causal links, as happens in climate change litigation,[55] the judicial choice to allow a causal claim to proceed stems from legal causal theories, and hence, gets validated by law's own logic.

It is argued here that utilizing presumptions is a justifiable means for bridging the gap between scientific and legal concepts of certainty and causation. Importantly, presumptions are only legitimate argumentative tools as long as they are applied as *ultima ratio* solutions in absence of adequate scientific evidence. This is typically the case when available scientific knowledge makes the presumption probable on a general level, even if particularized evidence speaking to the individual case cannot be produced due to pervasive scientific uncertainty. In order to craft a legitimate presumption, adjudicators first should strive for attempting to engage with scientific evidence substantively, and only if that were not possible, should they

---

[52]   Jasanoff, *The Fifth Branch*, pp. 61–79.

[53]   Fred Barbash, 'Major publisher retracts 43 scientific papers amid wider fake peer-review scandal' (27 March 2015), *Washington Post*, available at https://wapo.st/2XmtRHM (last accessed 25 June 2018).

[54]   Emphasis added, Charles Jennings, 'Quality and value: the true purpose of peer review' (2006) *Nature*, available at www.nature.com/nature/peerreview/debate/nature05032.html (last accessed 25 June 2018).

[55]   See in more detail in Chapter 9 Section IV, Subsection 2.2.2.

have recourse to purely legal reasoning. To take such an example from international case law, the presumption introduced by the ECtHR in *Fadeyeva* is triggered only if primary scientific proof of causation does not yield a conclusive answer as to the causal relations in a given case.[56] This observes the above requirement and, thus, it is argued to be an epistemically legitimate presumption.

Another way of ensuring respect for science's cognitive authority in the reasoning is by backing up presumptive causal links with scientific knowledge. This is illustrated by the practice of the Marshall Islands Nuclear Claims Tribunal, which utilized science-based presumptions in awarding compensation to victims of nuclear exposure. The list of compensable diseases has been drawn up and updated according to developing scientific knowledge about the adverse health effects of the exposure.[57] The diseases that were presumed to be causal upon the nuclear tests of the United States had, therefore, adequate scientific bases. This is purported here to be another convincing and legitimate way of crafting presumptions.

2.1.5 SUBSTITUTING THE LOGIC OF LEGAL FACT-FINDING FOR SCIENTIFIC EVALUATION
Commentators point out the possibility for adjudicators to justify ruling in favour of a party's scientific evidence by applying ordinary rules of standard and burden of proof.[58] Indeed, finding facts according to the preponderant position among experts is a perfectly legitimate solution according to legalistic logic. Yet, the WTO AB explicitly rejected the possibility to strike down a state's science-based measure only because it was based on minority views in the scientific community. It emphasized that a WTO panel 'need not, necessarily, reach a decision ... on the basis of the "preponderant" weight of the evidence'.[59] This strikes as a laudable approach, as deciding on science-based legal claims cannot always be simply a matter of a quantitative balancing. It is clear that judges should not regard the establishment of scientific facts as strictly a matter of adversarial exercise.[60]

3 *Reasoning with Intuitive Rationality*

When adjudicators choose to downplay science in their assessments, sometimes they turn to everyday knowledge and will reason with intuitive rationality. Although judicial reasoning has its own set of rules and conventions, it is deeply rooted in human psyche and therefore shares some fundamental characteristics with lay

---

[56] The ECtHR first reviewed causal evidence submitted by the applicant and only when it found it to be insufficient for purposes of establishing causation, did it apply the presumption of causality. See *Fadeyeva v. Russia*, paras. 80–8. For more details see Chapter 5 Section III, Subsection 3.2.

[57] For more details see Chapter 9 Section IV, Subsection 2.1.1.

[58] D'Aspremont and Mbengue, 'Strategies of engagement with scientific fact-finding in international adjudication', 266–7.

[59] *EC – Asbestos*, Report of the AB, WT/DS135/AB/R (12 March 2001), para. 178.

[60] Foster, 'The consultation of independent experts by international courts and tribunals in health and environmental cases', 392.

reasoning. Inductive, deductive, extensional, and intuitive forms of reasoning all appear outside the courtroom as well. This segment will focus on those judicial justification methods that are rooted in intuitive inferential strategies shared by every reasoner. Judges occasionally refer to intuitive rationality and rely on everyday experience in selecting relevant information to form the premises of their decisions. These argumentative practices are therefore not peculiar to the legal language, as their application falls within the epistemic competence of everyone. These tools are often appealing to judicial reasoners as they enable them to bypass the detailed inferential process necessary to evaluate the merits of scientific arguments.[61] Specific examples from international case law will be discussed in the coming section. Suffice it to note here that these intuitive reasoning methods all function as inferential shortcuts in the assessment of factually complex situations.

3.1 Perils and Benefits of Intuitive Reasoning

Intuitive yardsticks undoubtedly confer certain benefits on the reasoner. This form of reasoning scores high on both epistemic non-arbitrariness and preserving the judicial monopoly over the dispute resolution. Moreover, commonsense rationality is usually intuitively persuasive to judges and relevant audience alike as a means of locating legitimate knowledge claims. Intuitive reasoning techniques constitute a heterogeneous category. Certain forms of intuitive reasoning are epistemically legitimate, albeit these are not available in every context, hence their practical feasibility is somewhat limited. In contrast, other intuitive yardsticks may either run against scientific realities or invite epistemic trespassing, which weaken their epistemic legitimacy.

It is submitted here that intuitive reasoning style can be a perfectly legitimate way of reasoning provided that it is utilized as auxiliary means of justification, that is, when scientific rationality is not available for legal reasoners to scaffold findings in a given case. Each peculiar type of intuitive reasoning generates more specific benefits and downsides. The remainder of this section will address these in relation to the typical intuitive reasoning techniques of international courts.

3.1.1 SUBSTITUTING INTUITIVE PROXIES FOR SCIENTIFIC ASSESSMENT. Rule-of-thumb balancing is a specific type of inferential shortcut rooted in intuitive rationality.[62] An apposite example of making a rough assessment of all factual circumstances manifests in the proxy-based causal inquiry of the ECtHR, which is known for substituting non-scientific proxies for a thorough scientific evidence-based inquiry. A significant drawback of this justification method stems from the fact that rule-of-thumb inferences often yield inaccurate results.[63] Indeed, it has been shown above

---

[61] Dwyer, *The Judicial Assessment of Expert Evidence*, p. 68.
[62] Dwyer, *The Judicial Assessment of Expert Evidence*, p. 67.
[63] Dwyer, *The Judicial Assessment of Expert Evidence*, p. 67.

that the overwhelming majority of these proxies cannot be justified scientifically, because they are overly simplified representations of the underlying causal processes leading from toxic pollution to health injuries.[64] Consequently, they are either under-inclusive or over-inclusive in the sense that they are not capable of singling out with precision those sources of pollution that had, scientifically speaking, a causal role in bringing about the respective health injury. This aptly illustrates the reasons why this mode of intuitive reasoning scores low on factual accuracy.

What is more, common sense considerations may justify refuting a causal claim even in clear contradiction with established scientific knowledge. For instance, the distance proxy in the Strasbourg Court's case law suggests that only those emitters are regarded as 'causes' of the injury that are located in close proximity of the applicant's home. This goes clearly against scientific consensus holding that certain pollutants may travel long-range without losing their toxic potential. Nevertheless, such a reasoning could be deemed convincing for many scientifically lay reasoners, as at first glance, it appears intuitively logical. This well illustrates the main risk of the proxy-based intuitive reasoning, that is it is all too often at odds with scientific knowledge and factual realities of a case. Consequently, such judicial reasoning runs the risk of losing convincing force in light of developing scientific knowledge.

3.1.2 SEMANTIC ANALYSIS. Grammatical interpretation is a common form of argumentation shared by every reasoner, and a fundamental method in the reasoning toolkit of international courts and tribunals. More particularly, judges often have recourse to a semantic analysis and reasoning when they interpret scientific legality criteria embedded in elaborate legal rules. Simply put, in such cases judges provide mainly grammatical explanations for their findings. For instance as has been discussed in detail above, WTO panellists frequently use semantic analysis in scrutinizing as to whether a trade measure is regarded to be 'based on' a certain scientific international standard.[65] Similarly, the ICJ also used such technique in *Whaling in the Antarctic*, when it had to interpret the scope of exemption under ICRW granted to a whaling programme conducted 'for purposes of scientific research'.[66]

A common thread underlying these reasoning methods is the decisive force attached to grammatical interpretation of ordinary textual elements surrounding scientific notions in relevant legal rules. Grammatical interpretation fits neatly within the epistemic competence and mandate of international judges,[67] and

---

[64] For a more detailed discussion on the proxies and their drawbacks see Chapter 5 Section III, Subsections 3.2 and 3.3.

[65] See related discussion in Chapter 6 Section III, Subsection 5.3 and Chapter 9 Section V, Subsection 2.4.

[66] *Whaling in the Antarctic*, Judgment, para. 30, see in more detail Chapter 3.

[67] See Vienna Convention on the Law of Treaties, Vienna, 23 May 1969, in force 27 January 1980, 1155 UNTS 331, Article 31.

hence, this argumentative technique yields an altogether persuasive reasoning style. It also observes the requirement of epistemic non-arbitrariness as judicial reasoners need not interpret scientific evidence speaking to the technical terms of art enshrined in the text in order to appraise the scientific narratives advanced by the parties. Instead, judges can comfortably discharge their task via a descientized grammatical interpretation.

The only downside of this convenient solution is rooted in its limited availability. It is only applicable where express scientific legality criteria are enshrined in the legal text subject to adjudicatory review. It is true that MEAs, WTO law, and EU law commonly provide rules incorporating scientific notions, where semantic analysis may be a useful interpretative tool. However, science often enters the adjudicative process in less formalized manner when it is not couched or embedded in express legal rules. In such cases, this type of intuitive reasoning would not be available.

3.1.3 SECOND-ORDER INDICATORS TO ASSESS EXPERT EVIDENCE. On certain occasions international adjudicators rely on second-order indicators to justify their science-based conclusions.[68] These involve techniques where the reliability of a certain piece of expert evidence is evaluated based on the experts' credentials, their perceived independence or impartiality, or the peer reviewed or uncontested nature of scientific evidence. A common element in these reasoning techniques is that they interrogate the value of first-order evidence, that it, the expert opinion, only indirectly through so-called higher-order justifications.[69] Furthermore, they allow judges to reason their way out of a direct interaction with the first-order scientific evidence via drawing intuitive inferential shortcuts.

Yet this particular type of intuitive reasoning has its own blind spots and shortcomings too. To begin with the most straightforward, attaching higher evidentiary value to well-known sources of information is an ordinary cognitive fallacy. From an analytical point of view the reputation of scientists says in fact little, if at all, about the scientific merit of their scientific opinion. Even most eminent scientists may fall prey to good faith cognitive, or even express economic, bias,[70] which would go unnoticed under a formalistic assessment built only on second-order indicators.

Occasionally, international adjudicators use peer review as a higher-order indicator of reliable scientific opinions.[71] Peer review, although it forms an integral and important part of scientific knowledge production, is not immune to failures either, as it has been argued in Section II, Subsection 2.1.3 in this chapter. Other second-order evidence, such as impartiality and independence of experts, is also vulnerable

---

[68]   Specific examples have been examined in Chapter 3 Section III, Subsection 2.2.2, and Chapter 9 Section III, Subsection 1.5.

[69]   Perez, 'Judicial strategies for reviewing conflicting expert evidence'.

[70]   Perez, 'Judicial strategies for reviewing conflicting expert evidence', 85–8.

[71]   See for example the *Methanex* Arbitration, *Methanex v. The United States of America* (NAFTA) Final Award (3 August 2005), in more detail in Chapter 7 Section V, Subsection 2.1.

to epistemic challenge. These qualities constitute vague and inherently subjective standards, which also points to a larger problem of building judicial reasoning exclusively on second-order indicators. Psychological experiments show that reasoners are prone to make intuitive judgments first, for which they seek rational justifications only subsequently.[72] Against this backdrop, relying on intuitive rationality renders it dangerously easy for judicial reasoners to hide their subjective appraisals from public scrutiny, which is especially problematic considering that judges are suspected of being inclined not to reveal their real motivations behind particular decisions.[73]

For all these reasons relying exclusively on subjective second-order justifications may lead to obscure reasoning and, thus, is not satisfactory for purposes of securing legitimacy for adjudicatory findings. Combining intuitive rationality with closer engagement with the scientific evidence could remedy these shortcomings. This is confirmed by psychological research suggesting that experts' credentials carry less weight for lay decision-makers, when the scientific evidence is presented in a form intelligible to non-scientists.[74]

To conclude this appraisal on a more positive tone, certain forms of higher-order evidence are less problematic. Attaching great weight to scientific evidence not contested by the opposing party[75] seems to strike a fair balance between the need for incorporating scientific evidence in the judicial decision-making process and the adjudicatory preference for making inferential shortcuts instead of conducting complex technical assessments. Their use may be especially justified, when judges have no institutional powers to increase their epistemic competence or have to operate under strict time and financial constraints. Overall, this form of intuitive rationality is likely to play a crucial role in rendering judgments, and will continue to provide a reasoning practice that is not *per se* objectionable from a legitimacy point of view.

4 Hybrid Concepts in Adjudicatory Reasoning

A peculiar category of judicial reasoning techniques was distinguished in the analytical chapters, which are built around concepts situated on overlapping areas of scientific and legal assessment. These have been dubbed 'hybrid' standards throughout this study, highlighting that these concepts enable judicial reasoners to

[72] J. Haidt, 'The emotional dog and its rational tail: a social intuitionist approach to moral judgment' in J. E. Adler and L. J. Rips (eds.), *Reasoning: Studies of Human Inference and Its Foundations* (Cambridge University Press, 2008), pp. 1024–52 pp. 1024–5.
[73] Griss, 'How judges think', 249; B. A. Spellman and F. Schauer, 'Legal reasoning' in K. J. Holyoak and R. G. Morrison (eds.), *The Oxford Handbook of Thinking and Reasoning* (Oxford University Press, 2012), pp. 719–35 p. 722.
[74] Dwyer, *The Judicial Assessment of Expert Evidence*, p. 69.
[75] The tendency of certain international fora to find non-contested scientific facts established has been examined in more detail in Chapter 9 Section III, Subsection 1.5.

answer legal questions through combining evidence from the scientific and the legal discipline.[76] As has been discussed earlier,[77] hybrid concepts yield a specific subset of legalistic reasoning techniques, which differ from purely legal benchmarks inasmuch as their application is inextricably linked to the underlying science. The hybridity of this reasoning style flags that this method is neither purely legal nor purely scientific in its epistemic character, since the notions that judicial reasoners interpret in such cases forge an interdisciplinary connection between the scientific and the legal fields of knowledge. Concrete examples will be discussed in the coming sections.

A consequential feature of this reasoning style lies in the fact that despite hybrid concepts being located on the interface of scientific and legal inquiry, they provide basis for a reasoning that neatly falls within the epistemic competence of legally trained judges. In essence, the primary focus of these benchmarks is on the *reasoning* of the risk assessor, or of the state appealing to the authority of science. Consequently, hybrid argumentative yardsticks enable adjudicators to craft a legalistic reasoning, which also closely reflects on the scientific subject matter of the dispute at hand. These dual-faceted benchmarks have emerged in the argumentative practice of various international fora representing convergent solutions for interpreting closely tied aspects of scientific and legal inquiry. The preceding analytical chapters have identified such tests in WTO case-practice as well as the ICJ jurisprudence; and structurally similar argumentation has been pointed out in decisions of an international arbitral tribunal and EU courts as well.[78]

The hybrid reasoning style appears to provide an efficient solution for several of the challenges inherent in legally adjudicating scientific dilemmas and, therefore, offers a potential adjudicatory good practice for approaching science-heavy disputes. Specific strengths of this reasoning method are elaborated on in the section that follows.

4.1 Benefits and Trade-Offs of Building a Reasoning on Hybrid Concepts

This comparative survey suggests that invoking hybrid concepts in the judicial analysis confers a number of benefits on judicial reasoners. Hybrid reasoning style provides a workable, pragmatic solution for adjudicators to live up to the requirements flowing from the interdisciplinary nature of the judicial mandate; most

---

[76]   To describe these argumentative techniques, this study purposefully crafted the term 'hybrid' reasoning, to invite connotations from the field of epistemology and Science and Technology Studies (STS). For an account on hybridized questions describing similar epistemic phenomena see Ballantyne, 'Epistemic trespassing', 372. The term hybrid has also been used by Bruno Latour in STS literature to describe constructs in which the scientific and the social aspects are inextricably entangled with each other see Latour, We have Never Been Modern, p. 3.

[77]   Chapter 9 Section V, Subsection 2.3.

[78]   For a discussion of relevant examples from international case law see Chapter 9 Section V, Subsection 2.3.

eminently, the need to craft epistemically legitimate reasoning, which conforms to both the logic of law and science.

To begin with, hybrid judicial analysis speaks the language of a legalistic evaluation and does not touch upon interrogating the validity of scientific data. Judges who engage in such an argumentative style, should only decide about the legally appreciable features of a science-based reasoning, such as its reasonable and coherent nature or its consistency. Ruling on these qualities says nothing about the scientific veracity or the robustness of the respective scientific findings put forth in the underlying science-based opinion. More concretely, reviewing the reasonableness of a science-based position does not compel judges to conduct a *de novo* appraisal as to the correct interpretation of the evidence.[79] This means that judges, who reason with hybrid concepts do not need to act as 'super-experts', or 'science courts'[80] and to decide whether the scientific claim is *the* single correct answer to the scientific controversy. They only need to ascertain that the respective claim can be regarded, for purposes of deciding the legal dispute, as *a* legitimate answer in light of the scientific evidence submitted.

It follows from the preceding considerations that legal adjudicators engaging in hybrid reasoning do not trespass epistemic boundaries. Emphatically, hybrid argumentative benchmarks do not invite mixing different rationalities, since they do not allow adjudicators to substitute legal rationality for scientific rationality when judging the acceptability of scientific knowledge claims. A central proposition of this study argues that applying hybrid yardsticks fits neatly within the competence of legal adjudicators. Even Judge Owada, who otherwise prefers construing a limited judicial purview in adjudicating scientific concepts, acknowledges that 'there may be certain elements in the concept [of scientific research] that the Court may legitimately and usefully offer as salient from the viewpoint of legal analysis'.[81] In the view of the present author, hybrid concepts as understood here capture these very aspects of a science-heavy analysis, as they lend themselves to legal evaluation. The reasonableness of implementing a research scheme, or the coherence of the reasoning provided by risk assessors all mark legally appreciable dimensions of inherently scientific notions. Owing to the very fact that hybrid reasoning focuses on such legalistic aspects of interdisciplinary concepts, this argumentative style effectively guards against epistemic trespassing.[82]

Another significant benefit of drawing on hybrid tests lies in retaining adequate judicial control over scientific expertise; consequently, judges can fully assume responsibility for the outcome of the dispute resolution. Formalistically speaking,

---

[79] For a similar position see *The Government of Sudan/The Sudan People's Liberation Movement/Army (Abyei* Arbitration) (Permanent Court of Arbitration), Final Award (22 July 2009), para. 537.

[80] This has been suggested by the respondent in *Glamis Gold* v. *US*, Award, para. 617.

[81] *Whaling in the Antarctic*, Dissenting Opinion of Judge Owada, para. 24.

[82] Ballantyne suggests that epistemic trespassing can be prevented by focusing on non-hybridized sub-aspects of interdisciplinary (i.e. hybridized) questions that can be answered by only one of the disciplines involved. See Ballantyne, 'Epistemic trespassing', 375–6.

legally trained reasoners could form an opinion about qualities such as reasonableness, consistency or coherence autonomously from the expert submissions.
Put differently, hybrid concepts function as points of translation on the law–science
interface, about which lawyers can formulate their own reading. This ensures that
scientific opinions put forth by experts do not dictate the judicial decision in
a dispute. To provide a concrete example, as has been addressed above regarding
the *Whaling in the Antarctic* judgment, the ICJ notably formed its own reading on
the notion of 'scientific research' without strictly following either parties' scientific
expert positions on the matter. Importantly, this is not to suggest that scientific
evidence is – or let alone should be – irrelevant for the legal interpretation of
these hybrid translation points. These concepts do have a scientific grounding to
which we shall return later. For present purposes, suffice it to illustrate this proposition by pointing readers to the specific segment of the ICJ's judgment, where the
lengthy application of the reasonableness test touched upon several of the features
that *ex parte* scientific experts described as essential for identifying the scientific
method.[83]

What is significant for retaining judges' epistemic control over scientific expertise
in a legal dispute is that the judicial as well as the scientific evaluation of these
attributes remain distinct processes, carried out by different authorities under
different rules or conventions. As has been aptly emphasized by the *Abyei*
Tribunal, scientific experts and judicial bodies 'are each programmed to assess the
facts using quite different methodologies, *i.e.* the methodology of science *vis-à-vis*
the methodology of law'.[84]

Looking at this reasoning style from a more theoretical standpoint, hybrid concepts can be described as 'boundary objects'[85] of scientific and judicial reasoning,
through which the scientific merit of an expert input can be translated into legal
determination. Philosophy of science literature uses the concept of boundary objects
to describe analytic notions that are present in different epistemic realms with
different meanings, while also satisfy the informational requirements of both social
worlds.[86] Their role is to *maintain coherence* across different fields of knowledge,
which interact in cross-disciplinary dialogue or co-operation – in our case, science-
intensive adjudication.

Against this backdrop, the gist of the argument that is proposed here is that
reasonableness, coherence, and consistency are qualities that are present in both
the scientific and the legal discipline with slightly different meanings. Yet these

---

[83] *Whaling in the Antarctic*, Judgment, paras. 147–222.
[84] *Abyei* Arbitration, para. 406.
[85] Star and Griesemer, 'Institutional ecology, "translations" and boundary objects: amateurs and profes-
      sionals in Berkeley's Museum of Vertebrate Zoology, 1907–39' (1989) 19 *Social Studies of Science*
      397–420, 393.
[86] Star and Griesemer, 'Institutional ecology, "translations" and boundary objects: amateurs and
      professionals in Berkeley's Museum of Vertebrate Zoology, 1907–39', 393.

concepts are robust enough to connect the two epistemic realms and to maintain coherence in the inevitable co-operation of law and science in the courtroom.

That reasonableness and coherence are fundamental concepts in law and legal reasoning[87] may warrant no further illustration. Perhaps less evident is the fact that they are also immanent in the scientific process. Philosophers of science argue that science is in fact a 'reasonable enterprise',[88] because scientific results are 'constructed from valid experimental evidence and from *reasoned and critical discussion*'.[89] Indeed, the need for critical review and falsifiability of scientific results by peers is a cornerstone of scientific knowledge production and the so-called scientific method. These qualities of scientific research presuppose that a chosen scientific methodology has to be justifiable, and thus, *reasonable* in light of the underlying data as well as consistent with accepted methods of the respective scientific field. Otherwise a given result would fail the statistical power analysis[90] and would preclude the possibility to be tested by fellow scientists.

The notion of coherence is similarly relevant for drawing inferences in both law and natural sciences. Argumentation theory, which interrogates how explanatory coherence is established in legal and scientific reasoning,[91] suggests that coherence is an integral part of reasoning in both realms, and it is evaluated based on the same cognitive principles, such as explanation, analogy, system coherence, and symmetry.[92]

Equally important is to emphasize that interpreting these translation points neither invites nor allows epistemic trespassing. Hybrid concepts do not render it to be the task of a judicial panel to judge the correct (and hence, scientifically reasonable) nature of a sample size of an alleged research programme for purposes of accepting it as part of the scientific discourse. Doing so requires a high level of literacy in ecology, statistics, and other specialized fields of sciences, which all fall out of the competence of lawyer judges. This particular line of inquiry into the reasonableness of a research project is a task epistemically fitting only to scientists. Yet, as the *Whaling in the Antarctic* judgment so pertinently shows, a court of law is suitable for conducting a reasonableness inquiry in relation to the same project, for purposes of evaluating the reasonableness of its sample size from the law's perspective. This, in contrast, requires expertise in abstract conceptual thinking, inferential reasoning and balancing, complemented by a basic understanding of the arguments

---

[87] A. Peczenik, *On Law and Reason* (Springer, 2009), p. 131.
[88] A. Franklin, *Can that Be Right?: Essays on Experiment, Evidence, and Science*, Boston Studies in the Philosophy of Science (Springer-Science, 1999), vol. 199 p. 1.
[89] Franklin, *Can that Be Right?: Essays on Experiment, Evidence, and Science*, p. 283. Emphasis added.
[90] The power analysis is also known as hypotheses testing. If the sample size is too small, it fails the statistical power analysis, that is, the hypothesis testing, see Chapter 2 Section I, Subsection 2.3.
[91] Thagard, 'Explanatory coherence'.
[92] Thagard, 'Explanatory coherence', pp. 473–5. Thagard suggests that symmetry, explanation, analogy, data priority, contradiction, acceptability, and system coherence are the principles that inform making cognitive evaluations on the coherence of an explanation.

provided by ecologists regarding their opinion on the scientific reasonableness of the sample size. The above can be condensed to a conclusion that, metaphorically speaking, hybrid concepts in the adjudicatory reasoning function as 'windows of evaluation' on the law–science interface enabling judicial reasoners to evaluate whether a certain science-based position can be accepted *for purposes of the legal analysis*.

On a practical level, hybrid reasoning style is beneficial for the dynamics of the adjudicatory analysis for at least two reasons. On the one hand, it yields a substantive assessment venturing beyond a strictly procedural review of the scientific process enabled by purely legalistic benchmarks. This boosts the output legitimacy of decisions, because an assessment that reflects on scientific expertise in a substantive way is generally regarded as more thorough and convincing.

On the other hand, applying hybrid concepts for giving content to the judicial review pressures scientists to pronounce their findings in a way that is accessible to lay decision-makers. When scientific evidence is presented in an intelligible form to non-scientists, judges are more likely to interact with it substantively.[93] This is seen as a favourable consequence of the hybrid reasoning style, as it assists judges in developing a basic understanding of their own of the scientific points of contention, which is, as we shall see below, a prerequisite to crafting a reasoning that respects science's cognitive authority.

This brings us to a more fundamental issue that needs to be addressed here in concluding this analysis. Perhaps the most consequential advantageous feature of the hybrid reasoning style is that it warrants an in-depth judicial reflection on the scientific profile of legal disputes. An adjudicatory body cannot form a solid opinion on the coherency between scientific facts and risk assessors' conclusions, or on the reasonableness of the implementation of a research scheme without understanding and engaging to certain extent with relevant scientific evidence. In fact, judging the above hybrid qualities *without* considering and evaluating scientific evidence, and based *solely* on legalistic logic, would constitute epistemic trespassing, and hence, would be illegitimate.

Instead, hybrid reasoning prompts international adjudicators to live up to the expectation articulated by judges of the ICJ, namely to 'improve their overall level of understanding of the science at play in the given case'.[94] This may sound like an overly ambitious construction of the judicial task, yet it is argued here that a science-intensive configuration of the judicial purview appears to be a necessary step in order to do justice to the complexity of the interdisciplinary judicial task. In order for judges to fully take responsibility for the resolution of science-intensive disputes, they ought to venture into previously uncharted waters of science. The preceding discussion sought to illustrate that by way of engaging in hybrid reasoning, they can safely do so. Such

---

93   Dwyer, *The Judicial Assessment of Expert Evidence*, p. 69.
94   *Pulp Mills*, Joint Dissenting Opinion of Judge Al-Khasawneh and Simma, para. 16.

a reasoning style guards against overstepping the red line judges are not supposed to cross, that is, to decide about the scientific veracity of underlying expert opinions. At the same time, hybrid reasoning promotes proactive reflection on the scientific bases of cases through the lenses of law, which supports the legitimacy of the judgment.

As a final remark, it remains to be pointed out that it is not only the epistemic benchmarks that are hybrid in nature. The legal questions entertained by scientific disputes are hybridized themselves too, in the sense that answering them requires combining insights and tools of more than one epistemic field.[95] What qualifies as scientific research in a litigious context? What is reliable expert evidence? What is a genuine environmental risk warranting regulation? What is a convincing causal link in a litigation? These questions are ubiquitous in environmental adjudication, but normally none of them can be answered correctly and responsibly only through a grammatical-legalistic reasoning. Therefore, they often invite essentially hybrid reasoning. Hybrid concepts embrace perhaps to the fullest extent that the judicial function itself has become hybridized, that is, the scientific and legal dimensions of adjudicatory dilemmas are so closely interwoven that their strict separation may, in fact, be analytically impossible.[96]

III GUIDANCE FOR SELECTING THE APPROPRIATE REASONING STYLE: SOME RECOMMENDATIONS

Readers may now wonder how international judges ought to reflect on science in a particular case to live up to the ideal of crafting a legitimate reasoning. How to choose between reasoning styles to respect the authority of science? What could be a solid argumentative approach to scientific evidence and arguments under the given circumstances? These are the ultimate questions to which this book seeks to offer some answers. It will therefore conclude with formulating some general recommendations to international adjudicators as to how to engage with science in order to respect and harness its cognitive authority to the maximum extent possible. Before turning to these concrete questions, some more general remarks are due on the nature of the judicial task that international courts and tribunals ought to fulfil in science-intensive cases.

1 *On the Interdisciplinary Nature of the Judicial Function*

The preceding discussion illustrated the many ways in which the interdisciplinary nature of the judicial task in environmental disputes warrants developing cross-disciplinary skills and understanding on the part of judges. And herein lies the real challenge for legal adjudicators. The roles assigned to judges in a litigious context

---

[95] Ballantyne, 'Epistemic trespassing', 372–3.
[96] Hybrids are defined by Bruno Latour as constructs in which the social and the scientific aspects cannot be strictly separated. Latour, *We Have Never Been Modern*, pp. 10–12.

confer an enormously arduous epistemic task on them. In contrast to an extra-judicial setting, where assistance from cross-disciplinary resources can be easily sought by primary decision-makers, in an adjudicatory setting judges cannot perform their duties by simply reaching out for epistemic support. The assistance they can ask from experts is essentially limited due to epistemic reasons. Even if respective procedural rules confer unrestricted powers on judges to seek expert advice, appointing experts does not absolve them from engaging with the scientific dimensions of disputes. Adjudicators thus are left with no choice but to develop a cross-disciplinary understanding of their own regarding the scientific profile of disputes if they wish to respect epistemic boundaries, discharge their judicial mandate meaningfully and retain their monopoly over the dispute resolution process.

Put differently, judges ought to recognize that they bear an 'epistemic responsibility'[97] to grasp and appreciate the scientific dimensions of legal disputes. Science cannot be hermeneutically sealed or contained in environmental adjudication, as it does permeate the adjudicatory process and impacts its legitimacy, in direct or indirect ways, even if adjudicators preferred ignoring science in their analysis. Fully discharging the judicial task in environmental disputes therefore compels a closer and more substantive engagement with the scientific subject matter of disputes, even if this fell outside the epistemic comfort zone of legal adjudicators. Should judges be willing to do so, their reward would lie in crafting epistemically legitimate and, therefore, more convincing judgments.

Better incorporation of science in the judicial analysis does not in any way imply that scientific opinions should dictate the judicial findings. Doing so would eliminate the normative aspects of environmental disputes, which would run against the core function of adjudication. Moreover, if adjudicators blindly followed science, their decisions could produce unjust results. Aryan science or phrenology are a few examples of how endeavours receiving transient recognition in parts of the scientific community as canonized 'science' promoted socially unacceptable and deeply immoral policies. Adjudicators deciding science-heavy disputes for this reason must be able to exert a critical epistemic control over scientific arguments raised in a legal dispute in order to guard against the abuse of science's cognitive authority.

Judges of science-based environmental disputes should inevitably become 'active borrowers'[98] of scientific findings in discharging their judicial function. Importantly, making sense of scientific debates from a legal point of view does not create a need for resolving scientific debates themselves.[99] Nevertheless, accepting this premise does not entail that the judicial task becomes any less complex, or less science-intensive. Notably, interdisciplinary questions that abound in scientific disputes

---

[97]   E. Fisher, 'Science, environmental law, and legal cultures: fostering collective epistemic responsibility' in E. Lees and J. E. Viñuales (eds.), *The Oxford Handbook of Comparative Environmental Law* (Oxford University Press, 2019), pp. 749–68 p. 761.

[98]   Faigman, 'Where law and science (and religion) meet', 1662.

[99]   Donoghue, 'Expert scientific evidence in a broader context', 382; Mbengue, 'International courts and tribunals as fact-finders', 76.

often invite epistemic trespassing, judicial paralysis, and surrendering the judicial function to experts – and thereby altogether threaten with delivering unconvincing and illegitimate judgments in scientific disputes. In answering such queries experts can undoubtedly be of assistance to judges by elucidating scientific facts, yet evaluating the legal relevance of those facts remains essentially a matter falling within the judicial purview.

At the outset of these final remarks it seems apt to recall that despite the plethora of pitfalls inherent in integrating science in a legal analysis, science may also prove to be an important ally, which, if treated properly, provides cognitive authority to well-reasoned judgments. In contrast, science would haunt adjudicators should they choose to dispose of it quickly by vague, inconsistent, or superficial reasoning. One must be mindful of the fact that the range of factors which confer legitimacy on a decision[100] are culturally embedded and are closely tied to the social practices, imaginaries, and expectations of a given community. Consequently, these factors are changing over time.[101] The reinterpreted reading of Solomon's judgment, as has been presented earlier,[102] warns that judges in the twenty-first century inevitably meet heightened expectations for their reflection on science should they aim to deliver respected, sound, and 'wise' decisions in scientific disputes. When science and technology pervade almost every side of modern existence, scientific aspects of legal disputes ought to be sufficiently addressed by adjudicators in order to render factually correct, epistemically non-arbitrary, and altogether persuasive decisions.

2 *General Recommendations for Selecting the Appropriate Reasoning Style*

The most appropriate reasoning style as well as the possible extent to which judges can engage with science directly may vary from case to case and across jurisdictions. As was seen in the previous sections, all types of benchmarks and corresponding adjudicatory reasoning methods have their own preconditions, trade-offs, and generate idiosyncratic risks regarding epistemic non-arbitrariness, persuasiveness, practical feasibility in terms of time and financial constraints in litigation, and preserving the judicial monopoly over the adjudicatory function. Available mitigation techniques to address the weaknesses of each reasoning style should also be borne in mind, when judges choose their preferred reasoning method in a given case. Before offering some recommendations for the selection of the most appropriate rationality with respect to concrete scenarios, an overview on each argumentative style is due, which is set out in the Table 10.1.

---

[100] For an overview see Grossman, 'Legitimacy and international adjudicative bodies', 115; Shany, 'Stronger together? legitimacy and effectiveness of international courts as mutually reinforcing or undermining notions', pp. 355–60.

[101] Grossman, 'Legitimacy and international adjudicative bodies', 117.

[102] See Chapter 9 Section II, Subsection 1.2.

TABLE 10.1 *Different scientific, legal, hybrid, and intuitive yardsticks used in the reasoning of international adjudicatory fora*

Reasoning style	Adjudicatory techniques	Relevant fora	Epistemic trade-offs	Remedy/solutions
Scientific rationality	relying on expert evidence	virtually all	inadvertent delegation of judicial task, partisan evidence	capacity building in science/training, ex curia experts, expert arbitrators
	using independent experts, expert arbitrators	WTO, PCA, UNCC	inadvertent delegation of judicial task	capacity building in science, ex curia experts, expert arbitrators
	accepting mathematical models as proof	PCA, UNCC, U.S. toxic tort law	epistemic competence is needed for the bench	capacity building in science, ex curia experts, expert arbitrators
	accepting probabilistic evidence	US toxic tort law	epistemic competence is needed for the bench	capacity building in science, ex curia experts, expert arbitrators
	almost *de novo* inquiry	WTO (initially)	epistemic competence is needed for the bench	capacity building in science, ex curia experts, expert arbitrators
	evidence must meet scientific and methodological rigor	WTO	inadvertent delegation of judicial task	
	prescribing expert-led consultations of the parties	ITLOS, PCA		
Legal rationality	scientific standards issued by international organizations	WTO, investment tribunals, ECtHR	not specific enough standards	using them only as complementary means of justification when scientific benchmarks are not available
	international regulatory trends	ECtHR, investment tribunals	'first regulator' problem, potential for abuse (deregulation)	
	scientific due process requirements	investment tribunals	culturally dependent criteria	
	causal presumption	ECtHR, Marshall Islands Claims Tribunals		

	Method	Fora	Disadvantage	Remedy
	relaxing causal tests	climate change litigation, toxic torts, ECtHR	leaves adverse third-party effects unabated	
	prioritizing procedural obligations over substantive ones	virtually all fora	epistemic trespassing	
	decoupling the notion of risk from scientific risk assessments			
'Hybrid' rationality	coherence test	ICJ		
	consistency test	WTO, EU courts, ICJ, PCA	epistemic competence is needed for the bench	scientific capacity building
	reasonableness test	ECtHR		
Intuitive rationality	causal proxies	ICJ, WTO	detached from scientific realities may not always be available	
	semantic analysis	ICJ, ITLOS, human rights courts	many are too vague or misleading indicators	using this reasoning style only as a last resort
	second-order indicators			

The absence of an abstract, a priori hierarchy between legal, hybrid, intuitive, and scientific standards used in judicial reasoning does not preclude setting out some generalized guidelines for selecting the most appropriate benchmarks in concrete cases. Under particular circumstances certain forms of reasoning do appear to be more suitable than others for delivering a legitimate outcome. Some recommendations to that effect are offered in the remainder of this chapter.

2.1 When We Do Need More Science

Increasing the scientific profile of adjudicatory reasoning via direct engagement with scientific evidence and a closer reflection on science-based arguments is beneficial for the epistemic legitimacy of every judicial decision. In this vein, applying framing techniques that put science duly on the table and incorporate such dimensions in the legally relevant ambit of a case projects a picture of a thorough adjudicatory analysis. As to the fact-finding stage, adequately considering scientific evidence is critical to the input legitimacy of judicial decisions, since properly consulting with experts makes a decision seem more legitimate in the eyes of the public. In light of the currently prevailing evidentiary techniques of international fora, judges ought to take more visible efforts to account for the scientific aspects of disputes in their fact-finding procedures. Lastly, scientific rationality can enhance the persuasive nature of causal findings too. In this vein, adjudicative fora would benefit from using scientific reasoning to showcase that their inquiry resembles factual realities as close as possible. As a precondition for such a more thorough scientific engagement, judicial fora should be equipped with advanced scientific fact-finding capacities. This also points to the need for more extensive use of independent experts by thus far reluctant courts and tribunals.

Using scientific reasoning better legitimizes adjudicatory conclusions especially when the parties themselves deem scientific facts relevant to their controversy. In such scenarios, not evaluating the evidence submitted seriously undermines the legitimacy of decisions. Equally vulnerable to legitimacy challenges are those judgments that provide only a superficial and opaque overall assessment as to why they accept or reject a given party-submitted scientific claim. At its extreme, if adjudicatory analysis fails to scrutinize the evidence and builds on scientifically flawed expert input, it will compromise the legitimacy of the resulting decision.

Relying on the cognitive authority of science in the inquiry is also preferable, because argumentative styles that automatically or exclusively reason with legal or intuitive yardsticks jeopardize the perceived legitimacy of decisions. If the reasoning offers only vague justification for its scientific findings, it can easily be suspected as concealing arbitrary decision-making. In the WTO context, one commentator explicitly referred to the use of a 'smell test',[103] signalling decisions that are

---

[103]   Palmeter, 'The WTO standard of review in health and safety disputes', p. 234.

seemingly based on a rough assessment with no adequate references to the under-lying facts. Indeed, adjudicatory balancing in which actual scientific evidence plays saliently little role may easily be regarded as illegitimate. A possible antidote lies in judges rolling up their sleeves and utilizing existing procedural powers as well as their possible argumentative space more strategically to increase the scientific flavour and profile of their assessment.

Importantly, the probabilistic and uncertain nature of scientific input should not be regarded as an insurmountable obstacle to exercise adjudicatory functions. Various forms of uncertainty have always been ubiquitous in law and in legal adjudication, which have long called for appropriate judicial solutions. The survey of international jurisprudence confirms that some adjudicative bodies could suc-cessfully integrate uncertain scientific knowledge in their legal analysis and render legitimate decisions while not using the peculiarities of science as an excuse for judicial paralysis.

Even though the extra-legal epistemic authority of science may intimidate legally trained adjudicators from forging judicial techniques that allow for a closer scientific engagement, the above factors do compel an in-depth judicial interaction with, and consideration of, scientific knowledge speaking to the legal dispute at hand. In fact, a wide array of reasoning practices is available to offer various solutions for a more meaningful judicial interaction with science. Emphatically, these are not mere theoretical possibilities. The comparative overview set forth in Chapter 9 has revealed a good number of such reasoning techniques in international environmen-tal case law at every stage of the adjudicatory process. As has been emphasized earlier, integrating scientific knowledge in the adjudicatory inquiry and reasoning is not only warranted but is also perfectly in line with the judicial function in science-intensive disputes.

2.2 When We Cannot Have More Science

It is worth recalling that nothing in the above analysis suggests that science alone is always capable of providing the ultimate, factually correct answer to adjudicatory dilemmas. There will be several instances when uncertainty and ambiguity in the sciences will be insurmountable and pervasive, coupled with time and budgetary constraints due to which interrogating the scientific aspects of the case would be impossible in a particular dispute. On such occasions, when relying on scientific rationality is not possible for judicial reasoners, legal or intuitive benchmarks may provide for satisfactory argumentation. Legal benchmarks enable adjudicators to pronounce judgments in science-intensive cases without the need for developing scientific capacities for the bench. When the relevant textual environment permits, intuitive rationality may also yield a legitimate semantic reasoning. These argu-mentative solutions are of special importance in institutional settings, where scien-tific capacity-building is precluded for some reason.

Moreover, non-scientific principles such as equity or good faith may be crucial for settling respective disputes. Importantly, deciding legal controversies as dictated by expert opinions is not the way of resolving disputes that is advocated for in this study. Quite the contrary, in certain legal contexts it may even be desirable that states address and regulate environmental risks even if these are not corroborated by a majority view of scientists.[104] Therefore not adopting an extremely deferential approach to scientific rationality can be deemed desirable in certain scenarios.

To sum up, judicial fora do have to deploy legalistic logic. When it is utilized correctly, that is, not in lieu of available scientific information, legal rationality can be instrumental in closing the science–law gap in the judicial analysis. Suffice it to refer to causal presumptions that tackle irreducible uncertainties in complex causal scenarios by legally attributing effects to toxic agents. Furthermore, relaxation of rigid legal doctrines through legalistic reasoning could be particularly significant in remedying climate change risks and damage in the face of considerable technical difficulties inherent in attributing, scientifically speaking, the adverse impacts to particular GHG sources.

2.3 When a Hybrid Approach Is Necessary

The hybrid reasoning style may yield the most solid approach to the interpretative exercise when scientific aspects cannot be circumvented in the judicial appraisal either due to the centrality of scientific dimensions to the legal dispute or on account of the specificities of the governing substantive law, for example, when express scientific legality criteria are applicable.

Situations are most amenable to hybrid analysis and reasoning whenever the scientific dilemma put before legal adjudicators concerns more than a binary question of scientific validity with regard to a piece of expert evidence, but is one that combines scientific and socio-legal aspects. Due to the presence of such non-scientific dimensions, outsourcing such questions entirely to scientific experts and scientific rationality would not yield an epistemically satisfactory result. Questions that combine a scientific 'core' with a normative 'cloak' abound in science-intensive adjudication. This is typically the case in the judicial review of regulatory decisions that avowedly constitute a mixture of scientific facts and value judgments; and as such they invite a hybrid assessment. Appraising the legality of risk assessment decisions inevitably drags scientific considerations into the ambit of judicial scrutiny, as judges have to look closely at what inferences were drawn based on what type of scientific information. Facing these queries, hybrid concepts such as coherence and consistency assist judges in analysing the essentially social aspects of the science-based decision-making, that is, the adequacy of reasoning.

---

[104]   The WTO dispute settlement bodies as well as certain investment tribunals accept minority scientific views as basis for legitimate regulation. For more details see Chapter 6 Section III, Subsection 5.2, and Chapter 7 Section V, Subsection 1.

Hybrid reasoning in this context is also the most appropriate avenue for realizing the 'informational catalyst'[105] function of courts. This conception of the judicial task sees the essential mandate of judges in ensuring that competent expert authorities properly discharge their obligations to carefully examine complex scientific matters. By reviewing whether primary decision-makers have provided explanations that fully accounted for possible interpretations of underlying data,[106] judges in fact 'prompt responsible actors to engage in effective problem solving'.[107] Hybrid concepts thus allow judges to fully assume their catalyst function as reviewing the logical coherence and consistency of reasoning ensures an ambitious standard of judicial review.

There are a number of further legal contexts where science-intensive legal questions cannot be boiled down to a single factual validity inquiry, but necessitate a judicial balancing concerning social and/or normative dimensions of disputes. The reasonableness standard provides an apt illustration for relying on hybrid reasoning for playing out such a balancing. The *Abyei* Tribunal for instance employed it to review whether a scientific expert body had exceeded its mandate in delineating a geographical area relevant for a peace process. This question has not been simply a matter of scientific evaluation either. It concerned whether the experts drew acceptable inferences from their mandate and, thus, whether their own construction of their task could be deemed reasonable.[108] Introducing the hybrid concept of reasonableness enabled the tribunal to conduct an assessment that was essentially decoupled from scientific rationality and could duly account for the legalistic aspects of the underlying dilemma, such as the historical context and the appropriate textual interpretation of said mandate.

To take another example, the ICJ in *Whaling in the Antarctic* applied the reasonableness test to discern the meaning and requirements of conducting scientific research under the international whaling regime. Despite the undoubted scientific core of this term, when it has to be interpreted by a court of law in the context of a legal dispute, scientific research operates as a socio-legal construct that cannot be properly expounded based on purely scientific accounts offered by experts. In this context, the reasonableness standard enabled the Court to appraise the extra-scientific aspects of the question; most particularly to account for the socio-legal dimensions of appealing to the authority of science under an international treaty regime.

---

[105] This term was coined by Ellen Vos, see Vos, 'The European Court of Justice in the face of scientific uncertainty and complexity', p. 152.

[106] See in the WTO context *US – Safeguard Measures on Imports of Fresh, Chilled or Frozen Lamb from New Zealand*, Report of the AB, WT/DS177/AB/R (1 May 2001), para. 1086.

[107] J. Scott and S. Sturm, 'Courts as catalysts: re-thinking the judicial role in new governance' (2007) 13 *Columbia Journal of European Law* 565–94 at 575.

[108] *Abyei* Arbitration, paras. 537–43.

2.4 Concluding Remarks on the Argumentative Space of Judges

As is clear from the preceding discussion, judges of science-intensive disputes have a range of argumentative tools at their disposal to decide cases in a legitimate way. Epistemically illegitimate forms of reasoning are only located at the two extremes of a hypothetical spectrum; the lower end being repudiating scientific knowledge in the judicial appraisal, and the upper extreme being resolving the relevant scientific controversy itself. In between, one may find a wide array of legitimate reasoning techniques encompassing both scientific, intuitive, and legalistic arguments and inferences. The upper limit of acceptable and feasible judicial engagement with scientific rationality is marked by the terrain of hybrid reasoning, where adjudicators focus their review on legally appreciable notions situated on the law–science interface. Selecting among legitimate forms of argumentation is in the discretion of legal adjudicators, and the legitimacy of a chosen reasoning style will ultimately hinge on the circumstances of the particular case.

To conclude this inquiry, it remains to be emphasized that judges ought to think about their reasoning more strategically. In order to enhance the legitimacy of international environmental adjudication, judges first and foremost must be aware of the extent as well as the limits of their legitimate argumentative space. They must also craft their argumentative justifications more consciously, taking into account the epistemic risks of downplaying science in their assessments. If international judges pay due regard to the imperative of epistemic legitimacy, they can tame scientific knowledge and turn its authority into an important asset for the purposes of legal dispute resolution.

Conclusion

This book has sought to make a convincing case for the proposition that science-intensive disputes cannot be decided legitimately without properly investigating science-based arguments and reflecting on resulting scientific knowledge in the judicial reasoning. If adjudicators marginalize or downplay apparent scientific dimensions of legal disputes, science will haunt them as a powerful tool in the hands of those seeking to level criticism against their findings. Yet if treated properly, the cognitive authority of science can support the persuasiveness and legitimacy of adjudicatory decisions. Well-reasoned judicial engagement with science therefore underpins the acceptability of respective judgments, which ultimately supports the legitimacy of the adjudicatory body. Proper interaction with science is especially consequential in times of increasing competition between available international courts and tribunals, and heightened scrutiny and expectations for impartial and unbiased treatment of disputes.

Science, however, is not only a basis for claiming legitimacy, but is also a source of complications with respect to conferring legitimacy on a judicial decision. Engaging with science-based arguments warrants peculiar interpretative justifications from scientifically non-trained reasoners; moreover science also disrupts ordinary practices of accruing legitimacy for adjudicatory reasoning. This book traced these hardships to specific epistemic, legitimacy, and doctrinal challenges posed by the presence of scientific facts in the adjudicative process. With a view to these pervasive difficulties, it is no wonder that international fora have been experimenting with their approaches towards handling the scientific profile of disputes. The foregoing overview has seen some extreme positions either arguing for the non-justiciability of legal issues that touch upon scientific aspects or contending that adjudicators were required to assess the quality and validity of scientific evidence. Recent jurisprudence however reflects an emerging consensus that deems science-based disputes falling within the judicial purview and advocates that it is not the task of international courts and tribunals to decide underlying scientific controversies nor 'to give a scientific assessment',[1] but to resolve the legal conflict referred to them.

---

[1] *Pulp Mills on the River Uruguay (Argentina v. Uruguay)* (Judgment) (2010) ICJ Rep 14, Joint Dissenting Opinion of Judge Al-Khasawneh and Simma, para. 4.

In other words, adjudicators are not supposed to act as 'science courts'[2] or 'super-experts' by deciding the underlying scientific controversy, for example whether an alleged risk is indeed established *from a scientific point of view*. Instead, judges need to ascertain whether they have a legitimate basis for accepting a piece of scientific evidence or science-based argument *from the perspective of the relevant legal rule*. In other words, legal adjudicators have to decide which among the rival science-based arguments is legitimate enough to be accepted to answer the legal question put before them. This is a highly interdisciplinary task; one that cannot be simply delegated to experts to have them distil a single answer that can be readily fed into the machine of adjudicatory decision-making. Accordingly, judges who decide environmental disputes need to become 'sophisticated consumers'[3] of scientific facts in order to exert control over scientific expertise and to single out the scientific bases relevant for answering the underlying legal question. Judges, hence, do have an epistemic responsibility to understand the main points of contention in the scientific controversy dragged into the courtroom. In other words, they have to take science seriously.

It is also crucial that legal adjudicators recognize and accept what science can and cannot deliver for the adjudicative process. If judges acknowledge the inescapably probabilistic nature of scientific knowledge, strong arguments can be made in favour of not construing scientific uncertainty as an ultimate obstacle to exercising the judicial function. Indeed, evaluating scientific evidence calls for idiosyncratic epistemic rules. While the traditional canon of epistemology defines knowledge as 'justified true belief', in the context of evaluating uncertain scientific evidence judges ought to strive for 'justifiable acceptance'[4] of scientific opinions. Simply put, the goal in a science-intensive dispute is to 'convince, not to prove',[5] which means that respective scientific data can form a legitimate basis of judicial conclusions even if they are surrounded with a level of scientific uncertainty.

The preceding chapters have shown that the entering of science into the course of adjudication fundamentally impacts the ways in which adjudicatory reasoning can be crafted in a persuasive and, thus, legitimate way. A main tenet of this study is that 'de-scientized' judicial assessment and reasoning often threaten with eroding the acceptability of a particular decision. Apart from concerns for the epistemic legitimacy of decisions, which warns that scientifically poorly reasoned judgments may easily prove unconvincing, thoroughly reflecting on the scientific dimensions of disputes in the judicial decision is also crucial for accounting for the significant third-party effects of environmental disputes. In the age when humanity puts the

---

[2]   This has been suggested by the respondent in *Glamis Gold Ltd. v. US* (UNCITRAL) Award (June 8, 2009), para. 617.

[3]   Faigman, 'Where Law and Science (and Religion) Meet', 1679.

[4]   Walton and Zhang, 'The epistemology of scientific evidence', 174.

[5]   Quotation from Tony Blackshield, cited by R. French, 'Conference on Judicial Reasoning: Art or Science?' (2010) 42 *Australian Journal of Forensic Sciences* 5–9 at 6.

earth's systems on the brink of collapse, legal proceedings revolving around conducts that degrade ecosystems, discharge pollution, and deplete finite natural resources affect and interest a far wider community than the litigants. Duly considering scientific knowledge therefore also provides a vehicle for representing these community interests in the litigation.

This is not to suggest here, however, that relying on *more* science would necessarily result in better reasoned, and hence, *more legitimate* judgments in every dispute. The judicial task is more nuanced. The key to legitimate reasoning lies in choosing the most appropriate epistemic rationality as a basis for judicial reasoning in light of the specific circumstances. In this respect, this study identified legal, scientific, intuitive, and hybrid reasoning styles in the case law of international adjudicative bodies. Each of these reasoning methods are suggested to have their own strengths and weaknesses in terms of underpinning the legitimacy of the judgment. Besides scientific rationality, legalistic logic and everyday reasoning certainly have their place in the adjudicatory toolkit in science-intensive disputes, but only if they do not serve to replace scientific knowledge that speaks to the scientific subject-matter of the dispute.

The comparative part of this study highlighted that international courts and tribunals entertain science in their inquiry to differing extents. Therefore, the role that science is allowed to play in the judicial analysis of major jurisdictions is also remarkably different. Instances of downplaying or marginalizing scientific evidence and arguments are still widespread in contemporary judicial practice in terms of how disputes are framed, the process of scientific fact-finding is conducted, causal nexus are assessed, and scientific claims are scrutinized by judicial bodies. This book ultimately points out that adjudicating scientific disputes without duly considering apparent scientific dimensions runs the risk of losing convincing force in the twenty-first century. Rendering Solomonic judgments that set aside science in the reasoning was only appropriate in the past, when the absence of in-depth scientific knowledge justified substituting non-scientific logic for a science-based inquiry. Yet international adjudicators are in a very different position nowadays as they are usually equipped with a range of options to have recourse to scientific expertise to thoroughly assess factually intricate cases. Courts therefore cannot be immune to the irrepressible intrusion of techno-scientific progress into society and social institutions.

Since the second half of the twentieth century, international law itself 'is becoming a more and more complex and many-sided subject',[6] and international adjudication must follow suit. Scientific complexity is not a matter of choice, neither is it an inconvenience that one may neglect or disregard in the long term. Uncertainty and ambiguity remain inherent in science and, therefore, science-intensive adjudication as well, thus judges must design ways of interacting with science

---

[6] W. Friedmann, *The Changing Structure of International Law* (Stevens & Sons, 1964), p. 70.

meaningfully. International judges bear the burden of making creative but episte-mically legitimate choices to reflect on science in their inquiry as well as to integrate scientific knowledge in their reasoning.

While the majority of adjudicatory tools seem to foster an evasive approach to science, this study also flagged adjudicatory attempts at better engaging with the scientific profile of disputes. This suggests a promising trend, even though it is far from being uniform across every international jurisdiction, resulting in a piecemeal approach to science underlying environmental disputes. This book has put scientific engagement of international adjudicators into the limelight hoping that scholarly and judicial awareness would provide further impetus for developing epistemically legitimate tools for bridging the science–law divide in adjudicating environmental claims. Undoubtedly there is still a long way to go for international jurisdictions in order to duly consider science in their analysis and to provide well-reasoned justi-fications for scientific findings of judges. Many shortcomings notwithstanding, the fact that international courts and tribunals have already improved in terms of their scientific engagement provides grounds for cautious optimism.

Bibliography

Adler, J. E., 'Introduction: Philosophical Foundations' in J. E. Adler, L. J. Rips (eds.), *Reasoning: Studies of Human Inference and Its Foundations* (Cambridge University Press, 2008), pp. 1–34.

Ahmad, J., 'Indus Waters Kishenganga Arbitration and State-to-State Disputes' (2013) 29 *Arbitration International* 507–38.

Alemanno, A., 'EU Risk Regulation and Science: The Role of Experts in Decision-Making and Judicial Review' in E. Vos (ed.), *European Risk Governance: Its Science, Its Inclusiveness and Its Effectiveness*, Connex Report Series No. 6 (2008), pp. 37–88.

Allott, P., 'Interpretation: An Exact Art' in A. Bianchi, D. Peat, M. Windsor (eds.), *Interpretation in International Law* (Oxford University Press, 2015), pp. 373–92.

Allum, J. R., '"An Outcrop of Hell": History, Environment, and the Politics of the Trail Smelter Dispute' in R. Bratspies, R. Miller (eds.), *Transboundary Harm in International Law* (Cambridge University Press, 2006), pp. 13–26.

Alter, K. J., L. R. Helfer, and M. R. Madsen (eds.), *International Courts Authority* (Oxford University Press, 2018).

Alvarez, J. E., 'Are International Judges Afraid of Science? A Comment on Mbengue' (2011) 34 *Loyola of Los Angeles International & Comparative Law Review* 81–98.

Alvarez, J. E., 'The Search for Objectivity: The Use of Experts in *Philip Morris* v. *Uruguay*' (2018) 9 *Journal of International Dispute Settlement* 411–22.

Ambrus, M., R. Rayfuse, and W. Werner, 'Risk and International Law' in M. Ambrus, R. Rayfuse, W. Werner (eds.), *Risk and the Regulation of Uncertainty in International Law* (Cambridge University Press, 2017), pp. 3–9.

Ambrus, M., R. Rayfuse, and W. Werner (eds.), *Risk and the Regulation of Uncertainty in International Law* (Cambridge University Press, 2017).

Ambrus, M., K. Arts, E. Hey, and H. Raulus (eds.), *The Role of 'Experts' in International and European Decision-Making Processes* (Cambridge University Press, 2014).

Amiott, J. A., 'Environment, Equality, and Indigenous Peoples' Land Rights in the Inter-American Human Rights System: *Mayagna (Sumo) Indigenous Community of Awas Tingni* v. *Nicaragua*' 32 *Environmental Law* 873–904.

Andersen, S., 'The Role of Scientific Expertise in Multilateral Environmental Agreements: Influence and Effectiveness' in M. Ambrus, K. Arts, E. Hey, H. Raulus (eds.), *The Role of 'Experts' in International and European Decision-Making Processes* (Cambridge University Press, 2014), pp. 105–25.

Andersen, S. and J. B. Skjærseth, 'Science and Technology from Agenda Setting to Implementation' in D. Bodansky, J. Brunnée, E. Hey (eds.), *The Oxford Handbook of International Environmental Law* (Oxford University Press, 2008), pp. 183–202.

Anderson, D., 'Scientific Evidence in Cases under Part XV of the LOSC' in M. H. Nordquist, R. Long, T. Heidar, J. N. Moore (eds.), Law, Science and Ocean Management (Martinus Nijhoff Publishers, 2007), pp. 503–18.

Asteriti, A., 'Climate Change Policies and Foreign Investment: Some Salient Legal Issues' in Y. Levashova, T. Lambooy, I. Dekker (eds.), *Bridging the Gap between International Investment Law and the Environment* (Eleven Publishing, 2015), pp. 145–86.

Asteriti, A., 'Environmental Law in Investment Arbitration: Procedural Means of Incorporation' (2015) 16 *The Journal of World Investment & Trade* 248–73.

Babione, J. C., 'Mission Accomplished? Fifty-Four Years of Suffering for the People of the Marshall Islands and the Latest Round of Endless Reconciliation' (2000) 11 115–43.

Ballantyne, N., 'Epistemic Trespassing' (2019) 128 *MIND* 367–95.

Behn, D. and M. Langford, 'Trumping the Environment? An Empirical Perspective on the Legitimacy of Investment Treaty Arbitration' (2017) 18 *The Journal of World Investment & Trade* 14–61.

Benvenisti, E., 'Community Interests in International Law' in E. Benvenisti, G. Nolte (eds.), *Community Interests Across International Law* (Oxford University Press, 2018), pp. 70–85.

Berkes, A., 'A New Extraterritorial Jurisdictional Link Recognised by the IACtHR', EJIL Talk! (March 28 2018), available at www.ejiltalk.org/a-new-extraterritorial-jurisdictional-link-recognised-by-the-iacthr/.

Bertea, S., 'Certainty, Reasonableness and Argumentation in Law' (2004) 18 *Argumentation* 465–78.

Beven, K., 'Facets of Uncertainty: Epistemic Uncertainty, Non-Stationarity, Likelihood, Hypothesis Testing, and Communication' (2016) 61 *Hydrological Sciences Journal* 1652–65.

Bjorge, E., 'Been There, Done That: The Margin of Appreciation and International Law' (2015) 4 *Cambridge Journal of International and Comparative Law* 181–90.

Blackaby, N. and A. Wilbraham, 'Practical Issues Relating to the Use of Expert Evidence in Investment Treaty Arbitration' (2016) 31 *ICSID Review* 655–69.

Blackshield, T., 'Judicial Reasoning' in M. Coper, T. Blackshield, G. Williams (eds.), *The Oxford Companion to the High Court of Australia* (Oxford University Press, 2007).

Bodansky, D., 'Deconstructing the Precautionary Principle' in D. Caron, H. N. Scheiber (eds.), *Bringing New Law to Ocean Waters* (Martinus Nijhoff, 2004), pp. 381–91.

Bodansky, D., 'OSPAR Arbitration of the MOX Plant Dispute' (2008) 08–002 *University of Georgia School of Law Research Paper Series* 1–20.

Bodansky, D., 'Scientific Uncertainty and the Precautionary Principle' (1991) 33 *Environment* 4.

Bodansky, D., 'The Legitimacy of International Governance: A Coming Challenge for International Environmental Law?' (1999) 93 *American Journal of International Law* 596.

Bodansky, D., J. Brunnée, and E. Hey, 'International Environmental Law Mapping the Field' in D. M. Bodansky, J. Brunnée, E. Hey (eds.), *The Oxford Handbook of International Environmental Law* (Oxford University Press, 2008), pp. 6–25.

Bodansky, D., J. Brunnée, and L. Rajamani, *International Climate Change Law* (Oxford University Press, 2017).

Bogdandy, A. von and I. Venzke (eds.), *In Whose Name? A Public Law Theory of International Adjudication* (Oxford University Press, 2014).

Boisson de Chazournes, L., 'Plurality in the Fabric of International Courts and Tribunals: The Threads of a Managerial Approach: A Rejoinder – Fears and Anxieties' (2017) 28 *European Journal of International Law* 1275–81.

Boisson de Chazournes, L., M. M. Mbengue, R. Das, and G. Gros, 'One Size Does Not Fit All: Uses of Experts before International Courts and Tribunals – An Insight into the Practice' (2018) 9 *Journal of International Dispute Settlement* 477–505.

Boisson de Chazournes, L., H. Ruiz Fabri, M. M. Mbengue, R. Das, and G. Gros, 'The Expert in the International Adjudicative Process: Introduction to the Special Issue' (2018) 9 *Journal of International Dispute Settlement* 339–44.

Bossche, P. V. den and W. Zdouc, *The Law and Policy of the World Trade Organization* (Cambridge University Press, 2013).

Bottini, G. and M. Scheltema, 'Future Outlook: Bridging Gaps between Environment and International Investment Law or Juxtaposing Different Topics?' in Y. Levashova, T. Lambooy, I. Dekker (eds.), *Bridging the Gap between International Investment Law and the Environment* (Eleven Publishing, 2015), pp. 467–83.

Boyle, A., 'Forum Shopping for UNCLOS Disputes Relating to Marine Scientific Research' in M. H. Nordquist, R. Long, T. Heidar, J. N. Moore (eds.), *Law, Science and Ocean Management* (Martinus Nijhoff, 2007), pp. 519–40.

Boyle, A., 'Human Rights and the Environment: Where Next?' (2012) 23 *European Journal of International Law* 613–42.

Boyle, A., 'The Environmental Jurisprudence of the International Tribunal for the Law of the Sea Symposium to Mark the Tenth Anniversary ITLOS: The Jurisprudence of the International Tribunal of the Law of the Sea: Assessment and Prospects' (2007) 22 *International Journal of Marine and Coastal Law* 369–82.

Boyle, A. and J. Harrison, 'Judicial Settlement of International Environmental Disputes: Current Problems' (2013) 4 *Journal of International Dispute Settlement* 245–76.

Brennan, T. A., 'Causal Chains and Statistical Links: The Role of Scientific Uncertainty in Hazardous-Substance Litigation' (1987) 73 *Cornell Law Review* 469.

Brewer, S., 'Scientific Expert Testimony and Intellectual Due Process' (1998) 107 *Yale Law Journal* 1535–681.

Briggle, A. and C. Mitcham, *Ethics and Science* (Cambridge University Press, 2012).

Brown, J. D., 'Prospects for the Open Treatment of Uncertainty in Environmental Research' (2010) 34 *Progress in Physical Geography* 75–100.

Bruce, S., 'The Project for an International Environmental Court' in C. Tomuschat, R. P. Mazzeschi, D. Thürer (eds.), *Conciliation in International Law* (Brill, 2017), pp. 133–70.

Brunnée, J., 'ESIL Reflection: Procedure and Substance in International Environmental Law: Confused at a Higher Level?' June 2016. Available at: https://esil-sedi.eu/post_name-123/.

Brunnée, J., 'International Environmental Law and Community Interests: Procedural Aspects' in E. Benvenisti, G. Nolte (eds.), *Community Interests Across International Law* (Oxford University Press, 2018), pp. 151–75.

Brunnée, J. and S. J. Toope, *Legitimacy and Legality in International Law* (Cambridge University Press, 2010).

Brunner, L., 'The Rise of Peoples' Rights in the Americas: The Saramaka People Decision of the Inter-American Court of Human Rights' (2008) 7 *Chinese Journal of International Law* 699–711

Buchanan, A., 'The Legitimacy of International Law' in S. Besson, J. Tasioulas (eds.), *The Philosophy of International Law* (Oxford University Press, 2010), pp. 79–96.

Buergenthal, T., 'The Evolving International Human Rights System Centennial Essays: In Honor of the 100th Anniversary of the AJIL and the ASIL' (2006) 100 *American Journal of International Law* 783–807.

Cannizzaro, E., 'Proportionality and Margin of Appreciation in the *Whaling* Case: Reconciling Antithetical Doctrines?' (2016) 27 *European Journal of International Law* 1061–9.

Caron, D. and E. Shirlow, 'Dissecting Backlash' in A. Føllesdal, G. Ulfstein (eds.), *The Judicialization of International Law: A Mixed Blessing?* (Oxford University Press, 2018), pp. 159–82.

Carpenter, R. A., 'Uncertainty in Managing Ecosystems Sustainably' in J. Lemons (ed.), *Scientific Uncertainty and Environmental Problem Solving* (Blackwell Science, 1996), pp. 118–59.

Carruth, R. S. and B. D. Goldstein, 'Relative Risk Greater than Two in Proof of Causation in Toxic Tort Litigation' (2000) 41 *Jurimetrics* 195.

Ceder, M. A., 'Dose of Reality: The Struggle with Causation in Toxic Tort Litigation, A' (2013) 51 *Houston Law Review* 1381.

Chenwi, L., 'The Right to a Satisfactory, Healthy, and Sustainable Environment in the African Regional Human Rights System' in J. H. Knox, R. Pejan (eds.), *The Human Right to a Healthy Environment* (Cambridge University Press, 2018), pp. 59–85.

Chircop, A., 'Advances in Ocean Knowledge and Skill: Implications for the MSR Regime' in M. H. Nordquist, R. Long, T. H. Heidar, J. N. Moore (eds.), *Law, Science and Ocean Management* (Martinus Nijhoff, 2007), pp. 575–618.

Cohen, H. G., A. Føllesdal, N. Grossman, and G. Ulfstein, 'Legitimacy and International Courts: A Framework' in H. G. Cohen, A. Føllesdal, N. Grossman, G. Ulfstein (eds.), *Legitimacy and International Courts* (Cambridge University Press, 2018), pp. 1–40.

Colson, D. A. and B. J. Vohrer, 'In Re Chagos Marine Protected Area (*Mauritius* v. *United Kingdom*)' (2015) 109 *American Journal of International Law* 845–51.

Contesse, J., 'Contestation and Deference in the Inter-American Human Rights System Subsidiarity in Global Governance' (2016) 79 *Law and Contemporary Problems* 123–46.

Cook, C. N., M. B. Mascia, M. W. Schwartz, H. P. Possingham, and R. A. Fuller, 'Achieving Conservation Science that Bridges the Knowledge-Action Boundary: Achieving Effective Conservation Science' (2013) 27 *Conservation Biology* 669–78.

Cook, J. R., 'In re Indus Waters Kishenganga Arbitration (*Pakistan* v. *India*)' (2014) 108 *American Journal of International Law* 308–14.

Council of Europe, *Manual on Human Rights and the Environment*, 2nd ed. (Council of Europe Publishing, 2012).

Coustasse, J. G. S. and E. Sweeney-Samuelson, 'Adjudicating Conflicts Over Resources: The ICJ's Treatment of Technical Evidence in the Pulp Mills Case' (2011) 3 *Goettingen Journal of International Law* 447–71.

Craik, N. A., 'Recalcitrant Reality and Chosen Ideals: The Public Function of Dispute Settlement in International Environmental Law' (1998) 10 *The Georgetown International Environmental Law Review* 551–80.

Craik, N., 'Transboundary Pollution, Unilateralism, and the Limits of Extraterritorial Jurisdiction: The Second Trail Smelter Dispute' in R. Bratspies, R. A. Miller (eds.), *Transboundary Harm in International Law* (Cambridge University Press, 2006), pp. 109–24.

Cranor, C. F., 'The Challenge of Developing Science for the Law of Torts' in R. Goldberg (ed.), *Perspectives on Causation* (Hart, 2011), pp. 261–81.

Cranor, C. F., *Toxic Torts Science, Law and the Possibility of Justice* (Cambridge University Press, 2006).

Crawford, E., G. Hutton, and T. Stephens, 'Australian Cases before International Courts and Tribunals Involving Questions of Public International Law 2011' (2013) 31 *Australian Yearbook of International Law* 173–8.

Crawford, J., '*In Dubio Pro Natura*: The Dissent of Judge Herczegh' in P. Kovács (ed.), *International Law: A Quiet Strength* (Pázmány Press, 2011), pp. 251–69.

Crawford, J., *State Responsibility – The General Part* (Cambridge University Press, 2013).

Crawford, J., *The International Law Commission's Articles on State Responsibility* (Cambridge University Press, 2002).

D'Aspremont, J. and M. M. Mbengue, 'Strategies of Engagement with Scientific Fact-Finding in International Adjudication' (2014) 5 *Journal of International Dispute Settlement* 240–72.

Desgagné, R., 'International Decisions' (1995) 89 *American Journal of International Law* 788–91.

Desierto, D., 'Environmental Damages, Environmental Reparations, and the Right to a Healthy Environment: The ICJ Compensation Judgment in *Costa Rica* v. *Nicaragua* and the IACtHR Advisory Opinion on Marine Protection for the Greater Caribbean', EJIL Talk! (14 February 2018) Available at https://bit.ly/2LOvJT1.

Desierto, D., 'Evidence but Not Empiricism? Environmental Impact Assessments at the International Court of Justice in Certain Activities Carried Out by Nicaragua in the Border Area (*Costa Rica* v. *Nicaragua*) and Construction of a Road in Costa Rica along the San Juan River (*Nicaragua* v. *Costa Rica*)', EJIL Talk! (26 February 2016) Available at https://bit.ly/2ZsD2bi.

Donoghue, J. E., 'Expert Scientific Evidence in a Broader Context' (2018) 9 *Journal of International Dispute Settlement* 379–87.

Douhan, A., 'Liability for Environmental Damage' in R. Wolfrum (ed.), *Max Planck Encyclopedia of Public International Law*, 2013.

Dupuy, P.-M. and J. E. Vinuales (eds.), *Harnessing Foreign Investment to Promote Environmental Protection* (Cambridge University Press, 2013).

Dupuy, P.-M. and J. E. Vinuales, *International Environmental Law* (Cambridge University Press, 2018).

Durden, J. M., L. E. Lallier, K. Murphy, A. Jaeckel, K. Gjerde, and D. O. B. Jones, 'Environmental Impact Assessment Process for Deep-Sea Mining in "the Area"' (2018) 87 *Marine Policy* 194–202.

Duvic-Paoli, L.-A., *The Prevention Principle in International Environmental Law* (Cambridge University Press, 2018).

Duvic-Paoli, L.-A. and J. E. Vinuales, 'Prevention' in J. E. Vinuales (ed.), *The Rio Declaration on Environment and Development: A Commentary* (Oxford University Press, 2015), pp. 107–38.

Dwyer, D., *The Judicial Assessment of Expert Evidence* (Cambridge University Press, 2008).

Ebobrah, S. T., 'International Human Rights Courts' in C. Romano, K. J. Alter, Y. Shany (eds.), *The Oxford Handbook of International Adjudication* (Oxford University Press, 2014), pp. 225–49.

Esty, D. C., 'Good Governance at the World Trade Organization: Building a Foundation of Administrative Law' (2007) 10 *Journal of International Economic Law* 509–27.

Faigman, D. L., 'Where Law and Science (and Religion) Meet' (2014) 93 *Texas Law Review* 1659.

Farber, D. A., 'Uncertainty' (2011) 99 *Georgetown Law Journal* 901–59.

Faure, M. G. and A. Nollkaemper, 'International Liability as an Instrument to Prevent and Compensate for Climate Change' (2007) 43 *Stanford Journal of International Law* 123–79.

Feldman, R., 'Evidentialism, Higher-Order Evidence, and Disagreement' (2009) 6 *Episteme* 294–312.

Feldman, R., *The Role of Science in Law* (Oxford University Press, 2009).

Feldschreiber, P., L.-A. Mulcahy, and S. Day, 'Biostatistics and Causation in Medicinal Product Liability Suits' in R. Goldberg (ed.), *Perspectives on Causation* (Hart, 2011), pp. 179–94.

Fels, E. and T.-M. Vu, 'Introduction: Understanding the Importance of the Disputes in the South China Sea' in E. Fels, T.-M. Vu (eds.), *Power Politics in Asia's Contested Waters* (Springer, 2016), pp. 3–23.

Fisher, E., 'Science, Environmental Law, and Legal Cultures: Fostering Collective Epistemic Responsibility' in E. Lees, J. E. Vinuales (eds.), *The Oxford Handbook of Comparative Environmental Law* (Oxford University Press, 2019), pp. 749–68.

Fitzmaurice, M., 'International Responsibility and Liability' in D. M. Bodansky, E. Hey, J. Brunnée (eds.), *The Oxford Handbook of International Environmental Law* (Oxford University Press, 2008), pp. 1011–35.

Fitzmaurice, M., 'Principle 13 Liability and Compensation' in J. E. Vinuales (ed.), *The Rio Development on Environment and Development* (Oxford University Press, 2015), pp. 351–81.

Fitzmaurice, M., 'The European Court of Human Rights, Environmental Damage and the Applicability of Article 8 of the European Convention on Human Rights and Fundamental Freedoms: *Dubetska and Others* v. *Ukraine*, European Court of Human Rights (Application No. 30499/03), Judgment of 10 February 2011, Not Yet Reported' (2011) 13 *Environmental Law Review* 107–14.

Fitzmaurice, M., *Whaling and International Law* (Cambridge University Press, 2016).

Foerster, A. F. and C. Gregorski Rolph (eds.), *Toxic Tort Litigation* (American Bar Association Publishing, 2013).

Foster, C. E., 'Adjudication, Arbitration and the Turn to Public Law "Standards of Review": Putting the Precautionary Principle in the Crucible' (2012) 3 *Journal of International Dispute Settlement* 525–58.

Foster, C. E., 'International Adjudication – Standards of Review and Burden of Proof: Australia-Apples and Whaling in the Antarctic' (2012) *Review of European, Comparative & International Environmental Law* 80–91.

Foster, C. E., 'New Clothes for the Emperor? Consultation of Experts by the International Court of Justice' (2014) 5 *Journal of International Dispute Settlement* 139–73.

Foster, C. E., *Science and the Precautionary Principle in International Courts and Tribunals* (Cambridge University Press, 2011).

Foster, C. E., 'The Consultation of Independent Experts by International Courts and Tribunals in Health and Environmental Cases' (2009) 20 *Finnish Yearbook of International Law* 391–417.

Francioni, F., 'The Private Sector and the Challenge of Implementation' in P.-M. Dupuy, J. E. Vinuales (eds.), *Harnessing Foreign Investment to Promote Environmental Protection* (Cambridge University Press, 2013), pp. 24–49.

Franklin, A., *Can that Be Right?: Essays on Experiment, Evidence, and Science*, Boston Studies in the Philosophy of Science (Springer-Science, 1999), vol. 199.

Fravel, T., 'U.S. Policy towards the Disputes in the South China Sea Since 1995' in E. Fels, T.-M. Vu (eds.), *Power Politics in Asia's Contested Waters* (Springer, 2016), pp. 389–402.

Freestone, D., 'Responsibilities and Obligations of States Sponsoring Persons and Entities with Respect to Activities in the Area International Decisions' (2011) 105 *American Journal of International Law* 755–60.

French, R., 'Conference on Judicial Reasoning: Art or Science?' (2010) 42 *Australian Journal of Forensic Sciences* 5–9.

French, D., 'Environmental Dispute Settlement: The First (Hesitant) Signs of Spring?' (2006) 19 *Hague Yearbook of International Law* 3–32.

Friedmann, W., *The Changing Structure of International Law* (Stevens & Sons, 1964).

Fukunaga, Y., 'Standard of Review and "Scientific Truths" in the WTO Dispute Settlement System and Investment Arbitration' (2012) 3 *Journal of International Dispute Settlement* 559–76.

Fukushima, T., 'The Role of Science for Environmental Impact Evaluation Resulting from Ocean Mining' (2018) 14 *The Marine Environment and United Nations Sustainable Development Goal* 251–62.

Galaz, V., J. Tallberg, A. Boin, C. Ituarte-Lima, E. Hey, P. Ollson, and F. Westley, 'Global Governance Dimensions of Globally Networked Risks: The State of the Art in Social Science Research' (2017) 8 *Risk, Hazards & Crisis in Public Policy* 4–27.

Garrido-Munoz, A., 'Managing Uncertainty: The International Court of Justice, "Objective Reasonableness" and the Judicial Function' (2017) 30 *Leiden Journal of International Law* 457–74.

Gattini, A., 'Breach of International Obligations' in A. Nollkaemper, I. Plakokefalos (eds.), *Principles of Shared Responsibility in International Law: An Appraisal of the State of the Art* (Cambridge University Press, 2014), p. 25.

Gattini, A., 'Breach of the Obligation to Prevent and Reparation Thereof in the ICJ's Genocide Judgment' (2007) 18 *European Journal of International Law* 695–713.

Gautier, P., 'Environmental Damage and the United Nations Claim Commission: New Directions for Future International Environmental Cases?' in T. M. Ndiaye, R. Wolfrum (eds.), *Law of the Sea, Environmental Law and Settlement of Disputes: Liber Amicorum Judge Thomas A Mensah* (Martinus Nijhoff, 2007), pp. 177–214.

Gavouneli, M., 'Protection Standards for the Marine Environment: Updating Part XII of the Law of the Sea Convention?' in S. Minas and J. Diamond (eds.), *Stress Testing the Law of the Sea* (Brill Nijhoff, 2018), pp. 254–66.

Gerstetter, C., 'Substance and Style: How the WTO Adjudicators Legitimize Their Decisions' in A. Føllesdal, G. Ulfstein (eds.), *The Judicialization of International Law: A Mixed Blessing?* (Oxford University Press, 2018), pp. 64–85.

Ghaleigh, N. S., 'Science and Climate Change Law: The Role of the IPCC in International Decision-Making' in K. Gray, R. Tarasofsky, C. Carlarne (eds.), *The Oxford Handbook of International Climate Change Law* (Oxford University Press, 2016), pp. 56–72.

Gieryn, T., 'Boundaries of Science' in S. Jasanoff, G. E. Markle, T. Pinch (eds.), *Handbook of Science and Technology Studies* (SAGE Publications, 1995), pp. 393–443.

Gogarty, B. and P. Lawrence, 'The ICJ *Whaling* Case: Missed Opportunity to Advance the Rule of Law in Resolving Science-Related Disputes in Global Commons?' (2016) 77 ZaöRV 161–97.

Gogarty, B. and P. Lawrence, 'The ICJ *Whaling* Case: Science, Transparency and the Rule of Law' (2014) 23 *Journal of Law, Information and Science* 134.

Gold, S. C., 'The More We Know, the Less Intelligent We Are? How Genomic Information Should, and Should Not, Change Toxic Tort Causation Doctrine' (2010) 34 *Harvard Environmental Law Review* 369.

Gomula, J., 'Environmental Disputes in the WTO' in M. Fitzmaurice, D. M. Ong, P. Merkouris (eds.), *Research Handbook on International Environmental Law* (Edward Elgar, 2010), pp. 401–25.

Gray, C., 'The 2016 Judicial Activity of the International Court of Justice' (2017) 111 *American Journal of International Law* 415–36.

Green, M. D., 'The Future of Proportional Liability: The Lessons of Toxic Substances Causation' in M. S. Madden (ed.), *Exploring Tort Law* (Cambridge University Press, 2005), pp. 352–99.

Greenland, S., 'Relation of Probability of Causation to Relative Risk and Doubling Dose: A Methodological Error that Has Become a Social Problem' (1999) 89 *American Journal of Public Health* 1166–9.

Greenland, S. and J. M. Robins, 'Epidemiology, Justice, and the Probability of Causation' (2000) *Jurimetrics* 321–340.

Griss, I., 'How Judges Think: Judicial Reasoning in Tort Cases from a Comparative Perspective' (2013) 4 *Journal of European Tort Law* 247–58.

Grodsky, J. A., 'Genomics and Toxic Torts: Dismantling the Risk-Injury Divide' (2007) *Stanford Law Review* 1671–1734.

Grossman, D. A., 'Tort-Based Climate Litigation' in W. C. G. Burns, H. M. Osofsky (eds.), *Adjudicating Climate Change: State, National, and International Approaches* (Cambridge University Press, 2009), pp. 193–229.

Grossman, N., 'Legitimacy and International Adjudicative Bodies' (2009) 41 *George Washington International Law Review* 107–80.

Grossman, N., 'Solomonic Judgments and the Legitimacy of the International Court of Justice' in N. Grossman, H. G. Cohen, A. Føllesdal, G. Ulfstein (eds.), *Legitimacy and International Courts* (Cambridge University Press, 2018), pp. 43–61.

Grossman, N., H. G. Cohen, A. Føllesdal, and G. Ulfstein (eds.), *Legitimacy and International Courts* (Cambridge University Press, 2018).

Grubler, A., Y. Ermoliev, and A. Kryazhimskiy, 'Coping with Uncertainties: Examples of Modeling Approaches at IIASA' (2015) 98 *Technological Forecasting and Social Change* 213–22.

Gruszczynski, L., 'How Deep Should We Go? Searching for an Appropriate Standard of Review in the SPS Cases' (2011) 2 *European Journal of Risk Regulation* 111–14.

Gruszczynski, L., *Regulating Health and Environmental Risks under WTO Law: A Critical Analysis of the SPS Agreement* (Oxford University Press, 2010).

Gruszczynski, L., 'Science and the Settlement of Trade Disputes in the World Trade Organization' in B. Mercurio, N. Kuei-Jung (eds.), *Science and Technology in International Economic Law: Balancing Competing Interests* (Routledge, 2014), pp. 11–29.

Gruszczynski, L., 'Standard of Review and Scientific Evidence in WTO Law and International Investment Arbitration' in L. Gruszczynski, W. Werner (eds.), *Deference in International Courts and Tribunals: Standard of Review and Margin of Appreciation* (Oxford University Press, 2014), pp. 153–73.

Gruszczynski, L., 'Standard of Review of Health and Environmental Regulations by WTO Panels' in G. Van Calster, D. Prévost (eds.), *Research Handbook on Environment, Health and the WTO* (Edward Elgar, 2014), pp. 731–57.

Gruszczynski, L., 'The Role of Experts in Environmental and Health Related Trade Disputes in the WTO: Deconstructing Decision-Making Processes' in M. Ambrus, K. Arts, E. Hey, H. Raulus (eds.), *Irrelevant, Advisors or Decision-Makers? The Role of 'Experts' in International Decision-Making* (Cambridge University Press, 2014), pp. 216–37.

Gruszczynski, L., 'WHO Framework Convention on Tobacco Control as an International Standard under the TBT Agreement?' (2012) 9 *Transnational Dispute Management* 1–14.

Gruszczynski, L. and W. Werner (eds.), *Deference in International Courts and Tribunals: Standard of Review and Margin of Appreciation* (Oxford University Press, 2014).

Gruszczynski, L. and W. Werner, 'Introduction' in L. Gruszczynski, W. Werner (eds.), *Deference in International Courts and Tribunals: Standard of Review and Margin of Appreciation* (Oxford University Press, 2014), pp. 1–15.

Guarnieri, C. and P. Pederzoli, *The Power of Judges* (Oxford University Press, 2002).

Haack, S., *Defending Science within Reason: Between Scientism and Cynicism* (Prometheus Books, 2007).

Haas, P. M., 'Epistemic Communities' in J. Krieger (ed.), *The Oxford Companion to International Relations* (Oxford University Press, 2013), pp. 351–59.

Haas, P. M., 'Ideas, Experts and Governance' in M. Ambrus, K. Arts, E. Hey, H. Raulus (eds.), *The Role of Experts in International and European Decision-Making Processes* (Cambridge University Press, 2014), pp. 19–43.

Haidt, J., 'The Emotional Dog and Its Rational Tail: A Social Intuitionist Approach to Moral Judgment' in J. E. Adler, L. J. Rips (eds.), *Reasoning: Studies of Human Inference and Its Foundations* (Cambridge University Press, 2008), pp. 1024–52.

Hamamoto, S., 'From the Requirement of Reasonableness to a "Comply and Explain" Rule: The Standard of Review in the *Whaling* judgment' in M. Fitzmaurice, D. Tamada (eds.), *Whaling in the Antarctic: The Significance and Implications of the ICJ Judgment* (Brill Nijhoff, 2016), pp. 38–52.

Harker, D., *Creating Scientific Controversies* (Cambridge University Press, 2015) .

Harris, D., M. O'Boyle, E. Bates, and C. Buckley, *Law of the European Convention on Human Rights* (Oxford University Press, 2014).

Harrison, J., 'Addressing the Procedural Challenges of Environmental Litigation in the Context of Investor-State Arbitration' in Y. Levashova, T. Lambooy, I. Dekker (eds.), *Bridging the Gap between International Investment Law and the Environment* (Eleven Publishing, 2015), pp. 87–113.

Hart, H. L. A. and T. Honoré, *Causation in the Law*, 2nd ed. (Oxford University Press, 1985).

Harwood, J. and K. Stokes, 'Coping with Uncertainty in Ecological Advice: Lessons from Fisheries' (2003) 18 *Trends in Ecology & Evolution* 617–22.

Hey, E., 'International Institutions and Global Environmental Governance' (2006) 100 *American Society of International Law Proceedings* 303–16.

Hill, A. B., 'The Environment and Disease: Association or Causation?' (2015) 108 *Journal of the Royal Society of Medicine* 32–7.

Howse, R., 'The World Trade Organization 20 Years On: Global Governance by Judiciary' (2016) 27 *European Journal of International Law* 9–77.

Huguenin, M. T., M. C. Donlan, A. E. van Geel, and R. W. Paterson, 'Assessment and Valuation of Damage to the Environment' in C. Payne, P. H. Sand (eds.), *Gulf War Reparations and the UN Compensation Commission: Environmental Liability* (Oxford University Press, 2015), pp. 1–41.

Hunter, D., 'The Implications of Climate Change Litigation: Litigation for International Environmental Law-Making' in W. C. G. Burns, H. M. Osofsky (eds.), *Adjudicating Climate Change* (Cambridge University Press, 2010).

Ioannidis, M., 'Beyond the Standard of Review: Deference Criteria in WTO Law and the Case for a Procedural Approach' in L. Gruszczynski, W. Werner (eds.), *Deference in International Courts and Tribunals: Standard of Review and Margin of Appreciation* (Oxford University Press, 2014), pp. 91–112.

Irwin, A., 'STS Perspectives on Scientific Governance' in E. J. Hackett, O. Amsterdamska, M. Lynch, J. Wajcman (eds.), *The Handbook of Science and Technology Studies* (The MIT Press, 2008), pp. 583–607.

Jacur, F. R., 'Remarks on the Role of *Ex Curia* Scientific Experts in International Environmental Disputes' in N. Broschiero (ed.), *International Court and the Development of International Law: Essays in Honour of Tullio Treves* (T. M. C. Asser Press, 2013), pp. 441–55.

Jaeckel, A., 'An Environmental Management Strategy for the International Seabed Authority: The Legal Basis' (2015) 30 *International Journal of Marine and Coastal Law* 93–119.

Jaeckel, A., 'Deep Seabed Mining and Adaptive Management: The Procedural Challenges for the International Seabed Authority' (2016) 70 *Marine Policy* 205–11.

Jaeckel, A. and R. Rayfuse, *Conceptions of Risk in an Institutional Context: Deep Seabed Mining and the International Seabed Authority* (Oxford University Press, 2017).

Jarret, M., *Contributory Fault and Investor Misconduct in Investment Arbitration* (Cambridge University Press, 2019).

Jasanoff, S., 'Genealogies of STS' (2012) 42 *Social Studies of Science* 435–41.

Jasanoff, S., 'In a Constitutional Moment: Science and Social Order at the Millennium' in B. Joerges and H. Nowotny (eds.), *Social Studies of Science and Technology: Looking Back, Ahead* (Kluwer Academic Publishers, 2003), pp. 155–80.

Jasanoff, S., 'Ordering Knowledge, Ordering Society' in S. Jasanoff (ed.), *States of Knowledge: The Co-production of Science and Social Order* (Routledge, 2004), pp. 13–45.

Jasanoff, S., *The Fifth Branch* (Harvard University Press, 1990).

Jasanoff, S., 'The Practices of Objectivity in Regulatory Science' in C. Camic, N. Gross, M. Lamont (eds.), *Social Knowledge in the Making* (University of Chicago Press, 2011), pp. 307–38.

Jasanoff, S., *Science and Public Reason* (Routledge-Earthscan, 2012).

Jasanoff, S., 'Serviceable Truths: Science for Action in Law and Policy' (2014) 93 *Texas Law Review* 1723.

Jessup, P. C., *A Modern Law of Nations* (The Macmillan Company, 1948).

Johnston, D. M., 'Fishery Diplomacy and Science and the Judicial Function' (2000) 10 *Yearbook of International Environmental Law* 33–9.

Kammerhofer, J., *Uncertainty in International Law: A Kelsenien Perspective* (Routledge, 2011).

Kazazi, M., 'Environmental Damage in the Practice of the UN Compensation Commission' in M. Bowman, A. Boyle (eds.), *Environmental Damage in International and Comparative Law* (Oxford University Press, 2002), pp. 111–31.

Kazazi, M., 'The UNCC Follow-up Programme for Environmental Awards' in T. M. Ndiaye, R. Wolfrum (eds.), *Law of the Sea, Environmental Law and Settlement of Disputes: Liber Amicorum Judge Thomas A. Mensah* (Martinus Nijhoff, 2007), pp. 1109–29.

Kellner, M. and I. C. Durant, 'Causation' in A. Fenyves, E. Karner, H. Koziol, E. Steiner (eds.), *Tort Law in the Jurisprudence of the European Court of Human Rights* (De Gruyter, 2011), pp. 449–92.

Kheng, S. L., 'China's Nationalist Narrative of the South China Sea: A Preliminary Analysis' in E. Fels, T.-M. H. Vu (eds.), *Power Politics in Asia's Contested Waters* (Springer, 2016), pp. 159–72.

Kiss, A. C., 'Environmental Disputes and the Permanent Court of Arbitration' (2003) 16 *Hague Yearbook of International Law* 41–6.

Kiss, A., 'Present Limits to the Enforcement of State Responsibility for Environmental Damage' in F. Francioni, T. Scovazzi (eds.), *International Responsibility for Environmental Harm* (Graham and Trotman, 1991), pp. 3–14.

Klabbers, J., 'Changing Futures? Science and International Law' (2009) 20 *Finnish Yearbook of International Law* 211–13.

Klein, A. R., 'Causation and Uncertainty: Making Connections in a Time of Change' (2008) 49 *Jurimetrics* 5–50.

Knudsen, S. H., 'The Long-Term Tort: In Search of a New Causation Framework for Natural Resource Damages' (2014) 108 *Northwestern University Law Review* 1–67.

Koe, A., 'Damming the Danube: The International Court of Justice and the Gabcikovo-Nagymaros Project (*Hungary v. Slovakia*)' (1998) 20 *Sydney Law Review* 612.

Koh, T. and J. Lin, 'The Land Reclamation Case: Thoughts and Reflections Speech' (2006) 10 *Singapore Year Book of International Law* 1–8.

Koskenniemi, M., 'Peaceful Settlement of Environmental Disputes' (1991) 60 *Nordic Journal of International Law* 73.

Kritzer, H., 'The Arts of Persuasion in Science and Law: Conflicting Norms in the Courtroom' (2009) 72 *Law and Contemporary Problems* 41–61.

Kuhn, T., *The Structure of Scientific Revolutions*, 1970 ed. (The University of Chicago 1962).

Kulovesi, K., 'Fragmented Landscapes, Troubled Relationships: The WTO Dispute Settlement System and International Environmental Law' (2008) 19 *Finnish Yearbook of International Law* 29–62.

Kundis Craig, R., A. R. Klein, and J. Sanders, *Toxic and Environmental Torts Cases and Materials* (West, 2010).

Latour, B., 'Give Me a Laboratory and I Will Raise the World' in K. Knorr-Cetina, M. Mulkay (eds.), Science Observed: Perspectives on the Social Study of Science (Sage, 1983), pp. 141–70.

Latour, B., *We Have Never Been Modern* (Harvester Wheatsheaf, 1993).

Lauterpacht, H., *The Development of International Law by the International Court* (Stevens & Sons, 1958).

Lawrence, J., 'The Structural Logic of Expert Participation in WTO Decision-Making Processes' in M. Ambrus, K. Arts, E. Hey, H. Raulus (eds.), *The Role of 'Experts' in International and European Decision-Making Processes* (Cambridge University Press, 2014), pp. 173–93.

Lazarus, R. J., 'Super Wicked Problems and Climate Change: Restraining the Present to Liberate the Future' (2008) 94 *Cornell Law Review* 1153.

Lazarus, R. J., *The Making of Environmental Law* (The University of Chicago Press, 2004).

Lazarus, R. J., *The Rule of Five Making Climate History at the Supreme Court* (Harvard University Press, 2020).

Lefeber, R., *Transboundary Environmental Interference and the Origin of State Liability* (Kluwer Law International, 1996).

Legg, A., *The Margin of Appreciation in International Human Rights Law* (Oxford University Press, 2012).

Létourneau-Tremblay, L. and D. F. Behn, 'Judging the Misapplication of a State's Own Environmental Regulations' (2016) 17 *The Journal of World Investment & Trade* 823–32.

Lévesque, C., 'Science in the Hands of International Investment Tribunals: A Case for "Scientific Due Process"' (2009) 20 *Finnish Yearbook of International Law* 259–90.

Levashova, Y., 'Fair and Equitable Treatment and the Protection of the Environment: Recent Trends in Investment Treaties and Investment Cases' in Y. Levashova, T. Lambooy, I. Dekker (eds.), *Bridging the Gap between International Investment Law and the Environment* (Eleven Publishing, 2015), pp. 53–84.

Levine, M., 'Investor-State Arbitration and Domestic Environmental Governance: Recent Developments in Canada' in N. Craik, C. S. G. Jefferies, S. L. Seck, T. Stephens (eds.), *Global Environmental Change and Innovation in International Law* (Cambridge University Press, 2018), pp. 296–314.

Lin, J., 'Climate Change Litigation in Asia and the Pacific' in G. Van Calster, W. Vandenberghe, L. Reins (eds.), *Research Handbook on Climate Change Mitigation Law* (Edward Elgar, 2015), pp. 578–99.

Loewenstein, A. B., 'Adjudication of Environmental Impact Assessment Claims before International Courts and Tribunals' in C. Voigt (ed.), *International Judicial Practice on the Environment: Questions of Legitimacy* (Cambridge University Press, 2019), pp. 288–310.

Louka, E., *International Environmental Law Fairness, Effectiveness, and World Order* (Cambridge University Press, 2006).

Lowe, V., *International Law* (Oxford University Press, 2007).

Ludwig, D., M. Mangel, and B. Haddad, 'Ecology, Conservation, and Public Policy' (2001) 32 *Annual Review of Ecology and Systematics* 481–517.

Malintoppi, L., 'Fact Finding and Evidence before the International Court of Justice (Notably in Scientific-Related Disputes)' (2016) 7 *Journal of International Dispute Settlement* 421–44.

Malone, W., 'Ruminations on Cause-in-Fact' (1955) 9 *Stanford Law Review* 60.

Mangel, M., 'Whales, Science, and Scientific Whaling in the International Court of Justice' (2016) 113 *Proceedings of the National Academy of Sciences* 14523–7.

Marceau, G. Z. and J. K. Hawkins, 'Experts in WTO Dispute Settlement' (2012) 3 *Journal of International Dispute Settlement* 493–507.

Matheson, M. J., 'Eritrea-Ethiopia Claims Commission: Damage Awards' (2009) 13 *ASIL Insights*.

Mavroidis, P. C., 'The Gang That Couldn't Shoot Straight: The Not So Magnificent Seven of the WTO Appellate Body' (2017) 27 *European Journal of International Law* 1107–18.

Mbengue, M. M., 'International Courts and Tribunals as Fact-Finders: The Case of Scientific Fact-Finding in International Adjudication' (2011) 34 *Loyola of Los Angeles International & Comparative Law Review* 53.

Mbengue, M. M., 'Scientific Fact-Finding at the International Court of Justice: An Appraisal in the Aftermath of the *Whaling* Case' (2016) 29 *Leiden Journal of International Law* 529–50.

Mbengue, M. M., 'Scientific Fact-Finding by International Courts and Tribunals' (2012) 3 *Journal of International Dispute Settlement* 509–24.

Mbengue, M. M., 'The South China Sea Arbitration: Innovations in Marine Environmental Fact-Finding and Due Diligence Obligations' (2016) 110 *ASIL Unbound* 285–9.

Mbengue, M. M. and R. Das, 'The ICJ's Engagement with Science: To Interpret or Not to Interpret?' (2015) 6 *Journal of International Dispute Settlement* 568–77.

McCaffrey, S. C., 'Of Paradoxes, Precedents, and Progeny: The *Trail Smelter* Arbitration 65 Years Later' in R. Bratspies, R. A. Miller (eds.), *Transboundary Harm in International Law* (Cambridge University Press, 2006), pp. 34–45.

McIntyre, O., 'The Contribution of Procedural Rules to the Environmental Protection of Transboundary Rivers in Light of Recent ICJ Case Law' in Laurence Boisson de Chazournes (ed.), *International Law and Freshwater* (Edward Elgar, 2013), pp. 239–66.

Meetarbhan, M. J. N., 'Re-examining the Chagos Marine Protected Area Arbitration: The Lancaster House Undertakings' (2015) 45 *Environmental Policy and Law* 248–55.

Mensah, T. A., 'The International Tribunal for the Law of the Sea and the Protection and Preservation of the Marine Environment' (1999) 8 *Review of European, Comparative & International Environmental Law* 1–15.

Merton, R. K., 'The Normative Structure of Science' in N. W. Storer (ed.), *The Sociology of Science* (The University of Chicago Press, 1973), pp. 267–78.

Milanovic, M., *Extraterritorial Application of Human Rights Treaties* (Oxford University Press, 2011).

Miles, K., *The Origins of International Investment Law* (Cambridge University Press, 2013).

Moussa, J., 'Implications of the Indus Water Kishenganga Arbitration for the International Law of Watercourses and the Environment' (2015) 64 *International & Comparative Law Quarterly* 697–715.

Nedumpara, J., *Injury and Causation in Trade Remedy Law* (Springer, 2016)

Négre, C., 'Responsibility and International Environmental Law' in J. Crawford, A. Pellet, S. Olleson (eds.), *The Law of International Responsibility* (Oxford University Press, 2010), pp. 803–13.

Nollkaemper, A. and Burgers, L., 'A New Classic in Climate Change Litigation: The Dutch Supreme Court Decision in the *Urgenda* Case', EJIL Talk! (6 January 2020) Available at https://bit.ly/3c1XO4h.

Nollkaemper, A. and I. Plakokefalos (eds.), *Principles of Shared Responsibility in International Law* (Cambridge University Press, 2017).

'Note: Market Share Liability: An Answer to the DES Causation Problem' (1981) 94 *Harvard Law Review* 668.

O'Reilly, J., K. Brysse, M. Oppenheimer, and N. Oreskes, 'Characterizing Uncertainty in Expert Assessments: Ozone Depletion and the West Antarctic Ice Sheet: Characterizing Uncertainty in Expert Assessments' (2011) 2 *Wiley Interdisciplinary Reviews: Climate Change* 728–43.

Ogburn, W. F., 'How Technology Changes Society' (1947) 249 *The Annals of the American Academy of Political and Social Science* 81–8.

Oliphant, K., 'Uncertain Factual Causation in the Third Restatement: Some Comparative Notes' (2010) 37 *William Mitchell Law Review* 1599.

Oliphant, K. and K. Ludwichowska, 'Damage' in A. Fenyves, E. Karner, H. Koziol, E. Steiner (eds.), *Tort Law in the Jurisprudence of the European Court of Human Rights* (De Gruyter, 2011), pp. 397–448.

Oral, N., 'The South China Sea Arbitral Award, Part XII of UNCLOS, and the Protection and Preservation of the Marine Environment' in S. Jayakumar, T. Koh, R. Beckman, T. Davenport, H. Phan (eds.), *The South China Sea Arbitration: The Legal Dimension* (Edward Elgar, 2018), pp. 223–46.

Orellana, M. A., '*Saramaka People* v. *Suriname*' (2008) 102 *American Journal of International Law* 841–7.

Orellana, M. A., 'The EU and Chile Suspend the *Swordfish* Case Proceedings at the WTO and the International Tribunal of the Law of the Sea' (2001) 6(1) *ASIL Insights*.

Orellana, M. A., 'The Role of Science in Investment Arbitrations Concerning Public Health and the Environment' (2006) 17 *Yearbook of International Environmental Law* 48–72.

Orellana M. A., 'The *Swordfish* Dispute between the EU and Chile at the ITLOS and the WTO' (2002) 71 *Nordic Journal of International Law* 55–81.

Oreskes, N., *Why Trust Science?* (Princeton University Press, 2019).

Orford, A., 'Trade, Human Rights and the Economy of Sacrifice' in A. Orford (ed.), *International Law and Its Others* (Cambridge University Press, 2006), pp. 156–96.

Osofsky, H. M., 'Climate Change and Dispute Resolution Processes' in R. Rayfuse, S. V. Scott (eds.), *International Law in the Era of Climate Change* (Edward Elgar, 2012), pp. 350–70.

Osofsky, H. M., 'The Intersection of Scale, Science, and Law in *Massachusetts* v. *EPA*' in W. C. G. Burns, H. M. Osofsky (eds.), *Adjudicating Climate Change* (Cambridge University Press, 2010), pp. 129–44.

Osofsky, H. M., 'The Inuit Petition as a Bridge? Beyond Dialectics of Climate Change and Indigenous Peoples' Rights' in W. C. G. Burns, H. M. Osofsky (eds.), *Adjudicating Climate Change* (Cambridge University Press, 2010), pp. 272–90.

Paik, J.-H., 'South China Sea Arbitral Awards: Main Findings and Assessment' (2017) 20 *Max Planck Yearbook of United Nations Law Online* 367–407.

Palmeter, D., 'The WTO Standard of Review in Health and Safety Disputes' in G. A. Bermann, P. C. Mavroidis (eds.), *Trade and Human Health and Safety* (Cambridge University Press, 2006), pp. 224–34.

Palombino, F. M., 'Judicial Economy and Limitation of the Scope of the Decision in International Adjudication' (2010) 23 *Leiden Journal of International Law* 909–32.

Pascual, P., W. Wagner, and E. Fisher, 'Making Methods Visible: Improving the Quality of Science-Based Regulation' (2013) 2 *Michigan Journal of Environmental and Administrative Law* 429–72.

Patel, B. N., *Law of the Sea International Tribunal for the Law of the Sea Jurisprudence: Case Commentary, Case-Law Digest and Reference Guide (1994–2014)* (Eastern Book Company, 2016).

Paterson, J., 'Law's Approach to Harm under Uncertainty' in R. Goldberg (ed.), *Perspectives on Causation* (Hart, 2011), pp. 383–408.

Pauwelyn, J., 'Expert Advice in WTO Dispute Settlement' in G. A. Bermann, P. C. Mavroidis (eds.), *Trade and Human Health and Safety* (Cambridge University Press, 2006), pp. 235–56.

Pauwelyn, J., 'The WTO 20 Years On: "Global Governance by Judiciary" or, Rather, Member-Driven Settlement of (Some) Trade Disputes between (Some) WTO Members?' (2017) 27 *European Journal of International Law* 1119–26.

Payne, C., 'Environmental Claims in Context' in C. Payne, P. H. Sand (eds.), *Gulf War Reparations and the UN Compensation Commission: Environmental Liability* (Oxford University Press, 2015), pp. 1–39.

Payne, C., 'Mastering the Evidence: Improving Fact Finding by International Courts' (2011) *Environmental Law* 1191–220.

Payne, M. R. et al., 'Uncertainties in Projecting Climate-Change Impacts in Marine Ecosystems' (2016) 73 *ICES Journal of Marine Science: Journal du Conseil* 1272–82.

Peat, D., 'The Use of Court-Appointed Experts by the International Court of Justice' (2014) 84 *British Yearbook of International Law* 271–303.

Peczenik, A., *On Law and Reason* (Springer, 2009).

Pedersen, O. W., 'The European Court of Human Rights and International Environmental Law' in J. H. Knox, R. Pejan (eds.), *The Human Right to a Healthy Environment* (Cambridge University Press, 2018), pp. 86–98.

Peel, J., 'Changing Conceptions of Environmental Risk' in J. E. Vinuales (ed.), *The Rio Declaration on Environment and Development: A Commentary* (Oxford University Press, 2015), pp. 74–85.

Peel, J., 'Issues in Climate Change Litigation' (2011) 1 *Carbon and Climate Law Review* 15–24.

Peel, J., *Science and Risk Regulation in International Law* (Cambridge University Press, 2010).

Pellet, A., 'Should We (Still) Worry about Fragmentation?' in A. Føllesdal, G. Ulfstein (eds.), *The Judicialization of International Law: A Mixed Blessing?* (Oxford University Press, 2018), pp. 228–42.

Perez, O., 'Judicial Strategies for Reviewing Conflicting Expert Evidence: Biases, Heuristics, and Higher-Order Evidence' (2016) 64 *The American Journal of Comparative Law* 75–120.

Plakokefalos, I., 'Causation in the Law of State Responsibility and the Problem of Overdetermination: In Search of Clarity' (2015) 26 *European Journal of International Law* 471–92.

Plakokefalos, I., 'Seabed Disputes Chamber of the International Tribunal for the Law of the Sea Responsibilities and Obligations of States Sponsoring Persons and Entities with Respect to Activities in the Area Advisory Opinion' (2012) 24 *Journal of Environmental Law* 133–43.

Popper, K., *The Logic of Scientific Discovery* (Routledge, 2005).

Press, A., 'Science in the Court! The Role of Science in "Whaling in the Antarctic"' in M. Fitzmaurice, D. Tamada (eds.), *Whaling in the Antarctic* (Brill Nijhoff, 2016), pp. 346–86.

Preston, B. J., 'Climate Change Litigation (Part 1)' (2011) 1 *Carbon and Climate Law Review* 798–809.

Preston, B. J., 'The End of Enlightened Environmental Law?' (2019) 31 *Journal of Environmental Law* 399–411.

Proelss, A. (ed.), United Nations Convention on the Law of the Sea: A Commentary (C. H. Beck Hart Nomos, 2017).

Rainey, B., E. Wicks, and C. Ovey (eds.), *Jacobs, White and Ovey: The European Convention on Human Rights*, 6th ed. (Oxford University Press, 2014).

Ratliff, D. P., 'The PCA Optional Rules for Arbitration of Disputes Relating to Natural Resources and/or the Environment' (2001) 14 *Leiden Journal of International Law* 887–96.

Rayfuse, R., 'Precaution and the Protection of Marine Biodiversity in Areas beyond National Jurisdiction' (2012) 27 *International Journal of Marine and Coastal Law* 773–81.

Read, J. E., 'The Trail Smelter Dispute (Abridged)' in R. Bratspies, R. A. Miller (eds.), *Transboundary Harm in International Law* (Cambridge University Press, 2006), pp. 27–33.

Redgwell, C., 'International Environmental Law' in M. Evans (ed.), *International Law* (Oxford University Press, 2014), pp. 688–726.

Reed, L. and K. Wong, 'Marine Entitlements in the South China Sea: The Arbitration between the Philippines and China' (2016) 110 *American Journal of International Law* 746–60.

Regan, H. M., M. Colyvan, and M. A. Burgman, 'A Taxonomy and Treatment of Uncertainty for Ecology and Conservation Biology' (2002) 12 *Ecological Applications* 618–28.

Reid, E., 'Risk Assessment, Science and Deliberation: Managing Regulatory Diversity under the SPS Agreement' (2012) 4 *European Journal of Risk Regulation* 535–44.

Reinisch, A., 'Human Rights Extraterritoriality: Controlling Companies Abroad' in E. Benvenisti, G. Nolte (eds.), *Community Interests Across International Law* (Oxford University Press, 2018), pp. 396–413.

Ridell, A., 'Scientific Evidence in the International Court of Justice: Problems and Possibilities' (2009) 20 *Finnish Yearbook of International Law* 229–58.

Ridell, A. and B. Plant, *Evidence before the International Court of Justice* (British Institute of International and Comparative Law, 2009).

Roach, J. A., 'Marine Scientific Research and the New Law of the Sea' (1996) 27 *Ocean Development and International Law* 59–72.

Roach, J. A., 'Marine Scientific Research in the Area' in M. Lodge, M. H. Nordquist (eds.), *Peaceful Order in the World's Oceans* (Brill Nijhoff, 2014), pp. 265–81.

Roesch, R., 'The Ogiek Case of the African Court on Human and Peoples' Rights: Not So Much News After All?' *EJIL Talk!* (June 16, 2017) Available at https://bit.ly/3gLUjCn

Romano, C. P. R., *The Peaceful Settlement of International Environmental Disputes: A Pragmatic Approach* (Kluwer Law International, 2000).

Rosenberg, D., 'The Causal Connection in Mass Exposure Cases: A "Public Law" Vision of the Tort System' (1984) 97 *Harvard Law Review* 849.

Rothwell, D. R., 'The Contribution of ITLOS to Oceans Governance Through Marine Environmental Dispute Resolution' in T. M. Ndiaye, R. Wolfrum (eds.), *Law of the Sea, Environmental Law and Settlement of Disputes: Liber Amicorum Judge Thomas A. Mensah* (Martinus Nijhoff, 2007), pp. 1007–24.

Sand, P. H., 'Environmental Dispute Settlement and the Experience of the UN Compensation Committee' (2011) 54 *Japanese Yearbook of International aw* 151.

Sand, P. H. and J. K. Kammit, 'Public Health Claims' in C. Payne, P. H. Sand (eds.), *Gulf War Reparations and the UN Compensation Commission: Environmental Liability* (Oxford University Press, 2011), pp. 1–39.

Sands, P., 'Climate Change and the Rule of Law: Adjudicating the Future of International Law' (2016) 28 *Journal of Environmental Law* 19–35.

Sands, P., 'Human Rights, Environment and the Lopez-Ostra Case' (1996) *European Human Rights Law Review* 597–618.

Sands, P., 'International Environmental Litigation and Its Future' (1998) 32 *University of Richmond Law Review* 1619.

Sands, P., *Litigating Environmental Disputes: Courts, Tribunals and the Progressive Development of International Environmental Law* (OECD Global Forum on International Investment, 2008).

Schatz, V., 'Fishing for Interpretation: The ITLOS Advisory Opinion on Flag State Responsibility for Illegal Fishing in the EEZ' (2016) 47 *Ocean Development & International Law* 327–45.

Schill, S. W., 'Deference in Investment Treaty Arbitration: Re-conceptualizing the Standard of Review' (2012) 3 *Journal of International Dispute Settlement* 577–607.

Schill, S. W. and V. Djanic, 'International Investment Law and Community Interests' in E. Benvenisti, G. Nolte (eds.), *Community Interests Across International Law* (Oxford University Press, 2018), pp. 221–48.

Schrefler, L., 'Reflections on the Different Roles of Expertise in Regulatory Policy Making' in M. Ambrus, K. Arts, E. Hey, H. Raulus (eds.), *The Role of 'Experts' in International and European Decision-Making Processes* (Cambridge University Press, 2011), pp. 63–81.

Schreuer, C., 'Investment Arbitration' in C. Romano, K. J. Alter, Y. Shany (eds.), The *Oxford Handbook of International Adjudication* (Oxford University Press, 2014), pp. 295–315.

Scott, J. and S. Sturm, 'Courts as Catalysts: Re-Thinking the Judicial Role in New Governance' (2007) 13 *Columbia Journal of European Law* 565–94.

Shany, Y., *Assessing the Effectiveness of International Courts* (Oxford University Press, 2014).

Shany, Y., 'Stronger Together? Legitimacy and Effectiveness of International Courts as Mutually Reinforcing or Undermining Notions' in N. Grossman, H. G. Cohen, A. Føllesdal, G. Ulfstein (eds.), *Legitimacy and International Courts* (Cambridge University Press, 2018), pp. 354–71.

Shany, Y., 'The First MOX Plant Award: The Need to Harmonize Competing Environmental Regimes and Dispute Settlement Procedures' (2004) 17 *Leiden Journal of International Law* 815–27.

Shelton, D., 'Complexities and Uncertainties in Matters of Human Rights and the Environment: Identifying the Judicial Role' in J. H. Knox, R. Pejan (eds.), *The Human Right to a Healthy Environment* (Cambridge University Press, 2018), pp. 97–121.

Shelton, D. L., 'Developing Substantive Environmental Rights' (2010) 1 *Journal of Human Rights and the Environment* 89–120.

Shelton, D. L., 'Environmental Rights and Brazil's Obligations in the Inter-American Human Rights System' (2008) 40 *George Washington International Law Review* 733–77.

Shelton, D., 'Righting Wrongs: Reparations in the Articles on State Responsibility' (2002) 96 *American Journal of International Law* 833–856.

Simma, B., 'The International Court of Justice and Scientific Expertise' (2012) 106 *Proceedings of the Annual Meeting (ASIL)*, 230–3.

Singleton, B. E. and R. Lidskog, 'Science, Red in Tooth and Claw: Whaling, Purity, Pollution and Institutions in Marine Mammal Scientists' Boundary Work' (2018) 1 *Environment and Planning E: Nature and Space* 165–85.

Smith, C., 'Policy Implications of Uncertainty' (2011) 369 *Philosophical Transactions of the Royal Society A: Mathematical, Physical and Engineering Sciences* 4932–7.

Smyth, S. J., W. A. Kerr, and P. W. B. Phillips, 'Recent Trends in the Scientific Basis of Sanitary and Phytosanitary Trade Rules and Their Potential Impact on Investment' (2011) 12 *The Journal of World Investment& Trade* 5–26.

Spellman, B. A. and F. Schauer, 'Legal Reasoning' in K. J. Holyoak, R. G. Morrison (eds.), *The Oxford Handbook of Thinking and Reasoning* (Oxford University Press, 2012), pp. 719–35.

Squintani, L., J. Darpö, L. Lavrysen, and P.-T. Stoll, *Managing Facts and Feelings in Environmental Governance* (Edward Elgar, 2019).

Star, S. L. and J. R. Griesemer, 'Institutional Ecology, "Translations" and Boundary Objects: Amateurs and Professionals in Berkeley's Museum of Vertebrate Zoology, 1907–39' (1989) 19 *Social Studies of Science* 397–420.

Stec, S. and G. Eckstein, 'Of Solemn Oaths and Obligations: The Environmental Impact of the ICJ's Decision in the Case Concerning the Gabcikovo-Nagymaros Project' (1997) 8 *Yearbook of International Environmental Law* 41–57.

Steel, S., *Proof of Causation in Tort Law* (Cambridge University Press, 2015).

Steiner, E., 'Just Satisfaction under Art. 41 of ECHR: A Compromise in 1950 – Problematic Now' in A. Fenyves, E. Karner, H. Koziol, E. Steiner (eds.), *Tort Law in the Jurisprudence of the European Court of Human Rights* (De Gruyter, 2011), pp. 3–26.

Stephens, T., *International Courts and Environmental Protection* (Cambridge University Press, 2009).

Stephens, T., 'International Environmental Dispute Settlement' in J. E. Vinuales (ed.), *The Rio Declaration on Environment and Development: A Commentary* (Oxford University Press, 2015), pp. 599–616.

Stephens, T., 'The Settlement of Disputes in International Environmental Law' in S. Alam, M. J. H. Bhuiyan, T. Chowdhury, E. Techera (eds.), *Routledge Handbook of International Environmental Law* (Routledge, 2012), pp. 175–87.

Stewart, R. B., 'Remedying Disregard in Global Regulatory Governance: Accountability, Participation, and Responsiveness' (2014) *American Journal of International Law* 211–70.

Straus, M., 'Causation as an Element of State Responsibility' (1984) 16 *Law & Policy in International Business* 893.

Strauss, A., 'Climate Change Litigation: Opening the Door to the International Court of Justice' in W. C. G. Burns, H. M. Osofsky (eds.), *Adjudicating Climate Change* (Cambridge University Press, 2010), pp. 334–56.

Sulyok, K., 'Managing Uncertain Causation: Lessons for the Strasbourg Court from US Toxic Tort Litigation?' (2017) 18 *Vermont Journal of Environmental Law* 521–69.

Sulyok, K., Bögös, F., Paloniitty, T., and Eliantonio, M. Summary Report of the European Forum of Judges for the Environment – Answers to the questionnaire concerning the role of science in environmental adjudication, 2019. Available at https://bit.ly/2BnT8sB.

Sykes, A. O., 'Domestic Regulation, Sovereignty and Scientific Evidence Requirements: A Pessimistic View' in G. A. Bermann, P. C. Mavroidis (eds.), *Trade and Human Health and Safety* (Cambridge University Press, 2006), pp. 257–70.

Szabó, M., 'The Implementation of the Judgment of the ICJ on the Gabcikovo-Nagymaros Dispute' (2009) 5 *Iustum Aequum Salutare* 15–25.

Tanaka, Y., 'Obligations and Liability of Sponsoring States Concerning Activities in the Area: Reflections on the ITLOS Advisory Opinion of 1 February 2011' (2013) 60 *Netherlands International Law Review* 205–30.

Tanaka, Y., 'Provisional Measures Prescribed by ITLOS and Marine Environmental Protection' (2014) 108 *Proceedings of the Annual Meeting, published by the American Society of International Law* 365–8.

Telesetsky, A., 'The International Tribunal for the Law of the Sea: Seeking the Legitimacy of State Consent' in N. Grossman, H. G. Cohen, A. Føllesdal, G. Ulfstein (eds.), *Legitimacy and International Courts* (Cambridge University Press, 2018), pp. 174–215.

Thagard, P., 'Explanatory Coherence' in J. E. Adler, L. J. Rips (eds.), Reasoning: Studies of Human Inference and Its Foundations (Cambridge University Press, 2008), pp. 471–513.

The American Law Institute, *Third Restatement of the Law of Torts for Physical and Emotional Harm* (The American Law Institute Publishers, 2010), vol. i.

Thomas, C. A., 'Of Facts and Phantoms: Economics, Epistemic Legitimacy, and WTO Dispute Settlement' (2011) 14 *Journal of International Economic Law* 295–328.

Thomas, E. W., *The Judicial Process: Realism, Pragmatism, Practical Reasoning and Principles* (Cambridge University Press, 2005).

Thornburgh, D., G. Reichardt, and J. Stanley, 'The Nuclear Claims Tribunal of the Republic of the Marshall Islands: An Independent Examination and Assessment of Its Decision-Making Processes' (2003) available at www.bikiniatoll.com/ThornburgReport.pdf.

Thorson, E. J., 'The World Heritage Convention and Climate Change: The Case for a Climate-Change Mitigation Strategy beyond the Kyoto Protocol' in W. C. G. Burns, H. M. Osofsky (eds.), *Adjudicating Climate Change* (Cambridge University Press, 2010), pp. 255–71.

Tol, R. S. J. and R. Verheyen, 'State Responsibility and Compensation for Climate Change Damages: A Legal and Economic Assessment' (2004) 32 *Energy Policy* 1109–30.

Treves, T., 'Law and Science in the Interpretation of the Law of the Sea Convention' (2012) 3 *Journal of International Dispute Settlement* 483–91.

Treves, T., 'Law and Science in the Jurisprudence of the International Tribunal for the Law of the Sea' in M. H. Nordquist, R. Long, T. Heidar, J. N. Moore (eds.), *Law, Science and Ocean Management* (Brill Nijhoff, 2015), pp. 15–26.

Treves, T., 'The Settlement of Disputes and Non-Compliance Procedures' in T. Treves, L. Pineschi, A. Tanzi, C. Pitea, F. R. Jacur (eds.), *Non-Compliance Procedures and Mechanisms and the Effectiveness of International Environmental Agreements* (T. M. C. Asser Press, 2009), pp. 499–518.

Valles, C., 'Different Forms of Expert Involvement in WTO Dispute Settlement Proceedings' (2018) 9 *Journal of International Dispute Settlement* 367–78.

Van Damme, I., 'The Assessment of Expert Evidence in International Adjudication' (2018) 9 *Journal of International Dispute Settlement* 401–10.

Van Harten, G. and D. N. Scott, 'Investment Treaties and the Internal Vetting of Regulatory Proposals: A Case Study from Canada' (2016) 12 *Osgoode Legal Studies Research Paper Series*.

Viñuales, J. E., 'A Human Rights Approach to Extraterritorial Environmental Protection? An Assessment' in N. Bhuta (ed.), *The Frontiers of Human Rights* (Oxford University Press, 2016), pp. 177–221.

Viñuales, J. E., *Foreign Investment and the Environment* (Cambridge University Press, 2012).

Viñuales, J. E., 'Foreign Investment and the Environment in International Law: An Ambiguous Relationship' (2010) 80 *British Yearbook of International Law* 244–332.

Viñuales, J. E., 'Foreign Investment and the Environment in International Law: Current Trends' in K. Miles (ed.), *Research Handbook on Environment and Investment Law* (Edward Elgar, 2019), pp. 12–37.

Viñuales, J. E., 'Legal Techniques for Dealing with Scientific Uncertainty in Environmental Law' (2010) 43 *Vanderbilt Journal of Transnational Law* 437–503.

Viñuales, J. E., 'Observations sur le traitement des motifs scientifiques dans le contentieux environmental international' in F. Couveinhes Matsumoto, R. Nollez-Goldbach (eds.), *Les motifs non-juridiques des jugements internationaux. Actes de la 1ére journée de droit international de l'ENS* (Pedone, 2016), pp. 113–25.

Viñuales, J. E., 'The Contribution of the International Court of Justice to the Development of International Environmental Law: A Contemporary Assessment' (2008) 32 *Fordham International Law Journal* 232.

Viñuales, J. E., 'The Rio Declaration on Environment and Development' in J. E. Vinuales (ed.), *The Rio Declaration on Environment and Development: A Commentary* (Oxford University Press, 2015), pp. 1–60.

Voeten, E., 'International Judicial Behavior' in C. Romano, K. J. Alter, Y. Shany (eds.), *The Oxford Handbook of International Adjudication* (Oxford University Press, 2014), pp. 550–68.

Voigt, C., 'Climate Change and Damages' in C. Carlarne, K. Gray, R. Tarasofsky (eds.), *The Oxford Handbook of International Climate Change Law* (Oxford University Press, 2016), pp. 465–94.

Voigt, C. (ed.), *International Judicial Practice on the Environment: Questions of Legitimacy* (Cambridge University Press, 2019).

Voigt, C., 'State Responsibility for Climate Change Damages' (2008) 77 *Nordic Journal of International Law* 1–22.

Von Burg, R., 'The Supreme Court Cleans the Air: Legal and Scientific Standards for Argument in *Massachusetts v. EPA*' (2017) 53 *Argumentation and Advocacy* 41–58.

Vos, E., 'The European Court of Justice in the Face of Scientific Uncertainty and Complexity' in M. Dawson, B. De Witte, E. Muir (eds.), *Judicial Activism at the European Court of Justice* (Edward Elgar, 2013), pp. 142–66.

Vromman, P., 'Responsibilities and Obligations of Sponsoring States United Nations Activities: UNCLOS' (2012) 42 *Environmental Policy and Law* 90–6.

Walton, D. and N. Zhang, 'The Epistemology of Scientific Evidence' (2013) 21 *Artificial Intelligence and Law* 173–219.

Waseem, M. A., 'ITLOS at 20: Provisional Measures and the Precautionary Approach' in S. Minas, J. Diamond (eds.), *Stress Testing the Law of the Sea* (Brill Nijhoff, 2018), pp. 150–69.

Werner, W. G., 'The Politics of Expertise' in Ambrus, M., K. Arts, E. Hey, H. Raulus (eds.), *The Role of 'Experts' in International and European Decision-Making Processes* (Cambridge University Press, 2014), pp. 44–62.

Wilde, L., 'Scientific and Technical Advice' in C. Payne, P. H. Sand (eds.), *Gulf War Reparations and the UN Compensation Commission: Environmental Liability* (Oxford University Press, 2015), pp. 1–15.

Wilde, R., 'Socioeconomic Rights, Extraterritorially' in E. Benvenisti, G. Nolte (eds.), *Community Interests Across International Law* (Oxford University Press, 2018), pp. 381–95.

Will, G., 'Distant Partners: Europe and the South China Sea' in E. Fels, T.-M. Vu (eds.), *Power Politics in Asia's Contested Waters* (Springer, 2016), pp. 469–92.

Wolfrum, R., 'Taking and Assessing Evidence in International Adjudication' in T. M. Ndiaye, R. Wolfrum (eds.), *Law of the Sea, Environmental Law and Settlement of Disputes: Liber Amicorum Judge Thomas A. Mensah* (Martinus Nijhoff, 2007), pp. 341–56.

Wright, R. W., 'Causation, Responsibility, Risk, Probability, Naked Statistics, and Proof: Pruning the Bramble Bush by Clarifying the Concepts' (1987) 73 *Iowa Law Review* 1001.

Wright, R. W., 'Proving Causation: Probability versus Belief' in R. Goldberg (ed.), *Perspectives on Causation* (Hart, 2011), pp. 195–220.

Xue, H., *Transboundary Damage in International Law* (Cambridge University Press, 2003).

Yodzis, P., 'Diffuse Effects in Food Webs' (2000) 81 *Ecology* 261.

Yodzis, P., 'Must Top Predators Be Culled for the Sake of Fisheries?' (2001) 16 *Trends in Ecology & Evolution* 78–84.

Zander, J., *The Application of the Precautionary Principle in Practice* (Cambridge University Press, 2010).

Zupančič, B. M., 'Causation in Cases of Environmental Degradation: The Missing Link in Adjudicating Human Rights' (2011) 3 *The Yearbook of Polar Law Online* 113–28.

Index

Lightning Source UK Ltd.
Milton Keynes UK
UKHW022150061120
372964UK00002B/53